The Conflict of Laws

8th Edition

The Conflict of Laws

8th Edition

David McClean, C.B.E., Q.C., D.C.L., Hon.Litt.D, F.B.A.
Bencher of Gray's Inn
Membre de l'institut de droit international
Emeritus Professor of Law, University of Sheffield

Verónica Ruiz Abou-Nigm, LL.M, Ph.D
Lecturer in Law, University of Sheffield

Originally by:

The late J.H.C. Morris, Q.C., D.C.L., LL.D, F.B.A.
Honorary Bencher of Gray's Inn
Honorary Fellow of Magdalen College, Oxford
Emeritus Reader in the Conflict of Laws in the University of Oxford

SWEET & MAXWELL 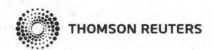 THOMSON REUTERS

Published in 2012 by Sweet & Maxwell, 100 Avenue Road, London NW3 3PF part of Thomson Reuters (Professional) UK Limited (Registered in England & Wales, Company No 1679046.
Registered Office and address for service: Aldgate House, 33 Aldgate High Street, London EC3N 1DL)

For further information on our products and services, visit *www.sweetandmaxwell.co.uk*

Typeset by Letterpart Ltd, Reigate, Surrey

Printed and bound in Great Britain by Ashford Colour Press, Gosport, Hampshire.

No natural forests were destroyed to make this product; only farmed timber was used and re-planted.

A CIP catalogue record of this book is available for the British Library.

ISBN: 978 0 414 02302 4

Thomson Reuters and the Thomson Reuters logo are trademarks of Thomson Reuters.

Sweet & Maxwell ® is a registered trademark of Thomson Reuters (Professional) UK Limited.

Crown copyright material is reproduced with the permission of the Controller of HMSO and the Queen's Printer for Scotland.

Preface

Barely three years have passed since the seventh edition of this book appeared. The principal events in the intervening period have been the coming into effect of three EU Regulations. In the last edition an account could be given of the Rome I Regulation on contractual obligations and the Rome II Regulation on non-contractual obligations (especially those in the area of tort or delict) but neither Regulation was in force. It will still be some time before decisions of the courts confirm or correct the opinions of commentators as to the precise effect of those instruments. These Regulations have been joined by Regulation 4/2009, the Maintenance Regulation, and the related work at The Hague (in which I was able to take an active part), the Convention on the International Recovery of Child Support and Other Forms of Family Maintenance and the Protocol on the Law Applicable to Maintenance Obligations. There has been a good deal of case law on the Brussels I (notably *West Tankers Inc v Allianz SpA*) and Brussels IIa Regulations, all duly incorporated in the text of this edition.

The EU continues to develop its system of private international law, but the United Kingdom has chosen not to be party to the instruments, actual or proposed, on choice of law in divorce, on matrimonial property and on wills and succession. These decisions are important for the future of our subject, for the approach and insights of the common law tradition were in danger of being all but eliminated in favour of those of the civil law. It is to be hoped that the coming recast of Brussels I Regulation may see the recovery of a little of the lost ground.

This book continues to seek to cover the principal areas of the conflict of laws. The tendency in some universities to reduce the scope of the subject to international commercial law (and so in practice for it to be almost wholly concerned with material from EU sources) deprives the student of the opportunity to see how this subject works across the whole field of law. We remain convinced that family law and property law remain important, not only in practice but to an understanding of the subject.

The Supreme Court of the United Kingdom has begun work. We share the general dismay that Lord Collins of Mapesbury, the doyen of our subject, had such a short tenure of office as a Justice. The court has already made some significant contributions, in decisions such as those in *Lucasfilm Ltd v Ainsworth*, *Granatino v Radmacher* and *Re E (Children) (International Abduction)*.

Another court, the European Court of Human Rights, has begun to have an impact on our subject. Its judgments in two child abduction cases, *Neulinger v Switzerland* and *Šneersone v Italy*, have caused a degree of consternation. The Hague Child Abduction Convention has its critics, but the voluminous body of case law (in England and elsewhere) provided clear guidance. The Strasbourg Court's decisions sadly create doubts and uncertainty.

New to this edition is the contribution of Verónica Ruiz Abou-Nigm. The birth of her third child prevented Verónica from taking as large a role in this edition as I had hoped. However, she did take the major responsibility for chapters 4, 5, 6 and 11, chapters most affected by the developments of the last three years. Every chapter has been carefully revised (who would have expected an important case on legitimacy?), with a deal of subtle re-writing and some re-ordering. The book still benefits from Kisch Beevers' contributions to the last two editions.

This is still John Morris's book in its scope and general approach. There are some lengthy passages, especially in the property chapters, which are virtually unchanged from his last (3rd) edition. He was a great, if occasionally terrifying, teacher and an exacting but generous colleague. As in each new edition, I salute his memory.

David McClean

TABLE OF CONTENTS

TABLE OF CASES

TABLE OF STATUTES

International

Australia

Austria

Canada

China

France

Germany

Ghana

Hong Kong

TABLE OF STATUTORY INSTRUMENTS

TABLE OF INTERNATIONAL CONVENTIONS

TABLE OF EUROPEAN INSTRUMENTS

TABLE OF CIVIL PROCEDURE RULES

CHAPTER 1

INTRODUCTION TO THE CONFLICT OF LAWS

On many an office or seminar-room wall, there hangs a political map of the   **1–001**
world. Each state, except the very smallest, has its own colour. Sixty years ago,
the colour scheme was rather simpler: pink for the British Empire, perhaps green
for the French possessions, and some other colour for the many republics which
made up the Soviet Union. The boundaries between the different colours once
meant a great deal. Many individuals lived and died without ever visiting a
foreign country. Patterns of trade and commerce tended to follow the Imperial
colour schemes, so that British companies would have their branches in the
colonies, where legal rules and commercial practice followed English models. All
this has now changed.

Mass tourism has made foreign travel commonplace. Students cross the world
in search of higher education, or to offer voluntary service, or simply for
adventure. Employees of British companies find themselves working in Tokyo or
the Gulf, and a trip to Brussels or Frankfurt has little novelty value. Many
national boundaries, such as those in "Schengenland" can be crossed without
formality. Love knows not national boundaries: tourist, student, or worker may
find romance and marry someone whose home is on the other side of the world.

Independence may increase the number of colours on the map, but the old
empires are replaced by regional common markets, such as those in Europe or the
Caribbean. The regional organisations soon move beyond a concern with
economic issues and acquire legislative powers. Each individual country
nonetheless retains its own body of law, its own system of courts, its own legal

personnel. Individual and corporate activity may be increasingly international, but there is no corpus of international law and no system of international courts to resolve any legal issues and disputes that arise. They have to be addressed through the courts of a particular national legal system and the legal rules which those courts choose to apply. Those rules are the rules of the conflict of laws.

THE SUBJECT DEFINED

1–002   The conflict of laws is that part of the private law of a particular country which deals with cases having a foreign element. "Foreign element" means simply a contact with some system of law other than that of the "forum", that is the country whose courts are seised of the case. Such foreign elements in the facts of a case are quite commonplace: a contract was made with a foreign company or was to be performed in a foreign country, or a tort was committed there, or property was situated there, or one of the parties is not English.

If a claim is made for damages for breach of a contract made in England between two English companies and to be performed in England, there is no foreign element: the case is not a case in the conflict of laws. It will be dealt with by the English court applying the English internal or domestic law of contract. But if the contract had been made in France between two French companies and was to be performed in France, then the case would be (for an English court, but not for a French court) a case in the conflict of laws, and an English court (in the unlikely event of litigation taking place in England) would apply French law to most of the matters in dispute before it, just as a French court naturally applies French law to all such matters.

1–003   If we change the facts once more, and assume that the contract was made in France between an English company and a French company and was to be performed in Belgium, then the case is a case in the conflict of laws not only for an English court but also for a French court and a Belgian court, and indeed for any court in the world in which the contract is litigated. That court will have to use its "choice of law" rules to decide whether to apply English, French or Belgian law, deciding in effect whether the French or English or Belgian elements are the most significant.

As Lord Nicholls of Birkenhead explained[1]:

> "Conflict of laws jurisprudence is concerned essentially with the just disposal of proceedings having a foreign element. The jurisprudence is founded on the recognition that in proceedings having connections with more than one country an issue brought before a court in one country may be more appropriately decided by reference to the laws of another country even though those laws are different from the law of the forum court."

---

[1] *Kuwait Airways Corpn v Iraqi Airways Co (Nos 4 and 5)* [2002] UKHL 19; [2002] 2 A.C. 883 at para.[15].

MEANING OF "COUNTRY"

In the conflict of laws, a foreign element and a foreign country mean a non-English element and a country other than England. From the point of view of the conflict of laws, Scotland and Northern Ireland are for most (but not all) purposes as much foreign countries as are France or Germany. More generally, a state in the political sense, or as understood in public international law, may or may not coincide with a country (or "law district" as it is sometimes called) in the sense of the conflict of laws. Unitary states such as Sweden, Italy and New Zealand, where the law is the same throughout the state, are "countries" in this sense. England or Scotland, New York or California, although merely component parts of the United Kingdom and the United States, are each a country in the sense of the conflict of laws, because each has a separate system of law.

1–004

England, Scotland, Northern Ireland, the Republic of Ireland, Guernsey, Jersey and the Isle of Man are each a separate country; so is each of the American and Australian states and each of the Canadian provinces, and each of the remaining dependencies of the United Kingdom. However, for some purposes larger units than these may constitute countries. Thus, the United Kingdom is one country for the purposes of the law of negotiable instruments,[2] and Great Britain is one country for most purposes of the law of companies.[3] In federal states, the greater use made of federal legislative powers has resulted in Australia being one country for the purposes of the law of marriage and matrimonial causes, and Canada one country for the purposes of the law of divorce. However, the mere fact that the Parliaments of the various Australian states and Canadian provinces decide to enact uniform legislation on technical legal subjects (as an exercise of state or provincial rather than federal competence) does not mean that they cease to be separate countries for those purposes.

On the other hand, Wales is not yet a country, because its system of law is still the same as that of England. The enactment of the Government of Wales Act 1998 did not change the position, for the Welsh Assembly was not given the power to enact primary legislation, but the additional powers conferred by the Government of Wales Act 2006 will in time create a body of Welsh law on some subjects. A country in the sense of the conflict of laws may exist without having a separate legislature: this was the case with Scotland between the Union in 1707 and the restoration of the Scottish Parliament by the Scotland Act 1998; and Northern Ireland did not cease to be a country when its legislature was suspended, originally in 1972.

1–005

In this book, "England" includes Wales; "Great Britain" means England (as so defined) and Scotland. "The United Kingdom" means England, Scotland, and Northern Ireland.

---

[2] Bills of Exchange Act 1882.
[3] Companies Act 2006.

The conflict of laws is sometimes known as private international law. This alternative title is potentially misleading, as the conflict of laws is not an international system of law. Public international law is a single system seeking primarily to regulate relations between sovereign states; in theory, at any rate, it is the same everywhere. But the rules of the conflict of laws differ from country to country. Nevertheless, some overlap exists between public international law and the conflict of laws: for instance, the topics of sovereign and diplomatic immunity from suit[4] and of governmental seizure of private property[5] are discussed in books on the conflict of laws as well as in books on public international law, and many rules of the conflict of laws are derived from international treaties or conventions.

1–006 The subject matter of this book is the English rules of the conflict of laws, which will not be identical with those of any other country. It is true that the common law countries of the Commonwealth adopt a similar approach, and the influence of English cases and textbooks persisted longer in the conflict of laws than in areas of law with more obvious political or economic importance. The work of law reform agencies and of appellate courts is causing the rules applied in different Commonwealth countries to diverge.[6] Even between England and Scotland there are some significant differences, and development of the subject in the United States has taken a rather different course.

The differences are much greater between the common law countries on the one hand and those in the civil law tradition. Civil law countries include most of the countries of mainland Europe, whose law is derived from Roman (and Napoleonic) sources; many of their former colonies in Latin America and elsewhere; and other countries which have chosen to use continental codes as models for their own. The common law uses "domicile" as a personal connecting factor[7]; the civil law tradition prefers nationality. The civil lawyers' devotion to the separation of powers leads to a distrust of judicial discretion, a concept much relied on by common lawyers in the context of jurisdiction. As we shall see, the development of European law is leading to a reception of civil law ideas to an ever-increasing extent in the English conflict of laws.

1–007 As an Advocate General of the European Court explained[8]:

> "Private international law, whatever its name may suggest, is not a body of international law. It is a branch of the domestic law of each legal system. It provides a mechanism or, more accurately, a series of interlocking mechanisms for determining, where legal situations or relationships have links to more than one legal system, what courts or other authorities should have jurisdiction, what substantive law should apply and what effects or recognition should be given to decisions taken, or legal acts accomplished, in accordance with other legal systems. Because the situations or relationships concerned are by definition inter-jurisdictional, the machinery of each legal system necessarily interacts with the machinery of other systems.

---

[4] Below, Ch.6.
[5] Below, Ch.13.
[6] See McClean, "A Common Inheritance? An Examination of the Private International Law Tradition of the Commonwealth", (1996) 260 *Recueil des Cours*, 1–98.
[7] See Ch.2.
[8] Sharpston A.G. in Case C-353/06 *Grunkin and Paul* at paras 37–38.

> Sometimes the gears mesh, sometimes they clash. When they mesh (which is preferable), it may be because the legal systems concerned have compatible rules from the outset, it may be because they have worked together to achieve compatibility in the context of a body such as ... the Hague Conference on Private International Law, or (within the European Union) it may be because they have had compatibility thrust upon them by Community legislation. There remain, however, many areas in which compatibility or harmonisation is incomplete."

Generally speaking, the conflict of laws is concerned much more with private than with public law.[9] It is traditional that English books on the conflict of laws do not discuss such topics as the jurisdiction of criminal courts to try crimes committed abroad, or the extradition of persons accused of crime, or mutual assistance between states in the conduct of criminal prosecutions, or the immigration or deportation of aliens.

THE QUESTIONS TO BE ANSWERED

The questions which the rules of the conflict of laws seek to answer are of two main types: first, has the English court jurisdiction to determine this case, and second, if so, what law will it apply? Logically, they must be addressed in that order, for if the English court has no jurisdiction it follows that the second, choice of law, question cannot arise. In practice, this logical purity does not quite hold: it can often make sense to ask the question "what law governs this contract?" quite independently of any jurisdictional issue.[10]   **1–008**

There may sometimes be a third question, namely, will the English court recognise or enforce a foreign judgment purporting to determine the issue between the parties? Of course, this third question arises only if there is a foreign judgment, and thus not in every case. But the first two questions arise in every case with foreign elements, though the answer to one of them may be so obvious that the court is in effect concerned only with the other. The law of every country has rules for dealing with these questions, the rules of the conflict of laws (or, less formally, "conflicts rules"), in contrast to its domestic or internal law.

In litigation practice, the issues as to jurisdiction feature very prominently. One reason is to be found in the fact that the rules of the conflict of laws found in England (and in many other common law countries) differ in one important respect from those adopted in many continental European countries (and others in the civil law tradition). There are many situations in which, if the English court has jurisdiction, it will apply English domestic law. This is true, for example, of most issues in the field of family law. Conversely, there are many situations in which, if a foreign court has jurisdiction according to English rules of the conflict of laws, its judgment or decree will be recognised or enforced in England, regardless of the grounds on which it was based or the choice of law rule which it applied. For a time, developments within the European Union also focused on jurisdictional issues. The negotiation of the Brussels Convention[11] (now replaced   **1–009**

---

[9] For the approach of the English courts to foreign public law, see below at para.3–014.

[10] Especially where all the countries concerned share the uniform choice of law rules of the Rome Convention or the Rome I Regulation; see Ch.11.

[11] Convention of 27 September 1968 on Jurisdiction and the Enforcement of Judgments in Civil and Commercial Matters.

by Council Regulation 44/2001,[12] referred to in this book as the Brussels I Regulation) and the related Lugano Convention[13] led to a re-examination (and in some cases the abandonment) of some of the more extensive assertions of jurisdiction which once passed largely unquestioned. The complexity of much civil litigation, which may involve a number of corporate parties each operating in many different countries, provides claimants with a range of possible forums and much consideration has to be given in practice to the relative advantages of one forum over another; though here the effect of European developments has been to limit the flexibility which was a feature of the common law approach to such matters.[14]

The attention of the European Union has now moved on the choice of law issues, especially in respect of contractual and non-contractual obligations dealt with in the Rome I and Rome II Regulations.[15] The interpretation of these Regulations is bound to feature prominently in the future case-law of the European Court and in national courts.

JUSTIFICATION

1–010 What justification is there for the existence of the conflict of laws? Why should the English courts trouble themselves with cases which are, to a greater or lesser extent, "foreign" cases? Why should we depart from the rules of our own law and apply those of another system? The justification for the conflict of laws can best be seen by considering what would happen if it did not exist. Theoretically, it would be possible for English courts to close their doors to all except English litigants. ("Theoretically" because this ignores the obligations of the United Kingdom under EU law and international conventions, and any question of "denial of justice" under the concepts of public international law.) But if they did so, grave injustice would be done not only to foreigners but also to the English. An English company, a party to a contract with a Scottish or French company, would be unable to enforce it in England; if the courts of other countries adopted the same principle, the contract could not be enforced in any country in the world.

Theoretically, it would be possible for English courts, while opening their doors to foreigners, to apply English domestic law in all cases. But if they did so, grave injustice would again be done to both foreign and English parties. For instance, if two English people married in France in accordance with the formalities prescribed by French law, but not in accordance with the formalities prescribed by English law, the English court, if it applied English domestic law to the case, would have to treat the parties as unmarried persons. This would have

---

[12] Council Regulation (EC) No 44/2001 of 22 December 2000 on jurisdiction and the recognition and enforcement of judgements in civil and commercial matters [2001] OJ L12/1.
[13] Convention of 16 September 1988 on jurisdiction and the enforcement of judgments in civil and commercial matters.
[14] See further, at para.5–047.
[15] Regulation (EC) No 593/2008 of the European Parliament and of the Council of 17 June 2008 on the law applicable to contractual obligations (Rome I), [2008] OJ L177/6; Regulation (EC) No 864/2007 of the European Parliament and of the Council of 11 July 2007 on the law applicable to non-contractual obligations (Rome II), [2007] OJ l199/40.

unexpected and unjust consequences in terms of matrimonial property rights and responsibility for the children of the supposed marriage.

Theoretically, it would be possible for English courts, while opening their doors to foreigners and while ready to apply foreign law in appropriate cases, to refuse to recognise or enforce a foreign judgment determining the issue between the parties. But if they did so, grave injustice would again be inflicted on both foreign and English parties. For instance, if a divorce was granted in a foreign country, and afterwards one party remarried in England, he or she might be convicted of bigamy. Or if an English claimant sued a foreigner in a foreign country for damages for breach of contract or for tort, and eventually obtained a judgment in his favour, the successful claimant might find that the defendant had surreptitiously removed all assets to England; the claimant would then have to start all over again.

    It was at one time supposed that the doctrine of comity was a sufficient basis for the conflict of laws; and even today references to comity are sometimes found in English judgments.[16] But it is clear that English courts apply French law in a particular context in order to do justice between the parties, not from any desire to show courtesy to the French Republic, nor even in the hope that if English courts apply French law in appropriate cases, French courts will be encouraged in appropriate cases to apply English law.

1–011

RANGE AND DIFFICULTY OF THE SUBJECT

Not the least interesting feature of the conflict of laws is that it is concerned with almost every branch of private law. "There is a sweep and range in it which is almost lyric in its completeness. It is the fugal music of law."[17] It is "one of the most baffling subjects of legal science", said the distinguished American judge Cardozo J.,[18] who also remarked on another occasion that "the average judge, when confronted by a problem in the conflict of laws, feels almost completely lost, and, like a drowning man, will grasp at a straw."[19] "The realm of the conflict of laws", said an American writer, "is a dismal swamp filled with quaking quagmires, and inhabited by learned but eccentric professors who theorise about mysterious matters in a strange and incomprehensible jargon."[20] Although the conflict of laws is highly controversial, the number of permutations and combinations arising out of any given set of facts is limited, as is the number of possible solutions. In any given case, the choice of law depends ultimately on considerations of reason, convenience and utility: e.g. how will the proposed choice of law work in practice, not only in this case, but also in similar cases in which a similar choice may reasonably be made? In the conflict of laws, to a

1–012

---

[16] *Spiliada Maritime Corp v Cansulex Ltd* [1987] A.C. 460 at 477; *Adams v Cape Industries Plc* [1990] Ch 433; *Airbus Industrie GIE v Patel* [1999] 1 A.C. 119. For a discussion of the doctrine of comity, see below, at para.19–008.

[17] Baty, *Polarized Law* (Stevens and Haynes, London, 1914), p.5.

[18] *Paradoxes of Legal Science* (Columbia University Press, New York 1928), p.67.

[19] Cited in Cook, *Logical and Legal Bases of the Conflict of Laws* (Harvard University Press, Cambridge MA, 1942), p.152.

[20] Prosser. (1953) 51 Mich.L.Rev. 959 at 971.

greater extent than in most other subjects, there is much to be learnt from the way in which similar problems have been solved in other countries with an historical and cultural background and legal tradition similar to our own. Hence no apology is needed for the occasional citation of Scottish, American and Commonwealth cases, even in a textbook for students.

THE TECHNIQUE OF THE SUBJECT

1–013   If you are learning to ride a bicycle, you gain little benefit from abstract instruction in matters of technique given before you have actually handled the machine. The same may be true of the conflict of laws; and the analogy has its comforting aspect, in that, once familiar with its workings, you wonder why the technique once seemed so intimidating. But there are some matters which require at least a preliminary airing at this stage, using a commercial illustration:

> A contract is made in Italy under which an English company will supply material to be used by the Italian party at its manufacturing plant in Belgium. The material supplied, it is claimed, is substandard, and the Italian company wishes to claim damages against the English supplier. Can the action be heard in the English courts? What law will be applied?

In tackling these questions, the conflict of laws uses legal categories and "localising" elements or "connecting factors".[21] On the facts of this problem, potential connecting factors include: to which country the parties belong; where the contract was entered into; where the legal duties it created, of making and delivering goods, were to be carried out.

Those factors may be of differing strength and may be allocated differing degrees of importance: for example, in these days of easy communication and electronic commerce it matters little where a contract is made. But the existence of the connecting factors makes it possible to devise rules which make sense of the infinite variety of possible fact-situations and discover to which country an issue "belongs". The rules will identify the legal category into which the issues fall (performance or breach of contract) and the connecting factor, or sometimes factors, appropriate to that category.

1–014   Typical rules of the conflict of laws state that succession to immovables is governed by the law of the country in which the property is situated (often referred to by the Latin expression *lex situs*)[22]; that the formal validity of a marriage is governed by the law of the place of celebration; and that capacity to marry is governed by the law of each party's antenuptial domicile. In these

---

[21] This expression (first suggested by Falconbridge) is the English equivalent of the French and German technical terms, respectively, "*point de rattachement*" and "*Anknüpfungspunkt*".

[22] An attempt (not wholly successful) has been made in this book to avoid unnecessary Latinisms, but they pervade much of the literature and are current tools in international debate. The principal expressions the reader may encounter are: *lex causae*, the law (usually but not necessarily foreign) which governs the question; *lex fori*, the domestic law of the forum, i.e. (if the forum is English) English law; *lex domicilii* (law of the domicile); *lex patriae* (law of the nationality); *lex loci contractus* (law of the place where a contract is made); *lex loci solutionis* (law of the place where a contract is to be performed or where a debt is to be paid); *lex loci delicti* (law of the place where a tort is committed); and *lex loci celebrationis* (law of the place where a marriage is celebrated).

examples, the categories are succession to immovables, formal validity of marriage and capacity to marry, and the connecting factors are situation, place of celebration and domicile.

In the example above, the connecting factors relevant to the jurisdictional issue will be that the defendant company has its "domicile" in England, and that the relevant obligation under the contract was to be performed principally in Belgium. In the choice of law context, the fact that the defendant's central administration is located in England may prove determinative. The reader will be able to give a fuller answer in due course; what is important here is the way in which connecting factors are used.

THE NEED TO PLEAD AND PROVE FOREIGN LAW

It is necessary at this point to introduce some features of English civil procedure **1–015** which complicate, even to some extent undermine, that part of the conflict of laws process by which the applicable law is chosen, the choice of law process.

It is a general principle of English procedure that in the pleadings, the documents which state the claimant's and defendant's position and so identify the issues in dispute, the parties plead only facts and not law. It is for the court, once the facts have been found, to apply the law; and "the law" means the law which the court knows, English law. Prima facie, therefore, even if the facts indicate the presence of foreign elements, the court will apply English law. If either party wishes the court to apply foreign law, it must say so in the pleadings. In that sense the possible relevance of foreign law is asserted amongst the pleaded facts, rather than argued as a point of law.[23]

The implications of this are that the rules of choice of law, that a certain issue is to be governed by a specified foreign law (for example, where the parties were at the time the contract was made), apply only if one or other of the parties chooses to raise the point in the pleadings. Application of the choice of law rules is, to a striking extent, "voluntary"; by remaining silent, the parties can avoid their application.[24] Shocking in theory, this result is perhaps less significant in practice: the nature of the dispute is likely to be such that the application of foreign law will be to the advantage of one party, who will take pains to plead it. If the application of foreign law has no advantage to either party, it will not feature and the case will, in practical effect, not be a case in the conflict of laws.

There is one statutory, and largely forgotten, exception to this principle. If a case is governed by the law of some "British territory", the court has power under the British Law Ascertainment Act 1859 to order that law to be ascertained in the manner prescribed in the Act, and has sometimes exercised this power on its own motion although the foreign law was not pleaded.[25]

---

[23] The origins of this rule are early: *Fremoult v Dedire* (1718) 1 P.Wms. 429; *Mostyn v Fabrigas* (1774) 1 Cowp. 161 at 174; *Nelson v Bridport* (1845) 8 Beav. 527. For a comparative study, see Hartley, "Pleading and proof of foreign law: the major European systems compared" (1996) 45 I.C.L.Q. 271.

[24] See Fentiman, *Foreign Law in English Courts* (Oxford University Press: Oxford, 1998); Geeroms, *Foreign Law in Civil Litigation* (Oxford University Press: Oxford, 2004).

[25] *Topham v Duke of Portland* (1863) 1 D.J. & S. 517.

1–016 However, that is not the end of the matter. If foreign law is pleaded, the English court is invited to apply law of which it is ignorant. English courts take judicial notice of the law of England and of "notorious" facts, but not of foreign law. An appellate court which has jurisdiction to determine appeals from the courts of several countries takes judicial notice of the laws of any of those countries when it hears an appeal from a court in one of them: so, the Supreme Court of the United Kingdom, when hearing an English appeal, takes judicial notice of Scots law,[26] and when hearing a Scottish appeal, takes judicial notice of the law of Northern Ireland[27] and of England. In other cases, foreign law must be proved (unless of course it is admitted).

A party seeking to rely on foreign law has, therefore, to produce evidence of the content of that foreign law. In this sense, too, foreign law is a matter of "fact" and has to be proved like any other fact. Here there is one more, rather startling, rule of practice: in the absence of proof to the contrary, the English court will assume that foreign law is the same as English law.[28] Foreign law must be both pleaded and proved before the court will do other than apply the familiar rules of internal English law. An English court will not conduct its own researches into foreign law. As the Court of Appeal put it in *Macmillan Inc v Bishopgate Investment Trust Plc (No.4)*[29]:

> "... the evidence of expert witnesses is necessary for the court to find that foreign law is different from English law. In the absence of such evidence, or if the judge[30] is unpersuaded by it, then he must resolve the issue by reference to English law, even if according to the rules of private international law the issue is governed by the foreign law."

No precise or comprehensive answer can be given to the question as to who, for this purpose, is a competent expert. A foreign judge or legal practitioner is of course always competent. But in civil proceedings there is no longer any rule of law (if indeed there ever was) that the expert witness must have practised, or at least be entitled to practise, in the foreign country.[31]

1–017 A witness may be competent, though his or her expertise is not that of a lawyer as such: any person who, by virtue of a profession or calling, has acquired a practical knowledge of foreign law may be a competent witness. Diplomatic and consular officers,[32] academic lawyers,[33] a bishop,[34] merchants and a bank

---

[26] *Elliot v Joicey* [1935] A.C. 209 at 236; *MacShannon v Rockware Glass Ltd* [1978] A.C. 795.

[27] *Cooper v Cooper* (1888) 13 App.Cas. 88. The question whether a similar rule applied to the Privy Council was noted but not resolved in *Oakely v Osiris Trustees Ltd* [2008] UKPC 2.

[28] This is how the courts state the matter. Fentiman cogently argues (p.147) that "to speak of [a presumption of similarity] at all, rather than admitting that English law applies as the *lex causae* where no other is proved, may rest on a conceptual mistake".

[29] Reported *sub nom MCC Proceeds Inc v Bishopsgate Investment Trust plc (No.4)* [1999] C.L.C. 417 at para.10

[30] Questions of foreign law, once decided by the jury are now reserved to the judge: Senior Courts (formerly Supreme Court) Act 1981 s.69(5).

[31] See the Civil Evidence Act 1972 s.4(1).

[32] *Lacon v Higgins* (1822) Dowl. & Ry. N.P. 38; *In the Goods of Dost Aly Khan* (1880) 6 P.D. 6.

[33] *Brailey v Rhodesia Consolidated Ltd* [1910] 2 Ch. 95 (Reader in Roman-Dutch Law to the Council of Legal Education); *McCabe v McCabe* [1994] 1 F.L.R. 410 (Professor in the School of Oriental and African Studies, giving evidence on Ghanaian customary law).

[34] *Sussex Peerage Case* (1844) 11 Cl. & F. 85.

manager[35] have all been held competent. Witnesses such as bishops, merchants and bank managers will, of course, be regarded as experts only in that part of the foreign law with which they are bound, by virtue of their profession or calling, to be familiar.

In *Macmillan Inc v Bishopgate Investment Trust Plc (No.4)* the Court of Appeal summarised the functions of the expert witness as being (1) to inform the English court of the relevant contents of the foreign law; identifying statutes or other legislation and explaining where necessary the foreign court's approach to their construction; (2) to identify judgments or other authorities, explaining what status they have as sources of the foreign law[36]; and (3) where there is no authority directly in point, to assist the English judge in making a finding as to what the foreign court's ruling would be were the issue to arise for decision there. The witness is there to predict the likely decision of a foreign court, not to press upon the English judge the witness's personal views as to what the foreign law might be.[37] Although matters of foreign law are issues of fact, they are factual issues "of a peculiar kind".[38]

The judge's role is not as passive as it may be in the case of issues of fact in the stricter sense. The foreign law, for example the law of an American state, may be in the English language, and it may make use of concepts and patterns of legal thought very similar to those of English law. In such a case, the English judge is entitled to make a legal input, using knowledge of the common law and of the rules of statutory construction. Unless the evidence shows that the foreign rules of construction are different, the English court interprets a foreign statute according to the English rules. If the expert witness advances an interpretation of a familiar concept which is "extravagant" or "impossible" the judge may decline to accept it.[39] More generally, if there is a conflict between the evidence of expert witnesses (as there may well be, the experts called by each side presenting differing opinions), the judge must look at the foreign material cited and form a judgment as best he or she may.[40]

---

[35] *Vander Donkt v Thellusson* (1849) 8 C.B. 812; *De Beeche v South American Stores Ltd* [1935] A.C. 148. But the court may refuse to admit the evidence of such a witness where that of a qualified lawyer is readily available: *Direct Winters Transport Ltd v Duplate Canada* (1962) 32 D.L.R. (2d) 278.

[36] For the weight to be given to foreign case law, see e.g. *Beatty v Beatty* [1924] 1 K.B. 807; *Re Annesley* [1926] Ch. 692; *Bankers and Shippers Insurance Co. of New York v Liverpool Marine & General Insurance Co Ltd* (1926) 24 Ll. L. Rep. 85; *Callwood v Callwood* [1960] A.C. 659; *In the Estate of Fuld (No. 3)* [1968] P. 675 at 701–702. Where foreign decisions conflict, the court may be asked to decide between them, even although in the foreign country the question still remains to be authoritatively settled: *Re Duke of Wellington* [1947] Ch. 506; *Breen v Breen* [1964] P. 144.

[37] *G. & H. Montage GmbH v Irvani* [1990] 1 W.L.R. 667; *Macmillan Inc v Bishopgate Investment Trust Plc (No.4)* at para.23.

[38] *Parkasho v Singh* [1968] P. 233 per Cairns J. at p.250. The implications of this for the role of the Court of Appeal, normally reluctant to differ from the trial judge on matters of fact, were discussed in *MacMillan Inc v Bishopgate Investment Trust Plc (No.4)*, citing Fentiman, above at pp.201–202.

[39] *Buerger v New York Life Assurance Co* (1927) 96 L.J.K.B. 930; *A/S Tallina Laevauhisus v Estonian State Steamship Line* (1947) 80 Ll.L.Rep. 99 at 108; *Macmillan Inc v Bishopgate Investment Trust Plc (No.4)*, above.

[40] *Bumper Development Corp v Commissioner of Police for the Metropolis* [1991] 1 W.L.R. 1362 (where the judge had wrongly rejected the agreed views of the expert witnesses).

1–018   There are three statutes and one international convention which provide alternative modes of establishing foreign law.[41] One statute, the British Law Ascertainment Act 1859, has already been mentioned; and a similar procedure exists as between parties to the European Convention on Information on Foreign Law, signed in 1968.[42] It is not well-known and is not used to obtain information for use in English cases. The certification of foreign law by a foreign authority, with no cross-examination of the author of the certificate, does not fit English procedures. The Convention is more attractive in civil law systems where typically the judge is responsible for ascertaining the content of foreign law and determining its application to the facts.[43]

By the Evidence (Colonial Statutes) Act 1907, copies of laws made by the legislature of any "British possession",[44] if purporting to be printed by its government printer, can be received in evidence in the United Kingdom without proof that the copies were so printed.

More significant is the Civil Evidence Act 1972. Section 4(2)–(5) of that Act provide that where any question of foreign law has been determined in civil or criminal proceedings at first instance in the High Court, the Crown Court, or in any appeal therefrom, or in the Privy Council on appeal from any court outside the United Kingdom, then any finding made or decision given on that question is admissible in evidence in any civil proceedings, and the foreign law shall be taken to be in accordance with that finding or decision unless the contrary is proved. The section does not apply if the subsequent proceedings are before a court which can take judicial notice of the foreign law. Thus a determination on a point of Scots law by the High Court or the Court of Appeal is not even prima facie evidence of that point in subsequent proceedings before the House of Lords. Nor is the determination prima facie binding if there are conflicting findings or decisions on the same question.

1–019   It may be that the harmonisation of law in the European Union may one day affect the English common law approach to proof of foreign law. In July 2007, at the time of the adoption of the Regulation known as "Rome II" on the law applicable to non-contractual obligations, the Commission issued a Statement[45]:

> "The Commission, being aware of the different practices followed in the Member States as regards the treatment of foreign law, will publish at the latest four years after the entry into force of the 'Rome II' Regulation and in any event as soon as it is available a horizontal study on the application of foreign law in civil and commercial matters by the courts of the Member States, having regard to the aims of the Hague Programme. It is also prepared to take appropriate measures if necessary."

---

[41] See also the possibilities presented by the European Judicial Network for informal consultation with foreign judges: *B.C. v A. C.* [2005] EWCA Civ 68, per Thorpe L.J. at para.44.

[42] Any information obtained under the Convention is not binding on the requesting court.

[43] Some countries have a mixed system; e.g. the Chinese Act on Application of Law in Civil Relationships with Foreign Contacts 2010 provides for the judge to find the content of foreign law unless the foreign law has been chosen as applicable by the parties; in the latter case the parties must prove the content of the chosen law.

[44] i.e. "any part of Her Majesty's dominions exclusive of the United Kingdom": s.1(3).

[45] [2007] OJ L 199/49. The matter is in the work programme of the Hague Conference on Private International Law as a global as opposed to a European approach is seen as preferable.

Some Technical Problems

In this book, some matters of fundamental importance and great difficulty have been reserved for discussion at the end, rather than at the beginning as they are in some other books. The reason for this treatment is that it would be daunting to the reader to embark on an examination of these matters before he or she knows enough about the subject to understand all their implications. Its disadvantage is that the reader is left in blissful ignorance of some fundamental matters until nearly the end of the book. Enough will be said here, by way of orientation, to enable the nature of the problems to be identified.

Characterisation

It has already been explained that the technique of the conflict of laws makes **1–020** much use of legal categories: before the correct connecting factors can be identified we need to know into which legal category the facts of the case, or the particular issues, are properly placed. In the international context of our subject, this process of categorisation or characterisation presents a special problem.

The nature of this problem can best be shown by two examples. Suppose that a person buys a ticket in London for a train journey to Edinburgh, and is injured in a railway accident in Scotland. Is the passenger's cause of action against the railway company for breach of contract, in which case English law might apply, as the law governing the contract, or for tort, in which case Scots law will apply? By which law, English or Scots, is this question to be answered? Or suppose that a marriage is celebrated in England between two French people domiciled in France. The marriage is valid by English law but invalid by French law because neither party has the consent of his or her parents as required by French law. If this rule of French law relates to formalities of marriage, it will not apply to a marriage celebrated in England; but if it relates to capacity to marry, it will invalidate the marriage of a French couple. By which law, French or English, is the nature of the French rule to be determined? These and other similar problems are discussed in a later chapter.[46]

Renvoi

We have already seen that where the significant elements in a case are divided **1–021** between two countries, e.g. France and England, the case is a case in the conflict of laws for any court in which it is litigated. If the English court applies French law, because it thinks that the French elements are more significant than the English ones, it may find that a French court would apply English law, because it thinks that the English elements are the more significant. The question then arises, does "French law" mean French domestic law, or does it mean the whole of French law, including its rules of the conflict of laws? This is the notorious problem of *renvoi*, possibly leading in this instance to a remission from French law to English law. If we change the facts and assume that the significant

---

[46] Below, at para.18–002.

elements are divided, not between England and France, but between France and Germany, then an English court, if it applies French law, may find that a French court would apply German law. This also is a *renvoi* problem, but it leads not to a remission from French to English law, but to a transmission from French to German law, and possibly to a further reference from German to English or French law.

Suppose, for example, that a British citizen domiciled in France dies intestate leaving movables in England. In order to determine who are his next of kin, an English court will apply French law because he was domiciled in France; but it may find that a French court would apply English law because he was a British citizen. If the intestate had been a German national instead of a British citizen, a French court might have applied German law. The problem is whether French law means French domestic law, or the whole of French law including its rules of the conflict of laws. If it means the latter, there may be a remission to English law in the first of these cases, and a transmission to German law in the second.

It may be said at once that in the vast majority of cases English courts interpret their reference to foreign law to mean its domestic rules only. But there are a few exceptional cases, to be discussed in a later chapter,[47] in which the reference has been interpreted to mean the whole of foreign law, including its rules of the conflict of laws.

The incidental question

1–022   The nature of this problem also can best be shown by two examples. Suppose that a testator domiciled in France gives movables in England to his "wife". The main question here is one of succession to the movables; and it is governed by French law, because the testator was domiciled in France. But a subsidiary or incidental question may arise as to the validity of the testator's marriage: should this question be referred to the English or the French rules of the conflict of laws relating to the validity of marriages? Or suppose that the English court has to determine the capacity of a domiciled Italian to contract a second marriage after obtaining a divorce from his first wife in Switzerland. The Swiss divorce is recognised as valid in England, but not in Italy. The main question here is the question of capacity to remarry, and it is governed by Italian law, because the husband was domiciled in Italy. The incidental question is the validity of the divorce: should this question be referred to the English or the Italian rules of the conflict of laws relating to the recognition of divorces?

The time factor

1–023   The conflict of laws deals primarily with the application of laws in space; but problems of time cannot altogether be ignored. In the conflict of laws, the time factor is significant in various situations. The most important of these is when there is a retrospective change in the applicable law after the events have happened which gave rise to the cause of action. Should the English court apply

---

[47] para.18–023.

the law as it was when the cause of action arose, or as it is at the date of the trial? This problem and others like it are also discussed in a later chapter.[48]

THE FUTURE OF THE SUBJECT

There is no doubt that in an era of globalisation our subject has a future, and one of growing importance.[49] This is reflected in the expanding membership of the specialist international body, the Hague Conference on Private International Law. For a century, the Hague Conference on Private International Law has had a leading role in the development of our subject.[50] Its title conceals the fact that it is an intergovernmental organisation, and not a "conference" in the more usual sense. It first met in 1893 under the leadership of T. C. M. Asser, a notable Dutch scholar, though it was the work of the Italian, Mancini, which first promoted the idea of such a meeting.

    1–024

The Hague Conference was originally very much a European, and a civil law, club. After an interruption in its activities from 1928 to 1951, it was revived and its present Statute declares it to have a permanent character, with the object of "the progressive unification of the rules of private international law".[51] The membership of the Conference is now much more representative of the various legal traditions, with a number of Eastern European countries and China representing the socialist legal tradition, with Australia, Canada, Cyprus, Ireland, Malta, New Zealand, the United Kingdom and the United States speaking from the common law perspective (though Cyprus, Ireland and the United Kingdom are bound to follow an agreed European Union line in negotiations), and with the Latin American countries taking a much more active role.

The significance of the work at The Hague lies primarily in the bridge it affords between common law and civil law traditions. Conventions drafted at The Hague and given statutory effect in the United Kingdom have made a significant contribution to the development of the English rules of the conflict of laws.

However, the work of the European Union is having an even greater impact on the English rules.[52] The provisions of the Treaty of Amsterdam on the "area of freedom, security and justice" have had particular importance. An Action Plan of the Council and Commission drawn up in 1998[53] suggested that within two years of entry into force of the Treaty of Amsterdam in 1999, work on the revision of the Brussels and Lugano Conventions should have been completed, a legal

    1–025

---

[48] para.18–048.

[49] See Harris and McClean in Hayton (ed.), *Law's Future(s)* (Hart Publishing, Oxford, 2000), Ch.9; McLachlan, (2004) 120 L.Q.R. 580.

[50] See Offerhaus, (1959) 16 *Annuaire Suisse de droit international* 27; van Hoogstraten, (1963) 12 I.C.L.Q. 148; North, (1981) 6 Dalhousie L.J. 417; McClean, (1992) 233 *Recueil des Cours* 271.

[51] Statute, Art.1.

[52] For the development of the Community's role in private international law, see Schockweiler in Borras (ed), *E Pluribus Unum; Liber Amicorum Georges A L Droz* (Martinus Nijhoff, The Hague, 1996), 391; Lowe, (2003) 56 *Current Legal Problems* 439; Borras, (2005) 317 Hague *Recueil des Cours* 313.

[53] Action Plan of the Council and Commission on how best to implement the provisions of the Treaty of Amsterdam establishing an area of freedom, security and justice, adopted on 7 December 1998 [1999] OJ C19/1.

instrument on the law applicable to non-contractual obligations drawn up ("Rome II"), and necessary revisions of the Rome Convention made. It was 10 years before those tasks were completed: the Brussels Convention has been converted, with improvements, into the Brussels I Regulation)[54]; the Lugano Convention has been revised to take account of those improvements[55]; this has been complemented by a Regulation on jurisdiction and the recognition and enforcement of judgments in matrimonial matters and in matters of parental responsibility ("Brussels II") agreed in 2000[56] and replaced by a revised Regulation agreed in 2003 ("Brussels IIa")[57]; "Rome II' has duly appeared, to be followed by "Rome I", replacing the Rome Convention. A Regulation dealing with maintenance has been agreed.[58] Other initiatives have led to a Regulation on taking evidence[59] and a revised Regulation on the service of judicial and extra-judicial documents in other Member States,[60] and the introduction of the European Payments Order[61] and the European Small Claims Procedure.[62] Many of these initiatives inevitably draw on work already done by the Hague Conference on Private International Law. The United Kingdom has a choice as to whether to "opt-in" to some proposed Regulations, and has chosen not to do so in respect of some other developments, as to the law applicable to divorce, and the private international law aspects of matrimonial property régimes and of succession and wills.

These European developments are referred to at appropriate places throughout the book. The reader will note not only the extent to which topics are now covered by legislation derived from European sources but also the extent to which approaches and practices traditional in common law countries are being supplanted.

A ROAD MAP

1–026   Following this introductory chapter, two chapters are devoted to necessary preliminary matters. Chapter 2 examines the complexities that lie behind seemingly simple statements that an individual or a company is English or French, and Chapter 3 deals with a number of doctrines which may enable the English courts to refuse to apply a rule of foreign law.

Questions of jurisdiction, undoubtedly the growth area of this subject, are treated next in Chapters 4 and 5; there are two sets of jurisdiction rules used by the English courts, and each requires separate treatment. Closely related to issues

---

[54] Council Regulation No 44/2001.
[55] See Council Decision 712/07.
[56] Council Regulation No. 1347/2000.
[57] Council Regulation No. 2201/2003.
[58] Council Regulation (EC) No 4/2009 of 18 December 2008 on jurisdiction, applicable law, recognition and enforcement of decisions and cooperation in matters relating to maintenance obligations, [2009] O.J. L 7/1.
[59] CCouncil Regulation No.1206/2001.
[60] European Parliament and Council Regulation 1393/2007, replacing the earlier Council Regulation No. 1348/2000.
[61] European Parliament and Council Regulation 1896/2006.
[62] European Parliament and Council Regulation 861/2007.

of jurisdiction are those relating to state immunity and the recognition and enforcement of foreign judgments and arbitral awards, the subject of Chapters 6 and 7.

Chapters 8 to 10 inclusive deal with international family law: the conflict of laws rules relating to marriage, matrimonial causes, the care of children, and issues of legitimacy and adoption.

Choice of law rules relating to claims in contract and "non-contractual   **1–027**
obligations" principally those in tort, both the subject of an EU Regulation, are the subject of Chapters 11 and 12. Four chapters deal with property issues, a relatively static area of the subject: Chapter 13 examines issues of title to property, Chapter 14 matrimonial property, Chapter 15 the rules of succession and the administration of estates, and Chapter 16 the choice of law rules as to trusts.

The last three chapters invite the reader to stand back from the rules dealing with specific topics and to consider some issues which concern the working of the conflict of laws as a whole: the conduct of international litigation, the technical problems outlined earlier in this introduction, and finally the theoretical basis and methodology of this most fascinating of all legal subjects.

CHAPTER 2

PERSONAL CONNECTING FACTORS

In the last chapter, a number of examples referred to "English" or "French"   **2–001**
parties, and the reader will have understood those terms as referring to people
who, in some sense "belong to" or are connected to England or France.
International travel means that some individuals move between countries very
frequently, and while they may at all times regard themselves as English or
French they have connections, stronger or weaker in character, with a range of
countries. An illustration will make this clear:

> Carlos is a Venezuelan businessman working in the oil industry. He has dealings with Shell,
> which has offices in London and in the Netherlands. He flies to Europe for lengthy
> negotiations with Shell executives. Suppose that his aircraft is diverted from its intended direct
> route to Amsterdam by an incident of 'air-rage'[1] to Heathrow for the malefactors to be
> deplaned; it stays there for 45 minutes before resuming its journey. Or, he had all along
> booked via Heathrow, and he has one and a half hours in the transit lounge before his onward
> flight to Amsterdam. Or, he has two days in London, having preliminary discussions with
> Shell executives based in London.
> He arrives in Amsterdam and spends a fortnight in a hotel. Or two months in an apartment
> hotel. Or six months in a company flat. Or, as his brother works in the Brazilian embassy in
> The Hague, he stays for those periods with his brother and sister-in-law.
> Suppose further that he arranges to stay on in the Netherlands because of an economic
> downturn in Venezuela; or because he fears arrest there for some political offence; or because
> he wishes to marry a Dutch girl. Ten years later, he is still in the Netherlands.

Each variation of the basic facts indicates a link of a certain strength between
Carlos ("a Venezuelan") and England or the Netherlands. At some point, the
strength of these links may be such that he may no longer be thought of, by others
or even by himself, as Venezuelan at all. The permutations are of course endless,
but if we are to have a manageable system of rules we have to make use of a
limited number of categories, which are explored in this chapter.

---

[1] Perhaps as in *Li v Quruishi*, 780 F Supp 117 (EDNY, 1992) where a drunken passenger exposed
himself and urinated over some of his fellow-passengers.

RESIDENCE

2–002   The most basic link between an individual and a country is mere physical presence, even if it be for 45 minutes spent wholly in an aircraft parked on an airport apron. Though factually clear-cut, it creates so limited a link as to have little or no significance in the conflict of laws. We will, however, hear rather more of "residence". Residence is basically a question of fact; in some contexts it means very little more than physical presence. But it does mean something more, for a person passing through a country as a traveller is clearly not resident there.[2] If someone becomes resident in a country, the link of residence may remain during brief periods of absence.[3]

It is difficult to be more specific, for a great deal depends on the context in which the term "residence" is used. In a case which held that university students were "resident" in their university town for electoral registration purposes,[4] Widgery L.J. pointed out that, "In any seaside town in the summer the population divides itself into the residents who live there all the year round and the visitors who merely come for a period"; but the visitors' hotel-keeper would expect those visitors to use a room called the "residents' lounge". In the same way, "residence" means different things for different legal purposes.[5] It may be that a person will relatively easily be held resident in a country if the issue is one of the jurisdiction of that country's courts,[6] but less easily if the context is one of residence during a fiscal year.[7] Even in a single context, "the pattern of, and reasons for, time being spent in the UK and elsewhere may be infinitely various. Decided cases illustrate a great variety of examples, and the result of one case cannot normally be used as a guide to how another should be decided, even if the two have some factors in common".[8]

ORDINARY RESIDENCE

2–003   Ordinary residence "connotes residence in a place with some degree of continuity and apart from accidental or temporary absences."[9] "If it has any definite meaning I should say it means according to the way in which a man's life is usually ordered."[10] It refers to a person's abode in a particular place or country which he has adopted voluntarily and for settled purposes, as part of the regular order of his or her life for the time being, whether of short or long duration.[11]

---

[2] *Matalon v Matalon* [1952] P. 233.
[3] *Sinclair v Sinclair* [1968] P. 189.
[4] *Fox v Stirk* [1970] 2 Q.B. 463.
[5] McClean, (1962) 111 I.C.L.Q. 1153.
[6] As in para.9 of the Civil Jurisdiction and Judgments Order 2001; see below at para.4–016.
[7] *Levene v IRC* [1928] A.C. 217; even there, relatively brief visits were held to amount to residence.
[8] *Grace v HMRC* [2009] EWCA Civ 1082 at [3] per Lloyd L.J.
[9] *Levene v IRC* [1928] A.C. 217 at 225, per Lord Cave.
[10] *Levene v IRC* [1928] A.C. 217 at 232, per Lord Warrington of Clyffe.
[11] *R. v Barnet LBC, Ex p. Nilish Shah* [1983] 2 A.C. 309. But see *R v West Middlesex University Hospital* [2008] EWHC 855 (Admin.) (2008) 11 C.C.L. Rep. 358 for the meaning of ordinary residence for the purposes of the National Health Service Acts of 1997 and 2006.

Ordinary residence can be changed in a day,[12] but there is no reason, on appropriate facts, for a person not to be held to be ordinarily resident in more than one country at the same time. Thus in *Inland Revenue Commissioners v Lysaght*,[13] a man whose home was in the Republic of Ireland, and who came to England for one week in every month for business reasons, during which time he stayed in an hotel, was held to be resident and ordinarily resident in England for income tax purposes. But clearly he was also resident and ordinarily resident in the Republic.

It has been said that a child of tender years "who cannot decide for himself where to live" is ordinarily resident in his or her parents' matrimonial home, and that this ordinary residence cannot be changed by one parent without the consent of the other. If the parents are living apart and the child is, by agreement between them, living with one of them, the child is resident in the home of that parent and that ordinary residence is not changed merely because the other parent takes the child away from that home.[14]

HABITUAL RESIDENCE

Habitual residence has long been a favourite expression of the Hague Conference on Private International Law. It appears in many Hague Conventions and therefore in English statutes giving effect to them; but it is increasingly used in other statutes as well. No definition of habitual residence has ever been included in a Hague Convention; this has been a matter of deliberate policy, the aim being to leave the notion free from technical rules which can produce rigidity and inconsistencies as between different legal systems. The expression is not to be treated as a term of art but according to the ordinary and natural meaning of the two words it contains.[15] However, there is a regrettable tendency of the courts, despite their insistence that they are not dealing with a term of art, to develop rules as to when habitual residence may and may not be established. The Law Commission has spoken of the "allegedly undeveloped state" of habitual residence as a legal concept, citing, in particular, uncertainties as to the place of intention and as to the length of time required for residence to become habitual.[16]

Although the courts have in the past sometimes taken a different view,[17] it seems that there is no real distinction between the two concepts of habitual residence and ordinary residence; or at least, they share "a common core of

2–004

---

[12] *Macrae v Macrae* [1949] P. 397 at 403, per Somervell L.J.

[13] [1928] A.C. 234. It would be unfair to blame the House of Lords for this extraordinary decision, for they felt constrained to hold that a finding by the Special Commissioners was one of fact and so could not be disturbed on appeal.

[14] *Re P. (G.E.) (An Infant)* [1965] Ch. 568, 585–586.

[15] *Re J (A Minor) (Abduction)* [1990] 2 A.C. 562; *Re M (Minors) (Residence Order: Jurisdiction)* [1993] 1 F.L.R. 495; Clive, 1997 Jur. Rev. 137. See also Resolution (72)1 of the Committee of Ministers of the Council of Europe on the Standardisation of the Legal Concepts of "Domicile" and "Residence" Annex, r.9.

[16] *The Law of Domicile* (Law Com. No. 168), paras 3.5–3.8.

[17] *Cruse v Chittum* [1974] 2 All E.R. 940 at 943; *Oundjian v Oundjian* (1979) 1 F.L.R. 198 at 202–203.

meaning".[18] So the test to be applied in this context will again be that of a person's abode in a particular country which he or she has adopted voluntarily and for settled purposes as part of the regular order of life for the time being[19]; the burden of proof being on the party alleging the change.[20] However, it should be noted that the House of Lords has held that habitual residence "may have a different meaning in different statutes according to their context and purpose."[21]

2–005 It is consistent with that approach to hold that habitual residence cannot be acquired in a single day, as an appreciable period of time[22] and a settled purpose are required.[23] For many years it was thought that to acquire habitual residence, a person's residence must be lawful,[24] but the House of Lords in *Mark v Mark*[25] has confirmed that it is indeed possible to acquire habitual residence, at least for tax purposes, even though the residence is not lawful.[26] The person must live in the relevant country for a period which shows that the residence has become habitual[27]; the length of that period is not fixed; it must depend on the circumstances.[28] Habitual residence can, however, in appropriate circumstances, be lost in a day.[29] Habitual residence may continue during temporary absences,[30]

---

[18] *Nessa v Chief Adjudication Officer* [1999] 1 W.L.R. 1937. Lord Slynn reserved the question whether the terms were always synonymous; each might take a shade of meaning from the context in which it was used; but the Court of Appeal has held in *Ikimi v Ikimi (Divorce: Habitual Residence)* [2001] EWCA Civ. 873; [2002] Fam 72 that the two concepts are synonymous where family law statutes are concerned; and in the House of Lords case of *Mark v Mark* [2005] UKHL 42; [2006] 1 A.C. 98, Baroness Hale at para.33 stated that "It is common ground that habitual residence and ordinary residence are interchangeable concepts...".

[19] i.e.the test adopted in *R. v Barnet LBC, Ex p. Nilish Shah* [1983] 2 A.C. 309 at 344; *Kapur v Kapur* [1984] F.L.R. 920.

[20] *Re R (Wardship: Child Abduction)* [1992] 2 F.L.R. 481 at 487.

[21] *Mark v Mark* [2005] UKHL 42; [2006] 1 A.C. 98, per Baroness Hale at para.15.

[22] In *Ikimi v Ikimi (Divorce: Habitual Residence)* [2001] EWCA Civ. 873; [2002] Fam 72, residence for 161 days in the year was sufficient in the circumstances for the acquisition of habitual residence; whereas 71 days in *Armstrong v Armstrong* [2003] EWHC 777 (Fam); [2003] 2 F.L.R. 375 was not. cf. *Re A (Abduction; Habitual Residence)* [2009] EWCA Civ 1021; [2010] 1 F.L.R. 1146; (7–8 weeks sufficed; emphasis that movement between different EU countries).

[23] *Re J (A Minor) (Abduction)* [1990] 2 A.C. 562, obiter as the issue in the case was the loss rather than the acquisition of habitual residence; *Re M. (Minors) (Residence Order: Jurisdiction)* [1993] 1 F.L.R. 495.

[24] *R. v Barnet LBC, Ex p. Shah* [1983] 2 A.C. 309 at 343, Lord Scarman refusing unlawful ordinary residence on the grounds of public policy.

[25] *Mark v Mark* [2005] UKHL 42; [2006] 1 A.C. 98 at para.36.

[26] *Mark v Mark* [2005] UKHL 42. Baroness Hale did, however, leave open the caveat that a person's residence may need to be lawful for other purposes, for example, entitlement to State benefit. See *R v Secretary of State for Health* [2009] EWCA Civ 225; [2010] 1 W.L.R. 279 (entitlement to health services; failed asylum seeker held not ordinarily resident).

[27] *Nessa v Chief Adjudication Officer* [1999] 1 W.L.R. 1937.

[28] *Nessa v Chief Adjudication Officer* [1999] 1 W.L.R. 1937 citing the dictum of Butler-Sloss L.J. in *Re A.F. (a Minor) (Child Abduction)* [1992] 1 F.C.R. 269 at 277 that "a month can be ... an appreciable period of time".

[29] *Re M (Minors) (Residence Order: Jurisdiction)* [1993] 1 F.L.R. 495 at 500; *Al Habtoor v Fotheringham* [2001] EWCA Civ. 186; [2001] 1 F.C.R 385.

[30] *Oundjian v Oundjian* (1979) 1 F.L.R. 198 (habitual residence throughout period of one year despite absences totalling 149 out of 365 days); *Re H (A Child) (Abduction: Habitual Residence: Consent)* [2000] 2 F.L.R. 294; *C v FC (Brussels II: Freestanding Application for Parental Responsibility)* [2004] 1 F.L.R. 317, where an absence of two years was not fatal to the continuance of habitual residence.

but in most contexts a person can be without any habitual residence[31]; or have more than one habitual residence at any one time.[32] However, it is important not to treat the test as if it were the language of a statute. That habitual residence should be "adopted voluntarily" is not usually an issue; but in *Breuning v Breuning*[33] it was held that the continued presence in England of someone who had no choice but to remain in England for medical treatment did not constitute habitual residence. The Court of Session has doubted whether the element of voluntariness is always needed, using as examples the mythical case of Robinson Crusoe and the real example of Nelson Mandela as a prisoner.[34]

Although the "settled intent" has been identified as one to take up long-term residence in the country concerned,[35] the better view seems to be that evidence of intention or purpose may be important in particular cases (e.g. in establishing habituation when the actual period or periods of residence have been short) but is not essential. If long-term residence is established in a new country, the habitual residence will be there even if the individual concerned lives in an exclusively expatriate group (as in a forces' base) which simulates ordinary life in the individual's home country.[36]

Habitual Residence of a child

It is obvious that a young child will not have the necessary settled intent or purpose required of an adult but will still be treated as having a habitual residence. In many cases, the habitual residence of a child whose parents do not live together will be that of whichever parent has custody of the child.[37] In many cases, parents may share custody, and the way in which the day-to-day care of the child is shared may be more significant in such cases; though the number of cross border cases of this type is small. The courts have regularly held that a child's habitual residence cannot be changed by the unilateral action of one parent and remains unchanged unless circumstances arise which quite independently point to a change in its habitual residence.[38] Where the parents do have a

2–006

---

[31] *Hack v Hack* (1976) 6 Fam. Law 177: "unless one led a nomadic life" one had to have a habitual residence somewhere; *Re J (A Minor) (Abduction)* [1990] 2 A.C. 562. In some contexts, a piece of legislation may only be workable if there is no possibility of a gap in habitual residence: *Nessa v Chief Adjudication Officer* [1999] 1 W.L.R. 1937; *W. and B. v H. (Child Abduction: Surrogacy)* [2002] 1 F.L.R. 1008.

[32] *Ikimi v Ikimi (Divorce: Habitual Residence)* [2001] EWCA Civ. 873; [2002] Fam 72; *Armstrong v Armstrong* [2003] EWHC 777 (Fam); [2003] 2 F.L.R. 375; *C. v F.C. (Brussels II: free-standing application for parental responsibility)* [2004] 1 F.L.R. 317; *Mark v Mark* [2005] UKHL 42; [2006] 1 A.C. 98.

[33] [2002] EWHC 236 (Fam), [2002] 1 F.L.R. 888.

[34] *Cameron v Cameron* 1996 S.C. 17.

[35] *A v A (Child Abduction) (Habitual Residence)* [1993] 2 F.L.R. 225 at 235.

[36] *Re A (Minors) (Abduction: Habitual Residence)* [1996] 1 W.L.R. 25 (US. serviceman in Iceland).

[37] *Re A (Abduction: Habitual Residence)* [1996] 1 W.L.R. 25.

[38] For example, *Re A (A Minor) (Wardship: Jurisdiction)* [1995] 1 F.L.R. 767 (child taken to Pakistan); *Re S (Custody: Habitual Residence)* [1998] A.C. 750; *B v D* [2008] EWHC 1246 (Fam). There is also a more limited provision in Family Law Act 1986 s.41 that (in effect) the removal of a child to another part of the United Kingdom without the consent of all those having the right to determine its place of residence does not change the child's habitual residence until the expiry of one year from the date of the removal or retention.

common habitual residence, the court has also held that: "[t]he question of habitual residence of a child is not always determinable by reference to the combined intention of the parties. It ultimately depends upon whether, in all the circumstances, it can properly and realistically be said that the child is ...habitually resident in England and Wales."[39] However, in *Greenwich LBC v S*[40] three children were held to be habitually resident in England even after two year's residence in Canada since parental authority was vested in the Local Authority who placed them in foster care, not in the aunt who cared for them. As can be seen, the case law on the habitual residence of children has a tendency to be contradictory,[41] and this contradiction can be seen in the cases that consider the habitual residence of a newborn baby.

In *B v H (Habitual Residence: Wardship)*[42]:

> A pregnant mother was tricked by her husband into travelling to Bangladesh where the baby was born. Eventually the mother managed to flee back to England where she applied to the English court for her baby to be made a ward of court. Jurisdiction depended on whether the child was habitually resident in England.[43]

Charles J. held that the baby was habitually resident in England (where it had never lived) following the line of authority[44] that one parent cannot unilaterally change the habitual residence of a child without the consent or acquiescence of the other parent with rights of custody, and that the mother was habitually resident in England. With regard to the habitual residence of the baby, he said[45]:

> "[I]n the case of an infant child and *a fortiori* a new born baby his ... abode ... which has been adopted for him ... voluntarily and for settled purposes is as a matter of fact that of his ... parents who have parental responsibility for the child and with whom he ... will live ... It is the settled intentions of the parents that render that 'residence' of the baby habitual."

2–007   Charles J. distinguished the case from earlier Court of Appeal decisions,[46] and held that the baby could not have intentions as to residence independently of its parents, and that if the mother and father were habitually resident in England at the time of the child's birth, then so too was the child. The result of this, rather tortuous, reasoning is that a child who was, at the date of the judgment, nearly two years old, having been born in Bangladesh and having lived there all her short life, was habitually resident in England and, along with her siblings, was made a ward of the English court.

On the other hand, in *W v H (Child Abduction: Surrogacy)*[47]:

---

[39] *A (A Child)* [2006] EWHC 3338 (Fam) per Sir Mark Potter at para.49.
[40] [2007] EWHC 820 (Fam); [2007] 2 F.L.R. 154.
[41] Rogerson (2000) 49 I.C.L.Q. 86 at 88; Schuz, [2002] C.F.L.Q. 1, who identifies that there are three models of approach within the case law: the dependency model, the parent rights model, and the child-centred model.
[42] [2002] 1 F.L.R. 388.
[43] Family Law Act 1986 ss.1(1)(d), 2(3) and 3(1).
[44] As cited by Black J. in *Re N (Abduction: Habitual Residence)* [2000] 2 F.L.R. 899 at 907F–909D.
[45] At paras 108 and 109.
[46] *Re M (A Minor) (Abduction: Habitual Residence)* [1996] 1 F.L.R. 887; *Al Habtoor v Fotheringham* [2001] 1 F.L.R 951; *Re J (A Minor) (Abduction: Custody Rights)* [1990] 2 A.C. 562 at 578H–579A.
[47] [2002] 1 F.L.R. 1008.

The relationship between an English surrogate mother and the Californian prospective parents broke down when they discovered that the mother was carrying twins, and the surrogate mother returned to England where she gave birth. The Californian couple applied under the Hague Convention on International Child Abduction for the summary return of the babies to the jurisdiction of the Californian court. The Convention could only apply if the twins had been habitually resident in California immediately before being brought to England.

Hedley J. reiterated that habitual residence was a question of fact and that each case must stand alone,[48] but that it is not possible for someone to acquire a habitual residence in one country when they remain physically present in another at all times, and that the habitual residence of a young child is determined by whoever has legal responsibility for the child. Therefore, on the particular facts of the case, the twins were not habitually resident anywhere.[49]

In two further cases the courts have refused to acknowledge the habitual residence of child as being in a country in which they have never resided. In *Re G (Children) (Abduction: Withdrawal of Proceedings, Acquiescence, Habitual Residence)*[50] the younger child had been born in England following an abduction of the older child from Canada; the court found the baby was habitually resident in England since he had not been resident anywhere else. However, in this case the baby was in the physical care of his mother who the court accepted was at the time of the birth habitually resident in England. Similarly, in *Re F (Abduction: Unborn Child)*[51] a child born in Israel was considered habitually resident there for the same reasons: not having been resident anywhere else and in the physical care of the mother who was habitually resident in Israel at the time of the birth.

In the absence of higher authority, these cases raise various questions. Is it possible for a newborn baby to have a habitual residence? If so, does this habitual residence depend on the habitual residence of the parents? Can a baby be habitually resident in a country where he or she is resident but where neither parent is habitually resident? If not, may the English court find itself in a position of being unable to protect a most vulnerable child?[52] These questions arise from the development of principles that the courts have sought to impose on the concept of habitual residence and highlight the problems associated with the use of a connecting factor that is designed to be a question of fact rather than a question of law.

2–008

---

[48] At para.23.

[49] This meant that the application under the Hague Convention failed. W then brought an action for the summary return of the twins, and in *W. and W. v H. (Child Abduction: Surrogacy) (No 2)* [2002] 2 F.L.R 252 the children were returned to California as the *forum conveniens* for their future to be decided.

[50] [2007] EWHC 2807 (Fam).

[51] [2006] EWHC 2199 (Fam); [2007] 1 F.L.R. 627.

[52] EU Council Regulation 2201/2003 has now introduced an alternative connecting factor for children where their habitual residence cannot be determined; see below, para.10–006.

European autonomous meaning

2–009   The connecting factor of habitual residence has also been widely adopted by the legislators of EU law, and the leading ECJ case of *Swaddling v Adjudication Officer*[53] has held that, in the context of social security law, the term has a Community-wide meaning, being where the person's "habitual centre of their interests is to be found."[54] More recently, the English courts have been called upon to adjudicate on the habitual residence of adults and children in the family law context under the Brussels IIa Regulation.[55] In the absence of direct ECJ authority, the English courts have turned to the *Borrás* explanatory report,[56] which describes habitual residence as "the place where the person had established, on a fixed basis, his permanent or habitual centre of interest with all the relevant facts being taken into account for the purpose of determining such residence."[57] It appears that, under the autonomous Europoean meaning in contrast to the English concept of habitual residence, even though a person may be resident in more than one country at any one time, they may only be habitually resident in one.[58] The length of time a person is resident in the country is a relevant factor but not a conclusive factor and it appears that there is no minimum period for the establishment of habitual residence.[59]

    The ECJ has begun to explore the habitual residence of a child in the context of the Brussels IIa regulation. In *Mercredi v Chaffe*[60] such residence corresponds to the place which reflects some degree of integration by the child in a social and family environment. The duration, regularity, conditions and reasons for the stay on the territory of a Member State and the family's move to that State, the child's nationality, the place and conditions of attendance at school, linguistic knowledge and the family and social relationships of the child in that State must be taken into consideration.[61]

DOMICILE

2–010   In most systems of the conflict of laws the notion of "belonging to" a country in some strong sense is of great importance: it identifies an individual's personal law, which governs questions concerning the personal and proprietary relationships between members of a family. Place of birth is an inadequate criterion by which to identify the personal law. In many (but not all) continental European

---

[53] Case C-90/97 [1999] E.C.R. I-1075. The case concerned social security entitlement under Regulation 1408/71. See Lamont [2007] 3 J.Priv.I.L. 261 where it is questioned whether the *Swaddling* definition can be suitably adapted for use in the family law context.

[54] At para.29.

[55] See below para.9–006.

[56] OJ 1998 C 221/27; originally the explanatory report to the Convention on Jurisdiction and the Recognition and Enforcement of Judgments in Matrimonial Matters, but also applicable in general to the revised Brussels II Regulation.

[57] At para.32.

[58] *Marinos v Marinos* [2007] EWHC 2047 (Fam); [2007] 2 F.L.R. 1018; *Munro v Munro* [2007] EWHC 3315 (Fam); [2008] 1 F.L.R. 1613.

[59] *L-K v K (No. 2)* [2006] EWHC 3280 (Fam) at paras 36 and 44.

[60] Case C-497/10.

[61] Case C-523/07 *Proceedings brought by A* [2009] 2 E.C.R. I-2805 at [39].

countries, the personal law has traditionally been instead the law of an individual's nationality. In England and almost all common-law countries it is the law of the domicile.

Domicile is easier to illustrate than it is to define. The root idea underlying the concept is the permanent home. "By domicile we mean home, the permanent home", said Lord Cranworth,[62] "and if you do not understand your permanent home, I'm afraid that no illustration drawn from foreign writers or foreign languages will very much help you to it." The notion of home, or of permanent home, takes colour from particular facts. An Englishwoman aged 70 years, left a widow after living all her life in Somerset, goes to New Zealand to live with her married daughter; although that move may be, in practical terms, irreversible, is she not likely to regard England as her home country?

In fact, domicile cannot be equated with home, because as we shall see a person may be domiciled in a country which is not and never has been his home; a person may have two homes, but only have one domicile; a person may be homeless, but he or she must have a domicile. Indeed there is often a wide gulf between the popular conception of home and the legal concept of domicile. Domicile is "an idea of law".[63] Originally it was a good idea; but the once simple concept has been so overloaded by a multitude of cases that it has been transmuted into something further and further removed from the practical realities of life.[64] Important proposals for the reform of the law of domicile made by the Law Commission in 1987,[65] reflecting in part reforms adopted in a number of Commonwealth countries overseas[66] and examined at various points in this chapter, would narrow this gap; but unfortunately they were rejected by the Government in 1996. Partial reform has, however, been effected in Scotland with regard to the domicile of persons under the age of 16.[67]

Since the Civil Jurisdiction and Judgments Act 1982, there has been a further complication. This Act introduced a new concept which describes a certain type of link between an individual, or a company, and a country. It is called "domicile", but it is quite unlike the traditional, personal law, concept of domicile developed in English law and still important in many matters of family law and succession. It is very unfortunate that the same term had to be used to describe these two different concepts; in this chapter, it is the traditional concept which is to be examined.[68]

2–011

There are three kinds of domicile:

> *domicile of origin*, which is the domicile assigned by law to a child at birth is born;
> *domicile of choice*, which is the domicile which any independent person can acquire by a combination of residence and intention; and

---

[62] *Whicker v Hume* (1858) 7 H.L.C. 124 at 160.
[63] *Bell v Kennedy* (1868) L.R. 1 Sc. & Div. 307 at 320, per Lord Westbury.
[64] Anton, *Private International Law*, 2nd edn (Endinburgh: W. Green, 1990), p.125.
[65] The Law Commission and the Scottish Law Commission, *The Law of Domicile* (HMSO), Law Com. No.168, Cm.200.
[66] See McClean, (1996) 260 *Recueil des cours* 36–54.
[67] Family Law (Scotland) Act 2006 s.22. cf. McEleavy [2007] I.C.L.Q. 453.
[68] For domicile in the sense of the Civil Jurisdiction and Judgments Act 1982, see below, para.4–015.

domicile of dependency, which means that the domicile of dependent persons (children under 16 and mentally disordered persons) is dependent on, and usually changes with, the domicile of someone else, e.g. the parent of a child.

2–012 The object of determining a person's domicile is to connect that person with some legal system for certain legal purposes. To establish this connection it is sufficient to fix the domicile in some "country" in the sense of the conflict of laws, e.g. England or Scotland, California or New York. It is not necessary to show in what part of such a country an individual is domiciled[69]; but it is usually insufficient to show that he or she is domiciled in some composite state such as the United Kingdom, the United States, Australia or Canada, each of which comprises several "countries" in the conflict of laws sense. A person who emigrates, e.g. to the United Kingdom with the intention of settling either in England or Scotland, or to Canada with the intention of settling either in Nova Scotia or British Columbia, only acquires a new domicile by deciding in which country to settle and by actually settling there.[70]

This rule is unsatisfactory and the Law Commission recommended the adoption in England of rules based on those in the modern Australian legislation, so that a person who is present in a federal or composite state with the intention to settle in that state for an indefinite period should, if he is not held under the general rules to be domiciled in any country within that state, be domiciled in the country therein with which he is for the time being most closely connected.[71]

General principles

2–013 There are four general principles fundamental to the law of domicile.

(1) No person can be without a domicile.[72] This rule springs from the practical necessity of connecting every person with some system of law by which a number of legal relationships may be regulated.

(2) No person can at the same time have more than one domicile, at any rate for the same purpose.[73] This rule springs from that same necessity.

(3) An existing domicile is presumed to continue until it is proved that a new domicile has been acquired. Hence the burden of proving a change of domicile lies on those who assert it.[74] Varying views have been expressed as to the standard of proof required to rebut the presumption. According to Scarman J., the

---

[69] *Re Craignish* [1892] 3 Ch. 180 at 192.

[70] *Bell v Kennedy* (1866–69) L.R. 1 Sc. 307; *Att Gen of Alberta v Cook* [1926] A.C. 444 PC (Can); *Gatty and Gatty v Attorney General* [1951] P. 444.

[71] *The Law of Domicile*, paras 7.1–7.8.

[72] *Bell v Kennedy* (1868) L.R. 1 Sc. & Div 307 at 320; *Udny v Udny* (1869) L.R. 1 Sc. & Div 441 at 448, 453 and 457.

[73] *Udny v Udny* ((1869) L.R. 1 Sc. & Div 441 at 448; *Garthwaite v Garthwaite* [1964] P. 356 at 378–379 and 393–394.

[74] *Bell v Kennedy* (1868) L.R. 1 Sc. & Div. 307 at 310 and 319; *Winans v Att-Gen* [1904] A.C. 287; *Ramsay v Liverpool Royal Infirmary* [1930] A.C. 588; *In the Estate of Fuld (No.3)* [1968] P. 675 at 685; *Irvin v Irvin* [2001] 1 F.L.R. 178 at 185B; *Cyganik v Agulian* [2006] EWCA Civ. 129; [2006] 1 F.C.R. 406.

standard is that adopted in civil proceedings, proof on a balance of probabilities, not that adopted in criminal proceedings, proof beyond reasonable doubt.[75] There is little doubt that the test of balance of probabilities is applied in practice,[76] despite some dicta suggesting a higher standard.[77] However, as we shall see, the burden of proving that a domicile of origin has been lost is a very heavy one. Moreover, as Scarman J. himself added[78]:

> "two things are clear: first, that unless the judicial conscience is satisfied by evidence of change, the domicile of origin persists; and secondly, that the acquisition of a domicile of choice is a serious matter not to be lightly inferred from slight indications or casual words."

The presumption of continuance of domicile varies in strength according to the kind of domicile which is alleged to continue. It is weakest when that domicile is one of dependency[79] and strongest when the domicile is one of origin, for "its character is more enduring, its hold stronger, and less easily shaken off".[80] More recently, Cazalet J. reviewed this dictum and concluded that as far as the abandonment and acquisition of a domicile of choice is concerned:

2–014

> "... the standard is the civil standard of proof; but ... the judicial conscience will need particularly convincing evidence to be satisfied that the balance of probabilities has been tipped."[81]

Similarly, Arden L.J., dealing with the standard of proof, concluded:

> "... there is no need for any higher standard of proof ... because the civil standard has the inbuilt flexibility to take the seriousness of an allegation into account. Accordingly the more serious an allegation the more substantial will need to be the evidence to prove it on a balance of probabilities."[82]

The Law Commission's proposals for the reform of the law of domicile would leave unchanged the rule that the burden of proving the acquisition of a new domicile falls on the person alleging it. However, the normal civil standard of proof on a balance of probabilities would apply in all disputes about domicile and no higher or different quality of intention would be required when the alleged change of domicile was from one acquired at birth than when it was from any other domicile.[83]

---

[75] *In the Estate of Fuld (No.3)* [1968] P. 675 at 685–686; cf. *Re Flynn (No. 1)* [1968] 1 W.L.R. 103 at 115 Ch Div; *Re Edwards* (1969) 113 S.J. 108; *Buswell v Inland Revenue Commissioners* [1974] 2 All E.R. 520; [1974] S.T.C. 266; [1974] 1 W.L.R. 1631 at 1637.

[76] See, e.g. *Holliday v Musa* [2010] EWCA Civ 335 *Haji-Ioannou v Frangos* [2009] EWHC 2310 (QB), [2010] 1 All ER (Comm) 303.

[77] *Henderson v Henderson* [1967] P. 77 at 80 per Sir Jocelyn Simon P.: "the standard of proof goes beyond a mere balance of probabilities"; *Steadman v Steadman* [1976] A.C. 536 at 563.

[78] *In the Estate of Fuld (No .3)* [1968] P. 675 at 686.

[79] *Harrison v Harrison* [1953] 1 W.L.R. 865; *Re Scullard* [1957] Ch. 107; *Henderson v Henderson* [1967] P. 77 at 82–83. See below, para.2–035.

[80] *Winans v Att-Gen* [1904] A.C. 287 at 290, per Lord Macnaghten; cf. *Henderson v Henderson* [1967] P. 77 at 80 per Simon P.

[81] *Irvin v Irwin* [2001] 1 F.L.R. 178 at 189, per Cazalet J.

[82] *Henwood v Barlow Clowes* [2008] EWCA Civ 577; [2008] N.P.C. 61 at para.88.

[83] *The Law of Domicile*, paras 5.4, 5.6, 5.9.

2–015   (4) For the purposes of a rule of the conflict of laws, "domicile" means domicile in the English sense. The question as to where a person is domiciled is determined solely in accordance with English law. Thus, persons domiciled in England may acquire a French domicile of choice regardless of whether French law would regard them as domiciled there,[84] and English law alone determines when a Frenchman acquires a domicile in England.[85]

It is too wide a formulation to say that in an English court, domicile means domicile in the English sense. Under the *renvoi* doctrine,[86] English courts sometimes refer to the whole law of a foreign country, including its rules of the conflict of laws, and then accept a reference back to English law either because (i) the foreign conflict rule refers to the law of the nationality, and the person concerned is a British citizen; or (ii) because the foreign conflict rule refers to the law of the domicile, and the foreign court regards the person as domiciled in England. In the latter case, it is not true that domicile in an English court always means domicile in the English sense; but it is still true that it means domicile in the English sense for the purpose of an English rule of the conflict of laws.

Acquisition of a domicile of choice

2–016   The content of the notion of domicile is probably best understood from the rules governing the domicile of choice. Every independent person (i.e., one who is not a child under 16 or a mentally disordered person) can acquire a domicile of choice by the combination of (a) residence and (b) the intention of permanent or indefinite residence, but not otherwise.

These two factors must coincide before the law will recognise a change of domicile. Residence, however long, in a country will not result in the acquisition of a domicile of choice there if the necessary intention is lacking.[87] Conversely, intention, however strong, to change a domicile will not have that result if the necessary residence in the new country is lacking[88]:

> "A new domicile is not acquired until there is not only a fixed intention of establishing a permanent residence in some other country, but until also this intention has been carried out by actual residence there."[89]

---

[84] *Collier v Rivaz* (1841) 2 Curt, 855; *Bremer v Freeman*; (1857) 10 Moo.P.C. 306; *Hamilton v Dallas* (1875) 1 Ch. D. 257; *Re Annesley* [1926] Ch. 692. Article 13 of the Code Napoléon, which required a foreigner to obtain the authorisation of the French Government before he could establish a domicile in France, was repealed in 1927. See, by way of exception, Family Law Act 1986 s.46(5), which refers, in the alternative, either to domicile in a country in the English sense, or domicile in a country in the sense of that country's law.

[85] *Re Martin* [1900] P. 211.

[86] Below, para.18–023.

[87] *Jopp v Wood* (1865) 4 De G.J. & S. 616; *Winans v Att-Gen* [1904] A.C. 287; *Ramsay v Liverpool Royal Infirmary* [1930] A.C. 588; *IRC v Bullock* [1976] 1 W.L.R. 1178.

[88] *In the Goods of Raffenel* (1863) 3 Sw. & Tr. 49; *Harrison v Harrison* [1953] 1 W.L.R. 865; *Willar v Willar* 1954 S.C. 144 at 147 ("one cannot acquire a domicile of choice by wishful thinking").

[89] *Bell v Kennedy* (1868) L.R. 1 Sc. & Div. 307 at 319, per Lord Chelmsford.

Hence a domicile cannot be acquired *in itinere*[90]; it is necessary not only to travel, hopefully or otherwise, but to arrive.

It is very difficult to keep the two requirements of residence and intention in watertight compartments, but in the interest of clarity of exposition they must be considered separately.

Residence

The meaning of residence as an independent concept has already been examined.[91] A person can acquire a domicile in a country, if he or she has the necessary intention, after residence for even part of a day.[92] The length of the residence is not important in itself; it is only important as evidence of intention. Thus an immigrant can acquire a domicile in a country immediately after arrival there. "It may be conceded that if the intention of permanently residing in a place exists, residence in pursuance of that intention, however short, will establish a domicile."[93] In order to be resident in a country a person need not own or rent a house there. It is sufficient to live in an hotel,[94] or in the house of a friend,[95] or even in a military camp.[96] For many years it was held that a person could not acquire a domicile of choice if their residence was unlawful.[97] However, the House of Lords in *Mark v Mark*[98] has held that, although it may be a relevant factor in establishing the intention to permanently remain in a country, there is no reason why unlawful residence in itself would prevent the acquisition of a domicile of choice.[99]

2–017

In the Law Commission's proposed statutory reformulation of the rules as to domicile, the term "presence" was used in place of "residence".[100]

Intention

The intention which is required for the acquisition of a domicile of choice (often referred to as the *animus manendi*) is the intention to reside permanently or for an unlimited time in a particular country. "It must be a residence fixed not for a limited period or particular purpose, but general and indefinite in its future

2–018

---

[90] *Udny v Udny* (1869) L.R. 1 Sc. & Div 441 at 449–450 and 453–454.

[91] Above, para.2–003.

[92] For striking illustrations, see *White v Tennant* 31 W.Va. 790; 8 S.E. 596 (1888); *Miller v Teale* (1954) 92 C.L.R. 406. See the Law Commission's confirmation of the policy behind this rule: *The Law of Domicile*, para.5.7.

[93] *Bell v Kennedy* (1868) L.R. 1 Sc. & Div. 307 at 319, per Lord Chelmsford.

[94] *Levene v IRC* [1928] A.C. 217; *IRC v Lysaght* [1928] A.C. 234; *Matalon v Matalon* [1952] P. 233.

[95] *Stone v Stone* [1958] 1 W.L.R. 1287.

[96] *Willar v Willar* 1954 S.C. 144.

[97] *Puttick v Att-Gen* [1980] Fam. 1 (German terrorist in England on false passport). But query whether this is a rule of English public policy so that it would not apply to illegal residence in a foreign country. See Pilkington, (1984) 33 I.C.L.Q. 885.

[98] *Mark v Mark* [2005] UKHL 42; [2006] 1 A.C. 98.

[99] *Mark v Mark* [2005] UKHL 42; [2006] 1 A.C. 98. See *Henwood v Barlow Clowes* [2008] EWCA Civ. 577; [2008] N.P.C. 61 at 119 where Arden L.J. stated that the inability to live in Mauritius on a permanent basis without the permission of the Mauritian government made his residence there precarious and subsequently the acquisition of a domicile of choice less likely.

[100] *The Law of Domicile*, para.5.7.

contemplation."[101] If a person intends to reside in a country for a fixed period (e.g. an engineer accepts a three-year contract to work on a civil engineering project in Saudi Arabia), the intention necessary to acquire a domicile there is lacking, however long the fixed period may be.[102] The same is true where a person intends to reside in a country for an indefinite time (e.g. until passing an examination) but clearly intends to leave the country at some time.[103]

The result of these principles is that the burden of proving a change of domicile is a very heavy one. Indeed, if we confine our attention to cases decided by the House of Lords, there appears to be an almost irrebuttable presumption against a change, because in the 13 disputed cases of domicile that have reached the House since 1860, there are only two in which it was held that a domicile of origin had been lost.[104] Two leading decisions of the House of Lords in particular have attracted much criticism. These are *Winans v Att-Gen*[105] and *Ramsay v Liverpool Royal Infirmary*.[106]

2–019   In *Winans v Att-Gen*:

> Mr Winans was a man of eccentric ideas, self-centred and strangely uncommunicative. He was born in the United States in 1823 with a domicile of origin in Maryland or New Jersey. The two ruling passions of his life were hatred of England and the care of his health. As Lord Macnaghten described him: "He nursed and tended it" (i.e. his health, not England) "with wonderful devotion. He took his temperature several times a day. He had regular times for taking his temperature, and regular times for taking his various waters and medicines.

His opportunity for gratifying his hatred of England came in 1850, when he went to Russia and was employed by the Russian Government in equipping railways and in the construction of gunboats to be used against England in the Crimean War. But nemesis overtook him in 1859, when his health broke down. He was advised by his doctors that another winter in Russia would be fatal, and that he must spend the winter in Brighton. Very reluctantly he accepted this advice, spent the winter in a Brighton hotel, and in 1860 took a lease of a house there. However, he held aloof from English people, whom he continued cordially to dislike. From then on until his death in 1897 he spent more and more time in England, living in furnished houses and hotels, and less and less time elsewhere. From 1893 until 1897 he lived entirely in England.

He entertained a grandiose dream of constructing in Baltimore, Maryland, a large fleet of cigar-shaped vessels which, being proof against pitching and rolling (or so he thought), would gain for the United States the carrying trade of the

---

[101] *Udny v Udny* (1869) L.R. 1 Sc. & 441, at 458, per Lord Westbury. See *Cramer v Cramer* [1987] 1 F.L.R. 116.

[102] *Att-Gen v Rowe* (1862) 1 H. & C. 31.

[103] *Jopp v Wood* (1865) 4 D.J. & S. 616; *Qureshi v Qureshi* [1972] Fam. 173.

[104] *Casdagli v Casdagli* [1919] A.C. 145. The other cases are: *Aikman v Aikman* (1861) 3 Macq. 854; *Moorhouse v Lord* (1863) 10 H.L.C. 272; *Pitt v Pitt* (1864) 4 Macq. 627; *Bell v Kennedy* (1868) L.R. 1 Sc. & Div. 307; *Udny v Udny* (1869) L.R. 1 Sc. & 441; *Winans v Att-Gen* [1904] A.C. 287; *Huntly v Gaskell* [1906] A.C. 56; *Lord Advocate v Jaffrey* [1921] 1 A.C. 146 (where it was conceded that the husband had lost his domicile of origin, and the dispute was as to the domicile of dependency of the wife); *Ross v Ross* [1930] A.C. 1; *Ramsay v Liverpool Royal Infirmary* [1930] A.C. 588; *Wahl v Att-Gen* (1932) 147 L.T. 382; *Mark v Mark* [2005] UKHL 42; [2006] 1 A.C. 98.

[105] [1904] A.C. 287: the case of the anglophobe American millionaire.

[106] [1930] A.C. 588: the case of the human jellyfish (or sponge).

world and give her naval superiority over Great Britain. He also dreamed of acquiring control of 200 acres of wharves and docks in Maryland to accommodate the cigar-shaped vessels, and a large house in which he would live and superintend the whole scheme. He was working night and day on the scheme when he died, a millionaire several times over.

Mr Winans had thus lived mainly in England for the last 37 years of his life, and never revisited the United States after his departure in 1850.

On these facts, six judges held that he died domiciled in England; but a bare majority of two to one in the House of Lords held that he never lost his domicile of origin. "When he came to this country", said Lord Macnaghten,[107] "he was a sojourner and a stranger, and he was I think a sojourner and a stranger in it when he died." Lord Lindley, equally robust, said[108]: "He had one and only one home, and that was in this country; and long before he died I am satisfied that he had given up all serious idea of returning to his native country." Lord Halsbury was unable to make up his mind, and fell back on the presumption of continuance.

In *Ramsay v Liverpool Royal Infirmary*[109]:

2–020

> George Bowie was born in Glasgow in 1845 with a Scottish domicile of origin. In 1882, at the age of 37, he gave up his employment as a commercial traveller and did not work for the remaining 45 years of his life. At first he lived with his mother and sisters in Glasgow. In 1892 he moved to Liverpool and sponged on his brother and another sister. He died unmarried in 1927. Thus he lived in England for the last 36 years of his life. During all that time he left England only twice, once on a short visit to the United States, and once on a short holiday in the Isle of Man. Though he often said he was proud to be a Glasgow man, he resolutely refused to return to Scotland, even to attend his mother's funeral. On the contrary, he expressed his determination never to set foot in Glasgow again, and arranged to be buried in Liverpool. His will, which gave the residue equally between three Glasgow charities and one Liverpool one, was formally valid if he died domiciled in Scotland, but formally invalid if he died domiciled in England.

On these facts the House of Lords, affirming both the Scottish courts below, unanimously reached the astonishing conclusion that he died domiciled in Scotland. The *ratio decidendi* evidently was that he was such a low form of life as to be incapable of forming the necessary intent to change his domicile. "The long residence of George Bowie", said Lord Thankerton,[110] "is remarkably colourless, and suggests little more than inanition".

2–021

Unfortunately, we cannot dismiss these two cases as mere aberrations of the House of Lords, because in 1976 the Court of Appeal reached a similar decision. In *I.R.C. v Bullock*[111] it was held that a Canadian with a domicile of origin in Nova Scotia who had lived mainly in England for more than 40 years had not acquired an English domicile of choice, because he intended to return to Canada after the death of his English wife. Ironically, this decision meant that (as the law then stood) the wife also was domiciled in Nova Scotia at the time in question (1971–1973), although she disliked the place. On the other hand, in *Re Furse*[112]

---

[107] At p.298.
[108] At p.300.
[109] [1930] A.C. 588.
[110] At p.595.
[111] [1976] 1 W.L.R. 1178; criticised by Carter, (1976–77) 48 B.Y.I.L. 362.
[112] [1980] 3 All E.R. 838.

the home of an American for the last 39 years of his life was on a farm in England. He declared an intention to return to the United States if he became unable to lead an active physical life on the farm, where he remained until his death aged 80. The contingency was held to be so vague and indefinite that it did not prevent the acquisition of an English domicile of choice.

Fentiman has argued that *Re Furse* taken with some other cases can be read as indicating a shift towards an understanding of domicile as the place with which an individual has his most real and substantial connection.[113] Existing factual links, he argues, are becoming more important than reliance on intention as to future plans. This would effectively bring domicile closer to habitual residence, or at least to domicile as understood in many United States jurisdictions, but there is little sign that the courts intend to depart from the traditional English principles, which require a close examination of the evidence as to the propositus's intentions.

Evidence of intention

2–022   Most disputes about domicile turn on the question as to whether the necessary intention accompanied the residence; and this question often involves very complex and intricate issues of fact. This is because:

> "[T]here is no act, no circumstance in a man's life, however trivial it may be in itself, which ought to be left out of consideration in trying the question whether there was an intention to change the domicile. A trivial act might possibly be of more weight with regard to determining this question than an act which was of more importance to a man in his lifetime."[114]

There is, furthermore, no circumstance or group of circumstances which furnishes any definite criterion of the existence of the intention[115]; for example, naturalisation is not conclusive as "it is not the law either that a change of domicile is a condition of naturalisation, or that naturalisation involves necessarily a change of domicile".[116] A circumstance which is treated as decisive in one case may be disregarded in another, or even relied upon to support a different conclusion.

---

[113] (1991) 50 C.L.J. 445. The other cases he cites are *Brown v Brown* (1981) 3 F.L.R. 212 (US businessman resident in England for 14 years and belonging to London clubs held domiciled there; the links with English society were in sharp contrast with those in *Winans v Att-Gen* [1904] A.C. 287) and *Plummer v IRC* [1988] 1 W.L.R. 292.

[114] *Drevon v Drevon* (1864) 34 L.J.Ch. 129 at 133, per Kindersley V.C. See *Henwood v Barlow Clowes* [2008] EWCA Civ 577; [2008] N.P.C. 61 where the Court of Appeal criticised the trial judge for failing to consider certain elements of the propositus's life.

[115] As Mummery L.J. observed in *Cyganik v Agulian* [2006] EWCA Civ 129; [2006] 1 F.C.R. 406 at para.46: "...the court must look back at the whole of the deceased's life, at what he had done with his life, at what life had done to him and at what were his inferred intentions in order to decide whether he had acquired a domicile of choice in England..."

[116] *Wahl v Att-Gen* (1932) 147 L.T. 382 (H.L.) per Lord Atkin at 385. A decision to take British nationality when faced with a choice was held to be a "clear pointer" of the acquisition of a domicile of choice in England: *Bheekhun v Williams* [1999] 2 F.L.R. 229, per Chadwick L.J. at 239B; but the acquisition of British citizenship together with a British passport was not enough was not enough in *F v Inland Revenue Commissioners* [2000] W.T.L.R. 505 at 528.

The questions which the court has considered include the following: where did the propositus live and for how long? Was it in a fixed place or several different places? Did he build or buy a house, or live in furnished lodgings or hotels? What was his lifestyle? Was he accompanied by his wife, or unmarried partner, and children? Did he vote in elections there? Was he naturalised there? Did he arrange to be buried there? What churches did he attend? What clubs did he belong to? Of course, this list is far from being exhaustive: a person's "tastes, habits, conduct, actions, ambitions, health, hopes and projects" are all regarded as "keys to his intention."[117] Thus the law, instead of allowing long-continued residence to speak for itself, insists on proof of a person's intention, that most elusive of all factors. The resulting uncertainty has given rise to much criticism and to proposals for reform of the law.

Declarations of intention

The person whose domicile is in question may give evidence of his or her intention, but the court will view the evidence of an interested party with suspicion[118]; though in one case[119] such evidence was decisive. As Lord Buckmaster put it[120]:

2–023

> "Declarations as to intention are rightly regarded in determining the question of a change of domicile, but they must be examined by considering the persons to whom, the purposes for which, and the circumstances in which they are made, and they must further be fortified and carried into effect by conduct and action consistent with the declared expression".

A statement made for tax purposes may not be a cogent as entries in personal diaries showing a different intent.[121] The courts are particularly reluctant to give effect to declarations as to domicile made by testators in their wills, since the testator is unlikely to understand the meaning of the word, while to allow the solicitor drafting the will to determine the question of domicile would be to oust the jurisdiction of the court.[122]

---

[117] *Casdagli v Casdagli* [1919] A.C. 145 at 178, per Lord Atkinson, commenting on *Winans v Att-Gen* [1904] A.C. 287.

[118] *Bell v Kennedy* (1868) L.R. 1 Sc. & 307 at 313 and 322–323; *Re Craignish* [1892] 3 Ch. 180 at 190; *Qureshi v Qureshi* [1972] Fam. 173, 192; *Gaines-Cooper v Revenue and Customs Commissioners* [2007] S.T.C. (S.C.D.) 23 (decision upheld by the High Court [2007] EWHC 2617 (Ch); [2008] S.T.C., 1665); *Henwood v Barlow Clowes* [2008] EWCA Civ 335; [2008] N.P.C. 61 at para.81.

[119] *Wilson v Wilson* (1872) L.R. 2 P. & M. 435. The Scottish court arrived at an opposite conclusion on the same facts: *Wilson v Wilson* (1872) 10 M. 573; but the husband's evidence was not then admissible in Scotland.

[120] *Ross v Ross* [1930] A.C. 1 at 6–7. "Expression" the last word in the quotation, seems to be a misprint for "intention".

[121] *Holliday v Musa* [2010] EWCA Civ 335; [2010] 3 FCR 280.

[122] *Re Steer* (1858) 3 H. & N. 594; *Re Annesley* [1926] Ch. 692; *Att-Gen v Yule* (1931) 145 L.T. 9; *Re Liddell-Grainger* (1936) 53 T.L.R. 12; *Dellar v Zivy* [2007] EWHC 2266 (Ch); [2007] I.L.Pr. 868.

Motive and intention

2–024   It is important to distinguish between motive and intention. As a general rule it does not matter whether a person's motive in leaving one country and living in another is good or bad: the question is whether or not there is the requisite intention for a change of domicile. The motive may be, for instance, to enjoy the benefit of a lower rate of taxation,[123] or of a better climate, either for the person concerned or for a troupe of performing chimpanzees,[124] to get a divorce,[125] to prevent his wife from getting maintenance,[126] or to facilitate international travel[127]: in none of these cases has the particular motive prevented the acquisition of a new domicile. But if the motive is suspect, the court may be reluctant to concede a change of domicile. It may conclude that there really was no change at all, but merely the appearance of a change made to secure some personal advantage.[128]

Intention freely formed

2–025   In order that a person may acquire a domicile of choice, it has been said that "there must be a residence freely chosen, and not prescribed or dictated by any external necessity, such as the duties of office, the demands of creditors, or the relief from illness."[129] That is a somewhat misleading statement. It certainly does not mean that only a person able to exercise the most perfect freedom of choice can acquire a domicile of choice: if it did, the acquisition of a domicile of choice would be a rare event. It is submitted that the rules as to the acquisition of a domicile of choice apply to everyone, but that the position of certain groups of people who go to another country (persons liable to deportation; fugitives from justice; refugees; invalids; and employees, diplomats and members of the armed forces) is such that they are markedly less likely, as an observation of fact, to form the necessary intention to remain in that country.

(i)   Persons liable to deportation

2–026   A person who resides in a country from which he or she is liable to be deported may lack the necessary intention because the residence is precarious. But if in fact the necessary intention is formed, a domicile of choice will be acquired.[130] Once such a person has acquired a domicile of choice, it is not lost merely

---

[123] *Wood v Wood* [1957] P. 254.
[124] *Wood v Wood* [1957] P. 254.
[125] *Drexel v Drexel* [1916] 1 Ch. 251; *Wood v Wood* [1957] P. 254; *Chaudhary v Chaudhary* [1985] Fam. 19.
[126] *ibid.*
[127] *F v Inland Revenue Commissioners* [2000] W.T.L.R. 505.
[128] See *White v White* [1950] 4 D.L.R. 474, affirmed [1952] 1 D.L.R. 133.
[129] *Udny v Udny* (1869) L.R. 1 Sc. & 441 at 458, per Lord Westbury.
[130] *Boldrini v Boldrini* [1932] P. 9; *Zanelli v Zanelli* (1948) 64 T.L.R. 556; *Szechter v Szechter* [1971] P. 286 at 294; *Mark v Mark* [2005] UKHL 42; [2006] 1 A.C. 98.

because a deportation order has been made.[131] It is lost only when there is actual deportation *and* the deported person can no longer be said to have an intention to return as a lawful resident.

(ii)   Fugitives from justice

A person who leaves a country as a fugitive from criminal justice, or in order to evade creditors, has a special motive for leaving it, but no special motive for living in any other country. In the case of a fugitive from justice, the intention to abandon the previous domicile will readily be inferred, unless perhaps the punishment sought to be avoided is trivial, or by the law of that country a relatively short period of prescription bars liability to punishment. In *Re Martin*,[132] a French professor committed a crime in France in connection with his professorship[133] and fled to England where he remained for the next 20 years. Two years after the French period of prescription had expired, he returned to France. The Court of Appeal by a majority held that he had acquired an English domicile six years after his arrival in England. A similar conclusion was reached in *Moynihan v Moynihan (Nos. 1 and 2)*,[134] where a peer of the realm fled England to avoid arrest on serious fraud charges, and was held to have acquired a domicile of choice in the Philippines where he "was in the nature of a king", owning a hotel and at least one massage parlour. Similarly, a person who leaves a country in order to evade his creditors may lose a domicile there[135]; but if the debtor plans to return as soon as the debts are paid or have been cancelled, there is no change of domicile.[136]

2–027

(iii)   Refugees

If a political refugee intends to return as soon as the political situation changes, he or she remains domiciled there; there may, of course, come a point at which the prospect of return becomes so remote that the court will treat a declared intention to return as an exercise in self-deception, inconsistent with reality. A refugee who has decided *not* to return even when the political situation does change, may acquire a domicile of choice in the country of refuge.

2–028

Thus in *Re Evans*[137]:

> An Englishman with a Belgian domicile of choice returned to England very reluctantly in June 1940 because of the German invasion, and lived in furnished flats in England until he died in 1944. He always intended to return to Belgium after the war. It was held that he retained his Belgian domicile.

On the other hand, in *May v May*[138]:

---

[131]   *Cruh v Cruh* [1945] 2 All E.R. 545.
[132]   [1900] P. 211.
[133]   The report is tantalisingly silent as to what this might have been.
[134]   [1997] 1 F.L.R. 59 at 63.
[135]   *Udny v Udny* (1869) L.R. 1 Sc. & 441.
[136]   *Re Wright's Trusts* (1856) 2 K. & J. 595; *Pitt v Pitt* (1864) 4 Macq. 627.
[137]   [1947] Ch. 695.
[138]   [1943] 2 All E.R. 146.

A Jew fled from Germany to England in 1938 to escape persecution by the Nazis. He originally intended to emigrate to the United States, but his hope of doing so was frustrated by the outbreak of war in 1939. In 1941, the idea of going to the United States gradually faded from his mind. He declared that he would never return to Germany, even if the Nazis were overthrown. It was held that he had acquired an English domicile of choice by the beginning of 1942.

(iv) Invalids

2–029   If a person moves to live in a new country for health reasons, is there a change of domicile? Different judges have given different answers to this question. Since illnesses vary greatly in intensity, no general rule can be laid down. Each case turns on its own facts. A person who goes to a country for the temporary purpose of undergoing medical treatment there clearly lacks the necessary intention for a change of domicile. So does a person who is terminally ill and decides to move to a country to alleviate his last sufferings or to be cared for by relatives.[139] On the other hand, a person who moves to a new country in the belief that the move will ensure better health may well intend to live there permanently or indefinitely, but of course not necessarily.

In *Hoskins v Matthews*[140]:

> A man whose domicile of origin was English went to Florence at the age of 60, and lived there except for three or four months in each year in a villa that he had bought until he died 12 years later. He was suffering from an injury to the spine and left England solely because he thought that the warmer climate of Italy would benefit his health. His housekeeper gave evidence that he would have returned to England if he had been restored to health. Nevertheless it was held that he had acquired a domicile in Tuscany (as it then was), because he was "exercising a preference and not acting upon a necessity.[141]

(v) Employees

2–030   The question whether an employee who is sent to a country by his or her employer intends to reside there permanently or indefinitely remains in the last resort a question of fact. If someone goes to a country for the temporary purpose of performing the duties of office or employment,[142] he does not acquire a domicile of choice there; but if he goes not merely to work but also to settle,[143] he may acquire a domicile of choice.

The same principles apply to diplomats and members of the armed forces. It is a question of fact whether diplomats intend to reside permanently or indefinitely in the country to which they are accredited. Generally, of course, they form no such intention[144]; but occasionally they may do so and thus acquire a domicile of

---

[139] *Allen v Revenue and Customs Commissioners* [2005] S.T.C. (S.C.D.) 614.

[140] (1855) 8 D.M. & G. 13. See *Haji-Ioannou v Frangos* [2009] EWHC 2310 (QB); [2010] 1 All ER (Commm) 303 (medical treatment in Athens; domicile in Monaco retained).

[141] cf. *Re James* (1908) 98 L.T. 438 where the continued ownership of a farm in Wales seems to have been decisive.

[142] For example *Att-Gen v Rowe* (1862) 1 Hurl. & C. 31 (English barrister appointed Chief Justice of Ceylon).

[143] For example *Gunn v Gunn* (1956) 2 D.L.R. (2d) 351.

[144] *Niboyet v Niboyet* (1878–79) L.R. 4 P.D. 1 CA.

choice there.[145] Members of the armed forces are likely to have even less freedom of choice as to where they are stationed. Nonetheless, a member of the armed forces can, during service, acquire a domicile of choice in the country in which he is stationed[146] or elsewhere,[147] provided he has established the necessary residence and formed the necessary intention. But in the great majority of cases he does not intend to make his permanent home where he is stationed, and retains the domicile which he had on entering service.[148]

Loss of a domicile of choice

A person abandons a domicile of choice in a country by ceasing to reside there and by ceasing to intend to reside there permanently or indefinitely, and not otherwise.[149] It is not necessary to prove a positive intention not to return: it is sufficient to prove merely the absence of an intention to continue to reside.[150] A domicile of choice is lost when both the residence and the intention necessary for its acquisition are given up. It is not lost merely by giving up the residence,[151] nor merely by giving up the intention.[152]

2–031

Domicile of origin

"It is a settled principle", said Lord Westbury in a leading case,[153] "that no man shall be without a domicile, and to secure this result the law attributes to every individual as soon as he is born the domicile of his father, if the child be legitimate, and the domicile of the mother if illegitimate".[154] This has been called the domicile of origin, and is involuntary. In many cases, the domicile of origin will be in the country in which the child is born but this is coincidental as the place of birth is in no way determinative.[155]

2–032

Since the domicile of the child's father may be the father's domicile of origin which itself may be derived from the father's father, it follows that a domicile of origin may be transmitted through several generations no member of which has ever lived in the country of his or her domicile of origin,[156] and during which

---

[145] As in *Naville v Naville* 1957 (1) S.A. 280.
[146] *Donaldson v Donaldson* [1949] P. 363; *Willar v Willar* 1954 S.C. 144.
[147] *Stone v Stone* [1958] 1 W.L.R. 1287.
[148] *Cruickshanks v Cruickshanks* [1957] 1 W.L.R. 564; *Sellars v Sellars* 1942 S.C. 206.
[149] *Udny v Udny* (1869) L.R. 1 Sc. & Div. 441 at 450; *IRC v Duchess of Portland* [1982] Ch. 314.
[150] *Re Flynn (No. 1)* [1968] 1 W.L.R. 103 at 113–115; *Qureshi v Qureshi* [1972] Fam. 173 at 191; *Morgan v Cilento* [2004] EWHC 188 (Ch); [2004] W.T.L.R. 457.
[151] *Bradford v Young* (1885) L.R. 29 Ch.D. 617; *Re Lloyd Evans* [1947] Ch. 695; *Breuning v Breuning* [2002] EWHC 236 (Fam); [2002] 1 F.L.R. 888.
[152] *In the Goods of Raffenel* (1863) 3 Sw. & Tr. 49; *Zanelli v Zanelli* (1948) 64 T.L.R. 556.
[153] *Udny v Udny* (1869) L.R. 1 Sc. & Div. 441 at 457.
[154] There is no English authority on the domicile of origin of a posthumous child or of a foundling; but it is generally assumed that the former takes the domicile of the mother and that the latter has domicile of origin in the country where he or she is found.
[155] See, e.g. cases of children born to expatriates working away from the country of their domicile such as *M v M (Divorce: Domicile)* [2010] EWHC 982 (Fam); [2011] 1 F.L.R. 919 (child born in Kenya had English domicile of origin).
[156] See *Peal v Peal* (1930) 46 T.L.R. 645; *Grant v Grant* 1931 S.C. 238.

time national borders may have changed.[157] The Law Commission proposed new rules for determining the domicile of a child, under which the concept of the domicile of origin would disappear.[158]

No person can legally be without a domicile, but a person may in fact be without a home, being for instance a wanderer or a sailor, with no home except a cabin. To meet such situations, the law has to resort to fictions; and it draws a sharp distinction between the domicile of origin and a domicile of choice.

2–033   A domicile of origin possesses a very adhesive quality[159] and cannot be lost by mere abandonment. It can only be lost by the acquisition of a domicile of choice. Thus in *Bell v Kennedy*[160]:

> Mr Bell was born in Jamaica of Scottish parents domiciled in Jamaica. In 1828 he married in Jamaica. In 1837, at the age of 35, he left Jamaica for good and went to Scotland, where he lived with his mother-in-law and looked around for an estate on which to settle down. He found one in 1839, and from then on was admittedly domiciled in Scotland. But until then he was undecided whether to settle in Scotland or in England or elsewhere. He was dissatisfied with Scotland, mainly due to the bad weather – so different from what he was used to in Jamaica. The question was where was he domiciled in September 1838 when his wife died? The House of Lords held that he had not lost his Jamaican domicile of origin.

2–034   On the other hand, a domicile of choice can be lost by abandonment; and if it is, and a new domicile of choice is not simultaneously acquired, the domicile of origin revives to fill the gap.[161] The reasons given for this rule (often referred to as "the rule in *Udny v Udny*") are not very convincing,[162] and its artificiality has often been criticised. If, for instance, an Englishman emigrates to New York at the age of 25, remains there for the next 40 years and then decides to retire to California, but is killed in an air crash en route, it does not make much sense to say that he died domiciled in England, especially as an American court would undoubtedly hold that he died domiciled in New York. Yet the opposite American rule, that a domicile of choice continues until a new one is acquired, sometimes produces equally bizarre results. For instance, in the leading American case, *Re Jones' Estate*[163]:

> Evan Jones was born in Wales in 1850 with an English domicile of origin. In 1883, he put a Welsh girl in the family way and she threatened him with affiliation proceedings. To escape this prospect he emigrated to the United States, where he acquired a domicile of choice in

---

[157] See *Al-Bassam v Al-Bassam* [2004] EWCA Civ 857; [2004] W.T.L.R. 757.

[158] This reform has been implemented in Scotland, Family Law (Scotland) Act 2006 s.22; see below 2–038.

[159] *Winans v Att-Gen* [1904] A.C. 287; *Ramsay Liverpool Royal Infirmary* [1930] A.C. 588. See above para.2–014; *R v R (Divorce: Jurisdiction: Domicile)* [2006] 1 F.L.R. 389; *Cyganik v Agulian* [2006] EWCA Civ. 129; [2006] 1 F.C.R. 406.

[160] (1868) L.R. 1 Sc. & Div. 307.

[161] *Udny v Udny* (1869) L.R. 1 Sc. & Div. 441; *Harrison v Harrison* [1953] 1 W.L.R. 865; *Re Flynn (No. 1)* [1968] 1 W.L.R. 103 at 117; *Tee v Tee* [1974] 1 W.L.R. 213; *Henwood v Barlow Clowes* [2008] EWCA Civ 577; [2008] N.P.C. 61.

[162] In *Udny v Udny* (1869) L.R. 1 Sc. & Div. 441, Lord Westbury said (at 458): "as the domicile of origin is the creature of law, and independent of the will of the party, it would be inconsistent with the principles on which it is by law created and ascribed, to suppose that it is capable of being by the act of the party entirely obliterated and extinguished."

[163] 192 Iowa 78, 182 N.W. 227 (1921).

Iowa, became a naturalised American citizen, and married an American wife. He was "a coal miner, an industrious, hardworking, thrifty Welshman who accumulated a considerable amount of property. In 1915, after the death of his wife, he decided to return to Wales for good and live there with his sister. He sailed from New York on May 1 in the *Lusitania*, and was drowned when she was torpedoed by a German sub-marine off the south coast of Ireland. He died intestate. By English law, his brothers and sisters were entitled to his property; by the law of Iowa, it went to his illegitimate daughter, from whom he had fled over 30 years ago, and with whom he had never had anything to do. The Supreme Court of Iowa held that he died domiciled in Iowa and that the daughter was entitled.

Short of holding that he died domiciled in the *Lusitania*, and therefore (since she was registered at Southampton) in England, there would appear to be no satisfactory solution to this problem. The truth is that the American rule is as much a fiction as the English one.

Domicile of dependency

Dependent persons cannot acquire a domicile of choice by their own act. As a general rule, the domicile of such persons is the same as, and changes with, the domicile of the person (if any) on whom they are legally dependent. For this purpose, the category of dependent persons now comprises children and the mentally disordered; it formerly included all married women, and it is still necessary to know something of a rule which now seems a prime example of political incorrectness.

The rules applying to each group will be examined in turn.

2–035

Children

At common law, the domicile of a child below the age of majority was the same as, and changed with, the domicile of the appropriate parent, the father in the case of a legitimate child, and the mother in the case of an illegitimate child or a legitimate child whose father was dead.[164] One decision suggests that the rule was not quite so strict in the case of an illegitimate or fatherless child as it was in the case of a legitimate child whose father was alive. In *Re Beaumont*,[165] a widow, domiciled in Scotland with her minor children, remarried and went to live with her second husband in England, taking all but one of the children with her, leaving the one behind in Scotland in the care of an aunt; it was held that the domicile of this child continued to be Scottish. Although there is no authority on the point, it seems likely that the domicile of a legitimated child would be dependent on that of its father, at any rate if the legitimation was effected by the subsequent marriage of the parents.

2–036

---

[164] A female minor who married took her husband's domicile in place of her father's or mother's.
[165] [1893] 3 Ch. 490. Given that at that date a married woman had no power over her own domicile, the suggestion that she might have a discretion as to that of her children is surprising.

The modern law is contained in the Domicile and Matrimonial Proceedings Act 1973 ("the 1973 Act") s.3(1) of which provides that a child becomes capable of having an independent domicile when he or she attains the age of 16 or marries under that age.[166]

2–037   At common law, the child was treated as dependent upon the father even if the parents had separated and the child was living with the mother. Section 4 of the 1973 Act sought to introduce greater flexibility into the rules as to dependency, enabling the child to be dependent upon its mother in appropriate circumstances. It provides that the domicile of a dependent child whose parents are alive but living apart shall be that of his mother if (a) he has his home with her and no home with his father, or (b) he has at any time had her domicile by virtue of (a) above and has not subsequently had a home with his father. "Living apart" does not imply any breakdown in the relationship between the parents, who may be living apart because of the demands of one parent's job. "Home" is also undefined: the home of a pre-school child[167] may be more easily identifiable than that of a young teenager being educated at a boarding school. Section 4(3) provides that the domicile of a dependent child whose mother is dead shall be that which she last had before she died if at her death he had her domicile by virtue of s.4(2) and he has not since had a home with his father. The main object of this enactment is to increase the number of cases in which the domicile of dependency of a child will be that of the mother; previously existing rules of law to that effect (e.g. those relating to illegitimate children and legitimate children whose fathers are dead) are preserved by s.4(4).

Adopted children are now treated in law as if they had been born as the legitimate child of the adopter or adopters.[168] Accordingly the domicile of an adopted child under 16 will be determined as if he or she were the legitimate child of the adopted parent or parents.

The domicile of a legitimate child whose parents are both dead, or of an illegitimate child whose mother is dead, probably cannot be changed at all. But there is no authority on the point.

2–038   When the domicile of a dependent child is changed as a result of a change in the parents' domicile or as a result of its legitimation, the new domicile acquired by the child in this way is a domicile of dependency and not a domicile of origin.[169] Hence, it is not this domicile but the one acquired at birth that will revive if in later life he or she abandons one domicile of choice without at the same time acquiring another. On the other hand, it would seem to follow from what has been said above about adopted children, that the domicile of origin of an adopted child is deemed to be the domicile of the relative adoptive parent at the time of the

---

[166] In English domestic law, a marriage between persons either of whom is under 16 is void (Marriage Act 1949 s.2); but a child may be regarded as validly married under foreign law even if under that age.

[167] "Where the child keeps its toys" may once have been a relevant question to ask in the days when toys were few and treasured, but for today's children this is less likely to be a determinative factor; some families may have children's toys in different countries.

[168] Adoption and Children Act 2002 s.67.

[169] *Henderson v Henderson* [1967] P. 77.

child's birth[170] since s.67(1) of the Adoption and Children Act 2006 provides that an adopted person is to be treated in law as if born as the child of the adopters or adopter. It is submitted that this extends the fiction of the domicile of origin too far. If domicile is based on the concept of 'permanent home' and the domicile of origin denotes being born to a family, a community, then if the domicile of origin is to change at all upon adoption, it should be to the domicile of the relevant parent at the time of adoption, not changed retrospectively to whatever domicile the adoptive parent may have had at the time the child was born to his biological parents.

In its 1987 report,[171] the Law Commission recommended new and simpler rules to replace those in the 1973 Act. A child should be domiciled in the country with which he or she is, for the time being, most closely connected. Where the child's parents were domiciled in the same country and the child had its home with either or both of them, it would be presumed, unless the contrary were shown, that the child was most closely connected with that country. Where the child's parents were not domiciled in the same country and the child had its home with one of them, but not with the other, it would similarly be presumed that the child was most closely connected with the country in which the parent with whom it had its home was domiciled. No presumption would apply in cases in which the parents were domiciled in separate countries and the child had a home with both of them; nor in cases where the child had a home with neither parent. For the purposes of these rules, "parent" would include parents who are not married to one another; there would no longer be separate rules applying to legitimate, illegitimate and legitimated children.

Mentally disordered persons

A mentally disordered person cannot acquire a domicile of choice and, as a general rule, retains the domicile which he or she had when becoming mentally incapable.[172] Since such a person cannot exercise any will, he or she lacks the capacity to acquire or lose a domicile; nor can the domicile be changed by a person taking charge of or caring for the mentally disordered person,[173] nor by the court.[174] The rules governing who lacks the mental capacity to form the necessary intention to change their domicile are now contained in the Mental Capacity Act 2005. Had the Law Commission's proposals[175] been accepted, special rules would have applied to mentally incapable adults. Such persons would be domiciled in the country with which they were for the time being most closely connected. When that capacity was restored, they would retain the

2–039

---

[170] If this is correct, it is the only instance in English law in which a domicile of origin can be changed.

[171] *The Law of Domicile*, Pt VI.

[172] *Bempde v Johnstone* 30 E.R. 967; (1796) 3 Ves. Jr. 198; *Urquhart v Butterfield* (1887) 37 Ch.D. 357; *Crumpton's Judicial Factor v Fitch-Noyes* 1918 S.C. 378.

[173] However, if a dependent child becomes insane and remains so after attaining the age of 16, the appropriate parent has power to change his or her domicile even after he or she attains that age: *Sharpe v Crispin* 1869) L.R. 1 P. & M. 611; *Re G* [1966] N.Z.L.R. 1028.

[174] See *Westminster City Council v C* [2008] EWCA Civ 198; [2009] Fam. 11 at 14–15.

[175] *The Law of Domicile*, Pt VI.

domicile held immediately before it was restored, but could of course then acquire a new domicile under the rules applying to adults generally.

Married women

2–040
Before 1974 there was an absolute rule, to which there were no exceptions, that the domicile of a married woman was the same as, and changed with, the domicile of her husband.[176] This rule reflected social conditions and attitudes of a past age, and it was abolished by s.1(1) of the 1973 Act.

Section 1(1) of the 1973 Act is retrospective in the sense that it applies to women married before as well as after January 1, 1974. Hence, a transitional provision was needed. Section 1(2) provides that where immediately before that date a woman was married and then had her husband's domicile by dependence, she is to be treated as retaining that domicile (as a domicile of choice, if it is not also her domicile of origin) unless and until it is changed by acquisition of another domicile either on or after that date.

2–041
In *Inland Revenue Commissioners v Duchess of Portland*[177]:

> A woman with a domicile of origin in Quebec married a domiciled Englishman in 1948. She lived with her husband in England but retained links with Quebec, visiting it for ten to 12 weeks every summer, keeping a house which she owned there ready for immediate occupation, and retaining Canadian citizenship. She intended to return permanently to Quebec with her husband when he retired from business, but continued to live in England. It was held that the effect of s.1(2) was that she retained her English domicile of dependency as a domicile of choice. In effect, the pattern of her own life before 1974 was given no weight.

The Law Commission subsequently recommended a much more satisfactory form of transitional provision, that the domicile of any person at any date after the enactment of the new rules should be determined as if those rules had always been in force.[178]

Section 1(1) of the 1973 Act is not retrospective in any other sense. Hence, in considering the domicile of a married woman as at any time before January 1, 1974, the old law will still apply.

DOMICILE OF CORPORATIONS

2–042
The English law of domicile was evolved almost entirely with individuals in mind. It can only be applied to corporations with a certain sense of strain. A corporation is not born (though it is incorporated); it cannot marry (though it can be amalgamated with or taken over by another corporation); it cannot have children (though it can have subsidiaries); it does not die (though it can be dissolved or wound up). Hence in the case of corporations, most of the occasions for determining the domicile of an individual do not arise. But it may be important to know whether a so-called corporation possesses corporate

---

[176] *Lord Advocate v Jaffrey* [1921] 1 A.C. 146; *Att-Gen of Alberta v Cook* [1926] A.C. 444.
[177] [1982] Ch. 314; criticised by Wade, (1983) 32 I.C.L.Q. 1 and by Thompson, *ibid.*, 237.
[178] *The Law of Domicile*, para.8.7.

personality, whether it has been amalgamated with another corporation, or whether it has been dissolved. These questions are determined by the law of its domicile.

A corporation is domiciled (for purposes other than those of the Civil Jurisdiction and Judgments Acts 1982 and 1991)[179] in its place of incorporation. Unlike an individual, it cannot change that domicile, even if it carries on all its business elsewhere.[180]

It may be asked, if questions concerning the existence, amalgamation, or dissolution of a corporation are governed by the law of its place of incorporation, why not say so and dispense altogether with the fiction that it has a domicile? That question is unanswerable; but the difficulty is that tax statutes sometimes speak of the domicile of a corporation, and the reference has to be given some meaning.

DOMICILE AND NATIONALITY[181]

Until the beginning of the nineteenth century, domicile was universally regarded as the personal law for purposes of the conflict of laws. The change from domicile to nationality on the continent of Europe started in France with the promulgation of the Code Napoléon in 1804. One of the principal objects of the codifiers was to substitute a uniform law throughout the whole of France for the different *coutumes* of the French provinces. In matters of personal status these *coutumes* applied to persons domiciled within the province, wherever they happened to be. It was natural that the new uniform law should apply to French people everywhere, and art.3(1) of the Civil Code provided that "the laws governing the status and capacity of persons govern Frenchmen even though they are residing in foreign countries." No provision was expressly made for the converse case of foreigners residing in France, but the French courts held that in matters of status and capacity foreigners too were governed by their own national law. The provisions of the French code were adopted in Belgium and Luxembourg; similar provisions were contained in the Austrian code of 1811 and the Netherlands code of 1829.

2–043

The change from domicile to nationality on the continent of Europe was accelerated by Mancini's famous lecture delivered at the University of Turin in 1851. In his lecture, he advocated the principle of nationality on the ground that laws are made more for an ascertained people than for an ascertained territory. A sovereign (he said) in framing laws for his people should consider their habits and temperament, their physical and moral qualities, and even the climate, temperature and fertility of the soil. This was heady wine for a people preparing to throw off a foreign yoke and unify all the small states of Italy into a new nation. Under Mancini's influence, art.6 of the Italian Civil Code of 1865 provided that "the status and capacity of persons and family relations are governed by the laws of the nation to which they belong." Mancini's ideas also proved extremely influential outside Italy, and in the second half of the nineteenth

---

[179] See below, para.4–019.
[180] *Gasque v IRC* [1940] 2 K.B. 80.
[181] See Nadelmann, (1969) 17 Am.Jo.Comp. Law 418.

century the principle of nationality replaced that of domicile in code after code in continental Europe, until today only Norway and Denmark retain the principle of domicile. The result is that the nations of the world have become divided in their definition of the personal law; and it is this fact more than any other which impedes international agreement on uniform rules of the conflict of laws. What then are the arguments in favour of nationality or domicile as the personal law?

2–044   The advocates of nationality claim that it is more stable than domicile because nationality cannot be changed without the formal consent of the State of new nationality. However, as has been well said,[182] "the principle of nationality achieves stability, but by the sacrifice of a man's personal freedom to adopt the legal system of his own choice. The fundamental objection to the concept of nationality is that it may require the application to a man, against his own wishes and desires, of the laws of a country to escape from which he has perhaps risked his life."

It is also claimed that nationality is easier to ascertain than domicile because it involves a formal act of naturalisation and does not depend on the subjective intentions of the person concerned. This is undoubtedly true, though there may be difficult cases of double nationality or of statelessness. But it does not follow that the most easily ascertained law is the most appropriate law. Many immigrants who have no intention of returning to their country of origin do not take the trouble to apply for naturalisation.

The decisive consideration for countries such as the United Kingdom, the United States, Australia and Canada is that, save in a very few respects, there is no such thing as United Kingdom, American, Australian, or Canadian law. Since the object of referring matters of status and capacity to the personal law is to connect a person with one legal system for legal purposes, nationality breaks down altogether in the case of a federal or composite state containing more than one country.[183]

---

[182] Anton, *Private International Law* (Edinburgh: W. Green, 1970), p.123.
[183] See *Re O'Keefe* [1940] Ch. 124, and below at para.18–045.

THE EXCLUSION OF FOREIGN LAW

In any system of the conflict of laws, and the English system is no exception, the courts retain an overriding power to refuse to enforce, and sometimes even to refuse to recognise, rights acquired under foreign law on grounds of public policy. This notion is related to that of mandatory rules[1]; however, mandatory rules operate in priority to the normal conflicts process, whereas public policy operates when that process has led to an unacceptable result. In the English conflict of laws we need to consider first the general doctrine of public policy, which is necessarily somewhat vague; and secondly, some more specific applications of it.   **3–001**

PUBLIC POLICY

The nature and scope of the public policy doctrine was fully examined by Lord Nicholls of Birkenhead in *Kuwait Airways Corp v Iraqi Airways Co (Nos 4 and 5)*.[2] The case concerned the seizure by the Iraqi Government, in the immediate aftermath of the Iraqi invasion of Kuwait in 1990, of aircraft belonging to the claimant company, and the effect of an Iraqi Government Resolution transferring the ownership of the aircraft to the defendants.   **3–002**

Lord Nicholls described the normal workings of the conflict of laws, which often lead to the application of the laws of another country even though those laws are different from the law of the forum.[3] That was "overwhelmingly" the normal position, but "blind adherence to foreign law can never be required of an English court".[4] He continued:

---

[1] These are examined below at para.11–022.

[2] [2002] UKHL 19; [2002] 2 A.C. 883. See Rogerson, "Kuwait Airways Corp V Iraqi Airways Corp: The Territoriality Principle in Private International Law – Vice or Virtue?" (2003) *56 Current Legal Problems 265*; Briggs, "Choice of Law for Tort Claims" (2002) 73 B.Y.B.I.L. 487.

[3] See *Harding v Wealands* [2004] EWHC 1957 (New South Wales rules as to calculation of damages differed from those in England; but not contrary to English public policy).

[4] *In the Estate of Fuld (Deceased) (No.3)* [1968] P. 675 at 698, per Scarman J.

"Exceptionally and rarely, a provision of foreign law will be disregarded when it would lead to a result wholly alien to fundamental requirements of justice as administered by an English court. A result of this character would not be acceptable to an English court. In the conventional phraseology, such a result would be contrary to public policy. Then the court will decline to enforce or recognise the foreign decree to whatever extent is required in the circumstances".[5]

3–003 In English domestic law it is now well settled that the doctrine of public policy "should only be invoked in clear cases in which the harm to the public is substantially incontestable, and does not depend upon the idiosyncratic inferences of a few judicial minds".[6] In the conflict of laws it is even more necessary that the doctrine should be kept within proper limits, otherwise the whole basis of the system is liable to be frustrated. As Justice Cardozo, a distinguished American judge once said:

"[T]he courts are not free to refuse to enforce a foreign right at the pleasure of the judges, to suit the individual notion of expediency or fairness. They do not close their doors unless help would violate some fundamental principle of justice, some prevalent conception of good morals, some deep-rooted tradition of the common weal".[7]

Lord Nicholls held that the English courts had a residual power, to be exercised exceptionally and with the greatest circumspection, to disregard a provision in the foreign law when to do otherwise would affront basic principles of justice and fairness which the English courts seek to apply. Gross infringements of human rights were an important example, but the principle could not be confined to one particular category of unacceptable laws. In the *Kuwait Airways* case, the seizure of Kuwaiti assets was held to involve flagrant violations of rules of international law of fundamental importance; the breach of established principles of international law was plain and ultimately acknowledged by the Iraqi Government. In those circumstances, recognition of the Iraqi Government Resolution was contrary to public policy.

3–004 The doctrine of public policy has assumed far less prominence in the English conflict of laws than have seemingly corresponding doctrines, often referred to as *ordre public*, in the laws of some continental European countries.[8] One reason for this may be that English courts invariably apply English domestic law in many types of family proceedings, such as those involving divorce, maintenance, or the care or adoption of children. Thus, foreign law is inapplicable in many important departments of family law in which, in continental European countries, it is frequently excluded on grounds of public policy.

It is only on the rarest occasions that a foreign law itself can be regarded as contrary to English public policy.[9] What is usually in question is not the foreign law in the abstract, but the results of its enforcement or recognition in England in

---

[5] *Kuwait Airways Corpn v Iraqi Airways Co (Nos 4 and 5)* [2002] UKHL 19; [2002] 2 A.C. 883, at para.[16].
[6] *Fender v St. John Mildmay* [1938] A.C. 1 at 12, per Lord Atkin.
[7] *Loucks v Standard Oil Co.* (1918) 224 N.Y. 99 at 111; 120 N.E. 198 at 202, cited with approval in *Kuwait Airways Corpn v Iraqi Airways Co (Nos 4 and 5)* [2002] UKHL 19; [2002] 2 A.C. 883, at para.[17].
[8] See Mills, "The Dimensions of Public Policy in Private International Law" (2008) 4 J.Priv.I.L. 201.
[9] Traditional illustrations are laws licensing slavery and (perhaps now more arguable) prostitution.

the concrete case. Everything turns on the nature of the question which arises. Thus, until 1972, no polygamously married spouse could obtain a divorce from the English courts but the spouses were treated as married persons and thus incapable of contracting a valid marriage in England and the children were regarded as legitimate; and the wife was entitled to assert rights of succession and other rights on the footing that she was a wife.[10] Again, to take an improbable but striking example, if a foreign law allowed a bachelor aged 50 to adopt a spinster aged 17, an English court might hesitate to give the custody of the girl to her adoptive father; but that is no reason for not allowing her to succeed to his property as his "child" on his death intestate.[11] In other words, public policy is not absolute but relative; the recognition of a foreign status is one thing, and the recognition of all its incidents another.

The doctrine of public policy may not only lead a court to refuse to enforce or recognise, for example, a contract or a marriage when it would be valid under the appropriate foreign law. It may also produce the opposite effect, leading to the enforcement or recognition of a contract or a marriage that under the applicable foreign law would be invalid. Thus, a foreign law that invalidates a marriage will be disregarded if it is discriminatory and so adjudged penal.[12] On the other hand, the effect of the doctrine of public policy is always to exclude the application of foreign law that would otherwise be applicable. In one case,[13] the doctrine was anomalously applied so as to invoke the application of a foreign law which would otherwise have been inapplicable; but this case has since been held to have been wrongly decided.[14]

3–005

The reservation of public policy in conflict of laws cases is a necessary one, but "no attempt to define the limits of that reservation has ever succeeded".[15] All that can be done, therefore, is to enumerate the cases in which the recognition or enforcement of rights arising under foreign laws has been refused on this ground. It will be found that the doctrine has been usually invoked in two classes of case, namely those involving foreign contracts; and those involving a foreign status.

Contracts

Under Article 21 of the Rome I Regulation,[16] the application of a rule of law otherwise applicable by virtue of the Convention may be refused if its application is manifestly incompatible with the public policy *(ordre public)* of the forum.[17] So in *Duarte v Black & Decker Corp*,[18] the English court would have refused to

3–006

---

[10] See below, para.8–051.

[11] See below, para.10–081.

[12] Below, para.8–031.

[13] *Lorentzen v Lydden & Co Ltd* [1942] 2 K.B. 202.

[14] *Bank voor Handel en Scheepvart NV v Slatford (No.2)* [1953] 1 Q.B. 248 at 263–264 CA; *Peer International Corp v Termidor Music Publishers Ltd* [2003] EWCA Civ 1156; [2004] 2 W.L.R. 849 (noted Briggs, (2003) 74 B.Y.B.I.L. 522).

[15] Westlake, *Private International Law* (London: Sweet and Maxwell, 1925), p.51.

[16] See below, para.11–074. The same provision was in the predecessor provision, Rome Convention art.16.

[17] The English text of the Regulation includes the French term.

[18] [2007] EWHC 2720; [2008] 1 All E.R. (Comm) 401.

apply a covenant in restraint of trade had it been enforceable under the law governing the contract. In earlier cases, English courts refused to enforce champertous contracts,[19] contracts entered into under duress or coercion,[20] contracts involving collusive and corrupt arrangements for a divorce,[21] or trading with the enemy,[22] or breaking the laws of a friendly country.[23] On the other hand, they enforced contracts for the loan of money to be spent on gambling abroad,[24] and for foreign loans which contravened the English Moneylenders Acts.[25]

Status

3–007   English courts will not give effect to the results of any status existing under a foreign law which is penal, i.e. discriminatory. Examples are the status of slavery or civil death,[26] and the disabilities or incapacities which may be imposed on priests, nuns, Protestants, Jews, persons of alien nationality, persons of certain ethnic groups,[27] and divorced persons. Some of the disabilities referred to above are obviously imposed as a punishment,[28] e.g. the inability under some systems of law of persons divorced for adultery to remarry while the innocent spouse remains single,[29] or the disabilities imposed on Jews by the Nazi regime in Germany.[30] Others equally obviously are not, e.g. the inability under the laws of some Catholic countries of priests and nuns to marry at all.[31] None of these disabilities will be recognised in England, the true reason being that recognition would be contrary to English public policy.

The treatment of "prodigals" in civil law systems has sometimes been treated by the English courts as contrary to public policy, but it is arguable that the limitation of a person's normal powers of dealing with property to prevent it being dissipated is protective in nature not penal.[32]

---

[19] *Grell v Levy* (1864) 10 C.B. (N.S.) 73.
[20] *Kaufman v Gerson* [1904] 1 K.B. 591, a much-criticised decision.
[21] *Hope v Hope* (1857) 8 D. M. & G. 731.
[22] *Dynamit A/G v Rio Tinto Co.* [1918] A.C. 260.
[23] *Foster v Driscoll* [1929] 1 K.B. 470; *Regazzoni v KC Sethia* [1958] A.C. 301 (in both of which the contract was governed by English law).
[24] *Saxby v Fulton* [1909] 2 K.B. 208.
[25] *Schrichand v Lacon* (1906) 22 T.L.R. 245.
[26] *Re Metcalfe's Trusts* (1864) 2 D. J. & S. 122.
[27] See *Wolff v Oxholm* (1817) 6 M. & S. 92; *Re Fried Krupp AG* [1917] 2 Ch. 188; *Re Helbert Wagg & Co. Ltd's Claim* [1956] Ch. 323 at 345–346.
[28] See *Sottomayor v De Barros (No.2)* (1879) 5 P.D. 94 at 104
[29] *Scott v Att Gen* (1886) 11 P.D. 128, as explained in *Warter v Warter* (1890) L.R. 15 P.D. 152 at 155; below, para.8–031.
[30] See *Frankfurther v W L Exner Ltd* [1947] Ch. 629; *Novello & Co Ltd v Hinrichsen Edition Ltd* [1951] Ch. 595; *Oppenheimer v Cattermole* [1976] AC 249 at 277–278; *Kuwait Airways Corpn v Iraqi Airways Co (Nos 4 and 5)* 2002] UKHL 19; [2002] 2 A.C. 883, at para.[19]. cf. *Oppenheimer v Rosenthal & Co.* [1937] 1 All E.R. 23; *Ellinger v Guinness Mahon & Co.* [1939] 4 All E.R. 16.
[31] *Sottomayor v De Barros (No.2)*(1879) 5 P.D. 94 at 104.
[32] Compare *Worms v De Valdor* (1880) 49 L.J.Ch. 261 (Frenchman declared a prodigal and unable in French law to sue without approval of his *conseil judiciaire* held free to sue in England) and *Re Selot's Trusts* [1902] 1 Ch. 488 (French status of prodigal apparently not recognised). See also *Re Langley's Settlement* [1962] Ch. 541 (status of "incompetent" under Californian law did not prevent dealings in

Public policy may sometimes require that a capacity existing under foreign law should be disregarded in England[33] but the circumstances have to be extreme before such a course is taken. An example of such extreme circumstances is provided by *Westminster City Council v C*[34]:

> C had very limited mental capacity. In many respects his intellectual functioning was below that of an average three-year-old. At the behest of his family, he was married in an Islamic ceremony conducted by telephone, the bride being in Bangladesh. The marriage was valid under the law of Bangladesh.

> The English court received evidence that the marriage was potentially highly injurious to C, and noted that any sexual activity he was encouraged to engage in would be a criminal offence under English law. In its duty to prevent abuse to C, the marriage was refused recognition on the ground of public policy. Although marriages by proxy had been held not contrary to public policy,[35] some qualification was required were such a procedure to be used for abusive purposes.

3–008

English courts do recognise the validity of polygamous marriages,[36] and of marriages within the prohibited degrees of English law,[37] provided of course they are valid under the applicable foreign law. But they might refuse to recognise a marriage between persons so closely related that sexual intercourse between them was incestuous by English criminal law,[38] or with a child below the age of puberty.[39]

The mere fact that a foreign status or relationship is unknown to English domestic law is not a ground for refusing to recognise it.[40] Thus, legitimation by subsequent marriage was recognised and given effect to in England long before it became part of English domestic law.[41] The recognition of polygamous marriages is another example.

Other cases

Apart from cases of contract and status, examples of the exclusion of foreign law on the grounds of public policy are rare. It is not contrary to public policy to recognise foreign decrees confiscating private property,[42] but it may be otherwise if the decree is "penal" in the sense of being directed against the property of a

3–009

England); criticised by Grodecki, (1962) 11 I.C.L.Q. 578; Collier, [1962] C.L.J. 36. In all these cases, English law seems to have been the *lex causae,* and the results might have been different if the foreign law had been the *lex causae.*

[33] *Cheni v Cheni* [1965] P. 85 at 98.

[34] [2008] EWCA Civ 198; [2009] Fam. 11.

[35] *Apt v Apt* [1948] P. 83.

[36] See below, para.8–041.

[37] *Re Bozzelli's Settlement* [1902] 1 Ch. 751 (marriage in 1880 with deceased brother's widow); *Re Pozot's Settlement Trusts* [1952] 1 All E.R. 1107 at 1109 (marriage with step-daughter); *Cheni v Cheni* [1965] P. 85 (marriage between uncle and niece).

[38] *Brook v Brook* (1861) 9 H.L. Cas. 193 at 227–228; *Cheni v Cheni* [1965] P. 85 at 97.

[39] cf. *Alhaji Mohamed v Knott* [1969] 1 Q.B. 1, where such a marriage was recognised. See Karsten, (1969) 32 M.L.R. 212.

[40] *Phrantzes v Argenti* [1960] 2 Q.B. 19; *Shahnaz v Rizwan* [1965] 1 Q.B. 390 at 401.

[41] Below, para.10–063.

[42] *Luther v Sagor* [1921] 3 K.B. 532 at 559; *Princess Paley Olga v Weisz* [1929] 1 K.B. 718.

particular individual or a particular company or a particular family or persons of a particular race or a particular alien nationality.[43] It is not contrary to public policy to recognise foreign exchange control legislation,[44] but it may be otherwise if the legislation, even though originally passed with the genuine object of protecting the state's economy, has become an instrument of oppression and discrimination.[45] The recognition of a foreign decree of divorce or nullity of marriage[46] and the enforcement of a foreign judgment in personam[47] may be refused on grounds of public policy, but instances are extremely rare. There is no general principle that the application of a foreign law is contrary to public policy merely because it operates retrospectively.[48] However, the *Kuwait Airways* case[49] established that breaches of public international law could attract the public policy doctrine.

PENAL LAWS

3–010 It is well settled that English courts will not directly or indirectly enforce a foreign penal law. "The courts of no country execute the penal laws of another",[50] said Chief Justice Marshall of the United States. The reason has been thus explained by the Privy Council[51]:

> "The rule has its foundation in the well-recognised principle that crimes, including in that term all breaches of public law punishable by pecuniary mulct or otherwise, at the instance of the State Government, or of someone representing the public, are local in this sense, that they are only cognisable and punishable in the country where they were committed. Accordingly no proceeding, even in the shape of a civil suit, which has for its object the enforcement by the State, whether directly or indirectly, of punishment imposed for such breaches by the *lex fori*, ought to be admitted in the courts of any other country."

Although this principle is almost universally accepted, modern state practice requires some qualification of its more expansive formulations. There is a growing number of international treaties under which states, including the United Kingdom, provide mutual assistance in the conduct of criminal prosecutions. For example, compulsory measures available under the law of one state may be exercised at the request of a foreign state to search and seize evidence, or to freeze and confiscate the profits of drug-trafficking. International practice is reflected in English law in legislation such as the Crime (International Co-operation) Act 2003.

A "penal" law, in the present context, is a criminal law imposing a penalty recoverable at the instance of the State or of an official duly authorised to

---

[43] Below, para.13–058.
[44] *Kahler v Midland Bank Ltd* [1950] A.C. 24; *Zivnostenska Banka National Corpv Frankman* [1950] A.C. 57.
[45] *Re Helbert Wagg & Co. Ltd's Claim [1956]* [1956] Ch. 323 at 352.
[46] Below, para.9–060.
[47] Below, para.7–035.
[48] Below, para.18–061.
[49] *Kuwait Airways Corpn v Iraqi Airways Co (Nos 4 and 5)* [2002] UKHL 19; [2002] 2 A.C. 883.
[50] *The Antelope* (1825) 10 Wheat. 66 at 123.
[51] *Huntingdon v Attrill* [1893] A.C. 150 at 156.

prosecute on its behalf.[52] The fact that a particular piece of legislation contains provisions creating criminal offences does not mean that the whole Act is necessarily penal.[53] The word "penal" here has quite a different meaning from that which it bears in the contexts examined earlier in this chapter, where "penal" means merely discriminatory. It is for the English court to determine for itself whether the foreign law in question is a penal law, and it is not bound by the interpretation placed upon the law by the courts of the foreign country.[54]

Since "the essential nature and real foundation of a cause of action are not changed by recovering judgment upon it",[55] the court will not enforce a foreign judgment based upon a foreign penal law.[56] A striking illustration of the rule is afforded by *Banco de Vizcaya v Don Alfonso de Borbon y Austria*[57]:

3–011

> The King of Spain deposited securities with the Westminster Bank in London. A decree of the Constituent Cortes of Spain declared the ex-King to be guilty of high treason, and ordered all his properties, rights and grounds of action to be seized for its own benefit by the Spanish State. An action by a nominee of the State to recover the securities was dismissed.

An important distinction was drawn by the Irish courts in *Larkins v National Union of Mineworkers*[58]:

> A part of the funds of the National Union of Mineworkers was transferred to Ireland during the miners' strike of 1984. After the Union had refused to obey English court orders, its assets were made the subject of sequestration, and the sequestrators began proceedings in Ireland to recover sums in Irish bank accounts. A receiver was later appointed by the English court with general powers to take control of the Union's assets; the receiver began similar proceedings in the Irish courts. It was held that the sequestrator's action was a means of enforcing a penal process of English law, and could not be allowed; the receivership rested on other grounds, and the receiver's action could continue.

REVENUE LAWS

"No country ever takes notice of the revenue laws of another", said Lord Mansfield in *Holman v Johnson*[59]; and though (as will be seen below) this proposition is too widely stated, it has ever since been assumed by English lawyers that foreign revenue laws will not be enforced in England. Authority for this more limited proposition was sparse until the decision of the House of Lords

3–012

---

[52] *Huntingdon v Attrill* [1893] A.C. 150 at 157–158.
[53] *Islamic Republic of Iran v Barakat Galleries Ltd* [2007] EWCA Civ 1374; [2008] 3 W.L.R. 486.
[54] *Huntingdon v Attrill* [1893] A.C. 150
[55] *Wisconsin v Pelican Insurance Co* 127 U.S. 265 at 292 (1888).
[56] *Huntingdon v Attrill* [1893] A.C. 150.
[57] [1935] 1 K.B. 140. Compare *Huntingdon v Attrill* [1893] A.C. 150 (New York statute making company directors signing certificates false in any material respect personally liable for company debts held not to be penal). See the decision of the US Supreme Court in *Huntingdon v Attrill* 146 US 657 (1892).
[58] [1985] I.R. 671; cf. the distinction drawn in a rather different context in *Williams & Humbert Ltd v W&H Trade Marks (Jersey) Ltd* [1986] A.C. 368; below, para.13–057.
[59] (1775) 1 Cowp. 341 at 343.

in *Government of India v Taylor*[60] placed the matter beyond doubt. The reason for non-enforcement is that "tax-gathering is not a matter of contract but of authority and administration as between the state and those within its jurisdiction".

A foreign revenue law is a law requiring a non-contractual payment of money to the state or some department or sub-division thereof. It includes income tax,[61] capital gains tax,[62] customs duty,[63] death duties,[64] local rates or council taxes,[65] compulsory contributions to a State insurance scheme[66] and a profits levy.[67]

3–013 English courts will not enforce foreign revenue laws either directly or indirectly. Direct enforcement occurs when a foreign state or its nominee seeks to recover the tax by action in England. Indirect enforcement occurs, for example, where a company in liquidation seeks to recover from one of its directors assets under the director's control which the liquidator would use to pay foreign taxes due from the company,[68] or where a debtor pleads that the debt has been attached by a foreign garnishee order obtained by a foreign state claiming a tax.[69] But where neither direct nor indirect enforcement arises, foreign revenue laws are freely recognised.[70] Thus Lord Mansfield's proposition that "no country ever takes notice of the revenue laws of another" is now seen to be too widely stated. The difference between enforcement and recognition was explained by Lord Simonds in *Regazzoni v K.C. Sethia Ltd*[71]:

> "It does not follow from the fact that today the court will not enforce a revenue law at the suit of a foreign State that today it will enforce a contract which requires the doing of an act in a foreign country which violates the revenue law of that country. The two things are not complementary or co-extensive. This may be seen if for revenue law penal law is substituted. For an English court will not enforce a penal law at the suit of a foreign State, yet it would be surprising if it would enforce a contract which required the commission of a crime in that State".

---

[60] [1955] A.C. 491 at 514. The coming of the Brussels and Lugano Conventions (and now the Judgments Regulation) has made no difference: it remains a fundamental principle: *QRS 1 ApS v Frandsen* [1999] 1 W.L.R. 2169 (see Briggs, "Indirect Enforcement of Foreign Revenue Laws" (1999) 70 B.Y.I.L. 341).
[61] *USA v Harden* (1963) 41 D.L.R. (2d) 721.
[62] *Government of India* [1955] A.C. 491.
[63] *Att Gen for Canada v Schulze* (1901) 9 S.L.T. 4.
[64] *Re Visser* [1928] Ch. 877.
[65] *Municipal Council of Sydney v Bull* [1909] 1 K.B. 7.
[66] *Metal Industries (Salvage) Ltd v Owners of ST Harle* 1962 S.L.T. 114; cf. *The Acrux (No.3)* [1965] P. 391, where this point was overlooked.
[67] *Peter Buchanan Ltd v McVey* [1954] I.R. 89.
[68] *Peter Buchanan Ltd v McVey* [1954] I.R. 89.
[69] *Rossano v Manufacturers Life Assurance Co. Ltd* [1963] 2 Q.B. 352.
[70] *The State of Norway's Application (Nos 1 and 2)* [1990] 1 A.C. 723.
[71] [1958] A.C. 301 at 322.

OTHER PUBLIC LAWS

English courts will not enforce other public laws of a foreign state but the scope   **3–014**
of this principle is unclear.[72] In *Att Gen of New Zealand v Ortiz*,[73] which
concerned the unauthorised export of an ancient Maori carving from New
Zealand, Lord Denning M.R. recognised the existence of this "other public law"
category, but when the decision was affirmed in the House of Lords the
discussion of this point was regarded as obiter.[74]

It is perhaps best to limit the scope of "other public law" to the enforcement of
claims by the foreign state relating to the exercise of its governmental power.
That it is so limited is suggested by a number of decisions in several jurisdictions.
The High Court of Australia recognised the existence of such a principle in *Att
Gen v Heinemann Publishers Australia Pty Ltd*[75]:

> Mr Wright, a former member of the British Civil Service, wrote his memoirs under the title
> *Spycatcher*. The British Government sought to restrain their publication, relying on the duty of
> confidentiality arising from his employment.

The Australian court refused to grant the British Government an injunction, a
decision which has been trenchantly (and, it is submitted, rightly) criticised[76] as
going beyond the proper limits of the principle. The court regarded the principle
as including an action to protect and enforce the "interests" of the British
Government, a marked and undesirable extension of a principle which, as one
limiting access to the courts, should be cautiously applied.

The *Spycatcher* principle was examined in the Court of Appeal in *Mbasogo v*   **3–015**
Logo Ltd (No.1)[77]:

> After what was alleged to have been a conspiracy to overthrow the Government of Equatorial
> Guinea, the President of that state and the Republic itself sought remedies in the English
> courts against the conspirators. The defendants argued that this would be to enforce the public
> laws of a foreign state.
> The Court of Appeal sought to go behind the language of "public law". In its judgment, the
> critical question was whether in bringing a claim, a claimant was doing an act which was of a
> sovereign character or which was done by virtue of sovereign authority; and whether the claim
> involved the exercise or assertion of a sovereign right. If so, then the court would not
> determine or enforce the claim. On the other hand, if in bringing the claim the claimant was
> not doing an act which was of a sovereign character or by virtue of sovereign authority and the
> claim did not involve the exercise or assertion of a sovereign right and the claim did not seek
> to vindicate a sovereign act or acts, then the court would both determine and enforce it.

---

[72] See Collins, "Revolution and Restitution: Foreign States in National Courts", Collected Courses of
the Hague Academy of International Law 326 (Leiden: Brill Publishing, 2007) 11.
[73] [1984] A.C. 1. See now the Dealing in Cultural Objects (Offences) Act 2003.
[74] [1984] A.C. 1 at 41.
[75] (1988) 165 C.L.R. 30.
[76] Mann, "Spycatcher in the High Court of Australia" (1988) 104 L.Q.R. 497.
[77] [2006] EWCA Civ 1370; [2007] QB 246. For earlier related proceedings, see *President of the
Republic of Equatorial Guinea v Bank of Scotland International* [2006] UKPC 7.

That distinction was central to *Iran v Barakat Galleries Ltd.*[78] Like *Att Gen of New Zealand v Ortiz*[79] it involved the unlawful export of antiquities, and the Republic claimed remedies in conversion. The Court of Appeal found that the goods were the property of the Republic under Iranian law, and held that where the foreign state had acquired title under its law to property within its jurisdiction in cases not involving compulsory acquisition of title from private parties, so that it owned property in the same way as a private citizen, there was no reason in principle for the English court not to recognise its title in accordance with the general principle that the *lex situs* governed.[80]

3–016   It is increasingly the case that states, including the United Kingdom, use what are ostensibly civil proceedings to recover the proceeds of crime. The courts have had to examine how this practice relates to the rule about foreign penal laws. In *United States Securities & Exchange Commission v Manterfield*[81] the applicant for a freezing order was a United States regulator which was seeking in United States civil proceedings both the "disgorgement" of huge profits made in what was alleged to be a fraudulent scheme, the sums obtained to be returned to the victims of the fraud, and also a monetary penalty. The Court of Appeal upheld the freezing order in respect of the disgorgement, the applicant having given an undertaking not to enforce any penalty. However, that case was distinguished in *Pocket Kings Ltd v Safenames Ltd.*[82] The judge held that a foreign order requiring the forfeiture of assets used in the commission of crime under local foreign law, even if categorised by the foreign state as a civil remedy under its law, was "distinctly penal in nature, requiring the confiscation without compensation of an asset on the ground that the owner, or user of it, was guilty of a criminal offence"; the fact that the purpose of the forfeiture was ostensibly to protect the public rather than to punish the wrongdoer did not alter the position.

It is still difficult to be sure how this part of the law will develop. It would be wise for the courts to maintain a flexible approach which recognises the great variety and the continuing capacity for development within the field of "governmental power".

---

[78] [2007] EWCA Civ 1374; [2008] 3 W.L.R. 486.
[79] [1984] A.C. 1. See now Council Directive 93/7/EEC of 15 March 1993 on the return of cultural objects unlawfully removed from the territory of a Member State [1993] OJ L74 74, the Return of Cultural Objects Regulations 1994 (SI 1994/501), and the Dealing in Cultural Objects (Offences) Act 2003.
[80] On that principle, see para.13–052.
[81] [2009] EWCA Civ 27,; [2010] 1 W.L.R. 172.
[82] [2009] EWHC 2529 (Ch); [2010] Ch. 438.

CHAPTER 4

JURISDICTION: THE EUROPEAN REGIME

The rules as to jurisdiction determine whether or not a court can hear a case. **4–001** More precisely, they identify the country or countries whose courts can appropriately deal with a case.

The notion of an "appropriate forum" for the resolution of a dispute is a complex one, and is understood in different ways in different legal traditions. Clearly there must be limits to the jurisdiction of the courts of any country. It would be entirely appropriate for the English court to have jurisdiction over an action arising out of a fight between two English students in the middle of an English city. It would be entirely inappropriate for that court to deal with an action arising out of a fight between two Chinese students in the middle of Beijing. In practice, cases seldom have the simplicity of such textbook examples: they may concern corporations operating in several countries, or events causing loss or damage in several countries. There is also the time factor: if a claim is brought against a defendant now based wholly within a single country, and having assets solely in that country, it may well be appropriate to have the claim heard there. That will be true even if the underlying dispute has no connection with that country and neither party had any such connection when the dispute first arose.

Before the rules as to jurisdiction are examined more closely, it should be noted **4–002** that in federal countries, and countries which have courts operating on a regional basis, similar issues may arise in deciding how cases are to be allocated between the various regions. As we shall see, many rules give jurisdiction to the courts of the United Kingdom, but it is then necessary to decide whether the case is to be heard in England, Scotland or Northern Ireland. Students of legal history may recall the old rules as to "venue" which identified the English county within which a trial was to be held. There are still some rules assigning cases to particular local courts but they are regarded as domestic rules and not part of the conflict of laws.

By far the greater part of this chapter is concerned with jurisdiction on actions in personam; a brief mention of the effects of the Brussels I Regulation[1] in relation to English actions in rem follows.[2] An action in personam is an action brought against a person to compel him or her to do a particular thing, e.g. the payment of a debt or of damages for breach of contract or for tort, or the specific performance of a contract; or to compel a person not to do something, e.g. when an injunction is sought. It does not include Admiralty actions in rem, probate actions, administration actions, petitions in matrimonial causes, or cases concerning guardianship or custody of children, or proceedings in bankruptcy or for the winding up of companies.

CONCURRENT JURISDICTION: CHOICE BY THE CLAIMANT

4–003   In many cases, there will be two or more countries with jurisdiction, each of which could properly provide the forum in which the matter could be tried. It is the claimant who decides whether and where to begin legal proceedings, and the claimant's choice of forum may have a crucial effect on the outcome of the case. The choice is influenced by a whole series of factors of greater or lesser sophistication.

One is simply a wish to "play on one's home ground". Particularly to the individual or small firm claimant, it seems only natural to sue in the local courts down the road. Litigation is never comfortable, but it seems less alarming in one's home town, or at least one's home country, before local judges, speaking one's own language. There is perhaps the subconscious feeling that the court is more likely to be on your side if you are the local party, a feeling that may even be justified.

The home ground factor shades into considerations of convenience. It is easier to sue locally in most cases – but not always. It may depend on the location of the evidence and of potential witnesses. A corporate claimant may have in-house lawyers: if not, much may depend on the location of the legal firm which understands the special features of the particular company or the particular business.

4–004   A more sophisticated analysis will take into account differences in the substantive law applied in the possible fora including, of course, their choice of law rules. The law that would be applied might, for example, make liability strict or require a claimant to prove negligence; it might provide for compensatory damages only or exemplary ("punitive") damages as well. There might be a difference in the limitation periods applicable in the different countries, and different categories of persons eligible to sue, as a result, for example, of varying definitions of "relatives" able to claim in fatal accident cases, or the existence of strict privity of contract rules, or the availability of claims by "third-party beneficiaries".

Other relevant factors include differences in procedural law, including the law of evidence and pre-trial procedures such as the extensive rights of "discovery"

---

[1] Council Regulation (EC) No 44/2001 of 22 December 2000 on jurisdiction and the recognition and enforcement of judgements in civil and commercial matters [2001] OJ L12/1.
[2] See below, para.4–085.

available to claimants and potential claimants in United States jurisdictions, and differences in professional practices, such as rights of audience and the rules as to costs or contingent fees.

All these factors put the claimant in a strong position. It is natural to assume that the claimant is the person asserting that someone else is liable for a particular act or omission, but that is not necessarily the case. Someone who appears to be the potential defendant may attempt a pre-emptive strike by seeking a negative declaration, a ruling that there is no liability to the claimant, and the proceedings for such a declaration would be in a forum chosen by the applicant, the potential defendant.

Can the claimant's choice be challenged?

The claimant is able to take many matters into account so as to select the most favourable forum. The forum which is most favourable to the claimant may not be the forum which is, on more objective criteria, the most appropriate for the trial of the case. A defendant may well feel that the claimant, by selecting a forum which is relatively inappropriate, is "playing the system", manipulating it to the claimant's own advantage. In the common law tradition, various devices were developed which enabled defendants to influence the choice of forum, and which enabled the judges themselves to steer a case to what they considered the most appropriate court.[3]

4–005

Under the doctrine of *forum non conveniens*, originating in Scots law,[4] a defendant might ask the court chosen by the claimant not to exercise its jurisdiction on the ground that the case could more appropriately be tried elsewhere.[5] In some cases the defendant could prevent the claimant suing in a foreign court by obtaining an anti-suit injunction.[6] As we shall see, developments within the European Union have greatly limited the use that can be made of these procedures.

General and special jurisdiction

This classification was first coined more than forty years ago.[7] It distinguishes, on the one hand, jurisdictional grounds based on the relationship between the forum and the person or persons whose legal rights are to be affected (general jurisdiction) and, on the other hand, jurisdictional grounds based on the

4–006

---

[3] See *Stonebridge Underwriting Ltd v Ontario Municipal Insurance Exchange* [2010] EWHC 2279 (Comm); [2011] Lloyd's Rep. I.R. 171.

[4] The doctrine took various tags when it first appeared: *forum non conveniens, forum conveniens* and *forum non competens*. The earliest cases identified as the origins of the doctrine date from the 1830s. In *Sim v Robinow* (1892) 19 R. 665 Lord Kinnear, at 668, made the doctrine "fit for export", providing the world with a valuable device to secure the ends of justice; and particularly, to contain far-reaching general jurisdictional bases. The doctrine was successfully developed in the United States; see among the leading cases *Canada Malting Co Ltd v Paterson Steamships Ltd* 285 U.S. 413 (1932); and later on, in England.

[5] See below, para.5–044.

[6] See below, para.5–053.

[7] von Mehren and Trautman, (1966) 79 Harvard L. Rev. 1121.

relationship between the forum and the dispute (special jurisdiction).[8] The universal assertion *actor sequitur forum rei* is the most accepted general jurisdictional ground internationally. This is because of the advantages generally possessed by the claimant; this basic rule of "general jurisdiction"[9] requires a link between the *defendant* and the chosen court, for example the habitual residence of the defendant and not of the claimant. In the United States this has been elevated to a constitutional rule, as an application of the Due Process clause.

This principle of resort to what is sometimes called "the defendant's forum" is qualified in a number of ways. What is an appropriate jurisdiction may depend on the subject matter as much as on the identity and characteristics of the parties, so there are additional rules of "special jurisdiction",[10] for example taking into account where an obligation was to be performed. In international civil and commercial litigation in Europe, this other category – special jurisdiction – includes the jurisdictional grounds based on an objective link between the forum and the dispute, such as the place of the characteristic performance in contractual matters,[11] the place where the harmful event occurred or may occur for tort/delict claims,[12] or the place where the res is situated for jurisdiction regarding proceedings concerning rights in rem in relation to immovable/heritable property.[13] A court exercising special jurisdiction "may adjudicate only disputes which are related to the particular connecting factor on which jurisdiction is based".[14] Choice of court agreements can also be considered as a source of special jurisdiction: the agreement of the parties determines the scope of competence of the chosen court, so that it may adjudicate only disputes that are within the competence attributed to the court by the choice of court agreement.[15]

4–007 Furthermore, some categories of claimant deserve special consideration: consumers seeking to sue commercial firms with which they have had unhappy dealings; employees in dispute with their employers (though some employees may be rich and powerful: labels can mislead); policy-holders with a claim against an insurance company. In many of these cases, there may be "protective" jurisdiction.[16] Contrary to the usual rule, such a claimant may be allowed to sue in his or her home jurisdiction even if the defendant is based elsewhere. Finally, because in some cases, notably disputes about title to land, the location of the

---

[8] de Winter, (1968) 17 I.C.L.Q. 706 at 718. Note that in the US "special jurisdiction" is known as "specific jurisdiction". The term used in the Brussels I Regulation, i.e. special jurisdiction (art.5), is the one used throughout this book.

[9] Jurisdiction *ratione personae*.

[10] Subject-matter jurisdiction or jurisdiction *ratione materiae*.

[11] Brussels I Regulation art.5(1).

[12] Brussels I Regulation art.5(3).

[13] Brussels I Regulation art.22(1).

[14] Hill, "The Exercise of Jurisdiction in Private International Law" in Capps, Evans and Konstadinidis (eds), *Asserting Jurisdiction -International and European Legal Approaches* (Oxford: Hart Publishing, 2003), p.52.

[15] Fentiman, *International Commercial Litigation* (Oxford: Oxford University Press, 2010); para.5–061.

[16] See paras 4–051 to 4–059.

subject matter is of more importance than any other factor, there may be rules giving "exclusive jurisdiction" to the courts of the country in which the property is to be found.[17]

In the context of the Brussels I Regulation, the ECJ stressed in *Falco Privatstiftung v Weller-Lindhorst*[18] that "the broad logic and scheme of the rules governing jurisdiction laid down by Regulation No 44/2001 require ... a narrow interpretation of the rules of special jurisdiction[19]... which derogate from the general principle that jurisdiction is based on the defendant's domicile".[20]

THE APPLICABLE SETS OF JURISDICTIONAL RULES

The Brussels I Regulation

Four different sets of rules govern the jurisdiction of the English courts. The first is the Brussels I Regulation. Provisions making the necessary adjustments to the law of the United Kingdom were made in the Civil Jurisdiction Order 2001.[21] The Brussels I Regulation now applies in every Member State of the European Union, Denmark having accepted its terms in a special Agreement which came into effect on July 1, 2007. The Regulation contains the latest version of rules first established in the Brussels Convention of 1968.[22] The 1968 text reflected, as one would expect, the civil law traditions of the original signatory Member States, and it was adjusted in 1978 to facilitate the accession of the United Kingdom, Ireland, and Denmark, states whose legal traditions are not in the classical civil law form.

4–008

The Lugano Convention

On 16 September 1988, a new Convention, closely based upon but not identical to the then current text of the Brussels Convention, was signed at Lugano. The signatories were Member States of the European Union and of the European Free Trade Association ("EFTA"), and the object of what was sometimes called "the Parallel Convention" was to apply the principles of the earlier Convention throughout the wider area covered by the two groups of States. As most of the

4–009

---

[17] Advocate General Jacobs, writing in Case C-37/00 *Weber v Universal Ogden Services* [2002] Q.B. 1189 of the application of the basic principles of jurisdiction in the European legislation, could not resist tracing their ancestry to a national source: "The principles ... are not new. Already in the sixteenth century, Sir James Balfour of Pittendreich wrote in his *Practicks*: 'Na man may be Judge in ony cause, bot gif defendar be within his jurisdiction, be resson of his dwelling place within the same, or in respect of contract of obligation made thair; or be resson of tresspas committit within the boundis thairof, or in respect of the thing that is askit and clamit, quhilk is and lyis within his jurisdictioun; because the persewar sould follow the defendar's jurisdictioun, and persew him befoir his awin competent Judge' (*Of jugeis* , Ch.15, p.284 in the printed editions)".

[18] Case C-533/07, [2010] Bus L. R. 210.

[19] See also Case C-462/06 *Glaxosmithkline v Rouard* [2008] E.C.R. I-3965.

[20] Case C-462/06 *Glaxosmithkline v Rouard* [2008] E.C.R. I-3965 at [37].

[21] SI 2001/3929.

[22] Formally the Convention on Jurisdiction and the Enforcement of Judgments in Civil and Commercial Matters of 27 September 1968; it came into force on February 1, 1973.

EFTA signatories have since become Member States of the European Union, the Lugano Convention now applies only as between the Member States and Iceland, Norway and Switzerland. It was given effect in the UK by the Civil Jurisdiction and Judgments Act 1991. A revised version of the Convention was agreed on October 30, 2007. The Lugano Convention 2007 entered into force for the European Union (including Denmark) and Norway on January 1, 2010; for Switzerland on January 1, 2011 and for Iceland on May 1, 2011.[23] The new Convention's text is for the most part identical to that of the Brussels I Regulation.[24]

Intra-United Kingdom jurisdictional rules

4–010   There is one more variant of the European rules, based on Chapter II of the Brussels I Regulation, allocating jurisdiction as between different parts of the United Kingdom.[25] It is considered further below,[26] but as a general rule the position before the English courts of a person domiciled in another part of the United Kingdom is similar to that of one domiciled in another Contracting State.

English traditional rules of jurisdiction

4–011   So far, all the sets of rules are derived from European initiatives. When the United Kingdom joined the European Union, it had to decide whether to apply the principles underlying the European instruments universally, in all cases coming before the English courts. A contrary position prevailed: there should be no change in the existing practice of the English courts in what could broadly be described as "non-European" cases.[27] So, the fourth set of rules governing the jurisdiction of the English courts contains the "traditional rules" developed by the judges and now stated in the Civil Procedure Rules. The Rules of Court of many Commonwealth countries are based on the principles underlying these traditional rules. The technical basis on which the English courts apply the traditional rules is art.4 of the Brussels I Regulation: that allows national law to apply in cases not caught by the other provisions of the Regulation. The traditional rules are examined in the next chapter.

At one time it seemed likely that the Hague Conference on Private International Law would produce a potentially world-wide convention on jurisdiction and the recognition and enforcement of judgments, but after a decade of work the project had to be abandoned. This initial failure is instructive, for it

---

[23] The Civil Jurisdiction and Judgments Regulations 2009 (SI 2009/3131), has amended the Civil Jurisdiction and Judgments Act 1982 to reflect the entry into force of the 2007 Lugano Convention.

[24] See the Explanatory Report by Pocar ("the Pocar Report"), [2009] OJ C319/1; for the relationship between the Brussels I Regulation and the 2007 Lugano Convention, see art.64 of the latter and the Pocar Report at paras 18–22.

[25] Civil Jurisdiction and Judgments Act 1982 Sch.4 as substituted by the Civil Jurisdiction Order 2001 (SI 2001/3929) and amended by the Civil Jurisdiction and Judgments Regulations 2009 (SI 2009/3131).

[26] See para.4.083.

[27] cf. the situation in Scotland: Maher and Rodger, *Civil Jurisdiction in the Scottish Courts* (Edinburgh: W. Green, 2010).

reveals continuing tensions between the approaches adopted in the common law and civil law traditions and between the jurisdictional rules developed in the United States and those found in almost all other countries.[28] In the EU these tensions can be gradually lessened by reviewing the working of the jurisdictional rules every so often. The Brussels I Regulation made provision for the European Commission to report on its functioning after five years from its entry into force, and to make the necessary proposals for its amendment.[29] A revised Brussels I Regulation is expected to be adopted in 2012–2013. The United Kingdom has decided to opt into the revised Regulation.

THE BRUSSELS I REGULATION

Interpretation

Under the Treaty on the Functioning of the European Union ("TFEU"), where a court of final appeal in any Member State finds that a decision on the interpretation of the Regulation is necessary for it to give judgment, it must refer the matter to the ECJ.[30] Other courts, trial or appellate, may make such a reference[31] and will apply the principles laid down by the ECJ.[32] The courts must also consider the explanatory reports published in the *Official Journal*.[33]

4–012

Scope

Article 1 provides that the Brussels I Regulation is to apply in civil and commercial matters whatever the nature of the court or tribunal but that it is not to extend, in particular, to revenue, customs or administrative matters.[34] It does not apply to (1) the status or legal capacity of natural persons, rights in property

4–013

---

[28] See McClean, in Fawcett (ed), *Reform and Development of Private International Law* (Oxford: Oxford University Press, 2002), p.255ff.; O'Brian, "The Hague Convention on Jurisdiction and Judgments: The Way Forward, (2003) 66 M.L.R. 491.

[29] Brussels I Regulation art.73. The revision process started in 2009 (see the Report from the Commission (COM (2009) 174 final); see also the Green Paper (COM (2009) 175 final) and a proposal for a revised Regulation was published on the December 14, 2010 (COM (2010) 748) (hereafter "the EU Commission Proposal"). Where appropriate in this chapter and in the following one, reference will be made to some of the issues raised by the EU Commission Proposal.

[30] Treaty on the Functioning of the European Union (TFEU) art 267.

[31] This is a possibility introduced by the Treaty of Lisbon, in force since December 1, 2009.

[32] See the express provision to that effect in the context of the Brussels Convention: Civil Jurisdiction and Judgments Act 1982 s.3(1). The Lugano Convention is not subject to interpretation by the ECJ, but an English court is obliged to "take account of" any principles laid down in a relevant decision in another Contracting State: Civil Jurisdiction and Judgments Act 1982 s.3B(1) inserted by Civil Jurisdiction and Judgments Act 1991 s.1(1).

[33] Civil Jurisdiction and Judgments Act 1982 ss.3(3) (as amended by SI 1989/1346 and S.I. 1990/2591) and 3B(2) (inserted by Civil Jurisdiction and Judgments Act 1991 s.1(1)). The reports are the Jenard report on the 1968 text (O.J. 1979, C59); the Schlosser report on the 1978 Accession Convention (*ibid.*); the reports on the 1982 and 1989 Accession Conventions (O.J. 1986 C298 and 1990 C189); and that on the Lugano text (O.J. 1990 C189).

[34] art.1(1).

arising out of a matrimonial relationship, wills and succession; (2) bankruptcy, the winding-up of insolvent companies and analogous proceedings[35]; (3) social security; or (4) arbitration.[36]

The category of "rights in property arising out of a matrimonial relationship", excluded from the scope of the Regulation, is to be distinguished from maintenance which is within it.[37] In *Van den Boogard v Laumen*[38] an English divorce court ordered a lump sum payment and the transfer of certain property, and enforcement was sought in the Netherlands. The ECJ drew a distinction between orders made for the purpose of providing support for the wife, which would be a maintenance matter, and orders effecting the division of property, which would relate to "rights in property arising out of a matrimonial relationship". This distinction is not always clearly drawn in English court orders made after a divorce, especially where large sums of money are involved.

In *West Tankers Inc v Allianz SpA*[39] the exclusion of arbitration from the scope of application of the Brussels I Regulation was considered. The claimant applied in English courts for an anti-suit injunction to restrain the defendant from pursuing legal proceedings in the Italian courts, proceedings which were allegedly brought in breach of an arbitration agreement between the parties. As the purpose of the anti-suit injunction was to enforce the arbitration agreement, the claimant argued that the English proceedings fell outside the scope of the Regulation. However, the ECJ ruled that despite the arbitration agreement, the Italian proceedings, involving a claim based on non-contractual obligations, concerned civil and commercial matters within the scope of Brussels I.[40] Hence, the claim was within the scope of the Regulation (and the requested anti-suit injunction, whose purpose was to obstruct those proceedings, was held to be incompatible with the Regulation).[41]

Civil and commercial matters

4–014   The text of the Regulation does not define the key term, "civil and commercial matters". In common law countries, this term is not in general use. To a common lawyer, it appears to cover everything that is not a criminal matter, and its use in international conventions such as those negotiated at the Hague Conference on Private International Law has given rise to difficulties as a result.[42] In civil law

---

[35] See Case 133/78 *Gourdain v Nadler* [1979] E.C.R. 733; *Polymer Vision R&D Ltd v Van Dooren* [2011] EWHC 2951 (Comm).
[36] Case C-190/89 *Marc Rich & Co. AG v Societa Italiana Impianti pA, The Atlantic Emperor* [1991] E.C.R. I-3855. Provisional measures in support of arbitration are not excluded: Case C-391/95 *Van Uden Maritime BV v Deco-Line* [1999] 2 W.L.R. 1181.
[37] See art.5(2), considered below, para.4–037; see also paras 9–067 to 9–087.
[38] Case C-220/95, [1997] E.C.R. I-1147; [1997] Q.B. 759.
[39] Case C-185/07, [2009] E.C.R. I-663; [2009] 1 A.C. 1138.
[40] See also *Youell v La Réunion Aérienne* [2009] 1 Lloyd's Rep. 586.
[41] Not surprisingly, this decision has been severely criticised in England, see e.g. Briggs, [2009] L.M.C.L.Q. 161; Peel, (2009) 125 L.Q.R. 356; Fentiman, [2009] C.L.J. 278. A European Parliament non-legislative resolution of September 7, 2010 (T7-0304/2010, para (M)) on the review of the Brussels I Regulation favoured the state of affairs prior to the *West Tankers* decision which might one day pass into history.
[42] See *Re the State of Norway's Application (Nos. 1 and 2)* [1990] 1 A.C. 723; below, para.17.018.

countries, the more usual contrast is with public law, though the precise boundary is an unclear and shifting one. For this reason, the ECJ held that the concept was among what has become quite a long list of terms which must be given an "autonomous" meaning, not tied to the understanding of any one legal system. The rationale behind "autonomous interpretation" is the aim to attain uniformity in the allocation of jurisdiction throughout the European area of justice. So in the *Eurocontrol* case[43]:

> Eurocontrol, an international agency supplying air traffic control services to civil aviation in Western Europe, claimed route charges allegedly owed by Lufthansa. Eurocontrol was clearly a public body, but that did not necessarily take the claim outside the "civil and commercial" category. The Court held that the question had to be asked whether the public body was acting in the exercise of its powers. If it were *not*, the matter would be a "civil and commercial" one.

The reference to the public body acting in the exercise of its powers is not to the English law notion of acting intra or ultra vires. The contrast is between a claim arising out of the primary purposes of a public authority, in the *Eurocontrol* case the provision of air traffic control services, and a claim arising out of activities not specific to those purposes, for example the purchase of food for consumption in the organisation's staff canteen. It is not surprising that issues concerning the acts of German armed forces in Greece during the Second World War should be regarded as outside the scope of "civil and commercial matters" as military operations are a direct exercise of state sovereignty.[44] Other cases are more difficult.[45] So it has been held that claims relating to clearance of a wreck in a public waterway by the public authority charged with that responsibility[46] and a claim against a central bank charged with supervisory duties over the registration of companies[47] were not civil or commercial matters; but a claim concerning the actions of a teacher in a state school taking pupils on climbing trip was, as it did not involve an exercise of public authority powers.[48] In *Realchemie Nederland BV v Bayer Cropscience AG*[49] the ECJ held that a party's right to exclusively exploit the invention protected by its patent was clearly within the autonomous concept.

---

[43] Case 29/76 *LTU GmbH v Eurocontrol* [1976] E.C.R. 1541.
[44] Case C-292/05 *Lechouritou v Dimisio tis Omospondiakis Dimokratias tis Germanias* [2007] 2 All E.R. (Comm) 57.
[45] See Betlem and Bernasconi, (2006) 122 L.Q.R. 124.
[46] Case 814/79 *Netherlands State v Ruffer* [1980] E.C.R. 3807.
[47] *Grovit v Nederlandesche Bank* [2007] EWCA Civ 953; [2008] 1 W.L.R. 51.
[48] Case C-172/91 *Sonntag v Waidmann* [1993] E.C.R. I-1963. See also Case C-435/06 *C* [2008] 3 W.L.R. 419 (taking child into care a "civil matter" for purposes of Brussels II Revised (Regulation 2201/2003 concerning jurisdiction and the recognition and enforcement of judgments in matrimonial matters and matters of parental responsibility).
[49] Case C-406/09, October 18, 2011, [2012] I.L.Pr.1.

Domicile

4–015   The concept of domicile has a very important place in the scheme of the Regulation, but a definition is given only in the case of companies and other "legal persons".[50]

Individuals

4–016   Article 59 provides that in order to determine whether a party is domiciled in the Member State whose courts are seised of a matter, the court is to apply its internal law. So, if the English court has to determine whether an individual party is or is not domiciled in England, it is English law that supplies the applicable definition of domicile. It was recognised that it would be unsatisfactory, indeed absurd, to use in this context the traditional understanding of domicile. Domicile in that sense can be very artificial, notably as a result of its emphasis on permanent home and on the domicile of origin, and it is often difficult to ascertain. It describes a long-term association between an individual and a country: there is no reason to insist on such an association before an individual can, for example, be sued for breach of contract. Instead a definition of domicile was needed that could be applied more readily and would be closer to the understandings of domicile in the states of mainland Europe as something not dissimilar from habitual residence. So, s.41 of the Civil Jurisdiction and Judgments Act 1982 supplied a new definition in the context of the Brussels Convention, and the same rules are applied to the Regulation in the Civil Jurisdiction and Judgments Order 2001.[51]

The rules provide that an individual is domiciled in the United Kingdom if and only if he or she is resident in the United Kingdom and the nature and circumstances of the residence indicate that the individual has a substantial connection with the United Kingdom.[52] There is no definition of 'residence' or of 'substantial connection' but the English courts speak of a 'settled or usual place of abode'.[53] This can involve a time-consuming assessment of all the circumstances. To minimise the need for this, the rules provide that in the case of an individual who is resident in the United Kingdom and has been so resident for the last three months or more, the requirement of substantial connection is presumed to be fulfilled unless the contrary is proved.[54] This, very convenient, rule resolves most domicile issues, but the "substantial connection" test is relevant if it sought either to defeat the presumption or to establish the acquisition of a domicile within the three month period. *Petrotrade Inc. v Smith*[55] provides an illustration of that last type of case:

---

[50] It has been suggested that the revised Brussels I Regulation should include an autonomous rule for determining the domicile of individuals as it does for companies in art.60 (see European Commission, Brussels I Green Paper, COM (2009) 175 final, p.10).

[51] SI 2001/3929 Sch.1, para.9.

[52] Civil Jurisdiction and Judgments Order 2001 Sch.1, para.9(2).

[53] *Bank of Dubai Limited v Fouad Haji Abbas* [1997] I.L.Pr. 308 (C.A.).

[54] Civil Jurisdiction and Judgments Order 2001 Sch.1, para.9(6).

[55] [1998] 2 All E.R. 346.

Mr Smith, born in England and of British nationality, had lived for some eight years in Switzerland; his work was there and he had a Swiss wife. He came to England on what was intended to be a four-day visit. He was arrested and was bailed on condition that he remained in England. He remained on bail for two years, and once the criminal proceedings were dropped decided to stay on in England. The issue was his domicile 21 days after his initial arrival in England, and it was held that his enforced presence in England did not indicate a substantial connection.

It is almost always necessary to show that someone is domiciled not merely in the **4–017** United Kingdom as a whole but in a particular part of it, for example in England. An individual is domiciled in a particular part of the United Kingdom if, and only if, he or she is resident in that part and the nature and circumstances of the residence indicate that the individual has a substantial connection with that part.[56] The presumption based on residence for three months applies in this context.[57]

There may well be cases in which the three-month rule is unhelpful. Suppose D is appointed by his German company to come to the United Kingdom to set up a marketing and distribution network for the company's products. He has been in the United Kingdom for six months, dividing his time as to two-fifths in England, two-fifths in Scotland, and one-fifth in Northern Ireland. He has never spent a continuous period of three months in any of them, and may well be found not to have a substantial connection with any one part. To deal with this type of case, the rules provide that if an individual is domiciled in the United Kingdom but has no substantial connection with any particular part, he is to be treated as domiciled in the part of the United Kingdom in which he is resident.[58]

Under the Brussels I Regulation, it is sometimes necessary to determine the "place" where an individual is domiciled.[59] An individual is domiciled in a particular place in the United Kingdom if, and only if, he or she is (a) domiciled in the part of the United Kingdom in which that place is situated; and (b) is resident in that place.[60]

The Regulation provides that if a party is not domiciled in the state whose courts are seised of the matter, then, in order to determine whether the party is domiciled in another Member State, the court is to apply the law of that state.[61] This contrasts with the approach under the traditional domicile rules, where English law is always applied. There is another contrast: under the Regulation an individual may have more than one domicile. It may be, for example, that French law would regard an individual as domiciled in France, and Belgian law would accept him or her as a Belgian domiciliary. In such a case, an action may be begun in either country. For the purposes of the Regulation, the ECJ has held that defendants with unknown domicile are domiciled at their last known domicile.[62] The Regulation does not address the determination of the domicile of a person in a state other than a Member State. The rules in the Civil Jurisdiction and Judgments Order 2001 provide that an individual is domiciled in such a state if

---

[56] Civil Jurisdiction and Judgments Order 2001 Sch.1, para.9(4).
[57] Civil Jurisdiction and Judgments Order 2001 Sch.1, para.9(6).
[58] Civil Jurisdiction and Judgments Order 2001 Sch.1, para.9(5).
[59] e.g. under art.5(2) (maintenance claims).
[60] Civil Jurisdiction and Judgments Order 2001 Sch.1, para.9(3).
[61] art.59(2).
[62] Case C-327/10 *Hypotecni banka a.s. v Lindner* (November, 17 2011).

and only if he is resident in that state and the nature and circumstances of his residence indicate that he has a substantial connection with that state.[63] In this case, there is no presumption based on three months' residence.

Corporations and associations

4–019   A different approach is taken in the case of a company or other legal person or association of natural or legal persons; this will include partnerships[64] and clubs with a defined membership. Article 60(1) provides that, for the purposes of the Regulation, such an entity is domiciled at the place where it has its statutory seat, or central administration, or principal place of business. Although it is unlikely in practice, this can mean that the entity is domiciled in three different countries.[65]

The notion of "statutory seat" is unknown in common law countries, so the Regulation has a special rule that for the purposes of the United Kingdom and Ireland: "statutory seat" means the registered office or, where there is no such office anywhere, the place of incorporation or, where there is no such place anywhere, the place under the law of which the formation took place.[66]

There is one further complication. Article 22(2) of the Regulation, considered below,[67] gives exclusive jurisdiction over certain disputes about the constitution, dissolution or acts of a company or association to the courts for the "seat" of that entity. In order to determine the seat, a court is to apply its rules of private international law.[68] The relevant English rules are set out in the Civil Jurisdiction and Judgments Order 2001.[69] For the purposes of art.22(2), a company, legal person or association has its seat in the United Kingdom if and only if (a) it was incorporated or formed under the law of a part of the United Kingdom; or (b) its central management and control is exercised in the United Kingdom. A company, legal person or association has its seat in another state to which the Regulation applies if and only if (a) it was incorporated or formed under the law of that state; or (b) its central management and control is exercised in that state. But it will not be regarded as having a seat in such a state if it was incorporated or formed under the law of a part of the United Kingdom or if the courts of that other state would not regard it as having its seat there for the purposes of art.22(2).

Trusts

4–020   Article 60(3) provides that in order to determine whether a trust is domiciled in the Member State whose courts are seised of the matter, the court shall apply its rules of private international law. The 2001 Order provides that a trust is domiciled in a part of the United Kingdom if the system of law of that part is the

---

[63] Civil Jurisdiction and Judgments Order 2001 Sch.1, para.9(7).
[64] *Phillips v Symes* [2001] 1 W.L.R. 853.
[65] For example, *The Deichland* [1990] 1 Q.B. 361 (Brussels Convention case: company incorporated in the Republic of Panama, but its central management and control exercised in Germany).
[66] Regulation, art.60(2). For cases under the Brussels and Lugano Conventions, see the Civil Jurisdiction and Judgments Act 1982 s.42.
[67] See para.4–022.
[68] art.22(2).
[69] Civil Jurisdiction and Judgments Order 2001 Sch.1, para.10.

system of law with which the trust has its closest and most real connection.[70] The Court of Appeal has indicated that where there is a choice of English law to govern a trust, it is very difficult to see what other circumstance would be sufficient to outweigh it in assessing which was the system of law which the trust had its closest and most real connection.[71] Of course it is artificial and novel to speak of the domicile of a trust at all. But it is a convenient form of shorthand.

Exclusive jurisdiction

The Regulation sometimes gives "exclusive jurisdiction" to the courts of a particular country. The term has a special meaning in the Regulation, reflecting the fact that the Member States have agreed that where a case concerns a particular subject matter the courts of one country within the European Union, and one country only, can hear the case. The allocation of exclusive jurisdiction operates regardless of the defendant's domicile.[72] If a court of one Member State finds itself seised of a claim which is principally concerned[73] with a matter over which the courts of another Member State have exclusive jurisdiction, it must declare of its own motion that it has no jurisdiction.[74] The types of case in which there is exclusive jurisdiction are set out in art.22.

    Before that Article is examined, it is necessary to identify and distinguish two other situations arising under the Regulation. The first is where the parties have reached a choice-of-court agreement, under which a court is identified as having exclusive jurisdiction over the dispute. Rather different rules apply in this type of case, and they are considered below.[75] The second situation is one in which the Regulation provides that a certain claims (by an insurer, or against a consumer or employee) may only be brought in the country in which the defendant is domiciled. This is not strictly a case of exclusive jurisdiction, not least because, as we have seen, the defendant may be domiciled in more than one country.

4–021

In considering whether any particular claim falls within the jurisdictional rules of the Regulation, it is wise to begin with art.22 on exclusive jurisdiction. This Article applies regardless of the domicile of the defendant; that means that it is relevant even if the defendant is domiciled in, say, New Zealand, a non-Member State. The cases in which a court has exclusive jurisdiction under art.22 are defined by reference to the "object" of the relevant proceedings, which refers to

4–022

---

[70] Civil Jurisdiction and Judgments Order 2001 Sch.1, para. 12(3).

[71] *Gomez v Encarnacion Gomez-Monche Vives* [2008] EWCA Civ 1065; [2009] Ch. 245.

[72] For example, Case C-73/04 *Klein v Rhodos Management Ltd* [2005] E.C.R. I-8667.

[73] What is the principal issue in a case may be difficult to determine, especially at the outset; see *Newtherapeutics Ltd v Katz* [1991] Ch. 226 (issue of whether a resolution of a Board of Directors authorised acts appeared the principal issue, not the issue of breach of duty involved in the acts themselves).

[74] art.25.

[75] At paras 4–060 to 4–069.

the nature of the subject matter,[76] not to the purpose of the claimant in bringing the action.[77] Exclusive jurisdiction is given to the following courts:

(1) *Immovable property*: in proceedings which have as their object rights in rem in, or tenancies of, immovable property; the courts of the Member State in which the property is situated; this is subject to qualifications in respect of certain short-term lettings, and the matter is more fully examined in the context of immovables.[78]

(2) *Corporations*: in proceedings which have as their object the validity of the constitution, the nullity or the dissolution of companies or other legal persons or associations of natural or legal persons, or the validity of a decision of their organs[79]; the courts of the Member State in which the company, legal person or association has its seat.[80]

This head of jurisdiction includes proceedings for the winding-up of solvent companies, but the winding-up of insolvent companies is outside the scope of the Regulation.[81] Where the proceedings have as their object a decision of an organ, the jurisdiction of the English courts is not exclusive as against the courts of other parts of the United Kingdom.[82] In *Hassett v South Eastern Health Board*,[83] the ECJ held that proceedings where the subject matter was whether a decision adopted by the organ of a company had infringed the rights of one of the parties under that company's articles of association did not concern the "validity of a decision" for the purposes of art.22(2). In *Berliner Verkehrsbetriebe (BVG) v JP Morgan Chase Bank NA*,[84] the ECJ explained that art.22(2) did not apply to proceedings in which a company pleaded that a contract could not be relied upon against it because the contract's conclusion by its organs was invalid on account of infringement of its statutes. It is apparent from the case law of the ECJ that, as in the case of other "special" jurisdictional grounds that represent an

---

[76] See Case C-103/05 *Reisch Montage AG v Kiesel Baumaschinen Handels GmbH*, [2006] E.C.R. I-6827; Case 73/77 *Sanders v Van del Putte*, [1977] E.C.R. 2383; Case C-8/98 *Dansommer A/S v Gotz*, [2000] E.C.R. I-393; [2001] 1 W.L.R. 1069; Case C-343/04 *Land Oberosterreich v CEZ*, [2006] E.C.R. I-4457.

[77] *Newtherapeutics Ltd v Katz* [1991] Ch. 226.

[78] See below, paras 13–005ff. In the context of the review of the Brussels I Regulation, the Commission's Green Paper suggests that jurisdiction clauses in contracts for the rent of office space should be allowed, and also that in relation to the rent of holiday homes the need for some flexibility might be advantageous; see COM (2009) 175 final.

[79] Note also in COM (2009) 175 final the possible extension of the scope of exclusive jurisdiction under art.22(2) to some other matters related to the organisation and decision-making of companies.

[80] An example is a dispute about the appointment of directors: *Speed Investments Ltd v Formula One Holdings Ltd (No 2)* [2004] EWCA Civ 1512; [2005] 1 W.L.R. 1936. For the seat, see above, para.4–019.

[81] art.1(2)(g). See the Schlosser report, paras 57–58.

[82] See Civil Jurisdiction and Judgments Act 1982 Sch.4, r.11(b) as substituted by SI 2001/3929.

[83] Case C-372/07 [2008] ECR I-7403.

[84] Case C-144/10 *Berliner Verkehrsbetriebe (BVG) v JP Morgan Chase Bank NA* [2011] 1 W.L.R. 2087. See also *UBS AG v Kommunale Wasserwerke Leipzig GmbH* [2010] EWHC 2566 (Comm); [2010] 2 CLC 499.

exception to the "general" rule of jurisdiction based on the defendant's domicile, the interpretation given to art.22(2) is narrow and should not be extended.

(3)   *Public registers*: in proceedings which have as their object the validity of   **4–023** entries in public registers, the courts of the Member State in which the register is kept. The scope of this head is limited in the English situation, given that cases involving the registration of land will usually be covered by the first head; an example might be a case involving the Register of Aircraft Mortgages kept by the Civil Aviation Authority.

(4)   *Intellectual property*: in proceedings which concern the registration or validity of patents, trade marks, design or other similar rights required to be deposited or registered,[85] the courts of the Member State in which the deposit or registration has been applied for or has taken place (or is deemed by virtue of a European instrument or an international convention to have taken place), or in which a European patent has been granted. Infringement proceedings may be included, where the substance of the dispute is the validity of the patent or other right allegedly infringed, regardless of which party raises the validity issue.[86] In *Lucasfilm Ltd v Ainsworth*[87] the United Kingdom Supreme Court decided that art.22(4) did not apply to infringement actions where there was not a validity issue.[88] Copyrights actions are likely to be outside the scope of this provision.[89]

(5)   *Enforcement of judgments*: in proceedings which concern the enforcement of judgments, the courts of the Member State in which the judgment has been or is to be enforced.[90]

Jurisdiction based on domicile

The principal basis for jurisdiction is that set out in art.2(1), that persons   **4–024** domiciled in a Member State shall, whatever their nationality, be sued in the courts of that state. This accords with what we have already identified as a basic rule of "general jurisdiction", requiring a link between the defendant and the chosen court. The domicile of the defendant in England is thus the primary basis for the jurisdiction of the English courts under the Brussels I Regulation. The defendant must have a domicile in the Member State at the time of the issue of

---

[85] In the EU Commission Proposal the words "irrespective of whether the issue is raised by way of an action or as a defence" are inserted into art.22(4) at this point. This addition follows from the ECJ's decision in Case C-4/03 *Gesellschaft fur Antriebstechnik mbH & Co KG (GAT) v Lamellen und Kupplungsbau Beteiligungs KG (LuK)*, [2006] E.C.R. I-6509; [2007] I.L.Pr. 34 and has already been added to the wording of the same article in the 2007 Lugano Convention.

[86] *Coin Controls Ltd v Suzo International (U.K.) Ltd* [1999] Ch. 33; Case C-4/03 *Gesellschaft für Antriebstechnik mbH & Co KG v Lamellen und Kupplungsbau Beteilings KG* [2006] E.C.R. I-6509.

[87] [2011] UKSC 39; [2011] 3 W.L.R. 487.

[88] *ibid.*, paras 105–110.

[89] *ibid.*

[90] See *Kuwait Oil Tanker Co. SAK v Qabazard* [2003] UKHL 31; [2004] 1 A.C. 300; *Masri v Consolidated Contractors International (UK) Ltd (No 2)* [2009] QB 450.

proceedings, which in England means the time of the issue of the claim form rather than its service on the defendant.[91]

If the proposed defendant is domiciled in another Member State, he or she may be sued in England only in accordance with the rules set out in ss.2 to 7 of Ch.II of the Regulation, i.e. arts 5 to 24 inclusive.[92] These rules, shortly to be examined, include cases where the defendant submits to the jurisdiction, various cases of "special" jurisdiction, and cases in which there is a jurisdiction agreement within art.23. Reliance on the traditional English rules as to service of process on a defendant during the defendant's temporary presence in England is expressly excluded by art.3, along with bases for jurisdiction under other legal systems judged equally exorbitant[93]; England is not the only villain.

Where the defendant is *not* domiciled in another Member State, the jurisdictional rules applicable are those of the national law of the forum, in England, the traditional rules, subject always to art.22 which confers exclusive jurisdiction on the courts of particular Member States regardless of the domicile of the parties.[94]

Special jurisdiction

4–025   Article 5 deals with a number of cases of "special" jurisdiction, in which a person domiciled in one Member State such as France may nonetheless be sued in England because the subject matter of the dispute is closely connected with England.

Contract[95]

4–026   The Brussels I Regulation provides:

> A person domiciled in a Member State may, in another Member State, be sued in matters relating to a contract, in the courts for the place of performance of the obligation in question.[96]

The first phrase to be considered is "matters relating to a contract". This will include cases where there is a disagreement as to the very existence of the

---

[91] *Canada Trust Co. v Stolzenberg (No.2)* [2002] 1 A.C. 1.
[92] art.3(1).
[93] Even though there is no definition of what constitutes an exorbitant jurisdictional basis, it can be said that when the balance between the interests of the claimant and the defendant is not even, and one or the other is put into a position which is close to a practical denial of justice, the situation is unacceptable from an international point of view. See Fernández Arroyo, *Compétence exclusive et compétence exorbitante dans les relations privées internationales*, (2006) 323 Recueil des cours (Martinus Nijhoff, Leiden, 2008).
[94] art.4.
[95] For insurance, consumer and employment contracts, see paras 4–051 to 4–059.
[96] art.5(1)(a). For art.6(4) (action in contract combined with one relating to rights *in rem* in immovable property), see para.13–010.

contract,[97] but not cases in which the subject matter is a duty to conduct pre-contractual negotiations in good faith.[98]

What is a contract?

The notion of "contract" is not identical in every legal system, with different understandings of the boundary between contract and tort or property law. For this reason, "contract" in the text of the Regulation is given an autonomous meaning, independent of the categories in national legal systems; it covers any matters having their basis in an agreement.[99] So, in *Peters v Zuid Nederlandse Aannemers Vereniging*,[100] the dispute was between a Dutch trade association and one of its members. Under the association's rules, a percentage of any earnings within the association's area was to be paid to the association. The issue would clearly be contractual in English law, but Dutch law treated the relationship between members of an association as *sui generis*. The ECJ held that, as membership of an association creates between the members close links of the same kind as those which are created between the parties to a contract, their obligations should be regarded as contractual for the purpose of the application of art.5(1).

4–027

The case-law emphasises the existence of a direct relationship between the parties. The ECJ has ruled that the phrase "matters relating to a contract" is not to be understood as covering a situation in which there is no obligation freely assumed by one party towards another.[101] That suggests that benefits conferred on others, as third party beneficiaries or as sub-purchasers, under some national legal systems will not be treated as arising under a contract. However, the Court of Appeal held in *WPP Holdings Italy Srl v Benatti*,[102] without any full examination of the European case-law, that where two contracting parties confer a benefit on a stranger to the contract, intending that the stranger may enforce the benefit in his own right, the claim by the stranger under the Contracts (Rights of Third Parties) Act 1999 was a contractual matter for the purposes of the Brussels I Regulation.

A difficult issue was addressed by the House of Lords in *Kleinwort Benson Ltd v Glasgow City Council*[103]:

4–028

> Financial dealings called "interest swap agreements had been undertaken by a number of local authorities until the House of Lords in a separate decision held that they were all void as *ultra vires* the local authorities. The plaintiff bank claimed the return of the money it had paid to the

---

[97] Case 38/81 *Effer SpA. v Kantner* [1982] E.C.R. 825.

[98] Case C-334/00 *Fonderie Officine Meccaniche Tacconi SpA v Heinrich Wagner Sinto Maschinenfabrik GmbH* [2002] E.C.R. I-7357. cf. the position where an insurance contract is challenged for non-disclosure: *Agnew v Länsförsäkringsbolagens AB* [2001] 1 A.C. 223.

[99] Case 9/87 *Arcado Sprl v Haviland SA* [1988] E.C.R. 1539 (agency dispute involving allegations of bad faith held contractual).

[100] Case 34/82, [1983] E.C.R. 987.

[101] Case C-26/91 *Ste Handte et Cie GmbH v Traitements Mecano-Chimiques des Surfaces* [1992] E.C.R. I-3967 (sub-purchaser unable to sue the original manufacturer-supplier of goods).

[102] [2007] EWCA Civ 263; [2007] 1 W.L.R. 2316.

[103] [1999] 1 A.C. 153.

Council under the invalid contract, a claim classified in English law as one for restitution, or for unjust enrichment. The issue was whether the claim for restitution fell within art.5(1).[104]

A bare majority (Lords Goff, Clyde and Hutton) held that the claim did not fall within art.5(1): it had already been decided there was no contractual obligation on which the claim could be founded, and that was not now in dispute between the parties. Because of that unusual feature of the case, it is not authority for a general proposition that restitution claims can never be within art.5(1). Lords Mustill and Nicholls dissented, principally to avoid having to draw awkward distinctions depending on how claims were worded: the view taken by the majority means that a claim for damages for non-performance is within art.5(1) but an additional claim in the same case for the return of sums paid in advance will not be.

The obligation in question

4–029   It would seem obvious that "the obligation in question" means that which is relied upon as the basis for the claim. This was the interpretation placed upon the text by the ECJ in *De Bloos Sprl v Bouyer SA,*[105] where the claim concerned an alleged breach of the condition of exclusivity in an agreement appointing the claimant sole distributor of the defendant's products in Belgium. It was immaterial that other obligations under the contract fell to be performed in France.

It is of course possible for a claim to relate to several distinct obligations, with different places of performance. When in trouble, lawyers revert to Latin: *accessorium sequitur principale*, which means that the court has to identify the principal obligation and let those other obligations accessory to the principal obligation be swept up with it.[106]

Identifying the principal obligation may not be at all easy. An example is *Union Transport Group plc v Continental Lines SA*[107]:

> The plaintiffs claimed that the defendant ship owners had agreed to nominate a vessel suitable for the carriage of telegraph poles from Florida to Bangladesh and then to execute the carriage. The defendants had failed to do so. When sued in England, the defendants argued that the English courts had no jurisdiction: they were domiciled in Belgium, and the place of performance must be the port of loading, in Florida.

4–030   The House of Lords held that under a "tonnage to be nominated" charter, the principal obligation is to nominate the vessel, and on the facts that had to be done in London. Jurisdiction therefore existed under art.5(1).[108]

---

[104] The issue arose under Sch.4 of the 1982 Act, the Convention as applied to intra-UK cases rather than the Convention text itself; the ECJ had for that reason refused to rule on the matter.

[105] Case 14/76 [1976] E.C.R. 1497.

[106] Case 266/85 *Shenavai v Kreischer* [1987] E.C.R. 239.

[107] [1992] 1 W.L.R. 15.

[108] For other examples, see *Source Ltd v Rheinland Holding A.G.* [1998] Q.B. 54 (English company prepared to grant credit on imported goods, subject to inspection in country of origin; principal obligation in that country); *A.I.G. Group (U.K.) Ltd v The Ethniki* [2000] 2 All ER 566 (reinsurance of earthquake risks in Greece; notification of damage to be in England, and that held principal obligation).

The ECJ has had to recognise that there can be cases in which the claim concerns obligations of equal importance, where it is impossible to identify one as "principal" and the others as "accessory".[109] In such a case, a court can take jurisdiction under art.5(1) only in respect of the obligation the place of performance of which is within its territory. Although this can produce inconvenience, the claim being divided between two or more courts, the claimant always has the option of relying on art.2 and bringing action in the country of the defendant's domicile.

Place of performance

Although the notion of contract itself is given an autonomous interpretation, it is for national law (including its rules of the conflict of laws) to identify "the place of performance".[110] The courts can find this a surprisingly difficult task. Take the apparently simple facts of *Barry v Bradshaw*[111] which was decided under the Brussels Convention:

4-031

> Mr and Mrs Barry retired from business in 1989 and went to live in the Republic of Ireland. Mr and Mrs Barry employed tax advisers, including Mr Young. They sued Mr Young for negligence and breach of contract in failing to secure capital gains tax retirement relief in respect of certain years. Mr Young argued that the English courts had no jurisdiction: he was domiciled in Ireland and the place of performance under art.5(1) was also in Ireland.

However, the Court of Appeal held that, as the tax claim had to be delivered to the Inland Revenue in England, the place of performance was there.

Another, and more difficult, case involving an exclusive distributorship agreement is *Boss Group Ltd v Boss France SA*.[112]:

> An English company, manufacturers of fork-lift trucks, set up a French subsidiary to act as sole distributor of its products in France. Both companies were later sold, the English manufacturing company to a German corporation which had its own distribution network in France, and the French company to a French businessman. He claimed that the distribution of the fork-lift trucks was now routed through the distribution net-work of the German parent company, in breach of the exclusive distributorship agreement.

The English company applied to the English court for a negative declaration, that there was no distributorship contract or, if there were, it had been terminated. At first sight, a contract for exclusive distributorship rights in France is to be performed there. The court, however, finding that the trucks were delivered to the distributors at the factory gates, held that the obligation was to be performed either in England (the place of delivery) or possibly everywhere (because it was a duty not to deliver to anyone else), and "everywhere" included England. The last

4-032

---

[109] Case C-420/97 *Leathertex Divisione Sintetici SpA v Bodetex BVBA* [1999] E.C.R. I-6747 (agency contact; commission payable in Italy, notice of termination to be given in Belgium).
[110] Case 12/76 *Industrie Tessili Italiana Como v Dunlop A.G.* [1976] E.C.R. 1473; Case C-288/92 *Custom Made Commercial Ltd v Stawa Metallbau GmbH* [1994] E.C.R. I-2913; Case C-440/97 *GIE Groupe Concorde v The Suhadiwarno Panjan* [1999] E.C.R. I-6307.
[111] [2000] I.L.Pr. 706.
[112] [1996] 4 All E.R. 970.

idea now seems untenable: the ECJ has held that a negative obligation applying everywhere cannot be located in a Member State at all.[113]

Dissatisfaction with art.5(1) as it stood in the text of the Brussels Convention grew: in too many cases, it seemed to identify an inappropriate forum. It was redrafted in the Brussels I Regulation, with an additional provision as art.5(1)(b)[114]:

> for the purpose of this provision and unless otherwise agreed, the place of performance of the obligation in question shall be:
> – in the case of the sale of goods, the place in a Member State where, under the contract, the goods were delivered or should have been delivered,
> – in the case of the provision of services, the place in a Member State where, under the contract, the services were provided or should have been provided.[115]

4–033 This additional provision has been the object of further interpretation by the ECJ in the cases of *Car Trim GmbH v KeySafety Systems Srl*[116] and *Electrosteel Europe sa v Edil Centro SpA*.[117] In *Car Trim* the ECJ held that art.5(1)(b) of the Regulation had to be interpreted:

> "as meaning that contracts for the delivery of goods to be produced or manufactured are to be classified as a sale of goods, notwithstanding specific requirements by the customer with regard to the provision, fabrication and delivery of the components to be produced, including a guarantee of the quality of production."[118]

Furthermore, where a sale involved the carriage of goods, the place where the goods were or should have been delivered under the contract was to be determined on the basis of the provisions of that contract; or, if it was not possible to do so, then that place was the place of physical transfer of the goods to the buyer. *Car Trim* was followed in *Electrosteel* where the ECJ further clarified the application of the provision for cases of distance selling.

The case involved proceedings arising out of a contract for the sale of goods by an Italian company (C) to a French company (E). The contract was concluded in Italy, and the goods were delivered to E's headquarters in France. C claimed that E had failed to pay for the goods and began proceedings in the Italian court. The issue was whether the Italian court had jurisdiction as the "place of delivery". C claimed that the court had to take account of a clause in the contract which contained the words "delivered free ex our business premises". It asserted that those words corresponded to the "ex works" clause in the Incoterms. On that basis it argued that Italy was the place of delivery.

4–034 The ECJ held that in the case of distance selling, in order to verify whether the place of delivery was determined "under the contract", the national court had to

---

[113] Case C-265/00 *Besix AG v Wasserreinigungsbau Alfred Kretzschmar GmbH & Co. KG* [2003] 1 W.L.R. 1113. It followed that there was no jurisdiction under art.5(1).

[114] For the effects of this innovation in the allocation of jurisdiction in complex contracts, see Grušić (2011) 7 J.Priv.Int.L. 321.

[115] In cases to which this new provision does not apply, the matter is governed by the general words of art.5(1)(a): see art.5(1)(c).

[116] Case C-381/08, [2010] E.C.R. I-1255.

[117] Case C-87/10, June 9, 2011, [2011] I.L.Pr. 28.

[118] See paras 16–26 of judgment.

take account of all the relevant terms and clauses of the contract that were capable of clearly identifying that place, including terms that were generally recognised and applied through the usages of international trade or commerce, such as the Incoterms. If it was impossible to determine the place of delivery on that basis, without referring to the substantive law applicable to the contract, the place of delivery was the place where the physical transfer of the goods took place, as a result of which the purchaser obtained, or should have obtained, actual power of disposal over those goods.[119]

In relation to contracts for the provision of services the ECJ held in *Falco Privatstiftung v Weller Lindhorst*[120] that a contract under which the owner of an intellectual property right granted its contractual partner the right to use that right in return for remuneration was not a contract for services within the meaning of that provision.

Article 5(1)(b) has a particular significance in cases in which the obligation in question is an obligation to pay. Under English law and in the absence of a relevant contractual term, that obligation is located in the creditor's country, so that under the original Convention text the English court would often have jurisdiction over a claim by an unpaid English seller against a foreign purchaser. This is less likely under the Regulation, for it is the place of delivery, commonly in the purchaser's country, that provides the forum in the absence of agreement.

More generally, by locating the various obligations arising under contracts to which it applies in a single country, the new provision minimises some of the difficulties discussed above: it may no longer be necessary to struggle with the identity of the "principal" and "accessory" obligations, as all will have a common location attributed to them. But some problems remain. They can be illustrated by the facts of a Brussels Convention case, *Viskase Ltd v Paul Kiefel GmbH*[121]: **4–035**

> Eight machines were to be supplied for a particular purpose. In the case of seven of the eight machines, delivery had taken place in Germany, but in the case of one machine delivery was at the National Exhibition Centre in Birmingham, England. The Court of Appeal held that the place of the obligation to deliver goods fit for the purpose was the place of delivery. The English court had jurisdiction only in respect of that machine.

In *Color Drack GmbH v Lexx International Verbriebs GmbH*[122] the ECJ held that where there are several places of delivery all within the same Member State, the "principal place of delivery" is the relevant one, failing which the claimant could sue at any delivery place.[123] The rationale behind this approach, sometimes referred as the "*Color Drack* test" is to attribute jurisdiction to the courts with the "closest linking factor" with the contract in question; in the case of contracts for

---

[119] *ibid.*
[120] Case C-533/07, [2009] E.C.R. I-3327.
[121] [1999] 1 W.L.R. 1305, noted Briggs, (2000) 70 B.Y.B.I.L. 336. See also *M.B.M. Fabri-Clad Ltd v Eisen Und Huttenwerke Thale AG* 2000] I.L.Pr. 505.
[122] Case C-386/05, [2007] E.C.R. I-3699; see Harris, (2007) 123 L.Q.R. 522.
[123] See also *Scottish & Newcastle International Ltd v Othon Ghalanos Ltd* [2008] UKHL 11; [2008] 2 All E.R. 768 (place of shipment is place of delivery in F.O.B. contracts); see Merrett [2008] C.L.J. 244 and Hare and Hinks [2008] L.M.C.L.Q. 353.

the provision of services, the place where, pursuant to that contract, the main provision of services was to be carried out.[124]

4–036 This approach was followed in *Wood Floor Solutions Andreas Domberger GmbH v Silva Trade SA*,[125] a case involving a contract for services in which the defendant had to perform services in more than one country. The proceedings related to a contract of commercial agency under the terms of which the agent undertook to provide services in more than one Member State. The ECJ held that the court which has jurisdiction is the court of the place where the "main provisions of services" is performed. However, in many types of case, including a commercial agency contract, that criterion may link the case with more than one jurisdiction; hence the ECJ added, with no basis for such addition in the text of the Brussels I Regulation, that where that place cannot be established, the courts that have jurisdiction are the courts of the place where the agent is domiciled[126]:

> "if the place of the main provision of services cannot be determined on the basis of the provisions of the contract itself or its actual performance, the place must be identified by another means which respects the objectives of predictability and proximity pursued by the legislature. For that purpose, it will be necessary for the purposes of the application of the second indent of article 5(1)(b) to consider, as the place of the main provision of the services provided by a commercial agent, the place where that agent is domiciled. That place can always be identified with certainty and is therefore predictable. Moreover, it has a link of proximity with the dispute since the agent will in all likelihood provide a substantial part of his services there."

In relation to the same question in the context of air travel, the ECJ held in *Rehder v Air Baltic Corp*[127] that the only places which had a direct link to those services were those of the departure and arrival of the aircraft. Accordingly, the claimant had an option to sue the defendant in the court in whose jurisdiction one of those places was situated. Hence, it seems that in the case of provision of services related to an air transport contract, there would be always concurrent jurisdiction at the courts of the place of departure and arrival and the claimant has the option of suing at the courts of either place.

Maintenance

4–037 The provisions in art.5(2) of the Brussels I Regulation dealing with matters relating to maintenance are considered in a later chapter.[128]

Tort

4–038 The Brussels I Regulation provides:

---

[124] Case C-204/08, *Rehder v Air Baltic Corp*, [2009] E.C.R. I-6073.
[125] Case C-19/09, [2010] 1 W.L.R. 1900. See Costas Stamatiou [2010] ICCLR 43.
[126] at paras 41–42.
[127] Case C-204/08, [2009] E.C.R. I-6073. See George and Harris [2010] L.Q.R. 30, arguing that there is a fundamental difference between contracts of sale and contracts for the provisions of services and that extension of the *Color Drack* test to services performed in cross-border cases militates against predictability.
[128] Below, paras 9–067 to 9–087.

A person domiciled in a Member State may, in another Member State, be sued in matters relating to tort, delict or quasi-delict in the courts for the place where the harmful event occurred or may occur.[129]

The phrase "tort, delict or quasi-delict" uses the varying terms found in national legal systems. Despite this, the phrase has an autonomous meaning unrelated to those in national systems. It covers actions calling into question the liability of the defendant outside the field of matters relating to contract.[130] The effect of so defining the scope of actions in tort is to exclude the possibility, which exists in English domestic law, of the action being available in either contract or tort at the claimant's option; if the claim arises out of an agreement, it must be pursued as a claim in contract.

One aspect of *Kleinwort Benson Ltd v Glasgow City Council,*[131] the restitution claim after the invalid "interest swap" agreements considered above in the context of the contract head, art.5(1), was whether the claim could be brought under art.5(3) as a claim in tort. The House of Lords answered in the negative because a claim based on unjust enrichment "does not, apart from special circumstances, presuppose either a harmful event or a threatened wrong". The result is to leave at least some restitution claims wholly outside art.5, and the claimant must sue under art.2 in the country of the defendant's domicile.[132]

The place of the tort

Article 5(3) is imprecise in respect of the vexed question of the place of the tort. In *Bier v Mines de Potasse d'Alsace*[133]:

    4–039

> A market gardener in the Netherlands complained that his plants were damaged by pollutants in the Rhine water he used for irrigation purposes. He brought an action in the Dutch courts against the defendants, a company domiciled in France, alleging that the damage was caused by their pumping chlorides into the river from its French bank. The ECJ held under art.5(3) the claimant has an option to sue either at the place where the damage occurred or the place of the event giving rise to it.

The ruling in the *Bier* case has been applied repeatedly by the ECJ in several different contexts, e.g. in *Zuid-Chemie BV v Philippo's Mineralenfabriek NV/SA*[134] it was decided that "the place where the damage occurs" was the place where the initial damage occurred as a result of the normal use of a product for the purpose for which that product was intended.

Bier was a case of physical damage. The ECJ has confirmed that it need not be read as limited to that type of damage, and can be applied to (for example) damage to reputation in a defamation context, as in *Shevill v Presse Alliance*[135]:

---

[129] art.5(3).
[130] Case 189/87 *Kalfelis v Shroder, Munchmeyer, Hengst & Co.* [1988] E.C.R. 565.
[131] [1999] 1 A.C. 153.
[132] See *Casio Computer Co. Ltd v Sayo (No. 3)* [2001] EWCA Civ 661; [2001] I.L.Pr. 694, noted Yeo, (2001) 117 L.Q.R. 560 (constructive trust based on knowing assistance; claim held within art.5(3)).
[133] Case 21/76, [1976] E.C.R. 1735; [1978] Q.B. 708.
[134] Case C-189/08, [2009] ECR I-6917.
[135] Case C-68/93, [1995] E.C.R. I-415; [1995] 2 A.C. 18.

A Yorkshire woman, the plaintiff, worked in a bureau de change in Paris. *France Soir* carried a story that that bureau was used for money laundering in the drugs trade. The plaintiff's name was mentioned. The paper sold 200,000 copies in France, and some 230 in England (perhaps 10 of them in Yorkshire). S sued in England relying on art.5(3), and it was held that jurisdiction existed under art.5(3) both where the article was originally published (the place of the event giving rise to the damage)[136] and where damage to reputation was sustained.

4–040 The ECJ explained that the *Bier* principle was essential if art.5(3) was to have any real effect. If jurisdiction under that provision were limited to the place the defendant acted, it would so often overlap with art.2 as to be worthless. But the court placed a new limitation on the effect of art.5(3). If the action was brought in the Member State where the publisher of the libel was established, the court could award damages for all the damage sustained by the plaintiff, wherever it occurred; if the action were in one of the states where her reputation was damaged (on the periphery, as it were), the court could award damages only in respect of the damage sustained in that state.

The place of damage for this purpose is where the relevant physical damage or economic loss is *directly* sustained. For example, had the claimant in the *Bier* case been a company with English shareholders, it could not have invoked art.5(3) as giving the English court jurisdiction even though it might have suffered consequential financial loss. Had the rule been otherwise, almost every business claim could be brought in the claimant's forum.[137] So in *Dumez France v Hessische Landesbank*[138]:

> D, a French company, had German subsidiary companies engaged in a building project, financed by loans from the defendant bank. After a dispute, the bank suspended the loans and the project came to a halt. D sued in France, arguing that it sustained loss at its registered office in Paris.

4–041 The ECJ held that jurisdiction must be limited to where the harmful event "directly produced its harmful effect on the person who is the immediate victim of that event" and would not normally cover the domicile of an indirect victim.

The same principle applies to further losses suffered by the original victim. In *Henderson v Jaouen*[139]:

> The claimant, an Englishman, was injured in a road traffic accident in France and was awarded damages by a French court in an action against the other driver and his insurers. He began fresh proceedings in England some 17 years later, claiming that his state of health had deteriorated in the ensuing years as a direct result of the accident: this, he argued, was a "harmful event" occurring in England.

The Court of Appeal applied the *Dumez France* principle. The only "harmful event" was that which occurred in France.

---

[136] For similar results in a misrepresentation context, see *Domicrest Ltd v Swiss Bank Corp.* [1999] Q.B. 548 and *Sunderland Marine Mutual Insurance Co Ltd v Wiseman (The "Seaward Quest")* [2007] EWHC 1460 (Comm); [2007] 2 Lloyd's Rep. 308.

[137] See Case C-364/93 *Marinari v Lloyd's Bank plc* [1995] E.C.R. I-2719.

[138] Case 220/88, [1990] E.C.R. I-49.

[139] [2002] 1 W.L.R. 2971, noted Briggs, (2002) 73 B.Y.B.I.L. 458.

The notion of the "harmful event" itself is, however, to be given a broad interpretation.[140] It has been held to include the "undermining of legal stability" by the use of unfair contract terms, a ruling coloured by the need to give practical effect to the Directive on unfair terms in consumer contracts. In cases where the "harmful event" is the lack of payment to which the claimant was entitled, the harm occurs at the place where the payment should have been made.[141]

The final words of art.5(3), "or may occur", have no counterpart in the earlier Convention texts but probably reflect their intent. It is now clear that an action to prevent a tort occurring is within art.5(3).

4–042

The ECJ has clarified the concept in cases involving an alleged infringement of personality rights by means of content placed online on an internet website.[142] The Court recognized that the placing online of content on a website is to be distinguished from the regional distribution of media e.g. in a physical newspaper, in that it is intended, in principle, to ensure the ubiquity of that content.

> "Consequently, … in the event of an alleged infringement of personality rights by means of content placed online on an internet website, the person who considers that his rights have been infringed has the option of bringing an action for liability, in respect of all the damage caused, either before the courts of the Member State in which the publisher of that content is established or before the courts of the Member State in which the centre of his interests is based. That person may also, instead of an action for liability in respect of all the damage caused, bring his action before the courts of each Member State in the territory of which content placed online is or has been accessible. Those courts have jurisdiction only in respect of the damage caused in the territory of the Member State of the court seised".

Civil claims in criminal proceedings

The Brussels I Regulation provides:

4–043

> A person domiciled in a Member State may, in another Member State, be sued as regards a civil claim for damages or restitution which is based on an act giving rise to criminal proceedings, in the court seised of those proceedings, to the extent that that court has jurisdiction under its own law to entertain civil proceedings.[143]

This relates to such claims as those of a *partie civile* intervening in French criminal cases; there is no direct English equivalent.

Branches and agencies

Of greater importance is the provision in the Brussels I Regulation about branches and agencies:

4–044

---

[140] Case C-167/00 *Verien fur Konsumenteninformation v Henkel* [2002] E.C.R. I-8111. See *Future Investments SA v FIFA* [2010] EWHC 1019 (Ch); [2010] I.L.Pr. 34.

[141] *Dolphin Maritime & Aviation Services Ltd v Sveriges Angfartygs Assurans Forening* [2009] EWHC 716 (Comm); [2009] 2 Lloyd's Rep. 123.

[142] Case C-509/09 *eDate Advertising GmbH v X* and Case C-161/10 *Martinez v MGN Ltd*, October 25, 2011 (joined cases).

[143] art.5(4).

A person domiciled in a Member State may, in another Member State, be sued as regards disputes arising out of the operations of a branch, agency or other establishment, in the courts for the place where the branch, agency or other establishment is situated.[144]

It is an entirely familiar feature of economic life that businesses established in one country will also operate in other countries. This is true by definition of the big multinationals, but a relatively small company may decide to set up a manufacturing, assembly or distribution plant abroad, or at least to have a representative office in a foreign capital to help in marketing its products. It may operate in the foreign country directly, or through the agency of another company, or it may establish its own subsidiary company for the purpose. A fundamental aim of those who created the European Economic Community was the facilitation of just this type of activity. The question is how many of these arrangements are within the scope of this part of the Regulation. It is important to note that it applies only where the defendant is domiciled in a Member State, and not, for example, to a branch of a United States corporation.[145]

The terms "branch, agency or other establishment" have autonomous meanings. The court must ask whether a particular entity acts as an extension of the parent body, is subject to its direction and control of the parent body, and has "the appearance of permanence".[146] A mere sales agency, especially where the agent may represent several firms and merely transmits orders to the relevant principal, will not qualify.[147] In this context, the corporate structure of a group of companies may not be decisive; an entity may be an extension of the "parent" body in this sense even though the "parent" body is actually one of its subsidiaries; commercial realities are to be examined.[148]

4–045   Article 5(5) refers to claims arising out of the "operations" of the branch, agency or other establishment. This notion includes matters concerning the management of the agency or branch itself, such as those concerning the situation of its premises or the local engagement of staff to work there; to undertakings entered into there in the name of the parent body; and to non-contractual obligations arising from the activities in which the branch or agency has engaged.[149]

It was once held by the ECJ[150] that art.5(5) had to be limited to contracts which were to be performed within the state in which the branch, agency or other establishment was to be found, but the Court later recognised that such an interpretation had no basis in text, and would make art.5(5) largely redundant as it would overlap almost wholly with art.5(1). So in *Lloyd's Register of Shipping v Soc. Campenon Bernard*[151] the Court upheld the jurisdiction of a French court

---

[144] art.5(5).

[145] Contrast the position under the special rules for insurance, consumer and employment contracts (arts 9(2), 15(2) and 18(2)), all considered below.

[146] Case 14/76 *De Bloos Sprl v Bouyer SA* [1976] E.C.R. 1497; Case 33/78 *Somafer SA v Saar-Ferngas AG* [1978] E.C.R. 2183.

[147] *De Bloos Sprl v Bouyer SA* [1976] E.C.R. 1497; Case 139/80 *Blanckaert and Willems PVBA v Trost* [1981] E.C.R. 819.

[148] Case 218/86 *SAR Schotte GmbH v Parfums Rothschild* [1987] E.C.R. 4905.

[149] Case 33/78 *Somafer S.A. v Saar-Ferngas A.G.* [1978] E.C.R. 2183.

[150] In the *Somafer* case, above.

[151] Case C-439/93, [1995] E.C.R. I-961. For the application of the same approach to a claim in tort, see *Anton Durbeck GmbH v Den Norske Bank ASA* [2003] EWCA Civ 147; [2003] Q.B. 1160.

over a dispute as to quality-control duties undertaken by Lloyd's, domiciled in England, at their Paris office but to be carried out in Spain through another Lloyd's office there.

Trusts

There were no provisions as to trusts in the original Brussels Convention as the trust device was unknown in the law of the signatory States. The text has made provision for trusts since the Accession Convention of 1978, and the Regulation now provides that:

4–046

> A person domiciled in a Member State may, in another Member State, be sued in his capacity as settlor, trustee or beneficiary of a trust created by the operation of a statute, or by a written instrument, or created orally and evidenced in writing, in the courts of the Member State in which the trust is domiciled.[152]

The trust must have been created by statute or by a written instrument: resulting or constructive trusts are not included. Nor are trusts arising under wills or intestacies, because wills and intestacies are outside the scope of the Regulation.[153] Article 5(6) applies to disputes relating to the internal relationships of the trust, such as disputes between beneficiaries or between trustees and beneficiaries, and not to disputes relating to its external relations, such as the enforcement by third parties of contracts made by trustees.[154] It must be restrictively interpreted, and while the word "trustee" has an autonomous meaning under the Regulation that meaning will be strongly influenced by the understanding of the concept in the common law countries which gave birth to the trust.[155]

The domicile of a trust has already been considered[156]; it is tested as at the time when proceedings are commenced.[157]

Shipping cases[158]

Article 5(7) provides that where by virtue of the Regulation a court of a Member State has jurisdiction in actions relating to liability from the use or operation of a ship, that court, or any other court substituted for this purpose by the internal law of that Member State, shall also have jurisdiction over claims for limitation of such liability.

4–047

---

[152] art.5(6).
[153] art.1; Schlosser, para.52.
[154] Schlosser, para.120.
[155] *Gomez v Encarnacion Gomez-Monche Vives* [2008] EWCA Civ 1065; [2009] Ch. 245.
[156] See above, para.4–020.
[157] *Chellaram v Chellaram (No.2)* [2002] EWHC 632 (Ch); [2002] 3 All E.R. 17.
[158] See Jackson, *Enforcement of Maritime Claims* (LLP 2005).

Multi-party cases and counterclaims

Co-defendants

4–048 A person domiciled in another Member State who is one of a number of co-defendants may also be sued in the courts for the place[159] where any one of them is domiciled,[160] provided the claims are so closely connected that it is expedient to hear and determine them together to avoid the risk of irreconcilable judgments resulting from separate proceedings.[161] Although the text of the Regulation says nothing about the basis of the claims, there was a suggestion in one judgment of the ECJ that a claim in contract could not be "connected" for the purposes of art.6(1) to one in tort.[162] In a later decision, *Freeport plc v Olle Arnoldsson*,[163] the ECJ held, on facts which involved claims on those two bases, that the fact that claims brought against a number of defendants had different legal bases did not preclude the application of art.6(1).

It will be seen that art.6(1) may operate so as to allow a claimant to sue a foreign defendant in the domicile of another, less important, defendant. But art.6(1) cannot always be relied upon. The ECJ has held that it cannot be interpreted in such a way as to allow a claimant to make a claim against a number of defendants for the sole purpose of removing one of them from the jurisdiction of the courts of the Member State in which that defendant is domiciled[164]; but in the *Freeport* case the Court seemed to qualify this statement: if the required degree of connection between the claims was established, there was no further need to establish separately that the claims were not brought for that sole purpose.

If the case falls within the special rules relating to individual employment contracts, those rules apply to the exclusion of art.6(1).[165] The Advocate General in *Painer v Standard Verlags GmbH*[166] recognised that the ECJ's overall approach to the issue of connection remained unclear.[167] The opinion stressed that the first requirement for the existence of a close connection was that the anchor claim and the other claim arose in the context of a single factual situation where it was clear to a defendant that he was likely to be sued as the co-defendant of an anchor defendant. That minimum requirement was not met where the two claims were similar yet had arisen in separate and independent circumstances. Secondly,

---

[159] One of the few points in the Regulation at which domicile at particular place must be established.

[160] At the time of the issue of the claim form rather than its service: *Canada Trust Co. v Stolzenberg (No.2)* [2002] 1 A.C. 1.

[161] art.6(1); the proviso was new in the Regulation, but it reflects earlier case-law: Case 189/87 *Kalfelis v Schroder, Munchmeyer, Hengst & Co.* [1988] E.C.R. 5565. See also, e.g. *Shetty v Al Rushaid Petroleum Investment* [2011] EWHC 1460 (Ch).

[162] Case C-51/97 *Réunion européenne SA v Spliethoff's bevrachtingskantoor BV* [1998] I-E.C.R. 6511. The proposition was doubted by the English Court of Appeal *Watson v First Choice Holidays and Flights Ltd* [2001] 2 Lloyd's Rep. 339; the issue was referred to the ECJ but the claim was settled.

[163] Case C-98/06, [2007] E.C.R. I-8319.

[164] Case C-103/05 *Reisch Montage AG v Kiesel Baumaschinen Handels GmbH* [2006] E.C.R. I-6827.

[165] Case C-462/06 *Glaxosmithkline v Rouard* [2008] E.C.R. I-3965. The EU Commission Proposal amends art.18 to allow for the application of art.6(1). It has been suggested that the use of art.6(1) in this context should be limited to employees suing multiple defenders (Beaumont and McEleavy, *Anton's Private International Law*, (3rd edn 2011) at 284.

[166] Case C-145/10, opinion of Trstenjak AG, April 12 2011.

[167] *ibid.*, paras 71 and 78–85.

there had to be a sufficiently close legal connection between the two claims such that inconsistencies between them would not be acceptable.[168]

Third parties

A person domiciled in a Member State may also be sued as a third party in an action on a warranty or guarantee or in any other third party proceedings in the court seised of the original proceedings,[169] unless these were instituted solely with the object of removing the original defendant from the jurisdiction of the court which would otherwise be competent.[170] Given the purpose of this provision in the Regulation, to avoid the risk of irreconcilable judgments, it is necessary for there to be a close connection between the original claim and the third party proceedings (in English practice, a "Part 20 claim", referring to the relevant provisions in the Civil Procedure Rules). That a mere factual link is not enough is shown by the facts of *Barton v Golden Sun Holidays Ltd*[171]:

4–049

> The claimants, a group of holidaymakers on a holiday arranged by the defendant company, stayed at a hotel in Cyprus. Its low standards of hygiene led to the claimants suffering gastrointestinal infections. The defendants admitted liability and agreement was reached on the damages payable and the basis on which costs were to be quantified. At that point the defendants sought leave to bring a Part 20 claim against the hotel operators.

It was held that the case fell outside art.6(2). The main claim had been entirely a matter of English law, but the claim against the hotel company also involved the law of Cyprus. The main claim was now effectively dealt with, so that there was no realistic possibility of the two claims being heard together and no risk of irreconcilable judgments.

Counterclaims

A person domiciled in a Member State may also be sued on a counterclaim arising from the same contract or facts on which the original claim was based, in the court in which the original claim is pending.[172]

4–050

---

[168] *ibid.*, paras 86–99.
[169] Whether the basis for jurisdiction in the original proceedings was the defendant's domicile or some other basis: Case C-365/88 *Kongress Agentur Hagen GmbH v Zeehage B.V.* [1990] E.C.R. I-1845.
[170] art.6(2). The provisions of art.6(2) cannot be relied upon to deprive the third party of the benefit of a jurisdiction agreement under art.23: *Hough v P & O Containers Ltd* [1999] Q.B. 834.
[171] [2007] EWHC 3455 (QB), [2007] I.L.Pr. 57.
[172] art.6(3).

Insurance

4–051   The original Brussels Convention text made special provision for jurisdiction in matters of insurance[173] in order to protect the policy-holder, the supposedly weaker party. As Schlosser says,[174] the accession of the United Kingdom introduced a totally new dimension to the insurance business as it had hitherto been practised within the European Union. This was because the London insurance market has such a large share of worldwide insurance business, particularly in the international insurance of large risks. In such business the policy-holder is likely to be a powerful multinational corporation which does not need the protection given by the original Convention to an individual policy-holder insuring his or her house, car, or life. Changes to take account of the new situation were made at the time the United Kingdom acceded and again when the Brussels I Regulation was formulated. The result is the very complicated law contained in arts 8 to 14.

These provisions provide an almost exclusive code governing jurisdiction "in matters relating to insurance"[175] and with two exceptions other bases of jurisdiction cannot be relied upon: the exceptions are arts 4 (application of national jurisdictional rules in certain cases) and 5(5) (disputes concerning the operations of a branch, agency or other establishment). In addition, the general rule giving jurisdiction to the court of a Member States before which a defendant enters an appearance[176] applies to insurance as to other cases.[177]

The basic rule is that an insurer domiciled in a Member State may be sued (a) in the courts of the Member State where the insurer is domiciled (a basis corresponding to that in art.2, or (b) in the case of a co-insurer, in the courts of a Member State in which proceedings are brought against the leading insurer (a provision similar to the "co-defendants" provision in art.6(1), but distinguishing between "leading" and other insurers), or (c) in another Member State, in the case of actions brought by the policyholder, the insured or a beneficiary, in the courts for the place where the plaintiff is domiciled.[178] The effect of these rules is enlarged by the provision that an insurer who is not domiciled in a Member State but has a branch, agency or other establishment in one of the Member States is, in disputes arising out of the operations of the branch, agency or establishment, deemed to be domiciled in that Member State.[179]

---

[173] For the scope of this phrase, see Case C-412/98 *Universal General Insurance Co. v Group Josi Reinsurance Co. S.A.* [2001] 1 Q.B. 68; *Agnew v Länsforsäkringsbølagens* [2001] 1 A.C. 223.

[174] para.136.

[175] As between insurer and insured: actions between insurers are not covered and the general rules apply: *Youell v La Réunion Aérienne* [2008] EWHC 2493 (Comm); the issue was not taken on appeal.

[176] art.24. See Case C-111/09 *Ceska Podnikatelska Pojistovna as,Vienna Insurance Group v Bilas* [2010] Lloyd's Rep IR 734.

[177] In the EU Commission Proposal a new safety-net is proposed for the operation of art.24 in relation to insurance, consumer and employment contracts (considered to be contracts with a weaker party), that is for the court before assuming jurisdiction to inform the weaker party on his right to contest the jurisdiction of the court and the consequences of entering an appearance.

[178] art.9(1). See *Jones v Assurances Générales de France (AGF) SA* [2010] ILPr 4 (English victim of road accident in France entitled to sue French insurer of Irish negligent driver in England).

[179] art.9(2).

In respect of liability insurance or insurance of immovable property, the insurer **4–052** may in addition be sued in the courts for the place where the harmful event occurred. The same applies if movable and immovable property are covered by the same insurance policy and both are adversely affected by the same contingency[180]; and in respect of liability insurance the insurer may also, if the law of the court permits it, be joined in proceedings which the injured party has brought against the insured.[181]

On the other hand, an insurer[182] may bring proceedings against a policyholder, the insured or a beneficiary only in the courts of the Member State in which the defendant is domiciled.[183] This rule is subject to a number of exceptions: where the applicable rules governing direct actions between injured party and insurer so provide[184]; when a counterclaim is brought against the original plaintiff[185]; and in certain cases in which the parties have given jurisdiction to a court by agreement.[186]This last possibility is hedged about by complex rules designed to protect individuals: cases of marine, aviation and "large risks" insurance are treated differently.[187]

Consumer contracts

Section 4 (arts 15–17) of the Regulation contains special provisions for **4–053** jurisdiction over consumer contracts in order to protect consumers, the economically weaker party. These provisions provide an almost exclusive code, and other bases of jurisdiction cannot be relied upon, with two exceptions: the exceptions are arts 4 (application of national jurisdictional rules in certain cases) and 5(5) (disputes concerning the operations of a branch, agency or other establishment). In addition, the general rule giving jurisdiction to the court of a Member State before which a defendant enters an appearance[188] applies in the consumer context as elsewhere.

There are important definitions of "consumer" and "consumer contract" in art.15. A person is a "consumer" only if he or she concluded the contract for a purpose which can be regarded as being outside his or her trade or profession.[189] The ECJ has held that this brings within the consumer contract category only

---

[180] art.10.

[181] art.11(1). For direct actions between injured party and insurer, see art.11(2)(3) and Case C-463/06 *FBTO Schadeverzekeringen NV v Odenbreit* [2007] E.C.R. I-11321. See also Case C-347/08 *Vorarlberger Gebietskrankenkasse v WGV-Schwabische Allgemeine Versicherungs AG* [2009] E.C.R. I-8661.

[182] Whether or not domiciled in a Member State: *Jordan Grand Prix Ltd v Baltic Insurance Group* [1999] 2 A.C. 127.

[183] art.12(1); *New Hampshire Insurance Co. v Strabag Bau A.G.* [1992] 1 Lloyd's Rep. 361.

[184] arts 11(3), 12(1).

[185] art.12(2); *Jordan Grand Prix Ltd v Baltic Insurance Group* [1999] 2 A.C. 127.

[186] art.13.

[187] See arts 13(5), 14.

[188] art.24.

[189] art.15(1). Assignees of the original consumer are not included: Case C-89/91 *Shearson Lehman Hutton Inc v TVB Treuhandgesellschaft fur Vermogensverwaltung* [1993] E.C.R. I-139; nor are consumer associations: Case C-167/00 *Verien fur Konsumenteninformation v Henkel* [2002] E.C.R. I-8111.

contracts concluded[190] for the purpose of satisfying an individual's own needs in terms of private consumption.[191] In many cases an item is bought for mixed purposes: a professor may buy a computer partly to use in editing a student textbook but also for playing computer games. The professor could claim the benefit of the special rules as to consumer contracts only by showing that the trade or professional purpose was so limited as to be negligible in the overall context of the supply, and even in that case not if he or she had acted in such a way as to lead the supplier reasonably to believe that the supply was for business purposes.[192]

4–054   A "consumer contract" includes a contract for the sale of goods on instalment credit terms[193]; a contract for a loan repayable by instalments, or any other form of credit, made to finance the sale of goods; or any other contract (wherever concluded) with:

> a person who pursues commercial or professional activities in the Member State of the consumer's domicile or, by any means, directs such activities to that Member State or to several states including that Member State, and the contract falls within the scope of such activities.[194]

The idea behind this provision is that a business which seeks to enter the consumer market in a particular country cannot complain if it finds itself exposed to litigation there. This applies even if the transactions which the business seeks to promote have effects in another country: for example, a French company advertising in the English press time-share arrangements for the use of apartments in Spain could be sued by an English consumer. Although United States law does not have this type of protective jurisdiction for consumers, the Regulation has echoes of the American notion of jurisdiction based on "doing business" in a State. The Regulation provision caused much controversy, primarily because of its effect on e-commerce. The European Commission observed, in making the proposal on which the Regulation is based,[195] that:

> "The concept of activities pursued in or directed towards a Member State is designed to make clear that [art.15(1)(c)] applies to consumer contracts concluded via an interactive website accessible in the State of the consumer's domicile. The fact that a consumer simply had knowledge of a service or possibility of buying goods via a passive website accessible in his country of domicile will not trigger the protective jurisdiction. The contract is thereby treated in the same way as a contract concluded by telephone, fax and the like . . ."

---

[190] Case C-96/00 *Gabriel v Schlank & Schick GmbH* [2000] E.C.R. I-6367; Case C-27/02 *Engler v Janus Versand GmbH* [2005] E.C.R. I-481; Case C-180/06 *Ilsinger v Dreschers* [2009] E.C.R. I-3961.

[191] Case C-269/95 *Benincasa v Dentalkit SRL* [1997] E.C.R. I-3767.

[192] Case C-464/01 *Gruber v BayWa AG* [2006] Q.B. 204 (E.C.J.) (tiles for a farmhouse which was used both as a private house and for farm purposes).

[193] See Case 150/77 *Société Bertrand v Paul Ott KG* [1978] E.C.R. 1431 (decided under an earlier text of the Convention).

[194] art.15(1)(c). Contracts of transport are excluded (art.15(3)) (but not packages covering both transport and accommodation) because there are specific rules in the various international transport conventions.

[195] See O.J. C 376E/1, 28.12.1999; Kennett, (2001) 50 I.C.L.Q. 725 and, more generally, Øren, (2003) 52 I.C.L.Q. 665.

The European Commission admitted that some of the concepts were in fact difficult to apply, and noted the anxiety of commercial parties that a website accessible from anywhere in the world could lay them open to litigation in any country unless they were able to refuse to deal with consumers resident in stated countries, so that, for example, an English company could indicate that it would not accept orders from New Zealand. There is concern in some, geographically isolated, countries such as New Zealand that their consumers may find themselves excluded from the new forms of commerce altogether.[196]

In *Pammer v Reederei Karl Schlüter GmbH*[197] and *Hotel Alpenhof GmbH v Heller*[198] (joined cases) the ECJ was asked for a preliminary ruling on inter alia the interpretation of directing activities in the context of art.15 of the Brussels I Regulation. Both cases involved consumers purchasing services via the internet from companies based in different Member States, having obtained information about them from the internet. One of the questions referred was whether the fact that the website of an intermediary, or of a party with whom a consumer had concluded a contract, could be consulted on the internet was sufficient to justify a finding that activities were being "directed" to the Member State of the consumer's domicile within the meaning of art.15(1)(c). The Court held that the protection afforded by art.15(1)(c) and art.16 was not absolute because the directing of activities to a Member State had been laid down as a condition for the application of the rules relating to consumer contracts, not the mere existence of a website.[199] In order to determine whether the rule applied to a particular trader, it had to be ascertained whether, before the conclusion of any contract with the consumer, it was apparent from the trader's websites and the trader's overall activity that the trader envisaged doing business with consumers domiciled in one or more Member States, including the Member State of that consumer's domicile, "in the sense that it was minded to conclude a contract with them". The ECJ went on to enumerate a non-exhaustive list of matters capable of constituting evidence from which it might be concluded that the trader's activity was directed to the Member State of the consumer's domicile: the international nature of the activity; mention of itineraries from other Member States for going to the place where the trader was established; use of a language or currency other than the language or currency generally used in the Member State where the trader was established; mention of telephone numbers with an international code; outlay of expenditure on an Internet referencing service in order to facilitate access to the trader's site by customers domiciled in other Member States; use of a top-level domain name other than that of the Member State in which the trader was established; and mention of an international clientele composed of customers domiciled in various Member States. However, the mere accessibility of the trader's or intermediary's website in the Member State where the consumer was domiciled was insufficient,

4–055

---

[196] See Øren, (2003) 52 I.C.L.Q. 665; Farah, (2008) E.L.Rev.257; Cachia, (2009) E.L.Rev. 476.
[197] Case C-585/08, [2012] All ER (EC) 34.
[198] Case C-144/09, [2012] All ER (EC) 34.
[199] See paras 60–61, 63–64, 66–68, 70–71 of the ECJ's decision.

as was mention of an email address or other contact details and use of the language or currency generally used in the Member State where the trader was established.[200]

4–056 The effect of art.16 is that a consumer may bring proceedings against the other party to a contract either in the courts of the Member State in which that party is domiciled or in the courts of the Member State in which the consumer is domiciled.[201] Proceedings may be brought against a consumer by the other party to the contract only in the courts of the Member State in which the consumer is domiciled.[202] A consumer who enters into a contract with a party who is not domiciled in a Member State but who has a branch, agency or other establishment in one of the Member States, has the benefit of a special rule: that party is, in disputes arising out of the operations of the branch, agency or establishment, deemed to be domiciled in that state.[203]

There is further protection of the consumer, against the effect of jurisdiction clauses. The rules as to jurisdiction over consumer contracts may be departed from only by an agreement (a) which is entered into after the dispute has arisen; or (b) which allows the consumer to bring proceedings in courts other than those indicated in those rules; or (c) which is entered into by the consumer and the other party to the contract, both of whom are at the time of conclusion of the contract domiciled or habitually resident in the same Member State, and which confers jurisdiction on the courts of that state, provided that such an agreement is not contrary to the law of that state.[204]

Individual contracts of employment

4–057 The earlier Convention texts contained no special provisions governing employment contracts, so that jurisdiction was given to the court of the defendant's domicile (under art.2) or the place of performance of the obligation in question (under art.5(1)). In a series of cases,[205] the ECJ ignored the plain language of the text and held that in the case of individual contracts of employment there had to be a single place of performance: that in which the employee's duties were performed. The justification offered for this exercise of judicial creativity was that contracts of employment have special features, notably the existence of mandatory rules designed to protect employees and of collective agreements, which made the fragmentation of employment cases between jurisdictions especially undesirable. In the Brussels I Regulation, provisions reflecting the earlier case-law form s.5 (arts 18–21).[206]

As is the case with the comparable provisions as to insurance and consumer contracts, the Section provides an almost exclusive code, and with two exceptions

---

[200] *ibid.*, paras 69, 76–77, 80–84, 89–94.
[201] art.16(1).
[202] art.16(2). Article 16 does not affect the right to bring a counterclaim in the court in which, in accordance with s.4, the original claim is pending: art.16(3).
[203] art.15(2).
[204] art.17.
[205] Beginning with Case 133/81 *Ivenel v Schwab* [1982] E.C.R. 1891.
[206] See Grusic, (2012) 61 I.C.L.Q. 91.

other bases of jurisdiction cannot be relied upon: the exceptions are arts 4 (application of national jurisdictional rules in certain cases) and 5(5) (disputes concerning the operations of a branch, agency or other establishment).[207] In addition, the general rule giving jurisdiction to the court of a Member States before which a defendant enters an appearance[208] applies in the employment context as elsewhere.

Claims against an employer are governed by art.19. An employer domiciled in a Member State may be sued in the courts of the Member State where the employer is domiciled (a rule corresponding to that in art.2). If an employee works at different times for two companies, in the same group but with different domiciles, it might be expected that the co-defendants rule of art.6[209] would be available, but the ECJ has held, for frankly unconvincing reasons, that it is not.[210]

The scope of the jurisdiction over actions against employers is extended by the rule that where an employee enters into an individual contract of employment with an employer who is *not* domiciled in a Member State but has a branch, agency or other establishment in one of the Member States, the employer is, in disputes arising out of the operations of the branch, agency or establishment, deemed to be domiciled in that Member State.[211] The employer may also be sued in a Member State other than that of the employer's domicile:

    4–058

(a)   in the courts for the place where the employee habitually carries out his work or in the courts for the last place where he did so, or
(b)   if the employee does not or did not habitually carry out his work in any one country, in the courts for the place where the business which engaged the employee is or was situated.[212]

The approach taken to the rule in sub-paragraph (a) reflects a concern that where work is performed in more than one Member State, it is important to avoid any multiplication of courts having jurisdiction, so that the rule should not be read as conferring concurrent jurisdiction on the courts of each of the states involved.[213]

The reference to the place where the business is situated will often point to the country in which the employer is domiciled, at least in those cases in which the employee is recruited by the employing firm's head office, so adding nothing to the domicile basis of jurisdiction under art.19(1). That no doubt influenced the ECJ to adopt another bold interpretation of the text and especially of the phrase "if the employee does not habitually carry out his work in any one country", so as to maximise the number of cases in which art.19(2)(a) applies. In *Rutten v Cross*

---

[207] art.18(1).
[208] art.24.
[209] See para 4–048.
[210] Case C-462/06 *GlaxoSmithKline v Rouard* [2008] ECR I-3965; see Harris, (2008) 124 L.Q.R. 523.
[211] art.18(2).
[212] art.19(2).
[213] Case C-125/92 *Mulox IBC Ltd v Geels* [1993] ECR I-4075.

Medical Ltd[214] the plaintiff had an office in the Netherlands to which he returned after each business trip, but spent only two-thirds of his time in that country, the rest in other States. The Court equated the place where the employee habitually carries out his work with the place in which the employee had "established the effective centre of his working time and where, or from which, he in fact performs the essential part of his duties *vis-à-vis* his employer" (in that case, the Netherlands). The Court noted that that is the place where it is least expensive for the employee to commence proceedings against the employer or to defend himself in such proceedings. The courts for that place are also best placed and, therefore, the most appropriate to resolve the dispute relating to the contract of employment.

4–059   This development of the text of the provision was taken further in *Weber v Universal Ogden Services*[215] where the Court held that the place where the employee actually performed the essential part of his duties was normally the place where, the whole of the term of employment being taken into account, the employee spent most of his working time engaged on the employer's business, but that it could be otherwise if there were circumstances showing that the subject matter of the dispute was more closely connected with a different place. That might involve looking at the nature and importance of the work done in each place.

The employee is further protected by the rule that an employer may bring proceedings only in the courts of the Member State in which the employee is domiciled.[216] The employee is also protected against the effect of jurisdiction clauses. The rules as to jurisdiction over employment contracts may be departed from only by an agreement (a) which is entered into after the dispute has arisen; or (b) which allows the employee to bring proceedings in courts other than those indicated in those rules.[217] In *Glaxosmithkline v Rouard*[218] the ECJ held that the protective jurisdiction rules laid down in the Regulation in relation to individual contracts of employment, on account of their specific and exhaustive nature, could not be amended or supplemented by other rules of jurisdiction laid down in that Regulation unless specific reference was made thereto in arts 18–21 of the Regulation.

Choice of court or jurisdiction clauses[219]

4–060   Any well-drafted contract which has factual links with more than one country will contain a choice of court or jurisdiction clause. This is often in an "exclusive" form, providing that all disputes between the parties arising out of the

---

[214] Case C-383/95, [1997] E.C.R. I-57 (dealing with the equivalent phrase which then formed part of art.5(1) of the Brussels Convention.

[215] Case C-37/00, [2002] Q.B. 1189.

[216] art.20(1). But the provisions of s.5 do not affect the employer's right to bring a counter-claim in the court in which, in accordance with the section, the original claim is pending: art.20(2).

[217] art.21.

[218] Case C-462/06, [2008] ECR I-3965.

[219] There is an international convention, the Convention of 30 June 2005 on Choice of Court Agreements, drawn up under the auspices of the Hague Conference on Private International Law. See

contract *must* be referred to a named court or the courts of a named country. Less frequently it takes a "non-exclusive" form, the parties agreeing that disputes *may* be referred to such a court, without seeking to preclude any other possible forum. Whether a jurisdiction clause is exclusive or "non-exclusive" is a matter of construction of the contractual terms and in principle this construction should be done according to the law governing the agreement.[220] The court selected may be the English court or a foreign court. Different considerations apply to these different categories of case.

Clauses selecting the courts of an EU Member State

A clause giving jurisdiction to the English courts or those of another Member State will often fall within art.23 of the Brussels I Regulation.[221] Article 23(1) applies to agreements as to jurisdiction between parties one or more of whom is domiciled in a Member State and which meet certain formal requirements. These are that the clause must be (a) in writing or evidenced in writing, any communication by electronic means which can provide a durable record of the agreement being treated as in writing[222]; or (b) in a form which accords with practices which the parties have established between themselves[223]; or (c) in international trade or commerce, in a form which accords with a usage of which the parties are, or ought to be, aware and which in such trade or commerce is widely known to, and regularly observed by, parties to contracts of the type involved in the particular trade or commerce concerned.[224] National law may not invalidate agreements by requiring additional formalities to those prescribed by Article 23.[225]

4–061

The meaning of "evidenced in writing" has exercised the courts.[226] The courts have repeatedly emphasised that the real issue is that of consensus between the parties; the written material is evidence of that consensus.[227] General references to standard conditions of contract will not suffice; more specific evidence of agreement is required.[228]

Schulz, (2006) 2 J.Priv.Int.L. 243; Beaumont, (2009) 5 J.Priv.Int.L. 125.The Convention has been signed by the EU and the US, and ratified by Mexico, but it is not yet in force.

[220] See *Bank of New York Mellon v GV Films* [2010] 1 Lloyd's Rep 365.

[221] See Camilleri, (2011) 7 J.Priv.Int.L. 297; Steinle and Vasiliades, (2010) 6 J.Priv.Int.L. 565.

[222] art.23(2).

[223] This possibility eases some practical problems, e.g. that of the tacit renewal of written clauses which have in their own terms expired; see Case 313/85 *Iveco Fiat SpA v Van Hool NV* [1986] E.C.R. 3337.

[224] See Case C-106/95 *Mainschiffahrts-Genossenschaft eG v Les Gravieres Rhenanes SARL* [1997] E.C.R. I-911.

[225] Case 150/80 *Elefanten Schuh v Jacqmain* [1981] E.C.R. 1671.

[226] There is no material difference between art.17 of the Brussels Convention, examined in the earlier cases, and art.23 of the Regulation: *Bols Distilleries BV v Superior Yacht Services Ltd* [2007] 1 W.L.R. 1 (P.C.).

[227] *Deutsche Bank AG v Asia Pacific Broadband Wireless Communications Inc* [2008] EWCA Civ 1091; [2008] 2 Lloyd's Rep 619.

[228] Case 24/76 *Estasis Salotti de Colzani Amo e Giammario Colzani v RUWA Polstereimaschinen GmbH* [1976] E.C.R. 1831; Case 25/76 *Galeries Segoura sprl v Rahim Bonakdarian* [1976] E.C.R. 1851.

So, in *Estasis Salotti de Colzani Amo e Giammario Colzani v RUWA Polstereimaschinen GmbH*[229]:

> A German company, R, wrote to C, an Italian company, offering for sale a number of machines used in making furniture. The letters referred to R's general conditions of sale which were printed on the back. Those conditions permitted R to bring any claim in the courts of Cologne. The offer was accepted and a written contract drawn up, again with the conditions on the reverse. C refused to take delivery of the machines. R began proceedings in Cologne, where the court held it had no jurisdiction.

4–062   The ECJ held that where a clause conferring jurisdiction is included among the general conditions of sale of one of the parties, printed on the back of a contract, the requirement of a writing under what is now art.23(1) is fulfilled only if the contract signed by both parties contains an express reference to those general conditions.

In *Crédit Suisse Financial Products v Société Générale d'Entreprises*[230] and *7E Communications Ltd v Vertex Antennentechnik GmbH*[231] the Court of Appeal applied that decision, holding that a guarantee that the relevant party has "really consented to the clause" exists where there is an express reference to the terms and conditions which include the jurisdiction clause. It is not necessary for there to be a specific reference to the jurisdiction clause itself. The second is that the fact that the relevant party does not have a copy of the terms and conditions or the jurisdiction clause in his possession is not relevant.[232]

A case in which agreement could not be shown is *Lafarge Plasterboard Ltd v Fritz Peters & Co KG*[233]:

> L was an English company making gypsum plasterboard. F was a German company, supplying liner paper for gypsum plaster-board. F approached L offering to supply liner paper. An order was placed. On the back were L's terms of trade including a clause giving exclusive jurisdiction to the English courts. There was nothing on the face of the order form drawing attention to the fact that there were conditions printed on the back. L had different conditions in other documents; F's conditions conflicted with L's. L sued in England and F contested the jurisdiction; L relied on (what is now) art.23.

4–063   The court noted that if art.23 were satisfied, it was mandatory.[234] Before it could apply, the court had to be satisfied that there had been a consensus between the parties; the detailed requirements as to formalities were designed to help the court in making that assessment. On the facts, there was no consistent practice on which the parties could rely. There was no document in which the defendant had expressed in writing consent to the conditions containing the jurisdiction clause: the mere printing of a jurisdiction clause on the reverse of a bill of lading did not satisfy the requirements of the Regulation, as such a procedure gave no guarantee

---

[229] Case 24/76, [1976] E.C.R. 1831
[230] [1997] CLC 168.
[231] [2007] EWCA Civ 140; [2007] 1 W.L.R. 2175.
[232] See *Coys of Kensington Automobiles Ltd v Pugliese* [2011] EWHC 655 (QB); [2011] 2 All ER (Comm) 664; *Sherdley v Nordea Life and Pension SA* [2012] EWCA Civ 88.
[233] [2000] 2 Lloyd's Rep. 689.
[234] See also *Equitas Ltd v Allstate Insurance Co* [2009] 1 All ER (Comm) 1137; *UBS AG v HSH Nordbank AG* [2009] 2 Lloyd's Rep 272.

that the other party had actually consented to the clause derogating from the ordinary jurisdiction rules of the Regulation.

A written document confirming the oral agreement need not be produced by the party bound by the clause so long as there is evidence of acceptance by that party[235]; in one case the articles or statutes of a company were relied upon.[236] A more common practice where the agreement is essentially oral is for one party to confirm the agreement by fax or e-mail; if the other party receives the confirmation and does not object, agreement may be established.[237] The choice of forum may be upheld even if the contract within which it is contained, or by which it is evidenced, is void or vitiated by misrepresentation or want of authority.[238] An agreement meeting these requirements and specifying a court or courts of a Member State[239] gives that court or those courts jurisdiction for the purposes of the Regulation. Unless the parties have agreed otherwise, such jurisdiction is exclusive.

If none of the parties is domiciled in a Member State, the courts of other Member States have no jurisdiction unless the chosen court declines jurisdiction.[240] This appears to apply even if the agreement is non-exclusive in its terms.

It remains unclear how a claim that apparent consent to the clause was vitiated by fraud or duress should be treated. The ECJ has asserted that the formal requirements of art.23 are a sufficient safeguard,[241] but that seems to fly in the face of logic: formal compliance can be secured by fraud. The case of *Deutsche Bank AG v Asia Pacific Broadband Wireless Communications Inc*[242] is illustrative in this context. The case involved a credit agreement including an exclusive jurisdiction clause in favour of the English courts. The claimant bank brought proceedings in England. The defendants argued that the credit agreement was void, alleging that it was part of a large scale fraud. Jurisdiction to consider certain claims which would be relied on by the bank were credit agreement found to be void only existed if the jurisdiction clause was valid. The Court of Appeal relied on the doctrine of severability or separability: a jurisdiction clause is a separable agreement from the agreement as a whole. It was only if the jurisdiction clause was itself under some specific attack (e.g. were fraud or duress to be alleged in relation specifically to the jurisdiction clause) that the jurisdiction clause might be challenged.

4–064

---

[235] Case 71/83 *Partenreederei MS Tilly Russ v Haven & Vervoebedrijf Nova NV* [1985] Q.B. 931; Case 221/84 *Berghoefer GmbH v ASA SA* [1985] E.C.R. 2699. See also *Calyon v Wytwornia Sprzetu Kommunikacynego PZL Swidnik SA* [2009] EWHC 1914 (Comm); [2009] 2 All ER (Comm) 603. cf. *Lafarge Plasterboard Ltd v Fritz Peters & Co KG* [2000] 2 Lloyd's Rep 689.

[236] Case 214/89 *Powell Duffryn v Petereit* [1992] E.C.R. I-1745.

[237] Case 221/84 *Berghoefer GmbH v ASA SA* [1985] E.C.R. 2699.

[238] *Deutsche Bank AG v Asia Pacific Broadband Wireless Communications Inc* [2008] EWCA Civ 1091; [2008] 2 Lloyd's Rep 619.

[239] See Case C-387/98 *Coreck Maritime GmbH v Handelsveem BV* [2000] E.C.R. I-9337 (clause named no country but referred to country where party had its principal place of business; that held sufficient to meet requirements of art.23).

[240] art.23(3). For provisions in trust instruments, see art.23(4)(5).

[241] Case C-159/97 Soc. *Trasporti Castelletti Spedizioni Internazionali SpA v Hugo Trumpy SpA* [1999] E.C.R. I-1597; and see Case C-269/95 *Benincasa v Dentalkit Srl* [1997] E.C.R. I-3767.

[242] [2008] EWCA Civ 1091; [2008] 2 Lloyd's Rep. 619.

In terms of the scope of jurisdiction clauses courts intend to give effect to the will of the parties as effectively[243] as possible, therefore, jurisdiction clauses are usually interpreted as to cover all disputes between the contracting parties.[244]

It is possible for a defendant to waive the clause, e.g. by submitting to the jurisdiction of another court.[245]

4–065　In *Bols Distilleries v Superior Yacht Services Ltd*,[246] the Privy Council considered what standard applied to an argument that an agreement under art.23(1) ousted the usual domicile rule of art.2. It endorsed the test of "a good arguable case". It explained:

> "The rule is that the court must be satisfied, or as satisfied as it can be having regard to the limitations which an interlocutory process imposes, that factors exist which allow the court to take jurisdiction. In practice, what amounts to a "good arguable case" depends on what requires to be shown in any particular situation in order to establish jurisdiction. In the present case, as the case law of the Court of Justice emphasises, in order to establish that the usual rule in art 2(1) is ousted by art 23(1), the claimants must demonstrate "clearly and precisely" that the clause conferring jurisdiction on the court was in fact the subject of consensus between the parties. So, applying the "good arguable case" standard, the claimants must show that they have a much better argument than the defendants that, on the material available at present, the requirements of form in art 23(1) are met and that it can be established, clearly and precisely, that the clause conferring jurisdiction on the court was the subject of consensus between the parties."

Consumer, insurance and employment cases

4–066　There are special rules in respect of choice of court agreements related to consumer, insurance and employment contracts. These provisions are within the "protective" rules of jurisdiction of the Brussels I Regulation, the rationale of which is to protect the weaker party in those cases.

In consumer cases, an agreement as to jurisdiction departing from the rules in s.4 of the Brussels I Regulation (i.e., arts 15–16) is effective only if it is entered into after the dispute has arisen; or allows the consumer to bring proceedings in courts other than those indicated in s.4; or which is entered into by the consumer and the other party to the contract, both of whom are at the time of conclusion of the contract domiciled or habitually resident in the same Member State, and which confers jurisdiction on the courts of that Member State, provided that such an agreement is not contrary to the law of that Member State.[247]

In insurance cases, an agreement as to jurisdiction departing from the rules in s.3 of the Brussels I Regulation (i.e., arts 8 to 14) is effective only if it is entered into after the dispute has arisen; or allows the policyholder, the insured or a beneficiary to bring proceedings in courts other than those indicated in s.3; or

---

[243] See *Deutsche Bank AG v Asia Pacific Broadband Wireless Communications Inc* [2008] EWCA Civ 1091; [2008] 2 Lloyd's Rep. 619.

[244] *ibid.*; *UBS AG v HSH Nordbank AG* [2009] EWCA Civ 585; [2009] 2 Lloyd's Rep. 272; *Cinnamon European Structured Credit Master Fund v Banco Commercial Portugues SA* [2009] EWHC 3381 (Ch); [2010] I.L.Pr. 11.

[245] Case 150/80 *Elefanten Schuh v Jacqmain* [1981] E.C.R. 1671.

[246] [2006] UKPC 45; [2007] 1 W.L.R. 12.

[247] art.17. In some circumstances, a choice of court clause may be judged unfair within the Unfair Terms in Consumer Contracts Regulations 1999 (SI 1999/2083).

which is entered into by the policyholder and the insurer, both of whom are at the time of conclusion of the contract domiciled or habitually resident in the same Member State, and which confers jurisdiction on the courts of that Member State even if the harmful event were to occur abroad, provided that such an agreement is not contrary to the law of that Member State; or which is concluded with a policyholder not domiciled in a Member State, except in so far as the insurance is compulsory or relates to immovable property in a Member State; or which relates to a contract of insurance in so far as it covers certain types of risk listed in art.14.[248]

In individual employment cases, an agreement as to jurisdiction departing from the rules in s.5 of the Brussels I Regulation (i.e., arts 18–20) is effective only if it is entered into after the dispute has arisen, or allows the employee to bring proceedings in courts other than those indicated in Section 5.[249]

Exclusive jurisdiction clauses naming the English courts

An exclusive jurisdiction clause satisfying the requirements of art.23(1) and naming the English courts will plainly give those courts exclusive jurisdiction. There can be no question of the English court refusing to exercise jurisdiction. Should proceedings be begun in another Member State, the court in that state will be required to stay its proceedings, but there is no possibility of the English court restraining those proceedings by an anti-suit injunction.[250]

4–067

Non-exclusive jurisdiction clauses naming the courts of an EU Member State

Where the parties have agreed a non-exclusive choice of court clause, providing for example that the dispute may be referred to the courts of France or of England, art.23 of the Brussels I Regulation will not preclude proceedings in another Member State than that named in the clause, the courts of which have jurisdiction under the terms of the Regulation. There is no possibility of an English court granting an anti-suit injunction to restrain the proceedings brought in another Member State.[251]

4–068

Cases not within Article 23

The principles applying in cases which do not attract art.23 are dealt with in the following chapter.[252]

4–069

---

[248] art.13.
[249] art.21.
[250] Under the principle of Case C-111/01 *Erich Gasser GmbH v MISAT srl* [2003] E.C.R. I-14693; [2005] Q.B. 1; see para.4–076ff.
[251] Under the same principle.
[252] See para.5–061.

Submission to the jurisdiction

4–070   Article 24 provides that apart from jurisdiction derived from other provisions of the Regulation, a court of a Member State before which a defendant enters an appearance shall have jurisdiction. This rule does not apply where appearance was entered to contest the jurisdiction,[253] or where another court has exclusive jurisdiction under art.22. But it does apply where the parties have chosen another court under art.23[254]: thus, if there is a conflict, the provisions of art.24 prevail over those of art.23.

Competing jurisdictions

4–071   Within the framework of the Brussels I Regulation, it is plainly possible for the courts of two or more Member States to have jurisdiction (concurrent jurisdiction). In a contract case for example, one state may be the country in which the defendant is domiciled, and its courts will have jurisdiction under art.2, and the courts of another state may have special jurisdiction under art.5(1) as the place of performance of the obligation in question. The two parties may each seek to begin proceedings, selecting the courts of different Member States. In terms of legal technique, determining the most convenient jurisdiction in cases of concurrent jurisdiction is a difficult task for conflict of law rules. In most cases, as the previous example illustrates, the courts involved will be internationally competent to hear the merits due to a close connection between the forum and the parties, or the forum and the dispute. In the context of the Brussels I Regulation, the resulting problems are addressed in s.9 of Chapter II (arts 27–30). Articles 27 and 28 provide the courts with mechanisms to deal with the issues that may arise in these circumstances; these provisions apply regardless of the domicile of the parties[255] and independently of the basis of jurisdiction on which the proceedings are founded.[256]

Lis alibi pendens

4–072   The term *lis alibi pendens*, which is found in many of the older cases, refers to the situation in which what is essentially the same dispute is the subject of litigation in two or more countries. This is plainly undesirable, from the point of view of the courts as well as the parties, because of the extra costs involved and the risk that the two courts may make different and conflicting decisions.
Article 27 provides[257]:

---

[253] See Case 150/80 *Elefanten Schuh v Jacqmain* [1981] E.C.R. 1671 (but note that the Regulation, unlike the earlier texts does not speak of appearance entered *solely* to contest the jurisdiction).
[254] Case 150/80 *Elefanten Schuh v Jacqmain* [1981] E.C.R. 1671.
[255] Case C-351/89 *Overseas Union Insurance Ltd v New Hampshire Insurance Co.* [1991] E.C.R. I-3317.
[256] *Trademark Licensing Co Ltd v Leofelis SA* [2009] EWHC 3285 (Ch); [2010] I.L.Pr. 16.
[257] The same provision is to be found in art.21 of the Brussels and Lugano Conventions.

Where proceedings involving the same cause of action and between the same parties are brought in the courts of different Member States, any court other than the court first seised shall of its own motion stay its proceedings until such time as the jurisdiction of the court first seised is established. Where the jurisdiction of the court first seised is established, any court other than the court first seised shall decline jurisdiction in favour of that court.

The same parties

The two sets of proceedings must involve the same parties, and it is immaterial whether or not either party is domiciled in a Member State.[258] This rule is easy to apply where the parties are single companies or individuals, but much litigation involves multiple parties, and it is not uncommon for proceedings to be commenced in different countries by different groups of claimants with overlapping membership. The ECJ has held, logically but inconveniently, that art.27 has to be applied only where there is complete identity of parties.[259] This identity, it seems, is not entirely a question of names: an insurer and its insured, having identical interests, may be treated as the same party in this context[260] as may a company and its wholly-owned subsidiary.[261]

4–073

The Court of Appeal examined the interpretation of art.27 in *Kolden Holdings Ltd v Rodette Commerce Ltd*[262]:

> In March 2004, a group of companies sold their shareholdings in a Russian company to the defendants. A dispute arose, the seller companies maintaining that under the terms of the contract the defendants were obliged to pass on their newly-acquired shares to another company, but had not done so. In July 2006 the seller companies began an action in England seeking a declaration reflecting their position. On February 14, 2007 the defendants began proceedings in Cyprus (where all the relevant companies were incorporated) seeking a negative declaration on the same issues; the defendants were the seller companies and K. In November 2006 the seller companies assigned all their rights under the contract to K, and on February 16, 2007 (and so two days after the commencement of the Cyprus action) permission was given by the English court for K to be substituted as claimant in the English action.

The Court of Appeal held that the essential issue was whether there were on February 14, 2007 two sets of proceedings between "the same parties". If so, the subsequent substitution of K for the seller companies would not matter. It summarised the jurisprudence of the ECJ as saying that the term "between the same parties" in art.27 had an autonomous meaning. In considering whether two entities were the "same party", the court looked to the substance, and not the form. Although the parties had to be "identical", that identity was not destroyed by the mere fact of there being separate legal entities involved. Whether they were identical might depend on whether there was such a degree of identity between the interests of the entities that a judgment given against one of them

---

[258] Case C-351/89 *Overseas Union Insurance Ltd v New Hampshire Insurance Co.* [1991] E.C.R. I-3317.

[259] Case C-406/92 *The Tatry* [1994] E.C.R. I-5439 (actions by different groups of cargo-owners arising out of a single incident of cargo contamination). The Court suggested that flexible application of what is now art.28 (see below) would minimise the practical inconvenience of its decision.

[260] Case C-351/96 *Drouot Assurances SA v Consolidated Metallurgical Industries* [1998] E.C.R. I-3057.

[261] *Berkeley Administration Inc. v McClelland* [1995] I.L.Pr. 210. See *Turner v Grovit* [2000] Q.B. 345 (companies in same group treated as "same parties").

[262] [2008] EWCA Civ. 10; [2008] 1 Lloyd's Rep. 434.

would have the force of *res judicata* as against the other. It would also depend on whether the interests of the entities were identical and indissociable, and it was for the national court to ascertain whether that was in fact the case. The test to determine whether parties were "the same parties" for this purpose was the "good arguable case" test. On the facts, that test was satisfied. A decision against K or against the seller companies one would be *res judicata* as against the other; the interests of the seller companies and K were identical. It followed that the English court was the court first seised and the defendant's attempt to have the English proceedings stayed under art.27 failed.

The same cause of action

4–074   Another problem is that of deciding, given the variety of legal categories used in different states, when the proceedings do involve "the same cause of action". This must be interpreted independently of any one national system, and attention will be paid to the underlying issue rather than the forms in which it is presented. It is not necessary that the cause of action should be absolutely identical: proceedings for specific performance of a contract may be regarded as based on the same cause of action as proceedings seeking the annulment of the relevant contract.[263] Actions in personam and in rem may be treated as resting on the same cause of action if the subject matter and object of the proceedings do in fact coincide.[264] On the other hand, an action for infringement of a trademark and an action for passing off have been held not to be the same cause of action.[265]

When is a court seised of a case?

4–075   The approach of giving priority to the court first seised makes it crucial to discover when exactly a court is "seised". The Brussels and Lugano Conventions offered no definition of the term and the ECJ interpreted it as requiring the case to be "definitively pending", itself a matter to be determined by the national law of each court.[266] In England, although the issue of the claim form has considerable procedural significance, the claim was held not to be "definitively pending" until it had been served.[267] This is no longer the position: the Brussels I Regulation contains detailed rules in art.30,[268] which cater for the variant procedures found in Member States. A court is deemed to be seised: (1) in countries following procedures of the English type, at the time when the document instituting the

---

[263] Case 144/86 *Gubisch Maschinenfabrik AG v Palumbo* [1987] E.C.R. 4861.

[264] See Case C-406/92 *The Tatry* [1994] E.C.R. I-5439 (where there were claims *in rem* for compensation for damage to cargo and an action by the shipowner for limitation of liability); *Republic of India v India Steamship Co. Ltd (No.2)* [1998] A.C. 878.

[265] *Mecklermedia Corp. v DC Congress GmbH* [1998] Ch. 40.

[266] Case 129/83 *Zelger v Salintrini (No.2)* [1984] E.C.R. 2397.

[267] *Dresser (U.K.) Ltd v Falcongate Freight Management Ltd* [1992] Q.B. 502; *Neste Chemicals SA v DK Line SA, The Sargasso* [1994] 3 All E.R. 180; but cf. *Phillips v Symes (No. 3)* [2008] UKHL 1; [2008] 1 W.L.R. 180 (Lugano Convention; procedural defect in service later cured by court order).

[268] In *Debt Collect London Ltd v SK Slavia Praha-Fotbal AS*, [2010] EWCA Civ 1250; [2011] 1 W.L.R. 866 the English court was deemed to be the court first seised where Czech proceedings had been lodged first but there had been a failure to take a step required for effecting service within the Brussels I Regulation art.30(1): the Czech court fee had not been paid.

proceedings is lodged with the court, i.e., when the claim form is issued, provided that the claimant has not subsequently failed to take the steps required to have service effected on the defendant, or (2) in other countries, if the document has to be served before being lodged with the court, at the time when it is received by the authority responsible for service, provided that the claimant has not subsequently failed to take the steps required to have the document lodged with the court.

Practical implications

Article 27 is often referred to as the "court first seised" rule, and its critics see it as mechanical and as encouraging a race to the court-house: each party may see an advantage in "getting in first" in its chosen forum. It has encouraged the so-called "torpedo action" litigation tactic. In these respects it stands in sharp contrast to the highly discretionary practice in the common law tradition, no longer available in cases within the scope of the Regulation,[269] which enabled the courts to steer cases to the most appropriate forum regardless of the speed with which the various parties may have acted.

4–076

The "court first seised" rule is strictly applied. It may sometimes happen that the court first seised does not in fact have jurisdiction under the Regulation: it may be that another court has exclusive jurisdiction, either under art.22 or under a choice of court clause. This situation arose in *Erich Gasser GmbH v MISAT srl*.[270]:

> A contractual dispute arose between Italian and Austrian companies. The Italian company began proceedings in Italy, in effect for a negative declaration, asserting that the contract had been terminated and that it had not failed to carry out its obligations under the contract. Some eight months later, the Austrian company began proceedings in Austria, claiming sums due under the contract. The Austrian courts had exclusive jurisdiction by virtue of a clause in the contract.

The ECJ held that art.21 of the Brussels Convention, which corresponds to art.27 of the Regulation, must be interpreted as meaning that a court second seised whose jurisdiction has been claimed under an agreement conferring jurisdiction must nevertheless stay proceedings until the court first seised has declared that it has no jurisdiction.[271] The Court discussed and in effect overruled an English Court of Appeal decision to the contrary.[272]

Under art.27, even if England is the natural forum, the case may have to be heard in another Member State because the claimant chose to sue there. The facts of the *Gasser* case point to the remedy for a potential defendant in such a case: the

4–077

---

[269] See paras 5–044ff, below.

[270] Case C-111/01, [2003] E.C.R. I-14693; [2005] Q.B. 1, noted Mance, (2002) 120 L.Q.R. 357, Fentiman, [2004] C.L.J. 312; Hartley in *Mélanges en l'honneur de Paul Lagarde* (Dalloz, Paris, 2005) at p.383. See *J P Morgan Europe Ltd v Primacom* [2005] EWHC 508 (Comm); [2005] 2 Lloyd's Rep. 665.

[271] The ECJ also ruled that long delays in the court first seised could not be relied on as justifying a departure from the "court first seised" rule.

[272] *Continental Bank NA v Aeokos Cia Naviera SA* [1994] 1 W.L.R. 588.

device of the negative declaration.[273] The party against whom a claim alleging liability is likely to be brought may seek a declaration of non-liability in a court of its own choosing, for example the English court. If the application for such a declaration is made before the liability claim is commenced, the English court will be the "court first seised" and the courts in other Member States must stay any proceedings brought before them.[274] As a matter of domestic procedural law, the English courts may stay any proceedings for a negative declaration which are judged a misuse of the court's procedure.[275]

In reviewing the functioning of the Brussels I Regulation, the need to avoid the harmful consequences of the ECJ's decision in *Gasser* has become apparent. The report on the operation of the Brussels I Regulation adopted by the EU Commission recognises the difficulties generated by the application of the *lis pendens* rules.[276] One of the solutions proposed by the EU Commission is "to reverse the priority rule insofar as exclusive choice of court agreements are concerned...the court designated by the agreement would have priority to determine its jurisdiction and any other court seized would stay proceedings until the jurisdiction of the chosen court is established. ... Such solution would align to a large extent the internal Community rules with the international rules".[277] This would reinforce the efficacy of exclusive choice of court agreements. Moreover, the EU Commission Proposal[278] aims at improving the current situation by prescribing a six months time-limit for the court first seised to decide on its jurisdiction.[279]

Related actions

4–078 Article 28, unusual in the context of the Regulation in giving a discretion[280] to the court, provides as follows:

> Where related actions are brought in the courts of different Member States, any court other than the court first seised may stay its proceedings.
> Where these actions are pending at first instance, any court other than the court first seised may also, on the application of one of the parties, decline jurisdiction if the court first seised has jurisdiction over the actions in question and its law permits the consolidation thereof.
> For the purposes of this Article, actions are deemed to be related where they are so closely connected that it is expedient to hear and determine them together to avoid the risk of irreconcilable judgments resulting from separate proceedings.

The courts have sought to clarify the notion of a "risk of irreconcilable judgments". The ECJ has held that the risk is of conflicting decisions, even if

---

[273] See Bell (1995) 111 L.Q.R. 674.
[274] Case 144/86 *Gubisch Maschinenfabrik AG v Palumbo* [1987] E.C.R. 4861; Case C-406/92 *The Tatry* [1994] E.C.R. I-5439.
[275] See *Messier-Dowty Ltd v Sabena SA* (No 2) [2000] 1 W.L.R. 2040.
[276] See COM (2009) 174 final.
[277] COM (2009) 174 final, at p 5.
[278] See COM (2010) 748 final.
[279] Proposed art.29(2) (COM (2010) 748 final). In addition, the amendment introduced in the proposed art.29(2) provides for an exchange of information between the courts seized of the same matter.
[280] See *FKI Engineering Ltd v Stribog Ltd* [2011] EWCA Civ 622; [2011] 1 W.L.R. 3264.

there are no mutually exclusive legal consequences.[281] If two courts might give conflicting interpretations of identical contractual wording used in related transactions between different sets of parties, this would present a risk of irreconcilable judgments, even though each court's judgments could be executed. It is not always possible to predict the precise issues which a court may address, but in *Sarrio S.A. v Kuwait Investment Authority*[282] the House of Lords said that "a broad commonsense approach" should be taken, and that it was not essential for a party seeking to rely on art.28 to show that a court would inevitably deal with certain issues.

As the Court of Appeal explained in *Research in Motion UK Ltd v Visto Corporation*,[283] the effect of art.28 is not entirely mechanical:

> "It requires an assessment of the degree of connection, and then a value judgment as to the expediency of hearing the two actions together (assuming they could be so heard) in order to avoid the risk of inconsistent judgments. It does not say that any possibility of inconsistent judgments means that they are inevitably related. It seems to us that the article leaves it open to a court to acknowledge a connection, or a risk of inconsistent judgments, but to say that the connection is not sufficiently close, or the risk is not sufficiently great, to make the actions related for the purposes of the article. Mechanics do not, for once, provide a complete answer."[284]

Article 29 deals with the rare case in which two courts each have exclusive jurisdiction over the same case; the case must be heard by the court first seised.

Provisional and protective measures

Article 31 provides that application may be made to the courts of a Member State   **4–079** for such provisional, including protective, measures as may be available under the law of that State, even if, under the Regulation, the courts of another Member State have jurisdiction as to the substance of the matter.

International judicial co-operation in this field is two-fold. On the one hand, a court that has no jurisdiction to hear the merits of a case can still exercise jurisdiction for the sole purpose of granting provisional and protective measures in support of foreign proceedings or arbitration.[285] There is a clear distinction between jurisdiction on the merits and jurisdiction for the purposes of interim relief in the European jurisdictional scheme, introduced first by the original Brussels and Lugano Conventions, and currently established in the Brussels 1 Regulation and in the 2007 Lugano Convention.[286]

---

[281] Case C-406/92 *The Tatry* [1994] E.C.R. I-5439.

[282] [1999] 1 A.C. 32.

[283] [2008] EWCA Civ 153; [2008] 2 All E.R. (Comm) 560.

[284] See *FKI Engineering Ltd v Stribog Ltd* [2011] EWCA Civ 622; [2011] 1 W.L.R. 3264 where members of the Court of Appeal expressed rather different views as to way in which the courts should address the issue.

[285] The EU Commission Proposal prevents the free circulation within the European area of justice of measures ordered by a court other than the one having jurisdiction on the substance. According to the Proposal the effect of these measures should be limited to the territory of the Member State where they were granted (see Proposal, para.3.1.5.).

[286] See Council Decision 2009/430/EC of 27 November 2008 ([10.6.2009] OJ L147/1).

Typical of the protective measures contemplated by art.31 is the *saisie conservatoire* of French law, under which French courts have drastic powers to seize the defendant's property, put it under seal or freeze the defendant's bank account, even when the property or account is situated outside France. In that case the order of the French court, to be effective, would need to be enforced in the state where the property or account is situated. The courts of all the other original Member States have similar powers. The efficacy of such protective measures frequently depends on the element of surprise, so they are often made without notice to the defendant. But then they cannot be enforced under the Regulation in other Member States, because art.34(2) provides that a judgment shall not be recognised if it was given in default of appearance, if the defendant was not duly served with the document instituting the proceedings in sufficient time for him to arrange for his defence.[287]

4–080   Article 31 meets this situation by enabling protective measures to be applied for in, for example, the courts of the state where the property is situated. It may be important in the interests of the claimant to achieve a surprise effect; but it is equally important in the interests of the defendant (and of third parties) that such measures should be rapidly brought to the notice of all concerned and that they should have the opportunity to take immediate counter-measures.

In English practice the most important "protective measure" is the *Mareva* or freezing injunction,[288] which may be granted to a claimant who can show a good arguable case on the merits to restrain the defendant from dealing with, disposing of, or removing assets out of the jurisdiction in which they are to be found. Its purpose is to prevent the dissipation of the assets so as to prevent them being available to satisfy the judgment. Power to grant the injunction now rests upon s.37(3) of the Senior Courts (formerly Supreme Court) Act 1981 and, in the present context, on s.25 of the Civil Jurisdiction and Judgments Act 1982. Despite the reference in that provision to assets located within the jurisdiction, it is now clear that it may be granted in respect of assets abroad.[289]

In the Brussels I Regulation, the availability and the requirements concerning provisional, including protective measures are for the most part left to the law of the court granting the provisional measure (*lex fori*). The possibility of relying on national jurisdictional grounds, including exorbitant jurisdictional grounds, has generated real concern about the role of what is now art.31 of the Brussels I Regulation. It has been suggested that this provision has the potential to undermine the objectives pursued by the scheme, enabling circumvention of its core provisions.[290]

---

[287] See Case 123/79 *Denilauler v Couchet Frères* [1980] E.C.R. 1553, where art.27(2) was applied to orders for protective measures.

[288] Named after one of the first cases in which it was used, *Mareva Compania Naviera SA v International Bulkcarriers SA* [1975] 2 Lloyd's Rep. 509.

[289] This was established in a series of Court of Appeal decisions decided in a period of a few weeks in June and July 1989; it was treated as settled law in the third of the series, *Derby v Weldon (No.1)* [1990] Ch. 48.

[290] Dickinson (2010) 6 J.Priv.Int.L. 530.

Article 31 imposes no conditions on jurisdiction in the case of provisional, including protective measures. However, certain limitations have been established by the case law of the ECJ.[291]

The real connecting link

In *Van Uden Maritime BV v Firma Deco Line*[292] the ECJ developed the distinction between the powers of a court exercising merits jurisdiction according to the Brussels scheme and a court exercising its power to order provisional measures in support of proceeding on the merits in another court. Certain limitations were introduced by requiring the existence of a "real connecting link" between the subject-matter of the measures sought and the territorial jurisdiction of the court granting the measure. There has been much discussion about the appropriateness of this requirement of a link to the territorial jurisdiction of the court granting the measure. One view is that it may provide "a manageable (i.e., sufficiently flexible to reflect the variety of measures available and of the circumstances in which courts may be asked to grant them) outer limit upon the exercise of national rules of jurisdiction and procedure under Article 31".[293] A more prevalent view is that the *Van Uden* requirement should merely be a factor for consideration in the court's discretion.[294]

4–081

The Brussels I Regulation and non-Member States

One of the most controversial issues under the Brussels I Regulation is whether the English court may, in cases where its jurisdiction is based on the jurisdictional grounds provided for by Chapter II of the Regulation, stay proceedings or decline jurisdiction in favour of the courts of a non-Member State.[295]

4–082

In the EU Commission Proposal, the scope of the Brussels I Regulation is extended to defendants domiciled outside the European Union. This would eliminate the possibility of English courts applying the English traditional rules of jurisdiction altogether.[296] It is also proposed to create two new jurisdictional grounds that would only apply to non-EU defendants: one based on the non-EU

---

[291] See Case 143/78, *De Cavel v De Cavel I* [1979] ECR 1055 and Case 120/79, *De Cavel v De Cavel II* [1980] ECR 731; Case 125/79, *Denilauler v Couchet Frères* [1980] ECR 1553; Case C-261/90, *Reichert v Dresdner Bank II* [1992] ECR I-2149; Case C-391/95, *Van Uden Maritime BV v Firma Deco Line* [1998] ECR I-7091; Case C-99/96, *Mietz v Intership Yachting Sneek BV* [1999] ECR I-2277; Case C-80/00, *Italian Leather SpA v WECO Polstermöbel GmbH* [2002] ECR I-4995 and Case C-104/03, *St Paul Dairy Industries NV v Unibel Exser BVBA* [2005] ECR I-3481.

[292] Case C-391/95, *Van Uden Maritime BV v Firma Deco Line* [1998] ECR I-7091.

[293] Dickinson, (2010) 6 J.Priv.Int.L. 546. See also the suggestion of Hess, Pfeiffer and Schlosser, Report on the Application of Regulation Brussels I in the Member States (Study JLS/C4/2005/03) (the *Heidelberg Report*), para.783.

[294] See *Dicey, Morris & Collins* (14th edn, 2006) para 8.031; see also *Masri v Consolidated Contractors International (UK) Ltd (No 2)* [2009] Q.B. 450 *per* Collins L.J. (obiter) at para.106. Note that the proposed art.36 (an adaptation of current art.31) included in the EU Commission Proposal does not make any reference to the real connecting link, nor does the Proposal as a whole.

[295] See paras 5–048 to 5–051.

[296] The United Kingdom is opposed to this proposal.

defendant's movable or immovable property in the State[297]; and the other a *forum necessitatis*,[298] designed to prevent abuses of human rights through a denial of justice.

The EU Commission Proposal includes a discretionary *lis pendens* rule for disputes on the same subject-matter and between the same parties which are pending before the courts of a Member State and in a third country; under this proposal a Member State court would be entitled (in exceptional circumstances) to stay proceedings if a non-EU court were seised first, if it was expected that the foreign court would reach its decision within a reasonable time, and the decision would be capable of recognition and enforcement in that Member State.[299]

INTRA-UNITED KINGDOM CASES[300]

4–083   Section 16 of the Civil Jurisdiction and Judgments Act 1982[301] applies a modified form of the jurisdictional provisions of the Brussels I Regulation as between the different parts of the United Kingdom. This is set out in Sch.4. It applies where (a) the subject matter of the proceedings is within the scope of the Regulation and (b) the defendant is domiciled in the United Kingdom or the proceedings are of a kind mentioned in art.22 (exclusive jurisdiction).[302]

The principal differences between the rules set out in Sch.4 and those of the Brussels I Regulation are as follows:

(1)   The rules of special jurisdiction in matters relating to a contract refers simply to "the courts for the place of performance of the obligation in question"[303] and omits the words clarifying this notion which from part of the corresponding Regulation provision[304];

(2)   There is a new rule 3(h), the effect of which is to give the English court jurisdiction in proceedings to enforce a debt secured on immovable property or to determine proprietary or possessory rights or rights of security in or over movable property, in each case where the property is situated in England.

(3)   There is a new rule 4 which confers jurisdiction, in proceedings which have as their object a decision of an organ of a company or association, on the courts of that part of the United Kingdom in which the company or association has its seat.[305]

---

[297]   See art.25 of COM (2010) 748 final.

[298]   See art.26 of COM (2010) 748 final.

[299]   COM (2010) 748 final.

[300]   See Hood, *Conflict of Laws within the UK* (O.U.P., Oxford 2007).

[301]   As amended by the Civil Jurisdiction and Judgments Order 2001 (SI 2001/3929).

[302]   s.16(1).

[303]   See *MacRitchie Bros Ltd v Commercial Power Ltd* (unreported, Sh.Ct, 2010) (Scotland was not the place of performance of the obligation in question; the obligation in question was the providing of advice by the English defendants and the place of performance was not *solely* Scotland).

[304]   Sch.4, r.3(a).

[305]   The seat will be determined in accordance with para.10 of Sch.1 to the Order; see above, para.4–019.

(4)   There is no equivalent to s.3 of the Regulation on insurance contracts, and   **4–084**
        jurisdiction in such cases must be allocated under the other aspects of the
        Regulation system such as the domicile basis or the special jurisdiction
        rules as to contracts in general or the operations of a branch or agency.

(5)   Rule 11 corresponding to art.22 on exclusive jurisdiction omits any
        reference to patents, trade marks, etc.

(6)   In rule 12 corresponding to art.23 (jurisdiction agreements),[306] there is no
        requirement as to writing.

(7)   The provisions relating to *lis pendens* and related actions (arts 27–31) are
        omitted.

Rule 7 deals with allocation of jurisdiction in proceedings brought in the
United Kingdom by virtue of art.5(6) (trust domiciled in the United Kingdom) or
of art.16(1) (consumer domiciled in the United Kingdom), allocating jurisdiction
to the courts of the part of the United Kingdom in which the trust is domiciled
and the courts of the part of the United Kingdom in which the consumer is
domiciled.

The ECJ has no jurisdiction under art.267 of the Treaty on the Functioning of
the European Union in relation to the interpretation of Sch.4.[307] However, the
principles adopted by the ECJ in the interpretation of the rules contained in the
Brussels Convention and the Brussels I Regulation, which have been adopted as
part of Sch.4, must be considered by the United Kingdom courts when applying
these provisions.[308]

JURISDICTION IN ACTIONS IN REM

The precise effect of the Brussels jurisdictional rules on admiralty actions in rem   **4–085**
has exercised the courts in a number of cases.[309] It was established in *The
Deichland*[310] that the Brussels Convention was relevant despite the action being
brought in rem; the court would ascertain the identity of the person who was in
reality the defendant, and that person's domicile would affect the jurisdiction of
the English court in the matter. However, art.71 of the Brussels I Regulation
provides that the Regulation shall not affect any convention to which the Member
States are parties and which, in relation to particular matters, govern jurisdiction
or the recognition or enforcement of judgments. The Regulation does not prevent
a court of a Member State which is a party to a convention on a particular matter
from assuming jurisdiction in accordance with that convention, even where the
defendant is domiciled in another Member State which is not a party to that
convention.

It is important to discover whether the jurisdiction being invoked is in fact
derived from an international convention. Although it has been said in the House
of Lords that the most important part of the Admiralty jurisdiction is now derived

---

[306] See above, paras 4–060ff.
[307] Case C-346/93 *Kleinwort Benson Ltd v City of Glasgow District Council* [1995] ECR I-615.
[308] 1982 Act ss.16(3) and 20(5).
[309] See Hartley (1989) 105 L.Q.R. 640.
[310] [1990] 1 Q.B. 361. See also *Republic of India v India Steamship Co. Ltd (No.2)* [1998] A.C. 878.

from the 1952 International Convention on the Arrest of Seagoing Ships,[311] it was held in *The Deichland*[312] that jurisdiction was derived from that convention only when there was an actual arrest. It was inapplicable when security was given to avert arrest. The enhanced position of the *forum arresti* in the European regime has been possible through the *lex specialis* provision first included in the Brussels Convention and currently in the Brussels I Regulation (art.71). Article 7 of the 1952 International Arrest Convention is considered as *lex specialis* in this context and prevails over the jurisdictional rules of the Regulation.[313]

Where the action is concerned not with the ship itself but with the salvage of cargo or freight, a specific provision of the Brussels I Regulation applies, creating a form of special jurisdiction. Article 5(7) provides that claims for remuneration for the salvage of cargo or freight may be brought in the court under whose authority the cargo or freight (a) has been arrested or (b) could have been arrested, but bail or other security has been given: provided that the defendant has an interest in the cargo or freight or had such an interest at the time of the salvage. Article 7 further provides that where by virtue of the Regulation a court of a Member State has jurisdiction in actions relating to liability from the use or operation of a ship, that court, or any other court substituted for this purpose by the internal law of that Member State, also has jurisdiction over claims for limitation of such liability.

ARBITRATION[314]

4–086   Arbitration is one of the express exclusions of the scope of application of the Brussels I Regulation as it stands at present.[315] After extensive discussion on the relationship between arbitration and the Brussels I Regulation, the EU Commission Proposal does not change for the most part the scope of application of Brussels I in relation to arbitration. The position of the draft recast Regulation on arbitration is set out in a new Recital[316] where the aim is expressed as being to improve the effectiveness of arbitration agreements and to avoid parallel

---

[311] *The River Rima* [1988] 1 W.L.R. 758. For the International Convention of 1952 on Certain Rules concerning Civil Jurisdiction in Matters of Collision, see *The Po* [1991] 2 Lloyd's Rep. 206. For a detailed analysis of the jurisdictional aspects related to the arrest of ships see Ruiz Abou-Nigm, *The Arrest of Ships in Private International Law* (O.U.P., 2011).

[312] *Owners of Cargo Lately Laden on Board the Deichland v Owners and/or Demise Charterers of the Deichland (The Deichland)* [1990] 1 QB 361 (CA) 370; see also *The Tatry* [1995] 1 Lloyd's Rep 302 (ECJ); cf. *The Anna H* [1995] 1 Lloyd's Rep 11 (CA).

[313] The interface between the 1952 International Arrest Convention and the Brussels jurisdictional regime is analysed in Ruiz Abou-Nigm, *op.cit.*

[314] There is a vast amount of specialised commentary on the relationship between arbitration and the Brussels I Reg, *inter alia*, Van Houtte [2005] Arb. Int. 509; Pullen, (2009) 12 I.A.L.R. 56; Hess, [2010] P.J.I.A. 17; Schlosser, (2009) 12 I.A.L.R. 45; Pinsolle, (2009) 12 I. A. L.R. 62; Fentiman, (2007) 66 C. L. J. 493; Magnus and Mankowski, [2010] 1 Zeitschrift für Vergleichende Rechtswissenschaft 21; Radicati di Brozolo, [2010] IPRax 121 and (2011) 7 J.Priv.Int.L. 423.

[315] Brussels I Regulation, art.1(2)(d). There is a similar exclusion in the 2007 Lugano Convention and in Sch. 4 to the 1982 Act (intra-UK cases).

[316] Proposed Recital 20, COM (2010) 748 final. Recital 20 of the draft clarifies how the seat of the arbitration is to be established. The European Parliament has not received the proposed changes with enthusiasm and specifically requested the elimination of recital 20 and Art 29(4) (Committee on legal affairs 2010/0383 (COD), 28.06.2011 and 19.10.2011).

proceedings and abusive litigation tactics, where the seat of the arbitration is in a Member State. The main change is the introduction of a new provision related to the existence, validity or effects of an arbitration agreement, and giving priority to the "courts of the Member State where the seat of the arbitration is located" over the courts of any other Member State of the EU.[317] There is also a provision indicating when it is that an arbitral tribunal is deemed to be seised for the purposes of establishing that there are parallel proceedings.[318] It is also established, following the ECJ position in *Van Uden,*[319] that Member States courts are allowed to grant provisional, including protective measures to support arbitration proceedings.

---

[317] Proposed art.29(4), COM (2010) 748 final.

[318] Proposed art.33(3), COM (2010) 748 final.

[319] Case C-391/95 *Van Uden Maritime BV v Deco-Line* [1998] ECR I-7091.

CHAPTER 5

JURISDICTION: THE TRADITIONAL ENGLISH RULES

As we have seen, art.4 of the Brussels I Regulation enables the national courts of   **5–001**
Member States to apply their own jurisdictional rules in certain circumstances not
falling within the Regulation. These cases are where the defendant is not
domiciled in a Member State[1] and arts 22 (exclusive jurisdiction) and 23 (choice
of court agreements) do not apply. It is important to appreciate that the
jurisdictional rules of the Regulation and the "traditional rules" now to be
considered apply to different categories of case. The first step in considering the
issue of jurisdiction is always to decide which set of rules applies. If there turns
out to be no jurisdiction under the applicable rules, that is the end of the matter:
there can be no switching to the other (by definition inapplicable) set of rules.

The traditional rules, enshrined in the Civil Procedure Rules, base jurisdiction
on the presence of the defendant in England; the submission of the defendant to
the jurisdiction; and the service of process abroad. Within those principles, and in
associated practices, there is a degree of judicial discretion alien to the civil law
tradition underlying the European rules considered in the last Chapter. As we
shall see, the primacy of European law has had the effect of curtailing the
exercise of this type of discretion in a number of important respects.

PRESENCE

Every civil action governed by the Civil Procedure Rules, whether in the High   **5–002**
Court or a county court, is started when the court issues a claim form at the
request of the claimant.[2] The claim form must then be served on the defendant,

---

[1] Note that the European Commission has proposed the extension of the jurisdictional provisions of
the Regulation to defendants domiciled in non-Member States (European Commission, Brussels I
Revision Proposal, COM (2010) 748 final, para.3.1.2). This would greatly reduce the number of cases
to which the English courts would apply the traditional rules on jurisdiction. Not surprisingly, the UK
is opposed to such extension.
[2] CPR r.7.2.

within four months of the date of issue or six months if it is to be served out of the jurisdiction.[3] When a claim form cannot be served on a defendant, the court cannot exercise jurisdiction over the claim; conversely, when a defendant has been served with the claim form, the court can exercise jurisdiction.

Viewed critically, and especially through the eyes of foreign lawyers, these principles appear to rest upon a confusion of ideas. Service of a claim form serves a vital procedural purpose, that of putting the defendant upon notice of the claim being brought, and every legal system makes some provision to that end. But there is a distinct logical leap in moving from the proposition that a claim form is a necessary procedural step to that which makes it a sufficient basis for jurisdiction. As a basis for jurisdiction, it is widely regarded as exorbitant,[4] and its use is excluded under the Brussels I Regulation.

The rule that service of the claim form gives jurisdiction is, however, a central feature of the traditional rules. In general, therefore, in any case to which those traditional rules apply, any person who is in England and served there with the claim form is subject to the in personam jurisdiction of the court. The application of this principle depends on whether the defendant is an individual, a partnership firm, or a corporation.

Individuals

5–003   Any individual who is present in England is liable to be served with a claim form, however short may be the period for which he or she is present in England, and irrespective of nationality, or domicile, or usual place of residence, or of the nature of the cause of action.

Thus in *Maharanee of Baroda v Wildenstein*[5]:

> An Indian princess, resident in France, brought an action against an American art dealer, also resident in France, for rescission of a contract to sell her a picture. The contract was made in France and governed by French law. The writ (the document now known as the claim form) was served on the defendant at Ascot races during a temporary visit to England. It was held that the court had jurisdiction.

5–004   A claim form may be served on an individual by (a) personal service, by leaving it with that individual[6]; (b) first class post, document exchange or other service which provides for delivery on the next business day; (c) in certain cases, leaving it at the address of the defendant's solicitor or "European Lawyer" in any European Economic Area country, or at an address the defendant has given as an address at which service may be effected, or at the defendant's usual or last

---

[3] CPR r.7.5; the period may be extended: r.7.6.

[4] See Fernández Arroyo, *Compétence exclusive et compétence exorbitante dans les relations privées internationales*, (2006) 323 *Recueil des cours* 9 (Martinus Nijhoff, Leiden, 2008). But cf. Collins, (1991) 107 L.Q.R. 10, 13–14.

[5] [1972] 2 Q.B. 283. The actual decision would now be different because the case would fall under the Brussels I Regulation as a result of the defendant's domicile in France; cf. *Colt Industries Inc. v Sarlie* [1966] 1 W.L.R. 440.

[6] CPR r.6.5(3)(a).

known residence[7]; (d) fax or other means of electronic communication including e-mail.[8] In *Varsani v Relfo Ltd*[9] the determination of the defendant's "usual" residence for this purpose was not based on the consideration of duration of periods of occupation of that address as compared to the defendant's other residences. The defendant was a British citizen who had a business in Kenya. His family lived in a property owned by him and his wife in London and he visited as work permitted, staying for a month or two in each of the few years previous to the case. The court held that it was possible to have more than one "usual" residence; the fact that the premises were occupied permanently by the defendant's family was considered as material, hence the premises could be described as his "usual" residence.[10]

Where it appears to the court that there is a good reason to authorise service by some other method or at some other place, the court may make an order for "service by an alternative method",[11] for example publication in newspapers.

Partnerships

Where partners are being sued in the name of their firm, the claim form can be served on any partner or any other person who, at the time of service, has the control or management of the partnership business at its principal place of business.[12] A partnership without a place of business in England cannot be sued in the firm's name. A limited liability partnership may also be served by any of the methods of service permitted under the Companies Act 2006.[13]   **5–005**

Companies and other corporations

The notion of service on a defendant "present" in England is readily understood when the defendant is an individual, but the presence of a corporation is, like its nationality or domicile or residence, to some extent a fiction.[14] The Companies Act 2006 contains special rules as to service on companies. The Civil Procedure Rules preserve those statutory options,[15] but it is almost always preferable to use the simpler methods in the CPR.   **5–006**

---

[7] CPR rr.6.7 and 6.8; "European Lawyer" has a technical meaning set out in the European Communities (Services of Lawyers) Order 1978 (SI 1978/1910) art.2.

[8] CPR r.6.3(1) which needs to be read with Practice Direction 6A.

[9] [2010] EWCA Civ 560; [2010] 3 All E.R. (Comm)1045.

[10] See *Levene v Inland Revenue Commissioners* [1928] A.C. 217.

[11] CPR r.6.15 (formerly known as "substituted service").

[12] CPR r.6.5(3)(c).

[13] CPR r.6.3(3). For these modes of service see below; their application is subject to modification by regulations made under the Limited Liability Partnerships Act 2000.

[14] See Fawcett, (1988) 37 I.C.L.Q. 644, and the exhaustive treatment in *Adams v Cape Industries plc* [1990] Ch. 433.

[15] CPR r.6.3(2)(b).

Statutory methods

5–007   If the company is registered in England under the Companies legislation, it is present in England, even if it only carries on business abroad, and service of a claim form can always be effected by leaving it at, or sending it by post to, the company's registered office in England.[16] Similarly, if a company registered in Scotland carries on business in England, a claim form may be served on it by leaving it at, or sending it by post to, the company's principal place of business in England, with a copy to the company's registered office in Scotland.[17] An overseas company whose particulars are registered may be served by leaving the claim form at, or sending it by post to, the registered address of any person resident in the United Kingdom who is authorised to accept service of documents on the company's behalf, or if there is no such person, or if any such person refuses service or service cannot for any other reason be effected, by leaving it at or sending by post to any place of business of the company in the United Kingdom.[18]

Service under these provisions does not depend upon the subject matter of the action being substantially concerned with the activity of the place of business in the United Kingdom.[19]

Under the Civil Procedure Rules

5–008   Under the Civil Procedure Rules, a document is served personally on a company or other corporation by leaving it with a person holding a senior position within the company or corporation,[20] or by leaving it at the company's principal office or any place of business within the jurisdiction which has a real connection with the claim.[21] Service may be effected on a company other than one registered in England and Wales at any place within the jurisdiction where it carries on its activities, or at any place of business of the company within the jurisdiction.[22]

Service by contractually agreed method

5–009   Where a dispute arises out of a contract, and a claim form is issued containing only a claim relating to that contract, it may be served by any method specified in the contract.[23]

---

[16] Companies Act 2006 s.1139(1).
[17] Companies Act 2006 s.1139(4).
[18] Companies Act 2006 s.1139(2), (3).
[19] *Saab v Saudi Arabian Bank* [1999] 1 W.L.R. 1861.
[20] CPR r.6.5(3)(b); "person holding a senior position" is defined in Practice Direction 6A, para.6.2 as including, in the case of a company, a director, the treasurer, secretary, chief executive, manager or other officer of the company.
[21] CPR r.6.9(2). Similar rules apply to corporations which are not companies.
[22] CPR r.6.9(2); *Lakah Group v Al Jazeera Satellite Channel* [2003] EWHC 1231(QB).
[23] CPR r.6.11.

Service on agent of overseas principal

In respect of a particular contract entered into within the jurisdiction with or through an agent of a defendant who is overseas, the court may on application permit a claim form to be served on an agent of an overseas principal.[24] A copy of the claim form and of the order permitting service on the agent must be sent to the principal[25] but the effective service is that within the jurisdiction.

5–010

SUBMISSION

A person who would not otherwise be subject to the jurisdiction of the court may preclude him or herself by conduct from objecting to the jurisdiction, and thus give the court jurisdiction which, but for his or her submission, it would not possess.[26]

5–011

This submission may take place in various ways. A person who begins an action as claimant in general gives the court jurisdiction to entertain a counterclaim[27] by the defendant in some related matter, but not an action on an independent ground.[28] If the court considers that justice requires the counterclaim to be dealt with separately, it may so order; and in exercising this power it has in mind, amongst other factors, the connection between the Pt 20 claim and the claim made by the claimant.[29]

A defendant who wishes to dispute the court's jurisdiction to try the claim must first file an acknowledgment of service and then make the application, with supporting evidence, for an order by which the court declares that it has no jurisdiction.[30] The mere filing of the acknowledgment of service does not deprive the defendant of any right to dispute the court's jurisdiction,[31] but a defendant who does not make an application within the period prescribed in the Rules is treated as having accepted that the court has jurisdiction to try the claim.[32] If the court does not make the declaration applied for, the original acknowledgment of service ceases to have effect. If the defendant then files a further acknowledgment of service (to avoid a default judgment being given) that is treated as an acceptance that the court has jurisdiction to try the claim.[33] If a claim form has been validly served (including some method agreed in a contract to which the defendant is party) and no acknowledgement of service or defence is filed, the jurisdiction cannot be contested.

---

[24] CPR r.6.12.
[25] CPR r.6.12(4).
[26] cf. art.24 of the Brussels I Regulation; para.4–070.
[27] Under the C.P.R. classed as a "Part 20 claim".
[28] *South African Republic v Compagnie Franco-Belge du Chemin de Fer du Nord* [1987] 2 Ch. 487; [1898] 1 Ch. 190; *Factories Insurance Co. v Anglo-Scottish Insurance Co.* (1913) 29 T.L.R. 312; *High Commissioner for India v Ghosh* [1960] 1 Q.B. 134.
[29] CPR rr.3.1 and 20.9.
[30] CPR, r.11(1), (2), (4).
[31] CPR, r.11(3).
[32] CPR r.11(5).
[33] CPR r.11(7).

It must be emphasised that the principle of submission only applies to actions in personam: it does not apply, for instance, to petitions for a decree of divorce or nullity of marriage.[34]

5–012 At common law, if the defendant was not served with the claim form while present in England and did not submit to the jurisdiction, the court had no jurisdiction to entertain an action in personam. The Common Law Procedure Act 1852 modified the position and gave the court a discretionary power to permit service out of the jurisdiction.[35] The power to do so, which as we have seen is a power to assume jurisdiction, was until 2008 regulated by rules of court. Now, one short provision in the Civil Procedure Rules r.6.36, identifies the power but the detailed grounds for permitting service out of the jurisdiction are not contained in para.3.1 of Practice Direction B to Pt 6 of the Rules. When the first edition of this book was published, it would have been unthinkable that the jurisdiction of the Queen's courts would be defined by a European Regulation and a Practice Direction.

Before we consider the specific cases in which this discretionary power may be exercised, certain principles of general application must first be stated.

Applicable principles

5–013 There is an essential difference between cases where the defendant is in England and served there with the claim form, or where the defendant submits to the jurisdiction, and the cases which are about to be considered. If the defendant is in England, or submits to the jurisdiction, the claimant may proceed "as of right"; but under r.6.36 the jurisdiction of the court is essentially discretionary, and will only be exercised in a proper case.

The courts have spelt out carefully the considerations which govern the exercise of the discretion,[36] including the general cautionary point that the court ought to be exceedingly careful before it allows a claim form to be served on a foreigner outside England because of the apparent interference with the sovereignty of the foreign state concerned. In words dating from 1887[37] but repeatedly approved by later courts:

> "[I]t becomes a very serious question . . . whether this court ought to put a foreigner, who owes no allegiance here, to the inconvenience and annoyance of being brought to contest his rights in this country, and I for one say, most distinctly, that I think this court ought to be exceedingly careful before it allows a writ to be served out of the jurisdiction".

---

[34] Domicile and Matrimonial Proceedings Act 1973 s.5(2) and (3); below, paras 9–011ff.

[35] The power may be exercised retrospectively: *Kosa v Nesheim* [2006] EWHC 2710 (Ch).

[36] *Société Générale de Paris v Dreyfus Bros* (1887) 37 Ch.D. 215; *The Hagen* [1908] P. 189; *Re Schintz* [1926] Ch. 710.

[37] *Société Générale de Paris v Dreyfus Bros* (1885) 29 Ch.D. 239 at 242–243.

Perhaps this sort of consideration carries less weight with the much greater speed   **5–014**
of international travel and the growth of multinational corporations; but the
cautionary note is still relevant.

The modern approach of the English court was well summarised by Lord
Collins of Mapesbury in *AK Investment CJSC v Kyrgyz Mobil Tel Limited*,[38] a
Privy Council appeal from the Isle of Man:

> "On an application for permission to serve a foreign defendant . . . out of the jurisdiction, the
> claimant . . . has to satisfy three requirements.[39] First, the claimant must satisfy the court that
> in relation to the foreign defendant there is a serious issue to be tried on the merits, i.e. a
> substantial question of fact or law, or both. The current practice in England is that this is the
> same test as for summary judgment, namely whether there is a real (as opposed to a fanciful)
> prospect of success. Second, the claimant must satisfy the court that there is a good arguable
> case that the claim falls within one or more classes of case in which permission to serve out
> may be given. In this context 'good arguable case' connotes that one side has a much better
> argument than the other.[40] Third, the claimant must satisfy the court that in all the
> circumstances [England] is clearly or distinctly the appropriate forum for the trial of the
> dispute, and that in all the circumstances the court ought to exercise its discretion to permit
> service of the proceedings out of the jurisdiction. . . . However, if a question of law arises on an
> application in connection with service out of the jurisdiction, and the question of law goes to
> the existence of jurisdiction, the court will normally decide it, rather than treating it as a
> question of whether there is a good arguable case."[41]

So far as the various sub-heads set out in the Practice Direction are concerned,   **5–015**
the courts have held that if there is any doubt in the construction of any sub-head,
the doubt ought to be resolved in favour of the defendant. Since applications for
permission are made without notice to the defendant, the claimant must make a
full and fair disclosure of all relevant facts.[42]

The court will refuse permission if the case is within the letter but outside the
spirit of the Rule.[43] This is emphasised by a provision in the Rules that the court
must not give its permission unless the claimant satisfies it that England is a
proper place in which to bring the claim.[44] The court will consider whether
England is the *forum conveniens*,[45] taking into account the nature of the dispute,

---

[38] [2011] UKPC 7 at paras [71] and [81]. See also *Global 5000 Ltd v Wadhawan* [2012] EWCA Civ
13.
[39] *Seaconsar Far East Ltd v Bank Markazi Jomhouri Il,ami Iran* [1994] 1 A.C. 438 at 453–457.
[40] See *Canada Trust Co v Stolzenberg* (No 2) [1998] 1 W.L.R. 547 at 555–7 per Waller L.J.
(affd [2002] 1 A.C. 1); *Bols Distilleries BV v Superior Yacht Services* [2006] UKPC 45; [2007] 1
W.L.R. 12.
[41] *Hutton (EF) & Co (London) Ltd v Mofarrij* [1989] 1 W.L.R. 488 at 495 (CA); *Chellaram v
Chellaram (No 2)* [2002] EWHC 632 (Ch); [2002] 3 All E.R. 17 at 36.
[42] See, e.g., *Trafalgar Tours v Henry* [1990] 2 Lloyd's Rep. 298.
[43] *Johnson v Taylor Bros.* [1920] A.C. 144 at 153; *Rosler v Hilbery* [1925] Ch. 250 at 259–260;
George Monro Ltd v American Cyanamid Corporation [1944] K.B. 432 at 437 and 442.
[44] CPR r.6.37(3). See r.6.37(4) for special factors when service is to be in Scotland or Northern
Ireland.
[45] *Société Générale de Paris v Dreyfus Bros* (1887) 37 Ch.D. 215; *Rosler v Hilbery* [1925] Ch. 250;
Kroch v Rossell [1937] 1 All E.R. 725.

the legal and practical issues involved, such questions as local knowledge, availability of witnesses and their evidence, and expense.[46]

The test is substantially the same as that developed for the use of the power, formerly extensively used, to stay in English proceedings on the ground of *forum non conveniens*,[47] that England was *not* the appropriate forum. That the test was the same in both types of case was recognised in the leading House of Lords case, *Spiliada Maritime Corp. v Cansulex Ltd*.[48] This means that it is legitimate to draw on the *forum non conveniens* cases in the present context, but this must be done with care. Not only has the scope for pleas of *forum non conveniens* been drastically reduced since a decision of the ECJ in 2005,[49] but it has also to be remembered that in r.6.36 cases, unlike those dealing with pleas of *forum non conveniens*, the burden of proof is on the claimant: the claimant must persuade the court that the case is a proper one for service out of the jurisdiction and that England is clearly the appropriate forum.

5–016   In assessing the claimant's arguments, the court will seek to identify the "natural forum", meaning "that with which the action has the most real and substantial connection",[50] and will examine not only factors affecting convenience or expense (such as the availability of witnesses), but also such matters as the law governing the transaction, and the places where the parties reside or carry on business.[51] On the governing law, the courts take the common-sense view that difficult legal issues are best dealt with by judges familiar with them.[52] For example, in *Wright v Deccan Chargers Sporting Ventures Ltd*[53]:

> W had entered into a contract of employment with D, an Indian company. The contract stated that D required W's services in the development of a business model and plan to support an initial public offering of D's stock on the English market. It provided that W would be based initially in England and would travel to India and elsewhere as necessary and that D would establish an office in England for W. The contract also stated that it was to be governed by English law. The contract was terminated. W alleged there had been a breach of contract and sought to serve proceedings in England. D had never established an office in England for W.

5–017   It was held that the matters were relatively evenly balanced but marginally favoured English jurisdiction for two reasons: the English courts would be preferable in applying English law (as there were issues in the case that suggested

---

[46] *Spiliada Maritime Corp. v Cansulex Ltd* [1987] A.C. 460, adopting the approach of Lord Wilberforce in *Amin Rasheed Shipping Corp. v Kuwait Insurance Co.* [1984] A.C. 50 at 72; *Roneleigh Ltd v M.I.I. Exports Inc.* [1989] 1 W.L.R. 619; *Metall und Rohstoff A.G. v Donaldson Lufkin & Jenrette Inc.* [1990] Q.B. 391.

[47] See below, paras 5–044ff.

[48] [1987] A.C. 460.

[49] Case C-281/02 *Owusu v Jackson* [2005] E.C.R I-1383; [2005] Q.B. 801.

[50] A formulation used by Lord Keith in *The Abidin Daver* [1984] A.C. 398 at 415.

[51] e.g., *Chellaram v Chellaram (No 2)* [2002] EWHC 632; [2002] 3 All E.R. 17 (trusts probably governed by Hindu or Bermudan law; defendants domiciled in Bermuda, Gibraltar, Hong Kong, India and Spain; Indian forum more appropriate than English).

[52] e.g., *Smay Investments Ltd v Sachdev* [2003] EWHC 474; [2003] 1 W.L.R. 1973 (dispute over ownership of Indian company best dealt with by Indian courts.

[53] [2011] EWHC 1307 (QB); [2011] I.L.Pr 37.

the application of English law would not be straightforward); and D's agreement that W should remain resident in England and that it would establish an office in England.

It may be relevant that particular courts have special expertise in the relevant type of case. For example, if a city or region is known as the centre of a specialised industrial process, its courts may be more familiar with the types of damage that may be sustained by workers in that industry. In cases involving insurance policies negotiated in accordance with the practices of the London market, the English courts will usually be held to be the appropriate forum.[54] If a court has already dealt with a related aspect of some specialised or very complex litigation, it may well be appropriate that other aspects are dealt with by that court.[55] It is important in complex litigation involving multiple parties to identify where possible a forum in which all the issues can be resolved, and so minimise the risk of inconsistent judgments in different jurisdictions.[56]

Although every case must turn on its own facts, the natural forum for a claim in tort is likely to be held to be the country in which the tort occurred,[57] not least because the relevant evidence is likely to be there. The place of the tort will not always be the natural forum: in a case the apt name of which alone justifies its mention here, *The Forum Craftsman*,[58] the Angolan owners of a Panamanian ship with a Greek crew sued in respect of damage to cargo as the vessel was about to set sail from Yokohama, Japan; the argument that Japan was the natural forum failed.

If the parties have agreed to a choice of court clause, referring any dispute between them to the exclusive jurisdiction of a foreign court, permission will usually be refused.[59]

5–018

If the court gives permission for the service of the claim form out of the jurisdiction, the defendant has the opportunity to challenge the decision by applying for the service to be set aside.[60] The application will then be heard with both parties present, the initial decision having been made only on the submissions of the potential claimant.

---

[54] e.g., *Lincoln National Life Insurance Co v Employers Reinsurance Corp* [2002] EWHC 28; [2002] Lloyd's Rep I.R. 853. See also *Travelers Casualty and Surety Co of Europe Ltd v Sun Life Assurance Co of Canada (UK) Ltd* [2004] EWHC 1704 (Comm); [2004] Lloyd's Rep. IR 846 (relevance of involvement of regulatory authority in England).

[55] *Spiliada Maritime Corpn v Cansulex Ltd* [1987] A.C. 460, where there is discussion of the so-called "Cambridgeshire factor", the fact that related litigation involving a ship of that name had already been dealt with by the English court.

[56] See, e.g., *JSC BTA Bank v Granton Trade Ltd* [2010] EWHC 2577 (Comm); [2011] 2 All E.R. (Comm) 542.

[57] See *MacShannon v Rockware Glass Ltd* [1978] A.C. 795 (accident in factory in Scotland) and the line of cases following *Cordoba Shipping Co Ltd v National State Bank, Elizabeth, New Jersey, The Albaforth* [1984] 2 Lloyd's Rep 91 (negligent misstatement) and endorsed in *Berezovsky v Michaels* [2000] 1 W.L.R. 1004 (defamation); and *King v Lewis* [2004] EWCA CIV 1329 (internet material originating in New York downloaded in England and so published there).

[58] [1984] 2 Lloyd's Rep. 102.

[59] *Re Schintz* [1926] Ch. 710; *Mackender v Feldia* [1967] 2 Q.B. 590; contrast *Evans Marshall & Co Ltd v Bertola SA* [1973] 1 W.L.R. 349.

[60] CPR Pt 11.

Cases in which permission may be given

5–019　The various sub-heads of para.3.1 of the Practice Direction, listing the cases in which permission may be given for service out of the jurisdiction, will now be examined in turn.

General grounds

5–020　(1) a claim is made for a remedy against a person domiciled within the jurisdiction.[61]

"Domicile", here and throughout Pt 6 of the Civil Procedure Rules, is to be determined not in accordance with the rules of common law but in accordance with the provisions of the Brussels I Regulation and paras 9 to 12 of Sch.1 to the Civil Jurisdiction and Judgments Order 2001.[62] This means that the test for domicile is the same whichever set of jurisdictional rules applies. If the case falls within the scope of the Brussels I Regulation, the domicile of the defendant will give the English courts jurisdiction[63] and permission to serve the claim form will *not* be required.[64]

5–021　(2) a claim is made for an injunction ordering the defendant to do or refrain from doing an act within the jurisdiction.[65]

The injunction need not be the only relief sought, and it is immaterial whether or not damages are also claimed; but the injunction must be the substantial relief sought: permission will be refused if the claim for an injunction is not made bona fide but merely to bring the case within the sub-head.[66] Permission will also be refused if a foreign court can more conveniently deal with the question,[67] or if there is no real ground to anticipate repetition of the action complained of,[68] or if the injunction cannot be made effective in England.[69]

(3) a claim is made against a person ("the defendant") on whom the claim form has been or will be served and (a) there is between the claimant and the defendant a real issue which it is reasonable for the court to try; and (b) the claimant wishes to serve the claim form on another person who is a necessary or proper party to that claim.[70]

5–022　(4) a claim is an additional claim under Pt 20 and the person is a necessary or proper party to the claim or additional claim.[71]

These sub-heads are important, and have given rise to much litigation. The most obvious cases covered are cases where joint debtors or joint tortfeasors are

---

[61] Practice Direction 6A, para.3.1(1).
[62] CPR r.6.31(i); see above, paras 4–015ff.
[63] See above, para.4–024.
[64] CPR r.6.33(3).
[65] Practice Direction 6A, para.3.1(2).
[66] *De Bernales v New York Herald* [1893] 2 Q.B. 97n.; *Watson v Daily Record* [1907] 1 K.B. 853; contrast *Dunlop Rubber Co. Ltd v Dunlop* [1921] 1 A.C. 367.
[67] *Société Générale de Paris v Dreyfus Bros* (1887) 37 Ch.D. 215; *Rosler v Hilbery* [1925] Ch. 250.
[68] *De Bernales v New York Herald* [1893] 2 Q.B. 97n.; *Watson v Daily Record* [1907] 1 K.B. 853.
[69] *Marshall v Marshall* (1888) 38 Ch.D. 330.
[70] Practice Direction 6A, para.3.1(3).
[71] Practice Direction 6A, para.3.1(4).

alleged to be liable to the claimant[72]; or where the claimant has alternative claims against two persons, for example a claim against a principal for breach of contract, and against an agent for breach of warranty of authority.[73]

The person whom it is sought to serve out of the jurisdiction must be a "necessary or proper" party to the action. These terms are alternative, and a person may be a proper party although he or she is not a necessary party. The question whether B is a proper party to an action against A is simply answered: suppose both A and B had been in England, would they both have been proper parties to the action? If they would, and only one of them, A, is in England, then B is a proper party, and permission may be given to serve B out of the jurisdiction.[74] For instance, if defective goods are manufactured by B abroad, and supplied to A in England, and sold by A to the claimant, the claimant can bring an action for breach of contract against A and in tort against B.[75]

Claims for interim remedies

(5) a claim is made for an interim remedy under s.25(1) of the Civil Jurisdiction and Judgments Act 1982.[76]

In the past there were technical difficulties concerning applications for a freezing (*Mareva*) injunction in respect of the defendant's assets. Where permission to serve documents was needed, it was formerly sought under a sub-head dealing with injunctions. It was held at one time that this was not possible where the defendant was not otherwise amenable to the jurisdiction and the substantive proceedings had been brought, or were to be brought, in another country.[77] However, this limitation was removed, first in relation to proceedings in other Contracting States to the Brussels and Lugano Conventions,[78] and then in respect of proceedings in any country.[79] The application can now be made under this sub-head, first introduced in 2000.

5–023

Claims in relation to contracts

(6) a claim is made in respect of a contract where the contract:

5–024

(a) was made within the jurisdiction;
(b) was made by or through an agent trading or residing within the jurisdiction;
(c) is governed by English law; or

---

[72] *Williams v Cartwright* [1895] 1 Q.B. 142.
[73] *Massey v Heynes* (1888) 21 Q.B.D. 330.
[74] *Massey v Heynes* (1888) 21 Q.B.D. 330 at 338; *The Elton* [1891] P. 265; *Osterreichische Export etc. Co. v British Indemnity Co. Ltd* [1914] 2 K.B. 747; *The Goldean Mariner* [1990] 2 Lloyd's Rep. 215.
[75] *The Manchester Courage* [1973] 1 Lloyd's Rep. 386.
[76] Practice Direction 6A, para.3.1(5).
[77] *The Siskina v Distos Compania Naviera* [1979] A.C. 210; *Mercedes Benz AG v Leiduck* [1996] A.C. 284.
[78] Civil Jurisdiction and Judgments Act 1982 s.25(1).
[79] SI 1997/302, made under *ibid.*, s.25(3).

(d)   contains a term to the effect that the court shall have jurisdiction to determine any claim in respect of the contract[80]

There is an initial characterisation issue: is this a "contract" case? It has been held, for example, that the relationship between a company and a director of that company is not a matter of contract.[81] The text of the predecessor provision in the former Order 11 spoke of claims "brought to enforce, rescind, dissolve, annul, or otherwise affect a contract, or to recover damages or obtain other relief in respect of the breach of a contract": the current rule can be no less wide in scope and it has indeed been held that the current formulation is "deliberately wider" than its predecessor.[82] So this sub-head will be available where the claimant seeks a declaration that a contract has been frustrated,[83] and where the claim is for restitution, the repayment of money paid under a mistake of fact in circumstances related to, but not arising under, a contract.[84] The position was further clarified in *Greene Wood & McLean LLP v Templeton Insurance Ltd*[85]:

> Large numbers of miners brought claims in respect of lung disease and vibration white finger. Their solicitors, G, made an unsuccessful application in the course of the litigation and costs were ordered against the miners. The solicitors accepted liability to pay those costs but brought a claim against T, an insurance company based in the Isle of Man, for contribution. The claim alleged that G and T were liable for the same damage, G under their contract with the miners, T under an After The Event insurance policy taken out in the name of the miners. G argued that their contribution claim arose in respect of a contract (the insurance policy) which was governed by English law. T argued that there was no contractual relationship between G and T, and that the power to permit service out of the jurisdiction applied only where claimant and proposed defendant were parties to the relevant contract.

5–025   The Court of Appeal rejected T's argument. To say that, for a claim to be "in respect of a contract", it must be "in respect of a contract between the intended claimant and the intended defendant" would be to add words to the rule which were not there. Since the Contracts (Rights of Third Parties) Act 1999, there were cases in which a third party could sue on a contract made between two persons for his or her benefit; such a third party should be able to rely on the contractual aspects of the rules as to service out of the jurisdiction. The claim in the instant case clearly had a connection with a contract governed by English law, even though it was not a claim brought under the contract. No doubt some connections with contracts were more remote than others; that could be taken into account in considering whether England was the appropriate forum.

This sub-head is very important in practice: its four branches require separate discussion.

---

[80] Practice Direction 6A, para.3.1(6).
[81] *Newtherapeutics Ltd v Katz* [1991] Ch. 226.
[82] *Albon v Naza Motor Trading Sdn Bhd* [2007] EWHC 9 (Ch); [2007] 1 W.L.R. 2489; *Global 5000 Ltd v Wadhawan* [2011] EWHC 853 (Comm); [2011] 2 All E.R. (Comm) 190.
[83] *B.P. Exploration (Libya) Ltd v Hunt* [1976] 1 W.L.R. 788.
[84] *Albon v Naza Motor Trading Sdn Bhd* [2007] EWHC 9 (Ch); [2007] 1 W.L.R. 2489.
[85] [2009] EWCA Civ 65; [2009] 1 W.L.R. 2013.

(i)   Contracts made in England

A contract concluded by postal correspondence is made where the letter of acceptance is posted.[86] Many contracts are now made by "instantaneous" means of communication, telephone, fax or e-mail, in which case the contract is made where the acceptance is communicated to the offeror.[87] In *Brinkibon Ltd v Stahag Stahl und Stahlwaren-handelgesellschaft mbH*[88]:

> The contract concerned the supply of steel bars by S (an Austrian company) to B (an English company acting as agent (though it had not disclosed this fact) for a Swiss company. The steel was to be delivered by sea from Alexandria in Egypt. The contract was not performed after a dispute about the financial arrangements, and B sought to sue in England claiming that the contract was made in England. The acceptance of the terms was by a telex message from London to Vienna. The House of Lords confirmed that the postal communication rules did not apply to instantaneous communications. On the facts, the contract was made in Vienna.

5–026

The importance of the case lies in some qualifications mentioned by Lord Wilberforce. Indicating that there could be no "universal rule" he suggested facts which might render the communication less than instantaneous. The receiving machine might have a fault; it might be in a different building, or belong to a third party. Although he was speaking about telex machines, now outmoded, the same could be said about fax machines, and similar questions could be asked about e-mail or internet messages sent overnight and read in the morning, perhaps by a businessman in a hotel room far removed from his usual office and even in a different country. Lord Wilberforce referred to "business practice" and that appears to accept that all these cases are to be treated as covered by the "instantaneous" rule.

5–027

For a contract to be "made within the jurisdiction" it suffices that it is "substantially made" within the jurisdiction.[89] If a contract is made within the jurisdiction, a variation taking place abroad in the terms of the contract will not deprive the English court of jurisdiction, at least where the core obligations of the contract are untouched.[90]

(ii)   Contracts made by or through English agents of foreign principals[91]

This includes not only contracts made by agents but also contracts made through agents who have no authority to make contracts, but only to obtain orders and transmit them to the foreign principal for acceptance or rejection.[92] The sub-head applies only where the foreign principal is the intended defendant, and is not available to such a principal as claimant.[93] Rule 6.12 of the Civil Procedure Rules

5–028

---

[86] *Wansborough Paper Co. Ltd v Laughland* [1920] W.N. 344; *Benaim v Debono* [1924] A.C. 514 at 520.
[87] *Entores Ltd v Miles Far East Corporation* [1955] 2 Q.B. 327.
[88] [1983] 2 A.C. 34.
[89] *B.P. Exploration (Libya) Ltd v Hunt* [1976] 1 W.L.R. 788 at 798.
[90] *Sharab v Al-Saud* [2008] EWHC 1893 (Ch); [2009] 2 Lloyd's Rep 160.
[91] The Rules no longer state, as did the former Order 11, that the agent must be acting "on behalf of a principal trading or residing out of the jurisdiction" but this will still be the case.
[92] *National Mortgage and Agency Co. of New Zealand v Gosselin* (1922) 38 T.L.R. 832.
[93] *Union International Insurance Co. v Jubilee Insurance Co.* [1991] 1 W.L.R. 415.

provides an alternative method of service if the conditions laid down in (ii) are satisfied and also two further conditions, namely that the contract was made in England, and that the agent's authority has not been determined and he is still in business relations with his principal. The method is to issue the claim form against the principal and serve it with permission of the court on the agent in England.

(iii) Contracts governed by English law

5–029 Whether a contract is governed by English law is determined in accordance with the Rome I Regulation, the provisions of which are considered in detail elsewhere in this book.[94] It goes without saying that English judges are especially well qualified to apply the English law of contract, but nonetheless Lord Diplock observed in *Amin Rasheed Shipping Corp. v Kuwait Insurance Co.*[95] that jurisdiction exercised under this sub-head over a foreign corporation with no place of business in England was an exorbitant jurisdiction, one which an English court would not recognise as possessed by a foreign court in the absence of some treaty. For that reason, the judicial discretion to grant permission in such cases "should be exercised with circumspection". This part of Lord Diplock's speech was endorsed by the House of Lords in *Spiliada Maritime Corpn v Cansulex Ltd*,[96] where it was emphasised that the importance of the English governing law was something which varied greatly depending on the circumstances of the case.

So in *Novus Aviation Ltd v Onur Air Tasimacilik AS*[97] which concerned dealings between Bahamian and Turkish companies, the claimant's reliance on the choice of English law to govern the contract was unavailing: it was described as a simple case, concerning merely the evidential interpretation of one sentence in the minutes of a meeting. There was no important issue of English law. That case may be contrasted with *Stonebridge Underwriting Ltd v Ontario Municipal Insurance Exchange*.[98] In that case the implied choice of English law in a reinsurance contract, placed in London, by London brokers, with a London reinsurer, and incorporating a number of standard London market clauses was of considerable significance in determining that England was the proper place for hearing a dispute under the reinsurance contract; the issues were seen as "particularly suited" for determination by the English Commercial Court, whose habitual business includes the resolution of reinsurance disputes between reassureds and Lloyd's underwriters in accordance with well-developed principles of law and construction.

5–030 If the claimant has alternative remedies in contract and tort upon the same facts, he can choose his remedy. Thus, where the claimant was employed abroad under a contract governed by English law, and sustained personal injuries abroad in the course of his employment there, he was allowed to serve the claim form on his

---

[94] Below, Ch.11.
[95] [1984] A.C. 50.
[96] [1987] A.C. 460. See also *Ilyssia Cia. Naviera SA v Bamaodah, The Elli 2* [1985] 1 Lloyd's Rep. 107 for an explanation (endorsed in *Spiliada*) of related aspects of Lord Diplock's speech.
[97] [2009] EWCA Civ 122; [2009] 1 Lloyd's Rep. 576.
[98] [2010] EWHC 2279 (Comm); [2011] Lloyd's Rep IR 171.

employers out of the jurisdiction in an action for breach of an implied term in the contract, even though the facts also gave rise to a claim in tort, for which permission would have been refused because the tort was not committed in England.[99]

(iv)   Contracts containing a jurisdiction clause selecting the English court

Submission to the jurisdiction of the court may be inferred from the terms of a contract. If one party to a contract gives an address for service within the jurisdiction, service may be effected on the agent as of right.[100] Otherwise, the permission of the court under this sub-head is needed.

5–031

(7) a claim is made in respect of a breach of contract committed within the jurisdiction.[101]

For the purposes of this sub-head, it is immaterial where the contract was made or whether, in the language of the former Order 11, "the breach was preceded or accompanied by a breach committed out of the jurisdiction that rendered impossible the performance of so much of the contract as ought to have been performed within the jurisdiction".

A contract may be broken in one of three ways; namely by express repudiation, implied repudiation, or failure to perform.

Breach by express repudiation occurs when one party informs the other that he or she no longer intends to perform the contract. If X who is abroad writes a letter of repudiation to A in England, the breach is not committed in England.[102] On the other hand, if X who is abroad sends an agent to England, or writes to an agent who is in England, instructing the agent to repudiate a contract with A who is in England, and the agent does so, for example by letter posted in England, then the breach is committed in England.[103]

5–032

Breach by implied repudiation occurs when one party does an act that is inconsistent with the contract, for instance, when X promises to sell a house to A but sells it to B instead. Although there is no authority on the point, the breach in such a case presumably occurs where the inconsistent act is performed.

The normal form of breach is the failure by one party to perform one or more of his or her obligations under the contract. In such a case it is not necessary that the whole contract was to be performed in England by both parties, but it is necessary that some part of it was to be performed in England and that there has been a breach of that part.[104] It is not sufficient if the contract or part of it might be performed either in England or abroad; it is necessary that the contract or part

---

[99] *Matthews v Kuwait Bechtel Corporation* [1959] 2 Q.B. 57.

[100] CPR rr.6.3, 6.8.

[101] Practice Direction 6A, para.3.1(7).

[102] *Cherry v Thompson* (1872) L.R. 7 Q.B. 573 at 579; *Holland v Bennett* [1902] 1 K.B. 867, both approved by the Privy Council in *Martin v Stout* [1925] A.C. 359 at 368–369; but see *Cooper v Knight* (1901) 17 T.L.R. 299.

[103] *Mutzenbecher v La Aseguradora Espanola* [1906] 1 K.B. 254; *Oppenheimer v Louis Rosenthal & Co. AG* [1937] 1 All E.R. 23.

[104] *Rein v Stein* [1892] 1 Q.B. 753.

of it was to be performed in England and not elsewhere.[105] The contract need not contain an express term providing for performance in England[106]: it is enough if the court can gather that this was the intention of the parties by construing the contract in the light of the surrounding circumstances, including the course of dealing between the parties.[107]

5–033   In most of the reported cases, the breach complained of was the failure to pay money, a matter in which it is especially difficult to determine the place of performance in the absence of an express term in the contract. "The general rule is that where no place of payment is specified, either expressly or by implication, the debtor must seek out his creditor".[108] But this is only a general rule and, as stated, it only applies where no place of payment is expressed or implied in the contract. It certainly does not mean that a creditor can confer jurisdiction on the English court merely by taking up residence in England after the making of the contract, thus making England the place of performance.[109]

In a contract of employment, wages or salary would normally be payable where the service is to be performed, in the absence of an express or implied term in the contract.[110] But if the employee is employed in only a nominal or consultative capacity, and is free to reside where he likes, his salary may be payable in England, if that is where the employee decides to live.[111] In a contract for services, it may be possible to infer that the fee or commission is payable at the contractor's usual place of business in England, even if the work is to be performed abroad.[112]

5–034   In a contract for the sale of goods by a seller in England to a buyer abroad, it will, in the absence of a contractual term to the contrary, be easy to infer that the buyer's obligation was to pay for the goods in England.[113] The same is the case if a principal in England sends goods to an agent abroad to be sold on commission.[114] But it is otherwise if, on the true construction of the contract, the only duty of the foreign agent is to sell the goods and remit the proceeds to England from abroad in a specified manner, because it will be inferred that the agent's duty is at an end when the remittance is made.[115] If a foreign principal

---

[105] *Bell & Co. v Antwerp London and Brazil Line* [1891] 1 Q.B. 103; *The Eider* [1893] P. 119; *Comber v Leyland* [1898] A.C. 524; *Cuban Atlantic Sugar Sales Corporation v Compania de Vapores San Elefterio Lda* [1960] 1 Q.B. 187.

[106] *Reynolds v Coleman* (1887) 36 Ch.D. 453.

[107] *Rein v Stein* [1892] 1 Q.B. 753; *Fry & Co. v Raggio* (1891) 40 W.R. 120; *Charles Duval & Co. Ltd v Gans* [1904] 2 K.B. 685.

[108] *The Eider* [1893] P. 119 at 136–137, per Bowen L.J.

[109] *Malik v Narodni Banka Ceskoslovenska* [1946] 2 All E.R. 663.

[110] See *Malik v Narodni Banka Ceskoslovenska*, above.

[111] *Vitkovice Horni A Hutni Tezirstvo v Korner* [1951] A.C. 869.

[112] *Thompson v Palmer* [1893] 2 Q.B. 80.

[113] *Robey & Co. v Snaefell Mining Co. Ltd* (1887) 20 Q.B.D. 152; *Fry & Co. v Raggio* (1891) 40 W.R. 120.

[114] *Rein v Stein* [1892] 1 Q.B. 753; *Charles Duval & Co. Ltd v Gans* [1904] 2 K.B. 685.

[115] *Comber v Leyland* [1898] A.C. 524, a case "of a somewhat special character" per Stirling L.J. in *Charles Duval & Co. Ltd v Gans*, above, at p.691.

appoints an agent in England to sell goods on commission, it is usually inferred that the commission is payable in England.[116]

(8) a claim is made for a declaration that no contract exists where, if the contract was found to exist, it would comply with the conditions set out in sub-head (6).[117]

At one time it was doubtful whether an application for service out of the jurisdiction could be made where the claimant sought a declaration that there never was a contract. This is now the subject of the express provision in this sub-head.

Claims in tort

(9) a claim is made in tort where   **5–035**

(a)   damage was sustained within the jurisdiction; or
(b)   the damage sustained resulted from an act committed within the jurisdiction.[118]

The language of this sub-head was based on the approach adopted by the ECJ in interpreting art.5(3) of the Brussels Convention.[119] But difficulties remain. One is the question by what law is it determined whether the claim is "in tort" as opposed to any other type of action. This is essentially a characterisation exercise, which is appropriately carried out by reference to English law as the law of the forum.[120] That is consistent with the result but unfortunately not with the reasoning of the Court of Appeal in *Metall und Rohstoff A.G. v Donaldson Lufkin & Jenrette Inc.*[121] It is to be hoped that courts will adopt a straight-forward reading of the text of the sub-head, and ask themselves the question whether this claim is one English law would regard as sounding in tort. This seems to have been the approach taken by the Privy Council in a related context: sitting on appeal from the Bahamas, it considered only the law of that country in deciding that an action for contribution from a joint tortfeasor was to be classified as an action in tort.[122]

The other difficulty concerns the notion of "the damage" being sustained in England. It was argued in *Metall und Rohstoff A. G. v Donaldson Lufkin & Jenrette Inc.* that all the damage had to be in England. The court held, rightly it is submitted, that there was no justification for this reading of the text; it is enough if some significant damage occurs there. Similarly, if it is argued that the damage

---

[116] *Hoerter v Hanover etc. Works* (1893) 10 T.L.R. 103; *International Corporation Ltd v Besser Manufacturing Co.* [1950] 1 K.B. 488.
[117] Practice Direction 6A, para.3.1(8).
[118] Practice Direction 6A, para.3.1(9).
[119] Case 21/76 *Bier BV v Mines de Potasse d'Alsace SA* [1978] Q.B. 708; see above, paras 4–039ff.
[120] cf. the similar issue as to issues "relating to tort" under the Private International Law (Miscellaneous Provisions) Act 1995: below, para.12–010.
[121] [1990] Q.B. 391. See Carter, (1989) 60 B.Y.I.L. 485. The court seemed to treat the phrase in the former Order 11, "founded on a tort" as raising choice-of-law issues, which in turn led to a consideration of whether the tort had been committed within the jurisdiction, precisely the issue the revised language of the sub-head was designed to avoid.
[122] *FFSB Ltd v Seward & Kissel LLP* [2007] UKPC 16.

results from an act committed in England and the facts show acts both within and without the jurisdiction, the sub-head will apply if the damage results from substantial and efficacious (as opposed to minor and insignificant) acts of the defendant within the jurisdiction. It seems that the sub-head will apply to any sort of damage, provided it is significant; the *Dumez France* principle[123] has not been applied in this context. In the case of a claim relating to a death abroad, the sustaining in England of a loss of financial dependency and the incurring of funeral expenses will constitute "damage" for this purpose.[124]

As we have seen, if there are alternative causes of action in contract and tort on the same facts, the claimant may choose to rely on any of sub-heads (6), (7) or (9).

Enforcement

5–036 (10) a claim is made to enforce any judgment or arbitral award.[125]

This sub-head enables permission to be granted in a common law action on a foreign judgment or arbitration award against a debtor who remains out of England but has assets in England. This sub-head is all the more necessary now that s.34 of the Civil Jurisdiction and Judgments Act 1982 prevents the claimant from bringing a fresh action in England on the original cause of action.

Claims about property within the jurisdiction

5–037 (11) the whole subject matter of a claim relates to property within the jurisdiction.[126]

This sub-head replaced earlier provisions, with complex drafting, which dealt separately with land and movable property. It is not limited to claims relating to the ownership or possession of property, but extends to any claim for relief (whether for damages or otherwise) so long as it is related to property located within the jurisdiction.[127] It covers, for example, a claim in an insolvency context that property had been sold at an undervalue, a claim to recover rent due under a lease of land, and a claim for damages for breach of covenant.[128]

Claims about trusts, etc.

5–038 Under this heading, the Rules contain five distinct sub-heads:

---

[123] See paras 4–040 to 4–041, above.
[124] *Booth v Phillips* [2004] EWHC 1437.
[125] Practice Direction 6A, para.3.1(10).
[126] Practice Direction 6A, para.3.1(11).
[127] *Banca Carige SpA v Banco Nacional de Cuba* [2001] 1 W.L.R. 2039.
[128] See *Agnew v Usher* (1884) 14 Q.B.D. 78; *Kaye v Sutherland* (1887) 20 Q.B.D. 147; *Tassell v Hallen* [1892] 1 Q.B. 321; *Official Solicitor v Stype Investments Ltd* [1983] 1 W.L.R. 214; *Banca Carige SpA v Banco Nacional de Cuba* [2001] 1 W.L.R. 2039.

(12) a claim is made for any remedy which might be obtained in proceedings to execute the trusts of a written instrument where (a) the trusts ought to be executed according to English law; and (b) the person on whom the claim form is to be served is a trustee of the trusts.[129]

(13) a claim is made for any remedy which might be obtained in proceedings for the administration of the estate of a person who died domiciled within the jurisdiction.[130]

(14) a probate claim or a claim for the rectification of a will.[131]

(15) a claim is made for a remedy against the defendant as constructive trustee where the defendant's alleged liability arises out of acts committed within the jurisdiction.[132]

The predecessor provision of this sub-head was added to fill a lacuna revealed by the decision in *Metall und Rohstoff A. G. v Donaldson Lufkin & Jenrette Inc.*[133] that an action for breach of duty as a constructive trustee could not be regarded as "founded on a tort" and so within the sub-head dealing with claims in tort. It is not necessary to show that all the defendant's acts were committed within the jurisdiction[134]: and it may be that where the defendant did no act in England, some other link will suffice.[135]   **5–039**

(16) a claim is made for restitution where the defendant's alleged liability arises out of acts committed within the jurisdiction.[136]

The proper characterisation of restitution claims has given rise to difficulty under the Regulation rules.[137] This sub-head clarifies the position under the traditional rules.

Claims by HM Revenue and Customs

(17) a claim is made by the Commissioners for H.M. Revenue and Customs relating to duties or taxes against a defendant not domiciled in Scotland or Northern Ireland.[138]   **5–040**

Other claims

Other sub-heads cover claims made by a party to proceedings for an order that the court exercise its power under s.51 of the Senior Courts (formerly Supreme Court) Act 1981 to make a costs order in favour of or against a person who is not   **5–041**

---

[129] Practice Direction 6A, para.3.1(12).There is no requirement that the trust property be situated in England.
[130] Practice Direction 6A, para.3.1(13).
[131] Practice Direction 6A, para.3.1(14).
[132] Practice Direction 6A, para.3.1(15).
[133] [1990] Q.B. 391.
[134] *ISC Technologies Ltd v Guerin* [1992] 2 Lloyd's Rep. 430.
[135] *NABB Brothers International Ltd v Lloyds Bank International (Guernsey) Ltd* [2005] EWHC 405 (Ch); [2005] I.L.Pr. 506.
[136] Practice Direction 6A, para.3.1(16).
[137] *Kleinwort Benson Ltd v Glasgow City Council* [1999] 1 A.C. 153; see above, para.4–028.
[138] Practice Direction 6A, para.3.1(17).

a party to those proceedings[139]; certain salvage claims[140]; and claims made under an enactment which allows proceedings to be brought where those proceedings are not covered by any other sub-head or Directive No. 76/308/EEC (which concerns the European Agricultural Guidance and Guarantee Fund).[141]

Service abroad without permission

5–042   A claim form may be served on a defendant out of the jurisdiction without the permission of the court where (a) each claim included in the claim form made against the defendant to be served is a claim which the court has power to determine under the Brussels I Regulation; *and* no proceedings between the parties concerning the same claim are pending in the courts of any other part of the United Kingdom or any other Member State; *and* the defendant is domiciled in the United Kingdom or in any Member State, or (b) there is jurisdiction under art.22 (exclusive jurisdiction) or art.23 (jurisdiction agreements) of the Brussels I Regulation.[142]

A claim form may be also served on a defendant out of the jurisdiction without the permission of the court where each claim made against the defendant to be served is a claim which, under any other enactment, the court has power to determine, although (a) the person against whom the claim is made is not within the jurisdiction; or (b) the facts giving rise to the claim did not occur within the jurisdiction.[143] Most of the cases which fall under this rule involve statutes giving effect to international transport conventions which commonly contain special rules as to jurisdiction.

DISCRETIONARY POWERS IN THE COMMON LAW TRADITION

5–043   Reference has already been made to the procedural mechanisms developed in most common law countries which enable the judges to steer a case towards the most appropriate forum, and in the process off-set to some extent the initial advantage enjoyed by a claimant in selecting a forum likely to prove favourable to the claim. So, a court in a common law country typically has an inherent jurisdiction, reinforced in England by statute,[144] to stay an action brought in that country or to restrain by injunction (an "anti-suit injunction") the institution or continuation of proceedings in a foreign court, whenever it is necessary to do so in order to prevent injustice.[145] This, highly discretionary, jurisdiction came to

---

[139] Practice Direction 6A, para.3.1(18).

[140] Practice Direction 6A, para.3.1(19).

[141] Practice Direction 6A, para.3.1(20).

[142] CPR r.6.33(1); *DSG International Sourcing Ltd v Universal Media Corp (Slovakia) SRO* [2011] EWHC 1116 (Comm); [2011] I.L.Pr. 33.

[143] CPR r.6.33(3).

[144] Senior Courts (formerly Supreme Court) Act 1981 s.49(3); Civil Jurisdiction and Judgments Act 1982 s.49.

[145] See Fawcett, Declining Jurisdiction in Private International Law (Clarendon Press, Oxford, 1995); Bell, Forum Shopping and Venue in International Litigation (O.U.P., Oxford, 2003); Robertson (1987) 103 L.Q.R. 398; Slater, (1988) 104 L.Q.R. 398; Kennett, [1995] C.L.J. 552; Peel, (2001) 117 L.Q.R. 187.

play a very important part in English litigation practice, being invoked on the grounds that the availability of a more suitable forum elsewhere means that England is an inappropriate forum for the trial of the case *(forum non conveniens)*; that simultaneous actions are pending in England and in a foreign country between the same parties[146] and involving the same or similar issues *(lis alibi pendens)*; or that the parties have entered into a choice of court agreement. This approach to jurisdiction is characteristic of common law countries: the civil law tradition knows of jurisdiction clauses, but deals with cases of *lis alibi pendens* by a mechanistic rule giving priority to the action commenced first, and cannot accept the extensive degree of judicial discretion deployed in *forum non conveniens* cases. The adoption of the civil law approach in the Brussels I Regulation has greatly limited the use of the common law approach in the English courts.

Forum non conveniens

The power to stay actions on the ground that the forum chosen by the claimant was inappropriate for the trial of the action was known to the Scottish courts in the nineteenth century. It was much developed by the courts of the United States where it is now an essential part of litigation strategy as a means by which the defendant can resist the invocation by the claimant of what are often very widely-drawn (often styled "long-arm") bases of jurisdiction. The English courts eventually adopted a similar set of principles.[147]   5–044

The practice of the English courts was authoritatively stated by Lord Goff in *Spiliada Maritime Corpn v Cansulex Ltd*.[148] It can be stated as follows:

(a) The basic principle is that a stay will only be granted on the ground of *forum non conveniens* where the court is satisfied that there is some other available forum, having competent jurisdiction, which is the appropriate forum for the trial of the action, i.c., in which the case may be tried more suitably for the interests of all the parties and the ends of justice.

The defendant must show that another forum is "available". This means that the claimant must be able to begin proceedings against the defendant in the other forum as of right, either because the case falls within the jurisdiction regularly exercised by the courts of that country or as a result of a jurisdiction clause. It is not sufficient that an action could be brought in the named country on the basis of an undertaking proffered by the defendant to submit to its jurisdiction.[149]

---

[146] Very exceptionally, the power to stay English proceedings may be exercised where the outcome of the case is intimately bound up with foreign proceedings involving different parties: *Reichhold Norway ASA v Goldman Sachs International* [1999] 2 All E.R. (Comm) 174.

[147] The development of the doctrine can be traced in a number of landmark cases: *The Atlantic Star* [1974] A.C. 436; *MacShannon v Rockware Glass Ltd* [1978] A.C. 795; and *The Abidin Daver* [1984] A.C. 398.

[148] [1987] A.C. 460.

[149] *Lubbe v Cape plc* [1999] I.L.Pr. 113 (claim arising out of operations of defendant's subsidiaries in South Africa; defendant company itself not amenable to South African jurisdiction in absence of undertakings; stay of English action refused).

5–045   (b) The burden of proof is on the defendant to show not only that England is not the natural or appropriate forum, but also that there is another available forum which is clearly or distinctly more appropriate than the English forum.[150]

(c) In deciding whether there is another forum clearly more appropriate, the court will seek to identify the "natural forum", meaning "that with which the action has the most real and substantial connection",[151] and will examine not only factors affecting convenience or expense (such as availability of witnesses), but also such matters as the law governing the transaction, and the places where the parties reside or carry on business.

Although every case must turn on its own facts, the natural forum for a claim in tort is likely to be held to be the country in which the tort occurred, as illustrated by the facts of the *MacShannon* case[152]:

> M was a Scotsman resident in Scotland. He was injured in an accident at work in a factory in Scotland owned by his employers, a company registered in England. On the advice of the English solicitors to his London-based trade union, he brought his action in England and not in Scotland, because his solicitors believed that he would get higher damages in England and that proceedings in Scotland would take longer to come to trial. But when it was shown that medical and other expert witnesses were equally available in Scotland, and that therefore the comparative cost and inconvenience of a trial in England would be appreciably greater than those of a trial in Scotland, the House of Lords unanimously ordered the English action to be stayed.

5–046   (d) If there is another forum which prima facie is clearly more appropriate, the court will ordinarily grant a stay unless there are circumstances by reason of which justice requires that a stay should not be granted; at this point the burden of proof shifts to the claimant. It may be, for example, that for some reason the claimant could not obtain justice in the foreign country because of the weakness of,[153] or severe delays in,[154] the foreign legal system; the absence in the foreign country of the legal or other specialist assistance required for the fair hearing of the case[155]; or the existence of racial or political prejudice against the claimant.[156]

---

[150] cf. the approach adopted in Australia, of asking whether the Australian forum chosen by the claimant is "clearly inappropriate" which in effect means examining the choice of that forum for elements of vexation or oppression: *Voth v Manildra Flour Mills Pty Ltd* (1991) 171 C.L.R. 538; *Regie Nationale des Usines Renault SA v Zhang* [2002] HCA 10 ; (2003) 210 C.L.R. 491. Some American decisions arrive at a similar result by stressing the "deference" to be given to the claimant's choice of forum, especially if it is the claimant's "home forum".

[151] A formulation used by Lord Keith in *The Abidin Daver* [1984] A.C. 398 at 415.

[152] [1978] A.C. 795.

[153] *889457 Alberta Inc v Katanga Mining Ltd* [2009] I.L.Pr. 14, where in the alternative forum, the Republic of Congo, injustice was 'widespread and endemic' (at para.34).

[154] *The Jalakrishna* [1983] 2 Lloyd's Rep. 628 (five year delay in India in case of severe personal injuries).

[155] *Connelly v RTZ Corp. plc* [1998] A.C. 854 (but note the dissent of Lord Hoffman).

[156] e.g., *Mohammed v Bank of Kuwait* [1996] 1 W.L.R. 1483 (Iraqi citizen claiming arrears of salary for period including that of the Iraqi occupation of Kuwait); *Cherney v Deripaska (No 2)* [2009] EWCA Civ 849; [2010] 2 All ER (Comm) 456 (Russia was the natural forum, but the claimant feared that in Russia he would risk assassination or arrest on trumped-up charges, and that the defendant's government connections would prevent a fair trial; England held the appropriate forum); but cf. *Askin v Absa Bank Ltd* [1999] I.L.Pr. 471 (threats of assassination against claimant; stay nonetheless refused).

(e) The mere fact that the claimant has a legitimate personal or juridical advantage in proceeding in England cannot be decisive. As Lord Goff put it in *Connelly v RTZ Corp. plc*[157]:

> "If a clearly more appropriate forum overseas had been identified, generally speaking the plaintiff will have to take that forum as he finds it, even if it is in certain respects less advantageous to him than the English forum. He may, for example, have to accept lower damages, or do without the more generous English system of discovery. The same must apply to the system of court procedure, including the rules of evidence, applicable in the foreign forum".

Effect of the Brussels I Regulation and the Lugano Convention

There is, in general, no room for the operation of the doctrine of *forum non conveniens* in the context of the Brussels I Regulation. The European rules allocate jurisdiction and cannot be the subject of any general judicial discretion; it is seen as unnecessary, even unseemly, to argue that of the two or more courts in Member States competent to hear a particular case one is more appropriate than another. If an action is brought in England by a claimant domiciled in a Member State against a defendant domiciled in England, the English court clearly has jurisdiction under art.2 of the Regulation, and must exercise it; a plea of *forum non conveniens* cannot be heard.[158]

5–047

For many years after the Brussels Convention, the predecessor of the Regulation, first had legal effect in England, the courts continued to entertain pleas of *forum non conveniens* in the very common type of case involving an action by a claimant resident and domiciled in, say, New York (or any other country which is not a Member State) and begun by the service of process in England upon a defendant who was at the time of service present and domiciled in England. It will be seen that the English courts will undoubtedly have jurisdiction, by virtue either of the service of the claim form or of art.2 of the Regulation. After a number of first-instance decisions to the contrary, the Court of Appeal decided in *Re Harrods (Buenos Aires) Ltd*[159] that in such cases the Brussels Convention did not preclude the application of national law principles, including the *forum non conveniens* doctrine. The court's view was essentially that the purpose of the Brussels Convention was to set up an intra-Community mandatory system of jurisdiction, and that relations between individual Member States and non-Member States were outside that system. It followed that to consider a plea of *forum non conveniens*, and to uphold it in the appropriate cases, would be in no way inconsistent with the Convention.

---

[157] [1998] A.C. 854 at 872.
[158] See *Aiglon Ltd v Gau Shan Co. Ltd* [1993] 1 Lloyd's Rep. 164; Case C-288/92 *Custom Made Commercial Ltd v Stawa Metallbau GmbH.* [1994] E.C.R. I-2913. See also the reasoning of the ECJ in Case C-159/02 *Turner v Grovit* [2004] 3 W.L.R. 1193, considered below, para.5–058.
[159] [1992] Ch. 72. See Collins, (1990) 106 L.Q.R. 535, the argument in which is adopted by the Court of Appeal. *Re Harrods* was followed in a number of later Court of Appeal cases: *Ace Insurance SA-NV v Zurich Insurance Co.* [2001] Lloyd's Rep IR 504; *American Motorists Insurance Co. v Cellstar Corp.* [2003] EWCA Civ 206; [2003] Lloyd's Rep IR 295; *Anton Durbeck GmbH v Den Norske Bank ASA* [2003] EWCA Civ 147; [2003] Q.B. 1160 (a case on the Lugano Convention).

5-048   The ECJ eventually rejected the arguments adopted in *Re Harrods (Buenos Aires) Ltd*. It had previously held, in a different context, that the rules in the Brussels I Regulation were "in principle applicable where the defendant has its domicile or seat in a [Member] State, even if the plaintiff is domiciled in a non-member country".[160] The specific issue came before the Court in *Owusu v Jackson*[161]:

> O, a British national domiciled in the United Kingdom, hired a holiday villa in Jamaica from J, also domiciled in the United Kingdom. O was rendered tetraplegic by an accident while diving from the private beach belonging to the villa. O began proceedings in England, against J for breach of an implied term in their contract, and in tort against several Jamaican companies which were allegedly in breach of duties connected with the safety of the beach. J and several of the other defendants applied for a stay of the English proceedings under the *forum non conveniens* doctrine, arguing that in all the circumstances the case was more appropriately tried in Jamaica.

The ECJ held that the Brussels Convention precluded a court of a Contracting State from declining the jurisdiction conferred on it by art.2 of that Convention on the ground that a court of a non-Contracting State would be a more appropriate forum for the trial of the action even if the jurisdiction of no other Contracting State were in issue or the proceedings had no connecting factors to any other Contracting State.

5-049   In reaching this conclusion, the Court noted that nothing in the wording of art.2 suggested that its application was subject to the condition that there should be a legal relationship involving a number of Contracting States. The uniform rules of jurisdiction contained in the Convention were not intended to apply only to situations in which there is a real and sufficient link with the working of the internal market, by definition involving a number of Member States. The intention was to eliminate obstacles to the functioning of the internal market derived from disparities between national legislations on the subject. The *forum non conveniens* doctrine was recognised only in a limited number of Contracting States, and the objective of the Convention was precisely to lay down common rules to the exclusion of derogating national rules. Article 2 was mandatory in nature and, according to its terms, there could be no derogation from the principle it lays down except in the cases expressly provided for by the Convention and no exception on the basis of the *forum non conveniens* doctrine was provided for. Application of the *forum non conveniens* doctrine, which allowed the court seised a wide discretion as regards the question whether a foreign court would be a more appropriate forum for the trial of an action, was liable to undermine the predictability of the rules of jurisdiction laid down by the Convention, in particular that of art.2, and consequently to undermine the principle of legal certainty, which was the basis of the Convention.

The court recognised the concerns of the defendants, the negative consequences which would result in practice were the English courts be obliged to try the case, inter alia as regards the expense of the proceedings, the possibility of recovering their costs in England if the claimant's action were dismissed, the logistical difficulties resulting from the geographical distance, the need to assess

---

[160] Case C-412/98 *Universal Insurance Co. v Group Josi Reinsurance Co. SA* [2000] E.C.R. I-5925; [2001] Q.B. 68 (a case under the Brussels Convention).
[161] Case C-281/02, [2005] Q.B. 801; [2005] ECR I-1383.

the merits of the case according to Jamaican standards, the enforceability in Jamaica of a default judgment and the impossibility of enforcing cross-claims against the other defendants. But, said the court, "genuine as those difficulties may be, suffice it to observe that such considerations, which are precisely those which may be taken into account when *forum non conveniens* is considered, are not such as to call into question the mandatory nature of the fundamental rule of jurisdiction contained in Art.2".

Several questions were left unresolved. The actual decision is limited to cases in which the English court has jurisdiction on the domicile basis of art.2. What is the position if the jurisdictional basis is found not in that Article but in art.5, for example in a case in which England is the place for the performance of the contractual obligation in question? Given that art.5 only applies if the defendant is domiciled in another Member State, and given the connection with England which attracts the Article, it is relatively unlikely that the English courts would decide that the courts of a non-Member State offered a more appropriate forum. However, the reasoning of the ECJ in *Owusu v Jackson* is applicable in this context as in that of art.5.[162]   **5–050**

The reference to the ECJ in *Owusu v Jackson*[163] sought a ruling on the position where identical or related proceedings were already pending before a court of a non-Contracting State, where a choice of court clause gave jurisdiction to such a court, or where there was a connection with that state of the same type as those referred to in art.16 of the Convention (now art.22 of the Regulation). The Court refused to deal with these circumstances, which were not raised by the facts of the instant case.

These issues remain acutely controversial and the courts have shown a marked reluctance to resolve them,[164] although it has been held that *Owusu* does not apply in the very different context of family law.[165] In the context of the review of the Brussels I Regulation, the European Commission's Proposal has suggested a discretionary *lis pendens* rule where disputes on the same subject-matter and between the same parties are pending before the courts of a Member State and in a non-Member State: a Member State court would be entitled in exceptional circumstances to stay proceedings if a non-Member State court were seised first and it was expected that the foreign court would reach its decision within a reasonable time, and the decision would be enforceable in that Member State.[166]

The *forum non conveniens* doctrine does remain available in some types of case. One is where an English court is invited to hold that a Scottish or Northern Ireland court is a more appropriate forum. Although jurisdictional rules based   **5–051**

---

[162] *Gómez v Gómez-Monche Vives* [2008] EWHC 259 (Ch); [2008] 1 All E.R. (Comm) 973, reversed, but only on other aspects of the case [2008] EWCA Civ 1065; [2009] Ch. 245.

[163] Case C-281/02, [2005] Q.B. 801; [2005] ECR I-1383.

[164] See, e.g., *Lucasfilm Ltd v Ainsworth* [2011] UKSC 39; [2012] A.C. 208 at [111]–[113]; *UBS AG v HSH Nordbank* [2009] EWCA Civ 585; [2010] 1 All E.R. (Comm) 727 at [100]–[103]; *Choudhary v Bhatter* [2009] EWCA Civ 1176; [2010] 2 All E.R. (Comm) 419 at [54]; *Deutsche Bank AG v Sebastian Holdings Inc (No. 2)* [2010] EWCA Civ 998; [2011] 2 All E.R. (Comm) 245 at [71]–[72]. The reference to the ECJ envisaged in *Goshawk Dedicated Ltd v Life Receivables Ireland Ltd* [2009] IESC 7; [2009] I.L.Pr. 435 did not take place. See Fentiman, (2006) 59 Curr. Leg. Prob. 391.

[165] *JKN v JCN* [2010] EWHC 843 (Fam), [2011] 1 F.L.R. 826.

[166] See COM (2010) 748 final, para.3.1.2.

upon those of the Brussels I Regulation govern such cases,[167] the Regulation itself is inapplicable, at least in certain types of case, and there is no obstacle to the raising and consideration of the plea of *forum non conveniens*.[168] A possible qualification is where the regulation refers not to the courts of a Member State but to the court for a certain place; in that latter case the Regulation may be seen as applicable and the *forum non conveniens* plea would then be excluded.[169]

A second type of case involves an action brought in England against a defendant who is not domiciled in a Member State. Article 4 of the Brussels I Regulation allows the national law as to jurisdiction to be applied in such cases, so here the *forum non conveniens* plea can be raised, even if the alternative forum is that of a Member State.

Finally, the plea remains available in areas of law, such as succession, outside the scope of the Regulation.[170]

Lis alibi pendens

5-052 Although intervention on the ground of *lis alibi pendens* has a much longer history in English law than *forum non conveniens*, it came to be treated as a sub-set of the latter (and many of the leading cases in which that latter doctrine was developed rested also on *lis alibi pendens*).

The court may be asked to stay an action in England, or to enjoin an action abroad, where the same claimant sues the same defendant in England and abroad or where the roles of claimant and defendant are reversed in the two countries. It used to be said that it required a stronger case to induce the court to interfere in the second situation; surprisingly, the power of the court to interfere in the second situation was established as early as 1821,[171] but in the first situation not until 1882.[172] At common law, the English court might stay the English proceedings, or restrain the foreign proceedings by injunction, or require the claimant to elect which proceedings to pursue.[173]

The Brussels I Regulation deals with the cases in which actions are pending before the courts of different Member States, and has no express provision as to cases where actions are begun in England (or any other Member State) and in a non-Member State. The logic of the position taken by the ECJ in *Owusu v Jackson*[174] is that it is not open to an English court to stay proceedings begun in England on the basis of the domicile of the defendant even after proceedings raising the same issue have been commenced in a non-Member State; the ECJ declined to rule expressly on the matter.[175]

---

[167] See Civil Jurisdiction and Judgments Act 1982 Sch.4; and above, para.4–083.

[168] *Cumming v Scottish Daily Record and Sunday Mail Ltd*, The Times, 8 June 1995; noted Collins, (1995) 111 L.Q.R. 541.

[169] See Case C-386/05 *Color Drack GmbH v Lexx International Vertriebs GmbH* [2007] E.C.R. I-3699.

[170] e.g., *Dellar v Zivy* [2007] EWHC 2266 (Ch); [2007] I.L.Pr. 868 (interpretation of a will).

[171] *Bushby v Munday* (1821) 5 Madd. 297; *Beckford v Kemble* (1822) 1 S. & St. 7. See McClean (1969) 18 I.C.L.Q. 931.

[172] *McHenry v Lewis* (1882) 22 Ch.D. 397.

[173] *The Christianborg* (1885) 10 P.D. 141 at 152–153, per Baggallay L.J.

[174] Case C-281/02, [2005] Q.B. 801; [2005] ECR I-1383.

[175] See paras 5–048ff.

Anti-suit injunctions

In a number of contexts, the English court is asked on grounds similar to those   **5–053**
already examined not to stay its own proceedings but to enjoin the
commencement or continuation of proceedings abroad. This is not a case of
attempting to dictate to the foreign court, for "the injunction is not to the court,
but to the party".[176] The effect, nonetheless, is to interfere with proceedings in
another jurisdiction, so "the power should be exercised with great caution".[177]

The applicable principles were restated by the Privy Council in *Société
Nationale Industrielle Aérospatiale v Lee Kui Jak*[178]:

> A fatal helicopter crash in Brunei led to actions being commenced both in Brunei and in Texas
> against the manufacturers (A) and the company responsible for operating and maintaining the
> helicopter (B). It appeared highly likely that the Texas courts would have jurisdiction over A
> but not over B, and were A held liable in Texas, A would have to claim contribution from B in
> some other forum. Reversing the lower courts in Brunei, the Privy Council held that Brunei
> was the natural forum and granted an injunction restraining the continuation of the Texas
> proceedings.

The importance of the decision lies in its examination of the grounds upon which   **5–054**
the court should intervene. It had been suggested in earlier cases[179] that the
applicable principles corresponded to those elaborated in *Spiliada Maritime
Corpn v Cansulex Ltd.*[180] Those principles would, however, enable injunctions to
be granted too readily, and the Privy Council chose to go back to the language
used in earlier cases[181]: foreign proceedings would only be enjoined if they were
"vexatious" or "oppressive", and the court would not deprive the claimant of an
advantage in the foreign forum of which it would be unjust to deprive him.[182]

Subsequent cases, of which there is an abundance, have refined the tests to be
applied. In *Deutsche Bank AG v Highland Crusader Offshore Partners LP*,[183]
Toulson L.J. reviewed the authorities and set out a summary of the correct
approach:

(1)   Under English law the court may restrain a defendant over whom it has   **5–055**
       personal jurisdiction from instituting or continuing proceedings in a foreign
       court when it is necessary in the interests of justice so to do.
(2)   It is too narrow to say that such an injunction may be granted only on
       grounds of vexation or oppression, but, where a matter is justiciable in an

---

[176] *Love v Baker* (1665) 1 Cas. in Ch. 67; *Bushby v Munday* (1821) Madd. 297 at 306–307; *Societe Nationale Industrielle Aerospatiale v Lee Kui Jak* [1987] A.C. 871. For this reason, the use of the term "anti-suit injunction" has been criticised (see *Turner v Grovit* [2002] 1 W.L.R. 107 at 117 per Lord Hobhouse) but the usage is well established.

[177] *Cohen v Rothfield* [1919] 1 K.B. 410 at 413; *Settlement Corpn v Hochschild* [1966] Ch. 10 at 15.

[178] [1987] A.C. 871.

[179] Notably *Castanho v Brown & Root (U.K.) Ltd* [1981] A.C. 557.

[180] [1987] A.C. 460; see above, para.5–044.

[181] Especially in *St. Pierre v South American Stores* (Gath & Chaves) Ltd [1936] 1 K.B. 382.

[182] See *British Airways Board v Laker Airways Ltd* [1985] A.C. 58, decided before the Aerospatiale case (anti-trust remedies only available in United States courts). cf. the related case of *Midland Bank plc v Laker Airways Ltd* [1986] Q.B. 689.

[183] [2009] EWCA Civ 725; [2010] 1 W.L.R. 1023.

English and a foreign court, the party seeking an anti-suit injunction must generally show that proceeding before the foreign court is or would be vexatious or oppressive.

(3)   The courts have refrained from attempting a comprehensive definition of vexation or oppression, but in order to establish that proceeding in a foreign court is or would be vexatious or oppressive on grounds of *forum non conveniens*, it is generally necessary to show that (a) England is clearly the more appropriate forum (the natural forum), and (b) justice requires that the claimant in the foreign court should be restrained from proceeding there.

(4)   If the English court considers England to be the natural forum and can see no legitimate personal or juridical advantage in the claimant in the foreign proceedings being allowed to pursue them, it does not automatically follow that an anti-suit injunction should be granted. For that would be to overlook the important restraining influence of considerations of comity.

5–056   (5)   An anti-suit injunction always requires caution because by definition it involves interference with the process or potential process of a foreign court. An injunction to enforce an exclusive jurisdiction clause governed by English law is not regarded as a breach of comity, because it merely requires a party to honour his contract. In other cases, the principle of comity requires the court to recognise that, in deciding questions of weight to be attached to different factors, different judges operating under different legal systems with different legal policies may legitimately arrive at different answers, without occasioning a breach of customary international law or manifest injustice, and that in such circumstances it is not for an English court to arrogate to itself the decision how a foreign court should determine the matter. The stronger the connection of the foreign court with the parties and the subject matter of the dispute, the stronger the argument against intervention.

(6)   The prosecution of parallel proceedings in different jurisdictions is undesirable but not necessarily vexatious or oppressive.

(7)   A non-exclusive jurisdiction agreement precludes either party from later arguing that the forum identified is not an appropriate forum on grounds foreseeable at the time of the agreement, for the parties must be taken to have been aware of such matters at the time of the agreement. For that reason an application to stay on *forum non conveniens* grounds an action brought in England pursuant to an English non-exclusive jurisdiction clause will ordinarily fail unless the factors relied upon were unforeseeable at the time of the agreement.[184] It does not follow that an alternative forum is necessarily inappropriate or inferior.

(8)   The decision whether or not to grant an anti-suit injunction involves an exercise of discretion and the principles governing it contain an element of flexibility.

---

[184] cf. the position where there is an exclusive clause: *Donohue v Armco Inc* [2001] UKHL 64; [2002] 1 All E.R. 749: see para.5–061.

No proceedings in England

An attempt was made to extend the availability of anti-suit injunctions in *Airbus*   **5–057**
Industrie GIE v Patel[185]:

> An air crash in India involved an Airbus 320 manufactured by AI in France and used
> exclusively on internal Indian flights. The plaintiffs, representing the victims of the crash and
> their estates, commenced an action in Texas. An action in Texas, where liability was strict, was
> likely to succeed, and there was the added attraction to the plaintiffs of the possible award of
> punitive damages. An action in India, requiring proof of fault, would probably fail. The Indian
> courts had granted an anti-suit injunction, but that was not enforceable in England where the
> plaintiffs were resident. The applicants sought a similar injunction from the English court. The
> issue was whether an injunction could be granted, despite the fact that there were (and could
> be) no English proceedings, the natural forum being India.

The House of Lords ruled that in such circumstances an injunction was not
available; but the door was not firmly closed. It was recognised that there might
be "extreme cases" where the conduct of the foreign State exercising jurisdiction
was such as to deprive it of the respect normally required by comity. The refusal
of Texas to countenance *forum non conveniens* applications in personal injury
cases was not seen as bringing the case into that extreme category.

EU cases

The House of Lords in *Airbus Industrie* drew attention to the very different   **5–058**
approach of the civil law tradition as expressed in the Brussels and Lugano
Conventions. That was made clear in *Turner v Grovit*[186]:

> T was employed as an in-house lawyer by an English company, which was later taken over by
> H Ltd, a company in the C group of companies. For a period in 1997–1998, T was posted to
> Madrid, where CSA, another company in the C group, was based, but the English court held
> that he was still employed by H Ltd. After a dispute, T returned to England and successfully
> brought a claim against H Ltd in an Employment Tribunal for unfair and wrongful dismissal.
> Some six months after the commencement of those proceedings, CSA brought a claim against
> T in the Spanish courts alleging breach of contract.

The English tribunal was the "court first seised" and the Court of Appeal issued
an anti-suit injunction restraining the Spanish proceedings on the ground that they
were vexatious and had been begun in bad faith. On a reference by the House of
Lords, the ECJ emphasised that:

> " [T]he Convention is necessarily based on the trust which the Contracting States accord to one
> another's legal systems and judicial institutions. It is that mutual trust which has enabled a
> compulsory system of jurisdiction to be established, which all the courts within the purview of
> the Convention are required to respect, and as a corollary the waiver by those States of the
> right to apply their internal rules on recognition and enforcement of foreign judgments in
> favour of a simplified mechanism for the recognition and enforcement of judgments".[187]

---

[185] [1999] 1 A.C. 119; see Peel, (1998) 114 L.Q.R. 543.
[186] [2000] Q.B. 345, criticised Harris, (1999) 115 L.Q.R. 576. See also *Continental Bank NA v
Aeakos Compania Naviera SA* [1994] 1 W.L.R. 588 (where the proceedings were in breach of a
jurisdiction clause selecting the English courts).
[187] Case C-159/02, [2005] 1 A.C. 101 at [24].

5–059   It followed that any injunction prohibiting a claimant from bringing an action in another Convention State had to be seen as constituting interference with the jurisdiction of the foreign court which, as such, was incompatible with the system of the Convention.[188] These arguments appear equally applicable to the Brussels I Regulation. The effect is that it must be left to the court second seised, in the instant case the Spanish court, to stay its proceedings under arts 27 or 28. This ruling does not affect cases in which it is sought to restrain proceedings in a non-Member State.

Arbitration

5–060   As arbitration is excluded from the scope of the Brussels I Regulation, that Regulation does not prevent the English court from granting an injunction to restrain arbitral proceedings abroad, even in another Member State. This power will, however be exercised only in "exceptional circumstances": it must be shown, as a minimum, to establish that the applicant's legal or equitable rights have been infringed or threatened by a continuation of the arbitration, or that its continuation will be vexatious, oppressive or unconscionable.[189]

Choice of court agreements

5–061   We have already noted the provisions of art.23 of the Brussels I Regulation dealing with agreements as to jurisdiction between parties one or more of whom is domiciled in a Member State and specifying a court or courts of a Member State.[190]

The principles applying in cases which do not attract art.23 were fully examined by Lord Bingham in *Donohue v Armco Inc.*[191] He said:

> "If contracting parties agree to give a particular court exclusive jurisdiction to rule on claims between those parties, and a claim falling within the scope of the agreement is made in proceedings in a forum other than that which the parties have agreed, the English court will ordinarily exercise its discretion (whether by granting a stay of proceedings in England, or by restraining the prosecution of proceedings in the non-contractual forum abroad, or by such other procedural order as is appropriate in the circumstances) to secure compliance with the contractual bargain, unless the party suing in the non-contractual forum (the burden being on him) can show strong reasons for suing in that forum".

5–062   The ECJ refused in *Owusu v Jackson*[192] to decide whether the principles developed in that case prevented an English court from continuing to grant stays of English proceedings commenced in breach of an exclusive jurisdiction clause to favour the courts of a non-Member State. If it were decided that such stays were no longer possible, the English court's powers would be limited to possible intervention to restrain foreign proceedings commenced in a non-Member State

---

[188] *ibid.*, at [27].
[189] *Claxton Engineering Services Ltd v TXM Olaj-es Gazkutato Kft* [2010] EWHC 2567 (Comm); [2011] 2 All E.R. (Comm) 38.
[190] See paras 4–060 to 4–068, above.
[191] [2001] UKHL 64; [2002] 1 All E.R. 749.
[192] Case C-281/02, [2005] Q.B. 801; [2005] ECR I-1383.

in breach of a choice of court clause giving jurisdiction to the English courts and entered into by parties neither of who was domiciled in a Member State. In *Konkola Copper Mines plc v Coromin*,[193] it was held, however, that the *Owusu* case could be distinguished where foreign jurisdiction clauses were involved: such clauses created a degree of certainty missing from the normal *forum non conveniens* case the subject of the *Owusu* judgment.

Intervention would require "strong reasons". Lord Bingham approved a list of some of the matters which could be taken into account that was given by Brandon J. in *The Eleftheria*[194]:

"(a) In what country the evidence on the issues of fact is situated, or more readily available, and the effect of that on the relative convenience and expense of trial as between the English and foreign courts; (b) Whether the law of the foreign court applies and, if so, whether it differs from English law in any material respects; (c) With what country either party is connected, and how closely; (d) Whether the defendants genuinely desire trial in the foreign country, or are only seeking procedural advantages; (e) Whether the plaintiffs would be prejudiced by having to sue in the foreign court because they would – (i) be deprived of security for that claim, (ii) be unable to enforce any judgment obtained, (iii) be faced with a time-bar not applicable in England, or (iv) for political, racial, religious or other reasons be unlikely to get a fair trial.

Where the English court has power to intervene and the dispute is between two parties only, one party sues in a forum other than that specified in exclusive jurisdiction clause in their contract, and the interests of other parties are not involved, effect will in all probability be given to that clause.[195] However, where the interests of parties other than the parties bound by the exclusive jurisdiction clause are involved, or grounds of claim not the subject of the clause are part of the relevant dispute, there may be a risk of parallel proceedings and inconsistent decisions. In such a case, the English court may well decline to grant an injunction or a stay, as the case may be. This was the situation in *Donohue v Armco Inc.*[196]   **5–063**

The case concerned dealings between a group of companies and four individuals, and the heart of the case lay in allegations of fraud made by the companies against those four individuals. Mr Donohue was party, with some but not all the companies, to a clause giving exclusive jurisdiction to the English courts, but that clause did not bind all the claimant companies or all the defendants. The companies wished to sue in New York.

The House of Lords felt it right to give great weight to the danger of dividing the litigation between different courts.[197] Only the New York courts could hear all the issues in a single composite trial. An anti-suit injunction restraining proceedings

[193] [2005] EWHC 898 (Comm); [2005] 2 All E.R. (Comm) 637. The point was not taken on appeal: [2006] EWCA Civ 5; [2006] 1 All ER (Comm) 437.
[194] [1970] P. 94. As Lord Bingham recognised, this was a staying rather than an anti-suit injunction case, so the criteria to be applied in considering the listed matters would be different.
[195] See Lord Bingham in *Donohue v Armco Inc* [2001] UKHL 64; [2002] 1 All E.R. 749 at para.[25] citing authorities from England, Australia, Canada and the U.S.
[196] *Donohue v Armco Inc.* [2001] UKHL 64; [2002] 1 All E.R. 749, per Lord Bingham at para.[27].
[197] cf. *Astrazeneca UK Ltd v Albemarle International Corp* [2010] EWHC 1028 (Comm); [2011] 1 All E.R. (Comm) 510 (exclusive jurisdiction clause in favour of the courts of South Carolina in respect of certain claims; court accepted that different claims would have to be heard in different countries).

in New York was not granted, but the court accepted an undertaking by the claimant companies not to seek multiple or punitive damages in the New York proceedings.

5–064   The validity of a jurisdiction clause is a matter for the law governing the contract of which it forms part, and so is its interpretation, in particular whether it provides for the exclusive jurisdiction of the foreign court, or merely that the parties will not object to the exercise of jurisdiction by that court,[198] and is scope in terms of subject matter, for example whether it covers claims in tort as well as claims in contract.[199] Even if it is argued that the contract containing the choice of court clause is voidable (e.g., an insurance contract in relation to which there was a failure to disclose material facts) and that therefore the clause is not binding, the court will hold the parties to it[200]; but it might be otherwise if the contract is void, e.g., for mistake.[201]

Arbitration clauses

5–065   When the parties to a contract have agreed to submit any eventual dispute to arbitration, and one of the parties starts legal proceedings in England in breach of the terms of such a clause, the Arbitration Act 1996 applies. Section 9 of the Act implements art.2 of the New York Convention of 1958,[202] one of the purposes of which was to promote the enforceability of arbitration agreements. The English courts are required to grant a stay of proceedings if there is a valid[203] arbitration agreement "in writing" "in respect of a matter which under the agreement is to be referred to arbitration".[204] The defendant in the court proceedings loses the right to a mandatory stay under the Act if he submits to the jurisdiction.[205]

Very different considerations apply when the court is asked to exercise its discretionary powers to issue an anti-suit injunction in support of an arbitration agreement. In *AES Ust-Kamenogorsk Hydropower Plant LLP v AES Ust-Kamenogorsk Hydropower Plant JSCI*,[206] where no arbitration had been commenced, but a party asked the court to protect its interest in a right to have its disputes settled in accordance with its arbitration agreement, the Court of Appeal held that it was open to the court to consider whether, and how best, if at all, to protect such a right to arbitrate by way of an anti-suit injunction.

---

[198] *Evans Marshall & Co. Ltd v Bertola SA* [1973] 1 W.L.R. 349; *Sohio Supply Co. v Gatoil (USA) Inc.* [1989] 1 Lloyd's Rep. 588; *British Aerospace plc v Dee Howard Co.* [1993] 1 Lloyd's Rep. 368. Note that agreements on the choice of court are outside the scope of the Rome Convention.

[199] *The Sindh* [1975] 1 Lloyd's Rep. 372; *Continental Bank NA v Aeakos Cia Naviera SA* [1994] 1 W.L.R. 588; *The Pioneer Container* [1994] 2 A.C. 324.

[200] *Mackender v Feldia* [1967] 2 Q.B. 590.

[201] *ibid.*, p.598.

[202] United Nation Convention on the Recognition and Enforcement of Foreign Arbitral Awards (New York, 1958).

[203] The agreement must not be "null and void, inoperative or incapable of being performed" (Arbitration Act 1996 s.9(4)). The validity of the arbitration agreement is determined according to the applicable law to such agreement. See Parish, (2010) 76 Arbitration 661; see also Fentiman, (2010) 69 C. L. J. 242.

[204] Act 1996 s.9(1).

[205] *ibid.*, s.9(3).

[206] [2011] EWCA Civ 647; [2011] 2 Lloyd's Rep 233.

JURISDICTION IN ACTIONS IN REM

The only action in rem known to English law is an Admiralty action[207] against a ship or other *res*, such as cargo or freight, connected with a ship, or against an aircraft or hovercraft.[208] Its primary object is to satisfy the claim out of the *res*. For the essence of the procedure in rem is that the *res* may be arrested by the Admiralty marshal, and sold by the court to meet the claim, provided the claim is proved to the satisfaction of the court. It does not follow that the successful claimant will recover the full amount of the claim, for this may exceed the amount of the proceeds of sale of the *res*, or there may be other claimants with a higher priority. But in most actions in rem no arrest in fact takes place, because the owner of the *res* arranges for bail or for some other security to be given. The action then proceeds as an action in personam and the defendant's liability is not limited either to the amount of the bail or to the value of the *res*.[209]

5–066

Service of an in rem claim form issued in an action in rem is usually effected by serving it upon the property against which the claim in rem is brought by fixing the claim form, or a copy of it, on the outside of the property proceeded against in a position which may reasonably be expected to be seen.[210] Where the property is freight, service may be made either on the cargo in respect of which the freight was earned or on the ship upon which that cargo was carried.

Unlike a claim form beginning an action in personam, an in rem claim form cannot be served out of the jurisdiction. It is immaterial that the ship leaves the jurisdiction after the service of the claim form but before the execution of the warrant of arrest.[211]

Before 1956, an action in rem could not be brought against any ship other than the one in respect of which the cause of action arose. But under s.21(4) of the Senior Courts (formerly Supreme Court) Act 1981, re-enacting s.3(4) of the Administration of Justice Act 1956, which was passed to implement the 1952 International Convention on the Arrest of Seagoing Ships, such an action may be brought where the person who would be liable on the claim in an action in personam was, when the cause of action arose, the owner or charterer of, or in possession or in control of, the ship, against any other ship of which, at the time when the action is brought, that person is the beneficial owner as respects all the shares in it. There is no requirement that the sister ship must have been owned by that person at the time when the cause of action arose.[212] But the action may be brought against one ship only, either against the one in respect of which the cause of action arose, or against a sister ship, but not both.[213] However, this does not prevent the plaintiff from issuing a claim form against the ship in respect of

5–067

---

[207] A list of Admiralty actions is given in s.20 of the Senior Courts (formerly Supreme Court) Act 1981.

[208] Actions in rem against aircraft are practically unknown, but an instance is afforded by *The Glider Standard Austria SH 1964* [1965] P. 463.

[209] *The Dictator* [1892] P. 304; *The Gemma* [1899] P. 285; The Dupleix [1912] P. 8; *The August 8* [1983] 2 A.C. 450.

[210] See C.P.R. Part 61 and the relevant Practice Direction.

[211] *The Nautik* [1895] P. 121.

[212] See *The Tychy* [1999] 2 Lloyd's Rep. 11.

[213] *The Banco* [1971] P. 137.

which the cause of action arose and against several sister ships in the same ownership, and then serving it on one ship as soon as one whose value is sufficient to satisfy his claim comes within the jurisdiction.[214]

In Admiralty it was considered that the in rem proceedings were primarily a means of obtaining security for the claim and also a means of obtaining jurisdiction on the merits of the claim by arresting the ship within the jurisdiction. In 1997 the House of Lords in *The Indian Grace (No. 2)*[215] recognised that in reality an action in rem is an action against the owner, and not the ship. This decision of the House of Lords has been criticised both in England[216] and elsewhere.[217] However, in the opinion of other authors,[218] this decision helped significantly to replace fiction with reality: it contributed to the understanding that an in rem claim "is an action against a defendant with particular benefits for the claimant rather than an action against the ship as the 'wrongdoer'".[219] At first sight, considering an in rem claim as a claim against the owner goes against the traditional[220] and world-wide understanding that, as the literal expression itself indicates, an in rem claim is a claim against the *res*. In Admiralty, the distinctive feature of the old action in rem has always been the ability of the maritime claimant to proceed directly against the ship; if the person interested in defending the claim appears in the proceedings, or acknowledges service of the in rem claim form, an in personam claim may materialise in addition against the defendants.[221] This personal jurisdiction arises only in relation to the person liable for the claim; it does not extend to a bona fide purchaser of the ship. In relation to certain types of claim[222] it is possible to establish jurisdiction on the merits, even if there is no substantive link between the claim and the jurisdiction other than the presence of the arrested ship in the jurisdiction.[223]

---

[214] *The Berny* [1979] Q.B. 80; Senior Courts (formerly Supreme Court) Act 1981 s.21(8).

[215] *The Republic of India v India Steamship Co Ltd (No. 2) (The Indian Grace (No. 2))* [1998] 1 AC 878 (HL).

[216] See inter alia Teare, [1998] L.M.C.L.Q. 33; Derrington (2007) 123 L.Q.R. 358.

[217] See inter alia *Kuo Fen Ching v Dauphin Offshore Engineering & Trading Pte Ltd* [1999] 3 S L R 721; *The Irina Zharkikh and Ksenia Zharkikh* [2001] 2 N Z L R 801; [2001] 2 Lloyd's Rep 319; *Comandate Marine Corp v Pan Australia Shipping Pty Ltd* [2006] FCAFC 192.

[218] See Jackson, Enforcement of Maritime Claims (4th edn, L.L.P. 2005) 2–3.

[219] *ibid.*

[220] In the words of Sir George Jessel MR: "You may in England and in most countries proceed against the ship. The writ [now claim form] may be issued against the owner of such a ship, and the owner may never appear, and you may get your judgment against the ship without a single person being named from beginning to end. That is an action in rem, and it is perfectly well understood that the judgment is against the ship." (*The City of Mecca* (1881) 5 PD 106, 112). cf *The Indian Grace (No. 2)* [1988] AC 878 (HL).

[221] *The Dictator* [1892] P 304; *The Gemma* [1899] P 285 (CA); *The Burns* [1907] P 137; *The Dupleix* [1912] P 8; *The Joannis Vatis (No. 2)* [1922] P 213; *The Beldis* [1936] P 51; *The Banco* [1971] P 137; *The August 8* [1983] 1 Lloyd's Rep 351((PC) Singapore); *The Nordglimt* [1988] 1 QB 183; *The Maciej Rataj* [1992] 2 Lloyd's Rep 552; *The Anna H* [1995] 1 Lloyd's Rep 11.

[222] Senior Courts Act (formerly Supreme Court) 1981 s.20(2).

[223] On the jurisdictional effects of arrest of ships see Ruiz Abou-Nigm, The Arrest of Ships in Private International Law (O.U.P., 2011).

CHAPTER 6

SOVEREIGN AND DIPLOMATIC IMMUNITY

The courts of England are, generally speaking, open to the whole world. In   6–001
particular, the possession of foreign nationality is no bar to being a claimant or a
defendant. It is quite common for English courts to try disputes between
foreigners with no connection whatsoever with England. This is because the
parties have agreed to litigate in England, attracted no doubt by the high
reputation for impartiality which English justice enjoys among those who can
afford it.

There is, however, one class of persons who cannot sue, namely alien enemies,
and three classes of persons who cannot as a general rule be sued, namely foreign
sovereign States; foreign diplomats; and international organisations and their
members. These latter will now be discussed.

FOREIGN STATES

At common law, no foreign sovereign State could be sued in the English courts   6–002
without its consent.[1] The immunity was derived ultimately from the rules of
public international law and from the maxim of that law, *par in parem non habet
imperium*. These rules of public international law became part of the English
common law.[2] In the nineteenth century and for most of the twentieth century the
"absolute" rule of immunity prevailed, whereby foreign sovereign states were
accorded immunity for all activities, whether governmental or commercial. But
the increase in state trading in the twentieth century led a number of states
(including the United States) to develop what is generally known as the
"restrictive" theory of immunity, resting upon a distinction between acts of
government, *acta jure imperii*, and acts of a commercial nature, *acta jure
gestionis*.[3] Under the restrictive theory, states were immune in respect of acts of
government but not in respect of commercial acts. The United Kingdom was slow
to adopt the restrictive theory, and it was even said that "the English courts accord

---

[1] *Duke of Brunswick v King of Hanover* (1844) 6 Beav. 1; (1848) 2 H.L.C. 1.
[2] *The Cristina* [1938] A.C. 485 at 490, per Lord Atkin. See Marasinghe, (1991) 54 M.L.R. 664.
[3] See *Kuwait Airways Corp v Iraqi Airways Co* [1995] 1 W.L.R. 1147.

to foreign States immunity to an extent to which no other State would accord immunity either to this country or to any other State".[4]

In 1981, however, the House of Lords finally adopted the restrictive theory.[5] The Privy Council had earlier held that a foreign government was not entitled to immunity in an action in rem against a ship used for trading purposes,[6] and the Court of Appeal had held, by a majority, that a State was not entitled to immunity in respect of commercial transactions.[7] The judgment of Lord Denning M.R. in that case was later described as marking "the definitive absorption by the common law of the restrictive theory of sovereign immunity".[8]

6–003   Lord Wilberforce sought to define the effect of the new approach in *I Congreso del Partido*[9]:

> "In considering, under the 'restrictive' theory whether state immunity should be granted or not, the court must consider the whole context in which the claim against the state is made, with a view to deciding whether the relevant act(s) upon which the claim is based, should, in that context, be considered as fairly within an area of activity, trading or commercial, or otherwise of a private law character, in which the state has chosen to engage, or whether the relevant act(s) should be considered as having been done outside that area, and within the sphere of governmental or sovereign activity".

The boundary between the two areas is not a fixed one. In *Holland v Lampen-Wolfe,*[10] a professor of international relations at an American university was seconded to teach on a Master's course provided for US military personnel serving at a base in England. She alleged that the defendant, the educational services officer at the base, defamed her in a written report. He pleaded state immunity, arguing that he was acting as an official of the United States in an official capacity.

6–004   The House of Lords upheld the plea of immunity. As Lord Cooke of Thorndon put it:

> "changing concepts and circumstances may call on occasion for some extension of the field of the doctrine. At the present day, I think, a state may reasonably claim to have welfare and educational responsibilities towards the members of its armed forces. In turn the quality and efficiency of the forces may be strengthened if the state discharges those responsibilities. In their discharge the state may reasonably claim that it should not be subject to interference by other states or their courts".

In 1972 a comprehensive European Convention on State Immunity, severely restricting the scope of the doctrine, was concluded under the auspices of the

---

[4] Cohn, (1958) 34 B.Y.I.L. 260.

[5] *The I Congreso del Partido* [1983] 1 A.C. 244; see Fox, (1982) 98 L.Q.R. 94.

[6] *The Philippine Admiral* [1977] A.C. 373.

[7] *Trendtex Trading Corporation v Central Bank of Nigeria* [1977] Q.B. 529.

[8] *Alcom Ltd v Republic of Colombia* [1984] A.C. 580, per Lord Diplock.

[9] [1983] 1 A.C. 244.

[10] [2000] 1 W.L.R. 1573 (noted Yang, [2001] C.L.J. 17) (where the matter was still governed by the common law owing to the exclusion of cases related to visiting armed forces from Pt I of the State Immunity Act 1978 by s.16 of the Act).

Council of Europe and came into force in 1976.[11] It prompted legislation in the United Kingdom, the State Immunity Act 1978. The United Nations General Assembly adopted a Convention on Jurisdictional Immunities of States and Their Property on December 16, 2004, which adopts similar principles; it is not yet in force.[12]

State Immunity Act 1978

The law of sovereign immunity in the United Kingdom is now largely regulated by the State Immunity Act 1978, which was designed in part to implement the European Convention, but is worldwide in effect.[13] The Act goes considerably further than the Convention in restricting immunity. It applies to any foreign or Commonwealth State other than the United Kingdom, and it applies not only to the state itself but also to the sovereign or other Head of State in his or her public capacity,[14] to the government of the state, and any department of its government.[15]

6–005

There is no express reference to the servants and agents of foreign states, but as the House of Lords held in *Jones v Ministry of the Interior of Saudi Arabia*,[16] there is "a wealth of authority" to show that a foreign state is entitled to claim immunity for its servants as it could if sued itself, though in some cases there could be doubt whether the conduct of an individual, although a servant or agent of the state, had a sufficient connection with the state to entitle it to claim immunity for his conduct.

At common law a difficult question that often arose was whether a state corporation or agency could claim to be an emanation of the foreign state and thus entitled to immunity. The Act deals with this problem through the concept of a "separate entity". A separate entity which is distinct from the executive organs of the foreign government, and is capable of suing and being sued, is not entitled to immunity unless the proceedings relate to something done by it in the exercise of sovereign authority[17] and the circumstances are such that the State would have

---

[11] The text of the Convention is printed in Cmnd. 5081. For a commentary, see Sinclair, (1973) 22 I.C.L.Q. 254. The Convention has so far only eight ratifications, including that by the United Kingdom.

[12] The United Kingdom has signed but not ratified it. art.30 of the Convention provides that it will enter into force some time after the 30th ratification; at the time of writing it has only eleven ratifications. However, it has been considered as customary international law in *Cudak v Lithuania* [2010] E.H.R.R. 15 at paras 63 to 66. See also Gardiner, (2006) 55 I.C.L.Q. 407.

[13] See generally, Fox, *The Law of State Immunity* (O.U.P., Oxford, 2002).

[14] s.20 applies the Diplomatic Privileges Act 1964 (see para.6–018) to Heads of State, and this applies to a Head in both the public and private capacities: *Aziz v Aziz (Sultan of Brunei intervening)* [2007] EWCA Civ 712; [2008] 2 All E.R. 501. A former Head of State continues to enjoy immunity in respect of acts done as part of his official functions as Head of State: *R. v Bow Street Magistrate, Ex p. Pinochet Ungarte (No.3)* [2000] A.C. 147. See the Resolution of the *Institut de droit international* on immunities from jurisdiction and execution of Heads of State and Government in international law, (2000–2001) 69 Annuaire de l'Institut 742.

[15] s.14(1).

[16] [2006] UKHL 26; [2007] 1 A.C. 270.

[17] Which means an act *iure imperii*; see above, para.6–002 and *Kuwait Airways Corp v Iraqi Airways Co* [1995] 1 W.L.R. 1147.

been immune.[18] It may still be difficult for the courts to determine whether a "separate entity" was acting "in the exercise of sovereign authority".[19]

6–006 Provision is made for the application of the Act by Order in Council to the constituent territories of a federal state.[20] The effect of such an Order is that some or all of the Act's provisions apply to the constituent territory as they apply to a state. The position where no such Order has been made was examined in *Pocket Kings Ltd v Safenames Ltd*[21]:

> A court in the Commonwealth of Kentucky, a state of the United States of America, ordered the transfer to itself of a domain name, deemed to be a "gambling device" under Kentucky law. Proceedings were begun in England against the Commonwealth of Kentucky seeking a declaration that the court would not recognise or enforce the order.

The court held that the Commonwealth of Kentucky, being one of the constituent territories of the US, was not itself a state for the purposes of s.14(1)) of the Act. If it were to be treated as a "separate entity" it would have immunity in respect of "anything done by it in the exercise of sovereign authority" but it was held that this meant the sovereign authority of the entity recognised as a state, here the US. What had been done in Kentucky was an exercise of State and not federal authority; accordingly, the Commonwealth of Kentucky could not claim state immunity under the Act.

Exceptions to the immunity rule

6–007 Section 1 of the Act lays down what is still the general rule, namely that a state is immune from the jurisdiction of the courts of the United Kingdom, and that they must give effect to this immunity even though the state does not appear. The next 10 sections lay down exceptions to this general rule. It is important to bear in mind that none of these exceptions (except the first) confers jurisdiction on the English courts which otherwise they would not have: they merely remove an immunity which otherwise would exist.

A state is not immune in the following types of proceedings:

(1) Proceedings in respect of which the state has submitted to the jurisdiction of the courts of the United Kingdom.[22]
     At common law, sovereign immunity could be waived by or on behalf of the foreign state, but the doctrine was confined within very narrow limits. Waiver had to take place at the time when the court was asked to exercise jurisdiction[23]; it could not be inferred from a prior contract to submit to the

---

[18] s.14(1) and (2).

[19] See, e.g., *Koo Golden East Mongolia v Bank of Nova Scotia* [2007] EWCA Civ 1443; [2008] Q.B. 717 (central bank of Mongolia a separate entity but acted in bullion transaction in exercise of sovereign authority).

[20] s.14(5).

[21] [2009] EWHC 2529 (Ch); [2010] Ch. 438. See *Bank of Credit and Commerce International (Overseas) Ltd v Price Waterhouse* [1998] Ch. 84 (Ruler of Abu Dhabi); *R. (on the application of HRH Sultan of Pahang) v Secretary of State for the Home Department* [2011] EWCA Civ 616.

[22] s.2(1).

[23] *Mighell v Sultan of Johore* [1894] 1 Q.B. 149.

jurisdiction of the court[24] or to arbitration.[25] The Act has made a far-reaching and welcome change by providing that a state may submit after the dispute has arisen, or by a prior written agreement.[26] It will also be deemed to have submitted if it institutes the proceedings, or intervenes or takes any step in the proceedings, unless the intervention was solely for the purpose of claiming immunity, or unless it was in reasonable ignorance of facts entitling it to immunity, and immunity is claimed as soon as reasonably practical.[27] A submission in respect of any proceedings extends to an appeal, but not to a counterclaim unless it arises out of the same legal relationship or facts as the claim.[28] The submission must be in specific terms; a mere statement that a government would waive any right of sovereign immunity, with no reference to the jurisdiction of any country's courts, may not suffice.[29]

The Supreme Court considered a number of related issues in *NML Capital Ltd v Argentina*.[30] An action was brought in England on a New York judgment in favour of a "vulture fund"[31] and against the Republic of Argentina. The bonds issued by Argentina provided that any related judgment would be binding on Argentina and could be enforced in any court to whose jurisdiction Argentina could be subject by a suit upon the judgment. It was held that this constituted a waiver of state immunity applying to the proceedings in England.[32]   **6–008**

A written submission to arbitration by a state is submission to proceedings (including those in relation to enforcement) in the courts of the United Kingdom relating to the arbitration, unless contrary provision is made or the arbitration agreement is between states.[33]

(2) Proceedings relating to a commercial transaction entered into by the state.[34] This exception is extremely important and is much wider than the corresponding provision in the European Convention. "Commercial transaction" is defined to mean (a) any contract for the supply of goods or

---

[24] *Kahan v Pakistan Federation* [1951] 2 K.B. 1003; *Baccus S.R.L. v Servicio Nacional del Trigo* [1957] 1 Q.B. 438.

[25] *Duff Development Co v Government of Kelantan* [1924] A.C. 797.

[26] s.2(2).

[27] s.2(3), (4) and (5).

[28] s.2(6).

[29] *Svenska Petroleum Exploration AB v Government of the Republic of Lithuania (No 2)* [2006] EWCA Civ 1529; [2007] Q.B. 886.

[30] [2011] UKSC 31, [2011] 2 A.C. 495.

[31] A vulture fund buys at a discount the debts of sovereign states that are in acute financial difficulty then seeks to enforce the debt.

[32] At paras 57–61 and 127–130. A similar result was reached in corresponding proceedings in the Brussels Court of Appeal; but the French Cour de Cassation, basing itself on customary international law, held that Argentina was immune as waivers of sovereign immunity need not only to be express but also specially drafted as to cover diplomatic assets.

[33] State Immunity Act 1978 s.9. See Fox, (1988) 37 I.C.L.Q. 1 at 11–18; *Svenska Petroleum Exploration AB v Government of the Republic of Lithuania (No 2)* [2006] EWCA Civ 1529; [2007] Q.B. 886.

[34] s.3(1)(a). This confirms the decision of the Court of Appeal in *Trendtex Trading Corp v Central Bank of Nigeria* [1977] Q.B. 529.

services; (b) any loan or other transaction for the provision of finance (and any guarantee or indemnity in respect thereof or of any other financial obligation); and (c) any other transaction or activity (whether of a commercial, industrial, financial, professional or other similar character) into which a state enters otherwise than in the exercise of sovereign authority.[35] But it does not include a contract of employment: that is made a separate exception.[36] *In NML Capital Ltd v Argentina*,[37] the underlying transaction was clearly a "transaction for the provision of finance" but the Supreme Court decided, by a majority, that the exception did not extend to actions to enforce a foreign judgment, even if that judgment was itself based on a commercial transaction.

6–009   (3)   Proceedings relating to an obligation of the state which by virtue of a contract (whether a commercial transaction or not) falls to be performed wholly or partly in the United Kingdom.[38]

This would include contracts made in the exercise of sovereign authority provided they are to be performed here.

(4)   Proceedings relating to a contract of employment between the state and an individual where (a) the contract was made in the United Kingdom or (b) the work is to be wholly or partly performed there.[39]

This exception does not apply if either (a) at the time when the proceedings are brought, the employee is a national of the foreign state, or (b) at the time when the contract was made, the employee was neither a national of nor habitually resident in the United Kingdom.[40] But it does apply in each of these cases if the work is for an office, agency or establishment maintained by the state in the United Kingdom for commercial purposes, unless the employee was, at the time when the contract was made, habitually resident in the foreign state.[41] Nor does the exception apply to proceedings concerning the employment of members of a diplomatic mission or consular post.[42]

(5)   Proceedings in respect of death or personal injury, or damage to or loss of tangible property, caused by an act or omission in the United Kingdom.[43]

---

[35] s.3(3). On the phrase "the exercise of sovereign authority" see *Kuwait Airways Corp v Iraqi Airways Co* [1995] 1 W.L.R. 1147 and cf. *Littrell v Government of the United States (No.2)* [1995] 1 W.L.R. 82.
[36] Exception (4), below.
[37] [2011] UKSC 31; [2011] 2 A.C. 495.
[38] s.3(1)(b).
[39] s.4(1).
[40] s.4(2). For the meaning of "national of the United Kingdom" see s.4(5) as amended by British Nationality Act 1981 Sch.7.
[41] s.4(3). See *Egypt v Gamal-Eldin* [1996] 2 All E.R. 237 (drivers attached to medical office of embassy; not for a "commercial" purpose).
[42] s.16(1)(a).
[43] s.5. See *Nigeria v Ogbonna* (2011) UKEAT/0585/10; [2012] 1 W.L.R. 139 (personal injury includes mental ill-health; available even if consequent on a discrimination claim, and on facts to employee not within the exception as employed in a diplomatic mission).

(6) Proceedings relating to any interest of the state in, or its possession or use of, immovable property in the United Kingdom, or any obligation of the state arising therefrom.[44]

(7) Proceedings relating to any interest of the state in movable or immovable property by way of succession, gift or *bona vacantia*.[45]

The fact that a state claims an interest in any property does not preclude the court from exercising any jurisdiction relating to the estates of deceased persons or persons of unsound mind or to insolvency, the winding up of companies or the administration of trusts.[46]   **6–010**

(8) Proceedings relating to United Kingdom patents, trademarks and similar rights belonging to the state, or to the alleged infringement by the state in the United Kingdom of any such rights, including copyright.[47]

(9) Proceedings relating to the state's membership of a corporate or unincorporated body or a partnership which has members other than states and is incorporated or constituted under the law of the United Kingdom or is controlled from or has its principal place of business in the United Kingdom.[48]

(10) Actions in rem against a ship belonging to the state, or actions in personam for enforcing a claim in connection with such a ship, if at the time when the cause of action arose the ship was in use or intended for use for commercial purposes.[49]   **6–011**

A similar provision applies to actions in rem against a cargo belonging to the state if both the cargo and the ship were in use or intended for use for commercial purposes, and to actions in personam for enforcing a claim in connection with such a cargo.[50]

(11) Proceedings relating to a state's liability for value added tax, customs duty, agricultural levy, or rates in respect of premises occupied by it for commercial purposes.[51]

Indirect impleading

So far we have assumed (except in exception (10) above) that the question of sovereign immunity arises in proceedings in which the state is named as defendant in an action in personam, i.e. direct impleading. But at common law the doctrine of sovereign immunity protected a foreign state not only in direct proceedings against it but also in indirect proceedings against property in its   **6–012**

---

[44] s.6(1). See *Intro Properties (U.K.) Ltd v Sauvel* [1983] Q.B. 1019.
[45] s.6(2).
[46] s.6(2).
[47] s.7.
[48] s.8.
[49] s.10(1) and (2). This confirms the decision of the Privy Council in *The Philippine Admiral* [1977] A.C. 373. "Commercial purposes" are defined in s.17(1).
[50] s.10(4).
[51] s.11.

possession or control or in which it claimed an interest. Thus if a foreign state had an interest in property situated in England, whether proprietary, possessory or of some lesser nature, an action which affects its interest would be stayed, even though it was not brought against it personally but was, e.g. an action in rem against a ship[52] or an action in personam against its bailee[53] or agent.[54] The rule was not limited to ownership, and applied to lesser interests which might not merely be not proprietary but not even possessory, so that it applied to property under the control of the foreign state[55] and perhaps also to property in respect of which it had no beneficial interest but only the legal title.[56]

The Act implicitly assumes that these rules of the common law will continue to apply.[57] Moreover, it specifically provides that the court may entertain proceedings against a person other than a state notwithstanding that the proceedings relate to property in its possession or control, or in which it claims an interest, if the state would not have been immune had the proceedings been brought against it, or, in the case where the state merely claims an interest, if the claim is neither admitted nor supported by prima facie evidence.[58]

Enforcement of foreign judgments

6–013   Section 31(1) of the Civil Jurisdiction and Judgments Act 1982 provides that a foreign judgment against a foreign State (other than the United Kingdom or the State in which the foreign proceedings were brought) is to be recognised and enforced in England if (and only if) (a) the normal conditions for recognition and enforcement of judgments are fulfilled, and (b) *mutatis mutandis* the foreign State would not have been immune if the foreign proceedings had been brought in the United Kingdom.[59]

Execution

6–014   In general, even if a state is not immune under one of the exceptions, its property is not subject to execution for the enforcement of a judgment or arbitration award.[60] This is subject to two important exceptions: execution is allowed if (a) the state consents in writing, or (b) the property is for the time being in use or

---

[52] *The Parlement Belge* (1880) 5 P.D. 197; *The Jupiter* [1924] P. 236; *The Cristina* [1938] A.C. 485; *The Arantzazu Mendi* [1939] A.C. 256.
[53] *USA and Republic of France v Dollfus Mieg et Cie* [1952] A.C. 582.
[54] *Rahimtoola v Nizam of Hyderabad* [1958] A.C. 379.
[55] *The Cristina* [1938] A.C. 485; *The Arantzazu Mendi* [1939] A.C. 256.
[56] *Rahimtoola v Nizam of Hyderabad* [1958] A.C. 379 at p.403.
[57] See ss.2(4)(b), 6 and 10.
[58] s.6(4). See *Juan Ysmael & Co. Inc. v Indonesian Government* [1955] A.C. 75; *Rahimtoola v Nizam of Hyderabad* [1958] A.C. 379 at p.410; *Shearson Lehman Bros. Inc. v Maclaine Watson & Co. Ltd* [1988] 1 W.L.R. 16.
[59] See *NML Capital Ltd v Argentina* [2011] UKSC 31; [2011] 2 A.C. 495 (Argentina not entitled to immunity in New York had the 1978 Act's rules applied, because of the "commercial transactions" exception, so not immune from enforcement).
[60] s.13(2)(b).

intended for use for commercial purposes.[61] A central bank is accorded special treatment under the Act. If (as is likely) it is a "separate entity", its property is immune from execution, even if it is not entitled to immunity from suit; and its property is not regarded as in use or intended for use for commercial purposes.[62] In practice, therefore, the property of a state's central bank will only be liable to execution if it has waived, in writing, its immunity from execution.

Service of process

The Act provides for a method of service on a state by transmission of the claim form through the Foreign and Commonwealth Office to the state's Ministry of Foreign Affairs.[63] A state which appears in proceedings cannot thereafter object that service was not properly effected upon it.[64] Service by transmission of the claim form through the Foreign and Commonwealth Office is not necessary if the state has agreed to a different method of service.[65]

6–015

Miscellaneous

Provision may be made by Order in Council to restrict or extend the immunities of a state under the Act. If they exceed those accorded by the law of that state in relation to the United Kingdom, they may be restricted. If they are less than those required by any treaty or convention to which that state and the United Kingdom are parties, they can be extended.[66]

A certificate from the Secretary of State is conclusive evidence on any question whether any country is a state, whether any territory is a constituent territory of a federal state, or as to the person or persons to be regarded as the head or government of a state.[67]

6–016

The scope of the doctrine

The scope of the doctrine of sovereign or state immunity continues to attract controversy. In *Holland v Lampen-Wolfe*,[68] the House of Lords was pressed to declare that the doctrine was inconsistent with art.6 of the European Convention

6–017

---

[61] s.13(3) and (4). "Commercial purposes" are defined in s.17(1). See *A Co Ltd v Republic of X.* [1990] 2 Lloyd's Rep. 520; *Continental Tranfert Technique Ltd v Nigeria* [2010] EWHC 780 (Comm) at para.12.

[62] s.14(4).

[63] s.12(1); *Kuwait Airways Corp v Iraqi Airways Co* [1995] 1 W.L.R. 1147.

[64] s.12(3).

[65] s.12(6).

[66] s.15.

[67] s.21(a).

[68] [2000] 1 W.L.R. 1573 (where the matter was still governed by the common law owing to the exclusion of cases related to visiting armed forces from Pt I of the State Immunity Act 1978 by s.16 of the Act); *Jones v Ministry of Interior of the Kingdom of Saudi Arabia (Secretary of State for Constitutional Affairs intervening)* [2006] UKHL 26 at [14] and [64]; applied to the immunities of an international organisation in *Entico Corporation Ltd v United Nations Educational Scientific and Cultural Association* [2008] EWHC 531 (Comm); [2008] 2 All E.R. (Comm) 97.

on Human Rights which deals with the right of access to justice. It held that there was no inconsistency, principally because art.6 forbids a Contracting State from denying individuals the benefit of its powers of adjudication and cannot operate to give the courts additional powers of adjudication.

The House was referred to cases then pending before the European Court of Human Rights in which similar issues were being raised. One of those cases, *Al-Adsani v United Kingdom*,[69] which concerned an action against the Kuwaiti Government based on allegations of torture, was considered by the Grand Chamber of that court. It was held that art.6 was engaged but that the United Kingdom, in enacting the State Immunity Act, was within the "margin of appreciation" that States enjoy to limit Convention rights. The Act pursued a legitimate aim, compliance with international law, and was proportionate. The majority held that, while the prohibition of torture had achieved the status of a peremptory norm in international law, it was unable to discern a firm basis for concluding that, as a matter of international law, a state no longer enjoyed immunity from civil suit in the courts of another state where acts of torture were alleged. This decision was followed in a second House of Lords decision, *Jones v Ministry of the Interior of the Kingdom of Saudi Arabia*.[70]

In *Cudak v Lithuania*,[71] however, the Grand Chamber of the European Court of Human Rights held that there could be circumstances in which a national court's refusal to entertain a case on the ground of state immunity would violate art.6; this was where the national court, in failing to preserve a reasonable relationship of proportionality, had overstepped the margin of appreciation and had impaired the very essence of the applicant's right of access to a court.

FOREIGN DIPLOMATS

6–018   Before 1964, the immunity from suit of foreign ambassadors and members of their staffs was secured by the common law as reinforced by the Diplomatic Privileges Act 1708, which has always been treated as declaratory of the common law. That Act was passed in the following remarkable circumstances[72]:

> The Russian ambassador to the Court of St. James was arrested and removed from his coach in London for non-payment of a debt of £50. Tsar Peter the Great resented this affront so highly that he demanded that the Sheriff of Middlesex and all others concerned in the arrest should be punished with instant death. But, to the amazement of the Tsar's despotic court, Queen Anne informed him "that she could inflict no punishment upon the meanest of her subjects, unless it was warranted by the law of the land; and therefore she was persuaded that he would not insist upon impossibilities. To appease the wrath of Peter, a Bill was brought into Parliament and duly passed. A copy of this Act, elegantly engrossed and illuminated, accompanied by a letter from the Queen, was then sent to Moscow by ambassador extraordinary.

---

[69] (App. No. 35763/97) (2001) 34 E.H.R.R. 273. cf. *R. v Bow Street Metropolitan Stipendiary Magistrate and Others, Ex p. Pinochet Ugarte (No.3)* [2000] A.C. 147, which did not deal with state immunity from civil actions based on allegations of torture.

[70] [2006] UKHL 26; [2007] 1 A.C. 270. See Fox, (2006) 2 E.H.R.L.R.; Wright, (2010) 30 O.J.L.S. 143.

[71] [2010] E.C.H.R. 15869/02.

[72] *Taylor v Best* (1854) 14 C.B. 487 at 491–493.

The Act of 1708 has now been repealed and replaced by the Diplomatic Privileges Act 1964, which gives effect to the Vienna Convention on Diplomatic Relations 1961.[73] Section 1 of the Act provides that the following provisions of the Act shall have effect in substitution for any previous enactment or rule of law; and s.2 enacts those articles of the Convention which are set out in the First Schedule as part of the law of the United Kingdom. Hence, much of the old case law is now only of historical interest.

The most important single change effected by the Convention in the law of the United Kingdom is that it abolishes the principle of absolute immunity: diplomatic immunity, even that of the ambassador himself, is now only qualified. The Convention divides persons entitled to diplomatic immunity into three categories[74]:

6–019

(1) "diplomatic agents", namely, the head of the mission and members of his or her diplomatic staff;
(2) "members of the administrative and technical staff", i.e. persons employed in secretarial, clerical, communications and public relations duties, such as typists, translators, coding clerks and press and cultural representatives; and
(3) "members of the service staff", namely, members of the staff of the mission in its domestic service, such as cooks, cleaners, porters and chauffeurs. These three classes are each entitled to differing degrees of immunity from civil and criminal jurisdiction.

Foreign consuls

Foreign consuls and members of their staffs are not within the terms of the Vienna Convention on Diplomatic Relations. It appears to be accepted that they are entitled to immunity from suit at common law in respect of their official acts, but not in respect of their private acts.[75] This is confirmed by the Consular Relations Act 1968, which enacts as part of the law of the United Kingdom those articles of the Vienna Convention on Consular Relations 1963 which are set out in the First Schedule.[76] Under that Convention, consular officers and consular employees[77] are not amenable to jurisdiction in respect of acts performed in the exercise of consular functions, with some exceptions in civil actions.

6–020

---

[73] The full text of the Convention is printed in (1961) 10 I.C.L.Q. 600. For a commentary on the Act and the Convention, see Buckley, (1965–66) 41 B.Y.I.L. 321. See also Brown, (1988) 37 I.C.L.Q. 53.
[74] Diplomatic Privileges Act 1964 Sch.1, art.1.
[75] *Engelke v Musman* [1928] A.C. 433 at 437–438; Oppenheim, International Law, 8th edn, Vol. I. p.841; Beckett (1944) 21 B.Y.I.L. 34.
[76] s.1(1).The full text of the Convention is printed in (1964) 13 I.C.L.Q. 1214.
[77] For definitions, see Sch.1, art.1(d) and (e).

Evidence

6–021 If in any proceedings any question arises whether or not any person is entitled to immunity from suit, a certificate issued by or under the authority of the Secretary of State stating any fact relating to that question is conclusive evidence of that fact.[78]

Waiver

6–022 Diplomatic and consular immunity may be waived by the sending state.[79] A waiver by the head or acting head of a diplomatic mission is deemed to be a waiver by that state.[80] Waiver must always be express, except that the initiation of proceedings precludes the claimant from invoking immunity from jurisdiction in respect of any counterclaim directly connected with the principal claim.[81] There is no requirement that waiver must take place in the face of the court, as in waiver of sovereign immunity at common law. Waiver of immunity from jurisdiction in civil or administrative proceedings does not imply waiver of immunity in respect of execution of the judgment, for which a separate waiver is required.[82]

INTERNATIONAL ORGANISATIONS

6–023 The position of international organisations, much more recently arrived on the international scene than sovereigns and their diplomatic representatives, rests on statute rather than common law.[83] The International Organisations Act 1968 empowers the Crown by Order in Council to confer various degrees of immunity from suit and legal process upon any international organisation of which the United Kingdom is a member[84]; on representatives to the organisation or representatives on, or members of, any of its organs, committees or sub-committees, on specified high officers of the organisation, and persons employed by or serving as experts or as persons engaged on missions for the organisation[85]; and on specified subordinate officers or servants of the organisation.[86] No such

---

[78] Diplomatic Privileges Act 1964 s.4; Consular Relations Act 1968 s.11.

[79] Diplomatic Privileges Act 1964 Sch.1, art.32(1); Consular Relations Act 1968, Sch.1, art.45(1). See the curious case of *Fayed v Al-Tajir* [1988] Q.B. 712.

[80] Diplomatic Privileges Act 1964 s.2(3); Consular Relations Act 1968 s.1(5).

[81] Diplomatic Privileges Act 1964 Sch.1, art.32(2) and (3); Consular Relations Act 1968 Sch.1, art.45(2) and (3). See *High Commissioner for India v Ghosh* [1960] 1 Q.B. 134.

[82] Art.32(4) of Sch.1 of the 1964 Act; art.45(4) of Sch.1 of the 1968 Act.

[83] This seems to be clear from some of the issues in the litigation resulting from the collapse of the International Tin Council; see especially *J. H. Rayner (Mincing Lane) Ltd v Dept of Trade and Industry* [1989] Ch. 72, where the C.A. examines, inter alia, the European Community's lack of immunity.

[84] s.1(1), (2)(b), and Sch.1, Pt I, para.1. The International Organisations Act 1981 s.2 extends this to international commodity organisations of which the UK is not a member. For the capacity of international organisations of which the UK is not a party to sue as plaintiff, see *Arab Monetary Fund v Hashim (No.3)* [1991] 2 A.C. 114.

[85] s.1(2)(c), (3), and Sch.1, Pt II, para.9.

[86] s.1(2)(d), and Sch.1, Pt III, para.14.

immunity may be conferred on any person as the representative of the United Kingdom or as a member of his or her staff.[87]

The Act also empowers the Crown by Order in Council to confer immunity from suit on the judges, registrars or other officers of any international tribunal, on parties to any proceedings before any such tribunal, and their advocates and witnesses[88]; and on representatives of foreign states and their official staffs attending conferences in the United Kingdom.[89]

If in any proceedings a question arises whether any person is or is not entitled to any immunity, a certificate issued by or under the authority of the Secretary of State stating any fact relating to that question is conclusive evidence of that fact.[90] Orders in Council have been made under this and earlier Acts conferring immunity from suit on a large number of international organisations and (in most cases) on their representatives, officers and staffs. These organisations range from the United Nations Organisation to the International Coffee, Cocoa and Sugar Organizations. The possibility of waiver of the immunities thereby conferred is specifically provided for by these Orders in Council; but the term is not defined.

This type of immunity has been challenged as offending against the right guaranteed by art.6 of the European Convention on Human Rights which deals with the right of access to justice. As in the case of the similar challenge to state immunity,[91] this challenge has failed: the immunity of international organisations reflected generally recognised rules of public international law and could not be regarded as imposing a disproportionate restriction on the right of access to court as embodied in art.6.[92]

[87] s.1(6)(b).
[88] s.5(1), (2).
[89] s.6.
[90] s.8. See also *Zoernsch v Waldock* [1964] 1 W.L.R. 675.
[91] See above, para.6–017.
[92] *Entico Corp Ltd v United Nations Educational Scientific and Cultural Association* [2008] EWHC 531 (Comm); [2008] 1 Lloyd's Rep. 673.

CHAPTER 7

RECOGNITION AND ENFORCEMENT OF FOREIGN JUDGMENTS

It is sometimes easier to obtain a judgment than to enforce it. A claimant who, for example, successfully sues in Japan for breach of contract or for tort and is awarded damages may discover that the defendant has removed all his or her assets to England. The judgment cannot be enforced in Japan, because there are no assets there. The officers charged with the enforcement of judgments in the English legal system will not act on a Japanese judgment. The Japanese officials cannot act in England. What is the claimant to do? This chapter seeks to answer that question and deal with the sometimes difficult issues surrounding the recognition and enforcement of foreign judgments.[1]

7–001

There is an important distinction between the recognition of a judgment as one entitled to be given some weight in the court of the forum and the enforcement of that judgment. A court must recognise every foreign judgment which it enforces, but it need not enforce every foreign judgment which it recognises. Some foreign judgments do not lend themselves to enforcement, but only to recognition. Examples are a judgment dismissing a claim (unless it orders the unsuccessful claimant to pay costs, as it frequently does); or a declaratory judgment; or a decree of divorce or nullity.[2] But there may be orders ancillary to such decrees which, because they order the payment of money, are capable of enforcement: for example orders dealing with the financial consequences of divorce or orders as to costs.

This chapter is divided into two parts: the first deals with the modern rules as to the recognition and enforcement of judgments given in Member States of the European Union, principally to be found in the Brussels I Regulation[3]; the second deals with the much older and more complex rules, derived partly from common law and partly from statute, as to judgments from other countries.

---

[1] See, generally, Read, *Recognition and Enforcement of Foreign Judgments* (Harvard University Press, Cambridge MA, 1938); Patchett, *Recognition of Commercial Judgments and Awards in the Commonwealth* (Butterworths, London, 1984).

[2] For the recognition in England of foreign decrees of divorce and nullity, see Chapter 9. This chapter is concerned only with foreign judgments in personam.

[3] Council Regulation No. 44/2001 of 22 December 2000 on the recognition and enforcement of judgments in civil and commercial matters. See generally, Chapter 4.

The Brussels I Regulation

7–002   The jurisdictional provisions of the Brussels I Regulation were discussed in Chapter 4. For reasons of clarity of exposition, the provisions of the Regulation on jurisdiction and on the recognition and enforcement of judgments are dealt with in different chapters, but it cannot be stressed too strongly that the Regulation is one and indivisible and must be considered as a whole.

    The Regulation's rules on jurisdiction provide ample guarantees for the defendant: as a general rule the defendant can only be sued in the courts of his or her domicile[4]; if the defendant does not enter an appearance the court itself must declare of its own motion that it has no jurisdiction, unless its jurisdiction is derived from the provisions of the Regulation[5]; the court must stay the proceedings unless satisfied that the defendant had an opportunity to be heard.[6] The strictness of these provisions has its counterpart in the extreme liberality of the provisions on recognition and enforcement, which are designed to allow judgments given in one Member State to run freely throughout the European Union. The principles on which the Regulation is based seek to minimise the obstacles to the recognition and enforcement of judgments. As a general rule, a court of a Member State in which enforcement is sought may not investigate the jurisdiction of the court in another Member State which gave the judgment: it is for the original court to determine that it has jurisdiction and that determination cannot, in general, be questioned in another Member State at the recognition and enforcement stage.

    The provisions on recognition and enforcement apply only to judgments within the scope of the Regulation as defined in art.1.[7] Subject to that, "judgment" means any judgment given by a court or tribunal of a Member State, whatever the judgment may be called, including a decree, order, decision or writ of execution, as well as the determination of costs or expenses by an officer of the court[8]; and not only money judgments but also, for example, injunctions and orders for specific performance. Provisional or protective orders are included[9]; though not if they are granted without notice to the defendant.[10]

7–003   It is important to note that under the Regulation the enforcement procedures apply to all judgments within its scope, whether or not they are against persons domiciled in a Member State and whether or not the original court assumed jurisdiction on a ground set out in the Regulation or a ground to be found in its national law. So, an English judgment against a New York resident where the jurisdiction of the English court was based on the temporary presence of the defendant in England is enforceable in France; and a French judgment against a New York resident where the jurisdiction of the French court was based on the

---

[4] arts 2 and 3.
[5] art.26(1).
[6] art.26(2).
[7] See above, para.4–013.
[8] art.32.
[9] Case 143/78 *De Cavel v De Cavel (No.1)* [1979] E.C.R. 1055.
[10] Case 123/79 *Denilauler v Couchet Frères* [1980] E.C.R. 1553.

French nationality of the claimant under art.14 of the French Civil Code is enforceable in England. It is immaterial that the grounds for jurisdiction are "exorbitant", and that their use is prohibited as against defendants domiciled in a Member State by art.3(2) of the Regulation. Article 59 of the Brussels Convention allowed a Contracting State to enter into a binding agreement with a non-Contracting State that it will not recognise judgments given in other Contracting States on exorbitant grounds against defendants domiciled or habitually resident in that non-Contracting State. The United Kingdom took advantage of this provision to make agreements with Canada[11] and Australia.[12] The effect of those agreements is preserved under the Brussels I Regulation,[13] but no new agreements may be made.

Recognition

Article 33(1) of the Regulation provides simply that "a judgment given in a Member State shall be recognised in the other Member States without any special procedure being required". If an interested party raises the recognition of a judgment as the principal issue in a dispute, the Regulation provides that that party may apply for a decision that the judgment be recognised[14]: in England, this means applying for the registration of the judgment in the High Court.[15]   7–004

Grounds on which recognition may be refused

Recognition may be refused on certain limited grounds set out in arts 34 and 35. They are as follows: 7–005

(1) recognition is manifestly contrary to public policy in the Member State in which recognition is sought.

The case-law establishes that this ground is to be relied upon only in exceptional circumstances[16]; the word "manifestly", which was not in the equivalent Brussels Convention provision, was included here to emphasise this point. To safeguard the ready recognition of judgments, the Regulation must be interpreted so as to set limits on the use which may be made of national understandings of public policy. The ECJ has held that they can be used to deny recognition only where recognition or enforcement would be at variance to an unacceptable degree with the legal order of the state in which enforcement is sought; a manifest breach of a rule of law regarded as essential in the legal order of that state or of a right recognised as being fundamental within that legal

---

[11] By an Exchange of Notes of November 7, 1994 and February 17, 1995, published in the UK as Cmnd. 2894. For UK legislative provision, see Reciprocal Enforcement of Foreign Judgments (Canada) Order 1987 (SI 1987/468), as amended by SI 1995/2708.

[12] See Reciprocal Enforcement of Foreign Judgments (Australia) Order 1994 (SI 1994/1901) and *New Cap Reinsurance Corp Ltd (In Liquidation) v Grant* [2011] EWCA Civ 971.

[13] art.72.

[14] art.33(2). See also art.33(3) which removes any doubt as to the jurisdiction of a court to determine any incidental question of recognition.

[15] See, generally, Civil Procedure Rules, Pt 74.

[16] Case C-78/95 *Hendrickman v Magenta Dock & Verlag G.m.b.H.* [1996] E.C.R. I-4943.

order.[17] A judgment will be recognised even if the defendant was debarred from defending,[18] and even fraud in obtaining the judgment may not attract the defence, at least if there is a remedy in the foreign court.[19]

(2) where the judgment was given in default of appearance, if the defendant was not served with the document which instituted the proceedings or with an equivalent document in sufficient time to enable him to arrange for his defence, unless the defendant failed to commence proceedings to challenge the judgment when it was possible for him to do so.

7–006   The notion of "default of appearance" has an autonomous meaning and may be rather larger in scope than in the law of some Member States.[20] It is not enough simply to show that the defendant was aware of the proceedings; "service" must be understood in a way consonant with art.30 of the Brussels I Regulation itself[21] and with other Regulations, notably what is now Regulation 1393/2007 on the service in the Member States of judicial and extrajudicial documents in civil or commercial matters.[22] The final clause means that a defendant who becomes aware of the proceedings in a particular Member State or the ensuing judgment and decides not to take steps open to him or her in that state is debarred from alleging that there was no service or no opportunity to arrange a defence. If a defendant does seek to challenge a default judgment and fails in the challenge after a full hearing, the default nature of the original judgment can no longer be relied upon.[23]

(3) if the judgment is irreconcilable with a judgment given in a dispute between the same parties in the State in which recognition is sought.

(4) if the judgment is irreconcilable with an earlier judgment given in another Member State or a third State involving the same cause of action and between the same parties, provided that the earlier judgment fulfils the conditions necessary for its recognition in the Member State addressed.

In this context, "irreconcilable" means having mutually exclusive consequences.[24]

Other issues going to recognition

7–007   The court in which recognition is sought is not entitled to review the merits of the judgment.[25] Nor can it question the jurisdiction of the court which gave the judgment, and may not apply the test of public policy to rules relating to

---

[17] Case C-7/98 *Krombach v Bamberski* [2000] E.C.R. I-1935.
[18] Case C-394/07 *Gambazzi v Daimler Chrysler Canada Inc* [2009] E.C.R. I-2563.
[19] *Interdesco S.A. v Nullifire Lt*d [1992] 1 Lloyd's Rep. 180.
[20] Case C-78/95 *Hendrickman v Magenta Dock & Verlag GmbH* [1996] E.C.R. I-4943 (assertion by defendant that the lawyer who appeared for him was not authorised to do so: held "in default of appearance" for purposes of the Brussels Convention though not under the national law of the forum).
[21] See para.4–075.
[22] *Tavoulareas v Tsavliris (No 2)* [2006] EWCA Civ 1772; [2007] 1 W.L.R. 470.
[23] Case C-420/07 *Apostolides v Orams* [2009] E.C.R. I-3571.
[24] e.g. Case 145/86 *Hoffman v Krieg* [1988] E.C.R. 645 (maintenance order inconsistent with divorce granted in State of intended enforcement).
[25] art.36.

jurisdiction.[26] Recognition must be refused where the judgment conflicts with the provisions of arts 8 to 14 (insurance), 15 to 17 (consumer contracts) or 22 (exclusive jurisdiction).[27] But even in these cases, the court in which enforcement is sought is bound by the findings of fact on which the court of origin based its jurisdiction.[28] However, the court in which enforcement is sought is not bound by the findings of the original court as to whether the case is within the scope of the Regulation.[29]

An application for the recognition or enforcement of a judgment given in another Member State may (but need not) be stayed if an "ordinary appeal" against the judgment has been lodged.[30] It would seem that any form of appeal known to English law will be treated as an "ordinary appeal",[31] but "ordinary appeal" has an autonomous meaning not dependent on the procedural law of the Member State of origin.[32]

Enforcement

The general provision in the Regulation is that a judgment given in a Member State and enforceable in that state shall be enforced in another Member State when, on the application of any interested party, it has been declared enforceable there.[33] There is no equivalent of this declaration of enforceability in the law of any part of the United Kingdom, so the Regulation makes a special provision for enforcement there, requiring only the registration of the judgment in the relevant part of the United Kingdom on the application of any interested party.[34] In England, application for registration is made in the High Court. It is implicit in the decision of the European Court in *De Wolf v Cox*[35] that no other mode of enforcement is available, such as an action on the judgment at common law. 7–008

The party against whom enforcement is sought is not entitled to be heard at this stage of the proceedings,[36] or even to be informed of the application for registration. This is intended to preserve the element of surprise and to prevent the removal of assets from the State where enforcement is sought. Once registered, the judgment has, for the purposes of enforcement, the same force and effect as if it had been originally been given by the registering court, and enforcement powers and proceedings are available on that basis.[37] Either party

---

[26] art.35(3).
[27] art.35(1)(3). Note the surprising omission of individual employment cases (arts 18 to 21) from this list.
[28] art.35(2).
[29] Case 29/76 *LTU v Eurocontrol* [1976] E.C.R. 1541.
[30] art.37.
[31] See art.46(2), though that strictly applies only to that Article.
[32] See Case 43/77 *Industrial Diamond Supplies v Riva* [1977] E.C.R. 2175 ("ordinary appeal" must be understood as meaning any appeal which forms part of the normal course of an action and which, as such, constitutes a procedural development which any party must reasonably expect).
[33] art.38(1).
[34] art.38(2).
[35] Case 42/76, [1976] E.C.R. 1541.
[36] art.41.
[37] Civil Jurisdiction and Judgments Order 2001 (SI 2001/3929) Sch.1, para.2(2).

may appeal,[38] with a single further appeal on a point of law.[39] The court considering an appeal may set aside registration only on one of the grounds specified in arts 34 and 35, those already considered in the context of recognition; under no circumstances may the foreign judgment be reviewed as to its substance.[40]

European Enforcement Order

7–009   Steps were taken in 2004 to simplify enforcement procedures in respect of judgments in uncontested claims.[41] A claim is regarded as uncontested if:

(a)   the debtor has expressly agreed to it by admission or by means of a settlement which has been approved by a court or concluded before a court in the course of proceedings; or

(b)   the debtor has never objected to it, in compliance with the relevant procedural requirements under the law of the Member State of origin, in the course of the court proceedings; or

(c)   the debtor has not appeared or been represented at a court hearing regarding that claim after having initially objected to the claim in the course of the court proceedings, provided that such conduct amounts to a tacit admission of the claim or of the facts alleged by the creditor under the law of the Member State of origin; or

(d)   the debtor has expressly agreed to it in an authentic instrument.[42]

In these cases the requirement of *exequatur*, that is the need for a declaration of enforceability, is abolished and the judgment is to be recognised and enforced in other Member States without any possibility of the judgment-debtor opposing its recognition.[43]

European order for payment

7–010   International litigation, outside the area of family law, is typically between corporations and involves large sums of money. That is certainly true of the reported cases cited in this book. It tends to conceal the great volume of relatively low-value cross-border business. Unpaid bills are a major problem to small and medium enterprises and late payment of sums which are clearly due can drive small traders into insolvency. To address this problem the European Union established a European order for payment procedure available in every Member

---

[38] arts 42 and 43.
[39] art.44 and Annex IV.
[40] art.45.
[41] European Parliament and Council Regulation 805/2004 of 21 April 2004 creating a European Enforcement Order for uncontested claims (OJ L143/15, 30.4.2004) as amended by Regulation 1869/2005 (OJ L300/6, 17.11.2005) and Regulation 1103/2008 (OJ L304/80, 14.11.2008).
[42] art.3(1).
[43] art.5.

State (except Denmark) by adopting Regulation 1896/2006 of the European Parliament and of the Council of 12 December 2006 creating a European order for payment procedure.[44]

The declared purpose of the Regulation is to simplify, speed up and reduce the costs of litigation in cross-border cases concerning uncontested pecuniary claims, and to permit the free circulation of European orders for payment throughout the Member States by laying down minimum standards, compliance with which renders unnecessary any intermediate proceedings in the Member State of enforcement prior to recognition and enforcement.[45] It therefore lays down a harmonised procedure, as an alternative to whatever other procedures may be available under national law.[46] It applies when at least one of the parties is, when the application is submitted, domiciled or habitually resident in a Member State other than the Member State of the court seised.[47]

An application for a European order for payment is made using a standard form prescribed in the Regulation. It gives full details of the claim and a description of evidence supporting it.[48] The court to which application is made is required to examine, as soon as possible and on the basis of the application form, whether the requirements of the Regulation are met and whether the claim appears to be well founded. The Regulation states that this examination "may take the form of an automated procedure", and a judge will not usually be involved.[49] If need be, the applicant may be given an opportunity to complete or rectify an application.[50] At no stage in the procedure is legal representation required.[51]

If the application is in order, the court must issue, as soon as possible and normally within 30 days of the lodging of the application, a European order for payment in a prescribed standard form, which is accompanied by a copy of the application form. The order presents the defendant a choice between paying to the claimant the amount stated in the order and opposing the order by lodging with the court of origin a statement of opposition, to be sent within 30 days of service of the order on him, failing which the order becomes enforceable.[52] There is another standard form for opposition to the order; the defendant does not have to specify any reasons.[53] A statement of opposition has the effect of transferring

7–011

---

[44] For text, see OJ L399/1, 30.12.2006.

[45] art.1(1).

[46] See art.1(2).

[47] art.3. Domicile is determined under arts 59 and 60 of the Brussels I Regulation (Reg. No 44/2001 on jurisdiction and the recognition and enforcement of judgments in civil and commercial matters). Jurisdiction is governed by the rules in that Regulation; but if the claim relates to a contract concluded by a person, the consumer, for a purpose which can be regarded as being outside his trade or profession, and if the defendant is the consumer, only the courts in the Member State in which the defendant is domiciled have jurisdiction. See arts 3(2) and 6.

[48] art.7.

[49] art.8, and see Recital (16).

[50] art.9.

[51] art.24.

[52] art.12; for rules as to service of the order, see arts 13–15.

[53] art.16.

the proceedings to be dealt in accordance with the rules of ordinary civil procedure unless the claimant has explicitly requested that the proceedings be terminated in that event.[54]

If no statement of opposition has been lodged with the court of origin, that court must without delay declare the European order for payment enforceable and send the enforceable European order for payment to the claimant.[55] It is enforced under the same conditions as an enforceable decision issued in the Member State of enforcement.[56]

European small claims procedure

7–012   The process of developing harmonised claims procedures within the European Union was taken further with the adoption of Regulation 861/2007 of the European Parliament and of the Council of 11 July 2007 establishing a European Small Claims Procedure, applying from 1 January 2009 in all Member States except Denmark.[57] It is intended to simplify and speed up litigation concerning small claims in cross-border cases, and to reduce costs; the new procedure is available to litigants as an alternative to the procedures existing under national law.[58] It applies where the value of a claim does not exceed €2000.[59] The definition of a cross-border case and the rules as to jurisdiction are the same as in the European order for payment procedure.[60]

The European Small Claims Procedure is a written procedure. The court will hold an oral hearing if it considers it to be necessary or if a party so requests; it may refuse a request for an oral hearing if it considers that an oral hearing is obviously not necessary for the fair conduct of the proceedings.[61] The procedure is begun by the lodging of a prescribed standard form of claim, which includes a description of evidence supporting the claim and is accompanied, where appropriate, by any relevant supporting documents. A copy of the claim form, completed or rectified if necessary, is served, with its supporting documents and an answer form, on the defendant; these documents must be dispatched within 14 days of the receipt of a properly filled in claim form. The defendant must submit a response within 30 days of service of the claim form and answer form, by filling in the answer form and sending it, with any relevant supporting documents, to the court. Within 14 days of receipt of the response from the defendant, the court must send a copy, together with any relevant supporting documents, to the claimant.[62]

---

[54] art.17.
[55] art.18.
[56] art.21; note the translation requirements. There are very limited grounds on which enforcement may be refused: art.22.
[57] For text, see OJ L199/1, 31.7.2007.
[58] art.1.
[59] art.2(1).
[60] art.3.
[61] art.5. The hearing (and the taking of any evidence) may be by video conference or other communications technology: arts 8, 9.
[62] See art.5 generally; the procedure allows for counterclaims.

The court has 30 days after the receipt of the final document within which to give   7–013
judgment, to request further information, to take evidence (and the court, not the
parties, decides what evidence is required), or to summon the parties to an oral
hearing to be held within 30 days of the summons. The court must give the
judgment either within 30 days of any oral hearing or after having received all
information necessary for giving the judgment.[63] Legal representation is not
mandatory.[64] A judgment given in a Member State in the European Small Claims
Procedure is to be recognised and enforced in another Member State without the
need for a declaration of enforceability and without any possibility of opposing
its recognition.[65]

In the small claims procedure choice of law issues can arise, but the low value
of the claim and the simplicity of the issues will almost always mean that they are
effectively ignored. Even if they are raised, the applicable law is very likely to be
that of a Member State.

Mediation Directive

Various forms of mediation, in commercial and in family cases, are an   7–014
increasingly common feature of civil procedure in many countries. In 2008 the
European Union adopted a Directive dealing with mediation in cross-border
disputes,[66] to be transposed into national law by 21 May 2011.[67] Its declared aim
is to facilitate access to alternative dispute resolution and to promote the amicable
settlement of disputes by encouraging the use of mediation and by ensuring a
balanced relationship between mediation and judicial proceedings.[68] "Mediation"
is defined as "a structured process, however named or referred to, whereby two or
more parties to a dispute attempt by themselves, on a voluntary basis, to reach an
agreement on the settlement of their dispute with the assistance of a mediator".[69]
Mediation initiated by the parties or suggested or ordered by a court or prescribed
by the law of a Member State is included, as is mediation conducted by a judge
who is *not* responsible for any judicial proceedings concerning the dispute in
question.[70]

The effect of the Directive is limited to cross-border disputes, defined as those
in which at least one of the parties is domiciled[71] or habitually resident in a
Member State[72] other than that of any other party on the date on which the parties

---

[63] art.7.
[64] art.10.
[65] art.20(1).
[66] European Parliament and Council Directive 2008/52/EC of 21 May 2008 on certain aspects of
mediation in civil and commercial matters, OJ L136/3, 24.05.2008.
[67] art.12(1).
[68] art.1.
[69] art.3. Member States are to take certain steps to ensure the quality of mediation services: art.4; for
confidentiality of mediation, see art.7.
[70] *ibid.*
[71] Domicile is determined in accordance with arts 59 and 60 of the Brussels I Regulation; see
para.4 015, above: Directive, art.2(3).
[72] Denmark is not included in the term "Member State" for the purposes of the Directive.

agree to use mediation after the dispute has arisen, or mediation is ordered by a court, or an obligation to use mediation arises under national law, or the court invites the parties to use mediation.[73]

7–015   Member States must ensure that parties who choose mediation in an attempt to settle a dispute are not subsequently prevented from initiating judicial proceedings or arbitration in relation to that dispute by the expiry of limitation or prescription periods during the mediation process.[74]

Member States must ensure that it is possible for the parties, or for one of them with the explicit consent of the others, to request that the content of a written agreement resulting from mediation be made enforceable. The content of such an agreement is to be made enforceable unless, in the case in question, either the content of that agreement is contrary to the law of the Member State where the request is made or the law of that Member State does not provide for its enforceability.[75] The outcome, a judgment or decision or an authentic instrument, will be enforceable under the Brussels I Regulation.

Proposals for further changes

7–016   In its Green Paper on the revision of the Brussels I Regulation,[76] the Commission proposed the abolition of all intermediate measures to recognise and enforce foreign judgments, the *exequatur* requirement.

Noting that this had already been done for uncontested claims and in some cases under the Maintenance Regulation, the Commission declared that it was difficult to justify, in an internal market without frontiers, that citizens and businesses have to undergo the expense in terms of costs and time to assert their rights abroad. If, as the Commission thought, applications for declarations of enforceability were almost always successful and recognition and enforcement of foreign judgments was very rarely refused, aiming for the objective of abolishing the *exequatur* procedure in all civil and commercial matters could be seen as realistic.

JUDGMENTS RENDERED OUTSIDE THE MEMBER STATES

7–017   Where the judgment was given in a State outside the European Union, the recognition and enforcement of foreign judgments rest on common law developments with some statutory interventions.

English courts have recognised and enforced foreign judgments from the seventeenth century onwards.[77] It was at one time supposed that the basis of this enforcement was to be found in the doctrine of comity,[78] and a healthy fear that if

---

[73] art.2(1).

[74] art.8.

[75] art.6(1).

[76] COM (2009) 174 final, 21.4.2009.

[77] See Sack in *Law, a Century of Progress, 1835–1935* (1937), Vol. 3, pp.342, 382–384.

[78] On the decline, fall, but apparent survival of the notion of comity, see Collins, in Fawcett (ed), *Reform and Development of Private International Law* (Oxford University Press, Oxford, 2002) at 89–110.

foreign judgments were not enforced in England, English judgments would not be enforced abroad.[79] But later this theory was superseded by what is called the doctrine of obligation,[80] the best-known formulation of which is that of Blackburn J. in *Schibsby v Westenholz*[81]:

> "We think that . . . the true principle on which the judgments of foreign tribunals are enforced in England is . . . that the judgment of a court of competent jurisdiction over the defendant imposes a duty or obligation on the defendant to pay the sum for which judgment is given, which the courts in this country are bound to enforce".

The Court of Appeal examined afresh in *Adams v Cape Industries plc*[82] the reason foreign judgments should be recognised, adopting a more practical approach:

7–018

> "Underlying it all must be some notion of comity, but this cannot be comity on an individual nation-to-nation basis, for our courts have never thought it necessary to investigate what reciprocal rights of enforcement are conceded by the foreign country, or to limit their exercise of jurisdiction to that which they would recognise in others. The most one can say is that the duty of positive law first identified in *Schibsby v Westenholz* must stem from an acknowledgement that the society of nations will work better if some foreign judgments are taken to create rights which supersede the underlying cause of action, and which may be directly enforced in countries where the defendant or his assets are to be found. But this tells one nothing of practical value about how to identify the foreign judgments which have this effect".

Whatever the theoretical basis of the rules in this area, the English courts came to recognise the conclusiveness of foreign judgments, first those in favour of defendants[83] and then those in favour of claimants.[84]

At one time, it was always open to a claimant who had obtained a foreign judgment to sue all over again in England relying on the original cause of action. The Civil Jurisdiction and Judgments Act 1982[85] ended this possibility, so that a foreign judgment, like an English judgment, extinguished the original cause of action which is said to merge in the judgment-debt. The avenues now open to the judgment-creditor are to bring an action in England on the judgment-debt, or, where the relevant statutes apply, to register the foreign judgment in the High Court. Something will be said about each of these methods of proceeding, before a consideration of the principles followed by the English courts: they are largely, but not wholly, the same whichever method is used.

---

[79] See *Roach v Garvan* (1748) 1 Ves. Sen. 157 at 159; *Wright v Simpson* (1802) 6 Ves. 714 at 730; *Alves v Bunbury* (1814) 4 Camp. 28.
[80] See per Parke B. in *Russell v Smyth* (1842) 9 M. & W. 810 at 819 and *Williams v Jones* (1845) 13 M. & W. 628 at 633.
[81] (1870) L.R. 6 Q.B. 155, 159. See Ho, (1997) 46 I.C.L.Q. 443.
[82] *Adams v Cape Industries plc* [1990] Ch. 433.
[83] *Ricardo v Garcias* (1845) 12 Cl. & F. 368.
[84] *Godard v Gray* (1870) L.R. 6 Q.B. 139. cf. *Castrique v Imrie* (1870) L.R. 4 H.L. 414.
[85] s.34.

Action on the judgment-debt at common law

7–019   At common law, a judgment creditor seeking to enforce a foreign judgment in England may bring an action on the foreign judgment.[86] A creditor can apply for summary judgment under Pt 24 of the Civil Procedure Rules on the ground that the defendant has no real prospect of successfully defending the claim; and if the application is successful, the defendant will not be allowed to defend at all. The speed and simplicity of this procedure, coupled with the tendency of English judges narrowly to circumscribe the defences that may be pleaded to an action on a foreign judgment, mean that foreign judgments are in practice enforceable in England much more easily than they are in many civil law countries, where enforcement is easy in theory but difficult in practice because of the tendency of the courts to enlarge the scope of the defence that enforcement would be contrary to *ordre public* or public policy.[87] Thus it came about that foreign judgments are more easily enforceable in England than are English judgments in some foreign countries.[88]

Enforcement by registration under statute

7–020   A foreign judgment under which a sum of money is payable may be enforceable in England under statute by a slightly more direct process of registration. The two most important statutes are the Administration of Justice Act 1920, and the Foreign Judgments (Reciprocal Enforcement) Act 1933.

Part II of the Administration of Justice Act 1920 provides for the enforcement of judgments of superior courts in the United Kingdom by registration in designated Commonwealth countries and, conversely, for the enforcement of judgments of superior courts of those Commonwealth countries by registration in the United Kingdom. The Act has been applied by Order in Council to numerous countries of the Commonwealth. Registration is discretionary and not as of right, since it can be refused unless the registering court "in all the circumstances of the case . . . thinks it just and convenient that the judgment should be enforced in the United Kingdom".[89] Moreover, registration may not be ordered if the original court acted without jurisdiction (though no attempt is made to elucidate the meaning of this term), or if the defendant establishes any of a limited number of defences which are very similar to those available at common law.[90]

The Foreign Judgments (Reciprocal Enforcement) Act 1933 provides for the reciprocal enforcement by registration of judgments of courts in the United Kingdom on the one hand, and judgments of courts in politically foreign countries, and also in countries of the Commonwealth outside the United Kingdom, on the other. (The reason for including Commonwealth judgments was the intention that the regime of the 1933 Act would gradually replace that of the

---

[86] This does not apply in the context of insolvency, where special rules apply: *Rubin v Eurofinance SA* [2010] EWCA Civ 895; [2011] Ch. 133 (under appeal to the Supreme Court).
[87] See Gutteridge, (1932) 13 B.Y.I.L. 49; Graupner, (1963) 12 I.C.L.Q. 367.
[88] See the Report of the Foreign Judgments (Reciprocal Enforcement) Committee, Cmd.4213 (1932) at paras 2, 9, 10 and 14.
[89] s.9(1).
[90] s.9(2).

1920 Act). The 1933 Act is much more important than that of 1920. This is because the 1933 Act is drafted in much more detail, and contains specific rules on when foreign courts are deemed to have jurisdiction for the purposes of the Act, and on what defences the defendant may set up in opposition to an application to register a foreign judgment. These rules are modelled very closely on those of the common law. Registration of a judgment under the Act is available as of right instead of merely at discretion as under the Act of 1920.

Sections 18 and 19 of the State Immunity Act 1978 provide for the recognition (but not the enforcement) of judgments rendered against the United Kingdom in states which are parties to the European Convention on State Immunity.

Relationship of common law and statute

The Acts of 1920 and 1933 are of limited geographical application and the judgments of very many foreign countries are outside their scope. There thus remains a considerable area within which enforcement of a foreign judgment at common law is the only process possible. The provisions of the Act of 1933 were deliberately framed so as to reproduce the rules of the common law as closely as possible,[91] though, as the Foreign Judgments (Reciprocal Enforcement) Committee conceded, it was found desirable to make one or two very slight departures from the common law in order to secure international agreements which would be more likely to operate satisfactorily in practice.[92] The question therefore arises whether the provisions of the Act as to the jurisdiction of foreign courts, and as to the scope of the defences, can legitimately be invoked by a court which is asked to enforce a foreign judgment at common law, even though the Act has not been extended by Order in Council to the foreign country in question. After some fluctuation of opinion among judges of first instance, it was laid down by the Court of Appeal that "one cannot ascertain what the common law is by arguing backwards from the provisions of the Act".[93]

7–021

Jurisdiction of the foreign court

The most fundamental of all requirements for the recognition or enforcement of foreign judgments in England (whether at common law or under the 1920 or 1933 Acts) is that the foreign court should have had jurisdiction according to the English rules of the conflict of laws. These are "indirect jurisdiction rules", and there is no reason for them to mirror the ("direct jurisdiction") rules governing the jurisdiction of the English courts.

7–022

Where there is uniformity of direct jurisdiction rules, as within the European Union, there is no need for a separate set of indirect jurisdiction rules: it is enough that the judgment was given by a court in a Member State. The ill-fated Judgments Project of the Hague Conference on Private International Law set out

---

[91] Report of the Foreign Judgments (Reciprocal Enforcement) Committee, Cmd.4213 (1932), paras 2, 16, 18 and Annex V, para.7.
[92] *ibid.*, Annex V, para.7.
[93] *Henry v Geoprosco International Ltd* [1976] Q.B. 726, 751.

to achieve the same result on a global scale.[94] Where, however, national laws differ widely as to rules of direct jurisdiction, a court asked to recognise and enforce a foreign judgment has to have some criteria for determining whether the assumption of jurisdiction by the foreign court was proper. In a famous leading case[95]:

> The claimant brought an action in England on a judgment of a court in the island of Tobago. The defendant had never been in the island, nor had he submitted to its jurisdiction. There had been a substituted service, valid by the law of Tobago, effected by nailing a copy of the writ to the court-house door. Lord Ellenborough refused to enforce the judgment. He said: "Can the island of Tobago pass a law to bind the rights of the whole world? Would the world submit to such an assumed jurisdiction?"

Where jurisdiction exists

The defendant's residence or presence in the foreign country

7–023   In *Emanuel v Symon*[96] Buckley L.J. set out a list of circumstances in which a foreign court would be regarded as having jurisdiction. One was "where [the defendant] was resident in the foreign country when the action began". It is natural for the claimant to sue in the defendant's home country, and it is well settled that the residence of the defendant is a sufficient basis for recognition.[97]

International practice is coming to speak of habitual residence, preferred in the discussions during the Hague Judgments Project, or domicile, as in the European Union instruments. However, it was the term "residence" that was used by Buckley L.J. in *Emanuel v Symon*, and the same word is to be found in the Foreign Judgments (Reciprocal Enforcement) Act 1933, under which a foreign court is deemed to have had jurisdiction if "the judgment debtor, being a defendant in the original court, was at the time when the proceedings were instituted resident in, or being a body corporate had its principal place of business in, the country of that court".[98]

Residence has no precise definition: in most cases, it imports physical presence; but the two can be separated, so that the defendant is physically present in the foreign country but cannot be said to be resident there, or is a resident but was not physically present at the relevant time. The English courts have taken the view that at common law temporary residence and even mere presence in the foreign country suffices,[99] a rule which mirrors the extensive claims made for the jurisdiction of the English courts. As a matter of principle, it is not clear that the

---

[94] See McClean, in Fawcett (ed), *Reform and Development of Private International Law* (Oxford University Press, Oxford, 2002) at 255–271; Barcelo and Clermont (eds), *A Global Law of Jurisdiction and Judgments: Lessons from The Hague* (2002).

[95] *Buchanan v Rucker* (1809) 9 East 192; cf. *Sirdar Gurdyal Singh v Rajah of Faridkote* [1894] A.C. 670 at 683–684, per Lord Selborne.

[96] [1908] 1 K.B. 302 at 309. cf. *Schibsby v Westenholz* (1870) L.R. 6 Q.B. 155 at 161; *Rousillon v Rousillon* (1880) 14 Ch.D. 351 at 371.

[97] *Schibsby v Westenholz* (1870) L.R. 6 Q.B. 155 at 161. *Actor sequitur forum rei* is the time-honoured maxim.

[98] s.4(2)(a)(iv).

[99] See for early authority see *Carrick v Hancock* (1895) 12 T.L.R. 59 where, however, the defendant had submitted to the jurisdiction of the foreign court.

bases upon which the English courts take jurisdiction (especially as the doctrine of forum non conveniens moderated their effect) should be translated unchanged into bases for the recognition of the jurisdiction of a foreign court. However the Court of Appeal in *Adams v Cape Industries plc*[100] held that:

> "the voluntary presence of an individual in a foreign country, whether permanent or temporary and whether or not accompanied by residence, is sufficient to give the courts of that country territorial jurisdiction over him under our rules of private international law".

That case involved a corporate defendant, and the Court of Appeal sought to clarify the, necessarily artificial, concept of the presence of a corporation. It held that the English court was likely to treat a corporation as present in a country only if either (a) it had established and maintained at its own expense a fixed place of business of its own in that country and for more than a minimal period of time had carried on its own business there by its servants or agents, or (b) a representative of the corporation had for more than a minimal period of time been carrying on the corporation's business (not the representative's own business) at or from some fixed place of business in that country. The mere presence there of a representative of the corporation would not suffice.[101] Nor would it be sufficient if the corporation had a representative resident there who had authority to elicit orders from customers but not to make contracts on its behalf.[102]

7–024

None of this is affected by the appearance of internet trading. The fact that a company has a website accessible in a particular country and can and does accept orders placed via the website does not make it present there.[103] As the Court of Appeal observed:

> "It is true that the Internet and its uses take us into a new world, and that its existence as it were in the ether (but based on servers physically located in the real world) has in general presented novel difficulties to the law and to regulators. It is also true that a website can be both wonderfully expressive and can also, subject to change and removal, be found repeatedly at its web address. The question, however, is whether for current purposes the Internet or a website are fundamentally different from other matters which have enabled business persons to present themselves and their products where they are not themselves present: such as advertisements, salesmen, the post, telephone, telex and the like. We do not believe so ... On the contrary, it might be said that the sheer omnipresence of the Internet would suggest that it does not easily create, outside the jurisdiction or jurisdictions in which its website owners are on established principle already to be found, that presence, partaking in some sense of allegiance, which has been recognised by our jurisprudence and rules of private international law as a necessary ingredient in the enforceability of foreign judgments".[104]

The Foreign Judgments (Reciprocal Enforcement) Act 1933 requires that the corporation must have its principal place of business (and not merely carry on business) in the foreign country.[105] The Act also provides that the foreign court is deemed to have jurisdiction for the purposes of the Act if the defendant (not

---

[100] [1990] Ch. 433.

[101] *Littauer Glove Corporation v F. W. Millington Ltd* (1928) 44 T.L.R. 746.

[102] *Vogel v R. A. Kohnstamm Ltd* [1973] 1 Q.B. 133. cf. *Sfeir & Co. v National Insurance Co. of New Zealand Ltd* [1964] 1 Lloyd's Rep. 330, a case on the Administration of Justice Act 1920.

[103] *Lucasfilm Ltd v Ainsworth* [2009] EWCA Civ 1328; [2010] Ch. 503; the point was not raised in the Supreme Court.

[104] At paras 193–194.

[105] s.4(2)(a)(iv).

necessarily a corporation) had an office or place of business in the foreign country and the proceedings were in respect of a transaction effected through or at that office or place.[106] There does not appear to be any authority for this basis of jurisdiction at common law; but the Foreign Judgments (Reciprocal Enforcement) Committee regarded it as a rational extension of the common law rules.[107]

Submission

7–025 Submission to the jurisdiction of a foreign court can take place in various ways. In the language of the 1933 Act, they are where:

(i)   the judgment debtor, being a defendant in the original court, submitted to the jurisdiction of that court by voluntarily appearing in the proceedings; or

(ii)   the judgment debtor was the claimant in, or counter-claimed in, the proceedings in the original court; or

(iii)   the judgment debtor, being a defendant in the original court, had before the commencement of the proceedings agreed, in respect of the subject matter of the proceedings, to submit to the jurisdiction of that court (or to the jurisdiction of the courts of the relevant country).

The most obvious example is actually case (ii), where the claimant invokes the jurisdiction and thereby is rendered liable to a judgment for the defendant in respect of a counterclaim, cross-action or costs.[108]

7–026 A more frequent situation is that of case, (i) that in which the defendant voluntarily appears in, or takes part in, the foreign proceedings. By that action the defendant becomes subject to the foreign court's jurisdiction, both for the original claim and also for any others the original claimant may add in accordance with the procedural rules of the foreign forum.[109]

A defendant may, however, appear in the foreign proceedings solely to contest the jurisdiction. In those circumstances, it would be perverse to interpret the defendant's action as a submission to the very jurisdiction he or she actively repudiates. The courts showed themselves surprisingly reluctant to accept this glimpse of the obvious, and it was only as a result of the Civil Jurisdiction and Judgments Act 1982 that rationality was introduced into this corner of the law.[110] Section 33 of that Act provides that the defendant shall not be regarded as having submitted to the jurisdiction of an overseas court if he appeared (a) to contest the jurisdiction of the court; (b) to ask the court to dismiss or stay the proceedings on the ground that the dispute should be submitted to arbitration,[111] or to the

---

[106] s.4(2)(a)(v).

[107] Cmd. 4213 (1932), Annex V, para.8.

[108] *Schibsby v Westenholz* (1870) L.R. 6 Q.B. 155 at 161; Foreign Judgments (Reciprocal Enforcement) Act 1933 s.4(2)(a)(ii).

[109] *Murthy v Sivajothi* [1999] 1 W.L.R. 467.

[110] There was an earlier provision, Foreign Judgments (Reciprocal Enforcement) Act 1933 s.4(2)(a)(i), of limited scope.

[111] See *Tracomin S.A. v Sudan Oil Seeds Co. Ltd* [1983] 1 W.L.R. 662 at 1026.

determination of the courts of another country; or (c) to protect or obtain the release of property seized or threatened with seizure in the proceedings.

In some legal systems, an appearance to contest the jurisdiction must be accompanied by an appearance on the merits, although this can sometimes be merely *pro forma*, without substantive argument. Despite earlier authority to the contrary,[112] it is thought that such an appearance when unaccompanied by any positive act addressing the merits will not amount to submission.[113]

Another example of submission is case (iii), where a contract provides that all disputes between the parties shall be referred to the exclusive jurisdiction of a foreign tribunal. In such a case the foreign court is deemed to have jurisdiction over the parties.[114] An agreement to submit may also take the form of an agreement to accept service of process at a designated address. But English courts have stopped short of inferring an agreement to submit from a mere general provision in the foreign law (and not in a statute specifically referring to the particular company) that the shareholder must "elect a domicile" for the service of process,[115] unless the defendant does in fact elect such a domicile.[116]

7–027

As a general rule, an agreement to submit to the jurisdiction of a foreign court must be express: it cannot be implied.[117] If the parties agree, expressly or by implication, that their contract shall be governed by a particular foreign law, it does not follow that they agree to submit to the jurisdiction of the courts which apply it.[118] Nor can any such agreement be implied from the fact that the cause of action arose in a foreign country, nor from the additional fact that the defendant was present there when the cause of action arose.[119]

Where jurisdiction does not exist

The provisions of the Foreign Judgments (Reciprocal Enforcement) Act 1933 as to the jurisdiction of the foreign court are exclusive. That is to say, no judgment can be registered under the Act unless the jurisdiction of the foreign court can be brought under one of the five heads of s.4(2)(a).[120] But the rules of common law as to jurisdiction are not necessarily exclusive, and it has sometimes been suggested that other bases of jurisdiction, often relied on by foreign courts, might be available in England. It seems reasonably clear that this is not the case.

7–028

---

[112] *Boissiere & Co. v Brockner* (1889) 6 T.L.R. 85.

[113] *Marc Rich & Co. AG v Soc. Italiana Impianti PA (No.2)* [1992] 1 Lloyd's Rep. 624. cf. Case 150/80 *Elefanten Schuh GmbH v Jacqmain* [1981] E.C.R. 1671 (a case on submission under art.18 of the Brussels Convention).

[114] *Feyerick v Hubbard* (1902) 71 L.J.K.B. 509; *Jeannot v Fuerst* (1909) 25 T.L.R. 424; Foreign Judgments (Reciprocal Enforcement) Act 1933, s.4(2)(a)(iii).

[115] *Copin v Adamson* (1874) L.R. 9 Ex. 345 (the second replication). The point was reserved in the Court of Appeal: see 1 Ex.D. 17 at 19.

[116] *Vallée v Dumergue* (1849) 4 Exch. 290.

[117] *Sirdar Gurdyal Singh v Rajah of Faridkote* [1894] A.C. 670; *Emanuel v Symon* [1908] 1 K.B. 302; *Vogel v R. A. Kohnstamm Ltd* [1973] 1 Q.B. 133; *Adams v Cape Industries plc* [1990] Ch. 433 (a point not taken on appeal), not following dicta in *Blohn v Desser* [1962] 2 Q.B. 116 at 123, and in *Sfeir & Co. v National Insurance Co. of New Zealand Ltd* [1964] 1 Lloyd's Rep. 330 at 339–340.

[118] *Dunbee Ltd v Gilman & Co. Ltd* [1968] 2 Lloyd's Rep. 394.

[119] *Sirdar Gurdyal Singh v Rajah of Faridkote* [1894] A.C. 670; *Emanuel v Symon* [1908] 1 K.B. 302.

[120] *Société Co-opérative Sidmetal v Titan International Ltd* [1966] 1 Q.B. 828.

So, it is not sufficient that the judgment-debtor possessed property in the foreign country; this is relied upon in Scotland, but has been rejected in England.[121] Nor is it sufficient that the defendant was present in the foreign country at the time when the cause of action arose[122]; nor that the defendant was domiciled there.[123] There is a long chain of dicta extending from 1828 to 1948 suggesting that the courts of a country might have jurisdiction over a defendant who was a national of that country.[124] But there is no actual decision to this effect. On the contrary, nationality as a basis of jurisdiction has more recently been doubted by three High Court judges,[125] and definitely rejected by the Irish High Court.[126] It cannot, therefore, safely be relied upon today. It is obviously inappropriate when the defendant is a British citizen or an American citizen, since in neither case does the political unit (or state) coincide with the law district (or country).

7–029   A question which requires more discussion is whether the jurisdiction of the foreign court would be recognised if the situation were such that, mutatis mutandis, the English court might have assumed jurisdiction, e.g. under the Civil Procedure Rules.[127] The answer seems to be "no". In *Schibsby v Westenholz*,[128] the claimant brought an action in England on a French judgment. The defendant was not in France when the writ was issued (it was served on him in England), nor did he appear or submit to the jurisdiction. It was argued that as the English court would have power to order service out of the jurisdiction on similar facts, it should enforce the French judgment. In rejecting this argument, Blackburn J. said:

> "If the principle on which foreign judgments were enforced was that which is loosely called "comity", we could hardly decline to enforce a foreign judgment given in France against a resident in Great Britain under circumstances hardly, if at all, distinguishable from those under which we, *mutatis mutandis*, might give judgment against a resident in France; but it is quite different if the principle be that which we have just laid down" [i.e. the doctrine of obligation, quoted earlier in this chapter[129]]".

This refusal to include in rules governing recognition a principle found in the English jurisdiction rules may seem surprising. It is, however, clear that English courts do not concede jurisdiction in personam to foreign courts merely because

---

[121] *Emanuel v Symon* [1908] 1 K.B. 302.
[122] *Sirdar Gurdyal Singh v Rajah of Faridkote* [1894] A.C. 670; *Emanuel v Symon* [1908] 1 K.B. 302.
[123] For early dicta to the contrary, see *Turnbull v Walker* (1892) 67 L.T. 767 at 769; *Emanuel v Symon* [1908] 1 K.B. 302 at 308 at 314; *Jaffer v Williams* (1908) 25 T.L.R. 12 at 13; *Gavin Gibson & Co. v Gibson* [1913] 3 K.B. 379 at 385.
[124] *Douglas v Forrest* (1828) 4 Bing. 686; *Schibsby v Westenholz* (1870) L.R. 6 Q.B. 155, 161; *Rousillon v Rousillon* (1880) 14 Ch.D. 351, 371; *Emanuel v Symon* [1908] 1 K.B. 302 at 309; *Gavin Gibson & Co. v Gibson* [1913] 3 K.B. 379, 388; *Harris v Taylor* [1915] 2 K.B. 580 at 591; *Forsyth v Forsyth* [1948] P. 125, 132.
[125] *Blohn v Desser* [1962] 2 Q.B. 116 at 123, per Diplock J.; *Rossano v Manufacturers Life Insurance Co. Ltd* [1963] 2 Q.B. 352 at 382–383, per McNair J.; *Vogel v R. A. Kohnstamm Ltd* [1973] 1 Q.B. 133 at 141, per Ashworth J.
[126] *Rainford v Newell-Roberts* [1962] I.R. 95.
[127] Above, para.5–008.
[128] (1870) L.R. 6 Q.B. 155 at 159 followed in *Turnbull v Walker* (1892) 67 L.T. 767.
[129] Above, para.7–017.

English courts would, in converse circumstances, have power to order service out of the jurisdiction.[130] This means, of course, that in actions in personam English courts claim a wider jurisdiction than they concede to foreign courts.

Defences

The most usual defence pleaded to an action on a foreign judgment at common law is that the foreign court had no jurisdiction to give the judgment according to the recognition rules just examined. Several other defences are available. In considering these defences, it should be borne in mind that, unless otherwise stated, they may be pleaded as a defence to an action on the judgment at common law, or used as grounds for refusing to register the judgment under the Administration of Justice Act 1920 or for setting aside the registration of the judgment under the Foreign Judgments (Reciprocal Enforcement) Act 1933.

7–030

Jurisdiction contrary to a jurisdiction agreement between the parties

Section 32 of the Civil Jurisdiction and Judgments Act 1982 provides that a judgment given by a court of an overseas country cannot be recognised or enforced in the United Kingdom if (a) the bringing of the proceedings in the foreign court was contrary to a valid agreement under which the dispute was to be settled otherwise than by proceedings in the courts of that country; and (b) the judgment debtor did not agree to the bringing of those proceedings, counterclaim or otherwise submit to the jurisdiction of that court.[131] The latter condition means that jurisdiction based on submission is unaffected by s.32.

7–031

Fraud

It is settled that a foreign judgment, like any other, can be impeached for fraud.[132] Such fraud may be either fraud on the part of the court, for example where the judge deliberately made a false decision because of a personal interest in the outcome; or fraud on the part of the successful party in, for example, suppressing evidence or producing forged or perjured evidence; or fraud on the part of both court and party, as where one party bribes the court.

7–032

The difficult question is whether a foreign judgment can be impeached for fraud if, in order to prove the fraud, it is necessary to reopen the merits which have already been decided by the foreign court. Two principles are here in conflict: the principle that foreign judgments are impeachable for fraud, and the principle that the merits cannot be reopened. No English judgment can be impeached for fraud in the absence of fresh evidence: if the former principle

---

[130] *Re Trepca Mines Ltd* [1960] 1 W.L.R. 1273, 1280–1282; *Société Co-opérative Sidmetal v Titan International Ltd* [1966] 1 Q.B. 828.

[131] There was a similar provision (now repealed as redundant) in s.4(3)(b) of the Foreign Judgments (Reciprocal Enforcement) Act 1933, but no authority at common law.

[132] This does not apply to cases under the Brussels I Regulation, which has no defence of fraud; see para.7–005 for the public policy ground under the Regulation which may include some cases of fraud.

prevails, and it is now clear that it does, a foreign judgment is more susceptible to impeachment as no fresh evidence need be presented.

7–033   The leading case is *Abouloff v Oppenheimer & Co.*[133] where Lord Coleridge C.J. said:

> "where a judgment has been obtained by the fraud of a party to a suit in a foreign country, he cannot prevent the question of fraud from being litigated in the courts of this country, when he seeks to enforce the judgment so obtained. The justice of that proposition is obvious: if it were not so, we should have to disregard a well-established rule of law that no man shall take advantage of his own wrong".

The principle was reaffirmed by the House of Lords in *Owens Bank Ltd v Bracco.*[134] In that case:

> The claimant bank claimed to have lent nine million Swiss francs to the defendant, who received the money in cash against signed documents typed on the notepaper of a Geneva hotel. Bracco resisted a claim in the courts of Saint Vincent for the capital lent and interest, denying that he had ever entered into the transaction. The bank succeeded, and sought to register the judgment in England under the Administration of Justice Act 1920, to be met by an argument based on the bank's alleged fraud in making the claim.

Lord Bridge reviewed the cases which, although they have been criticised by academic writers, provided a consistent line of authority for the availability of the defence of fraud in such circumstances. They included four decisions of the Court of Appeal[135]; and there could have been added another Court of Appeal decision in which these cases had been regarded as authoritative but distinguished because the very issue of fraud had been addressed in a separate action in the courts of the foreign country concerned.[136]

7–034   Lord Bridge recognised that as a matter of policy there might be a strong case to be made, in the changed circumstances of the 1990s, for giving to foreign judgments the same finality accorded to English judgments. But both the Administration of Justice Act 1920,[137] applicable to the instant case, and the Foreign Judgments (Reciprocal Enforcement) Act 1933[138] provided for impeachment of the foreign judgment for fraud, and to alter the common law rule would produce such anomalies as to put that possibility out of the question.[139]

In a later Privy Council case, giving rise to similar issues, *Owens Bank Ltd v Etoile Commerciale SA,*[140] Lord Templeman said that "Their Lordships do not regard the decision in *Abouloff's* case with enthusiasm, especially in its application to countries whose judgments the United Kingdom has agreed to register and enforce. In these cases the salutary rule which favours finality in litigation seems more appropriate", but the old rule was not directly in issue.

---

[133] (1882) 10 Q.B.D. 295 at 300, followed in *Vadala v Lawes* (1890) 25 Q.B.D. 310.

[134] [1992] 2 A.C. 443. See also *Jet Holdings Inc. v Patel* [1990] 1 Q.B. 335.

[135] *Abouloff v Oppenheimer* (1882) 10 Q.B.D. 295; *Vadala v Lawes* (1890) 25 Q.B.D. 310; *Syal v Heyward* [1948] 2 K.B. 443; and *Jet Holdings Inc. v Patel* [1990] 1 Q.B. 335.

[136] *House of Spring Gardens Ltd v Waite* [1991] 1 Q.B. 241.

[137] s.9(2)(d).

[138] s.4(1)(a)(iv).

[139] For criticism, see Collier, [1992] C.L.J. 441.

[140] [1995] 1 W.L.R. 44 (P.C.).

Contrary to public policy

A foreign judgment can be impeached if its enforcement or recognition in   **7–035**
England would be contrary to public policy[141]: but there are very few reported
cases in which such a plea has been successful.

In *Re Macartney,*[142] a Maltese judgment ordering the personal representatives
of a deceased putative father to pay perpetual maintenance to the mother of his
illegitimate child was refused enforcement in England on three grounds: (1) it
was contrary to public policy to enforce an affiliation order not limited to the
child's minority[143]; (2) the cause of action, a posthumous affiliation order, was
unknown to English domestic law; and (3) the judgment was not final and
conclusive, because the Maltese court could vary the amount of the payments.[144]
The third ground by itself would have been sufficient to dispose of the case.
Under the second ground, the court relied heavily on an American case[145] in
which a French judgment awarding maintenance to a French son-in-law against
his American father-in-law and mother-in-law was refused enforcement in the
United States.

This American case and *Re Macartney* were disapproved or distinguished in
two later cases, one Canadian, the other English. In *Burchell v Burchell,* [146] an
Ontario court enforced a judgment of an Ohio divorce court ordering a wife to
make a lump-sum payment to her husband, although by the law of Ontario a wife
was not bound to support her husband. In *Phrantzes v Argenti*[147] (which was not
a case on a foreign judgment), Lord Parker C.J. refused to enforce a claim by a
Greek daughter against her father for the provision of a dowry on her marriage as
required by Greek law. His ground for doing so was not that the cause of action
was unknown to English domestic law, but that English law had no remedy for
awarding a dowry, the amount of which in Greek law was within the discretion of
the court and varied in accordance with the wealth and social position of the
father and the number of his children. Given that in some cases an English court
may entertain a claim on a cause of action unknown to English domestic law,
there seems no good reason, despite what was said in *Re Macartney,* for refusing
to enforce a foreign judgment based on such a cause of action. It is not contrary to
public policy to enforce a foreign judgment for what in England would be called
exemplary damages.[148]

On the other hand, the Supreme Court of the Republic of Ireland has refused to
enforce an English order for costs which was ancillary to a divorce decree.[149] The
grounds of this decision were partly that the cause of action was unknown to the

---

[141] See Administration of Justice Act 1920 s.9(2)(f); Foreign Judgments (Reciprocal Enforcement)
Act 1933 s.4(1)(a)(v). For public policy generally, see above, Ch.3.
[142] [1921] 1 Ch. 522.
[143] The notion was that it was undesirable that the illegitimate daughter should spend her whole life in
idleness basking in the Mediterranean sunshine, while father toiled in cloudy England to support her.
[144] See below, paras 7–045 and 9–082.
[145] *De Brimont v Penniman* (1873) 10 Blatchford Circuit Court Reports 436.
[146] [1926] 2 D.L.R. 595.
[147] [1960] 2 Q.B. 19, 31–34.
[148] *S.A. Consortium General Textiles v Sun and Sand Agencies Ltd* [1978] Q.B. 279, 300.
[149] *Mayo-Perrott v Mayo-Perrott* [1958] I.R. 336.

law of the Republic (where divorce was not then allowed), and partly that to enforce an order ancillary to a divorce decree was contrary to Irish public policy.

Contrary to natural justice

7–036   At common law, a foreign judgment can be impeached on the ground that the proceedings were opposed to natural justice; but the limits of this defence are even vaguer than those of public policy, and reported cases in which it has been successfully raised are rarer still. The proceedings are not opposed to natural justice merely because the judgment is manifestly wrong,[150] merely because the court admitted evidence which is inadmissible in England,[151] or did not admit evidence which is admissible in England,[152] for the admissibility of evidence is a matter of procedure and so governed by the *lex fori*.[153]

In *Adams v Cape Industries plc*[154]:

> A default judgment was entered by a United States court in a complex case in which some two hundred claimants claimed in respect of injury caused by exposure to asbestos. Damages were fixed, in effect, by counsel for the claimants after the judge had indicated, without hearing any evidence, that the average recovery should be at a given level and that individual claimants should be allocated to one of a number of broad categories; there was no judicial assessment of damages.

The Court of Appeal held that the concept of procedural natural justice was not limited to cases in which the defendant receives no notice[155] or is given no adequate opportunity to make a defence[156]; it extended to any circumstances which would constitute a breach of the English court's understanding of "substantial justice". Absence of a judicial determination of damages was such a breach.

7–037   It can be argued that reliance on the alleged breach of substantial justice should be excluded if the defendant took, or could have taken, the point in the foreign court. In *Adams v Cape Industries*, Scott J. at first instance regarded the possibility of appeal from, or collateral attack on, the judgment in the courts of the foreign country as immaterial. The Court of Appeal, by analogy with the fraud cases, held that the availability of remedies in the foreign country was indeed immaterial in cases where the defendant received no notice or was not given an adequate opportunity to make a defence; but in other cases it would be wrong in principle to ignore the possibility that there was a fair opportunity for remedy in the foreign country. What weight was to be given to that factor would

---

[150] *Godard v Gray* (1870) L.R. 6 Q.B. 139; *Castrique v Imrie* (1870) L.R. 4 H.L. 414; *Robinson v Fenner* [1913] 3 K.B. 835, 842.

[151] *De Cosse Brissac v Rathbone* (1861) 6 H. & N. 301 (the sixth plea).

[152] *Scarpetta v Lowenfeld* (1911) 27 T.L.R. 509; *Robinson v Fenner*, above.

[153] See below, para.17–010.

[154] [1990] Ch. 433.

[155] But note that "it is not contrary to natural justice that a man who has agreed to receive a particular mode of notification of legal proceedings should be bound by a judgment in which that particular mode of notification has been followed, even though he may not have had actual notice of them": *Vallée v Dumergue* (1849) 4 Exch. 290 at p.303, per Alderson B.

[156] cf. the position under the Brussels I Regulation: para.7–005, above.

depend on a number of matters: how far the defendant had known of the procedural defects and whether in all the circumstances it was reasonable to expect use to be made of the foreign remedy. On the particular facts, however, the defendants had no knowledge of (or reasonable means of knowing) the facts which could have prompted them to make an application for the foreign remedy, and were accordingly not precluded from relying on the ground of natural justice.

Neither the Administration of Justice Act 1920 nor the Foreign Judgments (Reciprocal Enforcement) Act 1933 mentions the defence that the proceedings were opposed to natural justice. Instead, the former Act provides that no judgment may be registered thereunder if the defendant was not duly served with the process of the court and did not appear[157]; and the latter Act provides that the registration of a judgment must be set aside if the defendant did not receive notice of the proceedings in sufficient time to enable him to defend them and he did not appear.[158]

Article 6 of the European Convention for the Protection of Human Rights and Fundamental Freedoms protects the right to a fair trial. The House of Lords held in *Government of the United States of America v Montgomery (No.2)*[159] that non-compliance with art.6 was a ground for refusing recognition or enforcement in the United Kingdom of a judgment obtained in another State, whether or not the latter is an adherent to the Convention.[160] This was applied in *Merchant International Co Ltd v Natsionalna Aktsionerna Kompaniya Naftogaz Ukrayiny*[161]:

7–038

> A judgment had been obtained in Ukraine and the successful claimant obtained an English judgment by a common law action on the judgment-debt. The foreign judgment was later set aside by the Supreme Commercial Court of Ukraine. Normally this would have destroyed the basis for the English judgment, but the English court held that the proceedings before the Ukrainian Supreme Commercial Court did not meet the standard required by art.6. Accordingly, the judgment of that court would be ignored and an application to set aside the English judgment was dismissed.

Judgments for multiple damages

Section 5 of the Protection of Trading Interests Act 1980 prohibits the enforcement in the United Kingdom of judgments for multiple damages or any judgment specified by the Secretary of State as concerned with the prohibition of restrictive trade practices. Section 6 goes much further and gives United Kingdom citizens, corporations incorporated in the United Kingdom, and persons carrying on business in the United Kingdom against whom multiple damages have been awarded, the right to recover so much of the damages as exceeds the sum assessed by the foreign court as compensation for the loss or damage sustained.[162] This section also contains the unusual provision that proceedings

7–039

---

[157] s.9(2)(c).
[158] s.4(1)(a)(iii).
[159] [2004] UKHL 37; [2004] 4 All E.R. 289.
[160] See Fawcett, (2007) 56 I.C.L.Q. 1.
[161] [2012] EWCA Civ 196.
[162] See *Lewis v Eliades* [2003] EWCA Civ 1758; [2004] 1 W.L.R. 692, noted Briggs, (2003) 74 B.Y.B.I.L. 549; Kellman, (2004) 53 I.C.L.Q. 1025 (compensatory element enforceable).

under it may be brought notwithstanding that the claimant in the foreign proceedings is not within the jurisdiction of the United Kingdom court. These two sections are aimed primarily at the tendency of American courts to interpret United States anti-trust legislation in such a way as to infringe the sovereignty of the United Kingdom and other states.

What are not defences

7–040   The above sub-heading is somewhat more dogmatic than the cases warrant. It is certain that the first matter about to be discussed is not itself a defence; but there is more doubt as to the status of the second.

Errors of fact or law

7–041   It is no defence that the foreign judgment is manifestly wrong either on the facts or on the law.[163] The merits cannot be reopened in England. But, as we have seen, this rule does not apply if it is alleged that the judgment was obtained by fraud.

In *Godard v Gray*,[164] it was held to be no defence that the foreign court, purporting to apply English domestic law, made an obvious mistake in doing so. It would seem to follow that it is no defence that the foreign court applied its own domestic law when according to English rules of the conflict of laws it should have applied English domestic law.

This finality of foreign judgments (subject to the grounds for impeachment already examined) is a form of estoppel *per rem judicatem*. The applicability of that doctrine, and in particular of issue estoppel, to foreign judgments has been recognised in two decisions of the House of Lords.[165] To attract this doctrine the decision must be a final and conclusive decision on the merits of a court of competent jurisdiction.

Lack of internal competence

7–042   Is it a defence that, though the foreign court had jurisdiction in the sense of the English rules of the conflict of laws, it lacked competence in the sense of its own domestic law? This is a difficult question, and the authorities are in a state of some confusion.

In *Vanquelin v Bouard*,[166] the defendant was sued in England on a French judgment in respect of a bill of exchange. The French court had jurisdiction according to the English rules of the conflict of laws; and the subject matter of the action (bills of exchange) was within its internal competence. But the defendant pleaded that this particular French court had no internal competence over him because he was not a trader. This plea was held bad.

---

[163] *Godard v Gray* (1870) L.R. 6 Q.B. 139; *Castrique v Imrie* (1870) L.R. 4 H.L. 414.
[164] (1870) L.R. 6 Q.B. 139.
[165] *Carl Zeiss Stiftung v Rayner & Keeler Ltd* (No.2) [1967] 1 A.C. 853; *The Sennar (No.2)* [1985] 1 W.L.R. 490.
[166] (1863) 15 C.B. (n.s.) 341; approved in *Pemberton v Hughes* [1899] 1 Ch. 781 at 791.

On the other hand, in *Castrique v Imrie,*[167] a case on a foreign judgment in *rem*, Blackburn J. regarded it as material "whether the sovereign authority of that state has conferred on the court jurisdiction to decide as to the disposition of the thing, and the court has acted within its jurisdiction". This could be taken to mean that a foreign judgment in *rem*, in order to be recognised in England, must have been pronounced by a court having internal competence as well as international jurisdiction. Further, in *Papadopoulos v Papadopoulos,*[168] one reason for refusing to recognise a Cypriot decree of nullity was that the Cypriot court had no internal competence to annul a marriage under the Order in Council which established it. And in *Adams v Adams,*[169] a Rhodesian divorce was not recognised because the judge who pronounced it had not taken the oath of allegiance and the judicial oath in the prescribed form.

In *Macalpine v Macalpine,*[170] there was some discussion whether fraud rendered a Wyoming decree of divorce void or merely voidable. It is believed that this distinction furnishes the key to the problem here discussed. If the foreign judgment is merely irregular, i.e. valid until set aside, it will be held valid in England unless and until it is set aside in the foreign country.[171] If, on the other hand, the foreign judgment is a complete nullity by the law of the foreign country, then it will be held invalid in England. A foreign judgment is, of course, much more likely to be irregular than void. Hence lack of internal competence is in practice hardly ever a good defence.

Enforcement

A foreign judgment can be enforced in England by action at common law or, in cases to which they apply, by registration under the Administration of Justice Act 1920, or the Foreign Judgments (Reciprocal Enforcement) Act 1933.

7–043

At common law

A foreign judgment in personam, given by a court having jurisdiction according to English rules of the conflict of laws, may be enforced by action in England, provided (a) it is for a debt, or definite sum of money, (b) it is not a judgment for taxes or penalties, and (c) it is "final and conclusive".

7–044

---

[167] (1870) L.R. 4 H.L. 414 at 429. Blackburn J.'s statement was approved by Lord Chelmsford at p.488.
[168] [1930] P. 55.
[169] [1971] P. 188.
[170] [1958] P. 35 at 41 and 45; cf. *Merker v Merker* [1963] P. 283 at 297–299. See below, para.9–060, for discussion of a similar problem in the recognition of foreign divorces.
[171] See, to this effect, *S.A. Consortium General Textiles v Sun and Sand Agencies Ltd* [1978] Q.B. 279 at 307.

The judgment must be for a debt, or definite[172] sum of money (including damages and costs[173]), and not, for example, a judgment ordering the defendant specifically to perform a contract.[174]

It must not be for taxes[175] or penalties.[176] It is well settled that an English court will not entertain an action for the enforcement, either directly or indirectly, of a foreign penal or revenue law.[177] Hence it will not enforce, either directly or indirectly, a foreign judgment ordering the payment of taxes or penalties. However, if the foreign judgment imposes a fine on the defendant and also orders the defendant to pay compensation to the injured party (called the *partie civile* in French proceedings), the latter part of the judgment can be severed from the former and enforced in England. Thus in *Raulin v Fischer*[178]:

> D, a young American lady, while recklessly galloping her horse in the Bois de Boulogne, Paris, ran into P, an elderly French colonel, and seriously injured him. D was prosecuted for her criminal negligence by the French authorities, and P intervened in the proceedings and claimed damages from D as allowed by French law. The court convicted D, fined her 100 francs, and ordered her to pay 15,000 francs to P by way of damages, and also costs. It was held that P could recover the sterling equivalent of the damages and costs in England.

7–045 The judgment must be "final and conclusive" in the court which rendered it.[179] "It must be shown that in the court by which it was pronounced, it conclusively, finally and for ever established the existence of the debt of which it is sought to be made conclusive evidence in this country, so as to make it res judicata between the parties".[180] So a summary judgment in which only a limited number of defences can be pleaded, and which is liable to be upset by the unsuccessful party in plenary proceedings where all defences may be set up, is not final and conclusive. However, at common law a foreign judgment may be final and conclusive even though it is subject to an appeal, and even though an appeal is actually pending in the foreign country where it was given.[181] But in a proper case, a stay of execution would no doubt be ordered pending a possible appeal.

The requirement that the foreign judgment must be final and conclusive usually makes it impossible to enforce a foreign maintenance order in England at common law, because the foreign court usually has power to vary the amount of the payments.[182] If, however, the foreign court has power to vary the amount of future payments, but not that of past payments, then an action may be brought in

---

[172] See *Sadler v Robins* (1808) 1 Camp. 253.

[173] *Russell v Smyth* (1842) 9 M. & W. 810.

[174] The restriction of the common law recognition rule to money judgments has been abandoned in Canada (*Pro Swing Inc v Elite Golf Inc* (2006) SCC 52) and seems to have been doubted by the Privy Council (on appeal from the Isle of Man) in *Pattni v Ali* [2007] 2 A.C. 85. See the Jersey case of *Brunei Investment Agency v Fidelis Nominees Ltd* [2008] JRC 152.

[175] *Government of India v Taylor* [1955] A.C. 491 at 514; *Rossano v Manufacturers Life Insurance Co. Ltd* [1963] 2 Q.B. 352 at 376–378. See Stoel, (1967) 16 I.C.L.Q. 663.

[176] *Huntington v Attrill* [1893] A.C. 150.

[177] See above, Ch.3.

[178] [1911] 2 K.B. 93.

[179] *Nouvion v Freeman* (1889) 15 App. Cas. 1; *Blohn v Desser* [1962] 2 Q.B. 116.

[180] *Nouvion v Freeman* (1889) 15 App. Cas. 1 at 9, per Lord Herschell.

[181] *Scott v Pilkington* (1862) 2 B. & S. 11; *Colt Industries Inc. v Sarlie* (No.2) [1966] 1 W.L.R. 1287.

[182] *Harrop v Harrop* [1920] 3 K.B. 386; *Re Macartney* [1921] 1 Ch. 522. The rule is criticised by Grodecki, (1959) 8 I.C.L.Q. 18 at 32–40.

England to recover the arrears.[183] And as we shall see,[184] provision is made by statute for the reciprocal enforcement in one part of the United Kingdom of maintenance orders made in another part, and for the reciprocal enforcement in England of maintenance orders made in the Commonwealth overseas and certain foreign countries and vice versa.

Under the Administration of Justice Act 1920

Where Pt II of this Act has been extended by Order in Council to any part of the Commonwealth outside the United Kingdom, a judgment creditor who has obtained a judgment in a superior court in that part of the Commonwealth may, if a sum of money is payable under the judgment, apply to the High Court in England or Northern Ireland or to the Court of Session in Scotland at any time within 12 months of the date of the judgment to have the judgment registered in that court; and the court may order the judgment to be registered accordingly,[185] in which case the judgment will be of the same force and effect as if it were a judgment of the court in which it is registered.[186]
    Registration of a judgment under the Act is not as of right, but discretionary: the Act provides that the court may order the judgment to be registered if the court thinks it just and convenient that the judgment should be enforced in the United Kingdom.[187] Moreover, registration may not be ordered if the original court acted without jurisdiction, or if the defendant establishes any one of a limited number of defences.[188] These accord very closely with those available at common law, except that no judgment can be registered if the judgment debtor satisfies the court either that an appeal is pending, or that he is entitled and intends to appeal against the judgment.[189]
    The judgment creditor remains free to bring an action on the foreign judgment in the ordinary way; but in that instance will usually not be awarded costs.[190]

7–046

Under the Foreign Judgments (Reciprocal Enforcement) Act 1933

When Pt I of this Act has been extended by Order in Council to any foreign country outside the United Kingdom, a judgment creditor under a judgment to which the Act applies may apply to the High Court in England or Northern Ireland or to the Court of Session in Scotland at any time within six years of the date of the judgment to have the judgment registered in that court, and on any such application the court must (not may) order the judgment to be registered.[191] A registered judgment has the same force and effect as if it had been a judgment

7–047

---

[183] *Beatty v Beatty* [1924] 1 K.B. 807.
[184] Below, para.9–087.
[185] s.9(1).
[186] s.9(3)(a).
[187] s.9(1).
[188] s.9(2).
[189] s.9(2)(e).
[190] s.9(5).
[191] ss.2(1), 12(a), 13(a).

originally given in the registering court.[192] The Act applies to any judgment of a court (not necessarily a superior court) of a country to which Pt I extends if it is final and conclusive as between the parties thereto, and there is payable thereunder a sum of money, not being a sum payable in respect of taxes or in respect of a fine or other penalty.[193] As at common law, a judgment is deemed to be final and conclusive notwithstanding that an appeal is pending against it.[194] But the court has a discretionary power to set aside the registration of a judgment on such terms as it thinks fit, if the defendant satisfies the court that an appeal is pending, or that he is entitled and intends to appeal.[195]

Registration must be set aside if the original court had no jurisdiction, or if the defendant establishes any one of a limited number of defences which accord very closely with those available at common law.[196] Registration may be set aside if the matter in dispute had, before the foreign judgment was given, been the subject of a final and conclusive judgment by a court having jurisdiction in the matter.[197] For instance, if a claimant sues a defendant in Switzerland and in Austria, and both courts have jurisdiction, and the Swiss court dismisses the action, but the Austrian court gives judgment for the claimant, the English court may set aside the registration of the Austrian judgment.

Unlike the Administration of Justice Act 1920, the Act of 1933 prevents the judgment creditor from bringing an action in England on the foreign judgment,[198] and from suing on the original cause of action.[199]

Recognition as a defence

7–048   A foreign judgment in personam in favour of the defendant given by a court having jurisdiction may be relied upon for defensive purposes by the defendant if the claimant sues in England on the original cause of action. A foreign judgment in favour of the defendant is a conclusive answer to an action in England on the original cause of action.[200] The judgment must be "final and conclusive" in the court which rendered it.[201] This last requirement applies when the judgment is

---

[192] s.2(2). Hence a stay of execution will not be ordered merely because an English action is pending between the same parties and raising similar issues: *Wagner v Laubscher Bros. & Co.* [1970] 2 Q.B. 313.
[193] s.1(2), as amended by Civil Jurisdiction and Judgments Act 1982 Sch.10, para.1. A sum payable by way of exemplary damages is not a penalty: *S.A. Consortium General Textiles v Sun and Sand Agencies Ltd* [1978] Q.B. 279 at 299–300 and 305–306.
[194] s.1(3).
[195] s.5.
[196] s.4(1)(a).
[197] s.4(1)(b).
[198] s.6.
[199] Civil Jurisdiction and Judgments Act 1982 s.34; above, para.7–018. For the relationship between the 1933 Act and the rules governing international co-operation in insolvency cases, see *New Cap Reinsurance Corp Ltd (In Liquidation) v Grant* [2011] EWCA Civ 971.
[200] *Ricardo v Garcias* (1845) 12 Cl. & F. 368; *Jacobson v Frachon* (1927) 138 L.T. 386. cf. Foreign Judgments (Reciprocal Enforcement) Act 1933 s.8.
[201] *Plummer v Woodburne* (1825) 4 B. & C. 625; *Frayes v Worms* (1861) 10 C.B. (n.s.) 149; *Carl Zeiss Stiftung v Rayner & Keeler Ltd (No.2)* [1967] 1 A.C. 853.

relied upon as a defence, just as it does when the claimant seeks to enforce it.[202] The foreign judgment is not a defence if the action was brought against a different party[203]; nor is it a defence unless it was given on the merits.

Section 3 of the Foreign Limitation Periods Act 1984 provides that where a court of a foreign country has determined any matter by reference to the law relating to limitation of that or any other country (including England), the court shall be deemed to have determined that matter on its merits.

Reciprocal enforcement within the United Kingdom

The reciprocal enforcement of judgments within the United Kingdom now depends on s.18 and Schs 6 and 7 of the Civil Jurisdiction and Judgments Act 1982, which apply equally to money and non-money judgments. Thus under the 1982 Act injunctions and orders for specific performance granted or made in one part of the United Kingdom are enforceable in other parts. Section 18 does not apply to judgments in proceedings other than civil proceedings, nor to maintenance orders or orders concerning the legal capacity of an individual, including judicial separation, guardianship and custody, nor to judgments in bankruptcy, the winding up of companies, or the administration of the estate of a deceased person.[204]

7–049

Enforcement is by way of registration in the court in which enforcement is sought of a certificate granted by the court which gave the judgment. Registration (even of certificates of judgments of inferior courts) is in superior courts only, i.e. the High Court in England or Northern Ireland, or the Court of Session in Scotland. Sch.6 contains the procedure for enforcement of certificates of money judgments, and Sch.7 for enforcement of certificates of non-money judgments. Registration of a certificate must be set aside if the registration was contrary to the provisions of the Schedules, and may be set aside if the registering court is satisfied that the matter in dispute had previously been the subject of a judgment by another court having jurisdiction in the matter.[205] It is not a ground for setting registration aside that the original court had no jurisdiction over the defendant, or that the judgment was obtained by fraud, or that its enforcement would be contrary to public policy, or that the proceedings were opposed to natural justice.

The judgment may not be enforced except by registration under Schs 6 or 7.[206] Section 19 contains provisions for the recognition, as opposed to enforcement, of judgments to which s.18 applies.

---

[202] Above, para.7–045.
[203] *Carl Zeiss Stiftung v Rayner & Keeler Ltd (No.2)* [1967] 1 A.C. 853 at 910–911, 928–929, 936–937 and 944–946. See *The Sennar (No.2)* [1985] 1 W.L.R. 490.
[204] s.18(3), (5) and (6).
[205] Sch.6 para.10; Sch.7 para.9.
[206] s.18(8).

7–050   International commercial arbitration is of enormous practical importance, and is a subject in its own right. Here we can examine only a limited topic: the enforcement of foreign arbitral awards. The issues are similar to those already considered, in the context of the enforcement of foreign judgments, but the answers are different as "arbitration" is excluded from the Brussels I Regulation (and from the Lugano Convention).[207] This means that a foreign arbitral award cannot be enforced under the Regulation or Convention; but if a foreign judgment has been obtained on the basis of the award it can be enforced under the usual rules relating to foreign judgments.

Foreign arbitral awards can be enforced in England in various ways. First, they can be enforced by action at common law; this mode of enforcement is always an option. Second, they can be enforced under the terms of international conventions, the earlier Geneva Convention for the Execution of Foreign Arbitral Awards of 1927, given effect by the Arbitration Act 1950 and not further considered here, and the much more important New York Convention on the Recognition and Enforcement of Foreign Arbitral Awards of 1958, given effect by the Arbitration Act 1996. Arbitration awards made in countries of the Commonwealth outside the United Kingdom to which Pt II of the Administration of Justice Act 1920 extends, or in countries to which Pt I of the Foreign Judgments (Reciprocal Enforcement) Act 1933 extends, can be enforced in England as if they were judgments, i.e. by registration,[208] and arbitration awards made in one part of the United Kingdom can be enforced in other parts by registration under the Civil Jurisdiction and Judgments Act 1982.

It is important, in reading what follows, to bear in mind that an arbitration clause in a contract is treated as if it were a separate contract. In English law, s.7 of the Arbitration Act 1996 provides:

> Unless otherwise agreed by the parties, an arbitration agreement which forms or was intended to form part of another agreement (whether or not in writing) shall not be regarded as invalid, non-existent or ineffective because that other agreement is invalid, or did not come into existence or has become ineffective, and it shall for that purpose be treated as a distinct agreement.

7–051   As Lord Hoffman explained in *Fiona Trust & Holding Corp v Privalov*[209]:

> "The invalidity or rescission of the main contract does not necessarily entail the invalidity or rescission of the arbitration agreement. The arbitration agreement must be treated as a 'distinct agreement' and can be void or voidable only on grounds which relate directly to the arbitration agreement. Of course there may be cases in which the ground upon which the main agreement is invalid is identical with the ground upon which the arbitration agreement is invalid. For example, if the main agreement and the arbitration agreement are contained in the same document and one of the parties claims that he never agreed to anything in the document and that his signature was forged, that will be an attack on the validity of the arbitration agreement. But the ground of attack is not that the main agreement was invalid. It is that the signature to

---

[207] See above, Ch.4.
[208] Certain arbitration awards made in pursuance of a contract for the international carriage of goods can also be enforced by registration under this Act: Carriage of Goods by Road Act 1965 ss.4(1) and 7(1). See also the Arbitration (International Investment Disputes) Act 1966.
[209] [2007] UKHL 40; [2008] 1 Lloyd's Rep. 254.

the arbitration agreement, as a "distinct agreement", was forged.... On the other hand, if ... the allegation is that the agent exceeded his authority by entering into a main agreement in terms which were not authorised or for improper reasons, that is not necessarily an attack on the arbitration agreement. It would have to be shown that whatever the terms of the main agreement or the reasons for which the agent concluded it, he would have had no authority to enter into an arbitration agreement."

At Common law

In the eyes of an English court, the jurisdiction of the arbitrators is derived from the agreement of the parties to arbitrate. Such an agreement may assume one of two forms, in that it may submit present or future disputes to arbitration. A contract may contain an arbitration clause by which the parties agree that if disputes arise under the contract they shall be referred to arbitration. Or parties may agree to submit a particular dispute between them (which need not necessarily stem from a contract) to the decision of a particular arbitrator.

7–052

The enforcement of foreign arbitral awards sometimes raises even more delicate questions than does the enforcement of foreign judgments. Moreover, the enforcement of foreign awards may be required more frequently than the enforcement of foreign judgments. This is because actions in personam are usually brought in the country where the defendant resides and keeps his or her assets, so that the need for enforcement elsewhere is the exception rather than the rule. But there is an increasing tendency for contracts between commercial parties from different countries to provide for arbitration in a third or "neutral" country, where neither resides or keeps assets, in which case the need for enforcement is the rule rather than the exception. On the other hand, parties may perhaps be more inclined to obey the award of a tribunal of their own choice than they are to obey the decision of a court.

Although English courts have enforced foreign judgments from the seventeenth century onwards, it is only since 1927[210] (so far as one can judge from reported cases) that they have enforced foreign arbitral awards, and so authority is relatively scanty. This is no doubt because arbitration is so ancient and well-developed an institution in England that for many years most disputes that had any connection with England, and many that had none,[211] were referred to arbitration in England, and so the enforcement of the award in England was a purely domestic matter.

Conditions for enforcement

A foreign arbitration award can be enforced by action in England at common law if (1) the parties submitted to the arbitration by an agreement which is valid by its governing law, and (2) the award is valid and final according to the law which governs the arbitration proceedings.

7–053

---

[210] *Norske Atlas Insurance Co. Ltd v London General Insurance Co.* Ltd (1927) 43 T.L.R. 541.

[211] For a striking and well-known example, see *Gilbert v Burnstine*, (1931) 255 N.Y. 348; 174 N.E. 706, where the New York Court of Appeals enforced an English award made in pursuance of an arbitration clause in a contract made and to be performed in New York between two residents of that state. See also Kerr J., (1978) 41 M.L.R. 1 at 5–6.

The validity, interpretation, and effect of the agreement to arbitrate are governed by the proper law of the agreement. The Rome I Regulation does not apply to arbitration agreements, so the common law rules as to the proper law of a contract remain applicable. This means that if there is an express choice of law in respect of the arbitration agreement, the chosen law will govern. The choice of the place where the arbitration is to be conducted (its "seat") may be treated as an implied choice of the governing law.[212] This is so even if the contract of which the arbitration clause forms part is governed by some other law.[213] Where there is neither an express nor an implied choice of law by the parties, regard must be had to all the circumstances in deciding with which law the agreement is most closely connected.

The parties can not only choose the law which governs their agreement to arbitrate but also the law which governs the arbitration proceedings. Normally the parties' choice of the place where the arbitration is to be conducted, its seat, will be accompanied by, or will imply, the choice of the law of that place as the law to govern the procedure. It is possible, however, for the parties to agree that state A shall be the seat of the arbitration but that the procedure shall be that of state B. In such a case, the parties' choice of procedural law will be respected but only subject to any mandatory provisions of the law of state A. In the absence of any choice by the parties, the law of the seat of the arbitration will govern the procedure.

If England is the seat of the arbitration, the provisions of the Arbitration Act 1996 will determine such issues as how the arbitrators are to be appointed, whether an arbitrator may be appointed by the court, whether the authority of an arbitrator can be revoked, what law the arbitrators are to apply, and whether they can decide *ex aequo et bono*.[214] The scheme of the Act, which cannot be examined in detail here, is to set out some provisions which are mandatory, applying notwithstanding any contrary agreement by the parties, and those which are non-mandatory, applying in the absence of any special agreement by the parties.

Finality of the award

7–054 To be enforceable in England, the award must be final and binding on the parties in the English sense, i.e. it must fulfil one of the conditions for the enforcement of foreign judgments in personam.[215] Whether the award is final in the English sense depends on the law governing the arbitration proceedings. The question to be answered is:

---

[212] *Hamlyn v Talisker Distillery* [1894] A.C. 202.
[213] *Deutsche Schachtbau v Shell International Petroleum Ltd* [1990] 1 A.C. 295 (a C.A. judgment, revd on other grounds at p.329).
[214] On the law to be applied in English arbitrations, see Arbitration Act 1996 s.46.
[215] See above, para.7–044.

"Has it become final, as we understand that phrase, in the country in which it was made? Of course the question whether it is final in [that country] will depend no doubt upon [the foreign] law, but the [foreign] law is directed to showing whether it is final as that word is understood in English".[216]

These remarks were made in a case where the award was enforced under Pt II of the Arbitration Act 1950, but it is thought that they are equally applicable to the enforcement of awards at common law.

Mode of enforcement

In order to enforce an arbitration award in England it is necessary to obtain an enforcement title from a court. A claimant seeking to enforce an English award can choose either to bring an action on the award or to apply for leave to enforce it under s.66 of the Arbitration Act 1996. This summary procedure is also available for the enforcement of a foreign award; but it should only be used where the validity of the award or the right to proceed upon it is "reasonably clear".[217]

    7–055

An award may be expressed in foreign currency, and such an award can be enforced under s.66.[218] Whether enforced by action or under s.66, it must be converted into sterling before it can be enforced in England by any process of execution. The date for conversion will be the date when the court authorises enforcement of the judgment or when leave to enforce the award in sterling under s.66 is given.[219]

A foreign arbitration award may be enforced in England whether or not the law governing the arbitration proceedings requires a judgment or order of the foreign court to make the award enforceable.[220] Provided the award is final in the English sense, it can be enforced in England even though by the law governing the arbitration proceedings it is not enforceable in the foreign country until a judgment of a court has been obtained. If the English court insisted on a foreign judgment in order to make the award enforceable in England, it would not be enforcing the award but the judgment, and the foreign award as such would be deprived of all effect in England. All doubts concerning this important principle were dispelled by the decision of the Court of Appeal in *Union Nationale des*

---

[216] *Union Nationale des Coopératives Agricoles v Catterall* [1959] 2 Q.B. 44 at 53, per Lord Evershed M.R.

[217] *Re Boks & Co. and Peters, Rushton & Co. Ltd* [1919] 1 K.B. 491; but see *Middlemiss and Gould v Hartlepool Corporation* [1972] 1 W.L.R. 1643 at 1647. In *Union Nationale des Coopératives Agricoles v Catterall* [1959] 2 Q.B. 44 at 52, this test was adopted and applied to the enforcement of a foreign award under Pt II of the Arbitration Act 1950.

[218] *Jugoslavenska Oceanska Plovidba v Castle Investment Co.* [1974] Q.B. 272. See below, para.17–021.

[219] *Miliangos v George Frank (Textiles) Ltd* [1976] A.C. 443 at 469, per Lord Wilberforce.

[220] *Union Nationale des Coopératives Agricoles v Catterall* [1959] 2 Q.B. 44. The decision to the contrary in *Merrifield Ziegler & Co. v Liverpool Cotton Association* (1911) 105 L.T. 97 should not now be followed: *Dalmia Dairy Industries Ltd v National Bank of Pakistan* [1978] 2 Lloyd's Rep. 223 at 249.

Coopératives Agricoles v Catterall.[221] That case was decided under Pt II of the Arbitration Act 1950, but it is thought that the principle applies equally to enforcement at common law.

However, if the party in whose favour a foreign award is made does obtain a judgment on it in the country where it was rendered, that judgment can be enforced in England in accordance with the principles on which foreign judgments are enforced.[222] By submitting to arbitration in a foreign country, the parties also submit to the jurisdiction of the foreign court which declares the award enforceable.[223]

Recognition as defence

7–056   The conditions under which a foreign arbitration award may be enforced in England at common law apply also to its recognition as a defence to an action on the original cause of action. A valid English award duly made in pursuance of a valid agreement to arbitrate is a defence to an action on the original cause of action, and there seems no reason for the same not to be true of a foreign award.

Defences to actions on foreign awards

7–057   There is very little authority on the grounds on which a foreign award can be challenged in England, notwithstanding that it was made in accordance with a valid agreement to arbitrate, and is valid and final according to the law governing the arbitration proceedings. But it can hardly be supposed that foreign arbitration awards will be more readily enforced or recognised in England than are foreign judgments. Hence the existence of the following grounds of challenge can probably be taken for granted:

(a)   that under the agreement to arbitrate the arbitrators had no jurisdiction to make the award[224];

(b)   that the award was obtained by fraud[225];

(c)   that the enforcement or recognition of the award would be contrary to English public policy in the limited sense in which that concept is deployed in conflicts cases[226]; and

(d)   that the proceedings in which the award was obtained were opposed to natural justice.

---

[221] [1959] 2 Q.B. 44.

[222] *East India Trading Co. Inc. v Carmel Exporters and Importers Ltd* [1952] 2 Q.B. 439.

[223] *International Alltex Corporation v Lawler Creations Ltd* [1965] I.R. 264.

[224] See *Kianta Osakeyhtio v Britain and Overseas Trading Co. Ltd* [1953] 2 Lloyd's Rep. 569; [1954] 1 Lloyd's Rep. 247; *Dalmia Dairy Industries Ltd v National Bank of Pakistan* [1978] 2 Lloyd's Rep. 223.

[225] See *Oppenheim & Co. v Mahomed Haneef* [1922] 1 A.C. 482 at 487; *Westacre Investments Inc. v Jugoimport-SDPR Holding Co. Ltd* [1999] 3 All E.R. 864 (refusing to extend to foreign arbitral awards the rule in *Abouloff v Oppenheimer & Co.* (1882) 10 Q.B.D. 295, above para.7–033).

[226] See *Dalmia Dairy Industries Ltd v National Bank of Pakistan*, above; cf. *Westacre Investments Inc. v Jugoimport-SDPR Holding Co. Ltd*, above (contract for purchase of personal influence contrary to domestic English public policy but not in international sense).

Under the New York Convention

Efforts to promote the international enforcement and recognition of commercial   **7–058**
arbitration awards have on a number of occasions been made by means of
multilateral international conventions. The United Kingdom is a party to the
Protocol on Arbitration Clauses 1923, and to the Geneva Convention on the
Execution of Foreign Arbitral Awards 1927 which has been almost entirely
replaced by the New York Convention 1958. Part II of the Arbitration Act 1950
(repealing and replacing earlier legislation) enacts the Protocol of 1923 as
supplemented by the Convention of 1927 as part of the law of the United
Kingdom. Part III of the Arbitration Act 1996 replaces earlier provisions in the
Arbitration Act 1975 which was passed to enable the United Kingdom to accede
to the New York Convention on the Recognition and Enforcement of Foreign
Arbitral Awards of 1958.[227]

The New York Convention applies to an award made in a State, other than the
United Kingdom, which is a party to the Convention.[228] The claimant seeking
enforcement merely has to produce the original award or a certified copy of it, the
original arbitration agreement or a certified copy of it, and (where the award or
agreement is in a foreign language) a certified translation.[229] Section 101of the
Arbitration Act 1996 provides that "A New York Convention award may, by leave
of the court, be enforced in the same manner as a judgment or order of the court
to the same effect ... Where leave is so given, judgment may be entered in terms
of the award." As Gross J. explained in *Norsk Hydro ASA v State Property Fund
of Ukraine*[230]:

> "There is an important policy interest, reflected in this country's treaty obligations, in ensuring
> the effective and speedy enforcement of such international arbitration awards, the corollary,
> however, is that the task of the enforcing court should be as 'mechanistic' as possible. Save in
> connection with the threshold requirements for enforcement and the exhaustive grounds on
> which enforcement of a New York Convention award may be refused ..., the enforcing court is
> neither entitled nor bound to go behind the award in question, explore the reasoning of the
> arbitration tribunal or second-guess its intentions."

The burden is then on the defendant resisting enforcement to prove any of the   **7–059**
following substantive circumstances under which the court may refuse
enforcement:

(a)   that a party to the arbitration agreement was (under the law applicable to
him or her) under some incapacity;

---

[227] For the text of the Convention, see Fifth Report of the Private International Law Committee, Cmnd. 1515 (1961).
[228] Arbitration Act 1996 s.100(1).
[229] *ibid.*, s.102.
[230] [2002] EWHC 2120 (Comm); [2009] Bus.L.R. 558 (judgment naming parties other than those in the award set aside); *West Tankers Inc v Allianz SpA (The Front Comor)* [2012] EWCA Civ 27 (declaratory award capable of being subject of an order in terms of the award).

(b)   that the arbitration agreement was not valid under the law to which the parties subjected it, or, failing any indication thereon, under the law of the country where the award was made[231];

(c)   that he or she was not given proper notice of the appointment of the arbitrator or of the arbitration proceedings or was otherwise unable to present his or her case;

(d)   that the award deals with a difference not contemplated by or not falling within the terms of the submission to arbitration or contains decisions on matters beyond the scope of the submission to arbitration (unless they can be separated);

(e)   that the composition of the arbitral authority or the arbitral procedure was not in accordance with the agreement of the parties, or, failing such agreement, with the law of the country where the arbitration took place; or

(f)   that the award has not yet become binding on the parties, or has been set aside or suspended by a competent authority of the country in which, or under the law of which, it was made.[232]

If the defendant proves any of these defences, the court retains a discretion nonetheless to enforce the award but will only do so in rare cases, where for example there has been some agreement to the contrary.[233]

7–060   Recognition or enforcement of an award may also be refused if the award is in respect of a matter which is not capable of settlement by arbitration, or if it would be contrary to public policy to recognise or enforce the award.[234] Recognition or enforcement may not be refused except in the cases mentioned above.[235]

A party who has obtained a Convention award may, if he or she chooses, enforce it either by action or by an application for leave to enforce the award summarily under s.66 of the Arbitration Act 1996.[236] As an order under s.66 will be a judgment capable of recognition under the Brussels I Regulation, obtaining such an order may benefit the applicant as it remove the possibility of a later

---

[231] See *Dallah Real Estate and Tourism Holding Co v Ministry of Religious Affairs of the Government of Pakistan* [2010] UKSC 46; [2011] 1 A.C. 763. *Renvoi* is inapplicable, but an English court will nonetheless recognise that a foreign court might apply different principles in an international as opposed to a purely domestic case: *ibid.*, at para [125].

[232] Arbitration Act 1996 s.103(2), (4).

[233] *Kanoria v Guinness* [2006] EWCA Civ 222; [2006] 1 Lloyd's Rep.701; The discretion must be exercised so as to give effect to the purposes of the Convention; where there was no valid arbitration agreement, a refusal of recognition will almost inevitably follow: *Dallah Real Estate and Tourism Holding Co v Ministry of Religious Affairs of the Government of Pakistan* [2010] UKSC 46; [2011] 1 A.C. 763.

[234] Arbitration Act 1996 s.103(3); *Westacre Investments Inc. v Jugoimport-SDPR Holding Co. Ltd* [2000] 1 Q.B. 288 and *Omnium de Traitement et de Valorisation SA v Hilmarton Ltd* [1999] 2 Lloyd's Rep. 222 (both dealing with illegality of the contract); *Kanoria v Guinness* [2006] EWCA Civ 222; [2006] 1 Lloyd's Rep.701 (party not given proper notice of case to be met); Case C-126/97 *Eco Swiss China Time Ltd v Benetton International NV* [1999] E.C.R. I-3055 (relevance of EU public policy).

[235] Arbitration Act 1996 s.103(1).

[236] Arbitration Act 1996 s.101(2).

inconsistent judgement of a court in another Member State.[237] The award may also be relied upon as a defence to an action on the original cause of action.[238]

Awards made in other parts of the United Kingdom

For the purposes of s.18 of the Civil Jurisdiction and Judgments Act 1982, which provides for the reciprocal enforcement of judgments within the United Kingdom,[239] "judgment" is defined so as to include an arbitration award which has become enforceable in the part of the United Kingdom in which it was given in the same manner as a judgment given by a court of law in that part.[240] The Act thus provides machinery for the reciprocal enforcement of such awards within the United Kingdom. Such awards made in Scotland or Northern Ireland can be enforced in England under Sch.6 of the Act (if they order payment of a sum of money) or under Sch.7 (if they order any relief or remedy not requiring payment of a sum of money). But registration under these Schedules is not the only way in which such awards can be enforced. They can also be enforced in England at the option of the claimant under the summary procedure of s.66 of the Arbitration Act 1996 or by action at common law.[241] But, for some obscure reason, the provisions of s.19 as to recognition as opposed to enforcement do not apply to arbitration awards.

7–061

Awards recognised or enforced under foreign judgments legislation

As we have seen,[242] the Administration of Justice Act 1920 provides for the direct enforcement in the United Kingdom of judgments of superior courts of other Commonwealth countries to which the Act has been extended by Order in Council. The Act defines a judgment so as to include an arbitration award if the award has, in pursuance of the law in force in the place where it was made, become enforceable in the same manner as a judgment given by a court in that place.[243] The claimant remains free to bring an action on the award at common law, but in that case may not be awarded costs.[244]

7–062

The Foreign Judgments (Reciprocal Enforcement) Act 1933 also provides[245] that the provisions of the Act, except ss.1(5) and 6, apply to an arbitration award which has become enforceable in the same manner as a judgment in the place where it was made. The effect of the exception for s.6 is that such an award can

---

[237] *West Tankers Inc v Allianz SpA (The Front Comor)* [2011] EWHC 829 (Comm); [2011] 2 Lloyd's Rep. 117 (the point not being argued on appeal); *African Fertilizers and Chemicals NIG Ltd (Nigeria) v BD Shipsnavo GmbH & Co Reederei KG* [2011] EWHC 2452 (Comm); [2011] I.L.Pr. 38.
[238] Arbitration Act 1996 s.101(1).
[239] See above, para.7–049.
[240] s.18(2)(e).
[241] s.18(8).
[242] Above, para.7–046.
[243] Administration of Justice Act 1920 s.12(1).
[244] *ibid.*, s.9(5).
[245] s.10A, added by Civil Jurisdiction and Judgments Act 1982 Sch.10, para.4.

be enforced at the option of the claimant either by registration under the Act or under the summary procedure of s.66 of the Arbitration Act 1996 or by action at common law.

CHAPTER 8

MARRIAGE

Despite the changes in society in recent decades, there remains much truth in   **8–001**
Lord Westbury's dictum in *Shaw v Gould*[1]:

> "Marriage is the very foundation of civil society, and no part of the laws and institutions of a
> country can be of more vital importance to its subjects than those which regulate the manner
> and conditions of forming, and if necessary of dissolving, the marriage contract".

Marriage is a contract in the sense that there can be no valid marriage unless each
party consents to marry the other.[2] But it is a contract of a very special kind.[3] It
can only be concluded (at least as a general rule) by a formal, public act, and not,
e.g. by an exchange of emails or (in English law at least) over the telephone; no
action for damages will lie for breach of the fundamental obligation to love,
honour and (optionally) obey; the contract cannot be rescinded by the mutual
consent of the parties: it may be dissolved (if at all) only by a formal, public act,
usually an order or decree of a divorce court. Marriage is a contract in the limited
sense indicated above, but it is in reality far more than that: it creates a status,
something affecting the community as well as the parties.

The validity of a marriage may arise in almost any context, and not merely in
judicial proceedings which raise the issue directly. On a matter of such
importance, there is need for certainty in the choice of law rule. As Lincoln J.
observed,[4] "Ideally, the conflict rules relating to the status of married and
divorced persons should be simple and easily understood". Unfortunately the
relevant English conflict of laws rules have yet to attain the necessary degree of
clarity and certainty. The Law Commission for long entertained hopes of
clarifying and simplifying these rules. Its consideration of the matter was
suspended for more than a decade in the hope that work under the auspices of the
Hague Conference on Private International Law might produce rules which

---

[1] (1868) L.R. 3 H.L. 55, 82.
[2] At common law a marriage was void for lack of consent, but voidable under the Matrimonial
Causes Act 1973 s.12.
[3] See *Mordaunt v Mordaunt* (1870) L.R. 2 P. & M. 109 at 126–127, per Lord Penzance.
[4] *Lawrence v Lawrence* [1985] 1 All E.R. 506 at 509.

would be internationally agreed. The relative failure of that work[5] led the Law Commission to publish its own Working Paper in 1985.[6] After consultation, however, the Commission reported, with a humility not always displayed by law reform agencies, that the law was still developing and that it was better, for the time being at least, to leave the process in the hands of the judges.[7]

8–002 The original rule was that the validity of a marriage depended on the law of the place of celebration (*lex loci celebrationis*). In 1861 the House of Lords drew a distinction between the formalities of marriage, governed by that law, and capacity to marry, governed by the law of each party's antenuptial domicile.[8] In 1866 Sir J. P. Wilde (later Lord Penzance) said that "marriage is the voluntary union for life of one man and one woman to the exclusion of all others".[9] He thus stressed that marriage is a consensual transaction, and seemed at first sight to deny that polygamous marriages could be recognised by English law, at least for certain purposes.

We need to consider, therefore, four topics: formalities; capacity to marry; consent of parties; and polygamous marriages.

FORMALITIES OF MARRIAGE

8–003 The term "formalities" includes such questions as whether a civil ceremony, or any ceremony at all, is required, the number of witnesses necessary, the permitted hours during which marriages can be celebrated, whether publication of banns is necessary, and so on.

It has been settled law since 1752[10] that the formalities of marriage are governed by the law of the place of celebration. It is sufficient to comply with the formalities prescribed by that law; and as a general rule it is also necessary so to do. *Locus regit actum* is the maxim; and in this context the maxim is imperative, not merely facultative.

The leading modern case is *Berthiaume v Dastous,*[11] where two Roman Catholics domiciled in Quebec were married in France in a Roman Catholic church. Owing to the carelessness of the priest who married them, there was no civil ceremony as required by French law. The Privy Council held that the marriage was void; and Lord Dunedin said[12]:

---

[5] The Hague Convention on Celebration and Recognition of the Validity of Marriages 1978 was much criticised and the United Kingdom has not ratified it.
[6] Working Paper No.89 (1985).
[7] *Choice of Law Rules in Marriage* (Law Com. No. 165, 1987); some changes were proposed, and later implemented, in the Foreign Marriage Act 1892, considered below. Choice of law rules were introduced in Scotland: Family Law (Scotland) Act 2006 s.38.
[8] *Brook v Brook* (1861) 9 H.L.C. 193.
[9] *Hyde v Hyde* (1866) L.R. 1 P. & M. 130, 133.
[10] *Scrimshire v Scrimshire* (1752) 2 Hagg. Con. 395; *Dalrymple v Dalrymple* (1811) 2 Hagg. Con. 54; *Simonin v Mallac* (1860) 2 Sw. & Tr. 67; *Berthiaume v Dastous* [1930] A.C. 79; *Apt v Apt* [1948] P. 83; *Kenward v Kenward* [1951] P. 124; *McCabe v McCabe* [1994] 1 F.L.R. 410.
[11] [1930] A.C. 79.
[12] *ibid.*, at 83.

"If there is one question better settled than any other in international law, it is that as regards marriage- putting aside the question of capacity – *locus regit actum*. If a marriage is good by the laws of the country where it is effected, it is good all the world over, no matter whether the proceeding or ceremony which constituted marriage according to the law of the place would or would not constitute marriage in the country of the domicile of one or other of the spouses. If the so-called marriage is no marriage in the place where it is celebrated, there is no marriage anywhere, although the ceremony or proceeding if conducted in the place of the parties' domicile would be considered a good marriage".

So well-established is the principle that compliance with the local form is sufficient, that it applies even though the marriage, originally invalid by the local law, has been subsequently validated by retrospective legislation in the country of the place of celebration, and even though the legislation does not take effect until after the parties have acquired an English domicile. Thus, in *Starkowski v Att-Gen*[13] two Roman Catholics domiciled in Poland were married without any civil ceremony in a Roman Catholic church in Austria in May 1945. At that time Austrian law did not recognise marriages without a civil ceremony; but a few weeks later a law was passed in Austria retrospectively validating such marriages if they were duly registered. By some oversight the marriage in question was not registered until 1949, by which time the parties had acquired an English domicile, and separated. In 1950, the wife married another man in England. The House of Lords held that the Austrian marriage was valid and therefore the English ceremony was bigamous and void. Their Lordships expressly left open the question what the position would have been if the English ceremony had preceded the registration of the Austrian marriage. It is thought that, in that case, the English ceremony would be held valid and the Austrian marriage void, because foreign retrospective legislation would hardly be held to invalidate a valid marriage celebrated in the country of the parties' domicile. There is Canadian authority which indirectly supports this view.[14]

8–004

For the *lex loci celebrationis* to be complied with, it is, of course, necessary to know where the marriage is celebrated. To date this has not presented a problem, but with certain cultures accepting marriage by telephone,[15] it may soon be necessary for the English courts to consider the place of celebration of marriage by a variety of electronic means.

Scope of the rule

Marriages by proxy

Thus far, it has been assumed that the place of celebration of a marriage is easily ascertained. In the usual case it is indeed wholly unproblematic, but not always: under some systems of law a marriage may be celebrated by proxy, one or both parties being represented at the ceremony by other persons whom they have duly authorised to make the necessary declarations. In *Apt v Apt,*[16] the Court of Appeal

8–005

---

[13] [1954] A.C. 155.
[14] *Ambrose v Ambrose* (1961) 25 D.L.R. (2d) 1. See below, para.18–062.
[15] *KC v City of Westminster Social and Community Services Dept* [2008] EWCA Civ. 198; [2008] 2 F.C.R. 146. See also the unsatisfactory Scottish case of *MRA v NRK* [2011] CSOH 101.
[16] [1948] P. 83.

upheld a marriage celebrated by proxy in Argentina between a man domiciled and resident there and a woman domiciled and resident in England, since it appeared that proxy marriages were valid by Argentine law.[17]

A more extreme set of facts presented themselves in *McCabe v McCabe*[18]:

> A man domiciled in the Republic of Ireland and a woman domiciled in Ghana were living together in England. They agreed to marry according to the tribal custom of the Akan, a people living in Ghana. The man provided a bottle of gin and some money (as "*aseda*"), which were taken to Ghana where a ceremony was held. Neither the man nor the woman was present at the ceremony, nor was either of them represented by proxy.

The Court of Appeal held that the couple were validly married, finding on the basis of expert evidence that the ceremony constituted a valid marriage under Akan customary law.[19] It does not seem to have been argued whether the place of celebration was Ghana (where, according to one expert witness, no ceremony was necessary at all) or England, the place where the couple gave their consent.

Parental consent

8–006
The most controversial question is whether lack of parental consent relates to formalities of marriage or to capacity to marry. The answer appears to be that it relates to the formalities, whether the requirement is imposed by English law or foreign law, and in the latter case no matter how stringently the requirement is expressed. However, the cases have been much criticised.

English law requires parental consent to the marriages of persons below the age of 18[20]; and there is some historical justification for treating this requirement as a formality. It was first imposed by Lord Hardwicke's Marriage Act of 1753. That Act also dealt with licences and publication of banns, matters which no one doubts are formalities. A marriage celebrated without parental consent is not invalid in English domestic law. The Act applied to England only and not to Scotland. Hence the practice arose of eloping English couples marrying without parental consent and without formal ceremony at Gretna Green, just across the border in Scotland. The validity of such marriages was established in a series of eighteenth-century cases[21] which were decided at a time when English courts did not distinguish between the formalities of marriage and capacity to marry, but referred both aspects to the law of the place of celebration. When that distinction was introduced in 1861, the Gretna Green cases were explained away as having turned on the formalities of marriage.[22]

---

[17] In *Apt v Apt* the Court of Appeal distinguished between the fact of consent and the method of giving consent; the acceptability of proxies went to the latter and was an aspect of formalities.

[18] [1994] 1 F.L.R. 410.

[19] The evidence was that the only (formal?) requirement of an Akan marriage was the consent of the parties and of their families, with some degree of publicity; even the "*aseda*" was not essential.

[20] Marriage Act 1949 ss.1, (as amended by the Family Law Reform Act 1987 Sch.2, para.9 and the Immigration and Asylum Act 1999 Sch.14, paras 3, 4) 1A,1B (as substituted by the Adoption and Children Act 2002 Sch.3, paras 1–3).

[21] The leading case is *Compton v Bearcroft* (1769) 2 Hagg. Con. 444n.

[22] *Brook v Brook* (1861) 9 H.L.C. 193 at 215, 228–229 and 236.

Of course it did not follow from this that foreign requirements of parental consent could also be treated as formalities. In *Simonin v Mallac,*[23] the English court was dealing with the more stringent rules of French law, which expressly applied to the marriages of Frenchmen and Frenchwomen, no matter where celebrated; non-compliance rendered the marriage voidable at the instance of the party who needed parental consent, or of his or her parents. Yet these rules were treated as inapplicable to a marriage between French persons celebrated in England. In that case a Frenchman aged 29 married a Frenchwoman aged 22 in England. The marriage was valid by English domestic law, but voidable by French law because neither party had obtained the consent of his or her parents as required by what was then art.151 of the French Civil Code. Although the marriage was annulled in France,[24] the country of the parties' domicile, it was held valid in England. The ground of the decision was that the validity of marriage generally is governed by the law of the place of celebration, but it was subsequently explained as having turned on formalities.[25] The court intimated[26] that art.148 of the French Civil Code, which imposed an absolute and not merely a qualified prohibition on marriages without parental consent, might receive a different interpretation.

However, the suggested distinction was ignored in *Ogden v Ogden,*[27] where a domiciled Frenchman aged 19 married in England a domiciled Englishwoman without the consent of his parents as required by art.148 which provided that a son who had not attained the age of 25 years could not contract marriage without the consent of his parents. The parties lived together in England for a few months, after which the husband returned to France, leaving the wife in England, and obtained a nullity decree from the French court on the ground of lack of parental consent. The Court of Appeal held that nevertheless the marriage was valid in England, because (among other reasons) the requirement of parental consent was a mere formality.[28] Although heavily criticised, *Ogden v Ogden* has since been followed in Scotland[29] and England.[30]

8–007

Renvoi

There is some reason to believe that if the marriage is formally invalid by the domestic law of the place of celebration, but formally valid by the system of law

8–008

---

[23] (1860) 2 Sw. & Tr. 67.

[24] The French nullity decree would now be recognised in England, but was not under the then English rules for the recognition of foreign decrees.

[25] *Brook v Brook* (1861) 9 H.L.C. 193, 218; *Sottomayor v De Barros (No. 1)* (1877) 3 P.D. 1 at 7.

[26] At p.77.

[27] [1908] P. 46. This case affords a striking example of characterisation in accordance with the *lex fori;* see below, para.18–008.

[28] At pp.57 and 75. The other reasons relate to capacity to marry and are considered below, para.8–026 The consequences of this decision were extremely awkward for the English woman, for both parties had remarried on the strength of the French nullity decree, but she was left married to a man who by the law of his domicile was not only not her husband but was the husband of someone else. She could not as the law then stood divorce her husband in England, since he was domiciled in France; nor was the French nullity decree recognised in England.

[29] *Bliersbach v McEwen,* 1959 S.C. 43.

[30] *Lodge v Lodge* (1963) 107 S.J. 437.

referred to by its conflict rules, the marriage would be held valid in England under the doctrine of *renvoi*.[31] In *Taczanowska v Taczanowski*,[32] two Polish nationals domiciled in Poland were married in Italy in a form which did not constitute a valid marriage by Italian domestic law. There was evidence that the Italian courts would recognise a marriage celebrated in Italy in accordance with the forms prescribed by the law of the parties' common nationality. But the marriage was not formally valid by Polish domestic law, and so it was not held valid in England on this ground. (It was held valid on another ground which is discussed later.[33]) It seems a safe deduction that it would have been held valid if it had been valid by Polish domestic law. Otherwise there would have been no point in admitting and discussing the evidence of the Italian conflict rule.

Exceptions to the rule

8–009 There is no exception to the proposition that a marriage, formally valid by the law of the place of celebration, is formally valid in England. But there are four real or apparent exceptions to the converse proposition that a marriage which is formally invalid by the law of the place of celebration, is also formally invalid in England. They are as follows: first, when it is impossible for the parties to use the local form; second, marriages in countries under belligerent occupation; third, marriages of members of H.M. Forces serving abroad; and fourth, marriages under the Foreign Marriage Act 1892, as amended.

Use of the local form impossible

8–010 There may be insuperable difficulties in using the local form. Quite how frequently such cases can arise in modern circumstances is open to question. The standard examples are of "desert islands" with no marriage procedures, and such islands may well exist only in the imagination; and while there may be states which insist on marriage in accordance with the rites of a single religious creed, which might be unacceptable to the parties, the notion of "insuperable difficulty" interpreted strictly might also involve an examination of the question as to whether the parties could travel to a neighbouring and more accommodating jurisdiction; and, in the light of modern social values, whether they should simply have waited until they could. However, it is thought that an English court would not be so accommodating of modern social ideas as was the Australian Family Court which excused compliance with the law of the Thai place of celebration because registration of the marriage would oblige the wife to take her husband's surname.[34]

If insuperable difficulties in using the local form do arise, a marriage will be formally valid if it is celebrated in accordance with the requirements of English common law. This means English law as it stood before Lord Hardwicke's

---

[31] For *renvoi*, see below, para.18–023. In Working Paper No.89 (1985), para.2.39, the Law Commission favoured the use of *renvoi* in this context; commentators were divided in their response.
[32] [1957] P. 301 at 305 and 318.
[33] Below, para.8–012.
[34] *Nygh and Kasey* [2010] FamCA 145.

Marriage Act 1753. That is to say, the marriage need not be celebrated in church, and no licence or publication of banns or witnesses are necessary: it is sufficient if the parties take each other as husband and wife.[35] At one time it was supposed that it was essential to the validity of an English common law marriage that it should be celebrated in the presence of an episcopally ordained clergyman. But the two decisions of the House of Lords[36] which laid down this rule have since been confined to marriages celebrated in England or Ireland[37]; and of course the principle under consideration could hardly apply to such a marriage, for ample facilities are provided for civil marriages in both countries, with or without such religious ceremony as the parties see fit to adopt. Hence a common law marriage celebrated abroad may be valid if celebrated before a minster of religion who is not episcopally ordained,[38] or before a layperson,[39] or (presumably) with no "officiant" of any sort, and merely the presence of others who could testify to what had taken place should the marriage need to be proved.

In many cases, marriages which have been held valid under this principle are not real exceptions to the general rule that the law of the place of celebration must be complied with. For their validity depends on the principle that the English common law, or so much of it as is applicable in the circumstances, applies to British subjects in a settled colony and also in some other colonies and places where Her Majesty once exercised extra-territorial jurisdiction.[40] Hence this law becomes, by a fiction of law, part of the *lex loci* itself.[41]

8–011

There is no English authority on the validity of marriages celebrated in merchant ships on the high seas.[42] It is thought that such a marriage would be held valid if celebrated in accordance with the formalities prescribed by the law of the ship's port of registration; and that, if this was English law, it would suffice if the parties took each other for husband and wife, provided the court was satisfied that it was impracticable for them to wait until the ship reached a port where sufficient facilities were available either by the local law or under the Foreign Marriage Act 1892. There would be no such element of emergency if the ship was lying in a foreign port, unless there was an insuperable difficulty in marrying ashore. However, a marriage celebrated in a British warship lying off Cyprus has been upheld.[43] The parties were British subjects domiciled in England

---

[35] However, for an analysis of the existence and effects of this type of pre 1753 "marriage", see Probert [2008] C.F.L.Q. 1.

[36] *R. v Millis* (1844) 10 Cl. & F. 534; *Beamish v Beamish* (1861) 9 H.L.C. 274. These two decisions have been much criticised: see Pollock and Maitland, *History of English Law*, Vol. 2, pp.370–372; Lord Hodson, (1958) 7 I.C.L.Q. 205 at 208–209; *Merker v Merker* [1963] P. 283 at 294, per Sir Jocelyn Simon P.

[37] *Wolfenden v Wolfenden* [1946] P. 61; approved by the Court of Appeal in *Apt v Apt* [1948] P.83 at 86, and by the Privy Council in *Penhas v Tan Soo Eng* [1953] A.C. 304, 319.

[38] *Wolfenden v Wolfenden* [1946] P. 61.

[39] *Penhas v Tan Soo Eng* [1953] A.C. 304.

[40] *Catterall v Catterall* (1847) 1 Rob. Ecc. 580; *Wolfenden v Wolfenden* [1946] P. 61; *Penhas v Tan Soo Eng* [1953] A.C. 304.

[41] *Taczanowska v Taczanowski* [1957] P.301 at 328 and 329.

[42] See Goddard, [2002] L.M.C.L.Q. 498 for a detailed consideration of marriages at sea.

[43] *Culling v Culling* [1896] P. 116.

and the ceremony was performed by the ship's chaplain in the presence of the captain, though without banns or licence.[44]

Marriages in countries under belligerent occupation

8–012   During the concluding weeks of the Second World War and its immediate aftermath, many thousands of marriages were celebrated in Germany and Italy between Roman Catholics or Jews domiciled in Poland and other Eastern European countries. These marriages were not valid by the local law, either because there was no civil ceremony or because some formality required by the local law was omitted. The validity of these marriages has been tested in a number of cases, and they have been held valid if they were celebrated in the form required by English common law and the husband was a member of belligerent occupying forces,[45] or of forces associated with them,[46] or (perhaps) of an organised body of escaped prisoners of war.[47] The status of the wife seems to have been treated as immaterial.[48] The leading case is the test case of *Taczanowska v Taczanowski,*[49] where the Court of Appeal upheld the validity of a marriage celebrated in 1946 in an Italian church by a Roman Catholic priest serving as a Polish Army chaplain; the husband was an officer of the Polish forces serving with the British Army in Italy and the wife a Polish civilian. The marriage was formally invalid by Italian law and also by Polish law. It was not valid under the previous exception (because there was no insuperable difficulty in complying with the local law), nor under the next exception (because the chaplain was not acting under the orders of the British Commander-in-Chief). The main ground of the decision appears to have been that, as the husband was not in Italy from choice but under the orders of his military superiors, he was exempt from the operation of the local law unless he submitted to it of his own volition. Widely construed, this could have been taken to include ordinary civilians who are present in a country from necessity and not from choice. But it is now clear that the principle does not extend to them.[50]

The decision in *Taczanowska v Taczanowski* has been followed[51] and distinguished[52] and has been heavily criticised by academic writers.[53] It is indeed a remarkable proposition that a marriage celebrated in a foreign country between

---

[44] Marriages on board British warships are now regulated by the Foreign Marriage Act 1892 s.22 as amended in 1947, 1988 and 2005.

[45] *Taczanowska v Taczanowski* [1957] P. 301.

[46] *Preston v Preston* [1963] P. 411.

[47] *Merker v Merker* [1963] P. 283 at 295.

[48] *Taczanowska v Taczanowski*, above; *Preston v Preston*, above, at pp.425 and 430.

[49] [1957] P. 301. According to contemporary press reports, this was a test case involving the validity of some 3,000–4,000 similar marriages.

[50] *Preston v Preston* [1963] P.411 at 426–427 and 434–435, disapproving *Kochanski v Kochanska* [1958] P. 147, where the principle was extended to the marriage of inmates of a Polish displaced persons' camp in Germany; but in *Preston v Preston*, above, the same camp was held to be a military one.

[51] *Kochanski v Kochanska* [1958] P. 147; *Merker v Merker* [1963] P. 283; *Preston v Preston* [1963] P. 411. It is a pity that the husband's conduct in this last case was so reprehensible that the Court of Appeal refused him leave to appeal to the House of Lords.

[52] *Lazarewicz v Lazarewicz* [1962] P. 171.

[53] Mendes da Costa, (1958) 7 I.C.L.Q. 217 at 226–235; Andrews, (1959) 22 M.L.R. 396 at 403–407.

persons domiciled in another foreign country who have never visited England in their lives, and may never do so, can derive formal validity from compliance with the requirements of English domestic law as it existed 200 years before the marriage. It cannot be supposed that such parties ever intended to submit to English common law. If the law of the place of celebration is inapplicable for any reason, it would seem more sensible to refer the formal validity of the marriage to the law of the parties' domicile, but this suggestion has found no favour with the courts.[54] It should be noted that these decisions belong to a very different social era, and the validity of such marriages today may be viewed more restrictively.

Marriages of members of H.M. Forces serving abroad

Such marriages are regulated by s.22 of the Foreign Marriage Act 1892, as substituted in 1947 and extended in 1988.[55] For this section to apply, at least one of the parties to the marriage must be a person who is: (a) a member of HM Forces serving in the foreign territory concerned; or (b) a civilian subject to service discipline (within the meaning of the Armed Forces Act 2006) of a description prescribed by Order in Council and who is employed in that territory; or (c) a child of such a person who has his home with that person in that territory.[56] A marriage may be celebrated under this provision by a chaplain serving with the naval, military, or air forces in the relevant territory or by anyone authorised by the commanding officer of such forces. Such marriages are as valid in law as if solemnised in the United Kingdom with due observance of all forms required by law. There is no requirement that either party must be a British citizen.[57] The term "foreign territory" does not include any part of the Commonwealth,[58] but it does include a ship in foreign waters.[59] The operation of the section depends very largely on Orders in Council.[60] Unlike the rest of that Act, s.22 is largely declaratory of the common law. It is a real exception to the principle that compliance with the formalities prescribed by the local law is necessary to the validity of a marriage; but of course its scope is limited.

8–013

Marriages under the Foreign Marriage Act 1892 s.8

A marriage solemnised in the manner provided by s.8 of the Foreign Marriage Act 1892, in any foreign country or place,[61] by or in the presence of a "marriage

8–014

---

[54] *Taczanowska v Taczanowski*, above, at pp.326 and 331; *Preston v Preston* [1963] P. 141 at and 152–153.
[55] See also Civil Partnership (Armed Forces) Order 2005 (SI 2005/3188).
[56] See s.22(1A) (1B) as inserted by Foreign Marriage (Amendment) Act 1988 s.6 as amended by SI 2005/3129 and SI 2009/812; a child of unmarried parents and one treated as a child of the family concerned are included.
[57] *Taczanowska v Taczanowski* [1957] P. 301 at 319–320 (with reference to the original s.22).
[58] s.22(2).
[59] s.22(3).
[60] See the Foreign Marriage (Armed Forces) Order, SI 1964/1000, as amended by SI 1965/137, SI 1990/2592 and SI 2009/2054.
[61] In the Act, a "foreign" country or place means one outside the Commonwealth.

officer", between parties of whom one at least is a United Kingdom national,[62] is as valid in law as if it had been solemnised in the United Kingdom with a due observance of all the forms required by law.[63] "Marriage officers" under the Act are British consuls and ambassadors and members of their diplomatic staff, provided in all cases that they hold a marriage warrant from the Secretary of State.[64] There is thus complete discretion to exclude any foreign country from the operation of the Act; and in some countries the marriage officers are only authorised to celebrate marriages between two British citizens.

Section 8 (as amended in 1988) provides that every marriage under the Act must be solemnised at the official house of the marriage officer, with open doors, between the hours of 8am and 6pm, in the presence of two or more witnesses. The ceremony may be in such form as the parties see fit to adopt; they must at some stage declare that they know of no lawful impediment to the marriage and utter the statutory words of consent.

The Act contains requirements as to notice of intended marriage,[65] the filing and entering of such notice,[66] parental consent,[67] the taking of an oath,[68] and the registration of the marriage.[69] But all these requirements are directory only and not mandatory: even if none of them is complied with, the marriage will still be valid provided the requirements of s.8 (which is the crucial section) have been met.[70] Moreover, the solemnisation of the marriage precludes subsequent inquiry as to whether the parties resided within the district of the marriage officer for the requisite three weeks, or whether parental consent was given[71]; and the solemnisation and registration of the marriage precludes subsequent inquiry as to the authority of the marriage officer.[72]

8–015 A marriage celebrated under the Act is valid in England as regards form (but not necessarily valid in other respects, e.g. capacity), though it may be invalid under the law of the place of celebration.[73] But although it may appear at first sight that the parties need not concern themselves with the formal requirements of the local law, in practice it is often essential that those requirements should be observed. For before a marriage is solemnised under the Act, the marriage officer must be satisfied (a) that at least one of the parties is a United Kingdom national; (b) that the local authorities will not object to the solemnisation of the marriage; (c) that

---

[62] Defined in s.1(2) as inserted in 1988 and amended by the British Overseas Territories Act 2002 s.2(3).

[63] Foreign Marriage Act 1892 s.1.

[64] *ibid.*, s.11. The solemnisation of marriages under the Act is regarded primarily as a consular function, and warrants are issued to ambassadors or members of their diplomatic staff only in exceptional circumstances.

[65] s.2.

[66] s.3.

[67] s.4 as substituted in 1988.

[68] s.7 as amended in 1988.

[69] s.9 as amended in 1988.

[70] *Collett v Collett* [1968] P. 482.

[71] Foreign Marriage Act 1892 s.13(1).

[72] *ibid.*, s.13(2) as amended in 1947.

[73] *Hay v Northcote* [1900] 2 Ch. 262, where a marriage celebrated in accordance with the Consular Marriage Act 1849 was held valid although it had been annulled by the courts of the parties' domicile, not then entitled to recognition in England.

insufficient facilities exist for the marriage under the local law; and (d) that the parties will be regarded as validly married by the law of the country in which each party is domiciled.[74] Moreover, the marriage officer need not solemnise a marriage, or allow one to be solemnised in his or her presence, if in the officer's opinion the solemnisation thereof would be inconsistent with international law or the comity of nations.[75] It is impossible to say what this imprecise phrase means; but it can hardly mean that the invalidity of the marriage by the local law is a sufficient ground for refusing to solemnise it.

Thus, in many cases, the advantage of the Act is not that it permits the parties to disregard the law of the place of celebration but that it enables them to obtain a certificate which will be evidence of the marriage in England.

CAPACITY TO MARRY

Capacity to marry (sometimes referred to as the essential validity of the marriage) concerns whether the parties to the marriage are legally able to contract a marriage, as opposed to *how* the marriage should be celebrated. Traditionally, this rubric includes the impediments of the prohibited degrees of consanguinity and affinity and lack of age; but there seems no reason for it not also to include the impediments of lack of parental consent, in so far as that is not treated as a mere formality; previous marriage; and physical incapacity: in short, all impediments to marriage, other than formal ones, which have already been considered, and lack of consent of parties, which is discussed later. This has the advantage of avoiding a multiplicity of categories: but it should be borne in mind that the social and policy reasons for the various impediments are not always the same, and that this may possibly justify the application of different conflict rules. 8–016

The rival theories

English textwriters have canvassed two theories as to what law governs capacity to marry. The theory of Dicey, which may be called the orthodox view, is that capacity to marry is governed by the law of each party's antenuptial domicile: the "dual domicile" theory.[76] Cheshire's theory was that the basic presumption is that capacity to marry is governed by the law of the husband's domicile at the time of the marriage, but that this presumption is rebutted if it can be inferred that the parties at the time of the marriage intended to establish their home in a certain country and that they did in fact establish it there within a reasonable time: the "intended matrimonial home" theory.[77] The difference between the two theories is that an incapacity imposed by the law of the wife's antenuptial domicile will invalidate the marriage according to Dicey, but will not generally invalidate it 8–017

---

[74] Foreign Marriage Order 1970 (1970/1539) art.3(1) as amended by SI 1990/598 arts 2 and 3.
[75] Foreign Marriage Act 1892 s.19.
[76] For other views, see Hartley, (1972) 35 M.L.R. 571; Jaffey, (1978) 41 M.L.R. 38; Fentiman, [1985] C.L.J. 256; Murphy, (2000) 49 I.C.L.Q. 643.
[77] It should be noted (a) that Cheshire's views have been virtually abandoned in the more recent editions edited by North and Fawcett; and (b) that neither *Dicey, Morris and Collins* nor *Cheshire and North* are discussing physical incapacity.

according to Cheshire. Thus, as a general rule, more marriages will be valid under Cheshire's theory than under Dicey's; but this is not invariably the case.[78]

Dicey's view is based on the idea that the community to which each party belongs is interested in his or her status, and that in these days of sex equality no preference should be shown to the laws of one community rather than to the laws of the other.

Cheshire's view is based on the idea that the community to which the parties belong after their marriage is more interested in their status than the communities to which they belonged before. At first sight this is a plausible view, but on closer examination it seems to prove too much. Suppose that a man domiciled in country A marries a woman domiciled in country B, and that at the time of the marriage the parties intend to establish their home in country C and do in fact establish it there within a reasonable time. According to Cheshire, the law of C is more interested in the status of these parties than the laws of A and B, and therefore the law of C and no other should determine whether they had capacity to marry. But now suppose that, ten years after the marriage, the parties abandon their domicile and matrimonial home in C and establish another in country D. By the same token, the law of D is now more interested in their status than any other law, and it alone should determine whether they had capacity to marry. Of course, nobody seriously suggests that the validity of a marriage should be reassessed every time the parties change their domicile: that would be unjust as well as quite impracticable.

8–018 Cheshire says that "whether the intermarriage of two persons should be prohibited for social, religious, eugenic or other like reason is a question that affects the community in which the parties live together as man and wife",[79] i.e. the intended matrimonial home. This may be true of the prohibited degrees of consanguinity, for the prohibition is based mainly on considerations of eugenics, and arguably this is a post-matrimonial matter. But it certainly is not true of the prohibited degrees of affinity, for such prohibitions can only be justified (if at all) by religious or moral considerations, and this is a pre-matrimonial matter. It would therefore be anomalous for English law to give effect to the religious or moral principles prevailing in a particular country when the man is domiciled there, but to ignore them in the case of a woman.

Cheshire says that principle supports the view that capacity to marry should be governed by the law of the intended matrimonial home, because capacity to make a commercial contract is governed by the system of law with which the transaction has the most substantial connection.[80] There is, however, all the difference in the world between a marriage (which as we have seen is like a contract only in the sense that it is a consensual transaction) and an ordinary commercial contract. To argue from one to the other seems quite unjustifiable.

---

[78] A case in point is *Schwebel v Ungar* (1964) 48 D.L.R. (2d) 644; below, para.8–030. There the validity of the marriage could only be sustained by an exclusive reference to the law of the wife's antenuptial domicile.

[79] Cheshire, North & Fawcett, *Private International Law* (Oxford University Press, Oxford, 14th edn., 2008), p.897.

[80] *ibid.*, at p.723. For capacity to make a commercial contract, see below, para.11–065.

Very serious practical difficulties are likely to arise if the validity of a marriage has to remain in suspense while we wait and see (for an unspecified period) whether or not the parties implement their (unexpressed) antenuptial intention to acquire another domicile. This is especially true if interests in property depend on the validity of a marriage, as, for instance, where a widow's pension ceases on her remarriage.

The two theories, together with a number of other possibilities, were fully canvassed by the Law Commission in its 1985 Working Paper; the arguments against the intended matrimonial home theory were adjudged "more cogent" than those in its favour,[81] and the Commission's provisional view was that the dual domicile test be adopted to govern all issues of legal capacity.[82] The ensuing consultations showed a substantial majority in favour of this view but, as we have seen, it was decided to take no legislative action.[83] The issue therefore remains a matter for the courts,[84] and it is to the case-law that we must now turn. We shall see that (apart from physical incapacity) with one exception[85] the cases strongly support Dicey's view, and that the more recent ones[86] expressly approve it.

Consanguinity and affinity

Changes in English domestic law

Before 1835, in English domestic law, a marriage between persons within the prohibited degrees of consanguinity or affinity was only voidable. This meant that the validity of the marriage could be attacked only during the joint lives of the parties, and then only by one party in a nullity suit against the other; and that, in the absence of a decree of nullity pronounced by a court of competent jurisdiction, the marriage was valid, the children were legitimate, and the devolution of property was not affected by the circumstance that the parties were married within the prohibited degrees. In 1835, however, Lord Lyndhurst's Marriage Act rendered such marriages not merely voidable, but void. This meant that the validity of the marriage could be attacked at any time, even after the death of the parties, by any person, in any proceedings; that if the marriage was void the children were illegitimate; and that the devolution of property often went awry. The Chancery reports of the Victorian and Edwardian reigns are full of cases in which gifts to children failed because their parents were married within the prohibited degrees.

8–019

---

[81] Working Paper, para.3.35.
[82] Working Paper, para.3.36.
[83] *Choice of Law Rules in Marriage* (Law Com. No. 165), para.2.6 (1987).
[84] Although an alternative reference test was rejected by the Law Commission's Working Paper No 89, para.3.37, Wall LJ expressed the view in *KC v City of Westminster Social and Community Services Dept* [2008] EWCA Civ. 198; [2008] 2 F.C.R. 146, at para.90 that: "… departures from the dual domicile rule designed to uphold the principle of marriage may be appropriate when the marriage in question is one which, on grounds of public policy, the courts will think it right to uphold."
[85] *Sottomayor v De Barros (No.2)* (1879) 5 P.D. 94; below, para.8–022.
[86] *Padolecchia v Padolecchia* [1968] P. 314, 336; *R. v Brentwood Marriage Registrar* [1968] 2 Q.B. 956 at 968; *Szechter v Szechter* [1971] P. 286, 295B. See however *Radwan v Radwan (No.2)* [1973] Fam. 35, discussed below, para.8–047.

The prohibited degrees of English law were, as a general rule, stricter than those of neighbouring European countries. For example, in English law a man could not marry his deceased wife's sister, nor a woman her deceased husband's brother, while in many European countries such marriages were valid. It therefore became the practice for English couples within the English prohibited degrees to marry during a temporary visit to some European country where the marriage was valid. Just as English couples in the eighteenth century managed to escape from the provisions of Lord Hardwicke's Marriage Act 1753 by marrying in Scotland, so their successors hoped to escape from the rigours of Lord Lyndhurst's Marriage Act 1835 by marrying in a suitable European country.

This practice was ended by the decision of the House of Lords in *Brook v Brook*,[87] with disastrous results for the family concerned. In that case a man and his deceased wife's sister, both British subjects domiciled in England, went through a ceremony of marriage during a temporary visit to Denmark, by whose law the marriage was valid. The husband, the wife, and one of the infant children of the marriage died within a few days of each other in an epidemic of cholera. It was held that the marriage was void, that the children were illegitimate, and that therefore the dead child's one-fifth share of the family property passed to the Crown as bona vacantia and not to his natural brothers and sisters.

8–020   In the decade which followed the decision in *Brook v Brook*, attempts to induce Parliament to legalise marriages between a man and his deceased wife's sister were almost annual events[88]; but it was not until 1907 that such marriages became lawful,[89] and not until 1921 that a marriage between a woman and her deceased husband's brother was legalised.[90] Marriages between a man and his deceased wife's niece or aunt, or between a woman and her deceased husband's nephew or uncle, were legalised in 1931.[91] But marriages between a man and his divorced wife's sister, niece or aunt, or between a woman and her divorced husband's brother, nephew or uncle, remained invalid until 1960.[92] It was only in 1986 that certain marriages between step-parent and step-child were allowed.[93] Most recently, the European Court of Human Rights held, in *B v United Kingdom*,[94] that it is a violation of art.12 ECHR to prohibit the marriage of a father-in-law and daughter-in-law after their previous marriages had been ended by divorce, and English law has been changed accordingly.[95]

The combined effect of these changes was greatly to reduce the discrepancy between English law and the laws of neighbouring European countries, and thus to reduce the practical importance of the English conflict rules about to be

---

[87] (1861) 9 H.L.C. 193.

[88] Devotees of Gilbert and Sullivan will recall that in *Iolanthe* (first produced in 1882), Strephon, whose mother was a fairy and whose father was a Lord Chancellor, was sent into Parliament by the Queen of the Fairies; and that one of the predictions she made about his career was: "He shall prick that annual blister, Marriage with deceased wife's sister".

[89] Deceased Wife's Sister's Marriage Act 1907.

[90] Deceased Brother's Widow's Marriage Act 1921.

[91] Marriage (Prohibited Degrees of Relationship) Act 1931. These three statutes are now consolidated in s.1 of the Marriage (Enabling) Act 1960.

[92] Marriage (Enabling) Act 1960.

[93] Marriage (Prohibited Degrees of Relationship) Act 1986.

[94] (2006) 42 E.H.R.R. 11; [2006] 1 F.L.R. 35.

[95] SI 2007/438, which repealed Marriage Act 1949 ss.1(4)–(8).

discussed. However, these rules still have some importance because, for example, a marriage between uncle and niece is void by English law but valid by the laws of many other countries, while on the other hand a marriage between first cousins is valid in English law but invalid by the laws of some Catholic countries.

The conflict of laws

In *Brook v Brook*,[96] the facts of which have already been stated, the House of Lords finally established that a distinction must be drawn between the formalities of marriage, governed by the law of the place of celebration, and capacity to marry, governed by the law of each party's antenuptial domicile. At about the same time it was held in *Mette v Mette*[97] that a marriage in Frankfurt between a man domiciled in England and a woman domiciled in Frankfurt was void because they were within the prohibited degrees of English law, although the marriage was valid by the law of Frankfurt. It was subsequently held in *Re Paine*[98] that a marriage in Germany between a man domiciled in Germany and a woman domiciled in England was void because they were within the prohibited degrees of English law, although the marriage was valid by the law of Germany.

8–021

In *Sottomayor v De Barros (No.1)*,[99] two first cousins supposedly domiciled in Portugal married in England. The marriage was valid by English law, but invalid by the law of Portugal, under which first cousins could not marry without papal dispensation. The parties were very young – the boy was aged 16 and the girl 14½. The marriage was one of convenience only, arranged for them by their parents; and though they lived together in the same house in England for six years, the marriage was never consummated. The girl then petitioned for a decree of nullity on the ground of consanguinity. The suit was undefended, but the Queen's Proctor intervened and alleged[100] (inter alia) that the parties were domiciled in England and not in Portugal; that they intended at the time of the marriage to live together in England and did so live for six years; and that the validity of the marriage was to be determined by English domestic law. The somewhat inconvenient course was taken of ordering that the question of law should be argued before the questions of fact. On the assumption, then, that the parties were both domiciled in Portugal at the time of the marriage, the Court of Appeal held that the marriage was void, because "as in other contracts, so in that of marriage, personal capacity must depend on the law of the domicile".[101] This seems a clear decision against the law of the intended matrimonial home.

The case was then remitted to the Divorce Division in order that the questions of fact raised by the Queen's Proctor's pleas might be determined. When it appeared that the husband's domicile at the time of the marriage was not in Portugal but in

8–022

---

[96] (1861) 9 H.L.C. 193. cf. *Re De Wilton* [1900] 2 Ch. 481, to the same effect.
[97] (1859) 1 Sw. & Tr. 416. The ratio decidendi was "There can be no valid contract unless each was competent to contract with the other" (p.423).
[98] [1940] Ch. 46. It is perhaps unfortunate that Cheshire's book (first published in 1935) was not cited to the court in this case.
[99] (1877) 3 P.D. 1.
[100] See the report of the case in the court below: 2 P.D. 81, 82.
[101] (1877) 3 P.D. 1 at 5.

England, Sir James Hannen P. pronounced the marriage valid[102] in reliance on a dictum in the judgment of the Court of Appeal that "Our opinion on this appeal is confined to the case where both the contracting parties are, at the time of their marriage, domiciled in a country the laws of which prohibit their marriage".[103] The judgment of Hannen P. seems to be based on the theory that capacity to marry is governed by the law of the place of celebration, which is, to put it mildly, difficult to reconcile with *Brook v Brook* and *Sottomayor v De Barros (No.1)*.

There is obvious difficulty in reconciling this decision with the other cases, and especially with *Mette v Mette*[104] and *Re Paine*.[105] Of the various attempts at reconciliation, the most significant are *(a)* that an incapacity imposed by English law is more important than an incapacity imposed by foreign law; and *(b)* that an incapacity imposed by the law of the husband's domicile is more important than an incapacity imposed by the law of the wife's domicile. Neither of these is satisfactory. Dicey found it necessary to make an exception to his general rule that capacity to marry is governed by the law of each party's antenuptial domicile, which exception he formulated as follows:

> "The validity of a marriage celebrated in England between persons of whom the one has an English, and the other a foreign, domicile is not affected by any incapacity which, though existing under the law of such foreign domicile, does not exist under the law of England".[106]

This exception is admittedly illogical, though it can be said to have a practical advantage in that it reduces the risk of a void marriage due to the ignorance of the provisions of the relevant foreign law by officiating clergy or registrars. The exception has been approved by the Court of Appeal,[107] and until *Sottomayor v De Barros (No.2)* is overruled, it must be taken to represent the law. But, as we shall see,[108] its scope is reduced by the Marriage (Enabling) Act 1960.

8–023   If the marriage is celebrated abroad and is valid by the law of each party's domicile, it will be held valid in England though the parties were within the prohibited degrees of English law.[109] At any rate this is true if the parties are not so closely related that intercourse between them would be incestuous by English criminal law.[110] On this ground, marriages celebrated in Italy between a woman and her deceased husband's brother,[111] and in Egypt between an uncle and niece,[112] have been held valid, even though the parties were within the prohibited degrees of English law.

---

[102] *Sottomayor v De Barros (No. 2)* (1879) 5 P.D. 94.
[103] (1877) 3 P.D. 1 at 6–7.
[104] (1859) 1 Sw. & Tr. 416.
[105] [1940] Ch. 46.
[106] See now Dicey, Morris & Collins, *The Conflict of Laws* (Sweet and Maxwell, London, 14th edn., 2006), exception 4 to Rule 67.
[107] *Ogden v Ogden* [1908] P. 46 at 74–77.
[108] Below, para.8–023.
[109] *Re Bozzellis Settlement*[1902] 1 Ch. 751; *Cheni v Cheni* [1965] P. 85.
[110] *Cheni v Cheni* [1965] P. 85 at 97.
[111] *Re Bozzellis Settlement*[1902] 1 Ch. 751.
[112] *Cheni v Cheni* [1965] P. 85.

Section 1 of the Marriage (Enabling) Act 1960 permits a marriage between a man and his former wife's sister, aunt or niece, or between a woman and her former husband's brother, uncle or nephew. Section 1(3) of the Act provides that the section does not validate a marriage if either party is at the time of the marriage domiciled in a country under whose law there cannot be a valid marriage between the parties. Hence the section implicitly accepts Dicey's view on capacity to marry and rejects that of Cheshire. The reference to "either party" means that neither Cheshire's intended matrimonial home theory nor Dicey's exception based on *Sottomayor v De Barros (No.2)*[113] can apply to any marriage mentioned in s.1, if one party was domiciled in England at the time of the marriage.

Relevance of the law of the place of celebration

Must the parties have capacity to marry by the law of the place of celebration as well as by the laws of their antenuptial domiciles? There is singularly little authority on this question. On principle it would seem that if the marriage is celebrated in England, the answer must be yes, because the English court could hardly disregard its own law on such a vital matter and hold valid a marriage which that law prohibited, even if it was valid by the law of the parties' domicile.[114] If the marriage is celebrated abroad, the question is more difficult.[115] There is no English authority,[116] but there is one early Australian case and one modern Canadian case, in each of which the marriage was held valid, despite the lack of capacity by the law of the place of celebration. In *Will of Swan,*[117] it was held that a will had been revoked by the testator's marriage in Scotland to his deceased wife's niece. The marriage was void by Scots law, but voidable in his lifetime by the Victorian law of his domicile, since Lord Lyndhurst's Marriage Act 1835 had not then been adopted in Victoria. Similarly, in *Reed v Reed,*[118] two first cousins domiciled in British Columbia wished to marry. The girl, who was aged 18, was unable to obtain the consent of her parents as required by the law of British Columbia. So the parties were married in the state of Washington, where such consent was not required. But unknown to them, first cousins were incapable of marriage by the law of Washington, though they were capable by the law of British Columbia. The marriage was held valid.

8–024

---

[113] (1879) 5 P.D. 94. See North (1980) I *Recueil des Cours* 57–65.

[114] This is now the case in Scotland; see Family Law (Scotland) Act 2006 s.38(3).

[115] The Law Commission examined this matter in its Working Paper No.89 (1985), paras 3.40–3.44; after receiving divided views in response, the Commission's view was that the law of the place of celebration, where it was not the forum, should be ignored: Law Com. No. 165, para.2.6 (1987).

[116] But see *Breen v Breen* [1964] P. 144, where, in the different context of bigamy, Karminski J. was prepared to hold that incapacity by the law of the place of celebration was fatal to the validity of a marriage.

[117] (1871) 2 V.R. (I.E. & M.) 47.

[118] (1969) 6 D.L.R. (3d) 617.

Lack of age

8–025   Section 2 of the Marriage Act 1949 (re-enacting the Age of Marriage Act 1929) provides that a marriage between persons either of whom is under the age of 16 is void. In other systems, the minimum age for marriage may be higher or lower. There is only one reported English case in which the law governing this impediment has been considered. In *Pugh v Pugh*,[119] a marriage was celebrated in Austria between a British officer domiciled in England but stationed in Austria, and a girl of 15 domiciled in Hungary. Four years later the parties came to England in accordance with their antenuptial intention, but parted almost at once. The marriage was valid by Austrian and Hungarian law, but it was held void. It therefore appears that no marriage is valid if either party is under 16, if either party (not necessarily the party under age) is domiciled in England. The law is different in Scotland, where s.1(1) of the Marriage (Scotland) Act 1977 provides that "no person domiciled in Scotland may marry before he attains the age of 16."

The court in *Pugh v Pugh* relied on *Brook v Brook*[120] and on the other cases on the prohibited degrees which have already been considered: this seems sufficient justification for treating lack of age as coming under capacity to marry.

It is thought that a marriage celebrated in England would be held void if one party was under sixteen, regardless of the domicile of the parties: and there is a dictum to this effect in *Pugh v Pugh*.[121] This is, indeed, the case in Scotland, where s.1(2) of the Marriage (Scotland) Act 1977 states that "A marriage solemnised in Scotland between persons either of whom is under the age of 16 shall be void."

Lack of parental consent

8–026   As we have seen, English courts seem committed to the view that lack of parental consent, whether imposed by English or by foreign law, and no matter how stringently the requirement is expressed, is a mere formality and therefore incapable of invalidating a marriage celebrated in England. In *Ogden v Ogden*,[122] however, the facts of which have already been stated, this was not the only ground of the decision. Other grounds were *(a)* that capacity to marry is governed by the law of the place of celebration and not by the law of the parties' domicile[123]; and *(b)* that a marriage celebrated in England between a person domiciled in England and a person domiciled abroad is not invalidated by any incapacity which, though existing under the foreign law, does not exist in English

---

[119] [1951] P. 482, cited, without disapproval, in *Re X (Children) (Parental Order)* [2008] EWHC 3030 (Fam); [2009] Fam. 71. cf. *Mohamed v Knott* [1969] 1 Q.B. 1, where the girl was only 13, but the marriage was held valid because it was valid by the law of each party's antenuptial domicile. The Domicile and Matrimonial Proceedings Act 1973 s.3(1), assumes that parties may be validly married under foreign law below the age of 16: see above, para.2–036.

[120] (1861) 9 H.L.C. 193.

[121] [1951] P. 482 at 491–492. The possible scope of the English statute is discussed by Beckett, (1934) 15 B.Y.I.L. 46 at 64–65, and Morris, (1946) 62 L.Q.R. at 170–171.

[122] [1908] P. 46.

[123] At pp.58–62.

law.[124] The first of these grounds is manifestly inconsistent with the decisions of the House of Lords in *Brook v Brook*[125] and of the Court of Appeal in *Sottomayor v De Barros (No.1)*.[126] The second reflects the illogical exception to the general rule on capacity to marry which was introduced by *Sottomayor v De Barros (No.2)*.[127]

These two additional grounds leave open the possibility that a foreign requirement of parental consent may one day be characterised as relating to capacity to marry and not to the formalities of marriage.

The decision in *Ogden v Ogden* can be defended on policy grounds. It is a strong thing to hold that a marriage, celebrated in England and valid by English law, is invalid because of its failure to comply with foreign law. Of course the decision left the woman in an unfortunate position, and for this reason it has been described as "grotesque from the social point of view."[128] But it was really fortuitous that she had remarried: the decision might not have seemed so grotesque if she had been seeking to uphold the marriage, e.g. by claiming maintenance from her French husband.

Previous marriage

It is submitted with some confidence that this impediment may properly be included under the heading of capacity to marry. There is high authority for placing it under this rubric[129]; nor does it seem an abuse of language to say that a monogamously married man or woman has no capacity to contract a second marriage until the first is dissolved.

8–027

If this is correct, the authority of the House of Lords may be cited for the proposition that capacity to marry is governed by the law of each party's antenuptial domicile and not by the law of the husband's domicile or that of the intended matrimonial home. In *Shaw v Gould,*[130] a man and a woman, both domiciled in England, married there and separated soon afterwards. The marriage was dissolved by the Court of Session in Scotland, and the woman then married a domiciled Scotsman and lived with him in Scotland. The divorce was not recognised in England because the first husband never lost his English domicile of origin. The House of Lords held that the second marriage was void, although it was valid by the law of the second husband's domicile and by the law of the intended matrimonial home. Lord Cranworth said: "If the first marriage here was not dissolved there could not have been a second marriage. Till the first was

---

[124] At pp.75–77.
[125] (1861) 9 H.L.C. 193.
[126] (1877) 3 P.D. 1.
[127] (1879) 5 P.D. 94.
[128] Falconbridge, *Selected Essays on the Conflict of Laws* (Canada Law Book, Toronto, 2nd edn, 1954), p.74.
[129] See, e.g., *Conway v Beazley* (1831) 3 Hagg. Ecc. 639 at 647 and 652, per Dr. Lushington; *Brook v Brook* (1861) 9 H.L.C. 193, 211–212, per Lord Campbell; *Shaw v Gould* (1868) L.R. 3 H.L. 55 at 71, per Lord Cranworth; *Padolecchia v Padolecchia* [1968] P. 314 at 336, per Sir Jocelyn Simon P.; *Wicken v Wicken* [1999] Fam. 224.
[130] (1868) L.R. 3 H.L. 55.

dissolved there was no capacity to contract a second."[131] It is submitted that this type of case demonstrates the impossibility of accepting any other view than that capacity to marry is governed by the law of each party's antenuptial domicile.

8–028   Again, in *Padolecchia v Padolecchia*[132] a man domiciled in Italy was divorced from his first wife in Mexico. This divorce was not recognised in Italy. He went to live in Denmark and, during a one-day visit to England, went through a ceremony of marriage with a woman domiciled in Denmark. They both returned to Denmark to live, and later the man (still domiciled in Italy) petitioned the English court for a decree of nullity on the ground of his own bigamy. Sir Jocelyn Simon P. held that since the Mexican divorce was not recognised in Italy, the man had no capacity to marry by the law of his domicile; and he expressly approved the Rule in Dicey and Morris's treatise stating the dual domicile test.[133] He declined to consider the possibility that the marriage might be valid by the law of the intended matrimonial home. This decision is thus a strong authority in favour of the orthodox view.

Three situations need to be discussed in greater detail. The first is where the remarriage of a person whose marriage has been validly dissolved or annulled has been held invalid. The second is where the remarriage has been held valid notwithstanding an invalid decree of divorce. The third is where the law of the country where a divorce was granted imposes some restriction on the right of a divorced person to remarry.

Remarriage after valid foreign divorce or nullity decree

8–029   This is one area which illustrates the Law Commission's confidence in the ability of the courts to develop the law and point the way for the legislators to follow.

It was at one time clear, but inconvenient, law that a person whose foreign divorce decree was entitled to recognition in England might be unable to remarry here if the law of his or her domicile refused recognition to the same decree[134]; in effect, the choice of law rules as to capacity to marry prevailed over those on the recognition of foreign decrees.[135] That particular type of case was dealt with by legislation in 1971,[136] in a provision limited to foreign divorces (as opposed to nullity decrees[137]) and to remarriage in England (and not elsewhere[138]).

The matter is now governed by s.50 of the Family Law Act 1986.[139] Where a divorce or annulment is granted, or is entitled to recognition, in any part of the United Kingdom, the fact that it may not be recognised elsewhere does not preclude either party to the marriage from forming a subsequent marriage or civil

---

[131] At p.71.
[132] [1968] P. 314.
[133] At p.336.
[134] *R. v Brentwood Marriage Registrar* [1968] 2 Q.B. 956.
[135] This is an example of the "incidental question"; see para.18–016.
[136] Recognition of Divorces and Legal Separations Act 1971 s.7 (since repealed).
[137] See *Perrini v Perrini* [1979] Fam. 84.
[138] See *Lawrence v Lawrence* [1985] Fam. 134.
[139] As amended by the Civil Partnership Act 2004 Sch.27, para.125.

partnership in that part of the United Kingdom or cause the subsequent marriage or civil partnership of either party (wherever it takes place) to be treated as invalid in that part.

Remarriage after void foreign divorce

The converse situation arose in the Canadian case of *Schwebel v Ungar.*[140] A husband and wife, both Jews, were domiciled in Hungary. They decided to emigrate to Israel. While en route to Israel they were divorced by a Jewish ghet (or extra-judicial divorce) in Italy. They then separately acquired domiciles of choice in Israel. The wife married a man domiciled in Ontario during a temporary visit to that province. The ghet was ineffective to dissolve the marriage by the law of Hungary (where they were domiciled at the time of the ghet) but was effective to do so by the law of Israel (where they were domiciled at the time of the remarriage). It was not recognised as a valid divorce in Ontario, since the parties were not domiciled in Israel when it was delivered. Nevertheless, the remarriage was held valid, because immediately prior to the remarriage the wife's status by the law of her domicile was that of a single woman.

8–030

Restrictions on the remarriage of divorced persons

Such restrictions are imposed for three main reasons: first, to punish the "guilty party"; second, to safeguard the unsuccessful party's right to appeal; and third, to prevent disputes about the paternity of children subsequently born to the woman.[141]

   In *Scott v Att-Gen*,[142] a husband obtained a divorce in Cape Colony, where he was domiciled, on the ground of his wife's adultery. By the law of the Cape, a person divorced for adultery was prohibited from remarrying so long as the injured party remained unmarried. After the divorce the wife came to England and married the co-respondent, who was domiciled in England. It was held that her remarriage was valid, because after the divorce she was a single woman and therefore free to acquire an English domicile separate from that of her first husband. But in the later case of *Warter v Warter*,[143] the same judge (Sir James Hannen P.) explained *Scott v Att-Gen* on the different ground that the prohibition on remarriage attached only to the guilty party and could therefore be disregarded in England because it was penal, i.e. discriminatory. The implication is that the remarriage in England would have been held valid even if the wife had remained domiciled in Cape Colony.

8–031

---

[140] (1963) 42 D.L.R. (2d) 622 (Ontario Court of Appeal); (1964) 48 D.L.R. (2d) 644 (Supreme Court of Canada); discussed by Lysyk (1965) 43 Can. Bar Rev. 363; approved by Simon P. in *Padolecchia v Padolecchia* [1968] P. 314 at 339. The case is another example of the incidental question: see below, para.18–018.

[141] See Hartley, (1967) 16 I.C.L.Q. 680, 694–699. As to the third reason, see *Lundgren v O'Brien (No.2)* [1921] V.L.R. 361.

[142] (1886) 11 P.D. 128.

[143] (1890) 15 P.D. 152 at 155. The decision in *Warter v Warter* was followed in *Miller v Teale* (1954) 92 C.L.R. 406 (High Court of Australia) and *Hellens v Densmore* (1957) 10 D.L.R. (2d) 561 (Supreme Court of Canada), but distinguished in *Buckle v Buckle* [1956] P. 181.

In *Warter v Warter*, a husband, domiciled in England but resident in India, divorced his wife in India for adultery.[144] She married in England a man domiciled in England less than six months after the decree absolute. Section 57 of the Indian Divorce Act 1869 provided that it should be lawful for the parties to remarry when six months from the date of the decree absolute had expired and no appeal had been presented, but not sooner. It was held that the remarriage was invalid.

The result of these two cases appears to be that if the restriction on remarriage imposed by the foreign law is an integral part of the proceedings by which alone both parties can be released from their incapacity to contract a fresh marriage, it will receive effect in England; but if the restriction on remarriage is imposed on one party only, it will be disregarded as penal.

Physical incapacity

8–032   In English domestic law, a marriage is voidable if one of the parties is incapable of consummating it,[145] or if it has not been consummated owing to the wilful refusal of the respondent to consummate it.[146] Wilful refusal is more likely than impotence to produce problems in the conflict of laws, because impotence renders a marriage invalid nearly everywhere, whereas wilful refusal is sometimes a ground for nullity, as in England, sometimes a ground for divorce, as in Canada, and is sometimes not an independent ground for relief at all, as in Scotland and Australia.

English courts have always applied English domestic law when deciding whether to grant divorces. Until 1947, it was assumed that the same applied to the annulment of marriages on the grounds of impotence and wilful refusal: and it may well be that this is still the law. For example, in two cases decided in 1944,[147] marriages were annulled on the ground of the wife's wilful refusal to consummate, although in each case the husband was domiciled abroad and there was no evidence that by the law of his domicile this was a ground for annulment. In neither case was foreign law pleaded.

In 1947, in *Robert v Robert*[148], the possible application of foreign law to this question was considered for the first time. The marriage was celebrated in Guernsey, between parties domiciled there; and Barnard J. held that the question as to whether it should be annulled for wilful refusal to consummate must be decided by the law of Guernsey, either because "wilful refusal to consummate a marriage . . . must be considered as a defect in marriage, an error in the quality of the respondent" (a matter for the law of the place of celebration)[149] or else because a question of capacity was involved, with the result that the law of the parties' domicile must be applied in accordance with the decision in *Sottomayor v*

---

[144] At that time it was supposed that the Indian courts had jurisdiction to grant divorces to persons domiciled in England and resident in India.

[145] Matrimonial Causes Act 1973 s.12(a) (a rule of great antiquity).

[146] *ibid.*, s.12(b). This was first made a ground for nullity by s.7 of the Matrimonial Causes Act 1937.

[147] *Easterbrook v Easterbrook* [1944] P. 10; *Hutter v Hutter* [1944] P. 95.

[148] [1947] P. 164.

[149] At pp.167–168. There is some difficulty in accepting Barnard J.'s view that wilful refusal as a ground for nullity depends upon error, for there is no requirement in s.13(3) of the Matrimonial

De Barros (No.1).[150] But *Robert v Robert* is not a very impressive authority for the application of foreign law: not only did the law of the place of celebration and the law of the parties' domicile coincide, but also no difference was shown to exist between the law of Guernsey and the law of England. Moreover, *Robert v Robert* was overruled in *De Reneville v De Reneville*[151] on the question of jurisdiction, although it was not expressly dissented from on the question of choice of law.[152]

In *Ponticelli v Ponticelli,*[153] Sachs J. held that English law, which was the *lex fori* and the law of the husband's domicile, and not Italian law, which was the law of the place of celebration and the law of the wife's antenuptial domicile, determined the question of wilful refusal to consummate. Had it been necessary to choose between the law of the husband's domicile and the *lex fori*, he would have preferred the former.   **8–033**

On the other hand, in *Ross Smith v Ross Smith*[154] the House of Lords held that the English court had no jurisdiction to annul a marriage for wilful refusal to consummate merely because it had been celebrated in England. Lord Reid and Lord Morris[155] both gave as one of their reasons for declining jurisdiction the undesirability of granting relief on grounds unknown to the law of the parties' domicile. This could be taken to imply that, had jurisdiction been held to exist, the *lex fori* would have been applied.[156]

In this confusing state of the authorities, it is very much an open question as to what law governs impotence and wilful refusal. It has been plausibly suggested[157] that the applicable law should be the law of the petitioner's domicile at the date of the marriage, on the ground that if the petitioner has no ground of complaint under his or her personal law, he or she ought not to be granted a decree. Certainly it seems that reliance on the law of the husband's domicile as such cannot survive s.1 of the Domicile and Matrimonial Proceedings Act 1973 which as we have seen, provides that a wife can have a domicile different from that of her husband.

There is however no reported case in which the court has applied a foreign law which differed from English domestic law. So far as wilful refusal is concerned, the whole problem would admit of a simple and rational solution if wilful refusal   **8–034**

Causes Act 1973 or its predecessors that the petitioner was at the time of the marriage ignorant of the facts alleged. Moreover, as we shall see (below, para.8–038) the effect of mistake is not a matter for the law of the place of celebration.

[150] (1877) 3 P.D. 1; above, para.8–021.
[151] [1948] P. 100 at 118.
[152] Much the same can be said of the Northern Ireland case of *Addison v Addison* [1955] N.Ir. 1, 30, overruled on the jurisdictional issue in *Ross Smith v Ross Smith* [1963] A.C. 280 at 307, 312 and 348.
[153] [1958] P. 204, following *Way v Way* [1950] P. 71 (below, para.8–039), and not following *Robert v Robert* [1947] P. 164, above.
[154] [1963] A.C. 280.
[155] At p.306 and pp.313, 322 respectively.
[156] In *Magnier v Magnier* (1968) 112 S.J. 233, a marriage was annulled for wilful refusal without reference to the law of the husband's domicile: but foreign law was not pleaded.
[157] Bishop, (1978) 41 M.L.R. 512.

were dealt with in the context of divorce rather than nullity. It is hard to justify the existence of wilful refusal as a ground for nullity, because it is necessarily a post-matrimonial matter.

Although a decree annulling a voidable marriage formerly declared the marriage to be and to have been absolutely void to all intents and purposes, nevertheless it seems that if the *lex fori* is applicable, it must be applied as it is at the date of the trial, and not as it was at the date of the marriage. For marriages have been annulled for wilful refusal to consummate even though they were celebrated before 1938,[158] when this first became a ground for annulment in English law.

Same-sex unions

8–035   A purported marriage between persons of the same sex is void under English law.[159] However, same-sex partners are able to marry in a growing number of countries, including Argentina, Belgium, Canada, Iceland, the Netherlands, Norway, Portugal, Spain, South Africa, Sweden and in some of the United States; the issue remains under discussion in the United Kingdom. In many other legal systems, partners of the same sex may enter into registered partnerships, with legal consequences similar to those of marriage. The Civil Partnership Act 2004 gave same-sex partners in the United Kingdom the right to formalise their union by registration conferring on them a legal status with rights similar to those of married heterosexual couples. The formalities to enter into a same-sex registered partnership or marriage are governed by the *lex loci celebrationis*, but, in contrast to heterosexual marriage, capacity to enter into a same-sex union is also governed by the *lex loci celebrationis*; the relevant law, however, being qualified where appropriate by certain English rules contained in the 2004 Act. Moreover, the relevant law includes its conflict of laws rules thereby permitting the application of *renvoi*.

The Civil Partnership Act 2004 provides for the registration of civil partnerships by same-sex partners[160] over the age of 16 who are not already married or a party to a civil partnership and are not within the prohibited degrees of relationship[161] and who have both resided in England and Wales for at least seven days before giving notice of their intended registration.[162] There are special rules for the registration of a civil partnership at a British Consulate overseas where one party must be a United Kingdom national,[163] and for armed forces personnel serving abroad.[164]

---

[158] *Cowen v Cowen* [1946] P. 36, overruled in *Baxter v Baxter* [1948] A.C. 274, but not on this point: see at p.282; *Dredge v Dredge* [1947] 1 All E.R. 29; but in none of these cases was the point argued. None of them had anything to do with the conflict of laws. cf. *De Reneville v De Reneville* [1948] P. 100, where the marriage was celebrated in 1935.

[159] Matrimonial Causes Act 1973 s.11(c).

[160] s.1; heterosexual couples cannot register a civil partnership.

[161] s.3(1). Parental consent is required for persons under the age of 18, s.4. The prohibited degrees are defined in Sch.1, para.1.

[162] s.8(1)(b).

[163] s.210.

[164] s.211.

The 2004 Act provides for recognition of overseas relationships[165] either as "specified relationships"[166] or under the "general conditions".[167] Specified relationships are a defined list of partnerships and same-sex marriages as listed in Sch.20. The general conditions provide for recognition of other relationships where, under the relevant law,[168] the parties are not already in such a relationship or married, the relationship is of indeterminate duration, and the parties are treated as a couple for general or specified purposes or treated as married. These relationships will be recognised and treated as civil partnerships in England and Wales[169] as long as the parties are same-sex partners,[170] have capacity to enter into the relationship under the relevant law and comply with the formalities of the law of the country of registration.[171] Additionally if one party is domiciled in England and Wales at the time of registration, neither party must be under the age of 16 or within the prohibited degrees of affinity.[172] If all these criteria are fulfilled, the relationship will be recognised subject to an exception that it would be manifestly contrary to public policy to recognise one or both parties' capacity under the relevant law to enter into such a relationship.[173]

Jurisdiction to grant a Declaration of Validity[174] is dependent on either party being domiciled or habitually resident for one year (or having died domiciled or habitually resident for one year) in England and Wales.

8–036

Transsexual marriages

Traditionally under English law, a transsexual has always lacked capacity to marry a partner of his or her original sex since a person's sex was declared at birth and could not be changed by artificial intervention[175] and a marriage can only be entered into by one man and one woman.[176] However, in 2002 the European Court of Human Rights declared that the United Kingdom was in breach of arts 8 and 12 of the European Convention for failing to recognise the transsexual's new gender,[177] and in *Bellinger v Bellinger*[178] the House of Lords declared that s.11(c) of the Matrimonial Causes Act 1973 was incompatible with the Convention. The legislature has sought to address this situation with the

8–037

---

[165] Partnerships that are registered outside the territory of the United Kingdom, s.212.

[166] s.213.

[167] s.214.

[168] s.54(10) defines the relevant law as the law of the country of registration including its conflict of laws rules.

[169] In *Wilkinson v Kitzinger (No 2)* [2006] EWHC 2022 (Fam); [2007] 1 F.L.R. 295 the High Court confirmed that the marriage, in British Colombia, of two women domiciled in England would be recognised as a civil partnership and not a marriage, and held further that this did not convene the women's human rights under the E.C.H.R arts 8 and 12; see Bamforth [2007] C.F.L.Q. 133, and on the recognition of foreign relationships: Norrie [2006] 2 J.P.I.L 137.

[170] s.216(1).

[171] s.215(1).

[172] s.217(2).

[173] s.218. The provisions contained in s.54(7) and (8) deal with void and voidable partnerships.

[174] s.58.

[175] *Corbett v Corbett* [1971] P. 110.

[176] Matrimonial Causes Act 1973, s.11(c).

[177] *Goodwin v UK* (2002) 35 E.H.R.R. 18; [2002] 2 F.L.R. 487.

[178] [2003] UKHL 22; [2003] 2 A.C. 467.

Gender Recognition Act 2004, under which transsexuals over the age of 18 who fulfil the medical criteria[179] and are living in the other gender or have changed gender[180] under the law of an approved country[181] will be able to apply for a gender recognition certificate which in turn will provide the legal status necessary in the acquired gender in order to marry a partner of the transsexual's former sex.[182] However, where the respondent was a person of "acquired gender" prior to the marriage, such a marriage is still voidable.[183]

It appears that there is no requirement for an applicant to be domiciled, habitually resident, resident or a national of the UK,[184] but the effect of s.21 is that the governing law is the *lex fori* as contained in the 2004 Act. There is no direct provision for recognising a change of gender that has taken place outside the United Kingdom[185] and any foreign post-recognition marriage will be considered void until such time as a full gender recognition certificate is issued to the party concerned in a part of the United Kingdom.[186]

CONSENT OF THE PARTIES

8–038   Marriage is a voluntary union; there can be no valid marriage unless each party consents to marry the other. The question of consent is often a question of fact, but sometimes it may be a question of law. Of course the laws of foreign countries may differ widely from English law, on for instance, the effect of fraud; the distinction between mistake as to the identity of the other party and mistake as to attributes, or between mistake as to the nature of the ceremony and mistake as to its effects; and whether duress or fear must emanate from the other party or can be extraneous.

In English law it was formerly a disputed question as to whether lack of consent rendered a marriage void or voidable. The question is set at rest (insofar as marriages taking place after 31 July 1971, are concerned) by s.12(c) of the Matrimonial Causes Act 1973, which provides that a marriage shall be voidable if either party did not consent to it, whether in consequence of duress, mistake, unsoundness of mind or otherwise. In addition to these common law instances of lack of consent, there are three situations where by statute a marriage is voidable on this ground. The first is where, at the time of the marriage, either party, though capable of giving a valid consent, was suffering from mental disorder within the meaning of the Mental Health Act 1983 of such a kind or to such an extent as to

---

[179] s.2.

[180] s.1(1).

[181] s.2.

[182] See Gilmore, (2004) 34 Fam L.J. 741.

[183] Matrimonial Causes Act 1973 s.12(h) as inserted by the Gender Recognition Act 2004 Sch.4(1), para.5. Similar provisions are contained in the Civil Partnership Act 2004 s.50(1)(e).

[184] Although certain conditions in the Act, such as the reports required from registered medical practitioners under s.7, may make it practically necessary to have a limited residential connection with a part of the United Kingdom.

[185] s.21(1).

[186] s.21(2), (3).

be unfitted for marriage.[187] The second is where the respondent was at the time of the marriage suffering from venereal disease in a communicable form. The third is where the respondent was at the time of the marriage pregnant by some person other than the petitioner.[188] In the second and third cases it is provided that the court shall not grant a decree of nullity unless it is satisfied that the petitioner was at the time of the marriage ignorant of the facts alleged[189] and this is why they are properly characterised as instances of lack of consent. They are cases of mistake as to the attributes of the other party – a kind of mistake which was inoperative at common law.

The issue of forced marriages, whereby an adult female or a child is taken abroad without their consent for the purposes of marriage,[190] is now the subject of pre-emptive legislation rather than purely being subject to the remedy of nullity under the Matrimonial Causes Act s.12(c). Part 4A of the Family Law Act 1996, as inserted by the Forced Marriage (Civil Protection) Act 2007, gives jurisdiction to the High Court or a county court to make a forced marriage protection order.[191] The order may contain any prohibitions, restrictions or requirements necessary to either prevent the marriage taking place or to protect the victim of a forced marriage, and the terms of an order may relate to conduct outside England and Wales. The protection orders may be made in any family proceedings including the High Court's inherent jurisdiction.[192]

8–039

There are a few reported cases which suggest, but do not conclusively answer, the question of what system of law governs the requirement of consent. In *Apt v Apt*,[193] where it was held that the validity of proxy marriages was a question of formalities, the Court of Appeal drew a distinction between the method of giving consent and the fact of consent. This observation enabled Hodson J. in *Way v Way*[194] to hold that "questions of consent are to be dealt with by reference to the personal law of the parties rather than by reference to the law of the place where the contract was made." But this case is not a clear-cut authority because no difference was shown to exist between English law (which was the law of the husband's domicile) and Russian law (which was the law of the wife's domicile and also the law of the place of celebration). It was followed in *Szechter v Szechter*,[195] where a Polish professor divorced his wife and married his secretary in order to rescue her from prison and enable her to escape to the West; and Sir Jocelyn Simon P. applied Polish law as the law of each party's antenuptial domicile. But this case also is not a clear-cut authority because the law of the

---

[187] Matrimonial Causes Act 1973 s.12(d). See, for example, *KC v City of Westminster Social and Community Services Dept* [2008] EWCA Civ. 198; [2008] 2 F.C.R. 146.
[188] s.12(e) and (f).
[189] Matrimonial Causes Act 1973 s.13(3).
[190] See, generally, Gaffney-Rhys [2008] I.F.L. 26.
[191] A forced marriage is one that has been entered into without the person's free and full consent, Family Law Act s.64A(4).
[192] Family Law Act 1996 s.63C.
[193] [1948] P. 83 at 88.
[194] [1950] P. 71 at 78. His judgment was reversed by the Court of Appeal, sub nom. *Kenward v Kenward* [1951] P. 124, but not on this point. Sir Raymond Evershed M.R. at p.133 was prepared to assume that Hodson J.'s view on the law governing consent was correct.
[195] [1971] P. 286.

parties' domicile and the law of the place of celebration coincided, and because, before pronouncing a decree, the learned President held that the marriage was also invalid by English domestic law.

8–040
On the other hand, the law of the place of celebration was applied in *Parojcic v Parojcic*[196]; but the decision would have been the same if the law of each party's antenuptial domicile had been applied, because they had lost their Yugoslav domicile of origin and acquired an English domicile of choice before their marriage in England. More recently, Singer J. in *Alfonso-Brown v Milwood*[197] seems to have applied the law of the place of celebration, Ghanaian customary law, to the question of consent to enter into a marriage instead of what the respondent understood to be an engagement; however, the legal point as to what law governed the giving of consent was not discussed. Moreover, it so happens that in all the reported cases,[198] English domestic law has been applied, either alone or cumulatively with the law of the domicile as in *Szechter v Szechter,*[199] even where the marriage was celebrated abroad and both parties were domiciled abroad at the time of their marriage.[200] However, this may have been because there was no evidence, or insufficient evidence, of the foreign law. It cannot be said, therefore, that the question is finally settled. But it is submitted that the best rule is that no marriage is valid if by the law of either party's domicile he or she does not consent to marry the other.

It may be that the rule in *Sottomayor v De Barros (No.2)*[201] applies to consent of parties as it applies to capacity to marry.[202]

POLYGAMOUS MARRIAGES

8–041
Even if the marriage complies with the law of the place of celebration as regards formalities and with the law of each party's antenuptial domicile as regards capacity to marry and consent of the parties, it will, for certain limited purposes only, not be regarded as a valid marriage in England if it is polygamous. Some systems of law, especially those following Islamic principles, allow a man to have several wives; fewer systems allow a woman more than one husband.[203] The

---

[196] [1958] 1 W.L.R. 1280; criticised by Webb, (1959) 22 M.L.R. 198.
[197] [2006] EWHC 642 (Fam); [2006] 2 F.L.R. 265 at para.53.
[198] See, in addition to the cases cited above, *Cooper v Crane* [1891] P. 369; *Valier v Valier* (1925) 133 L.T. 830; *Hussein v Hussein* [1938] P. 159 (in each of which the marriage was celebrated in England); and *Mehta v Mehta* [1945] 2 All E.R. 690; *Silver v Silver* [1955] 2 All E.R. 614; *Kassim v Kassim* [1962] P. 224 (in each of which the marriage was celebrated abroad). See also *Di Mento v Visalli* [1973] 2 N.S.W.L.R. 199 (a dramatic tale of the sacrifice of a young girl on the altar of family pride, calculated to bring tears to the eyes; its jurisprudential qualities are less marked).
[199] [1971] P. 286.
[200] *H. v H.* [1954] P. 258, discussed by Woodhouse, (1954) 3 I.C.L.Q. 454; *Buckland v Buckland* [1968] P. 296.
[201] (1879) 5 P.D. 94; above, para.8–021.
[202] *Vervaeke v Smith* [1981] Fam. 77. The House of Lords made no comment on this proposition: [1983] 1 A.C. 145.
[203] The former is technically polygyny, the latter polyandry.

importance of this topic is now much reduced because the former hostility of English law[204] to polygamous marriages has largely disappeared.

It is not often that an undefended divorce case becomes a leading case, not only in England but wherever the common law prevails: but such has been the fate of *Hyde v Hyde*[205]:

> The petitioner was an Englishman by birth, and in 1847, when he was about 16 years old, he joined a congregation of the Church of Jesus Christ of Latter Day Saints (the Mormons) in London, and was soon afterwards ordained a priest of that faith. In London he met the respondent and her family, all of whom were Mormons, and became engaged to her. In 1850, the respondent and her mother emigrated to Salt Lake City, in the Territory of Utah, in the United States, and in 1853 the petitioner joined them there. They were married in 1853, the marriage being celebrated by Brigham Young, the president of the Mormon church, and governor of the territory. They lived together in Utah until 1856, when the petitioner went on a mission to the Sandwich Islands (now called Hawaii), leaving the respondent in Utah. On his arrival in the islands the scales fell from his eyes and he renounced the Mormon faith and preached against it. A sentence of excommunication was pronounced against him in Utah in December 1856 and his wife was declared free to marry again, which she did in 1859 or 1860. In 1857 the petitioner resumed his domicile in England, where he became the minister of a dissenting chapel at Derby. He petitioned for divorce on the ground of his wife's adultery.

Lord Penzance refused to adjudicate on the petition on the ground that "marriage, as understood in Christendom, may for this purpose be defined as the voluntary union for life of one man and one woman to the exclusion of all others,"[206] and that this Mormon marriage was no marriage which the English Divorce Court could recognise, because there was evidence that polygamy was a part of the Mormon doctrine, and was the common custom in Utah. "It is obvious," he said, "that the matrimonial law of this country is adapted to the Christian marriage, and is wholly inapplicable to polygamy".[207] He pointed out that to divorce a husband at the suit of his first wife on the ground of his bigamy and adultery with the second, or to annul the second marriage on the ground that it was bigamous, would be "creating conjugal duties, not enforcing them, and furnishing remedies when there was no offence."[208]

8–042

At the end of his judgment Lord Penzance made the following important reservation[209]:

> "This court does not profess to decide upon the rights of succession or legitimacy which it might be proper to accord to the issue of polygamous unions, or upon the rights or obligations in relation to third persons which people living under the sanction of such unions may have created for themselves. All that is intended to be here decided is that as between each other they are not entitled to the remedies, the adjudication, or the relief of the matrimonial law of England".

---

[204] The history can be traced in the voluminous literature. See Fitzpatrick, (1900) 2 Jo.Comp.Leg. (2nd series) 359; Beckett, (1932) 48 L.Q.R. 341; Morris, (1953) 66 Harv.L.Rev. 961; Sinclair, (1954) 31 B.Y.I.L. 248; Mendes da Costa, (1966) 44 Can. Bar Rev. 293; Hartley, (1969) 32 M.L.R. 155; Poulter, (1976) 25 I.C.L.Q. 475; Jaffey, (1978) 41 M.L.R. 38; Shah, (2003) 52 I.C.L.Q. 369.
[205] (1866) L.R. 1 P. & M. 130.
[206] At p.133.
[207] At p.135. cf. *Baindail v Baindail* [1946] P. 122, 125, per Lord Greene M.R.
[208] At pp.35 and 136–137.
[209] At p.138.

What is a polygamous marriage?

8–043   The nature of the ceremony according to the law of the place of celebration, and not the personal law of either party, determines whether a marriage is monogamous or polygamous. Or, to adopt a more sophisticated statement, it is for the law of the place of celebration to determine the nature and incidents of the union and then for English law to decide whether the union is a monogamous or polygamous marriage.[210] The crucial question is whether the law under which the marriage is celebrated permits polygamy; if it does not, the marriage is monogamous. On this ground, Japanese marriages[211] have been treated as monogamous, and so has a composite ceremony at Singapore in mixed Chinese and Jewish form.[212] If a country has provision for both polygamous and monogamous marriages, as was formerly the case in India, the parties' choice of form of ceremony will determine the nature of the marriage. If the husband is not allowed to take more than one wife, but may have concubines, a marriage celebrated under such a law is polygamous, at any rate if concubinage is a status recognised by that law.[213]

The question which has to be asked is "What are the terms under which the parties enter into the marriage? Is it to the exclusion of other marriage partners or not?" If the husband may take other wives, the marriage is potentially polygamous even if the husband intends never to take further wives and never in fact does so.[214] (The marriage in *Hyde v Hyde* was not actually but only potentially polygamous because the petitioner never married more than one wife.) Subject to what is said below as to the effect of the Private International Law (Miscellaneous Provisions) Act 1995,[215] a potentially polygamous marriage is thus in the same category as an actually polygamous one.

Serial monogamy

8–044   The fact that under some systems of law divorces can be obtained at short notice and by mutual consent or at the will of either party, with merely formal conditions of official registration, so that new partners can be acquired with some frequency, is not to be equated with polygamy.[216] Polygamy requires a plurality of legal marriage partners at the same time.

---

[210] *Lee v Lau* [1967] P. 14.

[211] *Brinkley v Att-Gen* (1890) 15 P.D. 76.

[212] *Penhas v Tan Soo Eng* [1953] A.C. 304.

[213] *Lee v Lau* [1967] P. 14. Concubinage was abolished in Hong Kong in 1971: Marriage Reform Ordinance.

[214] *Hyde v Hyde* (1866) L.R. 1 P. & M. 130; *Sowa v Sowa* [1961] P. 70.

[215] See below, para.8–048.

[216] *Nachimson v Nachimson* [1930] P. 217 (Soviet divorce law).

Marriages in England

English domestic law makes no provision for polygamous marriages, and it follows that a marriage celebrated in England can only be monogamous.[217] Hence, if a Muslim domiciled, e.g., in Kuwait, goes through a ceremony of marriage in an English register office, he contracts a monogamous marriage. If the personal law of the husband had been applied, with the possibility of further wives, the effect would often be to defeat the expectations of English girls marrying Muslims in England. If a civil ceremony in an English register office is followed by a religious ceremony in Islamic form, the religious ceremony does not supersede or invalidate the prior civil ceremony and is not registered as a marriage in any marriage register book.[218] The only marriage is that created by the register office ceremony, necessarily monogamous. If there is a combined religious and civil ceremony in a Muslim mosque registered under s.41 of the Marriage Act 1949, the resulting marriage will again be monogamous. A "marriage" celebrated in England in accordance with polygamous forms and without any civil ceremony as required by English law is simply invalid, and that is true whatever the domicile of the parties.[219]

8–045

Change in the nature of the marriage

It was at one time supposed that the monogamous or polygamous character of the marriage had to be determined once and for all at its inception.[220] But now it is clear that a potentially polygamous marriage may become monogamous by reason of subsequent events. This may happen if, for instance, the parties (being domiciled in a country the law of which has both polygamous and monogamous marriages) change their religion from one which permits polygamy to one which does not[221]; or if the husband changes his domicile from a country whose law permits polygamy to a country (such as England) whose law does not[222]; or if the law under which the marriage is celebrated subsequently prohibits polygamy[223]; or (under some systems of law) if a child is born.[224] It was originally thought that

8–046

---

[217] *Chetti v Chetti* [1909] P. 67; *R. v Hammersmith Marriage Registrar* [1917] 1 K.B. 634; *Srini Vasan v Srini Vasan* [1946] P. 67; *Baindail v Baindail* [1946] P. 122; *Maher v Maher* [1951] P. 342; *Ohochuku v Ohochuku* [1960] 1 W.L.R. 183; *Russ v Russ* [1964] P. 315; *Qureshi v Qureshi* [1972] Fam. 173.

[218] Marriage Act 1949 s.46(2) as amended by Marriage Act 1983.

[219] However, in *A-M v A-M* [2001] 2 F.L.R. 6, the wife was entitled to the benefit of a presumption of marriage based on a long cohabitation coupled with a reputation of marriage, even where the original ceremony had taken place in polygamous Islamic form. Hughes J. found that there was no evidence to rebut the presumption that the parties had subsequently contracted a valid polygamous marriage in an Islamic country at a time when they were domiciled in Islamic countries. The contortions involved in this case underline the difficulties and discrimination in this area of law referred to in Shah, (2002) 52 I.C.L.Q. 369.

[220] *Hyde v Hyde* (1866) L.R. 1 P. & M. 130; *Mehta v Mehta* [1945] 2 All E.R. 690.

[221] *The Sinha Peerage Claim* (1939) 171 Lords' Journals 350; [1946] 1 All E.R. 348n., as explained in *Cheni v Cheni* [1965] P.85 at 90–91, and in *Parkasho v Singh* [1968] P.233 at 243 and 253.

[222] *Ali v Ali* [1968] P. 564; *R. v Sagoo* [1975] Q.B. 885. It is otherwise if the wife changes her domicile: *Onobrauche v Onobrauche* (1978) 122 S.J. 210.

[223] *Parkasho v Singh* [1968] P. 233; *R. v Sagoo* [1975] Q.B. 885.

[224] *Cheni v Cheni* [1965] P. 85.

a polygamous marriage could become a monogamous marriage if the parties, having gone through a polygamous ceremony in a country whose law permits polygamy, subsequently go through a monogamous ceremony in England.[225] However, in 1968[226] it was pointed out that if the polygamous marriage was valid, it is difficult to see how the registrar succeeded in marrying the parties again in England; and in *Mark v Mark*[227] the Court of Appeal assumed this not to be so; *per* Thorpe J.: "Given that the prior polygamous marriage was recognised in this jurisdiction as a valid marriage, the ... [Register] Office ceremony was a nullity."[228]

In all these cases of conversion, the marriage was only potentially polygamous; but there seems no reason for the principle not to be equally effective in converting an actually polygamous marriage into a monogamous one, after the number of wives has been reduced to one by death or divorce.

There is no English authority on the converse problem, namely, when does a monogamous marriage become polygamous.[229] The answer may be that the marriage has, so to speak, the benefit of the doubt: if it is monogamous at its inception, it remains monogamous although a change of religion or of domicile may entitle the husband to take another wife; if it is polygamous at its inception, it may become monogamous by reason of a change of religion, of domicile, or of law before the happening of the events which give rise to the proceedings.[230] Since a marriage celebrated in England in monogamous form between parties whose personal law permits polygamy is a monogamous marriage, it is difficult to see how a change of religion or of domicile could convert a monogamous marriage into a polygamous one.

Relevance of the personal law of the parties

8–047 Whether a marriage is monogamous or polygamous in form, it will be a valid marriage only if the usual rules are satisfied as to the formal requirements of the law of the place of celebration and those as to the capacity and consent of the parties. Capacity to marry is, as we have seen,[231] governed by the law of each party's antenuptial domicile. Hence it seems to follow that a man or woman whose personal law does not permit polygamy has no capacity to contract a valid polygamous marriage.[232] This was to some extent confirmed by s.11(d) of the Matrimonial Causes Act 1973 which, as originally enacted, provided that an

---

[225] *Ohochuku v Ohochuku* [1960] 1 W.L.R. 183.
[226] *Ali v Ali* [1968] P. 564 at 578.
[227] [2004] EWCA Civ. 168.
[228] *ibid.*, at para.7.
[229] The case of *Att-Gen of Ceylon v Reid* [1965] A.C. 720 was concerned solely with the law of Ceylon (now Sri Lanka); and in *Nabi v Heaton* [1983] 1 W.L.R. 626 the Court of Appeal presumed a second polygamous marriage to be valid without discussing the position of the first monogamous marriage, and Vinelott J. at first instance declined to express an opinion [1981] 1 W.L.R. 1052.
[230] See Simon P. in *Cheni v Cheni* [1965] P. 85.
[231] Above, para.8–016.
[232] *Re Bethell* (1887) 38 Ch.D. 220; *Risk v Risk* [1951] P. 50; *Ali v Ali* [1968] P. 564; *Crowe v Kader* [1968] W.A.R. 122; *contra, Kenward v Kenward* [1951] P. 124 at 145, per Denning L.J.; *Radwan v Radwan (No.2)* [1973] Fam. 35. "Personal law" is preferred to "domicile" because in many eastern countries the personal law is often a religious law. Hence a domiciled Englishman or Englishwoman

actually or potentially polygamous marriage entered into outside England after 31 July 1971 by a person domiciled in England was void.

Some doubt as to the correctness of this proposition was created by the surprising decision of Cumming-Bruce J. in *Radwan v Radwan (No.2)*.[233] This held that a woman domiciled in England had capacity to contract an actually polygamous marriage in 1951 with a man domiciled in Egypt at the Egyptian Consulate-General in Paris, because the parties intended to live together – and did live together for some years – in Egypt. In other words, it applied the test of the intended matrimonial home rather than the orthodox dual domicile test. The decision was the subject of heavy criticism by academic commentators,[234] and it is submitted that it was wrongly decided. It is inconsistent with the tenor of the argument in the later Court of Appeal case of *Hussain v Hussain*[235] and with the repeated references to domicile in the relevant provisions of the Private International Law (Miscellaneous Provisions) Act 1995.

Domicile in England

Hussain v Hussain[236] involved a marriage in Pakistan, the law of which permitted polygamy, between two Muslims, a man domiciled in England and a woman domiciled in Pakistan. It was argued that this must be a potentially polygamous marriage, and so void under s.11(d) of the Matrimonial Causes Act 1973. The Court of Appeal recognised that the acceptance of this argument would have repercussions for the Muslim community in this country which would be "widespread and profound", since many Muslim men domiciled in England return to the country of their birth to find a bride. It therefore held that a marriage is not potentially polygamous, even though celebrated in polygamous form, if neither spouse can under his or her personal law take another spouse during the subsistence of the marriage. In the instant case, the man could not lawfully take another wife under English law and the woman could not lawfully take another husband under the law of Pakistan. Had the woman been domiciled in England and the man in Pakistan, the decision would have been different, for then by the law of his domicile the man could take further wives.

It is important to understand what *Hussain v Hussain* did and did not decide. It did not change (indeed it proceeded on the basis of) the position that someone domiciled in England could not enter a polygamous marriage. It did decide that in the circumstances identified in the judgment, the marriage was a *monogamous* marriage, notwithstanding the law of the place of celebration; and this meant that the marriage did not fall within s.11(d) which applied only to actually or potentially polygamous marriages. This ingenuity was, however, accompanied by an element of injustice: it operated to the benefit of Muslim men domiciled in

8–048

who acquired a domicile of choice in, e.g., India, Pakistan or Sri Lanka could not contract a valid polygamous marriage without a change of religion.
[233] [1973] Fam. 35.
[234] Karsten, (1973) 36 M.L.R. 291; Pearl, [1973] C. L.J. 43; Wade, (1973) 22 I.C.L.Q. 571. It was defended by Jaffey, (1978) 41 M.L.R. 38.
[235] [1983] Fam. 26.
[236] [1983] Fam. 26. See Schuz, (1983) 46 M.L.R. 653.

England but not of Muslim women so domiciled. Legislation was plainly necessary to eliminate this discrimination.

Sections 5 to 8 of the Private International Law (Miscellaneous Provisions) Act 1995 are the result, based on the recommendations of the Law Commission in a report published ten years earlier.[237] Section 5(1) provides that:

> A marriage entered into outside England and Wales between persons neither of whom is already married is not void under English law on the ground that it was entered into under a law which permits polygamy and that either party is domiciled in England and Wales.

8–049 Section 11 of the Matrimonial Causes Act 1973 was amended[238] so that it now provides that, for the purpose of s.11(d), a marriage is not polygamous if, at its inception, neither party has any spouse additional to the other.

The result of these new provisions is that where the man or the woman is, or both parties are, domiciled in England, a marriage which would otherwise be potentially (as opposed to actually) polygamous is treated as a monogamous marriage. The fact of domicile in England cannot render it void on any ground relating to polygamy; though of course the marriage might be held void on some other basis such as age or affinity. Section 11(d) can apply only to actually polygamous marriages. In this context it is no longer the case that potentially polygamous and actually polygamous unions are treated alike; the distinction between the two is crucial.[239]

So, if a woman domiciled in England marries in a foreign country in polygamous form (that is a form of ceremony recognised by the law of the place of celebration as creating a marriage within which the husband may take a further wife or wives), then in the absence of any other legal defect the marriage is a valid monogamous marriage. If, however, the man is already married, so that the marriage would be actually polygamous, her domicile in England renders the marriage void under s.11(d) as amended.

Domicile abroad

8–050 If neither party is domiciled in England, the law of each party's antenuptial domicile determines their capacity to enter the marriage. So, if a man and a woman both domiciled in Pakistan marry there, the marriage will be a valid polygamous marriage. If they are domiciled in a country, for example New Zealand, the domestic law of which has no provision allowing polygamy, the validity of their marriage in polygamous form in Pakistan will depend on whether New Zealand law regards them as having capacity to enter that marriage (in effect

---

[237] *Capacity to Contract a Polygamous Marriage and Related Issues* (Law Com. No. 146).

[238] Private International Law (Miscellaneous Provisions) Act 1995 Sch.1, para.2(2).

[239] There are complex transitional provisions: Private International Law (Miscellaneous Provisions) Act 1995 s.6. In general the new rules apply retrospectively, but not so as to affect cases involving actual polygamy before 8 January 1996 or to reverse the effect of any nullity decree granted (or entitled to recognition) in England before that date.

whether New Zealand law resembles English law as it was understood to be before *Hussain v Hussain*, as it stood after that decision, or after the 1995 Act).[240]

Recognition of valid polygamous marriages in England

We come now to the important question: to what extent will English law recognise a valid polygamous marriage? It must be borne in mind that we are dealing with marriages that are both polygamous and valid, e.g. a marriage celebrated in Pakistan between Muslims domiciled there.   **8–051**

The present law can be summarised by saying that a polygamous marriage will be recognised in England as a valid marriage, even if it is actually polygamous, unless there is some strong reason to the contrary.[241] In spite of Lord Penzance's emphatic statement in *Hyde v Hyde*[242] that his decision was limited to the question of matrimonial relief, there was for many years a tendency to assume that all polygamous marriages were wholly unrecognised by English law. However, since 1939[243] it has become clear that they are recognised for many purposes. We shall now consider some typical situations.

Whether a bar to a subsequent monogamous marriage

A valid polygamous marriage will be recognised to the extent that it constitutes a bar to a subsequent monogamous marriage in England, and so entitles the second "wife" (or the husband) to a decree of nullity on the ground of bigamy.[244] Otherwise the husband would be validly married to his first wife in the country where he married her and to his second wife in England – a situation that would encourage rather than discourage polygamy.   **8–052**

Matrimonial proceedings

The rule in *Hyde v Hyde*,[245] that the parties to a polygamous marriage were not entitled to the remedies, the adjudication, or the relief of the matrimonial law of England, led to increasing hardship, especially after the influx of Commonwealth immigrants into the United Kingdom in the 1950s and 1960s. English judges did their best to mitigate its severity and restrict its scope by various devices, e.g. by holding that a potentially polygamous marriage could be converted into a   **8–053**

---

[240] See Private International Law (Miscellaneous Provisions) Act 1995 s.5(2): the section does not affect the determination of the validity of a marriage by reference to the law of another country (i.e., other than England) to the extent that it falls to be determined under the rules of private international law.

[241] See Winn J. in *Shahnaz v Rizwan* [1965] 1 Q.B. 390, 397 and Lord Parker C.J. in *Mohamed v Knott* [1969] 1 Q.B. 1 at 13–14.

[242] (1866) L.R. 1 P. & M. 130 at 138; quoted above, para.8–042.

[243] *The Sinha Peerage Claim* (1939) 171 Lords' Journals 350; [1946] 1 All E.R. 348n., is usually considered to mark the turning point.

[244] *Srini Vasan v Srini Vasan* [1946] P. 67; *Baindail v Baindail* [1946] P. 122; *Hashmi v Hashmi* [1972] Fam. 36; see Hartley, (1969) 16 I.C.L.Q. 680, 691–694.

[245] (1866) L.R. 1 P. & M. 130.

monogamous one by subsequent events.[246] Finally, the rule was abolished (on the recommendation of the Law Commission)[247] by s.1 of the Matrimonial Proceedings (Polygamous Marriages) Act 1972, now re-enacted as s.47 of the Matrimonial Causes Act 1973, which provides that English courts are not precluded from granting matrimonial relief or making a declaration concerning the validity of a marriage by reason only that the marriage was entered into under a law that permits polygamy. This applies whether the marriage is potentially or actually polygamous; in the latter case, rules of court may require notice of the proceedings to be served on any other spouse, and may give him or her the right to be heard.[248]

"Matrimonial relief" is widely defined[249] so as to include decrees of divorce, nullity of marriage, judicial separation, presumption of death and dissolution of marriage, divorce and separation orders under the Matrimonial Causes Act 1973, and orders for financial provision under s.27 of the 1973 Act, the variation of maintenance agreements, ancillary relief, and orders under Pt I of the Domestic Proceedings and Magistrates' Courts Act 1978. A "declaration concerning the validity of a marriage" is defined[250] to mean any declaration under Pt III of the Family Law Act 1986[251] involving a determination as to the validity of a marriage.

This enactment does not mean that a polygamously married wife could obtain a divorce on the ground of her husband's adultery with another wife, because adultery involves sexual intercourse with a person other than one's spouse. Since *ex hypothesi* both the marriages are valid and the other wife is a "spouse", the husband cannot commit adultery with her.[252] Nor does it mean that a later wife could get a decree of nullity on the ground of bigamy, because the earlier marriage is *ex hypothesi* valid.

Criminal law: bigamy

8–054   The question whether a valid polygamous marriage is a sufficient first marriage to support an indictment for bigamy was expressly left open in *Baindail v Baindail*.[253] It has subsequently been held not to be sufficient.[254] However, there seems no reason why a polygamously married man should not be convicted of perjury under s.3 of the Perjury Act 1911 if he obtained a certificate for an English marriage ceremony by falsely stating that he was an unmarried man and that he knew of no impediment to his marriage. (The maximum penalty for this

---

[246] See above, para.8–046.
[247] See Law Com. No. 42 (1971).
[248] s.47(4), (as substituted by Private International Law (Miscellaneous Provisions) Act 1995 Sch.1, para.2(3)(b). See Family Proceedings Rules 1991 r.3.11, (as amended).
[249] 1973 Act s.47(2).
[250] 1973 Act s.47(3).
[251] Below, para.9–015.
[252] *Onobrauche v Onobrauche* (1978) 122 S.J. 210.
[253] [1946] P. 122 at 130.
[254] *R. v Sarwan Singh* [1962] 3 All E.R. 612 (a decision of Quarter Sessions). This case was overruled in *R. v Sagoo* [1975] Q.B. 885, but only on the ground that the marriage had become monogamous under the principles stated above, para.8–046. The principle of the decision was not doubted.

offence is the same as that for bigamy.) It is one thing for a polygamist to marry two wives, and quite another thing for him to pose as an unmarried man.

Legitimacy of and succession by children

"It cannot, I think, be doubted now", said Lord Maugham, delivering the opinion of the Committee of Privileges of the House of Lords in *The Sinha Peerage Claim,*[255] "(notwithstanding some earlier *dicta* by eminent judges[256]) that a Hindu marriage between persons domiciled in India[257] is recognised by our courts, that the issue are legitimate, and that such issue can succeed to property in this country, with a possible exception which will be referred to later." Provided the marriages are valid by the law of the place of celebration and by the personal law of the parties, it is immaterial that the husband married more than one wife or that the succession is governed by English law. Thus, in *Bamgbose v Daniel,*[258] children of no fewer than nine polygamous marriages celebrated in Nigeria between persons there domiciled were held entitled to succeed to their father's property on his death intestate, although by a Nigerian Marriage Ordinance of 1884 the property was distributable in accordance with the English Statute of Distribution 1670. Similarly, each of the seven (or possibly eight) wives of a husband dying intestate domiciled in Ghana was held in *Official Solicitor v Yemoh*[259] to be a "spouse" for the purposes of the Administration of Estates Act 1925. The "possible exception" referred to by Lord Maugham in *The Sinha Peerage Claim* is the right to succeed as heir to real estate in England (which after 1925 is restricted to succession to entailed property and one or two other exceptional cases[260]). This exception was considered necessary because it was thought that difficulties might arise if there was a contest between the first-born son of the second wife and the later-born son of the first wife, each claiming to be the heir.

8–055

Succession by wives

It seems that the surviving wife of a polygamous marriage could succeed to the husband's property on his death intestate, whether he married one wife or several, and whether he died domiciled in a country whose law permits polygamy or in England. In *Coleman v Shang*[261] the widow of a potentially polygamous marriage celebrated in Ghana between parties domiciled there was held entitled to a grant of letters of administration to the husband's estate on his death intestate, although by a Ghana Marriage Ordinance of 1884 two-thirds of the property was

8–056

---

[255] (1939) 171 Lords' Journals 350; [1946] 1 All E.R. 348n. cf. *Baindail v Baindail* [1946] P. 122 at 127, per Lord Greene M.R.
[256] The reference is apparently to the decision of Stirling J. in *Re Bethell* (1887) 38 Ch.D. 220, which is usually explained away on the ground that the husband was domiciled in England and therefore lacked capacity to contract a valid polygamous marriage.
[257] The Hindu Marriage Act 1955 abolished polygamy among Hindus in India.
[258] [1955] A.C. 107.
[259] [2010] EWHC 3727 (Ch); [2011] 1 W.L.R. 1450.
[260] Law of Property Act 1925 s.131, (as amended by Trusts of Land and Appointment of Trustees Act 1996 Sch.3, para.4(14)); s.132; Administration of Estates Act 1925 s.51(2).
[261] [1961] A.C. 481; cf. *Baindail v Baindail* [1946] P. 122 at 127, per Lord Greene M.R.

distributable in accordance with the English Statute of Distribution 1670. Therefore, the word "wife" in that statute (and presumably the word "spouse" in the Administration of Estates Act 1925) is wide enough to cover the wife of a polygamous marriage, at any rate if there is only one.

In *Re Sehota*,[262] one of two surviving widows of a polygamous marriage was held to be a "wife" within the meaning of s.1(1)(a) of the Inheritance (Provision for Family and Dependants) Act 1975 and as such entitled to apply for financial provision under that Act. Moreover, the Privy Council has, without apparent difficulty, adopted the practice, in dealing with the estates of deceased Chinese who died domiciled in Malaysia, of assigning the one-third share of the widow under the Statute of Distribution equally between the several widows.[263] And there is Canadian and Zimbabwe authority for the proposition that gifts by will to a surviving wife attract succession duty at the lower rate applicable to a spouse, even if there is more than one wife.[264]

Social security legislation

8–057   The legislation governing social security benefits and allowances deals expressly with the rights of those who have married under a law which allows polygamy. Many Acts contain regulation-making powers and the regulations provide that a polygamous marriage is to be treated as having the same consequences as a monogamous marriage for any day, but only for any day, throughout which it is in fact monogamous.

Miscellaneous cases

8–058   The Divisional Court has recognised a potentially polygamous marriage celebrated in Nigeria between a man and a girl of thirteen domiciled there, and revoked a "fit person" order made in respect of the girl (on the basis that she was "exposed to moral danger") under the Children and Young Persons Act 1933.[265] The Privy Council has held that a husband and wife whose marriage is potentially polygamous cannot be guilty of a criminal conspiracy.[266] The wife of a potentially polygamous marriage has been allowed to assert a contractual claim against her husband for "deferred dower" under a marriage contract governed by Muslim law.[267] There is American authority for the proposition that the surviving spouse of a valid polygamous marriage can recover workmen's compensation for the death of her husband in an accident arising in the course of his employment.[268] If this case is followed in England, it would mean that the

---

[262] [1978] 1 W.L.R. 1506.
[263] *Cheang Thye Phin v Tan Ah Loy* [1920] A.C. 369; cf. *The Six Widows Case* (1908) 12 Straits Settlements L.R. 120.
[264] *Yew v Att-Gen for British Columbia* [1924] 1 D.L.R. 1166; *Estate Mehta v Acting Master*, 1958 (4) S.A. 252. In the latter case there was only one wife, but reliance on this fact was expressly disclaimed (at p.262).
[265] *Mohamed v Knott* [1969] 1 Q.B. 1.
[266] *Mawji v The Queen* [1957] A.C. 126.
[267] *Shahnaz v Rizwan* [1965] 1 Q.B. 390; *Qureshi v Qureshi* [1972] Fam. 173.
[268] *Royal v Cudahy Packing Co.*, 195 Iowa 759; 190 N.W. 427 (1922).

surviving spouse of a valid polygamous marriage would rank as a dependant under the Fatal Accidents Act 1976 (as amended) and could recover damages for the tortiously-inflicted death of her husband. In the law of immigration, the word "wife" includes each of two or more wives for the purposes of deportation,[269] and there are severe limitations on the extent to which a polygamous wife may exercise a right of abode in the United Kingdom if another wife of the same husband is already in the United Kingdom.[270] The summary remedy provided by s.17 of the Married Women's Property Act 1882 (as amended) applies to the spouses of a valid polygamous marriage.[271] Part IV of the Family Law Act 1996 (Family Homes and Domestic Violence) applies as between parties to a polygamous marriage.[272] A man who maintains his wife under a polygamous marriage is entitled to a deduction of tax under sections 257A and 257AB of the Income and Corporation Taxes Act 1988, even if there is more than one wife.[273]

Thus, a great deal of water has flowed under the bridge since 1866, when Lord Penzance denied matrimonial relief to the unfortunate Mr Hyde. It is now clear that English law does recognise valid polygamous marriages unless there is some strong reason to the contrary. The previous pages have shown that this reason has to be very strong indeed before recognition will be denied.

---

[269] Immigration Act 1971 s.5(4).
[270] Immigration Act 1988 s.2.
[271] *Chaudhry v Chaudhry* [1976] Fam. 148.
[272] s.63(5); a similar rule applied under the predecessor Matrimonial Homes Act 1983.
[273] *Nabi v Heaton* [1981] 1 W.L.R. 1052; appeal allowed by consent [1983] 1 W.L.R. 626.

CHAPTER 9

MATRIMONIAL CAUSES

Matrimonial causes include proceedings for divorce, separation, nullity of marriage, presumption of death and dissolution of marriage, or for a declaration as to status. Before 1858 jurisdiction in England over matrimonial causes (except divorce) was vested in the ecclesiastical courts. Their jurisdiction depended on the residence of the respondent within the relevant diocese. They had no power to dissolve a marriage[1]; that could only be done by private Act of Parliament. In 1857 the Matrimonial Causes Act introduced judicial divorce and transferred the matrimonial jurisdiction to the secular courts.   **9–001**

JURISDICTION

The Matrimonial Causes Act 1857 contained no rules as to jurisdiction in divorce. After a long period of uncertainty, the Privy Council held in *Le Mesurier v Le Mesurier*[2] that the only court which had jurisdiction to dissolve a marriage was the court of the common domicile of the parties. As the domicile of the wife during marriage was at common law the same as that of her husband, an Englishwoman whose husband had, or acquired, a foreign domicile would not have access to the divorce jurisdiction of the English courts. Legislation in 1937 and 1949[3] mitigated this hardship, but substantial reform came only with the reform of the law of domicile to allow married women an independent domicile.   **9–002**

The Domicile and Matrimonial Proceedings Act 1973 created a new set of jurisdictional principles applying to divorce and (with slight modifications) to

---

[1] References in early cases to "divorces" granted by the ecclesiastical courts can mislead. "Divorce *a mensa et thoro* [from bed and board]" is an old term for a separation.
[2] [1895] A.C. 517 at 540.
[3] Matrimonial Causes Act 1937 s.13 (deserted wives whose husbands had been domiciled in England) and Law Reform (Miscellaneous Provisions) Act 1949 s.1 (wives ordinarily resident for three years in England).

other matrimonial causes.[4] The English court had jurisdiction if either party was domiciled in England on the date on which proceedings were instituted or had been habitually resident in England for at least 12 months on that date.

9–003   These rules applied until the coming into force of a European Regulation on March 1, 2001.[5] That Regulation was later revised, though with no changes of substance so far as matrimonial matters were concerned, and jurisdiction in respect of most matrimonial causes is now governed by Council Regulation No. 2201/2003[6] (commonly known as the Brussels IIa Regulation) which came into force on March 1, 2005.[7] The Regulation contains a set of rules applicable in all Member States except Denmark ("the European Rules") but allows national law to apply in certain cases. The European Commission has already recognised the existence of problems with the jurisdictional criteria in the revised Regulation and in March 2005 issued a consultation paper,[8] which was followed in July 2006 by a Proposal for a new Regulation to amend Regulation 2201/2003, which however, failed to garner sufficient support for it to be taken further. The eventual outcome was limited to applicable law, and then only between certain Member States, not including the United Kingdom.[9]

European rules

Scope

9–004   The Brussels IIa Regulation provides a uniform set of jurisdictional rules and almost automatic recognition of matrimonial judgments throughout the European Union. It applies, whatever the nature of the court or tribunal, in civil matters relating to divorce, legal separation or marriage annulment as long as the matter is not excluded by art.1(3).[10]

Same-sex marriages are now available in a number of EU and non-EU countries. It has been questioned whether the provisions of the Regulation will extend to the dissolution of such marriages.[11] A similar question could be raised regarding the jurisdiction to grant a dissolution, separation or nullity order under

---

[4] For the background to this Act, see Law Com.No. 48 (1972).
[5] Council Regulation No. 1347/2000 of 29 May 2000 on jurisdiction and the recognition and enforcement of judgments in matrimonial matters and in matters of parental responsibility for children of both spouses, referred to as the "Brussels II Regulation". For text see O.J. 2000 L160/19. The Regulation was based on a draft Convention, agreed in 1998 but never brought into force.
[6] EU Council Regulation No. 2201/2003 of 27 November 2003 concerning jurisdiction and the recognition and enforcement of judgments in matrimonial matters and the matters of parental responsibility, repealing Regulation No. 1347/2000. For text see O.J. 2003 L338.
[7] See generally McEleavy, (2004) 53 I.C.L.Q. 605; Boele-Woelki and González Beilfuss (eds.), *Brussels IIbis: Its impact and application in the Member States* (Antwerp: European Family Law Series No.14, Intersentia). For a critique of the original Brussels II Convention and ensuing Regulation see: Karsten, [1998] I.F.L. 75; and Mostyn, [2001] Fam. Law 359.
[8] COM(2005)82 final.
[9] See para.9–026.
[10] art.1. Article 1(3) excludes maintenance obligations and trusts or succession. Recital (10) also explains that the Regulation does not apply to matters of social security, asylum and immigration.
[11] McEleavy, (2004) 53 I.C.L.Q. 605.

the Civil Partnership Act 2004.[12] However, the Civil Partnership (Jurisdiction and Recognition of Judgments) Regulations 2005[13] provide for the English court to have jurisdiction in the circumstances corresponding to art.3(a) of the Regulation.[14]

Grounds of jurisdiction

The Regulation bases jurisdiction primarily on habitual residence, deploying this connecting factor in a variety of ways, but also preserves jurisdiction based, so far as the United Kingdom and Ireland are concerned, on the common domicile of the parties – the traditional rule established in *Le Mesurier v Le Mesurier*,[15] and for other Member States on the common nationality of the parties – a feature of the traditional approach of many civil law States.

9–005

Article 3 of the Regulation contains a list of grounds on which the courts of a Member State have jurisdiction in divorce, legal separation and marriage annulment. Jurisdiction is given to the courts of the Member State:

(a)   in whose territory:
   (i)   the spouses are habitually resident, or
   (ii)   the spouses were last habitually resident, insofar as one of them still resides there, or
   (iii) the respondent is habitually resident, or
   (iv)   in the event of a joint application, either of the spouses is habitually resident, or
   (v)   the applicant is habitually resident if he or she resided there for at least a year immediately before the application was made,[16] or
   (vi)   the applicant is habitually resident if he or she resided there for at least six months immediately before the application was made and is either a national of the Member State in question or, in the case of the United Kingdom and Ireland, has his or her "domicile"[17] there;
(b)   of the nationality of both spouses or, in the case of the United Kingdom and Ireland, of the "domicile" of both spouses.

Additionally, where proceedings are pending in a court on the basis of art.3, that same court will also have jurisdiction to examine a counterclaim coming within the scope of the Regulation[18]; and where a court of a Member State has granted a legal separation, that court also has jurisdiction to convert the legal separation into divorce.[19] Article 20 allows for provisional, including protective, measures to

9–006

---

[12] See para.9–014.

[13] SI 2005/3334.

[14] The wisdom of extending the comprehensive régime of jurisdictional rules in matrimonial matters to civil partnerships has been strongly criticised. See Woelke [2004] I.F.L. 111.

[15] [1895] A.C. 517 at 540.

[16] As in *Sulaiman v Juffali* [2002] 1 F.L.R. 479, a case under the Brussels II Regulation.

[17] Domicile is declared to have the same meaning as it has under the legal systems of the United Kingdom and Ireland: art.3(2).

[18] art.4.

[19] art.5.

be taken in urgent cases even if the courts of another Member State have jurisdiction under the Regulation as to the substance of the matter, but this provisional jurisdiction ceases to apply when the court of the Member State having jurisdiction under the Regulation takes the measures it considers appropriate. The situation where the parties seek to begin proceedings in two different states is considered below.

Habitual residence The primary connecting factor of habitual residence is not defined in the Regulation. The Hague Conference has repeatedly declared the term a question of fact, but courts in England and many other countries have developed various legal criteria for the establishment of habitual residence depending on the nature of the claim under consideration. In the context of art.3 of the Brussels IIa Regulation, habitual residence is to be given an autonomous definition derived from the Borrás report on the preceding Brussels II Convention, from decisions of the European Court in other contexts,[20] and by the French Cour de Cassation.[21] The meaning derived from these authorities is that a person is habitually resident in the place which is the habitual centre of his or her interests. The interests to be weighed, the importance of which will vary from case to case, may include employment, educational, emotional, personal and family interests, a balancing exercise more difficult than the assessment undertaken by the English courts in considering habitual residence in other contexts. In this context, a person may only have one habitual residence.[22] The test is an objective one, the stated intentions of the parties being merely one factor in the assessment.[23]

9–007 The text of the fifth and sixth indents of art.3(1) of the Regulation use both "habitual residence" and "residence". The courts are divided as to whether in this context the latter term is to be interpreted as meaning habitual residence. In *Munro v Munro*[24] Bennett J. thought it should be so interpreted, relying essentially on the dominant role given to habitual residence in art.3 as stressed in the Borrás report on the equivalent material in the earlier draft Convention. In *Marinos v Marinos*[25] Munby J. took a different view, believing that the authors of the Regulation had deliberately distinguished between the two concepts, so that for the period of six or twelve months only residence *simpliciter* need be

---

[20] In Case C-523/07 *A (Applicant) (sub nom Re A (Area of Freedom, Security and Justice))* [2009] 2 F.L.R. 1 at [38], the European Court indicated that decisions on the meaning of habitual residence in one area of European Union law could not always be transposed so as to apply in another area (in the instant case the question of the habitual residence of a child). That case was distinguished in *Z v Z (Divorce: Jurisdiction)* [2009] EWHC 2626 (Fam); [2010] 1 FLR 694, where the context was art.3 of Brussels IIa rather than art.8.
[21] *L-K v K (No.2)* [2006] EWHC 3280 (Fam), [2007] 2 F.L.R. 729; *Marinos v Marinos* [2007] EWHC 2047 (Fam); [2007] 2 F.L.R. 1018; *Munro v Munro* [2007] EWHC 3315 (Fam); [2007] 1 F.L.R. 1613.
[22] *Marinos v Marinos* [2007] EWHC 2047 (Fam); [2007] 2 F.L.R. 1018 (not following *Armstrong v Armstrong* [2003] EWHC 777 (Fam); [2003] 2 F.L.R. 375); *Munro v Munro* [2007] EWHC 3315 (Fam); [2007] 1 F.L.R. 1613. See Lamont (2007) 3 J.Priv.Int.L. 261.
[23] *Z v Z (Divorce: Jurisdiction)* [2009] EWHC 2626 (Fam); [2010] 1 FLR 694; *V v V (Divorce: Jurisdiction)* [2011] EWHC 1190 (Fam); [2011] 2 F.L.R. 778.
[24] [2007] EWHC 3315 (Fam); [2007] 1 F.L.R. 1613 at [45] to [53].
[25] [2007] EWHC 2047 (Fam); [2007] 2 F.L.R. 1018 at [45] to [49].

established. In neither case was a resolution of this issue essential. In *V v V (Divorce: Jurisdiction)*,[26] where the issue was only lightly argued, Peter Jackson J. favoured the *Marinos* view.

The domicile basis   Article 3(b) of the Regulation gives jurisdiction on the basis of the common nationality, or in the case of the United Kingdom and Ireland, the common domicile of the spouses. In the case of the two named states, only domicile may be relied upon; nationality is irrelevant.[27]

In many cases the rules just considered are exclusive: no other jurisdictional rules   **9–008** can be relied upon. So, a spouse who is either habitually resident or a national of a Member State, or has his or her domicile in the United Kingdom or Ireland, may only be sued in accordance with the rules in arts 3 to 5 of the Regulation[28]; and only where none of the connecting factors in those provisions point to a Member State may a spouse be sued according to the traditional rules found in the national law of the forum State.[29] It follows that where the respondent is a national of a Member State but habitually resident in a non-Member State (and not domiciled in the United Kingdom or Ireland), and the applicant cannot satisfy one of the jurisdictional criteria in arts 3 to 5, no Member State will have jurisdiction to grant a divorce, legal separation or annulment.[30] It may be, of course, that the non-Member State will have jurisdiction, a matter governed by its national law.

Residual jurisdiction   Where the jurisdictional rules of arts 3 to 5 are not exclusive and no court of a Member State has jurisdiction under those rules,[31] jurisdiction may be exercised in accordance with the national law of the Member State before which the proceedings are begun.[32] The scope of national law is indeed extended by the Regulation: as against a respondent who is not habitually resident and is not a national of a Member State (or not domiciled in the United Kingdom or Ireland), any national of a Member State who is habitually resident within the territory of another Member State may, like the nationals of that State, avail him- or herself of the rules of jurisdiction applicable in that State.[33] The effect of these provisions is that as against such respondents, pre-existing national bases of jurisdiction remain in force and are available to nationals of other Member States, the resulting judgments having the benefit of the recognition

---

[26] [2011] EWHC 1190 (Fam); [2011] 2 F.L.R. 778 at [41] to [47].
[27] *Re N (Jurisdiction)* [2007] EWHC 1274 (Fam); [2007] 2 F.L.R. 1196. Where nationality is relevant and the parties are both dual nationals of the same two Member States, the parties may invoke the jurisdiction of either State: C-168/08 *Hadadi v Hadadi* [2009] E.C.R. I-6871.
[28] art.6. A pre-nuptial agreement including a clause that the parties will only litigate in a particular State has no effect; *C v C (Divorce: Jurisdiction)* [2005] EWCA Civ. 68; (2005) 149 S.J.L.B. 113 although the point was not expressly argued.
[29] Article 7; Case 68/07 *Lopez v Lizazo* [2007] E.C.R. I-10403; [2008] Fam. 21. See below for the English traditional rules.
[30] This was one of the problems that the rejected Proposal for a new Regulation amending the Brussels IIa Regulation aimed to remedy.
[31] Emphasised in Case 68/07 *Lopez v Lizazo* [2007] E.C.R. I-10403; [2008] Fam. 21.
[32] art.7(1).
[33] art.7(2).

provisions of the Regulation. This has rightly been described by one commentator as "a very unprincipled grab for excessive matrimonial jurisdiction."[34]

Traditional Rules

Divorce and judicial separation

9–009 Where the provisions of arts 6 and 7 of the Regulation allow for residual jurisdiction under the domestic laws of each Member State, s.5(2) of the Domicile and Matrimonial Proceedings Act 1973[35] provides that English courts have jurisdiction to entertain proceedings for divorce and judicial separation if (and, subject to s.5(5) considered below, only if):

(a)   the court has jurisdiction under the Brussels IIa Regulation; or
(b)   no court of a Contracting State has jurisdiction under the Brussels IIa Regulation and either of the parties to the marriage is domiciled in England and Wales on the date when proceedings are begun.

Thus the residual jurisdiction under the traditional rules will only arise if the respondent is not habitually resident in a Member State, is not a national of a Member State other than the United Kingdom and Ireland, and is not domiciled in the United Kingdom or Ireland, but the applicant is domiciled in England.

9–010 Section 5(5) of the Act is, on first reading, a complex provision, but is the counterpart under the traditional rules to art.4 of the Regulation regarding counterclaims. The basic idea is that once the English court is properly exercising jurisdiction over a marriage, it retains that jurisdiction even if the nature of the relief sought changes. Section 5(5) provides that the court has jurisdiction to entertain proceedings for divorce, judicial separation or nullity of marriage, notwithstanding that the jurisdictional requirements of the section are not (when those particular decrees are sought) satisfied, if they are begun at a time when proceedings which the court has jurisdiction to entertain[36] are pending in respect of the same marriage for divorce, judicial separation or nullity of marriage. This subsection contemplates (a) supplemental petitions by the petitioner for the same relief on a different ground, or for a different form of relief, and (b) cross-petitions by the respondent. The court will have jurisdiction to entertain the supplemental or cross-petition, even though the applicant is not domiciled in England, provided it had jurisdiction to entertain the original petition and that petition is still pending.

The exercise of the English courts' jurisdiction in proceedings for divorce is subject to rules requiring or enabling the court to stay those proceedings in certain circumstances. These rules are considered later in this chapter.

---

[34] Beaumont, in evidence to a House of Lords committee: H.L. Paper 19, Session 1997–98.

[35] As substituted by the European Communities (Matrimonial Jurisdiction and Judgments) Regulations 2001, SI 2001/3 10. Note that the definition of "Council Regulation" in s.5(1A) has been amended by the European Communities (Jurisdiction and Judgments in Matrimonial and Parental Responsibility Matters) Regulations 2005 (SI 2005/265).

[36] By virtue of s.5(2), (3) or (5).

Nullity of marriage

Before 1974 the jurisdiction of the English courts to entertain petitions for nullity **9–011** of marriage was one of the most vexed and difficult questions in the whole of the English conflict of laws. An enormous simplification of the law was effected by the Domicile and Matrimonial Proceedings Act 1973.[37] Section 5(3) of the Act[38] provides that English courts have jurisdiction to entertain such petitions[39] if (and, subject to s.5(5), only if):

(a)   the court has jurisdiction under the Brussels IIa Regulation; or
(b)   no court of a Contracting State has jurisdiction under the Brussels IIa Regulation and either of the parties to the marriage:
 (i)   is domiciled in England and Wales on the date when the proceedings are begun; or
 (ii)   died before that date and either was at death domiciled in England and Wales or had been habitually resident in England and Wales throughout the period of one year ending with the date of death.

Subsection (b)(ii) is intended to cover the rare but still theoretically possible case **9–012** where a person with sufficient interest petitions for a decree that a marriage is void after the death of one or both of the parties thereto. In theory, that can be done during the lives of the parties.

The provisions of s.5(5) of the 1973 Act on jurisdiction to entertain supplemental or cross-petitions apply to nullity of marriage as they apply to divorce and judicial separation. There is therefore no need to repeat here the earlier discussion.

The exercise of the English courts' jurisdiction in proceedings for nullity of marriage is subject to rules enabling the court to stay those proceedings in certain circumstances. These rules are considered later in this chapter.

"Non-marriages"

The English courts distinguish between a void marriage, which may be the **9–013** subject of a nullity decree with financial provisions, and "non-marriages" where no decree will be granted. An illustration is provided by *Hudson v Leigh*[40]:

> A religious ceremony was held in South Africa, which was intended by the parties and the officiant to have no legal effect and to be a precursor to a civil marriage in England (which did not in fact happen); the South African ceremony was held a "non-marriage".

It was held that questionable ceremonies are to be classified on a case by case basis, relevant factors including (but not being limited to): (a) whether the

---

[37] Implementing the recommendations of the Law Commission: Law Com. No. 48 (1972), paras 49–62.
[38] As substituted by the European Communities (Matrimonial Jurisdiction and Judgments) Regulations 2001 (SI 2001/3 10).
[39] The bases for jurisdiction are the same whether the marriage is alleged to be void or voidable.
[40] [2009] EWHC 1306 (Fam); [2009] 2 F.L.R. 1129.

ceremony or event set out or purported to be a lawful marriage; (b) whether it bore all or enough of the hallmarks of marriage; (c) whether the three key participants (most especially the officiating official) believed, intended and understood the ceremony as giving rise to the status of lawful marriage; and (d) the reasonable perceptions, understandings and beliefs of those in attendance. Other cases held to have been "non-marriages" include religious ceremonies with no attempt to comply with any legal formalities,[41] and social events which one party claimed to have been regarded as a marriage.[42]

Dissolution, separation or annulment of civil partnerships

9–014   Section 221 of the Civil Partnership Act 2004 makes provision for the English court to make dissolution, separation or nullity orders if it has jurisdiction under a s.219 regulation (i.e., regulations making provisions corresponding to the Brussels IIa Regulation),[43] or, where no court has jurisdiction under s.219, either party is domiciled in England on the date the proceedings are begun and the parties are registered as civil partners of each other in England, and it appears to the court to be in the interests of justice to assume jurisdiction in the case.[44] Similarly, if no court has jurisdiction under a s.219 regulation the English court will have jurisdiction to grant a nullity order, where either party is domiciled in England on the date when the proceedings are begun, or died domiciled or habitually resident for one year in England and the parties are registered as civil partners of each other in England, and it appears to the court to be in the interests of justice to assume jurisdiction in the case.[45] Additionally, where proceedings

---

[41] *A-M v A-M (divorce: jurisdiction: validity of marriage)* [2001] 2 F.L.R. 6 (Muslim ceremony); *Gandhi v Patel* [2002] 1 F.L.R. 603 (Hindu ceremony); *A v H* [2009] EWHC 636 (Fam); [2010] 1 F.L.R. 1 (Muslim ceremony).

[42] *Alfonso-Brown v Milwood* [2006] EWHC 642 (Fam); [2007] 2 F.L.R. 265 (event in Ghana found to be an engagement ceremony); *Al-Saedy v Musawi* [2010] EWHC 3293 (Fam); [2011] 2 F.L.R.287 (family gathering in England; event denied by one party, described as a 'religious agreement' by the other).

[43] The Civil Partnership (Jurisdiction and Recognition of Judgments) Regulations 2005 (SI 2005/3334), provide for the English court to have jurisdiction in the circumstances corresponding to art.3(a) of the Regulation, but not art.3(b) – the common domicile of the partners.

[44] s.221(1).

[45] s.221(2).

are pending and the court has jurisdiction in respect of one of the orders, the court may also take jurisdiction to make a different type of order even if jurisdiction was not exercisable at that time.[46]

Declarations as to status

Declarations as to status are not covered by the Brussels IIa Regulation. Accordingly, jurisdiction is governed by English law. Declarations as to status can be important as the procedural method of testing whether a foreign divorce or other matrimonial decree is entitled to recognition. Part III of the Family Law Act 1986,[47] implementing a report of the Law Commission,[48] enacted a comprehensive code of statutory rules as to declarations of status.[49] It applies to five types of declarations as to marital status specified in s.55(1) of the 1986 Act. These are declarations (a) that a marriage was at its inception a valid marriage; (b) that a marriage subsisted on a date specified in the application; (c) that a marriage did not subsist on a date so specified; (d) that the validity of a divorce, annulment or legal separation obtained in any country outside England in respect of a marriage is entitled to recognition in England; and (e) that the validity of a divorce, annulment or legal separation so obtained in respect of a marriage is not entitled to recognition in England. No court may make a declaration that a marriage was at its inception void[50]; such an allegation must be made in a petition for a decree of nullity of marriage.[51]

9–015

There is jurisdiction to make such a declaration if, and only if, either of the parties to the marriage concerned is domiciled in England on the date of the application, or was habitually resident in England throughout the period of one year ending with that date, or died before that date and either was at death domiciled in England, or had been habitually resident in England throughout the period of one year ending with the date of death.[52] The domicile and habitual residence of an applicant who is not a party to the marriage is immaterial; the court must, however, refuse to hear an application made by such a person if it considers that he or she does not have a sufficient interest in the determination of the application.[53]

The manner in which the court is to exercise its jurisdiction is dealt with in s.58(1) of the 1986 Act. Where the proposition to be declared is proved to the satisfaction of the court, the court must make the declaration unless to do so would be manifestly contrary to public policy. The Law Commission indicated that the reference to the court being satisfied was intended to make clear that the

9–016

---

[46] s.221(3).

[47] For a critique of the Family Law Act 1986, see Lowe, (2002) 32 Fam. Law 39.

[48] *Declarations in Family Matters*, Law Com. No. 132 (1984).

[49] The inherent jurisdiction of the High Court formerly relied on as a basis for making certain types of declarations as to status is excluded: Family Law Act 1986 s.58(4).

[50] Family Law Act 1986 s.58(5)(a).

[51] See, for example, *KC v City of Westminster Social and Community Services Dept* [2008] EWCA Civ. 198; [2008] 2 F.C.R. 146.

[52] Family Law Act 1986 s.55(2). These jurisdictional rules correspond to those which governed jurisdiction to grant a decree of nullity of marriage before the European Regulations were adopted.

[53] Family Law Act 1986 s.55(3).

standard of proof is high and that the evidence must be clear and convincing.[54] It may be doubted whether the statutory words actually convey that meaning.

At any stage in the proceedings, the court may, on its own motion or on the application of a party, send the relevant papers to the Attorney General; in any case, the Attorney General may intervene, and may argue any question which the court considers it necessary to have fully argued.[55] Whether or not the Attorney General is involved, a declaration made under the 1986 Act binds the Crown and all other persons.[56]

With regard to same-sex unions, s.58 of the Civil Partnership Act 2004 provides that any person with sufficient interest may apply to the English court for a declaration of validity or otherwise of a civil partnership, or the validity or otherwise of the dissolution of a civil partnership. However, the court may make such a declaration if, and only if, either of the partners is domiciled in England and Wales on the date of the application, or has been habitually resident throughout the period of one year ending with that date, or died domiciled or habitually resident for one year in England and Wales, and the two people concerned are civil partners of each other and it appears to the court to be in the interests of justice to assume jurisdiction.[57]

9–017   Despite the existence of this statutory code, other declarations relating to the validity of marriage are possible under the inherent jurisdiction of the High Court. So, declarations that an adult lacked capacity to enter a marriage on account of a mental condition have been made in a number of cases[58]; a declaration that the marriage was not recognised as a valid marriage in the jurisdiction of England and Wales (used in cases of forced marriages abroad)[59]; or that there never has been a marriage between the parties, when any ceremony or event involving the parties can be regarded as within the "non-marriage" category.[60]

STAYING OF MATRIMONIAL PROCEEDINGS

9–018   As a result of the many and various grounds of jurisdiction available for divorce, legal separation and nullity, it is quite possible that the parties may each start proceedings relating to the same matrimonial matters in the courts of different countries. The effect of the rules governing any possible stay of the English proceedings has been much reduced by the Regulation.

---

[54] Law Com. No. 132, para.3.57, fn.265.
[55] Family Law Act 1986 s.59.
[56] Family Law Act 1986 s.58(2).
[57] Civil Partnership Act 2004 s.224.
[58] *X City Council v MB* [2006] EWHC 168 (Fam); [2006] 2 F.L.R. 968; *Local Authority X v MM* [2007] EWHC 2003 (Fam); [2009] 1 F.L.R. 443; *Ealing LBC v S* [2008] EWHC 636 (Fam), sub nom *Re K* [2008] 2 F.L.R. 720.
[59] *SH v NB* [2009] EWHC 3274 (Fam); [2010] 1 F.L.R. 1927; *Re P (Forced Marriage)* [2010] EWHC 3467 (Fam); [2011] 1 F.L.R. 2060.
[60] *Hudson v Leigh* [2009] EWHC 1306 (Fam); [2009] 2 F.L.R. 1129; *B v I (Forced Marriage)* [2010] 1 F.L.R. 1721.

The Regulation provisions

The Brussels IIa Regulation, following the model first found in the 1968 Brussels   **9–019**
Convention on jurisdiction and the recognition and enforcement of judgments in
civil and commercial matters (now replaced by the Brussels I Regulation), adopts
a civil law approach to the question of *litispendence*, the existence of two (or
more) proceedings in relation to the same matter in different countries.

Article 19 provides that, where proceedings relating to divorce, legal
separation or marriage annulment between the same parties are brought before
courts of different Member States, the court second seised must of its own motion
stay its proceedings until such time as the jurisdiction of the court first seised is
established.[61] Where the jurisdiction of the court first seised is established, the
court second seised must decline jurisdiction in favour of that court. In that case,
the party who brought the relevant action before the court second seised may
bring that action before the court first seised.[62] For this purpose, a court is seised
(a) at the time when the document instituting the proceedings or an equivalent
document is lodged with the court, provided that the applicant has not
subsequently failed to take the steps he or she was required to take to have service
effected on the respondent; or (b) if the document has to be served before being
lodged with the court, at the time when it is received by the authority responsible
for service, provided that the applicant has not subsequently failed to take the
steps he or she was required to take to have the document lodged with the court.[63]
"Lodge" in this context means that the documentation was filed and proceeded
with in a manner accepted by the court and which led to the issue of a petition in
the proceedings by the court.[64] Proceedings are continuing in another jurisdiction
when they have been commenced there and have not been dismissed.[65]

Whether preliminary proceedings are proceedings relating to a divorce, legal   **9–020**
separation or marriage annulment, is a matter for the characterisation of the court
seised of those preliminary proceedings, and a court potentially second seised
should ascertain the decision of the court potentially first seised by direct judicial
cooperation.[66]

Although it could be argued that the absolute nature of the *lis pendens* rule
serves to promote a race to litigate in the country perceived to give the applicant
a particular advantage and in *L-K v L-K (No.3)*[67] Singer J. described the "first
past the post" régime as arbitrary and as having the potential be unfair to one

---

[61] art.19(1). See *Leman-Klemmers v Klemmers* [2007] EWCA Civ 919; [2008] 1 F.L.R. 692 (English
court first seised); *Re N (Jurisdiction)* [2007] EWHC 1274 (Fam); [2007] 2 F.L.R. 1196 (French court
first seised). cf. *Bentinck v Bentinck* [2007] EWCA Civ 175; [2007] 2 F.L.R. 1, decided under the
Lugano Convention 1988.

[62] art.19(3).

[63] art.16.

[64] See *L-K v L-K (No.3)* [2006] EWHC 3281 (Fam); [2007] 2 F.L.R. 741 (where failure to produce
marriage certificate did not prevent there being a sufficient "lodging" in the English court).

[65] See *C v S (Divorce: Jurisdiction)* [2010] EWHC 2676 (Fam); [2011] 2 F.L.R. 19 (where the
foreign court had rejected the petition before it and was held no longer seised).

[66] *C v C (Divorce: Jurisdiction)* [2005] EWCA Civ. 68; (2005) 149 S.J.L.B. 113, per Thorpe L.J. at
para.44. The case involved a French judicial hearing designed to enable the possibility of
reconciliation to be explored and seen as distinct from possible divorce proceedings.

[67] [2006] EWHC 3281 (Fam); [2007] 2 F.L.R. 741.

party or the other, it must be remembered that the jurisdictional rules do provide for a real connection between the applicant and the forum. A spouse who wishes to avail him- or herself of the jurisdiction of a Member State to which the respondent has no connection has to have been habitually resident in that state for one year, or for six months if also a national of that state (or domiciled in that state in the case of the United Kingdom and Ireland), thereby limiting the race to court to situations in which the marriage has true connections to more than one Member State.[68] It may, however, be doubted whether any sort of race to court is desirable in the context of matrimonial disputes, especially in the light of the promotion of mediation as a family dispute resultion mechanism.[69]

English law

Obligatory stays

9–021   Paragraph 8 of Sch.1 to the 1973 Act contains provisions obliging the English courts in certain circumstances to stay proceedings where other proceedings in respect of the same marriage are pending in a "related jurisdiction". Related jurisdictions are those within the British Isles.[70] They include Scotland and Northern Ireland[71]; but Guernsey, Jersey and the Isle of Man, not Member States, are also "related jurisdictions": if the English court has jurisdiction under art.7, the rules as to obligatory stays would be applicable.

Paragraph 8 provides that where before the beginning of the trial or first trial in any proceedings for divorce which are continuing in an English court it appears to the court:

(a)   that proceedings for divorce or nullity of marriage in respect of that marriage are continuing in another jurisdiction in the British Isles; and

(b)   that the parties to the marriage have resided together after its celebration; and

(c)   that the place where they resided together when the proceedings in the English court were begun, or last resided together before those proceedings were begun, is in that other jurisdiction; and

(d)   that either of the parties was habitually resident in that jurisdiction throughout the year ending with the date on which they last resided together before the date on which the proceedings in the English court were begun,

---

[68] See generally Truex, [2001] Fam. Law 233; Mostyn, [2001] Fam. Law 359.

[69] See, for example, Directive 2008/52/EC on certain aspects of mediation in civil and commercial matters; and see the earlier report *Parental Separation: Children's Needs and Parents' Responsibilities: Next Steps. Report of the Responses to Consultation and Agenda for Action*, Cm 6452 (2005), which stated at p.11: "The Government does not mean to make mediation compulsory but will strongly promote its use."

[70] Sch.1, para.3(2).

[71] It is unclear whether the Regulation allows the continued application of the rules as to obligatory stays in cases involving other proceedings in those countries. Article 19 giving priority to the court first seised speaks of the "courts of different Member States" but the effect of art.66 may be that the courts in England and Scotland are to be treated as if they were courts in different Member States.

the English court must order the proceedings to be stayed. The object of this provision was to give jurisdictional priority to the country most closely connected with the marriage, that is to say to the country to which the marriage may be said to "belong".[72]

Discretionary stays

Paragraph 9 of Schedule 1 to the Domicile and Matrimonial Proceedings Act 1973 makes provision for matrimonial proceedings in an English court to be stayed in favour of the court of another country in certain situations.[73]   **9–022**

Where before the beginning of the trial or first trial in any matrimonial proceedings, other than proceedings governed by the Brussels IIa Regulation, which are continuing in the court, it appears to the court:

(a)   that any proceedings in respect of the marriage in question, or capable of affecting its validity or subsistence, are continuing in another jurisdiction; and

(b)   that the balance of fairness (including convenience) as between the parties to the marriage is such that it is appropriate for the proceedings in that other jurisdiction to be disposed of before further steps are taken in the proceedings in the court,
the English court may, if it thinks fit, order that the proceedings before it be stayed.[74]

Paragraph 9 now applies only to proceedings other than those governed by the Brussels IIa Regulation[75]; the meaning of this exclusion is not wholly clear, for cases in which jurisdiction is taken under national law can be regarded as governed by the provision as to "residual jurisdiction" under art.7 of the Regulation. The intention appears to be that para.9 should continue to apply where that residual jurisdiction is invoked.[76]   **9–023**

The English courts have been reluctant to decide the question of the application in this context of the decision in *Owusu v Jackson*[77] which in the context of the Brussels I Regulation precluded the English courts from using the notion *forum non conveniens* to stay proceedings. The Court of Appeal refused an application for leave to appeal on the point in *Cook v Plummer*.[78] Thorpe L.J.

---

[72] Law Com. No. 48 (1972), para.85.
[73] Similar provisions exist for civil partnerships: Family Proceedings (Civil Partnership: Staying of Proceedings) Rules 2005/2921.
[74] Domicile and Matrimonial Proceedings Act 1973 Sch.1, para.9 as amended by the European Communities (Matrimonial Jurisdiction and Judgments) Regulations 2001 (SI 2001/310). See *Mytton v Mytton* (1977) 7 Fam. Law 244; *Shemshadfard v Shemshadfard* [1981] 1 All E.R. 726; *Thyssen-Bornemisza v Thyssen-Bornemisza* [1986] Fam. 1; *S v S (Matrimonial Proceedings: Appropriate Forum)* [1997] 1 W.L.R. 1200. For the discharge of stays, and the effect of a stay on powers to make orders as to financial and other ancillary matters, see Domicile and Matrimonial Proceedings Act 1973 Sch.1, paras 10 and 11.
[75] See SI 2001/310 reg.4.
[76] *JKN v JCN* [2010] EWHC 843 (Fam); [2011] 1 F.L.R. 826.
[77] Case 281/02 [2005] E.C.R. I-1383; [2005] Q.B. 801.
[78] [2008] EWCA Civ 484; [2008] 2 F.L.R. 989.

noted that the decision in *Owusu v Jackson* was "deeply unpopular in this jurisdiction" and that the United Kingdom was seeking "to mitigate its unattractive effect" by submissions in the review of the operation of the Brussels I Regulation; to admit the point for consideration by the full court would have "unpredictable consequences". The issue was squarely faced for the first time in *JKN v JCN.*[79] The court held that *Owusu v Jackson* did not apply to cases governed by the Brussels IIa Regulation, for a number of reasons. *Owusu v Jackson* did not address the position that arises under the Domicile and Matrimonial Proceedings Act 1973 where by definition there are concurrent proceedings. *Owusu v Jackson* should be limited to cases under the Brussels I Regulation, essentially a commercial Regulation, and not extended so as to apply to the Brussels IIa Regulation dealing with family law. Article 2 of the Brussels I Regulation had been described as "mandatory" by the European Court, but under art.3 of the Brussels IIa Regulation there was no corresponding obligation: art.3 envisaged a multiplicity of Member States having concurrent jurisdiction, art.2 of the Brussels I Regulation envisaged only one.

9–024 Assuming it survives, the discretionary power in para.9 may be exercised on the court's own motion as well as on the application of a party to the marriage. In considering the balance of fairness and convenience, the court must have regard to all factors appearing to be relevant, including the convenience of witnesses and any delay or expense which may result from the proceedings being stayed, or not being stayed. The court will exercise its discretion on the same basis as in *forum non conveniens* cases, using the principles set out in *Spiliada Maritime Corp. v Cansulex Ltd.*[80] That this was the correct approach was established in the House of Lords in *De Dampierre v De Dampierre,*[81] a case which illustrates the operation of the rules on discretionary stays:

> H was a French aristocrat whose family estates produced cognac. He married W, also a French national, in France in 1977. They moved to England in 1979, where their only son was born in 1982. In 1985, W took the child to New York and the marriage broke down. H began divorce proceedings in France in May 1985; W petitioned for divorce in England in July 1985, and H sought a stay of the English proceedings. Although unsuccessful in the lower courts, H succeeded in the House of Lords.

9–025 The decision in the lower courts was based on the fact that a maintenance order would be made in favour of W in the English proceedings, but that under French law a finding that she was responsible for the failure of the marriage would lead to a denial of any such order. The House of Lords, following the *Spiliada* approach, held that the financial advantage W might gain from proceeding in England was only one factor. Given the tenuous nature of her links with England, it was logical and not unfair to allow the litigation between the parties, both of whom were French and who had married in France, to be conducted in the courts of that country.[82]

---

[79] [2010] EWHC 843 (Fam); [2011] 1 F.L.R. 826.
[80] [1987] A.C. 460; see above, para.5–044.
[81] [1988] A.C. 92. Were the facts to recur, the outcome would now be different: the French proceedings, being in another Member State, would have priority under art.19.
[82] For other illustrations, see *R v R (Divorce: Stay of Proceedings)* [1994] 2 F.L.R. 1036 (stay refused); *T v T (Jurisdiction: Forum Conveniens)* [1995] 2 F.L.R. 660 (stay granted); *Otobo v Otobo*

The English court has power, which will be very sparingly exercised, to grant an interim injunction restraining the continuance of foreign matrimonial proceedings.[83] The principles applicable are again those developed in non-matrimonial cases, i.e., those in *S.N.I. Aerospatiale v Lee Kui Jak*.[84] It has been held that it is not necessary to show that England is the natural forum for a *Hemain* injunction to be granted,[85] since it is "merely an interim injunction to maintain the status quo ... pending the determination of an application for a stay ...".[86] Following the decision of the ECJ in *Turner v Grovitt*,[87] this power will only be available in the circumstances where the Regulation permits residual jurisdiction under the traditional rules.

CHOICE OF LAW

Divorce

The question of choice of law has never been prominent in the English rules of the conflict of laws relating to divorce, which has always been treated as primarily a jurisdictional question. English courts when deciding whether to recognise foreign divorces have never examined the grounds on which the decree was granted in order to see whether they were sufficient by English domestic law. On the other hand, when English courts have themselves assumed jurisdiction, they have never applied any other law than that of England. In marked contrast, courts on the continent of Europe have, since the beginning of this century, often applied foreign law, usually the law of the parties' nationality. This has sometimes involved them in very complicated problems, especially when the parties are of different nationalities.

9–026

The civil law approach is well illustrated by Council Regulation (EU) No 1259/2010 of December 20, 2010 implementing enhanced co-operation in the area of the law applicable to divorce and legal separation.[88] This sets out uniform applicable law rules for divorce and legal separation for the 14 participating Member States. The Regulation introduces an element of party autonomy, with the parties being able to designate the applicable law, subject to certain safeguards, from a list of options: (a) the law of the State of the spouses' habitual residence at the time of conclusion of the agreement; (b) the law of the State of the spouses' last habitual residence if one of them still resides there at the time of conclusion of the agreement; (c) the law of the State of nationality of one of the spouses at the time of conclusion of the agreement; and (d) the law of the

---

[2002] EWCA Civ 949; [2003] 1 F.L.R. 192 (stay refused); *Ella v Ella* [2007] EWCA Civ. 99, [2007] 2 F.L.R. 35 (stay granted, relevance of pre-nuptial agreement).

[83] e.g., *Hemain v Hemain* [1988] 2 F.L.R. 388.

[84] [1987] A.C. 871; see above, para.5–053.

[85] *R v R (Divorce: Hemain Injunction)* [2003] EWHC 2113 (Fam); [2005] 1 F.L.R. 386 at para.55.

[86] *ibid.*, per Munby J. at para.54.

[87] Case C-159/02; see above, para.5–058.

[88] [2010] O.J. L343, p. 10. For the discussions which led to the United Kingdom's decision not to participate the account given by Thorpe L.J. in *Radmacher v Granatino* [2009] EWCA Civ 649, [2009] 2 F.C.R. 645 at [6] to [9].

forum.[89] In the absence of a choice by the parties, a "cascade" of possibly applicable laws is established. Divorce and legal separation would be subject to the law of the State: (a) where the spouses are habitually resident at the time the court is seised; or, failing that, (b) where the spouses were last habitually resident, provided that the period of residence did not end more than one year before the court was seised, in so far as one of the spouses still resides in that State at the time the court is seised; or, failing that, (c) of which both spouses are nationals at the time the court is seised; or, failing that, (d) where the court is seised.[90] Where the law applicable under these rules makes no provision for divorce or does not grant one of the spouses equal access to divorce or legal separation on grounds of their sex, the law of the forum is to apply.[91]

9–027   In English law, the only possible alternative to the *lex fori* would be the law of the domicile. No difference between them could exist before 1938, because English courts did not exercise jurisdiction unless the parties were domiciled in England. When this did become possible, the Court of Appeal assumed without discussion that nevertheless English law was still applicable[92]; and this was confirmed by a legislative provision last enacted as s.46(2) of the Matrimonial Causes Act 1973.[93] This provided that in any proceedings in which the court had jurisdiction by virtue of that section, the issues should be determined in accordance with the law which would be applicable thereto if both parties were domiciled in England at the time of the proceedings, i.e., English law. This subsection was repealed in 1973, but this was not intended to alter the law.[94] Hence, if a spouse habitually resident in England but domiciled abroad wishes to obtain a divorce on a ground recognised by the law of his or her domicile but not by English law, the English court cannot assist. To require English courts to dissolve marriages on exotic foreign grounds would be distasteful to the judges and unacceptable to public opinion. Conversely, if the English court can grant a divorce under the terms of the 1973 Act, it is immaterial that the law of the domicile has no comparable ground of divorce. This approach can, of course, cause problems where the law of the parties' domicile does not recognise the divorce, but this has been held to be irrelevant.[95]

Separation

9–028   Unlike divorce *a vinculo matrimonii* (dissolving the marriage bond), judicial or legal separation was a remedy granted by the ecclesiastical courts before 1858. Its principal effect was (and is) to entitle the petitioner to live apart from the respondent, but not to dissolve their marriage nor enable either party to remarry. It is little used today; the remedy is sought chiefly by persons who have religious

---

[89] art.5. For provisions as to the formal and essential validity of the agreement, see arts 6 and 7.
[90] art.8.
[91] art.10.
[92] *Zanelli v Zanelli* (1948) 64 T.L.R. 556.
[93] Re-enacting earlier legislation going back to the Law Reform (Miscellaneous Provisions) Act 1949.
[94] Law Com. No. 48, paras 103–108.
[95] *Kapur v Kapur* [1984] F.L.R. 920; *Otobo v Otobo* [2002] EWCA Civ 949; [2003] 1 F.L.R. 192.

scruples about divorce. It has never been doubted that the English courts will apply English domestic law and no other, even if the parties are domiciled abroad.

Nullity of marriage

The question of what law governs the validity of a marriage was considered in the previous chapter. It was there pointed out that the formal validity of a marriage is governed (in general) by the law of the place of celebration, and capacity to marry (in general) by the law of each party's antenuptial domicile. There is more doubt about physical incapacity, which may be governed by the *lex fori* or possibly by the law of the petitioner's domicile, and consent of parties, which may be governed by the law of each party's antenuptial domicile or possibly by the *lex fori*. There is no need to repeat the former discussion of these matters in this chapter. But something should be said on the question of whether a marriage could be annulled in England on some ground unknown to English law.

9–029

The grounds on which a marriage is void or voidable in English law are clearly set out in ss.11 and 12 respectively of the Matrimonial Causes Act 1973 as amended, and the bars to relief in the case of voidable marriages in s.13. Section 14(1) provides that where, apart from the Act, any matter affecting the validity of a marriage would under the rules of private international law fall to be determined by reference to the law of a foreign country, nothing in ss.11, 12 or 13(1) shall preclude the determination of that matter by that foreign law, or require the application to the marriage of the grounds or bar to relief there mentioned. This subsection seems to leave open the question with which we are concerned.

Of course a marriage could be annulled for failure to comply with the formalities prescribed by the law of the place of celebration, however much those formalities might differ from those of English domestic law.[96] And a marriage could be annulled if the parties were within the prohibited degrees of the law of their antenuptial domicile, even though they might have capacity to marry by English domestic law.[97] But could a marriage be annulled in England on some ground quite unknown to English domestic law, e.g., lack of parental consent[98] or mistake as to the attributes of the other spouse?[99] In the former case, it is possible that the English court might fall back on tradition, characterise the impediment as a formality, and treat it as immaterial if the marriage was celebrated in England[100] or Scotland[101] but as invalidating the marriage if it was celebrated in the country by whose law the requirement of parental consent was imposed. But, as we have seen,[102] there are grave objections to this course. In the latter case, the impediment could not by any stretch of the imagination be characterised as a

9–030

---

[96] See, e.g. *Berthiaume v Dastous* [1930] A.C. 79 (marriage in church without civil ceremony).
[97] *Sottomayor v De Barros (No.1)* (1877) 3 P.D. 1 (first cousins).
[98] See *Ogden v Ogden* [1908] P. 46 (French law).
[99] See *Mitford v Mitford* [1923] P. 130 (German law).
[100] *Simonin v Mallac* (1860) 2 Sw. & Tr. 67; *Ogden v Ogden* [1908] P. 46.
[101] *Lodge v Lodge* (1963) 107 S.J. 437.
[102] Above, para.8–006.

formality, and the court would be squarely faced with the question whether a marriage could be annulled on some ground unknown to English law. There is no English authority on this question. All that can be said is that there is no reported case in which a marriage has been annulled on any such ground.

In *Vervaeke v Smith*,[103] the House of Lords refused to recognise a foreign decree annulling a marriage celebrated in England on the ground (unknown to English law) that it was a mock marriage. The implication is that the English court would not annul a marriage on such a ground.

RECOGNITION OF DIVORCES, SEPARATIONS AND ANNULMENTS

9–031 The simple statement in *Le Mesurier v Le Mesurier*[104] that domicile was the true test of jurisdiction did not exhaust the issues surrounding divorce. Many other countries, notably those in the civil law tradition, proceeded on a quite different basis, for example that of nationality. A failure on the parts of the courts of one country to recognise the decrees granted in another country creates a "limping marriage" valid in some parts of the world but invalid or dissolved elsewhere, with inconvenient consequences for the parties. The liberalisation of the bases on which jurisdiction could be assumed, a feature not only of English law but of that of many other countries in recent decades, requires a corresponding liberalisation of the rules governing the recognition of foreign decrees if the limping marriage syndrome is to be kept within bounds. Recognition cannot, however, be wholly automatic: the English courts need not accept every assertion of jurisdiction by a foreign court. Balancing these considerations makes for a certain necessary complexity in the law.

The law on the recognition and enforcement of decrees granted outside England and Wales depends in the first instance on where the decree was granted, and sometimes on the type of decree under consideration in the English court.

European rules: decrees granted in other Member States

9–032 Although the Brussels IIa Regulation[105] contains detailed rules as to jurisdiction in matrimonial causes, its most important role is ensuring the proper working of the internal market in the area of the free movement of persons by providing for the mutual recognition and enforcement of divorce, legal separation and marriage annulment throughout the European Union.[106]

Article 21(1) provides that a judgment given in a Member State must be recognised in the other Member States without any special procedure being required, a judgment being one for divorce, legal separation or marriage annulment whatever the judgment may be called, including a decree, order or

---

[103] [1983] 1 A.C. 145. See also *R (on the application of Baiai) v Secretary of State for the Home Department* [2008] UKHL 53; [2009] 1 A.C. 287 re-affirming the rule of public policy that a "sham" marriage is still a valid marriage in English law.
[104] [1895] A.C. 517 at 540.
[105] See generally McEleavy, (2004) 53 I.C.L.Q. 605 at p.633ff.
[106] With the exception of Denmark.

decision.[107] However, this automatic recognition is subject to the fact that any interested party may apply for a decision that the judgment not be recognised.[108] The grounds for non-recognition are limited to those listed in art.22:

(a)   that recognition is manifestly contrary to the public policy of the Member State in which recognition is sought;

(b)   where the judgment was given in default of appearance, that the respondent was not served with the document which instituted the proceedings, or not so served in sufficient time to enable him or her to arrange a defence; unless the respondent accepted the judgment unequivocally;

(c)   that the judgment is irreconcilable with a judgment in proceedings between the same parties in the Member State in which recognition is sought; or

(d)   that the judgment is irreconcilable with an earlier judgment given between the same parties in another Member State,

(e)   or in a non-Member State where the judgment is entitled to recognition in the Member State in which recognition is sought.

In practice, the availability of the public policy ground is extremely limited: neither the jurisdiction of the Member State granting the decree which is the subject of recognition[109] nor the substance of that decision[110] may be reviewed, and recognition may not be refused because the decree was granted on a basis unknown to the law of the recognising State.[111] This means that the public policy ground will be available only in extreme situations as the European jurisprudence under the Brussels I Regulation[112] demonstrates: **9–033**

> "Recourse to the public-policy clause . . . can be envisaged only where recognition or enforcement of the judgment delivered in another Contracting State would be at variance to an unacceptable degree with the legal order of the State in which enforcement is sought inasmuch as it infringes a fundamental principle . . . the infringement would have to constitute a manifest breach of a rule of law regarded as essential in the legal order of the State in which enforcement is sought or of a right recognised as being fundamental within that legal order".[113]

The second ground for refusal, relating to default of appearance of the respondent, is qualified by references to cases in which the respondent has accepted the judgment unequivocally. So, where the respondent has acted subsequently in such a way as to rely on that judgment, such as remarrying, the ground will not be available. This ground is mirrored in the non-recognition provisions of the Family Law Act 1986.[114]

The last two grounds deal with irreconcilable judgments. There is no requirement that the judgments contain the same cause of action so once the marriage has   **9–034**

---

[107]   art.2.
[108]   art.21(3).
[109]   art.24.
[110]   art.26.
[111]   art.25.
[112]   See para.7–035, above.
[113]   Case C-7/98 *Krombach v Bamberski* [2000] E.C.R. I-1935 at para.37.
[114]   See below paras 9–056 to 9–058.

been ended in one particular way, e.g., by annulment, a court may not recognise an alternative termination, e.g., a divorce. The ground is extended to earlier decrees of non-Member States as long as they fulfil the conditions necessary for recognition in the recognising state. However, since there are no provisions for a stay of proceedings in the courts of a Member State when the courts of a non-Member State are already seised, it is possible that irreconcilable judgments will be pronounced in the courts of a Member State and a non-Member State. The Regulation provides no answer to the resulting problem, but the spirit of the Regulation suggests that the judgment of the Member State would be preferred.

Decrees granted in the British Isles

9–035   The automatic recognition throughout the United Kingdom of decrees of divorce granted under the law of any part of the British Isles was first provided for, on the recommendation of the English and Scottish Law Commissions,[115] in the Recognition of Divorces and Legal Separations Act 1971. The Family Law Act 1986 extended the earlier provisions to nullity decrees and s.44(2) now provides for the automatic recognition throughout the United Kingdom of divorces, annulments and judicial separations granted at any time by a court of civil jurisdiction in any part of the British Isles, including the Channel Islands and the Isle of Man.

Such decrees cannot be questioned in England on any ground of lack of jurisdiction. Recognition may, however, be refused in the discretion of the court in limited circumstances examined below.[116]

The provisions in the Family Law Act 1986 as to the recognition or non-recognition of the validity of a decree granted elsewhere in the British Isles apply in relation to any time before the coming into effect of those provisions as well as in relation to any later time, but not so as to affect any property to which any person became entitled before that date,[117] or to affect the recognition of the validity of the decree if that matter had been decided by any competent court in the British Isles before that date.[118] In the latter case, the policy of the Act is not to disturb the position reached as a result of litigation.

9–036   Certain extra-judicial divorces granted in the British Isles before January 1, 1974 and recognised as valid under the common law rules applicable before that date remain entitled to recognition in England. The relevant pre-1974 recognition rule is that in *Armitage v Att-Gen,*[119] under which divorces recognised as valid under the law of the spouses' common domicile were recognised in England,[120] subject to a residual discretion not to recognise if justice so required.[121]

Apart from those exceptional cases, s.44(1) of the Family Law Act 1986 provides that no divorce or annulment obtained in any part of the British Isles

---

[115] Law Com. No. 34 (Scot. Law Com. No. 16) (1970), para.51.
[116] Below, para.9–054.
[117] April 4, 1988.
[118] Family Law Act 1986 s.52(2).
[119] [1906] P. 135.
[120] See *Har-Shefi v Har-Shefi (No. 2)* [1953] P. 220; *Qureshi v Qureshi* [1972] Fam. 173.
[121] *Qureshi v Qureshi* [1972] Fam. 173 at 201.

shall be regarded as effective in England unless granted by a court of civil jurisdiction. It is no longer possible for parties seeking a divorce to resort to the various ecclesiastical courts, such as that of the Greek Orthodox Church or the court of the Chief Rabbi. So far as annulments are concerned, this provision was new but stated what had been the position at common law. A nullity decree pronounced by a Roman Catholic diocesan tribunal has never had any effect on the civil, as opposed to the ecclesiastical, status of the parties.[122]

Decrees granted elsewhere[123]

In the period before 1972, English judges developed a number of rules for the recognition of foreign divorces. Over time, the rules became more and more liberal; in all of them, the basis on which the foreign court assumed jurisdiction,[124] and the grounds on which it pronounced a divorce,[125] were both equally irrelevant. Under the earliest rule, sometimes called the rule in *Le Mesurier v Le Mesurier*,[126] a foreign divorce was recognised in England if the parties were domiciled in the foreign country at the commencement of the proceedings. Under the rule in *Armitage v Att-Gen*,[127] a foreign divorce was recognised in England if it would be recognised by the courts of the country in which the parties were domiciled. The courts then came to recognise that "it would be contrary to principle and inconsistent with comity if the courts of this country were to refuse to recognise a jurisdiction which *mutatis mutandis* they claim for themselves."[128] As the English courts had been given jurisdiction to grant a divorce on the petition of a wife who had been ordinarily resident in England for three years, the principal effect of what was known as the rule in *Travers v Holley*[129] was to secure the recognition of a foreign divorce obtained by a wife after corresponding residence in the foreign country. Finally, under the rule in *Indyka v Indyka*,[130] a foreign divorce was recognised in England if there was a "real and substantial connection" between the petitioner or the respondent and the foreign country where the divorce was obtained, e.g. because of nationality or residence or both. The criterion of "real and substantial connection" proved difficult to interpret and large numbers of people simply did not know whether or not they were married, and if so, to whom.

9–037

Fresh legislative intervention was plainly required, and a model came to hand in 1968, when the Hague Conference on Private International Law produced a Convention on the recognition of divorces and legal separations.[131] The

9–038

---

[122] cf. *Di Rollo v Di Rollo*, 1959 S.C. 75 at 79.
[123] i.e., outside the European Union with the exception of Denmark.
[124] *Robinson-Scott v Robinson-Scott* [1958] P. 71 at 88; *Indyka v Indyka* [1969] 1 A.C. 33 at 66.
[125] *Bater v Bater* [1906] P. 209; *Wood v Wood* [1957] P. 254; *Indyka v Indyka* [1969] 1 A.C. 33.
[126] [1895] A.C. 517.
[127] [1906] P. 135.
[128] *Travers v Holley* [1953] P. 246 at 257, per Hodson L.J. See generally Hill, (2001) 50 I.C.L.Q. 144.
[129] [1953] P. 246.
[130] [1969] 1 A.C. 33.
[131] For the text of the Convention and comment thereon by Anton, see (1969) 18 I.C.L.Q. 620–643 and 657–664. The text and a commentary also appear in Law Com. No. 34 (Scot. Law Com. No. 16) (1970).

provisions of this Convention were originally implemented by the Recognition of Divorces and Legal Separations Act 1971 now replaced by more liberal provisions in the Family Law Act 1986. The Family Law Act 1986 provides in s.45 that an overseas divorce or legal separation must be recognised in the United Kingdom if, and only if, it is entitled to recognition under the Act or some other statutory provisions.[132] The effect of this important provision is retrospectively to abolish for all purposes the common law recognition rules, including those in *Armitage v Att-Gen; Travers v Holley* and *Indyka v Indyka* and also to preclude the courts from developing further judge-made rules of recognition.

Requirements for recognition

9–039 The Family Law Act 1986, though in almost all respects a distinct improvement on the legislation it replaced, makes use of a trouble-some distinction between divorces "obtained by means of judicial or other proceedings" and other divorces. The nature of this distinction between "proceedings" and "non-proceedings" divorces is more conveniently explored in a later context[133]; the rules now to be examined are those applicable to "proceedings" divorces, which are by far the most common. Such a divorce (or legal separation) obtained in a country outside the British Isles is entitled to recognition in England if (a) it is effective under the law of that country[134]; and (b) at the date of the commencement of the proceedings,[135] either party to the marriage was habitually resident or domiciled in, or was a national of that country.[136]

(i) Effective

9–040 The first requirement is that the divorce or separation must have been effective under the law of the foreign country in which it was obtained. A foreign divorce may of course be effective for some purposes but not for others: thus it may be effective to restore the spouses to the status of single persons, but ineffective to destroy the wife's right to maintenance from her husband. Presumably "effective" here means (in the case of a divorce) effective to dissolve the marriage. The divorce or separation would presumably not be effective if, e.g., the foreign court had no internal competence under its own law to grant it[137]; or if the foreign decree is not final until a specified period of time has elapsed, or until a decree absolute is pronounced, or while an appeal is pending. A divorce will be recognised as "effective" if the substantive rules of the foreign law have been

---

[132] These other statutory provisions, such as the Indian and Colonial Divorce Jurisdiction Act 1926 are of very limited importance. An argument that the Foreign Judgments (Reciprocal Enforcement) Act 1933 was relevant in the context of the recognition of overseas divorces was rejected, it is submitted rightly, in *Maples v Maples* [1988] Fam. 14 (not following dicta to the contrary in *Vervaeke v Smith* [1981] Fam. 77 at 125–126).

[133] See below, para.9–046.

[134] Family Law Act 1986 s.46(1)(a).

[135] s.46(3)(a).

[136] s.46(1)(b).

[137] See *Adams v Adams* [1971] P. 188, where a Southern Rhodesian divorce was refused recognition in England because the judge who pronounced it had not taken the oath of allegiance or the judicial oath in the prescribed form.

followcd; questions of proof which may arise, for example as to whether a letter of divorce had actually been delivered, are matters for English law,[138] "Effective" has been held to imply a less rigorous standard than "valid": it can mean a decree which, although invalid *per se* in the granting state, is none the less to be treated as valid by virtue of some supervening legal decision or equitable principle such as estoppel.[139] The requirement that the divorce or separation must have been effective under the law of the foreign country has important implications for the recognition in England of divorces granted in federal states where divorce is a matter for State as opposed to federal law, e.g., the United States. This matter is considered below.[140]

(ii)   Personal connecting factors

If the divorce or separation is in this sense effective, its recognition depends upon the existence at the date of the commencement of the proceedings of one of the specified links between one or both parties and the country in which it was obtained, i.e. habitual residence,[141] domicile, or nationality. For this purpose, "domicile" has two alternative meanings.[142] The first is that the party concerned was domiciled in the relevant foreign country under the normal rules as to domicile in English law. The second is domicile according to the law of the relevant foreign country "in family matters"; this last phrase ensures that if a country has differing concepts of domicile, as has England since the Civil Jurisdiction and Judgments Act 1982, it is that concept relevant to family law which will be used.

9–041

If there are cross-proceedings for divorce or separation, it is sufficient if the jurisdictional tests were satisfied at the date of commencement of either the original proceedings or the cross-proceedings, and it is immaterial which of them led to the decree. The decree must in other respects be entitled to recognition, e.g. it must be effective under the law of the country in which it is granted.[143]

In some countries, a legal separation can be converted into a divorce after a prescribed period, e.g., one year. The Act provides that in such a case if the original legal separation was entitled to recognition and is converted in the country in which it was obtained into a divorce effective under the law of that country, it will be recognised in England. It is immaterial that the spouses had lost the habitual residence, domicile or nationality of that country between the date of the original decree and its conversion into a divorce.[144]

(iii)   Findings of jurisdictional fact

If the foreign court makes a finding of fact, including a finding that either spouse was habitually resident or domiciled under the law of the foreign country, or a

9–042

---

[138] *Wicken v Wicken* [1999] Fam. 224; *K v R* [2007] EWHC 2945 (Fam).
[139] *Kellman v Kellman* [2000] 1 F.L.R. 785 ("mail order" decree in Guam).
[140] See para.9–044.
[141] As to the meaning of habitual residence, see above, para.2–004.
[142] Family Law Act 1986 s.46(5).
[143] s.47(1).
[144] s.47(2).

national of the foreign country, whether expressly or by implication, on the basis of which jurisdiction was assumed, that finding is conclusive evidence of that fact if both spouses took part in the proceedings, and in any other case is sufficient proof of that fact unless the contrary is shown.[145] If the proceedings are judicial in character, appearance in the proceedings is treated as taking part therein.[146]

(iv)   Retrospective application

9–043   In its application to overseas divorces and legal separations the Family Law Act 1986, like its predecessor, is retrospective. It applies to the recognition of divorces and legal separations obtained before or after the date of commencement of Pt II of the Act; and in the case of a decree obtained before that date it requires recognition in relation to any time before that date as well as in relation to any subsequent time.[147] There are two exceptions to this: s.52(2) provides that the provisions of Pt II of the Act do not affect any property to which any person became entitled before the date of commencement of that Part, or affect the recognition of the validity of the decree if that matter had been decided by any competent court in the British Isles before that date. In the latter case, that court decision will be followed.

(v)   Federal and other composite states

9–044   Special considerations arise where a divorce or legal separation is obtained in a federal or composite state in which the different territorial units have different systems of law in respect of matrimonial causes. The matter is complicated by the fact that while there is little difficulty in identifying the habitual residence or domicile of a party by reference to a particular territory or province, nationality is essentially a matter for the political state, the federation: one can speak of Australian citizenship but not of Tasmanian citizenship.

Accordingly, special provisions are contained in s.49 of the Family Law Act 1986. These provisions distinguish between cases in which recognition depends upon the habitual residence or domicile of a party and those in which the nationality criterion is used. Where the recognition of the decree depends upon habitual residence or domicile, s.46 of the Act[148] has effect as if each territory were a separate country. If, for example, a divorce is obtained in Nevada, it will be entitled to recognition if one party to the marriage is habitually resident or domiciled in Nevada[149] and the divorce is effective under the law of Nevada.[150] Where the divorce can be recognised only on the basis of nationality, a decree pronounced in any territorial unit of the state granting that nationality will be

---

[145]   s.47(1)(2). See *Torok v Torok* [1973] 1 W.L.R. 1066. But the Act does not require the recognition of any finding of fault made by the foreign court: s.51(5).
[146]   s.48(3).
[147]   s.52.
[148]   And s.47(2) which deals with the conversion of a legal separation into a divorce.
[149]   Satisfying s.46(1)(b)(i) or (ii).
[150]   Satisfying s.46(1)(a).

capable of recognition but only if the decree is effective throughout that state.[151] Were it possible to grant a divorce in Nevada to a United States citizen, neither party being habitually resident or domiciled in Nevada, the decree would be recognised in England only if it would be recognised in the other States of the Union. An *ex parte* divorce obtained in one state of the United States on the basis of the plaintiff's alleged domicile in the state is *prima facie* entitled to full faith and credit in the other states[152] but any other state may find that the plaintiff was not really domiciled in the divorce state and deny recognition on that ground.[153] A decree dissolving a same-sex union may similarly be denied recognition in some other states.

The difficulties discussed above do not arise in relation to every federal state, but only those in which divorce (or the relevant matrimonial remedy) is a provincial rather than a federal matter. In both Australia and Canada, for example, divorce is now a federal matter and s.49 of the Act does not apply.

Recognition of non-proceedings divorces

Some religious laws provide for divorce by the act of one party to a marriage (usually the husband) or of both parties. In Islamic law the process is called a talak and in Jewish law a ghet. In Jewish law a ghet is a form of divorce by mutual consent, expressed in a document prepared on the instructions of the husband, approved by a rabbinical court, and delivered to the wife before witnesses.[154] The court proceedings are "in no sense a judicial investigation."[155] In the Islamic law in force in Kashmir,[156] the Gulf States,[157] the Sudan and some other Islamic countries, the husband can divorce his wife by unilateral declaration, saying "I divorce you" three times. No reasons need be given, the presence of the wife is not necessary, and in some countries no notice need be given to her.[158] But in Egypt the divorce is usually registered with a court, though this is not essential for its validity.[159] Under the Pakistani Muslim Family Laws Ordinance 1961, the effect of the talak is suspended for 90 days to allow conciliation proceedings to take place before an arbitration council on which the wife is represented.[160] These conciliation proceedings may take place either in Pakistan or in a Pakistani embassy abroad.

9–045

---

[151] s.46(1)(a) as adapted by s.49(3)(a). A corresponding adaptation is made in s.47(2), the case of the conversion of legal separation into divorce.

[152] *Williams v North Carolina (No. 1)*, 317 U.S. 287 (1942).

[153] *Williams v North Carolina (No. 2)*, 325 U.S. 226 (1945).

[154] See Berkovits, (1988) 104 L.Q.R. 60.

[155] *Har-Shefi v Har-Shefi (No. 2)* [1953] P. 220 at 222.

[156] e.g., *Chaudhary v Chaudhary* [1985] Fam. 19.

[157] e.g., *Zaal v Zaal* (1983) 4 F.L.R. 284 (Dubai); *Z v Z (Financial Provision: Overseas Divorce)* [1992] 2 F.L.R. 291 (Bahrain).

[158] e.g., Lebanon, *El Fadl v El Fadl* [2000] 1 F.L.R. 175; and Saudi Arabia, *Sulaiman v Juffali* [2002] 1 F.L.R. 479.

[159] See the expert evidence given in *Russ v Russ* [1963] P. 87 at 95; [1964] P. 315 at 321–322.

[160] See *Quazi v Quazi* [1980] A.C. 744.

After early doubts, it became clear that such divorces could be recognised in England,[161] and this was held to be the case even where the ghet was obtained or the talak was delivered in England,[162] provided that the parties were domiciled in a country (e.g., Israel or Pakistan) the laws of which permit such a method. The reason was that if the grounds for divorce are immaterial, so should the method be.

9–046   This reasoning remains largely unaffected by the modern legislation, subject to the important qualification that extra-judicial divorces may no longer be obtained in England. Extra-judicial divorces may be recognised under the Family Law Act 1986, but, as has already been observed, s.46 of that Act draws a distinction between overseas divorces "obtained by means of proceedings" and those "obtained otherwise than by means of proceedings." Extra-judicial divorces may fall into either category and unfortunately the distinction between the two categories, a matter on which the Act departed from the recommendations of the Law Commission,[163] is unclear. "Proceedings" is defined in the Family Law Act 1986[164] to mean "judicial or other proceedings". The latter phrase appears in the Hague Convention and was also used in s.2 of the Recognition of Divorces and Legal Separations Act 1971.[165]

In *Quazi v Quazi*[166] the House of Lords considered the interpretation of the phrase "other proceedings" in s.2 of the 1971 Act. The House held that a Pakistani talak effective under the Pakistan Muslim Family Laws Ordinance 1961, which requires notification to the chairman of an arbitration council and postpones the coming into effect of the talak until the expiry of a 90-day period during which a reconciliation might be brought about, was within the phrase. It was not essential to the notion of "proceedings" that there be some state body having power to prevent the parties from dissolving their marriage as of right.[167] Lord Fraser expressed the view that the only limitation on the scope of "proceedings" was that they should be officially recognised and legally effective in that country.[168] Lord Scarman referred to "proceedings" as "any act or acts, officially recognised as leading to divorce in the country where the divorce was obtained".[169] The Law Commission, following Lord Scarman's approach, recommended that "judicial or other proceedings" should include acts which constitute the means by which a divorce may be obtained in a country and which are done in compliance with the law of that country[170] but this recommendation was not implemented in the Family Law Act 1986 nor was the same approach taken in later cases.

---

[161] *Sasson v Sasson* [1924] A.C. 10-07 (P.C.); *Har-Shefi Har-Shefi (No. 2)* [1953] P. 200; *Russ v Russ* [1964] P. 315; *Qureshi v Qureshi* [1972] Fam. 173; *Quazi v Quazi* [1980] A.C. 744.

[162] *Har-Shefi v Har-Shefi (No. 2)* [1953] P. 200; *Qureshi v Qureshi* [1972] Fam. 173.

[163] See Law Com. No. 137 (1984), para.6.11 and Young (1987) 7 Legal Studies 78.

[164] s.54(1).

[165] The term "proceedings" was also used in two other closely-related statutory provisions, s.6 of the 1971 Act as substituted by the Domicile and Matrimonial Proceedings Act 1973, and s.16 of the latter Act. These provisions are now repealed but are discussed in the cases cited in the text.

[166] [1980] A.C. 744.

[167] [1980] A.C. 744 at 814 and 823 rejecting the view of the Court of Appeal on this point.

[168] *Quazi v Quazi* [1980] A.C. 744 at 814.

[169] *Quazi v Quazi* [1980] A.C. 744 at 824.

[170] Law Com. No. 137, p.122.

The Court of Appeal in *Chaudhary v Chaudhary*[171] interpreted the speeches in **9–047** *Quazi v Quazi* as requiring the phrase "judicial or other proceedings" to be read as indicating a narrower category of divorces than all divorces obtained by any means whatever which are effective by the law of the country in which the divorce is obtained. This interpretation is based on the dubious ground that the House of Lords, while differing from the Court of Appeal, did not expressly dissent from a passage to that effect in the judgment of Ormrod L.J.[172] It was therefore possible to hold in *Chaudhary v Chaudhary*[173] that a "bare" talak, requiring nothing more than the making of a declaration by the husband, was not within the phrase "other proceedings" in s.2. Other forms of divorce by the private agreement of the parties would seem to be in the same position.[174]

The Family Law Act 1986 contains no direct guidance on the meaning of the phrase "judicial or other proceedings". Implicitly, however, it rejects the more liberal approach of Lords Fraser and Scarman, for effectiveness under the law of the country in which the divorce was obtained is a prerequisite to the recognition of any divorce whether or not obtained by means of proceedings, and cannot be a criterion for distinction between the two categories. A Jewish ghet, which involves the active participation of members of the rabbinical court, has been held to be "obtained by means of proceedings"[175]; the Japanese *kyogi rikon* divorce contained sufficient state regulation for the divorce to be a proceedings divorce[176]; the same would seem to apply to a foreign divorce obtained by a legislative or administrative process.[177] The position therefore is that Jewish ghets, Pakistani talaks[178] and Japanese *kyogi rikon* divorces fall to be treated as "proceedings" divorces, and so under the rules already examined, but "bare" talaks and similar divorces can only be recognised under the more stringent rules now to be examined applicable to "non-proceedings" divorces.

Requirements for recognition of non-proceedings divorces

Such a divorce or legal separation, provided it is obtained in a country outside the **9–048** British Isles, will be entitled to recognition in England if (a) it is effective under the law of that country[179]; and (b) on the date of which it was obtained[180] either each party to the marriage was domiciled in that country[181] or either party to the marriage was domiciled in that country and the other party was domiciled in a

---

[171] [1985] Fam. 19.
[172] *Quazi v Quazi* [1980] A.C. 744 at 788, in the Court of Appeal.
[173] [1985] Fam. 19, resolving a conflict of judicial opinion revealed in *Sharif v Sharif* (1980) 10 Fam. Law 216 and *Zaal v Zaal* (1983) 4 F.L.R. 284.
[174] e.g., Thai divorces of this type, as in *Ratanachai v Ratanachai*, The Times, 4 June 1960, and *Varanand v Varanand* (1964) 108 S.J. 693; *Chaudhary v Chaudhary* [1985] Fam. 19, 42.
[175] *Berkovits v Grinberg* [1995] Fam. 142.
[176] *H v H (Validity of Japanese Divorce)* [2006] EWHC 2989 (Fam); [2007] 1 F.L.R. 1318.
[177] *Manning v Manning* [1958] P. 112.
[178] *H v H (Talaq Divorce)* [2007] EWHC 2945 (Fam); [2008] 2 F.L.R. 857.
[179] Family Law Act 1986 s.46(2)(a).
[180] s.46(3)(b).
[181] s.46(2)(b)(i).

country under whose law the decree is recognised as valid.[182] However, recognition will not be extended to such a divorce or separation where either party to the marriage was habitually resident in the United Kingdom throughout the period of one year immediately preceding the date on which it was obtained.[183] This last provision is designed to prevent easy circumvention of the rule that no extra-judicial divorce can be obtained in England; an English resident obtaining such a divorce on a short trip abroad will find that it will not be recognised.

The country in which a divorce is obtained

9–049   Where a divorce is in the form of a court decree, there is no difficulty in identifying the country in which it is obtained. Extra-judicial divorces may not be so easily located, and can present the problem of the "transnational divorce". A "bare" talak would seem to be located where the husband speaks the required formula.[184] It was held in a case decided under the Recognition of Divorces and Legal Separations Act 1971[185] that if a talak is of the Pakistani variety, and so within *Quazi v Quazi*, it can only be recognised in England if the entirety of the relevant proceedings takes place in Pakistan. It was held that it is not possible to treat as an overseas divorce a talak pronounced by the husband in England even if it is then communicated to the wife and the appropriate procedures as to an arbitration council are completed in Pakistan. The principle of this decision was held applicable under the rather different language of the Family Law Act 1986 in a case involving a ghet.[186] The court held that the writing of the ghet and its delivery to the wife were each steps in the proceedings by which the dissolution of the marriage was obtained. As they had occurred in different countries, and as "proceedings" was held to be a concept territorial in nature, relating to the jurisdiction of a particular judicial authority within a specific geographical location, it was impossible to recognise a divorce as having been obtained in the country in which the ghet was delivered. The court recognised the strong policy considerations against the conclusion it felt bound to adopt: a wealthy man might find it easier to travel to the country in which his wife was living, to complete the whole process there, than a poorer man to whom the transnational procedure operated, with great care, by Beth Dins in different countries was attractive.

9–050   In Jewish law there are serious consequences for a woman who re-marries without a ghet having been delivered in respect of her first marriage, and that requires the co-operation of the first husband. In a number of cases in which the husband refused to co-operate, the courts refused to make a secular divorce decree absolute[187]; the matter has now been put on a statutory footing by s.10A of the Matrimonial Causes Act 1973, inserted by the Divorce (Religious Marriages)

---

[182] s.46(2)(b)(ii). For this purpose, domicile means domicile as understood in English law or the law of the relevant foreign country in family matters; see above, para.9–041.
[183] s.46(2)(c).
[184] *Sulaiman v Juffali* [2002] 1 F.L.R. 479.
[185] *R.v Secretary of State for the Home Department, ex p. Fatima* [1986] A.C. 527.
[186] *Berkovits v Grinberg* [1995] Fam. 142. See McClean, (1996) 112 L.Q.R. 230.
[187] *O v O (Jurisdiction; Jewish Divorce)* [2000] 2 F.L.R. 147.

Act 2002. Where the parties married in accordance with the usages of the Jews (or any other religious usages prescribed by statutory instrument) and the parties must co-operate if the marriage is to be dissolved in accordance with those usages, the court may order that the secular divorce decree may not be made absolute until both parties declare that steps have been taken to dissolve the marriage in accordance with those usages.

Federal and composite states

The requirements as to the recognition of "non-proceedings" divorces are adapted to the case of federal and composite states by s.49(4) of the 1986 Act. Each territory within such a State is treated for this purpose as a separate country.

9–051

Nullity decrees

Until the coming into force of Pt II of the Family Law Act 1986, the recognition of foreign nullity decrees was governed by common law rules which were as unsatisfactory in content as they were uncertain in scope; happily they are no longer of any relevance. On the recommendation of the English and Scottish Law Commissions, the 1986 Act provided a comprehensive statutory scheme which would include divorces and legal separations as well as annulments. The provisions of the 1986 Act applying to nullity decrees are retrospective: they apply to annulments granted or obtained before the date of commencement of these provisions as well as after that date,[188] so that it is no longer necessary to refer to the former common law rules. In their application to any time before the commencement date, however, the provisions do not affect any property to which any person became entitled before that date or affect the recognition of an annulment if that matter had been decided by any competent court in the British Isles before that date.[189]

9–052

Requirements for recognition

Here, as in the context of overseas divorces, the Act distinguishes between annulments obtained by means of judicial or other proceedings and "non-proceedings" annulments; but it is difficult to imagine actual cases which could fall within the latter category. An overseas annulment obtained by means of proceedings is entitled to recognition in England if (a) it is effective under the law of that country[190]; and (b) either at the date of the commencement of the proceedings,[191] either party to the marriage was habitually resident or domiciled

9–053

---

[188] Family Law Act 1986 s.52.
[189] s.52(2).
[190] s.46(1)(a).
[191] s.46(3)(a).

in, was a national of that country[192] or at the earlier date of the death of a party to the marriage, that party was habitually resident or domiciled in, or a national of, that country.[193]

It will be seen that, when compared with the rules as to overseas divorces and legal separations, there is here additional material to deal with the cases, which cannot arise in the divorce context, where nullity proceedings concern a marriage, a party to which is already dead. In such cases the connecting factors of habitual residence, domicile and nationality are taken as regards that party by reference to the date of the death rather than the date of the commencement of the proceedings.

The provisions of the Family Law Act 1986 as to cases of cross-proceedings,[194] the proof of facts relevant to recognition,[195] and the application of the recognition rules to decrees granted in federal and composite states,[196] all of which have been examined above, apply equally in the present context.

Grounds upon which recognition may be withheld

9–054   A divorce, annulment or judicial separation entitled to recognition under the principles examined thus far may in certain circumstances be refused recognition in England. At common law, the circumstances in which foreign decrees would be refused recognition were confined within narrow limits for fear of creating uncertainty in an area in which certainty was greatly to be desired. The Family Law Act 1986, building on earlier provisions in the Recognition of Divorces and Legal Separations Act 1971 and (in part) upon the recommendations of the Law Commissions,[197] sets out a clear set of grounds for non-recognition. They can be compared with those in art.22 of the Brussels IIa Regulation[198]; but unlike the grounds in the Regulation, all are discretionary; and all may be invoked not only by a party to the marriage but also by third parties, e.g., a second spouse or a person interested in property on the ground that the decree is invalid in England.[199]

(a)   Irreconcilable judgments

A divorce, legal separation or annulment may be refused recognition if it was granted at a time when it was irreconcilable with a previous decision given or entitled to recognition in England as to the subsistence or validity of the marriage of the parties.[200] So far as nullity is concerned this rule adopts the principle

---

[192] s.46(1)(b). For this purpose, domicile means domicile as understood in English law or the law of the relevant foreign country in family matters; see above, para.9–041.
[193] s.46(1)(b), (4).
[194] s.57(1).
[195] s.48.
[196] s.49.
[197] Law Com. No. 137 (1984), paras 4.6–4.10 and 6.62–6.68.
[198] See para.9–032, above.
[199] See *Pemberton v Hughes* [1899] 1 Ch. 781.
[200] Family Law Act 1986 s.51(1). See Law Com. No. 137 (1984), para.6.66.

established by the House of Lords in *Vervaeke v Smith*[201] where a foreign decree annulling a marriage for lack of consent was refused recognition in England because it was inconsistent with a prior English decision refusing to annul the same marriage on substantially the same grounds.

(b) No subsisting marriage

This ground applies to divorces or judicial separations, but not to annulments. A divorce or legal separation may be refused recognition in England if it was granted at a time when, according to English law (including the English rules of the conflict of laws) there was no subsisting marriage between the parties.[202] In some cases the facts will come within both grounds (a) and (b), e.g., where a nullity decree pronounced in one jurisdiction and entitled to recognition in England is followed by a divorce decree in respect of the same marriage granted in another jurisdiction: that divorce decree will be both inconsistent with the earlier decision (for a divorce decree can only be made where there is a subsisting marriage to dissolve) and granted at a time when English law considered there to be no subsisting marriage. Ground (b) will, however, cover cases in which an English court would treat the marriage purportedly dissolved by a foreign divorce decree as void *ab initio* (e.g. because under the English rules of the conflict of laws one party lacked capacity to marry) but no nullity decree has ever been pronounced.[203]

9–055

(c) Want of notice

An overseas divorce, annulment or judicial separation obtained by means of judicial or other proceedings may be refused recognition in England on the ground of want of proper notice of the proceedings to a party to the marriage, that is without such steps having been taken for giving notice of the proceedings to a party to the marriage[204] as, having regard to the nature of the proceedings and all the circumstances, should reasonably have been taken.[205] This ground has long been familiar to English judges; and since non-recognition on this ground is discretionary under the Act, some guidance may still be derived from the case law before the Act. It was at one time supposed that a foreign divorce could never be recognised in England if the respondent had insufficient notice of the proceedings to enable him or her to defend them.[206] But in each of the cases which appear to support this extreme proposition, the main ground for refusing recognition was that the parties were not domiciled in the country where the divorce was

9–056

---

[201] [1983] 1 A.C. 145.

[202] Family Law Act 1986 s.51(2).

[203] See Law Com. No. 137 (1984), paras 6.64–6.66.

[204] Not limited to the respondent spouse as was the predecessor provision: Recognition of Divorces and Legal Separations Act 1971, s.8(2)(a)(i) (repealed).

[205] Family Law Act 1986 s.51(3)(a)(i).

[206] *Shaw v Att-Gen* (1870) L.R. 2 P. & D. 156; *Rudd v Rudd* [1924] P. 72; *Scott v Scott* 1937 S.L.T. 632. Although see *Hornett v Hornett* [1972] P 255 where, even though the husband had not received notice, the French divorce was recognised since no injustice would be caused.

granted.[207] Under the Act the question is one of reasonableness, and involves an examination of the extent to which the respondent was actually prejudiced.[208] In the usual case, notice of the commencement of proceedings will suffice, but there may be special circumstances in which more is required.[209] Recognition is most likely to be refused if the want of notice is combined with fraud, as where the petitioner falsely tells the foreign court that he or she does not know the respondent's address.[210] On the other hand, recognition will not necessarily be obtained by proof that the petitioner complied with local procedure; that procedure may itself be unreasonable or contrary to natural justice.[211]

(d)   Want of opportunity to take part

9–057   An overseas divorce, annulment or judicial separation obtained by means of judicial or other proceedings may be refused recognition in England if it was obtained without a party to the marriage having been given (for any reason other than lack of notice) such opportunity to take part in the proceedings as, having regard to the nature of the proceedings and all the circumstances, he should reasonably have been given.[212] There are very few reported cases in which a party to foreign matrimonial proceedings, while receiving notice of the proceedings, was denied an opportunity to take part. In *Newmarch v Newmarch*,[213] failure by the wife's Australian solicitors to file an answer to the husband's petition as instructed, so that the suit went undefended, was treated as a ground for not recognising the decree under this head: but, in all the circumstances which included the fact that the petition could not have been successfully opposed, the decree was recognised. In *Mitford v Mitford*,[214] a German nullity decree was recognised in England, although the English respondent could not be personally heard because of war conditions. In two cases, a German court granted a divorce although the respondent was resident in England and could not be personally heard for the same reason: but in each case he received no notice of the proceedings.[215] In *Ashoor v Layass*,[216] divorce proceedings had been begun by the wife in England and by the husband in Egypt. The husband was restrained by a *Hemain* injunction from taking further steps in the Egyptian court but, having obtained an adjournment of the English

---

[207] See, to this effect, *Maher v Maher* [1951] P. 342 at 344–345.
[208] *Sabbagh v Sabbagh* [1985] F.L.R. 29; *D. v D.* [1994] 1 F.L.R. 38; *El Fadl v El Fadl* [2000] 1 F.L.R. 175.
[209] *Ashoor v Layass* (sub nom *A v L (overseas divorce)*) [2010] EWHC 460 (Fam), [2010] 2 FLR 1418.
[210] *Sabbagh v Sabbagh* [1985] F.L.R. 29 (compliance with foreign procedure not sufficient; but as no prejudice to respondent in all circumstances, decree recognised). cf. cases where decrees were recognised after compliance with foreign rules as to substituted service or dispensing with service: *Macalpine v Macalpine* [1958] P. 35. The court refused to recognise the Nigerian divorce in *Duhur-Johnson v Duhur-Johnson* [2005] 2 F.L.R. 1042 since the husband only provided the wife's Nigerian address knowing that she was living in England at the time.
[211] *Boettcher v Boettcher* [1949] W.N. 83; *Igra v Igra* [1951] P. 404; *Arnold v Arnold* [1957] P. 237; *Wood v Wood* [1957] P. 254 at 296; *Hornett v Hornett* [1971] P. 255.
[212] Family Law Act 1986 s.51(3)(a)(ii), 54(1).
[213] [1978] Fam. 79. cf. *Hack v Hack* (1976) 6 Fam. Law 177; *Joyce v Joyce* [1979] Fam. 93.
[214] [1923] P. 130.
[215] *Igra v Igra* [1951] P. 404; *Re Meyer* [1971] P. 298.

proceedings on spurious grounds, and despite the injunction, obtained an Egyptian divorce decree. The wife was deprived of the opportunity to take part in the Egyptian proceedings in which she could have raised issues of substance as well as the position reached in England.

The Act is concerned not only with the existence of an opportunity to take part but also with its quality. The court will consider whether, in all the circumstances, the party was given the opportunity to take an effective part in the proceedings, and a relevant question is whether he had the financial means to obtain appropriate legal representation. So, in *Joyce v Joyce,*[217] a husband who was in arrears in respect of payments to his wife under a maintenance order petitioned for divorce in Quebec; the wife was unable to afford to travel to Quebec, and could obtain no legal aid from either the English or the Quebec authorities. Despite the husband's remarriage, the divorce was refused recognition in England.

9–058

This ground applies to certain extra-judicial divorces, ghets and Pakistani talaks, which are obtained by "judicial or other proceedings" for the purposes of the Family Law Act 1986. The "nature of the proceedings" is a relevant consideration in deciding whether the steps taken to give notice of the proceedings were reasonable and whether the opportunity to take part in the proceedings was reasonable.[218] The English court will not require in relation to such proceedings precisely the length and form of notice and the opportunity to take part which would be appropriate to proceedings in an ordinary court of civil jurisdiction; the appropriate test would appear to be whether a party was prejudiced by conduct which, given the approach of the legal system under which the divorce was obtained, must be categorised as unreasonable. Compliance with the strict procedures required in the case of a ghet will fully protect the interests of the parties, and it is submitted that the Pakistani legislation will be similarly regarded. Little guidance can be found in case law, for the issue has been discussed in the context of "bare" talaks[219] to which the present ground does not apply.

(e) Want of documentation in non-proceedings cases

An overseas divorce, annulment or judicial separation obtained otherwise than by means of judicial or other proceedings may be refused recognition in England on the ground of the absence of an official document certifying (a) its effectiveness under the law of the country in which it was obtained; or (b) where relevant,[220] that it is recognised as valid in another country in which either party was

9–059

---

[216] *sub nom A v L (overseas divorce)* [2010] EWHC 460 (Fam); [2010] 2 FLR 1418. cf. *Golubovich v Golubovich* [2010] EWCA Civ 810; [2011] Fam. 88: the fact that a foreign decree was obtained in breach of a *Hemain* injunction issued by the English court will not in itself justify refusal of recognition on public policy grounds.

[217] [1979] Fam. 93. See also *Mamdani v Mamdani* [1984] F.L.R. 699; *Sabbagh v Sabbagh* [1985] F.L.R. 29.

[218] Family Law Act 1986 s.51(3)(a)(i) and (ii).

[219] See *Maher v Maher* [1951] P. 342 at 345; *Zaal v Zaal* (1983) 4 F.L.R. 284 at 288–9; *Chaudhary v Chaudhary* [1985] Fam. 19, 48.

[220] See Family Law Act 1986 s.46(2)(b)(ii) and above, para.9–048.

domiciled.[221] An "official" document is one issued by a person or body appointed or recognised for the purpose under the relevant law.[222] These provisions as to documentary proof are unusual (and were not recommended by the Law Commission); it is not clear what policy is served by requiring a particular form of proof. The absence of the necessary certificate is in any event only a discretionary ground for the refusal of recognition.[223]

(f) Recognition contrary to public policy

9–060   An overseas divorce, annulment or judicial separation may be refused recognition in England if its recognition would be manifestly contrary to public policy.[224] In *Kendall v Kendall*,[225] the wife was deceived by the husband's lawyers into applying for a divorce which she did not want in a language which she did not understand. It was held that recognition would be refused in England on the ground of public policy. This appears to be the only reported case in which a foreign divorce has been refused recognition solely on this ground. It was thought at one time that the public policy ground might be successfully invoked where a husband ordinarily resident in England obtained a divorce abroad (perhaps a talak, where the wife would have few if any procedural rights) in an attempt to avoid financial or other consequences attaching to a divorce obtained in England. It is now recognised that the enactment of Pt III of the Matrimonial and Family Proceedings Act 1984[226] prevents there being any public policy issue so far as financial consequences are concerned.[227] The recent case law evidences a very restrictive approach to the ground of public policy: in *Kellman v Kellman* it was held that "manifestly contrary to public policy" is "a very high hurdle to clear"[228]; in *Emin v Yeldag*[229] a divorce granted by a court of Northern Cyprus was entitled to recognition even though that state was not recognised by the United Kingdom government; and in *Golubovich v Golubovich*[230] it was said that to refuse recognition of a divorce decree pronounced by the court in another jurisdiction within the Council of Europe, in the absence of any breach of natural justice, must be regarded as truly exceptional.

---

[221] ss.51(3)(b), (4), 54(1).

[222] s.51(4).

[223] In the case of federal or composite states, it would appear to have been the intention of the draftsman to provide that these provisions were to have effect as if each territory in such a state were a separate country; s.49(4) refers in this context to s.52(3)(4) when s.51(3)(4) is plainly intended.

[224] s.51(3)(c).

[225] [1977] Fam. 208. See also *Joyce v Joyce* [1979] Fam. 93. cf. *Eroglu v Eroglu* [1994] 2 F.L.R. 287 where the public policy ground was not available, both parties having joined in a deception practised on the foreign court.

[226] See below, para.9–074.

[227] *Chaudhary v Chaudhary* [1985] Fam. 19; *Tahir v Tahir*, 1993 S.L.T. 194.

[228] [2000] 1 F.L.R. 785 at p.798E.

[229] [2002] 1 F.L.R. 956. See, however, the earlier case of *B v B (Divorce: Northern Cyprus)* [2000] 2 F.L.R. 707 where the opposite result was reached.

[230] [2010] EWCA Civ 810; [2011] Fam. 88.

Other grounds not available

These are the only grounds on which the court has discretionary power to refuse **9–061** recognition to an otherwise valid foreign divorce. The fact that it was obtained by fraud, or without the petitioner's consent, is not such a ground. At common law, it was doubtful whether a foreign divorce could be impeached on the ground that it was obtained by fraud: under the Act, a divorce obtained by fraud might in some circumstances be refused recognition in England on the ground that recognition would be manifestly contrary to public policy.

Same-sex unions

The Civil Partnership (Jurisdiction and Recognition of Judgments) Regulations[231] **9–062** contain provisions, in Pt 2, corresponding to the Brussels IIa Regulation for the dissolution or annulment of a civil partnership or the legal separation of civil partners, pronounced by a court of a Member State,[232] however termed by that State. Any interested party may apply for recognition or such recognition may arise as incidental issue to other proceedings.[233] Regulation 8 on the grounds for refusal of recognition is, however, curious. Even though the instrument purports to apply the Brussels IIa Regulation provisions to the recognition of dissolution or annulment of civil partnerships, the grounds for refusal of recognition mirror the grounds under the Family Law Act 1986, which apply to non-EU matrimonial judgments.

An order granted in one part of the United Kingdom will not be recognised in another part unless it has been obtained from a court of civil jurisdiction.[234] Recognition in the other part of the United Kingdom may only be refused where the judgment is irreconcilable with a judgment of that other part, or of a judgment that is entitled to recognition in that other part,[235] or where according to the law of that part there was no subsisting civil partnership.[236]

Recognition of overseas orders is governed by ss.235–237 of the Act.[237] Since the grounds for recognition and refusal of recognition mirror the provisions in the Family Law Act 1986 for the recognition of overseas matrimonial decrees in that they distinguish orders made by way of proceedings and orders otherwise than by way of proceedings, and provide for grounds on which recognition may be refused, it is not necessary to repeat the earlier examination of these provisions.

---

[231] SI 2005/3334.
[232] It is interesting to note the Regulation lists all Member States *including* Denmark.
[233] Regulation 7.
[234] s.233(1).
[235] s.233(3).
[236] s.233(4).
[237] As supplemented by SI 2005/3104.

Foreign declarations

9–063   No statutory provision is made for the recognition in England of foreign declarations as to status, e.g. that the parties were validly married. It is thought unlikely that an English court would regard such a declaration as binding. In *Al-Saedy v Musawi*[238] such a declaration was tendered but in an attempt to prove that a ceremony had in fact taken place. It was disregarded as the party obtaining the decree had misled the foreign court as to the respondent's whereabouts so that he had no notice of the application.

PRESUMPTION OF DEATH AND DISSOLUTION OF MARRIAGE

Jurisdiction of the English courts

9–064   Proceedings for presumption of death and dissolution of marriage were first introduced into English law by s.8 of the Matrimonial Causes Act 1937 and are now regulated by s.19 of the Matrimonial Causes Act 1973.[239] The relief provided is not primarily or in essence dissolution of marriage. Its object is to enable the petitioner to obtain a declaration that the other spouse is presumed to be dead. But a safeguard is added to guard against the awkward situation which would otherwise arise if the presumption turned out to be wrong. This safeguard takes the form of joining to the decree of presumption of death a decree of dissolution. But this is merely ancillary to the former decree and does not alter its essential character.[240] The subject receives separate treatment here not because it is particularly important but because of the clear doctrinal distinction drawn in *Wall v Wall*[241] between ordinary divorce decrees and decrees of presumption of death and dissolution of marriage.

Section 5(4) of the Domicile and Matrimonial Proceedings Act 1973 provides that English courts have jurisdiction to entertain proceedings for presumption of death and dissolution of marriage if (and only if) the petitioner (a) is domiciled in England on the date when the proceedings are begun, or (b) was habitually resident in England throughout the period of one year ending with that date.

In the case of same-sex unions,[242] s.222 of the Civil Partnership Act 2004 provides that English courts have jurisdiction to entertain proceedings for presumption of death if the applicant is domiciled in England and Wales on the date when the proceedings are begun, or habitually resident in England and Wales throughout the period of one year ending with that date, or if the two people concerned are registered as civil partners of each other in England and Wales and it appears to the court to be in the interests of justice to assume jurisdiction in the case.

---

[238] [2010] EWHC 3293 (Fam); [2011] 2 F.L.R. 287.
[239] As amended by Domicile and Matrimonial Proceedings Act 1973, Sch.6.
[240] For the strange consequences which sometimes ensue, see *Deacock v Deacock* [1958] P. 230, where a wife who was judicially presumed to be dead was subsequently awarded maintenance.
[241] [1950] P. 112.
[242] See para.9–014.

Choice of law

Section 19(5) of the Matrimonial Causes Act 1973 (re-enacting earlier legislation) provided that the issues should be determined in accordance with the law which would be applicable if both parties to the marriage were domiciled in England at the time of the proceedings, i.e., English law. This subsection has now been repealed, but this was not intended to alter the law.[243]

9–065

Recognition of foreign decrees

English courts are not bound to treat as conclusive a decree of presumption of death made by a foreign court, even a court of the domicile,[244] unless it is accompanied by an order vesting the deceased's property in someone, e.g. an administrator,[245] or (perhaps) by a decree of dissolution of marriage. But they will probably do so in order to avoid a limping marriage if the foreign court is that of the domicile, or if *(mutatis mutandis)* the English court would have had jurisdiction in the circumstances. Thus in *Szemik v Gryla*[246] the husband and wife were Polish nationals domiciled in Poland where they married in 1936. In 1947 the wife obtained a declaration from a Polish court that the husband died in 1942 and she remarried in 1953. By Polish law the declaration entitled the wife to remarry and her remarriage dissolved her first marriage. In fact the husband was not dead but was living in England where he had acquired an English domicile in 1946. Scarman J. recognised the Polish declaration and remarriage as having dissolved the first marriage.

9–066

FINANCIAL RELIEF

Jurisdiction of the English courts

This matter is largely, but not wholly, governed by Council Regulation 4/2009 of December 18, 2008 on jurisdiction, applicable law, recognition and enforcement of decisions and co-operation in matters relating to maintenance obligations, 'the Maintenance Regulation'.[247] The Regulation covers all maintenance obligations arising from a family relationship, parentage, marriage or affinity; "maintenance obligation" is interpreted autonomously.[248] The ECJ in *De Cavel v De Cavel (No.1)* distinguished, for the purposes of the Brussels I regulation which then governed maintenance, between "proprietary legal relationships between spouses resulting directly from the matrimonial relationship or the dissolution thereof"

9–067

---

[243] See Law Com. No. 48 (1972), para.108.

[244] *Inthe Goods of Wolf* [1948] P. 66.

[245] *In the Goods of Spenceley* [1892] P. 255; *In the Goods of Schulhof* [1948] P. 66; *In the Goods of Dowds* [1948] P. 256.

[246] (1965) 109 S.J. 175.

[247] [2009] O.J. L7, p 1; its provisions apply in relation to Denmark by virtue of the Agreement made on 19 October 2005 between the European Community and Denmark. The Lugano Convention, art.5(2) deals with jurisdiction in "maintenance" where it applies.

[248] See Recital (11) and art.1.

and "proprietary legal relations existing between them which have no connection with the marriage."[249] The question seems to be whether the rights in issue existed by virtue of the marriage or its dissolution, or independently; it is not correct to treat "maintenance" as an umbrella term for any financial award which was made in order to provide for the respective needs and resources of the parties.[250] The language in the Maintenance Regulation, "maintenance obligations arising from a family relationship" seems to reflect the same distinction.

The power of an English divorce court to make "financial provision" includes the making of orders not only for periodical payments but also orders for lump sum provision, property adjustment orders, pension sharing orders and pension compensation sharing orders.[251] It follows from the distinction drawn above that a property adjustment order made in consequence of the dissolution of a marriage is not within the scope of the Maintenance Regulation. Periodical payments between the former spouses are clearly within that scope as being "maintenance", and lump sum payments will be treated similarly so long as they are in place of periodical payments and take into account the needs or resources of the parties; it will be otherwise if they represent solely the money value of the divided property.[252]

Ancillary relief

9–068   The English courts have in their matrimonial jurisdiction wide powers under the Matrimonial Causes Act 1973 to make financial provision and property adjustment orders in favour of a party to a marriage or a child of the family. The jurisdiction is preserved by the Maintenance Regulation,[253] which confers jurisdiction on the court which, according to its own law, has jurisdiction to entertain proceedings concerning the status of a person if the matter relating to maintenance is ancillary to those proceedings, unless that jurisdiction is based solely on the nationality of one of the parties[254]; the concept of "domicile" replaces that of "nationality" in those Member States, such as the United Kingdom which use domicile as a connecting factor in family matters.[255]

A court exercising this jurisdiction will make an order for periodical payments by a husband even though he is domiciled and resident abroad and has no assets in England.[256] It will vary a settlement which comprises property situated abroad and is governed by foreign law and the trustees of which reside abroad.[257] It will

---

[249] Case 143/78, [1979] E.C.R. 1055 at p.1066.
[250] *JKN v JCN* [2010] EWHC 843 (Fam); [2011] 1 F.L.R. 826.
[251] Matrimonial Causes Act 1973 ss.21, 21A (as inserted by Welfare Reform and Pensions Act 1999 Sch.3, para.2), 21B and 21C (as inserted by Pensions Act 2008 Sch.6, para.2).
[252] Case C-220/95 *Van den Boogaard v Laumen* [1997] E.C.R. I-1147; [1998] Q.B. 759. See Schlosser, paras 93–5.
[253] And also by the Lugano Convention art.5(2).
[254] Maintenance Regulation art.3(c).
[255] Maintenance Regulation, art.2(3). "Domicile" will be determined in accordance with its traditional meaning in English family law: cf. Brussels IIa Regulation, art.3(2). For the application of the Regulation as between the parts of the United Kingdom see the Civil Jurisdiction and Judgments (Maintenance) Regulations 2011 Sch.6.
[256] *Cammell v Cammell* [1965] P. 467.
[257] *Nunneley v Nunneley* (1890) 15 P.D. 186; *Forsyth v Forsyth* [1891] P. 363.

order a settlement of a party's English property, although he is domiciled and resident abroad.[258] But it will decline to exercise its powers in cases where any order that it might make would be wholly ineffective.[259]

The Maintenance Regulation

The Maintenance Regulation provides that in matters relating to maintenance obligations in Member States, jurisdiction is to lie with:

9–069

(a)   the court for the place where the defendant is habitually resident[260]; or

(b)   the court for the place where the creditor is habitually resident[261]; or

(c)   the court which, according to its own law, has jurisdiction to entertain proceedings concerning the status of a person if the matter relating to maintenance is ancillary to those proceedings, unless that jurisdiction is based solely on the nationality (domicile in the case of the United Kingdom and Ireland) of one of the parties[262]; or

(d)   the court which, according to its own law, has jurisdiction to entertain proceedings concerning parental responsibility if the matter relating to maintenance is ancillary to those proceedings, unless that jurisdiction is based solely on the nationality (domicile in the case of the United Kingdom and Ireland) of one of the parties.[263]

The Maintenance Regulation adopts the principle of party autonomy, the parties being able to agree that certain courts chosen from a prescribed list are to have jurisdiction to settle any disputes in matters relating to a maintenance obligation which have arisen or which may arise between them. The agreement must be in writing, or by a communication by electronic means which provides a durable record of the agreement.[264] The parties may select:

9–070

(a)   a court or the courts of a Member State in which one of the parties is habitually resident;

(b)   a court or the courts of a Member State of which one of the parties has the nationality (in which one of the parties is domiciled in the case of the United Kingdom and Ireland);

(c)   in the case of maintenance obligations between spouses or former spouses:
(i) the court which has jurisdiction to settle their dispute in matrimonial

---

[258] *Hunter v Hunter and Waddington* [1962] P. 1.
[259] *Tallack v Tallack* [1927] P. 211; *Goff v Goff* [1934] P. 107; *Wyler v Lyons* [1963] P. 274.
[260] art.3(a).
[261] art.3(b).
[262] art 3(c).
[263] art.3(d).
[264] art.4(2).

matters; or (ii) a court or the courts of the Member State which was the Member State of the spouses' last common habitual residence for a period of at least one year.[265]

9–071   The relevant connecting factors have to be satisfied at the time the choice of court agreement is concluded or at the time the court is seised. The jurisdiction conferred by such an agreement is exclusive unless the parties have agreed otherwise.[266] As between the different parts of the United Kingdom, these choice of court provisions apply as if "part of the United Kingdom" replaced the term "Member State".[267]

Apart from jurisdiction derived from other provisions of the Regulation, a court of a Member State before which a defendant enters an appearance has jurisdiction. This rule does not apply where appearance was entered to contest the jurisdiction.[268]

Where no court of a Member State has jurisdiction under the above rules, and no court of a State party to the Lugano Convention which is not a Member State has jurisdiction pursuant to the provisions of that Convention, the courts of the Member State of the common nationality of the parties have jurisdiction.[269] In the case of the United Kingdom and Ireland, common domicile is substituted for common nationality; and a case in which the parties are domiciled in different territorial units of the same Member State amounts to common domicile in that Member State.[270] Where the parties are domiciled in different parts of the United Kingdom, the courts of either part may exercise jurisdiction under this provision.[271]

9–072   The Regulation also introduces a *forum necessitatis*. Where no court of a Member State has jurisdiction pursuant to any of the above rules, the courts of a Member State may, on an exceptional basis, hear the case if proceedings cannot reasonably be brought or conducted or would be impossible in a third State with which the dispute is closely connected. The dispute must have a 'sufficient connection', not further defined, with the Member State of the court seised[272]; in the United Kingdom this must be with the part of the United Kingdom in which the court seised is located.[273]

Where a decision is given in a Member State or a Contracting State to the Hague Convention of 2007 in which the creditor is habitually resident, proceedings to modify the decision or to have a new decision given cannot be brought by the debtor in any other Member State as long as the creditor remains habitually resident in the State in which the decision was given. This prohibition

---

[265] arts 2(3), 4(1). An agreement of this sort may not be made in the case of a dispute relating to a maintenance obligation towards a child under the age of 18: art.4(3). For cases in which the chosen court is in a State party to the Lugano Convention which is not also a Member State, see art.4(4).
[266] art.4(1).
[267] Civil Jurisdiction and Judgments (Maintenance) Regulations 2011 (SI 2011/1484) Sch.6, para.5.
[268] art.5; for application between the parts of the United Kingdom, see SI 2011/1484 Sch.6, para.6.
[269] art.6 "subsidiary jurisdiction".
[270] art.2(3).
[271] SI 2011/1484 Sch.6, para.7.
[272] art.8.
[273] SI 2011/1484 Sch.6, para.8.

does not apply in certain cases: (a) where the parties have agreed (in accordance with art.4) to the jurisdiction of the courts of that other Member State; (b) where the creditor submits to the jurisdiction of the courts of that other Member State; (c) where the competent authority in the Hague Convention Contracting State of origin cannot, or refuses to, exercise jurisdiction to modify the decision or give a new decision; or (d) where the decision given in the Hague Convention Contracting State of origin cannot be recognised or declared enforceable in the Member State where proceedings to modify the decision or to have a new decision given are contemplated.[274] This provision applies as between different parts of the United Kingdom, so that where a decision is given in a part of the United Kingdom where the creditor is habitually resident, proceedings to modify the decision or to have a new decision given cannot be brought by the debtor in any other part of the United Kingdom as long as the creditor remains habitually resident in the part of the United Kingdom in which the decision was given, unless the parties have the courts of that other part of the United Kingdom or the creditor submits to the jurisdiction of the courts of that other part.[275]

There are special rules as to the service of process when the defendant is habitually resident in a State other than the Member State where the action is brought and does not enter an appearance.[276] Application may be made to the courts of a Member State for such provisional, including protective, measures, as may be available under the law of that State even if the courts of another Member State have jurisdiction under the Maintenance Regulation to the substance of the matter.[277] The exercise of jurisdiction is subject to rules as to *lis pendens* and related actions.[278]   9–073

The Maintenance Regulation contains in Chapter VII (arts 49 to 63) detailed provisions, largely modelled on those in the Hague Convention of 2007, establishing a network of Central Authorities to facilitate the obtaining and enforcement of decisions as to maintenance. Chapter IV (arts 44 to 47) of the Regulation contain provisions as to legal aid. The Regulation gives parties who are involved in a dispute covered by this Regulation a qualified right to effective access to justice in another Member State, including enforcement and appeal or review procedures.

After a foreign decree

The English courts formerly had no jurisdiction to make an order for financial provision where the main decree was granted by a foreign court. The liberality of the English rules for the recognition of foreign decrees coupled with the restrictive approach of some foreign courts in considering financial provision produced cases of serious hardship to wives and children. Remedial legislation   9–074

---

[274] art.8.
[275] SI 2011/1484 Sch.6, para.9.
[276] art.11. For the position as between different parts of the United Kingdom, see SI 2011/1484 Sch.6, para.11.
[277] art.14. For the position as between different parts of the United Kingdom, see SI 2011/1484 Sch.6, para.14.
[278] arts 12 and 13.

based on recommendations by the Law Commission[279] was enacted as Pt III of the Matrimonial and Family Proceedings Act 1984.

The general effect of these provisions is to enable the English courts to exercise, after a foreign decree,[280] the full range of powers to make financial provision or property adjustment orders, including consent orders and orders for the transfer of tenancies, and to prevent or set aside transactions designed to defeat applications for financial relief.[281] The powers are only available if the marriage has been dissolved or annulled, or the parties to a marriage legally separated, by means of judicial or other proceedings in an overseas country and the decree is entitled to recognition in England.[282] In addition, there are a number of important qualifications affecting the exercise of this jurisdiction.

The first is the existence of a "filter mechanism". No application for an order for financial relief after a foreign decree may be made unless the applicant has first obtained the leave of the court, and leave may not be granted unless the court considers that there is substantial ground for the making of such an order,[283] and that the enforcement mechanisms in the foreign jurisdiction have been exhausted.[284] The applicant must satisfy the court that there are substantial grounds upon which the court could be invited to exercise its powers under s.12. Where the question of financial provision is currently before a court in the foreign country in which the decree was pronounced, the court will have to consider whether England is an appropriate forum.[285] The principal object of the filter mechanism is to prevent wholly unmeritorious claims being pursued to oppress or blackmail a former spouse. The Supreme Court has held that the threshold is not high, but is higher than "serious issue to be tried" or "good arguable case" found in other contexts. It is perhaps best expressed by saying that in this context "substantial" means "solid".[286] It is not necessary for the applicant to show the existence of hardship, nor that there was injustice as a result of whatever position emerged from the foreign proceedings: these are factors to be considered in exercising the jurisdiction and not preconditions on its exercise.[287]

9–075 Leave may be granted subject to such conditions as the court thinks fit[288]; for example, the applicant may be required to give an undertaking not to enforce any order made by a foreign court or to have any such order discharged.

---

[279] *Financial Relief after Foreign Divorce*, Law Com. No. 117 (1982).

[280] Even if granted before the 1984 Act: *Chebaro v Chebaro* [1987] Fam. 127.

[281] Matrimonial and Family Proceedings Act 1984 ss.17, 19, 22–24 and 34, as amended.

[282] s.12(1).

[283] s.13(1); *N. v N. (Foreign Divorce: Financial Relief)* [1997] 1 F.L.R. 900. The applicant for leave must make full disclosure of the material facts: *W. v W. (Financial Provision)* [1989] 1 F.L.R. 22.

[284] *Jordan v Jordan* [2000] 1 W.L.R. 210.

[285] *Holmes v Holmes* [1989] Fam. 47; *M. v M. (Financial Provision after Foreign Divorce)* [1994] 1 F.L.R. 399; *Hewitson v Hewitson* [1995] Fam. 10-0. The principles developed in *Spiliada Maritime Corp. v Cansulex Ltd.* [1987] A.C. 460 and applied in a matrimonial causes context in *De Dampierre v De Dampierre* [1988] A.C. 92 (see above, para.9–024) will be applied in considering the forum conveniens aspect.

[286] *Agbaje v Agbaje* [2010] UKSC 13; [2010] 1 A.C. 628 at [33].

[287] *Jordan v Jordan* [2000] 1 W.L.R. 210 (CA); *Agbaje v Agbaje* [2010] UKSC 13; [2010] 1 A.C. 628 at [60]–[61].

[288] Matrimonial and Family Proceedings Act 1984 s.13(3).

The second is that the parties must have a genuine connection with England; the jurisdiction is not available to those who are "birds of passage".[289] The jurisdictional requirements which reflect this policy are that the applicant must show that at one of two relevant dates, that of the initial application for the leave of the court or that on which the decree of divorce, nullity of marriage or legal separation took effect in the foreign country, either party was domiciled[290] in England or had been habitually resident there throughout the period of one year ending on that date.[291] Alternatively, it must be shown that either or both parties had, at the date of the application for leave, a beneficial interest in possession in a dwelling-house[292] situated in England which was at some time during the marriage a matrimonial home of the parties to the marriage[293]; where this is the only basis for jurisdiction the powers of the court are limited to the making of orders affecting an interest in the dwelling-house or as to lump sum payments, limited in amount to the value of that interest, to a party to the marriage or for the benefit of a child of the family.[294]

Even if the jurisdictional requirements are satisfied, the court is required, before making an order, to consider whether England is the appropriate venue.[295] If the court is not satisfied that it would be appropriate for such an order to be made by a court in England, it must dismiss the application. Factors are specified to which the court must in particular have regard:

9–076

(i)   the connection which the parties to the marriage have with England, with the foreign country in which the divorce, annulment or legal separation was granted, and with any other country;

(ii)   any financial benefits received or likely to be received, in consequence of the foreign decree, by virtue of any agreement or the operation of the law of any foreign country, or under a foreign order for the making of payments or the transfer of property;

(iii) any right which the applicant has, or has had, to apply for financial relief from the respondent under the law of any foreign country, and if the applicant has omitted to exercise that right, the reason for that omission[296];

(iv) the availability in England of any property in respect of which an order in favour of the applicant could be made;

9–077

(v)   the extent to which any order is likely to be enforceable; and

(vi) the length of time which has elapsed since the date of the foreign decree.[297]

---

[289] Law Com. No. 117, para.2.9.

[290] In the traditional family law sense.

[291] Matrimonial and Family Proceedings Act 1984 s.15(1)(a)(b).

[292] Defined, s.27.

[293] s.15(1)(c).

[294] s.20.

[295] s.16.

[296] The fact that the party seeking relief might have claimed in the foreign proceedings, though significant, is not to be treated as determinative: *Moore v Moore* [2007] EWCA Civ 361, [2007] 2 F.L.R. 339.

[297] *Lamagni v Lamagni* [1995] 2 F.L.R. 452 (delay of some 13 years due to lawyers' errors); *M v L* [2003] EWHC 328 (Fam), [2003] 2 F.L.R. 425 (after 33 years of voluntary contributions).

Although many of the factors to be considered have much in common with those which would be relevant in a *forum non conveniens* enquiry, the issue is not one of *forum non conveniens*. Section 16 does not require the court to determine the only appropriate forum where the case may be tried more suitably for the interests of the parties and the ends of justice; no choice between jurisdictions is involved.[298]

If an application or part of an application relates to a matter within the scope of the Maintenance Regulation, the jurisdictional rules in the 1984 Act are replaced by those in the Regulation (or of the Lugano Convention where it applies). If there has been a decision as to maintenance in Member State under the Maintenance Regulation (or in a Contracting State to the Lugano Convention), any application under Pt III of the 1984 Act so far as it related to matters falling within the scope of the Regulation or Convention would constitute an attempt to vary that order. It is thought that such a foreign order would not preclude an application for some other form of financial provision, e.g., a property adjustment order, under Pt III.[299]

Failure to maintain

9–078   Under s.27 of the Matrimonial Causes Act 1973,[300] the court has power to order either party to the marriage to make periodical payments (secured or unsecured) or pay a lump sum to the other or for the benefit of a child of the family on the ground that he has failed to provide reasonable maintenance for the applicant or has failed to provide, or to make a proper contribution towards, reasonable maintenance for any child of the family. This power is exercisable although no proceedings for divorce, separation or nullity of marriage are in train. The court has jurisdiction under this section only under the Maintenance Regulation (or the Lugano Convention).[301]

Maintenance in magistrates' courts

9–079   Special provisions are made for maintenance orders to be made by a combined operation involving magistrates' courts in England and certain Commonwealth countries; the arrangements governing the process are not affected by the Maintenance Regulation (or the Lugano Convention). If the respondent resides in any part of the Commonwealth to which the Maintenance Orders (Facilities for Enforcement) Act 1920 has been extended by Order in Council,[302] machinery is provided by s.3 of the Act[303] whereby a wife resident in England can get a

---

[298] *Agbaje v Agbaje* [2010] UKSC 13; [2010] 1 A.C. 628 at [50]; see also the discussion of "comity" at [51]–[54]. See also *Traversa v Freddi* [2009] EWHC 2101 (Fam); [2010] 1 F.L.R. 324.
[299] See *Agbaje v Agbaje* [2010] UKSC 13, [2010] 1 A.C. 628 at [55]–[57] where the issues were raised but not resolved.
[300] As amended by s.63 of the Domestic Proceedings and Magistrates' Court Act 1978.
[301] Matrimonial Causes Act 1973 s.27(2) as substituted by SI 2011/1484 Sch.7, para.6(2); and see para.15(b).
[302] The Act has been extended to a large number of Commonwealth countries: see the Maintenance Orders (Facilities for Enforcement) Order 1959 (SI 1959/377), as amended.
[303] As amended by Maintenance Order (Reciprocal Enforcement) Act 1992 Sch.1, para.1.

provisional maintenance order[304] from a magistrates' court in England, which will be enforceable against the husband if and when it is confirmed by a court in the country where he resides. It is immaterial that the applicant's cause for complaint did not arise in England.[305] Section 4 of the Act provides reciprocal machinery whereby a provisional order made in the absence of the husband in a country to which the Act extends may be confirmed by a magistrates' court in England if the husband resides there and has been served with a summons. Thus there are two hearings, one in the absence of the husband, and the other in the absence of the wife. The husband may raise any defence that he might have raised in the original proceedings, but no other defence. It is entirely within the discretion of the court whether to confirm the order with or without modifications, or refuse to confirm it, or remit the case to the court which made the order for the purpose of taking further evidence. This machinery is sometimes known as the "shuttlecock" procedure.[306] Of course the machinery is defective, in that the wife at the first hearing cannot be cross-examined on behalf of the husband, and the husband at the second hearing cannot be cross-examined on behalf of the wife. But it is better than no machinery at all.

Part I of the Maintenance Orders (Reciprocal Enforcement) Act 1972 as amended, which is intended ultimately to replace the Act of 1920,[307] makes similar and more elaborate provision for the reciprocal enforcement of maintenance orders, not confined to cases where the defendant is resident in any part of the Commonwealth. Pt I of the Act differs from the Act of 1920 in several respects, of which the following are the most important: **9–080**

(1)　It applies to Scotland as well as to England and Northern Ireland.
(2)　It can be extended to any country outside the United Kingdom which is prepared to grant reciprocal treatment to United Kingdom orders (called in the Act a "reciprocating country"[308]) and not merely to any part of the Commonwealth outside the United Kingdom.
(3)　It defines a maintenance order so as to include an affiliation order,[309] which the Act of 1920 did not.

---

[304] A "maintenance order" is defined by s.10 of the Act as an order (other than an affiliation order) for the periodical payments of sums of money towards the maintenance of the wife or other dependants of the person against whom the order is made. "Dependants" are defined to mean such persons as he is liable to maintain according to the law in force where the order was made.

[305] *Collister v Collister* [1972] 1 W.L.R. 54.

[306] See *Pilcher v Pilcher* [1955] P. 318 at 330.

[307] See s.22(2)(a), which repeals the Act of 1920. This subsection is not yet in force.

[308] s.1. The countries which have been designated as "reciprocating countries" (usually with a restricted definition of "maintenance orders") are listed in SI 1974/566, SI 1975/2187, SI 1979/115, SI 1983/1125, SI 2001/3501, SI 2002/788 and SI 2008/1202. Modified versions are applied to those Hague Convention countries which are not EU Member States (SI 1993/593, as amended by SI 1999/1318, SI 2002/2838 and SI 2011/1484); it applies only to Australia, Norway, Switzerland and Turkey); and to the United States (SI 2007/2005).

[309] s.21.

(4)   The "shuttlecock" procedure applies to orders varying or revoking maintenance orders.[310] The provisions of the Act of 1920 in this respect were found to be defective.[311]

(5)   It defines a maintenance order so as to include an order for the payment of a lump sum,[312] which the Act of 1920 did not.

Since the general scheme of Pt I of the Act is the same as that of the Act of 1920, there is no need to give a detailed exegesis here.

Part II of the Maintenance Orders (Reciprocal Enforcement) Act 1972 gives effect to the New York Convention on the Recovery of Maintenance Abroad, 1956, negotiated under the aegis of the United Nations.[313] It provides a procedure under which there is only one hearing, in the country where the defendant resides. The Convention is tersely drafted and this has given rise to considerable differences in interpretation, reducing its effectiveness.

Choice of law

9–081   Under the 1920 and 1972 Acts, there are some exceptional situations in which an English court has to apply the law of a reciprocating country. In all other cases, the English court will apply its own domestic law. This principle was re-affirmed by the Supreme Court in *Granatino v Radmacher*.[314] Although the court cited without disapproval an earlier case[315] in which it was said that there could be "a sideways look at foreign law as part of the discretionary analysis required by [English] substantive law", the Supreme Court emphasised that the weight to be given to a pre-nuptial contract governed by German law was entirely matter for English domestic law.

The Hague Conference on Private International Law adopted in November 2007 a Protocol on the Law Applicable to Maintenance Obligations.[316] The Protocol is essentially a revision of earlier Hague Conventions of 1956 and 1973, which had attracted support entirely from States in the civil law tradition. Article 15 of the Maintenance Regulation provides that the law applicable to maintenance obligations is to be determined in accordance with the Protocol in those Member States bound by the Hague Protocol. The United Kingdom is not, and will not be, so bound.

---

[310] ss.5 and 9.
[311] See *Pilcher v Pilcher* [1955] P. 318.
[312] s.21(1)(a), as amended by Civil Jurisdiction and Judgments Act 1982 Sch.11, para.4.
[313] A modified version of Pt II of the Act now applies to the whole of the USA: SI 2007/2006.
[314] [2010] UKSC 42; [2011] A.C. 534.
[315] *C v C (Ancillary Relief: Nuptial Settlement)* [2004] EWHC 742 (Fam); [2005] Fam. 250.
[316] See Bonomi, (2008) 10 Yb.P.I.L. 333.

Enforcement of foreign maintenance orders

Common law

A foreign maintenance order for periodical payments ranks at common law as a foreign judgment in personam. If, as is usually the case, the foreign court has power to vary the amount of the payments, the foreign order cannot be enforced in England at common law, because it is not "final and conclusive".[317] However, if the foreign court has power to vary the amount of future payments, but not that of past payments, then the arrears may be recovered in England by an action on the foreign judgment.[318]

9–082

This is the position at common law, and it usually prevents the enforcement of foreign maintenance orders in England. But the common law has been radically altered by the Maintenance Regulation and by statutes which provide for the reciprocal enforcement of maintenance orders within the United Kingdom, and also between England (and Northern Ireland) and countries of the Commonwealth overseas, and between the United Kingdom and designated countries overseas.

Orders made in Member States

The Maintenance Regulation contains provisions as to recognition and enforcement of maintenance decisions.[319] Many provisions of the Regulation are very similar to those of the Hague Convention on the International Recovery of Child Support and Other Forms of Family Maintenance and a Protocol on the Law Applicable to Maintenance Obligations agreed in November 2007, though the Regulation deals, as the Hague Convention does not, with jurisdiction as well as recognition and enforcement. The Hague Convention was designed to take account of important developments in the field (notably the move in countries such as Australia and the United Kingdom from court-based to administrative, formula-driven maintenance systems), to meet the specific needs of the United States which has a very large amount of "traffic" in this area, and to replace the United Nations Convention on the Recovery Abroad of Maintenance of 1956, the provisions of which have proved unsatisfactorily vague.[320] Subject to some transitional provisions,[321] the Maintenance Regulation applies only to proceedings instituted, to court settlements approved or concluded, and to authentic instruments established after June 18, 2011.

9–083

---

[317] *Harrop v Harrop* [1920] 3 K.B. 386; *Re Macartney* [1921] 1 Ch. 522; *Cartwright v Cartwright* [2002] EWCA Civ. 931, [2002] 2 F.L.R. 610. The rule is criticised by Grodecki (1959) 8 I.C.L.Q. 18 at 32–40; but it is well established. The rule is not followed in Ireland: *McC. v McC.* [1994] 1 I.R.L.M. 101 (Irish High Ct.).

[318] *Beatty v Beatty* [1924] 1 K.B. 807.

[319] "Decision" is defined (art.2(1)) as a decision in matters relating to maintenance obligations given by a court of a Member State, whatever the decision may be called, including a decree, order, judgment or writ of execution, as well as a decision by an officer of the court determining the costs or expenses.

[320] The United Kingdom has not signed the Hague Convention, although it was signed by the European Union on April 6, 2011; it is not yet in force.

[321] arts 75 and 76.

Different rules as to recognition and enforcement apply depending on the source of the decision. The rules in s.1 (Aarts 17 to 22) of Ch.IV of the Regulation applying to decisions given in a Member State bound by the Hague Protocol of November 23, 2007 on the law applicable to maintenance obligations; although the Hague Protocol is not itself in force, its provisions are applied provisionally as between the relevant Member States. Section 2 (arts 23 to 38) applies to decisions given in a Member State not bound by that Protocol; apart from the United Kingdom, the only Member State not bound by the Hague Protocol is Denmark.[322]

9–084   Section 3 (arts 39 to 43) of the Regulation contains provisions applying whatever the origin of a decision. So, the procedure for the enforcement of decisions given in another Member State is to be governed by the law of the Member State of enforcement. A decision given in a Member State which is enforceable in the Member State of enforcement must be enforced there under the same conditions as a decision given in that Member State of enforcement.[323] Under no circumstances may a decision given in a Member State be reviewed as to its substance in the Member State in which recognition, enforceability or enforcement is sought.[324] Recovery of any costs incurred in the application of the Regulation is not to take precedence over the recovery of maintenance.[325]

A decision given in a Member State other than Denmark will be recognised in England without any special procedure being required and without any possibility of opposing its recognition.[326] Such a decision which is enforceable in the Member State of origin is enforceable in England without the need for any declaration of enforceability.[327]

Jurisdiction in relation to applications for enforcement of such a maintenance decision lies with the courts for the part of the United Kingdom in which (a) the person against whom enforcement is sought is resident, or (b) assets belonging to that person and which are susceptible to enforcement are situated or held, or (c) any other matter relevant to enforcement arises.[328] In England, application is to be made to a magistrates' court. The claimant must provide the court with: (a) a copy of the decision which satisfies the conditions necessary to establish its authenticity; (b) what is referred to as an "extract from the decision" (actually a detailed form prescribed in Annex I to the Regulation setting out all relevant details) completed by the court of origin; (c) where appropriate, a document showing the amount of any arrears and the date such amount was calculated; (d) where necessary, a transliteration or a translation of the "extract of the decision".

---

[322] For therecognition and enforcement of maintenance decisions from Denmark (and to certain cases under the transitional provisions in art.75(2)(a) and (b)), see SI 2011/1484 Sch.1, Part 3.
[323] art.41(1).
[324] art.42. Under art.19, a defendant who did not enter an appearance in the Member State of origin has the right to apply for a review of the decision before the competent court of that Member State in certain circumstances.
[325] art.43.
[326] art.17(1).
[327] art.17(2).
[328] SI 2011/1484 Sch.1, para.4(3).

The court may require the claimant to provide a translation of the decision itself if, but only if, the enforcement of the decision is challenged.[329]

An enforceable decision carries with it by operation of law the power to proceed to any protective measures available in English law.[330] For the purposes of the enforcement of a maintenance decision, the decision has the same force and effect, the enforcing court has in relation to its enforcement the same powers, and proceedings for or with respect to its enforcement may be taken, as if the decision had originally been made by the enforcing court.[331]

9–085

The recognition and enforcement of a decision under the Maintenance Regulation does not in any way imply the recognition of the family relationship, parentage, marriage or affinity underlying the maintenance obligation which gave rise to the decision.[332]

By virtue of art.48, court settlements and authentic instruments which are enforceable in the Member State of origin are to be recognised and enforced in other Member States in the same way as decisions.[333]

Orders from other parts of the United Kingdom

Under Pt II of the Maintenance Orders Act 1950, a maintenance order made in one part of the United Kingdom may be registered in a court in another part of the United Kingdom if the person liable to make the payments resides there and it is convenient that the order should be enforceable there.[334] The registration of the order is therefore within the discretion of the court; but this discretion vests in the court which made the order and not in the court which is asked to register it.[335] An order so registered in a court in any part of the United Kingdom may be enforced in that part of the United Kingdom in all respects as if it had been made by that court and as if that court had had jurisdiction to make it.[336] When a maintenance order is registered in a magistrates' court, that court may vary the rate of the payments under the order on an application by either party but no such variation may impose on the person liable to make payments under the maintenance order a liability to make payments in excess of the maximum rate (if any) authorised by the law for the time being in force in the part of the United Kingdom in which the maintenance order was made,[337] and this power may not be exercised where the maintenance creditor remains habitually resident in the part of the United Kingdom in which the order was made.[338]

9–086

---

[329] art.20.

[330] art.18.

[331] SI 2011/1484 Sch.1, para.4(4). For limited powers to refuse or suspend enforcement, see art.21; SI 2011/1484 Sch.1, para.4(10).

[332] art.22.

[333] For the definitions of "court settlements" and "authentic instruments", see art.2(2), (3). See SI 2011/1484 Sch.3.

[334] ss.16(1), 17(2).

[335] s.17(2), (4).

[336] s.18(1).

[337] s.21(1) (as amended by Domestic Proceedings and Magistrates' Courts Act 1978 Sch.2, para.(14)) and (4).

[338] s.21(1ZA) as inserted by SI 2011/1484 reg.9, Sch 7, para 1(1), (3)(b).

Commonwealth arrangements

9–087 Under s.1 of the Maintenance Orders (Facilities for Enforcement) Act 1920, a maintenance order made in a country to which the Act extends may be registered in England or Northern Ireland. Section 2 provides reciprocal machinery whereby a maintenance order made in England or Northern Ireland may be registered in a country to which the Act extends. When an order has been registered, it has the same force and effect as if it had been an order originally obtained in the court in which it is registered. The court has no discretion to refuse to register an order, nor has the husband any right to be heard to show cause against the registration, or to appeal against it. Pt I of the Maintenance Orders (Reciprocal Enforcement) Act 1972 makes similar but more elaborate provision for the registration in the United Kingdom of maintenance orders made in reciprocating countries and vice versa.

CHAPTER 10

CHILDREN

Courts in many countries speak of parental rights and duties, and of the custody of and access to children. Similar terminology was used in England before the Children Act 1989. This substituted the concept of "parental responsibility" and introduced the present range of orders available to the courts in cases concerning children, including residence orders, contact orders, prohibited steps orders, and specific issue orders. The 1989 Act also sought to avoid the traditional term "wardship", preferring to speak of the "inherent jurisdiction with respect to children". The Adoption and Children Act 2002 introduced Special Guardianship Orders into the Children Act 1989, which granted more rights to unmarried fathers, and radically changed the law on adoption. These changes have to be borne in mind when reading the earlier cases on this branch of the law. **10–001**

Traditionally, the sovereign as *parens patriae* is interested in the welfare of his minor subjects who, because of tender years, are incapable of looking after themselves. The duty to protect their interests was delegated to the Lord Chancellor, from whom it passed first to the Court of Chancery and then to the High Court. This is the origin of the inherent jurisdiction of the High Court as to children, exercised since 1971 by the Family Division.[1] The inherent jurisdiction is usually invoked by making the child a ward of court. Under it, the court has very extensive powers in relation to the child: it can, for example, restrain him (more usually her) from marrying without the court's consent, prevent him from leaving the country, or send him abroad to be looked after by a foreign guardian. Anyone who disregards an order of the court made in the inherent jurisdiction is liable to severe penalties for contempt of court. **10–002**

---

[1] See generally, Cross J. (1967) 83 L.Q.R. 200; Lowe and White, *Wards of Court* 2nd edn, 1986 (Barry Rose, London,); Mitchell, (2001) 31 Fam. L.J. 130 and 212.

Quite apart from its inherent jurisdiction, the High Court has a statutory jurisdiction, which it shares with other courts, to make orders under the Children Act 1989 and in matrimonial proceedings.

A fundamental principle underlying the exercise of the courts' powers is now set out in s.1(1) of the Children Act 1989:

> When a court determines any question with respect to:
> (a)   the upbringing of a child; or
> (b)   the administration of a child's property or the application of any income arising from it, the child's welfare shall be the court's paramount consideration.

As we shall see, this welfare principle is qualified in a few contexts, notably in the application of international convention rules as to the abduction of children. Subject to that, the section applies whatever the nature of the dispute before the court, i.e., not only to disputes between parents, but also to disputes between parents and strangers, and between strangers.[2] It applies not only in domestic English cases but also in cases with a foreign element, where it may take precedence even over a guardianship or custody order made by a foreign court.[3] It should therefore be regarded as a rule of public policy applicable notwithstanding any rule of the conflict of laws.

JURISDICTION OF THE ENGLISH COURT

The European rules

10–003   EU Council Regulation No 2201/2003[4] (commonly known as the Brussels IIa Regulation)[5] provides uniform jurisdictional rules for the attribution, exercise, delegation, restriction or termination of parental responsibility,[6] and almost automatic recognition of judgments throughout the European Union.[7] Unlike its predecessor, which was limited to children of both spouses on the occasion of matrimonial proceedings, the Brussels IIa Regulation covers all decisions on parental responsibility, including measures for the protection of the child,[8] independent of any link with matrimonial proceedings, in order to ensure equality

---

[2] *J v C* [1970] A.C. 668.

[3] *Re B's Settlement* [1940] Ch. 54; *McKee v McKee* [1951] A.C. 352; below, para.10–033.

[4] EU Council Regulation No.2201/2003 of November 27, 2003 concerning jurisdiction and the recognition and enforcement of judgments in matrimonial matters and the matters of parental responsibility, repealing Regulation No.1347/2000. The relevant provisions of English domestic law are amended by the European Communities (Jurisdiction and Judgments in Matrimonial and Parental Responsibility Matters) Regulations 2005 (SI 2005/265).

[5] See generally, Lowe, [2004] I.F.L. 205; Lowe, Everall & Nicholls, *The New Brussels II Regulation: a supplement to International Movement of Children*, (Jordan Publishing Ltd, Bristol, 2005).

[6] art.1(1)(b). Parental responsibility is defined in art.2 as all rights and duties relating to the person or the property of a child which are given to a natural or legal person by judgment, by operation of law or by an agreement having legal effect, including rights of custody and rights of access.

[7] With the exception of Denmark.

[8] Normally thought of as public law measures in English law, but included in the Regulation under the concept of broadly defined "civil matters".

for all children.[9] The Regulation does not, however, apply to the establishment or contesting of a parent-child relationship, adoption, a child's name, emancipation, maintenance, trusts or succession, or criminal offences committed by children,[10] although it does apply to a public law decision to take a child into care.[11] With regard to the child's property, the Regulation only applies to measures for the protection of the child[12]: measures concerned with the child's property but not concerned with the protection of the child continue to be governed by the Brussels I Regulation.[13]

Article 8 establishes the primary jurisdictional rule in matters of parental **10–004** responsibility, giving jurisdiction to the Member State in which the child is habitually resident at the time the court is seised.[14] A child will be habitually resident for this purpose in the place which reflects some degree of integration by the child in a social and family environment.[15] The duration, regularity, conditions and reasons for the stay on the territory of a Member State and the family's move to that State, the child's nationality, the place and conditions of attendance at school, linguistic knowledge and the family and social relationships of the child in that State must be taken into consideration.[16]

This primary rule is supplemented by three additional grounds for jurisdiction, and is subject to two special rules. Provision is made for cases of *lis pendens*, and there exists a residual jurisdiction rule allowing the application of national law. These matters will be dealt with in turn.

Prorogation of jurisdiction

One additional ground, or set of grounds, for jurisdiction is established by art.12 **10–005** under the heading "prorogation of jurisdiction", though more is required than a simple choice of court by the parties. The courts of a Member State exercising jurisdiction in matrimonial proceedings under art.3 of the Regulation[17] also have jurisdiction for matters relating to parental responsibility where at least one of the spouses has parental responsibility for the child and the jurisdiction has been accepted[18] expressly or otherwise unequivocally by the spouses and any other

---

[9] Recital (5). There is no maximum age for a child in the Regulation; this is a matter for the internal law of each Member State.

[10] art.1(3).

[11] Case C-435/06 *C (A Child)* [2007] E.C.R. I-10141; [2008] Fam. 27.

[12] art.1(2)(e).

[13] Recital (9). For the Brussels I Regulation, see Ch.4.

[14] The definition of when a court is seised is found in art.16: when the document instituting the proceedings is lodged with the court, provided that the applicant has not subsequently failed to take the steps required to have service effected on the respondent.

[15] Case C-497/10 *Mercredi v Chaffe*.

[16] Case C-523/07 *Proceedings brought by A* [2009] 2 E.C.R. I-2805 at [39].

[17] See para.9–005, above.

[18] That is, jurisdiction over parental responsibility rather than over the matrimonial proceedings: *Bush v Bush* [2008] EWCA Civ. 865; [2008] 2 F.L.R. 1437. Members of the Supreme Court expressed different views in *Re I (A Child) (Contact Application: Jurisdiction)* [2009] UKSC 10; [2010] 1 A.C. 319 as to the time (whether before or after the court becoming seised) at which agreement had to be expressed; but once given, agreement could not be withdrawn. Acceptance cannot be limited to certain aspects of responsibility: *AP v TD* [2010] EWHC 2040 (Fam); [2011] 1 F.L.R. 1851.

holders of parental responsibility, and is in the superior interests of the child.[19] The courts of a Member State also have jurisdiction in matters relating to parental responsibility where the child has a substantial connection with that Member State (in particular because someone with parental responsibility is habitually resident in that State, or the child is a national of that State) and the jurisdiction has been accepted expressly or otherwise unequivocally by all the parties to the proceedings, and is in the best interests of the child.[20] In neither case is it essential that the child be resident in a Member State.[21]

Jurisdiction based on the child's presence

10–006   It is not always easy or even possible to determine the habitual residence of a child. The Brussels IIa Regulation addresses this difficulty by providing that where the child's habitual residence cannot be established and jurisdiction cannot be founded on art.12, then the courts of the Member State in which the child is present have jurisdiction.[22]

Provisional and protective measures

10–007   Article 20(1) of the Brussels IIa Regulation provides that in urgent cases its provisions do not prevent the courts of a Member State from taking such provisional, including protective, measures in respect of persons or assets in that State as may be available under the law of that Member State, even if, under the Regulation, the court of another Member State has jurisdiction as to the substance of the matter. Courts may be tempted to abuse this power in order to secure a final outcome which they judge desirable, but it has been held repeatedly that the provision is to be interpreted strictly and used only exceptionally.[23] The child must be protected from harm but the court must act so as to assist the foreign court in its task of making the final decision.[24]

---

[19] art.12(1); *Butt v Butt* [2010] EWHC 1989 (Fam); [2011] 1 FLR 54. *The Practice Guide for the application of the new Brussels II Regulation* (published by the European Commission in consultation with the European Judicial Network), p.17, makes it clear that the drafters did not intend there to be any distinction between the term "superior" and "best" interests of the child; and in fact other language versions use identical wording in arts 12(1)(b) and 12(3)(b); this has been accepted in *Bush v Bush* [2008] EWCA Civ. 865; [2008] 2 F.C.R. 139 and in *Re I (A Child) (Contact Application: Jurisdiction)* [2009] UKSC 10; [2010] 1 A.C. 319. For the termination of jurisdiction when a final judgment is given or the proceedings end for some other reason, see art.12(2).

[20] art.12(3). cf. *Re A (Children) (Removal Outside Jurisdiction: Habitual Residence)* [2011] EWCA Civ 265; [2011] 1 FLR 2025; *H v H* [2011] EWCA Civ 796. Article 12(4) adds that it will be deemed to be in the child's interest for the Member State to have jurisdiction under the provisions of the article where the child is habitually resident in a State that is not a Contracting State to the Hague Convention of 1996 on jurisdiction, if it is found impossible to hold proceedings in the state of the child's habitual residence.

[21] *Re I (A Child) (Contact Application: Jurisdiction)* [2009] UKSC 10; [2010] 1 A.C. 319 (Child in Pakistan).

[22] art.13.

[23] Case C-523/07 *Proceedings brought by A* [2009] 2 E.C.R. I-2805; Case C-403/09 PPU *Detiček v Sgueglia* [2009] E.C.R. I-12193; [2010] Fam. 104.

[24] *Re S (Care; Jurisdiction)* [2008] EWHC 3013 (Fam); [2009] 2 F.L.R. 550.

Qualifications on the general rule: transfer to a more appropriate forum

Forum non conveniens in the traditional common law sense is all but outlawed by the Brussels I Regulation[25] and arguably by the Brussels IIa Regulation so far as it deals with matrimonial proceedings. However, the Brussels IIa Regulation in its provisions on matters of parental responsibility enables a court with jurisdiction to stay its proceedings either in whole or in part on grounds that contain the principles of forum non conveniens. Article 15 contains detailed provisions under which a court may stay its proceedings, or request the court of another Member State to take jurisdiction, if the child has a particular connection with that other Member State, a court in that Member State would be better placed to hear the case (or a specific part of it), and the use of the power would be in the best interests of the child.[26] A court in one Member State may request a court in another Member State to exercise this power, so for example an English court may invite a Dutch court seised of a case to exercise its power under art.15 and transfer the case to England.[27] The child is to be considered to have a particular connection to a Member State for this purpose if that Member State: (a) has become the habitual residence of the child after the original court was seised; or (b) is the former habitual residence of the child; or (c) is the place of the child's nationality; or (d) is the habitual residence of a holder of parental responsibility; or (e) is the place where property of the child is located and the case concerns measures for the protection of the child relating to the administration, conservation or disposal of this property.[28] In order to determine whether there is a better forum in which to hear the case, the courts may co-operate either directly or through the Central Authorities.[29]

10–008

Qualifications on the general rule: continuing jurisdiction in certain access cases

Once the court of a Member State is seised under the primary rule, it may continue to have jurisdiction, even after a change in the child's habitual residence, for certain limited purposes connected with access rights. Where the proceedings as to parental responsibility in one Member State have led to a judgment on access rights, and the child acquires a new habitual residence by moving lawfully to another Member State, art.9 permits the courts of the former habitual residence to continue to exercise jurisdiction for a three month period[30] for the purpose of modifying the judgment on access rights. The courts of the child's new habitual residence do not have jurisdiction in this period, during which the holder of access rights, who will normally be still habitually resident in the Member State of origin, can apply to the same court for a variation when those access rights can no longer be exercised. However, art.9 does not apply if

10–009

---

[25] See para.5–047.
[26] art.15(1).
[27] The facts of *B v B* (Brussels II Revised: art.15) [2008] EWHC 2965 (Fam); [2009] 1 F.L.R. 517.
[28] art.15(3).
[29] art.15(6).
[30] Calculated from the date the child physically moves from the Member State of origin; *Practice Guide*, p.14.

the holder of access rights has accepted the jurisdiction of the new court by participating in proceedings before that court without contesting its jurisdiction.[31] It is important to stress that this provision only relates to access rights; it does not prevent the courts of the new Member State from deciding other matters as long as the proceedings in the first court have become final and not subject to appeal.[32]

However, it has been pointed out[33] that this provision is not without its problems since it appears to assume that the child will acquire a new habitual residence immediately on moving from one Member State to another. In English law the concept requires a period of time to have passed before the courts will find that a new habitual residence has been acquired. During the intervening period the court of the Member State of origin will not have jurisdiction under art.9 since the child will not be habitually resident anywhere. Presumably, then, during this time it will be the courts of the child's future habitual residence that will have jurisdiction under art.13 on the grounds of the child's presence, defeating the purpose of maintaining jurisdiction with the court originally seised to vary the original order during a short period of time.

Lis pendens

10–010   Where two sets of proceedings are initiated in the courts of different Member States, art.19 establishes the familiar rule of *lis pendens*. Where the proceedings for parental responsibility in different Member States relate to the same child and the same cause of action, the court second seised shall stay its proceedings in favour of the court first seised until such time as the court first seised establishes its jurisdiction, at which time the court second seised will decline jurisdiction,[34] unless the court first seised stays its proceedings on the forum non conveniens grounds described in art.15.

Residual jurisdiction

10–011   If no court of a Member State has jurisdiction under arts 8 to 12, then jurisdiction is to be determined in each Member State by the laws of that state,[35] and those decisions will also be recognised and enforceable in other Member States pursuant to the rules of the Regulation.[36] It has been argued that the provisions of the Regulation should be read as applying between different parts of the United Kingdom.[37] Other European instruments dealing with jurisdiction allocate jurisdiction to Member States as single units and do not seek to govern the allocation of jurisdiction as between the territorial units within Member States. In accordance with this approach, the European Communities (Jurisdiction and

---

[31]   art.9(2).
[32]   arts 17 and 19; *A v A (Jurisdiction: Brussels II)* [2002] 1 F.L.R. 1042, a case under the repealed Regulation 1347/2000.
[33]   McEleavy, (2004) 53 I.C.L.Q. 503 at p.508.
[34]   art.19(2) and (3). See Case 296/10 *Purrucker* [2011] I.L.Pr. 227 (test where court first seised deals with provisional measures only).
[35]   art.14.
[36]   arts 21 and 28; *Practice Guide*, p.18.
[37]   Lowe, [2004] I.F.L. 205 at 209.

Judgments in Matrimonial and Parental Responsibility Matters) Regulations 2005,[38] amending relevant statutory provisions to bring them into line with the Brussels IIa Regulation, have not materially altered the jurisdictional hierarchy between the countries of the United Kingdom. It is far from clear that this is a correct interpretation of the text of the Brussels IIa Regulation. Article 14 of the Regulation only applies "where no court of a Member State has jurisdiction", and that suggests that where the courts of Scotland have jurisdiction under the Regulation, the English courts may not take jurisdiction under the Family Law Act 1986.[39] Article 66, which deals with federal and other composite states and provides, in effect, that any reference to habitual residence, nationality or domicile is to be taken to refer not to the Member State as a whole but to the relevant territorial unit, also provides that any reference to "the authority" of a Member State refers to the authority of the relevant unit.[40] Had the Regulation made the same provision about the meaning of "court", it would be clear that the Regulation did deal with the allocation of jurisdiction within a Member State: the definition of "court" includes all "the authorities... with jurisdiction",[41] but art.66 refers only to "authority" and not "court". art.66 makes no reference to "presence", and it follows that the reference in art.13 to "the courts of a Member State" having jurisdiction based on presence must be interpreted by national law; to that extent at least, national law is relevant to determine the allocation of jurisdiction to the courts of different territorial units. The question as to whether the Brussels IIa Regulation determines jurisdiction within the UK has been considered by two Scottish cases with differing conclusions.[42] The outcome of this debate may one day fall to be decided by the European Court of Justice, determining whether or not the hierarchical provisions of the Family Law 1986 will continue to apply.

The Hague Convention of 1996

After a number of postponements, the United Kingdom is expected in the second half of 2012 to ratify the Hague Convention on Jurisdiction, Applicable Law, Recognition, Enforcement and Co-operation in respect of Parental Responsibility and Measures for the Protection of Children, signed in 1996. This has similarities to the EU provisions but also some significant differences which produce unwelcome complication. For ease of comparison what follows uses, as appropriate, the same sub-headings used for the EU Regulation.

10–012

The Convention defines "parental responsibility" as including "parental authority, or any analogous relationship of authority determining the rights, powers and responsibilities of parents, guardians or other legal representatives in

---

[38] SI 2005/265.
[39] See below, para.10–022.
[40] art.66(c).
[41] art.2(1).
[42] *S v D* [2007] S.L.T. (Sh. Ct.) 37; *MB v CB* (Sh. Ct). See also Beevers and McClean [2005] I.F.L. 129; Maher [2007] S.L.T. 117.

relation to the person or the property of the child".[43] Provision is made for a system of Central Authorities in each Contracting State with duties designed to facilitate international co-operation.[44]

Article 5 of the Convention gives jurisdiction to the state of the child's habitual residence, the same rule as is found in the Brussels IIa Regulation. The two instruments diverge in dealing with the qualifications on this general rule.

Prorogation of jurisdiction

10–013   The courts of a Contracting State exercising jurisdiction to decide upon an application for divorce or legal separation of the parents of a child habitually resident in another Contracting State, or for annulment of their marriage, have jurisdiction if at the time of commencement of the proceedings, one of his or her parents habitually resides in that State and one of them has parental responsibility in relation to the child, and the jurisdiction has been accepted by the parents, as well as by any other person who has parental responsibility in relation to the child, and is in the best interests of the child.[45] It will be seen that, in contrast to the position under Brussels IIa, this provision is limited to cases in which there are matrimonial proceedings, though the jurisdictional basis for those proceedings is not limited to those set out in art.3 of Brussels IIa.

Jurisdiction based on the presence of the child

10–014   Under the Convention, jurisdiction based on the presence of the child may be exercised not only where the child's habitual residence cannot be established, but also in the case of refugee children and children who, due to disturbances occurring in their country, are internationally displaced.[46]

Provisional, including and protective, measures

10–015   There are some fairly elaborate provisions in the Convention as to protective and other provisional measures. In all cases of urgency, the authorities of any Contracting State in whose territory the child or property belonging to the child is present have jurisdiction to take any necessary measures of protection.[47] The Explanatory Report gives examples: if it is necessary to ensure the representation of a child who is away from his or her habitual residence and who must undergo an urgent surgical operation, or it is necessary to make a rapid sale of perishable goods belonging to the child.[48] Subject to art.7, the authorities of a Contracting State in whose territory the child or property belonging to the child is present have jurisdiction to take measures of a provisional character for the protection of the person or property of the child which have a territorial effect limited to the

---

[43] art.1(2). Articles 3 and 4 set out in detail what is included and what excluded; the language is different but resulting scope seems the same as under the EU Regulation.
[44] arts 29 to 39.
[45] art.10.
[46] art.6.
[47] art.11.
[48] para.68.

State in question, in so far as such measures are not incompatible with measures already taken by authorities which have jurisdiction under arts 5 to 10.[49] All these measures lapse when the necessary steps have been taken by the authorities of the state of habitual residence.

Qualifications on the general rule: transfer to a more appropriate forum

Where the authority of a Contracting State having jurisdiction considers that the authority of another Contracting State would be better placed in the particular case to assess the best interests of the child, it may either request that other authority, directly or with the assistance of the Central Authority of its State, to assume jurisdiction, or suspend consideration of the case and invite the parties to introduce such a request before the authority of that other State. However, the Contracting States which may be approached in this way are limited. They are those of which the child is a national, in which property of the child is located, whose authorities are seised of an application for divorce or legal separation of the child's parents, or for annulment of their marriage, or with which the child has a substantial connection. The authority addressed may assume jurisdiction if it considers that this is in the child's best interests.[50] As in the EU Regulation, the initiative may be taken by a Contracting State qualified to take a transfer.[51]

10–016

Qualifications on the general rule: continuing jurisdiction in certain cases

In case of wrongful removal or retention of the child (defined as in the Hague Abduction Convention), the authorities of the Contracting State in which the child was habitually resident immediately before the removal or retention keep their jurisdiction until the child has acquired a habitual residence in another state, and *either* each person, institution, or other body having rights of custody has acquiesced in the removal or retention *or* the child has resided in that other state for a period of at least one year after the person, institution, or other body having rights of custody has or should have had knowledge of the whereabouts of the child, no request for return lodged within that period is still pending, and the child is settled in his or her new environment.[52] It will be seen that this provision speaks of the child acquiring a habitual residence in "another state", not necessarily a Contracting State. If that other state is in fact another Contracting State, then so long as the authorities of the Contracting State first mentioned retains jurisdiction, the authorities of the Contracting State to which the child has been removed or in which he or she has been retained can take only such urgent measures as are necessary for the protection of the person or property of the child.[53]

10–017

---

[49] art.12.

[50] art.8.

[51] art.9.

[52] art.7(1).

[53] art.7(3).

Which set of rules applies?

10–018   The inter-relationship of the Brussels IIa Regulation and the Hague Convention depends essentially on the habitual residence of the child. If the child is habitually resident in an EU Member State, the Regulation applies[54]; if the child is habitually resident in a non-EU Contracting State, the Convention will apply. In the case of a child abduction from one EU Member State to another, there is a special provision in the Regulation, considered below.[55] In the case of an abduction from a Member State to a non-EU Contracting State, art.7 of the Convention, considered above, applies.

The traditional rules

10–019   If no court of a Member State has jurisdiction pursuant to arts 8 to 13 of Regulation 2201/2003,[56] and the Hague Convention does not apply, the traditional rules of English law will govern jurisdiction. The same is true, it is thought, though the matter is not entirely clear, in intra-United Kingdom cases.

Inherent jurisdiction

10–020   The English courts still retain an inherent jurisdiction in children cases, although it is now very limited in scope. This jurisdiction is, as we have seen, derived from the sovereign as *parens patriae*. The sovereign accords protection to all who owe allegiance; and those who owe allegiance to the sovereign (and need his or her protection) include not only British citizens but also those who are present in England.

It was formerly asserted that the English court had jurisdiction if the child concerned is a British citizen, even though the child was not present in England.[57] This may have felt appropriate in the days of Empire but it now seems exorbitant. The courts have never entirely ruled out reliance on this basis for jurisdiction in truly exceptional cases, but their reluctance to exercise it means that it is all but obsolete.[58]

10–021   The High Court will also have jurisdiction in respect of a child if the child is present, or ordinarily or habitually resident, in England, even though the child is domiciled abroad and owns no property in England and even though guardians have already been appointed for the child by the courts of his or her domicile.[59]

---

[54]   See Brussels IIa Regulation, art.61 and the Convention, art.52.
[55]   See para.10–051.
[56]   See Brussels IIa Regulation, art.14 and Family Law Act 1986 s.2(1)(b).
[57]   *Hope v Hope* (1854) 4 D.M. & G. 328; *Re Willoughby* (1885) 30 Ch.D. 324; *Harben v Harben* [1957] 1 W.L.R. 261.
[58]   *Re P (GE) (An Infant)* [1965] Ch. 568, 582 at 587–588; *Al Habtoor v Fotheringham* [2001] EWCA Civ. 186 (C.A.); [2001] 1 F.L.R. 951; *Re A (A Child) (Wardship: Habitual Residence)* [2006] EWHC 3338 (Fam); [2007] 1 F.C.R. 390; *ES v AJ* [2010] EWHC 1113 (Fam).
[59]   *Johnstone v Beattie* (1843) 10 Cl. & F. 42; *Stuart v Marquis of Bute* (1861) 9 H.L.C. 440; *Nugent v Vetzera* (1866) L.R. 2 Eq. 704; *Re D* [1943] Ch. 305; *J v C* [1970] A.C. 668 at 720.

This basis of jurisdiction was re-affirmed by the House of Lords in *Re S (A Minor) (Custody: Habitual Residence)*[60]:

> S was the child of a Moroccan father and an Irish mother; the parents were not married. The day after the death of the mother in an English hospital, S was taken to Ireland by his maternal grandmother and an aunt. The next day, the father made S a ward of the English court. It was found as a matter of fact that the mother was habitually resident in England at the time of her death. S was therefore also habitually resident in England at that time.

The House of Lords held that the English courts had jurisdiction on the basis of the habitual residence of S, which continued despite the death of his mother, at the time the inherent jurisdiction was invoked. The House approved an earlier decision of the Court of Appeal[61] that the English courts had jurisdiction over a child (in that case, a stateless child) on the basis of its presence in England. In *Re S*, the child was an Irish citizen, but the House of Lords held that the English courts could exercise their jurisdiction even though, by the time of the order, the child had been removed from England and was now living in the country of its nationality. The courts have rejected domicile as an alternative basis for jurisdiction. In *Re P (GE) (An Infant)*[62] Russell L.J. said that "the whole trend of English authority on the parental jurisdiction of the Crown over infants bases the jurisdiction on protection as a corollary of allegiance in some shape or form. Domicile is an artificial concept which may well involve no possible connection with allegiance".

The Children Act 1989 and "section 8 orders"

Section 8 of the Children Act 1989 provides for the making of four types of what are known as "section 8" orders: residence orders, contact orders, prohibited steps orders and specific issue orders. The rules as to jurisdiction to grant s.8 orders are contained in Pt I of the Family Law Act 1986. English courts have jurisdiction to make such orders in four cases:

10–022

(a) in the course of proceedings for divorce, nullity of marriage or judicial separation ("the divorce basis");
(b) where the child was habitually resident in England ("the habitual residence basis");
(c) where the child was in England and the immediate intervention of the court was required for the child's protection ("the emergency basis"); and
(d) where the child was in England and was not habitually resident in any United Kingdom country ("the residual presence basis").[63]

To avoid conflicts of jurisdiction within the United Kingdom, priority would be given to jurisdiction on the divorce basis as against the habitual residence and residual presence bases. The emergency basis would always be available but

---

[60] [1998] A.C. 750.
[61] *Re P (GE) (An Infant)* [1965] Ch. 568.
[62] [1965] Ch. 568 at 592. cf. Lord Denning M.R. at p.583.
[63] Law Com. No.138 (1985), paras 4.1–4.92.

would be capable of being superseded by the exercise of jurisdiction on that or any other basis in another United Kingdom country.[64] The crucial date for determining priority is that of the application. So, for example, the court of the country of the child's habitual residence to which an application for an order has been made retains jurisdiction to consider that application even if divorce proceedings are later commenced in another part of the United Kingdom.[65] An order made by a court in any one part of the United Kingdom in reliance on these principles supersedes any earlier order made by any other such court.[66]

(i)   The divorce basis

10–023   The policy of the Family Law Act 1986 gives priority to the divorce basis.[67] The court can exercise these statutory powers even though the child is abroad.[68] This is in accordance with the general principle that the court has jurisdiction to make any ancillary orders in matrimonial proceedings whenever it has jurisdiction in the main suit.

Where the English court has jurisdiction to make an order under s.8 of the Children Act 1989 in matrimonial proceedings (and the Council Regulation does not apply), but considers that it would be more appropriate for such matters relating to the child to be determined outside England it may make an order which has the effect of disclaiming jurisdiction.[69] The effect of this provision within the United Kingdom is not entirely clear. The reference to the Council Regulation not applying cannot be read literally because even the residual jurisdiction under art.14 is created by the application of the Regulation; it presumably means that there is no jurisdiction under arts 8 to 13. However, as the purpose of the disclaimer provision within the United Kingdom is to allow a court in another part of the United Kingdom to exercise jurisdiction on the habitual residence basis, it is possible to argue that the court in the other part of the United Kingdom will have jurisdiction by virtue of art.8 (jurisdiction based on habitual residence) read with art.66(a) (habitual residence in composite states to be read as a reference to habitual residence in the relevant part of the state); accordingly, in that case the Council Regulation *would* apply.[70] At least to this extent, it is difficult to see how the Regulation principle of giving priority to the court of habitual residence can easily sit side by side with the Family Law Act 1986 giving priority to the court of matrimonial proceedings.

---

[64] *ibid.*, paras 4.91–4.115.

[65] *Dorward v Dorward*, [1994] S.C.L.R. 928.

[66] Family Law Act 1986 s.6(1)(2) (as amended by Children Act 1989 Sch.13, para.62).

[67] There are special provisions where the application is for judicial separation: Family Law Act 1986 s.2A (as substituted and amended).

[68] *Philips v Philips* (1944) 60 T.L.R. 395; *Harben v Harben* [1957] 1 W.L.R. 261; *Re P (GE) (An Infant)* [1965] Ch. 568, 581.

[69] Family Law Act 1986 s.2A(4) as amended. See *Re S (A Minor) (Application to Stay Proceedings)* [1995] 1 F.L.R. 1093 (child lived in Scotland; divorce proceedings in England a tactical ploy to defeat jurisdiction of Scottish court; English residence order application stayed); and *V v V* [2006] EWHC 3374 (Fam); [2007] 1 F.L.R. 1686 (the power to consider a residence order should be used sparingly where the issues had previously been resolved and jurisdiction over the child passed to another state).

[70] It is not possible to read art.15 as referring to the transfer of proceedings to a court in another part of the same Member State.

(ii)   The habitual residence and residual presence bases

English courts have jurisdiction to make a residence, contact, prohibited steps, or   **10–024**
specific issue order under the Children Act 1989 otherwise than in matrimonial
proceedings if the child is habitually resident in England, or is present in England
and not habitually resident in any part of the United Kingdom,[71] but this
jurisdiction is excluded if matrimonial proceedings in respect of the marriage of
the parents of the child concerned are continuing[72] in a court in Scotland or
Northern Ireland and that court has not declined jurisdiction in respect of
custody.[73]

In these cases jurisdiction rests on the "habitual residence" or "residual
presence" bases. If the "divorce basis" continues to take priority intra-United
Kingdom, the jurisdiction of the English courts is excluded if proceedings for
divorce, nullity of marriage or judicial separation are continuing in Scotland or
Northern Ireland unless the Scottish or Northern Ireland court has made an order
disclaiming its custody jurisdiction.[74]

Habitual residence is not defined in the 1986 Act but special provisions are
made in s.41. This deals with cases in which a child is removed from or retained
outside, or himself leaves or remains outside, the part of the United Kingdom in
which he or she was habitually resident before the change of residence, and this
takes place without the consent of all those persons having under the law of that
part of the United Kingdom the right to determine where the child is to reside, or
in contravention of an order of a court in any part of the United Kingdom.[75] In
such cases, the child is treated for the purposes of Pt I of the Act as continuing for
a period of one year to be habitually resident in the part of the United Kingdom in
which he or she was formerly habitually resident.[76] The effect is that in a case
where, for example, a child habitually resident with his mother in London is
taken to Belfast by his father without the mother's consent and becomes
habitually resident in Northern Ireland, the jurisdiction of the English court on the
habitual residence basis persists for a year after the abduction.[77] It has been held
that s.41 only applies where a child habitually resident in one part of the United
Kingdom becomes de facto habitually resident in another part; it has no
application where the child is removed to, but does not acquire a habitual
residence in that other part.[78]

---

[71] Family Law Act 1986 ss.2(1)(b)(ii) and 3(1).
[72] Proceedings that are stayed are not "continuing" proceedings, *Re B (Court's Jurisdiction)* [2004]
EWCA Civ. 681; [2004] 2 F.L.R. 741.
[73] Family Law Act 1986 ss.3(2), (3) as amended. However, Singer J. took jurisdiction to grant a
mirror order in *Re P (A Child: Mirror Orders)* [2000] 1 F.L.R. 435, where none of these criteria were
satisfied; see Beevers, (2000) 12 C.F.L.Q. 413.
[74] Family Law Act 1986 ss.3(2), (3) as amended.
[75] s.41(2).
[76] s.41(1).
[77] However, a residence order made in error of jurisdiction because of the continuance of habitual
residence for a period of one year is not a nullity: *Re B (Court's Jurisdiction)* [2004] EWCA Civ. 681;
[2004] 2 F.L.R. 741.
[78] *Re M (Minors) (Residence Order: Jurisdiction)* [1993] 1 F.L.R. 495. See Cretney, (1993) 109
L.Q.R. 538.

(iii)   The emergency basis

10–025   The High Court can also act in its inherent jurisdiction with respect to children and make an order as to the care or education of, or contact with, a child if the child concerned is present in England and the court considers that the immediate exercise of its powers is necessary for his or her protection.[79]

Power to stay proceedings

10–026   The English courts have a broad power to stay proceedings when the matter is being or could more appropriately be litigated in the court of another country.[80] The courts apply principles similar to those developed in the case of matrimonial proceedings in *De Dampierre v De Dampierre*.[81] An illustration is provided by *M v B (Child: Jurisdiction)*[82]:

> Both parents were United States citizens and the child was born in Texas. They came to England only because of the father's posting as part of his duties in the US Air Force. The parents separated, father and child returning to the United States. The mother commenced proceedings in England at a time when the child was with her under agreed shared custody arrangements, but took no steps to take those proceedings forward. The father began proceedings in a US court. The court recognised that whatever forum dealt with the matter, one parent would face inconvenience and expense. The English proceedings were stayed: the case was essentially about an American family and was best dealt with there.

It has been held that in these cases the welfare of the child is important but not paramount.[83]

Removal of child from England

10–027   Where a residence order under the Children Act 1989 is in force with respect to a child, no person may remove the child from the United Kingdom without either the written consent of every person who has parental responsibility for the child or the leave of the court.[84] This does not prevent the removal of a child, for a period of less than one month, by the person in whose favour the residence order is made.[85] A court making a residence order may grant leave for the removal of the child from the jurisdiction, and may do so generally[86] or for specified purposes[87] such as a holiday to get to know other members of the child's family.[88]

---

[79]   Family Law Act 1986 ss.1(1)(d) as amended.
[80]   Family Law Act 1986 s.5(2) as amended.
[81]   [1988] A.C. 92; see para.9–024. See also *Re D (Stay of Children Act Proceedings)* [2003] EWHC 565 (Fam); [2003] 2 F.L.R 1159.
[82]   [1994] 2 F.L.R. 819.
[83]   *Re S (Residence Order: Forum Conveniens)* [1995] 1 F.L.R. 314; *M v M (Stay of Proceedings: Return of Children)* [2005] EWHC 1159 (Fam); [2006] 1 F.L.R. 138.
[84]   Children Act 1989 s.13(1).
[85]   s.13(2).
[86]   *Payne v Payne* [2001] EWCA Civ. 166.
[87]   s.13(3).
[88]   *Re S (Leave to Remove from Jurisdiction: Securing Return from Holiday)* [2001] 2 F.L.R. 507, in which it was held that a child has rights under the European Convention on Human Rights to know both sides of its family.

The principles to be applied when considering whether to grant permission for a child to be permanently removed from the jurisdiction are contained in the Court of Appeal's judgments in *Payne v Payne*.[89] The principles have been much debated internationally and criticised as giving too much weight to the wishes of the relocating parent,[90] but have repeatedly been re-asserted.[91] In *Payne v Payne*, Thorpe L.J. summarised the effect of the earlier cases:

> "Relocation cases have been consistently decided upon the application of the following two propositions: (a) the welfare of the child is the paramount consideration; and (b) refusing the primary carer's reasonable proposals for the relocation of her family life is likely to impact detrimentally on the welfare of her dependent children. Therefore her application to relocate will be granted unless the court concludes that it is incompatible with the welfare of the children."

The issue often arises when the mother wishes to return to her own country or enters into a new relationship and wishes to move with her new partner to start a new life away from England. If she is to have her wish, the father may lose all contact with his child; there is simply no easy solution. As Dame Elizabeth Butler-Sloss put it in *Payne v Payne*, the welfare of young children is best met by bringing them up in a happy, secure family atmosphere. Their happiness and security, after the creation of a new family unit, will depend on becoming members of the new family. So, reasonable arrangements made by the mother or stepfather to relocate should not in principle be frustrated, since it would be likely to have an adverse effect upon the new family.[92]

The status of *Payne v Payne* was, however, clarified, and perhaps adjusted, by the Court of Appeal in *MK v CK*.[93] In that case Thorpe L.J. emphasised that the only principle to be extracted from *Payne v Payne* was the principle that the welfare of the child is paramount. All the rest was guidance as to factors to be weighed in search of the welfare paramountcy, which rendered the outcome of cases more predictable. *Payne v Payne* was also limited to cases in which one person, typically the mother, was the primary and virtually sole carer. Where there were two equally committed carers, one sought to relocate internationally, the judge should exercise the discretion to grant or refuse by applying the statutory checklist in s.1(3) of the Children Act 1989.[94]

Where the foreign country is one the legal system of which might not respect the rights of the parent remaining in England, great care will be taken before the court gives permission.[95] In cases involving countries following Islamic   **10–028**

---

[89] [2001] EWCA Civ. 166; [2001] 2 F.L.R. 1052.

[90] See Hayes, (2006) 18 C.F.L.Q. 351.

[91] For recent examples, see *Re G (Leave to Remove)* [2011] EWCA Civ 1497; [2008] 1 F.L.R. 1587; *Re D (A Child)* [2010] EWCA Civ 915; *Re W (Relocation; Removal from Jurisdiction)* [2011] EWCA Civ 345; [2011] 2 F.L.R. 409.

[92] For the special problems where siblings are involved, see *Re S (Relocation: Interests of Siblings)* [2011] EWCA Civ 454; [2011] 2 F.L.R. 678.

[93] [2011] EWCA Civ 293; [2011] 3 F.C.R. 111.

[94] *Re Y (leave to remove from jurisdiction)* [2004] 2 F.L.R. 330; *C v C (International Relocation: Shared Care Arrangement)* [2011] EWHC 335 (Fam).

[95] In the case of a country not party to the Hague Abduction Convention, expert evidence of the foreign law may be insisted upon: *Re M (Removal from Jurisdiction: Adjournment)* [2010] EWCA Civ 888; [2011] 1 F.L.R. 1943 (proposed holiday in Cameroon).

principles, the courts have sometimes required a notarised agreement to return the child backed by an order of the courts of the foreign country,[96] or a sworn declaration before a Sharia judge[97]; in the absence of such safeguards, permission may be refused.[98]

An order restricting the removal from the jurisdiction of a child who is still under 16 has effect in each part of the United Kingdom other than the part in which it was made, as if it had been made by the appropriate court in that other part. If it prohibits the removal of a child to a particular part, e.g., England, it has the effect in England of prohibiting the further removal of the child from England except to a place to which he or she could be moved consistently with the order.[99]

CHOICE OF LAW

10–029   Traditionally, an English court seeking to resolve issues concerning children applies English domestic law. This is qualified where an international convention so requires. Although the Brussels IIa Regulation contains no choice of law rules, the 1996 Hague Convention does. Article 15 provides that in exercising their jurisdiction under the Convention, the authorities of the Contracting States shall apply their own law. The implementing legislation in England applies the same rule when the court takes jurisdiction under the Regulation.[100] As the Explanatory Report to the Convention observes,[101] the principal argument which can be made in support of this rule is that it facilitates the task of the authority which has taken jurisdiction since it will thus apply the law which it knows best. To require the authority exercising jurisdiction in all circumstances to apply the law of the state of the child's habitual residence would have uselessly complicated the protection of the child. However, in so far as the protection of the person or the property of the child requires, the authority seised of the case may exceptionally apply or take into consideration the law of another State with which the situation has a substantial connection.[102]

The attribution or extinction of parental responsibility by operation of law, without the intervention of a judicial or administrative authority, is governed by the law of the State of the habitual residence of the child.[103] A change in the child's habitual residence does not affect existing parental responsibility but the law of the State of the new habitual residence may give parental responsibility by operation of law to a person who does not already have such responsibility.[104]

---

[96] *Re T (Staying Contact in Non-Convention Country)* [1999] 1 F.L.R. 262.
[97] *Re A (Security for Return to Jurisdiction)* [1999] 2 F.L.R. 1.
[98] As in *Re K (A Minor) (Removal from the Jurisdiction: Practice)* [1999] 2 F.L.R. 1084.
[99] Family Law Act 1986 s.36.
[100] Parental Responsibility and Measures for the Protection of Children (International Obligations) (England and Wales and Northern Ireland) Regulations 2010 (SI 2010/1898) reg.7.
[101] para.86.
[102] Convention, art.15(2).
[103] art.16(1).
[104] art.16(2)(3).

Similarly, the exercise of parental responsibility is governed by the law of the State of the child's habitual residence; if the child's habitual residence changes, it is governed by the law of the State of the new habitual residence.[105]

EFFECT OF FOREIGN ORDERS IN ENGLAND

European orders

The Brussels IIa Regulation provides that any judgment given by the courts of a Member State of the European Union[106] is to be recognised in the other Member States without any special procedure being required.[107] Any interested party may apply for recognition and enforcement in one Member State of a judgment on parental responsibility given by the courts of another Member State.[108]

Article 23 lists the grounds under which a court must refuse to recognise a judgment given in another Member State: if it is manifestly contrary to public policy taking into account the best interests of the child; if it was given, except in cases of urgency, without the child having been given the opportunity to be heard, in violation of fundamental principles of procedure of the Member State in which recognition is sought; if it was given in default of appearance of a party who was not served with the initiating document or not served in time to arrange a defence unless that person has accepted the judgment unequivocally; if a person with parental responsibility had not been given the opportunity to be heard; if it is irreconcilable with another judgment; or if art.56 had not been complied with where the court places a child in another Member State. The jurisdiction of the court of the Member State of origin may not be reviewed,[109] and under no circumstances may a judgment be reviewed as to its substance.[110]

In order for a judgment of another Member State to be enforced in a part of the United Kingdom, it must be an enforceable judgment in the Member State of origin and registered for enforcement in the relevant part of the UK.[111] The grounds for refusal of enforcement are the same as for refusal of recognition.[112] The grounds remain the same, but their application may differ: in a case under the original Brussels II Regulation, a court found that, since it was possible for facts to change between the two stages, what was not manifestly contrary to public policy at recognition stage could be so at enforcement stage.[113]

The Brussels IIa Regulation dispenses with this procedure in two types of cases: the return of a child following an abduction[114] and the recognition and enforcement of access rights. One of the main concerns of the Regulation is to ensure that the child continues to benefit from access to the non-custodial parent

10–030

10–031

---

[105] art.17.
[106] Except Denmark.
[107] art.21(1).
[108] art.21(3).
[109] art.24. See Case C-195/08 PPU *Inga Rinau* [2008] E.C.R. I-5271; [2009] Fam. 51.
[110] art.26.
[111] art.28(2).
[112] art.31(2).
[113] *X v Y* [2003] EWHC 2974 (Fam); [2004] 1 F.L.R. 582.
[114] See below para.10–051.

even where they live in different Member States. Therefore, holders of access rights may enforce them directly on production of a certificate issued by the court of origin.[115] Rights of access include in particular the right to take a child to a place other than his or her habitual residence for a limited period of time.[116] The *Practice Guide* makes it clear that access rights are a matter for national law and, therefore, may be held by the non-custodial parent, or other family members such as grandparents.[117]

Orders from Contracting States to the 1996 Hague Convention

10–032 Similarly, art.23 of the Hague Convention of 1996 provides that the measures taken by the authorities of a Contracting State shall be recognised by operation of law in all other Contracting States.

Recognition may however be refused if the relevant authority did not have jurisdiction under the rules in Chapter II of the Convention; if the measure was taken, except in a case of urgency, in the context of a judicial or administrative proceeding, without the child having been provided the opportunity to be heard, in violation of fundamental principles of procedure of the requested State; on the request of any person claiming that the measure infringes his or her parental responsibility, if such measure was taken, except in a case of urgency, without such person having been given an opportunity to be heard; if such recognition is manifestly contrary to public policy of the requested State, taking into account the best interests of the child; if the measure is incompatible with a later measure taken in the non-Contracting State of the habitual residence of the child, where this later measure fulfils the requirements for recognition in the requested State; or if in the case of the proposed transfer of the child to foster or institutional care in another state, the special procedure in art.33 of the Convention was not followed.

Orders from other states

10–033 A custody order made by a foreign court does not prevent the English court from making such custody orders in England with respect to the child as, having regard to the child's welfare, it thinks fit.[118] A striking illustration of this principle is afforded by *McKee v McKee*,[119] decided by the Privy Council:

> A husband and wife, American citizens resident in the United States, separated and agreed that neither should remove their minor son out of the United States without the written consent of the other. In 1945, in divorce proceedings in California, custody of the boy was awarded to the mother, and the father was allowed access. At that time the boy was living with the father under a previous custody order of the Californian court. On Christmas Eve 1946, when he heard that his last appeal against the custody order had failed, the father, in breach of his

---

[115] art.41.
[116] art.2(10).
[117] At p.24.
[118] *J v C* [1970] A.C. 668 at 700 per Lord Guest; *Re B's Settlement* [1940] Ch. 54; *McKee v McKee* [1951] A.C. 352; *Re Kernot* [1965] Ch. 217; *Re T (an Infant)* [1969] 1 W.L.R. 1608; *Re R. (Minors)* (1981) 2 F.L.R. 416.
[119] [1951] A.C. 352.

agreement and without the knowledge or consent of the mother, took the boy to Ontario and settled with him there. The mother then began habeas corpus proceedings in Ontario. In 1947, after a hearing lasting 11 days, the Ontario judge awarded the custody of the boy to the father. His decision was affirmed by a majority of the Ontario Court of Appeal, reversed by a majority of the Supreme Court of Canada, but restored by the Privy Council.

The entire process of litigation in *McKee v McKee* took many years, itself a matter for concern; and the end result did not produce clarity in the law. All that was decided was that a foreign custody order did not prevent the courts of Ontario from reviewing the matter, applying their understanding of the welfare of the child; but it was left open to the court to do so by way of a full review of the merits or in a more summary fashion, returning the child promptly where that seemed best.

In declining to be bound by foreign custody orders, English courts are prompted **10–034** by two considerations. The first is that a custody order by its nature is not final and is at all times subject to review by the court that made it. The second is that under the Children Act 1989 the welfare of the child is the first and paramount consideration.

This has been interpreted to apply not only to domestic English cases, but also to cases involving a previous custody order made by a foreign court. This approach has disadvantages: it can create uncertainty, and so instability, in the life of a child, and it can encourage litigation as a parent, denied custody by a foreign court, seeks a more favourable decision in England. A different approach is gaining support in international conventions and EU law, and the Family Law Act 1986 provides for the recognition in each part of the United Kingdom of custody orders made in any other part of the United Kingdom and for machinery for their registration and enforcement.[120] In cases not covered by these provisions, the weight to be given to a foreign custody order in England must depend on the circumstances of the case. An order made very recently, where no relevant change of circumstances is being alleged, will carry great weight.[121] Its persuasive effect is diminished by the passage of time and by a significant change in circumstances, for example the removal of the child to another country.[122] The effect of the foreign order will be weakest when it was made many years ago and has since been modified by consent and the child has nearly attained majority and so can make a personal decision as to with which parent he or she wishes to live.[123]

INTERNATIONAL CHILD ABDUCTION

The courts treat international abduction[124] (or "kidnapping") cases as a special **10–035** category, or at least one in which the special circumstances have a strong influence on the manner in which the welfare principle is to be applied. In many

---

[120] s.25 (as amended).
[121] *McKee v McKee* [1951] A.C. 352 at 364; *Re H (Infants)* [1966] 1 W.L.R. 381 at 399.
[122] *Re T (An Infant)* [1969] 1 W.L.R. 1608.
[123] *ibid.*
[124] See generally Lowe, Everall and Nicholls, *International Movement of Children* (Jordan Publishing Ltd, Bristol, 2004).

cases the kidnapping is in defiance of a custody order made by a foreign court,[125] but the same principles apply to any unilateral kidnapping of a child by one parent from the other.

The time factor is particularly important in kidnapping cases: a full consideration of the merits of the case may take a long time, since much of the evidence may have to come from abroad, and during that time the child may develop roots in England, a fact which will strengthen the claim of the kidnapper and threaten a grave injustice to the innocent parent. To minimise this risk, the English courts have been prepared to make orders for the peremptory return of a kidnapped child without making a full examination of the merits of the dispute.[126] Decisions of the European Court of Human Rights, made in the context of the Hague Abduction Convention and considered below,[127] have placed a question mark against that practice.

Judicial statements as to how this power to make a peremptory order should be exercised reveal a number of shifts of emphasis. At one time it was held that a peremptory order should not be made unless the court was satisfied beyond reasonable doubt that to do so would inflict serious harm on the child, but following the emphatic assertion of the welfare of the child as the first and paramount consideration by the House of Lords in *J v C*,[128] the Court of Appeal held that the principles to be applied in considering the making of a peremptory order were exactly the same as in all other decisions relating to the welfare of children.[129] The courts take into account the psychological damage to the child caused by a sudden removal from a familiar environment, at a time when his or her family life was disrupted; but also the risk of harm to the child if he or she were returned. For a period of time, the Court of Appeal held that decisions in international abduction cases should reflect the principles of the Hague Convention on the Civil Aspects of Child Abduction, even if the foreign country concerned were not a party to the Convention.[130] The normal result of applying those principles was that the child must be returned to the country of habitual residence; but subsequently the courts have now recognised that where the country concerned is not a Convention country, each decision must be based on the welfare principle.[131] Baroness Hale in the House of Lords case *Re J (A Child) (Custody Rights: Jurisdiction)*, confirming the paramountcy of the welfare of the

---

[125] For a case concerning contempt of court proceedings where a father defied the English court's order to return the child to England, see: *Re A (A Child)* [2008] EWCA Civ. 1138.

[126] *Re H (Infants)* [1966] 1 W.L.R. 381; *Re E. (D.) (An Infant)* [1967] Ch. 287 at 761; *Re C. (Minors)* [1978] Fam. 105. That the court does have the power to return the child immediately without a full examination of the merits was confirmed by the House of Lords in *Re J (A Child) (Custody Rights: Jurisdiction)* [2005] UKHL 40; [2006] 1 A.C. 80.

[127] See para.10–049.

[128] [1970] A.C. 688 (not an abduction case).

[129] *Re L (Minors)* [1974] 1 W.L.R. 250; *Re C (Minors)* [1978] Fam. 105; *Re R (Minors)* (1981) 2 F.L.R. 416.

[130] *G v G* [1991] 2 F.L.R. 506 (decided in May 1989); *Re F (A Minor) (Abduction: Custody Rights)* [1991] Fam. 25; *Re S (Minors) (Abduction)* [1993] 1 F.C.R. 789; *Re S (Minors) (Abduction)* [1994] 1 F.L.R. 6; *Re M (Abduction: Non-Convention Country)* [1995] 1 F.L.R. 89.

[131] *D v D (Child Abduction)* [1994] 1 F.L.R. 137; *Re P (A Minor) (Abduction: Non-Convention Country)* [1997] Fam. 45; *Re JA (Child Abduction: Non-Convention Country)* [1998] 1 F.L.R 231; *B v El-B (Abduction: Sharia Law: Welfare of Child)* [2003] 1 F.L.R. 811; McClean and Beevers (1995) 7 Ch. & F.L.Q. 128; *Re J. (A Child)* [2005] UKHL 40.

individual child, stated that "[t]he most one can say, in my view, is that the judge may find it convenient to start from the proposition that it is likely to be better for a child to return to his home country for any disputes about his future to be decided there. A case against his doing so has to be made. But the weight to be given to that proposition will vary enormously from case to case."[132]

In exercising this discretion, the English court will examine whether the courts of the country to which a child may be returned would apply the welfare principle. Differently constituted Courts of Appeal have taken opposite approaches when considering the welfare of a child from a very different legal system. In *Re JA (Child Abduction: Non-Convention Country)*,[133] Ward L.J. held that it was an abdication of responsibility and an abnegation of the duty of the English court to surrender the determination of the child's future to a foreign court whose regime may be inimical to the child's welfare. On that other hand, Thorpe L.J. in *Osman v Elasha (Abduction: Non-Convention Country)*[134] was of the opinion that "[w]hat constitutes the welfare of the child must be subject to the cultural background and expectations of the jurisdiction striving to achieve it." The House of Lords, preferring the approach taken by Ward L.J., has confirmed[135] that differences between legal systems cannot be irrelevant but that their relevance will depend on the facts of each individual case.[136] If the foreign court must follow the father's wishes rather than approach the mother's application with an open mind, then the English court must consider whether it is in the interests of the child for the dispute to be heard in the foreign court.

In cases where the abductor argues that, on return, the children would be taken **10–036** from her or she would be subject to criminal proceedings, the courts have attempted to safeguard the best interests of the child and the rights of the returning parent by requiring certain undertakings to be put in place before the return is effected.[137] In *Re S (Child Abduction: Asylum Appeal)*[138] two children were returned to India even though their mother was appealing against a refusal of asylum decision on the grounds that she was being persecuted by the father. Bennett J. accepted the father's undertakings that he would not institute any criminal proceedings against the mother, nor remove the children from the mother's care, would provide financially for her and the children, and undertake not to molest them.[139] Although accepting that the undertakings were not enforceable, the judge said: "[t]hey provide, in my judgment, if adhered to, proper and adequate protection and support, including financial support for the

---

[132] [2005] UKHL 40; [2006] 1 A.C. 80, at para.32.

[133] [1998] 1 F.L.R. 231.

[134] [2000] Fam 62. See also *Al Habtoor v Fotheringham* [2001] EWCA Civ 186; [2001] 1 F.L.R. 951; *Re S (Child Abduction: Asylum Appeal)*, [2002] EWHC 816; [2002] 2 F.L.R. 437; *B v El-B (Abduction: Sharia Law: Welfare of Child)* [2003] 1 F.L.R. 811; Beevers, [2003/4] Contemporary Issues in Law 302.

[135] *Re J (A Child) (Custody Rights: Jurisdiction)* [2005] UKHL 40; [2006] 1 A.C. 80.

[136] See, for example, *Re H (Abduction: Dominica: Corporal Punishment)* [2006] EWHC 199 (Fam); [2006] 2 F.L.R. 314 where the country concerned condoned treating children with physical violence.

[137] *Re Z (Abduction: Non-Convention Country)* [1999] 1 F.L.R. 1270; *Re S (Child Abduction: Asylum Appeal)* [2002] EWHC 816; [2002] 2 F.L.R. 437; *Re H (Child Abduction: Mother's Asylum)* [2003] EWHC 1820 (Fam); [2003] 2 F.L.R. 1105.

[138] [2002] EWHC 816; [2002] 2 F.L.R. 437.

[139] *ibid.*, at para.71.

mother and the children."[140] Although the courts are conscious of the fact that undertakings are not enforceable,[141] and research has shown that they are often broken,[142] they are still probably the best way of safeguarding the children's and returning parent's interests in the circumstances.

International instruments

10–037   The Child Abduction and Custody Act 1985 gives the force of law in the United Kingdom to two international conventions concluded in 1980. The first is the Luxembourg Convention, a product of the Council of Europe; it is essentially a convention for the enforcement of custody orders. The second, the Hague Child Abduction Convention, drawn up by the Hague Conference on Private International Law, has as its main object the return of a child abducted across national boundaries to the State of its habitual residence. Each convention seeks to protect existing rights of custody and to discourage the international abduction of children in breach of those rights. In consequence, where a child so abducted is to be found in England and one of the conventions applies, the powers of the English courts to review the merits and to form their own judgment as to what best serves the welfare of the child are largely eliminated. The Brussels IIa Regulation takes precedence over both these Conventions in its sphere of operation,[143] in effect replacing the rules of the Luxembourg Convention and supplementing the Hague Convention within the European Union.

In January 2003, the President of the Family Division and the Chief Justice of Pakistan signed a UK–Pakistan Protocol[144] in an attempt to protect children from the harmful effects of child abduction. Although the courts have started to apply the protocol in UK–Pakistan cases,[145] the legal effect of the document is unclear.[146]

The European (Luxembourg) Convention

10–038   A European Convention on Recognition and Enforcement of Decisions Concerning Custody of Children and on the Restoration of Custody of Children was prepared under the auspices of the Council of Europe and signed in Luxembourg on 20 May 1980.[147] The 1985 Act gives effect to the provisions of

---

[140] *ibid.*, at para.92.

[141] *ReJA (Child Abduction: Non-Convention Country* [1998] 1 F.L.R. 231 at p.244C; *W and W v H (Child Abduction: Surrogacy) (No.2)* [2002] 2 FLR 252. cf. *U v U* [2010] EWHC 1179 (Fam); [2011] 1 F.L.R. 354 where the undertakings were thought enforceable.

[142] McClean, [1997] C.F.L.Q. 387. See also Beevers [2003/4] C.I.L. 303.

[143] Brussels IIa Regulation, art.60(d).

[144] [2003] Fam Law 199; "Guidance from the President's Office—Implementation of the UK–Pakistan Judicial Protocol on Child Contact and Abduction" (2004) 34 Fam L.J. 609.

[145] *A v A* (Unreported, February 2, 2004); Binns, (2004) 34 Fam L.J. 359. For an example of circumstances in which the Protocol will not apply see *Re H (Child Abduction: Mothers Asylum)* [2003] EWHC 1820 (Fam); [2003] 2 F.L.R. 11-05.

[146] See Young, (2003) 66 M.L.R. 823.

[147] For full text, see Cmnd. 8155 (1981); a partial text forms Sch.2 to the Child Abduction and Custody Act 1985. For commentary, see Jones (1980) 30 I.C.L.Q. 467.

the Convention dealing with the recognition and enforcement of decisions,[148] with certain omissions,[149] but not those dealing with abduction where the provisions of the later Hague Convention are preferred. The adoption of successive European Regulations and the expansion of the European Union means that the Convention now has very limited effect, and it is not examined further here.

The Hague Child Abduction Convention

A Convention on the Civil Aspects of International Child Abduction was prepared under the auspices of the Hague Conference on Private International Law and signed on October 25, 1980.[150] Part I of the Child Abduction and Custody Act 1985 gives effect to this Convention, which deals with custody rights arising in another Contracting State by operation of law or by reason of an agreement having legal effect as well with custody decisions of judicial or administrative authorities.[151] The Convention deals with cases of wrongful removal or retention of a child in breach of rights of custody, and operates on the basis of a semi-automatic return of the child to the country of his or her habitual residence. The effective operation of the Convention relies heavily on a system of Central Authorities established in each Contracting State. The Convention is much used and has given rise to a great mass of case-law, most decisions turning on the particular facts; only a few illustrative cases can be cited here.

10–039

As Baroness Hale and Lord Walker explained in *Re E (Children) (International Abduction)*[152]:

> "The first objective of the Convention is to deter either parent (or indeed anyone else) from taking the law into their own hands and pre-empting the result of any dispute between them about the future upbringing of their children. If an abduction does take place, the next objective is to restore the children as soon as possible to their home country, so that any dispute can be determined there. The left-behind parent should not be put to the trouble and expense of coming to the requested state in order for factual disputes to be resolved there. The abducting parent should not gain an unfair advantage by having that dispute determined in the place to which she has come. And there almost always is a factual dispute, if not about the primary care of the children, then certainly about where they should live, and in cases where domestic abuse is alleged, about whether those allegations are well-founded. Factual disputes of this nature are likely to be better able to be resolved in the country where the family had its home."

The procedure under the convention is that the Central Authority of the state to which the child has been wrongfully removed, or in which it is wrongfully retained, on receiving an application for the return of the child either directly

10–040

---

[148] Child Abduction and Custody Act 1985 s.12.
[149] art.8 of the original text of the Convention is omitted and arts 9 and 10 are modified in consequence of a reservation made by the UK under art.17; see Child Abduction and Custody Act 1985 s.12(2).
[150] For detailed analysis of the Convention see: Beaumont and McEleavy, *The Hague Convention on International Child Abduction* (Oxford University Press, Oxford, 1999); Lowe, Everall and Nicholls, *op. cit.*
[151] Convention, art.3.
[152] [2011] UKSC 27 at para.[8].

from a person, institution or body concerned or from another Central Authority,[153] must take or cause to be taken all appropriate measures in order to obtain the voluntary return of the child; failing an amicable settlement it must initiate,[154] or facilitate the institution of, proceedings with a view to obtaining an order for the return of the child. The competent authorities are to act expeditiously[155] in such proceedings, and where there has been wrongful removal[156] or retention must order the return of the child forthwith, unless certain grounds for refusal are made out.[157] Where one of these grounds is made out, the court's consideration of the child's future is guided by the welfare test, taking into account the overall purpose and structure of the Convention.[158] The policy of the Convention is to secure the swift return of the child. A heavy burden therefore rests upon an abducting parent who seeks to invoke one of the grounds for refusal. We must now examine some of the terms used in the convention.

Rights of custody

10–041 The phrase "rights of custody" has a Convention meaning which will not necessarily coincide with the meaning of that term in the domestic law of either of the countries concerned, but draws its definition from the definitions, structure and purposes of the Convention. The rights include rights relating to the care of the person of the child and, in particular, the right to determine the child's place of residence.[159] This last phrase will include, for example, the right of a parent who does not have custody of a child to give or refuse consent to the removal of the child from the jurisdiction by the custodian parent,[160] but not a mere right to be consulted and to express views.[161]

The rights of custody may be attributed to a person, an institution, or any body,[162] either jointly or alone. They must exist under the law of the state in

---

[153] Although an application can be made to the court directly, *HA v MB* [2007] EWHC 2016 (Fam) at para.21.
[154] For the conflict between the two aims of speedy return and amicable settlement see Armstrong, (2002) 51 I.C.L.Q. 427.
[155] Indeed damages have been awarded by the European Court of Human Rights where the delay was excessive, *Deak v Romania and the United Kingdom* [2008] E.C.H.R. 19055/05; [2008] 2 F.C.R. 303.
[156] The High Court has the power to make a declaration that the removal or retention of a child in another country is wrongful; Convention art.15; Child Abduction and Custody Act s.8; *Re L (Children) (Abduction Declaration)* [2001] 2 F.C.R. 1; *Re G (Child Abduction) (Unmarried Father: Rights of Custody)* [2002] EWHC 2219 (Fam); [2003] 1 W.L.R. 493.
[157] Convention, arts 7–12.
[158] The principles to be applied in undertaking that discretion were spelt out by the House of Lords in *Re M (Children) (Abduction: Rights of Custody)* [2007] UKHL 55; [2008] 1 A.C. 1288.
[159] Convention, art.5.
[160] *C v C (Abduction: Rights of Custody)* [1989] 1 W.L.R. 654; *Re P (A Child) (Abduction: Acquiescence)* [2004] EWCA Civ 971; [2005] Fam. 85; *Re F (Children) (Abduction: Rights of Custody)* [2008] EWHC 272 (Fam); [2008] Fam. 75; *Re D (A Child) (Abduction: Rights of Custody)* [2006] UKHL 51; [2007] 1 A.C. 619. See *Neulinger v Switzerland* [2009] ECHR 41615/07; [2011] 1 F.L.R. 122 (Grand Chamber) at paras 65–74.
[161] *Re V-B (Abduction: Custody Rights)* [1999] 2 F.L.R. 192; *Re D (A Child) (Abduction: Rights of Custody)* [2006] UKHL 51; [2007] 1 A.C. 619.
[162] This term will include a court in cases where the child has been made a ward of court (*Re J. (Abduction: Ward of Court)* [1989] Fam. 85) and cases in which the court is currently seised of a custody dispute concerning the child (*B v B (Child Abduction: Custody Rights)* [1993] Fam. 32; *Re H*

which the child was habitually resident immediately before the removal or retention where those rights were actually exercised at the time of removal or retention (or would have been but for the removal or retention).[163] The reference to rights held jointly is important: in most countries parents will be joint custodians of the child in the absence of any order or agreement to the contrary, and either will be able to take steps under the Convention in respect of wrongful removal or retention of the child by the other.

Article 3 of the Convention provides, therefore, that for the removal or retention to be wrongful, it should be in breach of rights of custody that exist under the law of the child's habitual residence immediately before the abduction. The term "law of habitual residence", however, includes that country's rules of private international law[164] and it may be that the rights of custody ultimately fall to be decided by the law of another country to which the child is connected by some other means such as nationality.[165]

10–042

In English law a person with "parental responsibility" in the terms of the Children Act 1989 is a person with "rights of custody" for the purposes of the Convention, for "parental responsibility" includes the right to determine where the child shall live. It would seem to follow that where an unmarried father has no parental responsibility (or its equivalent under the law of the relevant foreign country) the removal of the child by the mother cannot be wrongful, even if the father has had joint de facto custody.[166] However, where the child was not in the care of the custodial parent immediately before the abduction because that parent had entrusted the child to the other parent or a family member, the English courts have developed a species of "inchoate rights"[167] so that the carer's rights are protected rights for the purposes of the Convention. Moreover, a right of custody, or at least an inchoate right, was found to exist where the mother, through a letter from her solicitors, had previously assured the father that she would not remove the child from the jurisdiction.[168] Although the courts have developed a very flexible approach to "rights of custody" under the Convention, they have not yet

---

(Child Abduction: Rights of Custody) [2000] 2 All E.R. 1); but not cases of the mere issue of proceedings for a residence order, where there had been no service on the other party, Re C (Child Abduction) (Unmarried Father: Rights of Custody) [2002] EWHC 2219 (Fam); [2003] 1 W.L.R. 493.
[163] Convention, art.3. See also art.13(a). These rights are not suspended even though a parent in temporarily incapable of exercising full day-to-day rights because of being in prison; Re A (Rights of Custody: Abduction: Imprisonment) [2004] 1 F.L.R. 1.
[164] Perez-Vera, "Explanatory Report of the Hague Convention on the Civil Aspects of International Child Abduction" Actes et Documents of the XIVe Session, Volume III, 1982, 426 at para.70.
[165] Re JB (Child Abduction) (Rights of Custody: Spain) [2003] EWHC 2130; [2004] 1 F.L.R 796; cf Beevers & Pérez-Milla [2007] J.P.I.L. 1 and see Kennedy v Kennedy [2009] EWCA Civ 986; [2010] 1 F.L.R. 782.
[166] Re J (A Minor) (Abduction: Custody Rights) [1990] 2 A.C. 562.
[167] Re B (A Minor) (Abduction) [1994] 2 F.L.R. 249; Re O (Child Abduction: Custody Rights) [1997] 2 F.L.R. 702. See McClean, (1997) 9 Ch.&F.L.Q. 387; Practice Note (Hague Convention: Applications by Fathers without Parental Responsibility) [1998] 1 F.L.R. 491; Re F (Abduction: Unmarried Father: Sole Carer) [2002] EWHC 2896 (Fam); [2003] 1 F.L.R. 839. cf. the views of Baroness Hale of Richmond in Re D (A Child) (Abduction: Rights of Custody) [2006] UKHL 51; [2007] 1 A.C. 619.
[168] Re H (Child Abduction) (Unmarried Father: Rights of Custody) [2003] EWHC 492 (Fam); [2003] 2 F.L.R. 153.

reached the point where the unmarried father who is jointly caring for his child can rely on that de facto custody to give him rights of custody to be protected.[169]

Wrongful removal and wrongful retention

10–043 The Convention refers to "wrongful removal" or "wrongful retention", meaning in each case removal or retention out of the jurisdiction of the courts of the state of the child's habitual residence.[170] The contrast between the two phrases is between an act of removal which at once breaches custody rights, and a keeping of the child which only breaches those rights when it is continued beyond the limits of lawfulness in terms of time; a typical example of wrongful retention occurs when a child is not returned after an agreed period of access.[171] In each case the removal or retention is an event which occurs once and for all on a specific occasion; "removal" and "retention" are mutually exclusive concepts, and it is impossible for them to overlap, or for either of them to follow the other in the same case.[172] For the purposes of the Convention, "retention" is not a continuing state of affairs, but something which occurs when the child should have been returned to his or her custodians, or when the person with rights of custody refuses to agree to an extension of the child's stay in a place other than that of his or her habitual residence. "Retention" does not necessarily entail physical restraint of any sort; the act of applying for a court order preventing the return of the child may amount to wrongful retention,[173] as may a firm decision not to return the child even if made before the expiry of the period for which it had been agreed that the child should remain with the abducting parent.[174]

Grounds for refusing return:

(i) Non-exercise of rights, consent or acquiescence

10–044 The first ground for refusal is that the person, institution or body concerned was not actually exercising the custody rights at the time of removal or retention, or had consented to or subsequently acquiesced in the removal or retention.[175] In the structure of the Convention text, "consent"[176] is something which occurs at or before the time of removal or retention, in contrast to subsequent acquiescence.[177] Consent can be inferred from the dealings between the parties some time before

---

[169] For criticism of this situation see: *Hunter v Murrow (Abduction: Rights of Custody)* [2005] EWCA Civ. 976; [2005] 2 F.L.R. 1119; Beevers [2006] C.F.L.Q. 499.

[170] *Re H (Abduction: Custody Rights)* [1991] 2 A.C. 476.

[171] *ibid.*

[172] *Re H (Abduction: Custody Rights)* [1991] 2 A.C. 476; *Re S (A Minor) (Abduction)* [1991] 2 F.L.R. 1.

[173] *Re B (Minors) (Abduction) (No.2)* [1993] 1 F.L.R. 993; *Re AZ (A Minor) (Abduction: Acquiescence)* [1993] 1 F.L.R. 682.

[174] *Re S (Minors) (Child Abduction: Wrongful Retention)* [1994] Fam. 70.

[175] Convention, art.13(a).

[176] For a detailed consideration of "consent" see *Re P (A child) (abduction: acquiescence)* [2004] EWCA Civ. 971; [2005] 2 W.L.R. 201.

[177] *Re C (Abduction: Consent)* [1996] 1 F.L.R. 414; *Re M (Abduction) (Consent: Acquiescence)* [1999] 1 F.L.R. 171; *Re H (Children) (Abduction: Children's Objections)* [2004] EWHC 2111 (Fam).

the removal or retention, but the question is always: what was the position at the time of the removal or retention?[178] Apparent consent obtained by deception will be disregarded.[179]

"Acquiescence" refers to a subjective state of mind of the wronged parent in which he or she has accepted, "gone along with", the abduction. It is a pure question of fact, and the court seeks to infer the parent's actual subjective state of mind from outward and visible acts and statements; the burden of proof is on the abducting parent. The court will be slow to infer an intention to acquiesce from attempts to effect reconciliation or to reach an agreed voluntary return of the abducted child.[180] If, however, the wronged parent so conducts himself (for example, by signing an agreement as to the child's future or taking part in proceedings in the country to which the child has been abducted to resolve its long-term future) as to lead the abducting parent to believe that no return is to be insisted upon, the wronged parent cannot be heard to say that his or her actual intention was all along to claim the summary return of the child.[181] Acquiescence may also be based on the conditional agreement for the children to live in another jurisdiction as long as satisfactory contact is established.[182] Express words will not amount to acquiescence where they are spoken without knowledge of the possibility of the rights being enforced; but awareness in general terms will suffice, and there is no need to show that the party concerned was aware of, for example, the expeditious and effective enforcement machinery provided by the Convention.[183]

In *Re A (Minors) (Abduction: Custody Rights)*[184] a letter from a father in Australia saying that his child's removal to England was illegal but that he would not insist on his rights was held to constitute acquiescence despite its retraction when the father learned of the existence of the Hague Convention. The courts have retreated somewhat from that rigorous approach[185]; acquiescence for a very short period may be disregarded if it is clearly withdrawn before the abducting

[178] Compare *Zenel v Haddow* 1993 S.C. 612 and *Re P-J (Children) (Abduction: Habitual Residence: Consent)* [2009] EWCA Civ 588; [2010] 1 W.L.R. 1237.
[179] *Re B (A Minor) (Abduction)* [1994] 2 F.L.R. 249; *Re O (Abduction: Consent and Acquiescence)* [1997] 1 F.L.R. 924; *Re L (Abduction: Future Consent)* [2007] EWHC 2181 (Fam); [2008] 1 F.L.R. 914.
[180] *Re H (Minors) (Acquiescence)* [1998] A.C. 72 (rejecting the distinction drawn between "active" and passive" acquiescence in *Re A (Minors) (Abduction: Custody Rights)* [1992] Fam. 106). See McClean, (1997) 9 Ch.&F.L.Q. 387. For the effect of without prejudice negotiations, see *P v P (Abduction: Acquiescence)* [1998] 2 F.L.R. 835. The withdrawal of Hague Convention proceedings to facilitate negotiation will not give rise to acquiescence: *Re G (Children) (Abduction: Withdrawal of Proceedings, Acquiescence, and Habitual Residence)* [2007] EWHC 2807; [2008] 2 F.L.R. 351.
[181] *Re H (Minors) (Acquiescence)* [1998] A.C. 72, citing as an example *Re AZ (A Minor) (Abduction: Acquiescence)* [1993] 1 F.L.R. 682; *Re D (Abduction: Acquiescence)* [1998] 2 F.L.R. 335.
[182] *T v T* [2008] EWHC 1169 (Fam); [2008] 2 F.L.R 972.
[183] *Re A (Minors) (Abduction: Custody Rights)* [1992] Fam. 106; *Re AZ (A Minor) (Abduction: Acquiescence)* [1993] 1 F.L.R. 682; *Re B (Abduction: Acquiescence)* [1999] 2 F.L.R. 818.
[184] [1992] Fam. 106; note dissent by Balcombe L.J.
[185] See *Re S (A Minor) (Abduction)* [1991] 2 F.L.R. 1 (child removed; custodial parent demanded not return but access; held no acquiescence in removal); *Re A (Minors) (Abduction)* [1991] 2 F.L.R. 241 ("emollient statements" to abducting parent inconsistent with conduct; expeditious application for return; acquiescence not made out); *Re I. (Abduction: Acquiescence)* [1999] 1 F.L.R. 778 (negotiations not to be equated with acquiescence).

parent has done anything in reliance upon it.[186] Where inactivity, in the sense of failure to make an application for the return of the child for a period of time, is relied upon as amounting to acquiescence, the court will pay some attention to the subjective motives and reasons of the party concerned.[187] It will, for example, take into account the fact that the applicant had initially received erroneous legal advice,[188] and will examine whether in all the circumstances the failure promptly to commence proceedings does point to an acceptance of the situation.[189]

(ii)   Grave risk of physical or psychological harm; intolerable situations

10–045   The second ground of refusal, and the one most commonly relied on in practice, is that there is a grave risk that the child's return would expose him or her to physical or psychological harm or otherwise place the child in an intolerable situation.[190] In recent years, the majority of international child abductions have been by the child's primary carer, usually its mother; there is often a history of domestic violence.[191] In such cases, this ground of refusal becomes of even more than usual importance. The violence may not have been directed at the child, so it may not appear to be a case in which there is a grave risk that return would expose the child to physical harm, so the court faces the more difficult issues of "psychological harm" and that of placing the child in an "intolerable situation".

It is sometimes said that art.13(b) is to be restrictively interpreted, but the Supreme Court has said that there is no need for the article to be "narrowly construed", as by its very terms, it is of restricted application. The court ruled that the words of art.13 are quite plain and need no further elaboration or "gloss".[192]

The English courts have taken a rather strict line when faced with allegations of domestic violence where the child has been the bystander, insisting that the

---

[186] *Re R (Minors: Child Abduction)* [1995] 1 F.L.R. 716. Compare *Re CT (A Minor) (Abduction)* [1992] 2 F.C.R. 92 (parent invoked Convention; later indicated would not press for return; acquiescence established) with *Re B (Minors) (Abduction) (No.2)* [1993] 1 F.L.R. 993 (consent by applicant to procedural steps in respect of custody proceedings in country in which child retained held not to be acquiescence when application for return made on same day).

[187] *H v H (Abduction: Acquiescence)* [1996] 2 F.L.R. 570.

[188] *Re S (Minors) (Abduction: Acquiescence)* [1994] 1 F.L.R. 819. See also *Re R (Minors) (Abduction)* [1994] 1 F.L.R. 190 (four-month delay while awaiting outcome of proceedings in foreign court held not to amount to acquiescence); *Re H (Children) (Abduction: Children's Objections)* [2004] EWHC 2111 (Fam) where a 12-month delay was not held to be acquiescence in the circumstances; likewise an 18-month delay in *M v M* [2007] EWHC 1820 (Fam); [2007] Fam. Law 888 (although the case was overturned by the House of Lords on other grounds: *Re M (Children) (Abduction: Rights of Custody)* [2007] UKHL 55; [2007] 3 W.L.R. 975).

[189] *Re K (Abduction: Child's Objections)* [1995] 1 F.L.R. 977 (inactivity for six to seven months held on facts not to amount to acquiescence); *H v H (Abduction: Acquiescence)* [1996] 2 F.L.R. 570 (delay of five months, during which other proceedings, not involving a demand for the immediate return of the child, pursued; acquiescence established); *Re M (Abduction: Acquiescence)* [1996] 1 F.L.R. 315 (delay of 14 months; acquiescence made out) *Re B. (Abduction: Acquiescence)* [1999] 2 F.L.R. 818 (proceedings taken for contact, and only when that proved difficult was Convention invoked; acquiescence established).

[190] art.13(b).

[191] Lowe and Perry, (1999) 48 I.C.L.Q. 127; see *Re E (Children) (International Abduction)* [2011] UKSC 27 at [7].

[192] *Re E (Children) (International Abduction)* [2011] UKSC 27 at [31].

grave risk of harm must be to the child and not just to the returning parent,[193] and that parents should take their problems to the courts,[194] and seek the protection of the authorities,[195] of habitual residence rather than abduct their children. Moreover, requested authorities should trust in the capability of requesting states to protect the children on return, and where situations are particularly problematic, courts should insist on undertakings[196] that make a return feasible.[197]

The courts have recognised that some psychological harm to the child may be inherent in the very conflict which is before the court or might normally be expected to occur on the transfer of a child from one parent to another; the Convention envisages more substantial harm, a severe degree of harm hinted at by the later reference to the child being "otherwise... in an *intolerable* situation".[198] There must be "clear and compelling evidence of the grave risk of harm or other intolerability which must be measured as substantial and not trivial".[199]

The Supreme Court has commented on the working of art.13 and especially **10–046** art.13(b).[200] It emphasised that the burden of proof, on the ordinary balance of probabilities, lies with whoever opposes the child's return. There are, however, limitations involved in the summary nature of the Hague Convention process; it is rarely appropriate to hear oral evidence which could be tested in cross-examination. The risk to the child must be "grave", and not merely "real". Although the words "physical or psychological harm" are not qualified, they gain colour from the phrase "an intolerable situation". Every child had to put up with a certain amount of rough and tumble, discomfort and distress; it was part of growing up. But there were some things which it was not reasonable to expect a child to tolerate including, of course, physical or psychological abuse or neglect of the child him- or herself and also exposure to the harmful effects of seeing and hearing the physical or psychological abuse of his or her own parent. Article 13(b) is looking to the future: the situation as it would be if the child were to be returned forthwith to the home country. That situation depended crucially on the protective measures which could be put in place to secure that the child would not be called upon to face an intolerable situation when he or she gets home. The appropriate protective measures and their efficacy would obviously vary from case to case and from country to country.

Where there have been allegations of a risk of harm, the courts have adopted the practice in a number of cases of requiring the applicant, before return will be

---

[193] *K v K (Child Abduction)* [1998] 3 F.C.R. 207; *Re W (Abduction: Domestic Violence)* [2004] EWHC 1247; [2004] 2 F.L.R. 499.

[194] *N v N (Abduction: art.13 Defence)* [1995] 1 F.L.R. 107.

[195] *TB v JB (Abduction: Grave Risk of Harm)* [2001] 2 F.L.R. 515.

[196] See para.10–046, below.

[197] *N v N (Abduction: art.13 Defence)* [1995] 1 F.L.R. 107; *K v K (Child Abduction)* [1998] 3 F.C.R. 207; *Re H (Abduction: Grave Risk)* [2003] EWCA Civ. 355, [2003] 2 F.L.R 141; *Re W (Abduction: Domestic Violence)* [2004] EWHC 1247; [2004] 2 F.L.R. 499.

[198] *Re A (A Minor) (Abduction)* [1988] 1 F.L.R. 365; *C v C (Abduction: Rights of Custody)* [1989] 1 W.L.R. 654 at 664; *Re N (Minors) (Abduction)* [1991] 1 F.L.R. 413; *B v B (Abduction: Custody Rights)* [1993] Fam. 32.

[199] *Re C (Abduction: Grave Risk of Psychological Harm)* [1999] 1 F.L.R. 1145.

[200] *Re E (Children) (International Abduction)* [2011] UKSC 27 at [32]ff.

ordered, to accept conditions or to give undertakings, for example as to the maintenance and accommodation of the child and the abducting parent after their return.[201] Undertakings of this sort may have a clear tactical advantage to the parent seeking the return of the child, for they may effectively undermine any argument that the return of the child would expose it to a grave risk of harm.[202] It is not in itself an objection to this practice that the undertakings will be unenforceable,[203] but the court may investigate the likely attitude of the foreign court to the undertakings as part of its assessment of the risk of harm to the child if return is ordered.[204] There are, however, dangers in the practice of accepting undertakings of this sort. The practice can come close to qualifying the clear duty of the court to order the child's return; and the court "must be careful not to usurp or be thought to usurp the functions of the court of habitual residence".[205]

(iii)   The child's objections to return

10–047   A third ground for refusal in this type of case is that the child objects to being returned and has attained an age and a degree of maturity at which it is appropriate to take account of his or her views.[206] The child's age and maturity are first assessed; if it is judged appropriate to take the child's views into account, the court must then decide what weight to give to them in the light of the return policy of the Hague Convention other facts of the case,[207] and bearing in mind the possibility that the child could have been coached by the abducting parent.[208] There is no minimum age stipulation; each child will be looked at as an individual; so in *Re R (Child Abduction: Acquiescence)*[209] siblings of seven-and-a-half- and six years old were judged to be mature enough that their

---

[201] For examples of terms which may be agreed, see *Re W (Abduction: Domestic Violence)* [2004] EWHC 1247; [2004] 2 F.L.R. 499. For a case where undertakings were not considered sufficient to protect the child, see: *Re M (A Child)* [2007] EWCA Civ. 260; [2007] 3 F.C.R. 631.

[202] See the Australian case of *McOwan v McOwan* (1994) FLC 92–451 (M. had taken the child to England, claiming that F. was a violent alcoholic, who failed to support his family; F. undertook to provide home for sole use of M. and the child, and to allow issues to be raised in proceedings already pending before the Australian Family Court; on M.'s return to Australia, F. reneged on his promises on both counts); *Re J (Children) (Abduction: Child's Objections to Return)* [2004] EWCA Civ 428; [2004] 2 FLR 64 where previous undertakings had been breached.

[203] In *Re E (Children) (International Abduction)* [2011] UKSC 27 at [37] the Supreme Court urged the Hague Conference to consider whether machinery could be put in place to ensure that protective measures identified by the court in the requested state could be enforceable in the requesting state, for a temporary period at least, before the child was returned.

[204] *Re O (Child Abduction: Undertakings)* [1994] 2 F.L.R. 349.

[205] *Re M (Abduction: Undertakings)* [1995] 1 F.L.R. 1021; *Re K (Abduction: Psychological Harm)* [1995] 2 F.L.R. 550; McClean, (1997) 9 Ch.&F.L.Q. 387.

[206] Convention, art.13(2); *Re S (A Minor) (Abduction: Custody Rights)* [1993] Fam. 242; *Re J (Children) (Abduction: Child's Objections to Return)* [2004] EWCA Civ. 428; [2004] 2 F.L.R. 64; *Re H (Children) (Abduction: Children's Objections)* [2004] EWHC 2111. See generally, McEleavy [2008] I.C.L.Q. 230.

[207] *Re S (Minors) (Abduction: Acquiescence)* [1994] 1 F.L.R. 819 (describing the three stage approach: were the objections made out, was the child of an age and maturity, should the discretion not to return be exercised; an older child being returned against his wishes.)

[208] *Re P (Abduction: Minor's Views)* [1998] 2 F.L.R. 825.

[209] [1995] 1 F.L.R. 716; where despite the objections, their return was ordered.

objections gave the court discretion as to their return,[210] as was a girl of eight in *Re M (A Child) (Abduction: Child's Objections to Return)*.

Cases involving two or more siblings can present special problems. A rigorous approach to the application of the Convention in such cases has been adopted in a Canadian case.[211] In that case, the return of one child, a spina bifida sufferer, was refused but a step-sister returned despite evidence that the first child was suicidal at the thought of their separation. The court took the view that art.13 had to be applied to each child separately. Even on that approach, however, it may be possible to find that the return of one child without his or her sibling would place one or other in an intolerable situation, and English courts have reached such a conclusion.[212] However, in *Re HB (Abduction: Children's Objections)*[213] a finding that only one child strongly objected to being returned meant that both children were ordered to return on the grounds it is not usually advisable to separate siblings who are close in age and in their relationship to each other.

The issue as to whether a child should be made a party to the proceedings with separate legal representation was discussed in the judgment of Baroness Hale in *Re M (Children) (Abduction: Rights of Custody)*.[214] To order separate representation in all cases would send the wrong messages to children since they should not be given an exaggerated impression of the relevance and importance of their views, but it would not send the wrong messages to so order in settlement cases under art.12,[215] cases where the views of the child are particularly important. The question the judge should consider is whether separate representation would add enough to the understanding of the case to justify the intrusion, expense and delay that may result.

(iv)   Additional ground after 12 months

Where an application for the return of a child is made after the passage of one year from the date of the wrongful removal or retention, return may also be refused if it is demonstrated that the child is now settled in his or her new environment.[216] "Settled" is to be given its natural meaning, which includes an examination of the existing facts demonstrating the establishment of the child in a community and an environment,[217] and a consideration of the perceived stability of the position into the future. The "new" features of the situation are to be examined: they will include place, home, school, friends, activities and opportunities, but not as such the continuing relationship with the abducting

10–048

---

[210] [2007] EWCA Civ. 260; [2007] 2 F.L.R. 72.

[211] *Chalkley v Chalkley* (1995) 10 R.F.L. (4th) 442 (Man. C.A.); the Supreme Court of Canada refused leave to appeal: (1995) 11 R.F.L (4th) 376.

[212] *B v K (Child Abduction)* [1993] 1 F.C.R. 382 (disapproved but not on this point, *Re M (A Minor) (Child Abduction)* [1994] 1 F.L.R. 390).

[213] [1997] 1 F.L.R. 392 (order later set aside for other reasons: [1998] 1 F.L.R. 422); cf *Re W (Minors)* [2010] EWCA Civ 520.

[214] [2007] UKHL 55; [2008] 1 A.C. 1288 at para.57, endorsed as superseding earlier cases in *C v C* [2008] EWHC 517 (Fam); [2008] 2 F.L.R. 6.

[215] See below at para.10–048

[216] Convention, art.12.

[217] The meaning of these terms are considered in *Re C (A Child) (Child Abduction: Settlement)* [2006] EWHC 1229 (Fam); [2006] 2 F.L.R. 797.

parent.[218] It is not enough for the courts to consider only the physical characteristics of the settlement, but must also take into account the emotional and psychological elements.[219] A long delay in the proceedings will not of itself excuse compliance with the Convention but it may mean that its provisions designed to protect the best interests of the child by a return to the country of habitual residence would be rendered completely unworkable.[220] It is in this type of case that the views of the children concerned are of particular importance.[221]

Effect on the Hague practice of the European Convention on Human Rights

10–049   The emphasis on a swift return of the child to the more appropriate venue to resolve the underlying issues faced an unexpected challenge from the Grand Chamber of the European Court of Human Rights in *Neulinger v Switzerland*.[222] A mother removed the child from Israel to Switzerland. There was a history of difficulties between the parents, with Israeli social services finding that the father created a hostile environment at home, an atmosphere of verbal aggression and threats that terrorised the mother, such that maintaining a common home was harmful to the child. The father's application for the return of the child under the Hague Convention was rejected under art.13(b), the Swiss court finding that there was a grave risk that return would expose the child to physical or psychological harm, but the Swiss Federal Court ultimately allowed an appeal by the father, holding that art.13(b) was not satisfied. The father made an application, which he later withdrew, for enforcement of the return order and was no longer in contact with the Swiss authorities.

On an application by the mother the European Court of Human Rights considered art.8 of the European Convention which protects the right to respect for an individual's private and family life. There is to be no interference by a public authority with the exercise of this right except such as is in accordance with the law and is necessary in a democratic society in the interests of national security, public safety or the economic well-being of the country, for the prevention of disorder or crime, for the protection of health or morals, or for the protection of the rights and freedoms of others.

The Grand Chamber held that the decisive issue was whether a fair balance between the competing interests at stake – those of the child, of the two parents, and of public order – had been struck, within the margin of appreciation afforded to States in such matters, bearing in mind, however, that the child's best interests must be the primary consideration. There was held to a broad consensus in support of the idea that in all decisions concerning children, their best interests

---

[218] *Re N (Minors) (Abduction)* [1991] 1 F.L.R. 413 (where an inoperative fax machine in the Lord Chancellor's Department took the case over the 12-month limit).
[219] *Cannon v Cannon* [2004] EWCA Civ. 1330; [2005] 1 W.L.R. 32, where the mother abducted the child and managed to evade the authorities seeking her and the child for four years; the court held that where the parent engages in concealment and subterfuge it will be difficult for her to demonstrate that the child is settled.
[220] *Re D (A Child)(Abduction: Rights of Custody)* [2006] UKHL 51; [2007] 1 A.C. 619 at paras 4–5, where a child had been living in England for more than half his life.
[221] See above at para.10–047; *Re M (Children) (Abduction: Rights of Custody)* [2007] UKHL 55, [2007] 3 W.L.R. 975; cf Schuz [2008] C.F.L.Q. 64.·
[222] [2010] ECHR 41615/07; [2011] 1 F.L.R. 122. See Walker, (2010) 6 J.Priv.I.L. 649.

must be paramount. The child's interest comprised two limbs. On the one hand, it dictated that the child's ties with his or her family must be maintained, except in cases where the family has proved particularly unfit. It followed that family ties might only be severed in very exceptional circumstances and that everything must be done to preserve personal relations and, if and when appropriate, to "rebuild" the family. On the other hand, it was clearly also in the child's interest to ensure his or her development in a sound environment, and a parent cannot be entitled under art.8 to have such measures taken as would harm the child's health and development. This philosophy was declared to be inherent in the Hague Convention. The judgment of the Grand Chamber then contains a crucial passage:

> "138. It follows from Art.8 that a child's return cannot be ordered automatically or mechanically when the Hague Convention is applicable. The child's best interests, from a personal development perspective, will depend on a variety of individual circumstances, in particular his age and level of maturity, the presence or absence of his parents and his environment and experiences . . . . For that reason, those best interests must be assessed in each individual case. That task is primarily one for the domestic authorities, which often have the benefit of direct contact with the persons concerned. To that end they enjoy a certain margin of appreciation, which remains subject, however, to a European supervision whereby the Court reviews under the Convention the decisions that those authorities have taken in the exercise of that power . . .
> 139. In addition, the Court must ensure that the decision-making process leading to the adoption of the impugned measures by the domestic court was fair and allowed those concerned to present their case fully . . . To that end the Court must ascertain whether the domestic courts conducted an in-depth examination of the entire family situation and of a whole series of factors, in particular of a factual, emotional, psychological, material and medical nature, and made a balanced and reasonable assessment of the respective interests of each person, with a constant concern for determining what the best solution would be for the abducted child in the context of an application for his return to his country of origin."

On the facts, the Grand Chamber noted that the domestic courts and psychologists agreed that the child's return could only be envisaged with his mother, who was refusing to return to Israel. The question was seen as being "whether the forced return of the child accompanied by his mother, even though she seems to have ruled out this possibility, would represent a proportionate interference with the right of each of the applicants to respect for their family life". Relying in particular on events since the return order was made, the Grand Chamber was not convinced that it would be in the child's best interests for him to return to Israel. As to the mother, she would sustain a disproportionate interference with her right to respect for her family life if she were forced to return with her son to Israel. Consequently, there would be a violation of art.8 in respect of both mother and child if the decision ordering the second applicant's return to Israel were to be enforced.

The effect of *Neulinger* was examined by the Supreme Court in *Re E (Children)* **10–050** *(International Abduction)*.[223] Baroness Hale and Lord Walker in a joint judgment noted that *Neulinger* had been greeted with "concern, nay even consternation" in some quarters, because of its possible impact upon the application of the Hague Convention. The Supreme Court addressed the "best interests" issue, considering first art.3(1) of the UN Convention on the Rights of the Child, that "in all actions

---

[223] [2011] UKSC 27; [2012] 1 A.C. 144.

concerning children, whether undertaken by public or private social welfare institutions, courts of law, administrative authorities or legislative bodies, the best interests of the child shall be a primary consideration." However, Hague Convention proceedings were not proceedings in which the upbringing of the child was in issue; they were proceedings about where the child should be when that issue was decided.

The judgment explains the role of "best interests" in the Hague Convention. The Convention assumed that the best interests of the child will be served by a prompt return to the country where she is habitually resident. That assumption might be rebutted in the circumstances set out in arts 12 and 13; all of them are inspired by the best interests of the child. In that sense, the Hague Convention was designed with the best interests, not only of children generally, but also of the individual child concerned as a primary consideration.

Having quoted paragraphs 138 and 139 of the *Neulinger* judgment, the Supreme Court notes as follows[224]:

> "As the President of the Strasbourg court has acknowledged extra-judicially (in a paper given at the Franco-British-Irish Colloque on family law on May 14, 2011), it is possible to read para 139 of *Neulinger* as requiring national courts to abandon the swift, summary approach that the Hague Convention envisages and to move away from a restrictive interpretation of the art 13 exceptions to a thorough, free-standing assessment of the overall merits of the situation. But, he says:
>
>> 'that is over-broad – the statement is expressly made in the specific context of proceedings for the return of an abducted child. The logic of the Hague Convention is that a child who has been abducted should be returned to the jurisdiction best-placed to protect his interests and welfare, and it is only there that his situation should be reviewed in full.'
>
> *Neulinger* 'does not therefore signal a change of direction at Strasbourg in the area of child abduction'. The President has therefore gone as far as he reasonably could, extra-judicially, towards defusing the concern which has been generated by, in particular, para 139 of *Neulinger.*'[225]

The Supreme Court held that the violation of art.8 in *Neulinger* arose, not from the proper application of the Hague Convention, but from the effects of subsequent delay.[226] However, a later case in the European Court, *Šneersone v Italy,*[227] seemed to re-assert *Neulinger* without any qualification; as it arose under the Brussels IIa Regulation, it is considered below.

---

[224] para.[25].
[225] This assurance was welcomed by the 6th Special Commission of the Hague Conference in 2011; see para.49 of its conclusions and recommendations.
[226] para.[26].
[227] [2011] ECHR 14737/09. See also *Raban v Romania* [2011] ECHR 25437/08 (not a Hague Convention case).

The Brussels IIa Regulation and child abduction

In an attempt to further deter parental child abduction within the European Union, **10–051** the Brussels IIa Regulation provides that the Hague Child Abduction Convention will continue to be applicable but as supplemented by certain provisions that take precedence over the Convention[228] in cases of child abduction between Member States.[229]

The Regulation provides that where a child was habitually resident in a Member State immediately before a wrongful removal or retention,[230] the courts of that Member State will continue to have jurisdiction over the child until the child has acquired a habitual residence in another Member State and certain further requirements are met. It will be sufficient if every person, institution or other body having rights of custody has acquiesced in the removal or retention. Otherwise, the child must have resided in that other Member State for a period of at least one year after the person, institution, or other body having rights of custody has had or should have had knowledge of the whereabouts of the child and the child is settled in his or her new environment and at least one of the following conditions is met: (i) within that period of one year no request for return has been lodged before the competent authorities of the Member State where the child has been removed or is being retained; (ii) a request for return lodged by the holder of rights of custody has been withdrawn and no new request has been lodged within the one year time limit; (iii) a case before the court in the Member State where the child was habitually resident immediately before the wrongful removal or retention has been closed pursuant to art.11(7) (where no submissions have been made to challenge a non-return order made in the other Member State); (iv) a judgment on custody[231] that does not entail the return of the child has been issued by the courts of the Member State where the child was habitually resident immediately before the wrongful removal or retention.[232] It has been held that this continuing jurisdiction allows the court of origin to determine contact for the non-custodial parent or deal with matters under the Children Act 1989 or the inherent jurisdiction even if it does not order the child's return.[233]

When an application to the authority of a Member State is made by a person, institution or other body having rights of custody seeking the return of a child to

---

[228] Regulation art.60(e).

[229] For detailed explanation and criticism, see: McEleavy, [2005] J.P.I.L. 5; Lowe, [2004] I.F.L.J. 205; McEleavy, (2004) 53 I.C.L.Q. 503, asserting that the inclusion of these provisions is controversial since an equal number of States opposed European legislative intervention; Lowe, Everall & Nicholls, *The new Brussels II Regulation: a supplement to international movement of children*, (Jordan Publishing Ltd, Bristol, 2005); Lowe [2007] I.F.L. 182.

[230] Defined in art.2(11) of the Regulation in similar terms to art.3 of the Convention. See, however, Case 400/10 PPU *McB v E* (whether a child's removal is wrongful for the purposes of applying the Regulation is entirely dependent on the existence of rights of custody, conferred by the relevant national law.

[231] A final order, not merely an interim one: Case C-211/10 PPU *Povse v Alpago* [2010] 2 F.L.R . 1343.

[232] art.10.

[233] *HA v MB (Brussels II Revised: art.11(7) Application)* [2007] EWHC 2016 (Fam); [2008] 1 F.L.R. 289.

its Member State of habitual residence under the Hague Child Abduction Convention, art.11 of the Regulation sets out various supplementary and qualifying provisions. When applying arts 12 and 13 of the Convention (grounds for refusing return) the court must ensure that the child is given the opportunity to be heard unless this is inappropriate for reasons of age or maturity.[234] The court to which an application for return is made must act expeditiously and issue its judgment within six weeks from application except in exceptional circumstances,[235] a timescale that includes any appeal the original decision.[236]

10–052   A court cannot refuse to return a child unless the applicant has been given an opportunity to be heard,[237] nor on the basis of art.13(b) of the Convention (grave risk of physical or psychological harm, or placing the child in an intolerable situation) if it is established that adequate arrangements have been made to secure the protection of the child after return.[238] This ground-breaking provision reinforces the principles of the immediate return of the child by minimising the application of the art.13(b) defences. This means that even though the court of refuge believes the child to be in grave risk of danger if returned, the discretion not to return is removed if it can be established that there are adequate protective measures in place in the Member State of habitual residence.[239] It is questionable whether the concept of judicial comity and mutual trust has been taken one step too far. It is one thing for a State to have sophisticated protective mechanisms in place but quite another for a violent parent to comply with them.[240]

Where the court of the Member State to which the child has been abducted issues a non-return order pursuant to art.13 of the Convention,[241] that court must immediately transmit a copy of the order and all the relevant documents to the court or Central Authority of the Member State of the child's habitual residence.[242] The court or Central Authority of habitual residence will then notify the parties and invite them to make submissions to that court regarding custody of the child within three months of the date of notification.[243] If no submission is made within the three month period, the case will be considered closed. This provision precludes the Member State of refuge from assuming jurisdiction for

---

[234] art.11(2). Failure to hear the child will lead to a rehearing being ordered: *Re F* [2007] EWCA Civ 468; [2007] 2 F.L.R. 697.

[235] art.11(3); see *Re K (Rights of Custody: Spain)* [2009] EWHC 1066 (Fam); [2010] 1 F.L.R. 57.

[236] The *Practice Guide* at p.33 makes it clear that six weeks is a strict deadline and one possibility of adhering to the six weeks is for national law to preclude the possibility of an appeal.

[237] art.11(5). For a discussion as to possible methods of hearing the child, see *Re D (A Child) (Abduction: Rights of Custody)* [2006] UKHL 51; [2007] 1 A.C. 619 at para.60.

[238] art.11(4). However, see *Re D (A Child) (Abduction: Rights of Custody)* [2006] UKHL 51; [2007] 1 A.C. 619 at para.52 where adherence to this provision would have turned the Regulation into an instrument of harm itself.

[239] For a very difficult case under art.11(4) coupled with the potential for an art.11(8) order (see below), see *K v K* [2007] EWCA Civ. 533; [2007] 2 F.L.R. 996.

[240] For example, in 2003 a father applied under the Convention for the return of his children from Spain (SAP Baleares of April 23, 2003). The Spanish court found that the father had been imprisoned for domestic violence and was subject to an English non-molestation order, but that on release from prison he had gone to the mother's address and kicked down the front door, threatening the mother and children.

[241] Not under art.12.

[242] art.11(6).

[243] art.11(7).

substantive custody arrangements as soon as the non-return order is granted. Most importantly, the court of the child's habitual residence may make an order requiring the child to be returned, an order which is enforceable via the fast track system contained in art.42 of the Regulation, without the need for a declaration of enforceability and without any possibility of opposing its recognition. So the court of the child's habitual residence before the abduction has the final say. Such "trumping" orders seem out of line with the mutual trust and respect that the Regulation endeavours to engender between the authorities of Member States.[244]

Where the English court is considering making an order for return despite the non-return order in the state of refuge, it is exercising a welfare jurisidiction, the best interest of the child are paramount and a peremptory order can be made in appropriate circumstances.[245]

However, in this context issues arise similar to those in *Neulinger*, considered earlier. In *Šneersone v Italy*,[246] a child was wrongfully removed by its mother from Italy to Latvia. The Latvian court considered evidence from a psychologist that severance of contact between Marko and his mother could negatively affect the child's development and could even create neurotic problems and illnesses; it also received an assurance from the Italian Central Authority that if any of the circumstances mentioned in art.13(b) of the Hague Convention arose, Italy would be able to activate a wide-ranging child protection network which could ensure that Marko and his father received psychological help. The court refused to order the child's return, relying on art.13(b). The Latvian court noted art.11(4) of the Brussels IIa Regulation, precluding a return if it were established that adequate arrangements had been made to secure the protection of the child after his return; it held that as the mother could not afford to return to Italy, the arrangements would not protect the child from psychological harm.

The father applied to the Italian courts for an order under art.11 of the Regulation, proposing detailed arrangements which the court found satisfactory; it made the requested return order. The mother applied to the European Court of Human Rights alleging breach of art.8 of the European Convention. In the light of evidence that the child was suffering psychological stress and anxiety in connection with his potential return to Italy, the court held that the Italian court's order constituted an interference with the applicants' right to respect for family life. Such interference would be allowed where it was "necessary in a democratic society" within the meaning of art.8(2) of the European Convention. It noted that the Italian court had failed to address the risks that had been identified by the Latvian authorities, viewed the arrangements accepted by the Italian court as inadequate, and noted further that the Italian courts had not considered any alternative solutions for ensuring contact between Marko and his father. The court

10–053

---

[244] McEleavy, (2004) 53 I.C.L.Q. 503; for an alternative view, see Lowe, [2004] I.F.L.J. 205 at p.215.
[245] *M v T (Abduction: Brussels II Revised, art.11(7))* [2010] EWHC 1479 (Fam); [2010] 2 FLR 1685; *D v N* [2011] EWHC 471 (Fam); [2011] 2 F.L.R. 464; *AF v T (Brussels II Revised; art.11(7) Application)* [2011] EWHC 1315 (Fam); [2011] 2 F.L.R. 891.
[246] [2011] ECHR 14737/09. See also *Raban v Romania* [2011] ECHR 25437/08 (not a Hague Convention case).

concluded that the interference with the applicants' right to respect for their family life was not "necessary in a democratic society" and that art.8 had been violated.

STATUS: LEGITIMACY AND LEGITIMATION

10–054 Legitimacy is the status which a legitimate child acquires at the time of his or her birth. Legitimation means that a child who is illegitimate at the time of birth becomes legitimate by reason of subsequent events.

Legitimacy

10–055 Since the Family Law Reform Act 1987, the marital status of a person's parents at the time of his or her birth is of almost no relevance if the child is claiming to succeed to property under an English deed or will or intestacy. It might be thought that the whole question of legitimacy could be ignored in a modern textbook. But succession is not the only context in which the issue can arise.[247] It will be recalled that the domicile of dependency of a child depends on whether the child is legitimate or illegitimate; the status may be relevant under a particular deed or will if restrictive words are used; and the issue of legitimacy may be raised specifically in an action for a declaration as to status. That the issue is a live one can be seen from the attention paid to it in recent legislation on civil partnerships and assisted reproduction.[248]

There is also the situation in which the succession is governed by foreign law. This is the classic case of the incidental question,[249] much discussed by the jurists: should the legitimacy of the child be determined by the conflict rules of the forum, or by the conflict rules of the foreign *lex successionis?* There is no English authority on this question. One may hazard the guess that English courts would probably permit the foreign *lex successionis* to determine not only what classes of children were entitled to succeed, but also (if legitimacy were a necessary qualification under the foreign law) whether any individual was or was not legitimate, and what law governed that question.[250]

Recognition of the status

10–056 Here we are confronted not by the familiar question, what is the English conflict rule, but by a more fundamental question: is there an English conflict rule at all?

According to the first and oldest answer, a child is legitimate if (and only if) he or she is born or conceived in lawful wedlock, within a marriage which is valid by English rules of the conflict of laws. Until 1959, this was the traditional test of legitimacy in English domestic law, and the theory under discussion projects that

---

[247] For this reason the view of Welsh, (1947) 63 L.Q.R. 65, that the sole question is one of construction of words like "children" or "issue" in deeds, wills and statutes, cannot be accepted.

[248] Family Law Reform Act 1987 s.1, Legitimacy Act 1976 s.2A and Family Law Act 1986 s.56 all as inserted or amended by the Human Fertilisation and Embryology Act 2008 Sch.6.

[249] See below, para.18–016.

[250] See *Baindail v Baindail* [1946] P. 122, 127.

test into the conflict of laws. It follows from this approach that English law has no conflict rule for legitimacy, only a conflict rule for the validity of marriage.[251] This is supported by all the English reported cases before 1947, including two in the House of Lords.

In *Brook v Brook*[252]:

> A man and a woman, both domiciled in England, went through a ceremony of marriage in Denmark and immediately afterwards returned to England. The marriage was valid by Danish law but void by English domestic law because the woman was the sister of the man's deceased wife. A child of the marriage died intestate and unmarried, domiciled in England.

The House of Lords held that the marriage was void, that the child was illegitimate, and that his brothers and sisters could not succeed to his property, which went to the Crown as bona vacantia. The validity of the marriage was the only question discussed by the House of Lords.

In the famous case of *Shaw v Gould*[253]:

> A testator domiciled in England devised land in England on trust for the sons lawfully begotten of his great-niece Elizabeth Hickson, and bequeathed movables on trust for her children. Elizabeth, while domiciled in England, and aged 16, was induced by the fraud of Thomas Buxton (also domiciled in England) to go through a ceremony of marriage with him. The marriage was valid by English law, and at that time could only have been dissolved by private Act of Parliament; but it was never consummated, and Buxton was sent to prison for fraud. Some years later, Elizabeth fell in love with a law student, one John Shaw, who was eating his dinners at Gray's Inn. Her still-subsisting marriage with Buxton was of course an impediment to their union. So Buxton was persuaded to go to Scotland and stay there for 40 days so that Elizabeth could divorce him in the Court of Session. After the divorce Elizabeth married John Shaw, who was now domiciled in Scotland, lived with him in Scotland and had children by him.

The House of Lords held that these children were illegitimate, and could take neither the land nor the movables under the testator's will. The reason was that the marriage of their parents was void, because the Scottish divorce could not be recognised in England, since Buxton (and therefore Elizabeth) was domiciled in England.

It is the case that according to some systems of law, including now English domestic law, a child may be legitimate even though his parents were not, and could not be, validly married. This is the doctrine of "putative marriage", invented by the canon lawyers in order to preserve the legitimacy of the children when they multiplied the grounds on which a marriage could be annulled. From the canon law it passed into the law of most continental European countries, and a variation of it was first enacted in England in 1959. The current provision, section 1(1) of the 1976 Act[254] provides that the child of a void marriage[255] shall be treated as the legitimate child of his parents, if at the time of the insemination

10–057

---

[251] For the validity of marriage, see above, Ch.8
[252] (1861) 9 H.L.C. 193. See also *Re Paine* [1940] Ch. 46, another deceased wife's sister case, where only the wife was domiciled in England.
[253] (1868) L.R. 3 H.L. 55.
[254] As amended by the Family Law Reform Act 1987 ss.28(1), 34(5).
[255] Whether born before or after the commencement of the Act. But not a child born before the parents entered into the void marriage: *Re Spence* [1990] Ch. 652.

resulting in the birth or, where there was no such insemination, the child's conception (or at the time of the celebration of the marriage if later) both or either of his parents reasonably believed that the marriage was valid. This applies notwithstanding that the belief that the marriage was valid was due to a mistake as to law.[256] This enactment is retrospective as to status but not as to rights of succession.[257] Section 28 of the Family Law Reform Act 1987 developed the law further, inserting a new sub-section providing for a rebuttable presumption that one of the parties to a void marriage did reasonably believe at the relevant time that the marriage was valid.[258] Section 1(2) of the Legitimacy Act 1976 provides that the section only applies where the father of the child was domiciled in England at the time of the birth, or, if he died before the birth, was so domiciled immediately before his death.

Given this development, the approach based on *Shaw v Gould* cannot be expressed as a simple rule that the child must be born or conceived in lawful wedlock: the rule must be stated so as to include cases in which the parents are deemed to have been in lawful wedlock as a result of the statutory rules just set out.

10–058 Law can never be divorced from its social context, and the social attitude to questions of legitimacy has changed utterly since the 1860s when the House of Lords addressed the matter. Down to 1947 there appears to be no reported English case in which a child not born or conceived in lawful wedlock was held to be legitimate. But in *Re Bischoffsheim*[259] Romer J. adopted a new approach, in the following proposition:

> "Where succession to personal property depends on the legitimacy of the claimant, the status of legitimacy conferred on him by his domicile of origin (i.e. the domicile of his parents at his birth) will be recognised by our courts, and if that legitimacy be established, the validity of his parents' marriage should not be entertained as a relevant subject for investigation."

In that case a testator, presumably domiciled in England, gave a share of residue to the children of his granddaughter, Nesta. In 1917, Nesta, whose domicile of origin was England, was married in New York to the brother of her first husband, and in 1920 she had a son, Richard. The marriage was valid by the law of New York, but void by English domestic law. Romer J. was unable to hold that Nesta and her second husband had acquired a New York domicile by 1917, when they were married, but he did decide that they had acquired a New York domicile by 1920, when Richard was born: and he held that Richard was entitled to share with Nesta's children by her first marriage in the testator's residuary estate.

This decision seems difficult to reconcile with earlier authority,[260] and with *Shaw v Gould* itself. The facts involved two parents with the same domicile; if

---

[256] Legitimacy Act 1976 s.1(3) as inserted by Family Law Reform Act 1987 s.28(2). For children born by artificial insemination with the semen of a man other than the mother's husband, see Family Law Reform Act 1987 s.27.

[257] Legitimacy Act 1976 s.11(1) and Sch.1, paras 3, 4(1).

[258] Legitimacy Act 1976 s.1(4) as inserted by Family Law Reform Act 1987 s.28(2). This presumption applies only in relation to a child born after April 4, 1988, the date of the coming into force of that section.

[259] [1948] Ch. 79 at 92; approved by the Privy Council in *Bamgbose v Daniel* [1955] A.C. 107 at 120.

[260] *Re Paine* [1940] Ch. 46, which was not cited.

their domiciles differed, then the case would be caught in a vicious circle: a child's domicile of origin is that of its father if the child is legitimate and that of his mother if illegitimate; and the legitimacy of the child cannot depend on the law of its domicile of origin if that depends on its legitimacy. There were previous dicta favouring reliance on the child's domicile of origin[261]: they were all delivered in cases on legitimation by subsequent marriage, not legitimacy itself.

The question arose again in *Green v Alexander*[262]:

> The 13th Duke of Manchester went through a ceremony of marriage in California with a woman domiciled in that State in May 1993, a week before the birth of the couple's son; a daughter was born in 1999. His Grace had not mentioned the fact that he was still married to another woman, whom he had married in Australia, so the Californian marriage was void for bigamy. The children were held to be legitimate.

The second wife of course thought her marriage valid, so that the doctrine of putative marriage in the Legitimacy Act 1959 would have applied, provided the Duke was domiciled in England at the relevant time. That issue was not resolved, but the court noted that by the domestic law of all possible domiciles (England, Australia and California) the children would be legitimate. The court considered that the children were legitimate without reliance on that doctrine. *Re Bischoffsheim* was followed; and the *dicta* in the legitimation case of *Re Goodman's Trusts*[263] were held to be equally applicable to legitimacy.

There was the difficult question of *Shaw v Gould*. Floyd J. noted that that case merely addressed the question of the recognition of the Scottish divorce. He asserted, incorrectly, that it was decided at a time when a marriage in England was not dissoluble by a court order but required an Act of Parliament; hence the concentration on the question whether a Scottish court could do what an English court could not. He also stated, with an equally fine disregard for history, that the notion of legitimacy as a status, capable of recognition in private international law, "is now, but was not at the time of that decision, well established". He held that *Shaw v Gould* must "now be regarded as a case very closely confined to its own particular facts, and as deciding only a question concerned with the recognition of a divorce, an issue which would not arise now". In applying the rule that legitimacy depended on the domicile of both parents, the judge added that that rule might be too restrictive; that presumably suggests that the domicile of one parent might suffice, but the remark is not explained.

10–059

Although the judgments in both *Re Bischoffsheim* and *Green v Alexander* can be regarded as flawed, the notion of identifying a number of bases upon which legitimacy can be established is welcome in policy terms. As matters now stand, the position seems to be that a child is legitimate in England if born or conceived in lawful wedlock, or during a putative marriage, or he or she is legitimate by the law of the domicile of each parent at the time of the child's birth.

---

[261] *Birtwhistle v Vardill* (1835) 2 Cl. & F. 571 at 573–574; *Re Don's Estate* (1857) 4 Drew. 194 at 197; *Re Goodman's Trusts* (1881) 17 Ch.D. 266 at 291–292; *Re Andros* (1883) 24 Ch.D. 637 at 638.
[262] [2011] EWHC 1856 (Ch).
[263] (1881) 17 Ch D 266.

Declarations of parentage or legitimacy

10–060 Under s.55A of the Family Law Act 1986[264] the English courts have jurisdiction to grant a declaration of parentage if, and only if, either of the persons named in the application (that is, the claimed parent and child) is domiciled in England on the date of the application or was habitually resident in England throughout the period of one year ending with that date, or was so connected to England at the date of death.[265] If the applicant is not the child, one of the parents of the child,[266] the Secretary of State or the person with care,[267] then the court will only hear the application if the applicant has sufficient personal interest in the determination of the application.[268] The court may also refuse to hear the application if it considers that it would not be in the best interests of the child.[269]

Similarly, under s.56 of the 1986 Act,[270] the court has jurisdiction to grant a declaration of legitimacy if the applicant (*not* the child) is domiciled in England on the date of the application or was habitually resident in England throughout the period of one year ending with that date. The declaration may take the form that the applicant is the legitimate child of its parents (a declaration of legitimacy); or that the applicant has or has not become a legitimated person (a declaration of legitimation).[271] This statutory declaration is exclusive; it is not possible to invoke the inherent jurisdiction of the High Court.[272]

Questions relating to the parentage or legitimacy of a person may, of course, arise in proceedings other than an application for a declaration, for example in a succession case. The courts decide such questions whenever they arise as between the parties to the proceedings, whether the person whose parentage or legitimacy is in question is alive or dead,[273] and whether or not that person is a party to the proceedings. But such decisions do not bind anyone except the parties or those claiming under them, and they do not declare that the person in question is or was legitimate for all purposes, but only for the particular purpose in question.[274]

---

[264] As inserted by the Child Support, Pensions and Social Security Act 2000 Sch.9, para.1. See *M v W (Declaration of Parentage)* [2006] EWHC 2341 (Fam); [2007] 2 F.L.R. 270 for a consideration of the issues that apply in deciding whether to grant such an application.

[265] s. 55A(2).

[266] s. 55A(4).

[267] See Child Support Act 1991 s.27 as substituted by the Child Support, Pensions and Social Security Act 2000 s.83(5), Sch 8, paras 11, 13.

[268] Family Law Act 1986 s.55A(3).

[269] s.55A(5).

[270] As substituted by Family Law Reform Act 1987 s.22 and amended by the Human Fertilisation and Embryology Act 2008 Sch.6.

[271] Family Law Act 1986 s.56(1)(2) as substituted by Family Law Reform Act 1987 s.22.

[272] Family Law Act 1986 s.58(4).

[273] *Brook v Brook* (1861) 9 H.L.C. 193.

[274] *Skinner v Carter* [1948] Ch. 387.

Legitimation

The law on this subject is needlessly complicated because there are two conflict   **10–061**
rules for the recognition of foreign legitimations, a rule of common law and a
statutory rule contained in s.3 of the Legitimacy Act 1976.

Legitimation in English domestic law

Section 2 of the Legitimacy Act 1976,[275] provides that where the parents of an   **10–062**
illegitimate person marry or have married one another,[276] the marriage shall, if
the father was or is at the date of the marriage domiciled in England, render that
person, if living, legitimate from January 1, 1927, or from the date of the
marriage, whichever last happens. So, a child is now legitimated by subsequent
marriage in English domestic law; but, if the marriage was celebrated before
1927, only from January 1, 1927. If the marriage was celebrated before that date,
there is nothing in the section which requires that the father should be domiciled
in England, or even alive, on January 1, 1927.

Statutory recognition of foreign legitimations

Section 3(1) of the Act of 1976[277] deals with the recognition of foreign   **10–063**
legitimations. It provides that where the parents of an illegitimate person marry or
have married one another, and the father of the illegitimate person was or is, at
the time of the marriage, domiciled in a foreign country by the law of which the
illegitimate person became legitimated by virtue of such subsequent marriage,
that person, if living, shall be recognised in England as having been so
legitimated from January 1, 1927, or from the date of the marriage, whichever
last happens, notwithstanding that, at the time of the child's birth, the father was
domiciled in a country the law of which did not permit legitimation by
subsequent marriage.[278] It has been held in Australia that, under s.90 of the
Marriage Act 1961 (which was closely modelled on s.8(1) of the English Act of
1926), it is not necessary for the marriage to legitimate the child immediately.
Effect will be given to a later change in the law of the foreign country which
legitimates the child by virtue of the marriage, even if the father is no longer
domiciled in the foreign country at the date of the subsequent change in its law.[279]

Even before the 1926 Act introduced the concept of legitimation into English
domestic law, the courts had been prepared to recognise legitimations under
foreign law. The intention was, no doubt, that the new statutory rule as to the

---

[275] Re-enacting section 1(1) of the Legitimacy Act 1926. Provisions dealing with civil partnership
cases were inserted by the Human Fertilisation and Embryology Act 2008 Sch.6.
[276] Whether before or after January 1, 1927 (the commencement date of the 1926 Act). Technically,
s.2 of the 1976 Act only applies to marriages celebrated after its commencement (August 22, 1976):
but the rights of children legitimated by s.1 of the 1926 Act are preserved by Sch.1, para.1(1) to the
1976 Act.
[277] Re-enacting s.8(1) of the Legitimacy Act 1926.
[278] Whether before or after January 1, 1927. Technically, s.3 of the 1976 Act only applies to
marriages celebrated after its commencement (August 22, 1976); but the rights of children recognised
as legitimated by s.8 of the 1926 Act are preserved by Sch.1, para.1(1) to the 1976 Act.
[279] *Heron v National Trustees Executors and Agency Co of Australasia Ltd.* [1976] V.R. 733.

recognition of foreign legitimations would replace the previously existing common law rule altogether. But the courts have held that it still continues to exist side by side with the new statutory rule. It may still be necessary to fall back on it in some cases where it is necessary to show legitimation at a date before 1976. The section only applies to legitimation by subsequent marriage; the common law rule, as we shall see,[280] applies also to other modes of legitimation.

The common law rule: legitimation by subsequent marriage

10–064   In a rule developed long before 1926, the English courts recognise foreign legitimations if the father was domiciled both at the time of the child's birth and at the time of the subsequent marriage in a country the law of which recognised legitimation by subsequent marriage.[281] The place of the child's birth, the place of celebration of the marriage, and the domicile of the mother are all irrelevant. All that matters is the domicile of the father on the two critical dates. If the father was domiciled in England at the time of the child's birth[282] or at the time of the subsequent marriage,[283] the child was not recognised as having been legitimated. It will be seen that the main difference between the statutory rule and the older common law rule is that the latter refers to *two* dates, including the date of the child's birth which is irrelevant under the statutory rule. The common law rule of double reference was based on the argument that "the domicile at birth must give a capacity to the child of being made legitimate; but then the domicile at the time of the marriage, which gives the status, must be domicile in a country which attributes to marriage that effect".[284]

The requirement that the father must be domiciled in a country whose law recognises legitimation by subsequent marriage at the time of the child's birth as well as at the time of the subsequent marriage rests (apart from dicta) on two cases only, *Re Wright's Trusts*[285] and *Re Luck's Settlement.*[286] The former was decided at a time when the English courts were still disinclined to allow foreign-legitimated children to succeed to property under English wills; and it is surprising that the majority of the Court of Appeal did not take the opportunity of overruling it in *Re Luck's Settlement.* Instead, they extended it to a case of legitimation, not by subsequent marriage, but by parental recognition. They held that the child of a father who was domiciled in England at the time of the child's birth, but in California at the time of the parental recognition, was not recognised in England as having been legitimated, and could not take as a "child" under an English marriage settlement and will, although by Californian law the effect of the parental recognition was to render the child legitimate as from the date of its birth.

---

[280] Below, para.10–064.
[281] *Goodman v Goodman* (1862) 3 Giff. 643; *Skottowe v Young* (1871) L.R. 11 Eq. 474; *Re Goodman's Trusts* (1881) 17 Ch.D. 266; *Re Andros* (1883) 24 Ch.D. 637; *Re Grey's Trusts* [1892] 3 Ch. 88; *Re Askew* [1930] 2 Ch. 259; *Re Hurll* [1952] Ch. 722.
[282] *Re Wright's Trusts* (1856) 2 K. & J. 595.
[283] *Re Grove* (1888) 40 Ch.D. 216.
[284] *Re Grove* (1888) 40 Ch.D. 216 at 238.
[285] (1856) 2 K. & J. 595.
[286] [1940] Ch. 864.

In that case, owing to the rule against perpetuities, it was necessary for the child to prove that the legitimation was retrospective. In such a case there may perhaps be some justification for looking to the law of the father's domicile at the time of the child's birth. There can be no such justification if, as in the normal case, it is not necessary to prove that the legitimation is retrospective. The majority of the Court of Appeal pointed out that legitimation affects the status of the father as well as the status of the child; and they refused to allow a foreign law retrospectively to alter the status of a father who, at the time of the child's birth, was domiciled in England. But this reasoning has subsequently been weakened by the decision of the House of Lords in *Starkowski v Att-Gen,*[287] where they held that foreign law can retrospectively alter the status of a person domiciled in England.

The decision of the Court of Appeal is also weakened by the vigorous dissenting judgment of Scott L.J., who confessed that: **10–065**

> "the very idea of attributing to a newly born child, to *alius nullius*, a sort of latent capacity for legitimation at the hands of the natural father to whom he is denied any legal relation, seems to me an even more absurd legal fiction, and even less convincing, than the mythical contract of marriage supposed by the canonists to have been entered into at the moment of procreation".[288]

He could "see no warrant for applying a rule, originating in the special reasons for the doctrine of legitimation by subsequent marriage, and justified by various legal fictions invented to support it, to the simple and straightforward case of a direct command of legitimation by the statute law of the father's domicile".[289]

Legitimation by parental recognition

Re Luck's Settlement is the only reported case in which the English court has had to consider the effect of legitimation otherwise than by subsequent marriage. In that case, counsel for the appellant conceded[290] that if the father had been domiciled in California at the time of the child's birth as well as at the time of the parental recognition, the child would have been recognised in England as having been legitimated. The majority of the Court of Appeal made no comment on this concession; but they did cite with approval[291] Dicey's view[292] that in such a case the child would be recognised in England as legitimate. Moreover, s.10(1) of the Legitimacy Act 1976 assumes that the common law rule is not limited to legitimation by subsequent marriage. **10–066**

---

287 [1954] A.C. 155; above, para.8–004. In that case Lord Tucker at pp.175–176 and Lord Cohen at pp.180–181 attempted to distinguish *Re Luck's Settlement*, but on very slender grounds.
288 [1940] Ch. 864 at 912.
289 *ibid.*, at pp.912–913.
290 *ibid.*, at pp.871–872.
291 *ibid.*, at p.884.
292 3rd ed., p.532.

Legitimation by foreign statute

10–067 Statutes very similar to s.2 of the Legitimacy Act 1976 are in force in other countries, e.g. Northern Ireland.[293] What, then, is the position if the English court is asked to recognise the legitimation under one of these statutes of a person whose father was dead, or no longer domiciled in the country in question on the date when the statute came into operation, the marriage having taken place earlier? The Legitimacy Acts 1926 and 1976 do not in terms answer this question, and one may therefore be thrown back on the rule of common law. Unfortunately, the common law rule for legitimation by subsequent marriage is not well adapted to this situation.

The English courts have not yet been confronted by a case of this sort, but it has arisen in the Republic of Ireland and also in Australia and New Zealand with reference to children legitimated by the English Act of 1926. The Australian and New Zealand courts apparently recognise the legitimation of the child only if the father was domiciled in England on three critical dates, the date of the child's birth, the date of the subsequent marriage, and the coming into operation of the Act on January 1, 1927.[294] On the other hand, the Irish court has recognised the legitimation when the father was domiciled in England at the date of the child's birth and at the date of the subsequent marriage, even though he was dead on January 1, 1927.[295] The view of the Irish court seems preferable to that of the Australasian courts, and it is to be hoped that it will be followed in England. It seems unduly onerous to force the child to prove that his father was domiciled in the country in question at three critical dates; and of course it is an impossible task if the father was dead when the Act came into operation. It seems much better to apply the law of the country where the father was domiciled at the date of the child's birth and at the date of the subsequent marriage, as that law stands at the date of the proceedings in England. This would do much to prevent a person being held legitimate in one country and illegitimate in another. This was in effect the test applied by the Irish court and by the Supreme Court of Victoria in the most recent Australian case on the subject.[296]

Declarations of legitimation

10–068 The English courts have jurisdiction to grant a declaration that the applicant has or has not become a legitimated person if (and only if) the applicant is domiciled in England on the date of the application or was habitually resident in England

---

[293] Legitimacy Act (Northern Ireland) 1928 as amended. The status of illegitimacy was abolished in Scotland by the Family Law (Scotland) Act 2006 s.21.

[294] *Re Williams* [1936] V.L.R. 223; *Re Davey* [1937] N.Z.L.R. 56; *Re Pritchard* (1940) 40 S.R.N.S.W. 443; *Re James* [1942] V.L.R. 12; *Thompson v Thompson* (1951) 51 S.R.N.S.W. 102; *In the Estate of Taylor* [1964–65] N.S.W.R. 695; *Re Beatty* [1919] V.L.R. 81 (decided with reference to a New York statute of 1895).

[295] *Re Hagerbaum* [1933] I.R. 198.

[296] *Heron v National Trustees Executors and Agency Co. of Australasia Ltd.* [1976] V.R. 733, which (unlike the cases cited in n.294, above) was decided under s.90(1) of the Australian Marriage Act 1961. The cases cited in n.294, above, were accepted as stating the position at common law.

throughout the period of one ending with that date.[297] The expression "legitimated person" means a person legitimated by the Legitimacy Act 1976 (or by Legitimacy Act 1926) or recognised as legitimated at common law.[298] The applicant may also seek a declaration that he or she has not become a legitimated person[299]; this form of declaration was first introduced in 1987 and is designed to deal particularly with cases where there is uncertainty as to the effect of an alleged legitimation as a result of formal acknowledgement or governmental act in a foreign country.[300] This statutory jurisdiction is exclusive; it is not possible to seek such a declaration by invoking the inherent jurisdiction of the High Court.[301]

It will be seen that the jurisdictional requirements are the same as those applying to declarations as to legitimacy.[302]

ADOPTION

Adoption may give rise to complicated problems in the conflict of laws, because the laws of different countries differ widely as to the objects that adoption should serve, the methods by which it is effected, the requirements necessary for adoption (especially the age of the adopter and of the adopted person), and the effects of adoption (especially in the matter of succession). In England, adoption can only be effected by court order after a judicial inquiry directed mainly to ensuring that it will be for the welfare of the child. In some foreign systems, adoption can be effected by agreement between the parties, sometimes with and sometimes without judicial approval, or even by religious ceremony. In many foreign systems the adoption of adults is possible.

10–069

It was not until the Adoption of Children Act 1926 that English law made any provision for adoption, and not until the Adoption Act 1950 that an adopted child acquired rights of succession as a child of its adoptive parents and not of its natural parents. Adoption is now governed by the Adoption and Children Act 2002, which also implements the Hague Convention on Intercountry Adoption.

The effect of an English adoption order is to vest parental responsibility for the child in the adopters.[303] This in effect transfers to the adopters all the rights and duties which by law the mother and father have in relation to a legitimate child and its property.

---

[297] Family Law Act 1986 s.56(2)(3) (as substituted by Family Law Reform Act 1987 s.22).
[298] Family Law Act s.56(5) (as substituted by Family Law Reform Act 1987 s.22).
[299] Family Law Act 1986 s.56(2)(b) (as substituted by Family Law Reform Act 1987 s.22).
[300] Law Com. No. 132 (1984), para.3.14.
[301] Family Law Act 1986 s.58(4).
[302] See above, para.10–060.
[303] Adoption and Children Act 2002 s.46(1).

Jurisdiction to make an adoption order

10–070   The Adoption and Children Act 2002 sets out in detail the requirements to be met before an English adoption order can be made. An application to adopt may be made by a couple[304] or by one person if the applicant or one of the couple is domiciled in a part of the British Islands or has been habitually resident in a part of the British Islands for at least one year prior to the date of application.[305]

There is no jurisdictional requirement that the child must be domiciled or even resident in England. However, s.42 states that an adoption order may not be made unless that child has had a home with the applicant(s) for between 10 weeks and three years depending on the category of applicant(s), and the adoption agency must have had sufficient opportunity to see the child with the adoptive parent(s) in their home.[306]

Similar provisions existed under the previous governing statute, the Adoption Act 1976, and it was held in *Re Y (Minors) (Adoption: Jurisdiction)*[307] that the requirement that the agency have sufficient opportunity to see the child in the adoptive home was mandatory and the "home" therefore must be in the area of the local authority to which the applicant was required to give notice of the intent to adopt. However, in *Re S.L. (Adoption: Home in Jurisdiction)*[308] Mumby J. distinguished the facts of *Re Y* and held that although the child had to have a home with the applicants in the area of a particular local authority at the time of giving notice (to allow sufficient opportunity for the agency to see the child with the adoptive parents in their home), this did not mean that the "home" had to be the one and only home that the child had with the adopters for the required period of time immediately prior to the making of the adoption order, the two tests having different statutory purposes.[309] So, in *Re SL*, the fact that the applicant moved from England to Scotland part way through the required one year period prior to the adoption was not fatal to the jurisdiction of the court to grant an adoption order.

---

[304] The definition of a couple is either a married couple, or a couple living as partners in an enduring family relationship: s.144(4).
[305] *ibid.*, s.49.
[306] *ibid.*, s.42(7).
[307] [1985] Fam. 136.
[308] [2004] EWHC 1283 (Fam); [2005] 1 F.L.R. 118.
[309] *Re SL (Adoption: Home in Jurisdiction)* [2004] EWHC 1283 (Fam); [2005] 1 F.L.R. 118.

Convention adoptions

The Hague Convention of May 29, 1993 on Protection of Children and   **10–071**
Co-operation in respect of Intercountry Adoption[310] is implemented in the United
Kingdom by the Adoption and Children Act 2002, the Intercountry Adoption
(Hague Convention) Regulations 2003,[311] and the Adoptions with a Foreign
Element Regulations 2005.[312]

The Convention applies where a child[313] who is habitually resident in one
Contracting State ("the State of origin") has been, is being, or is to be moved to
another Contracting State ("the receiving State") either after his or her adoption
in the State of origin by spouses or a person habitually resident in the receiving
State, or for the purposes of such an adoption in the receiving State or in the State
of origin.[314] It only applies to adoptions that create a permanent parent-child
relationship.[315]

The connecting factor employed in this Convention to identify the child and
the adoptive parents with a Contracting State is that of habitual residence[316]
rather than nationality or domicile. This connecting factor is not without its
problems in the area of adoption. A child may well be habitually resident in a
Contracting State but a national of a State where adoption is considered to be
contrary to domestic law,[317] and a subsequent adoption may lead to a difference
in the recognition of the child's status depending on the law of the State
addressed. Considerations of this possibility and how it affects the adoption
process, however, fall to be dealt with both under the principle of the best
interests of the child, and the requirement that if the state of origin is satisfied that
a child is adoptable, it must "give due consideration to the child's upbringing and
to his or her ethnic, religious and cultural background."[318]

The Convention requires that each Contracting State designate a Central   **10–072**
Authority to discharge the duties which are imposed by the Convention upon
such authorities[319] but allows Central Authorities to delegate much of the actual
workload to public authorities or other accredited bodies.[320] In the respective

---

[310] cf. Parra-Aranguren, Explanatory Report to the Convention of May 29, 1993 on protection of Children and Co-operation in respect of Intercountry Adoptions; Van Loon, [1993] VII Recueil des Cours, 195; Murphy, International Dimensions in Family Law (Manchester University Press, Manchester, 2005), Ch.7.
[311] SI 2003/118.
[312] SI 2005/392 as amended by SI 2009/2563.
[313] The Convention ceases to apply if the child reaches the age of 18 before the agreement of all parties has been obtained; art.3.
[314] art.2(1).
[315] art.2(2); i.e., full adoptions as opposed to simple adoptions which do not extinguish all ties to the biological family.
[316] art.2. See *Greenwich LBC v S* [2007] EWHC 820; [2007] 2 F.L.R. 154 for a discussion of when a child being placed for intercountry adoption gains a new habitual residence. For a general discussion of the term "habitual residence", see para.2–004.
[317] Most Islamic countries fall into this category. However, see Beevers and Ebrahimi, [2002] I.F.L. 166.
[318] art.16(b).
[319] art.6. For England the Central Authority is the Secretary of State; for Wales, the National Assembly for Wales; SI 2005/392, reg.2.
[320] Intercountry Adoption Convention, art.9.

countries reports are prepared on the eligibility of the adoptive parents and on the child.[321] The Central Authority of the state of origin has the responsibility of considering these two reports and determining if the proposed intercountry adoption is indeed in the best interests of the child. Once the decision has been made to proceed with the intercountry adoption and the necessary consents have been obtained, the child may only be entrusted to the prospective adoptive parents if both Central Authorities and the adoptive parents agree to the adoption and the Central Authority of the Receiving State has determined that the child will be authorised to enter and reside permanently in that state.[322]

Adoptions may be made in England as "convention adoptions" when the procedure set out in the Convention has been followed.[323]

Choice of law

10–073　　When deciding whether or not to grant an adoption order, the English court will apply the *lex fori* as contained in the detailed provisions of the 2002 Act. Although the court is required to have regard to the child's background,[324] there is no reference in the Act to the consideration of any foreign law. It is, therefore, always possible that a child may be considered the child of the adoptive parents in England but the child of its biological parents in the child's country of origin. However, as more and more states ratify the Hague Convention of 1993 on Intercountry Adoption, such cases will decrease.

Bringing children into the United Kingdom

10–074　　The relevant provisions of the 2002 Act, supplemented by the Children and Adoption Act 2006 and by regulations,[325] restrict the conditions under which a child who is habitually resident in country outside the British Islands can be brought in to the United Kingdom either for the purpose of adoption, or subsequent to an external adoption otherwise than a Convention adoption.[326] Failure to comply with the prescribed conditions is a criminal offence which carries penalties of up to one year in prison.[327] Further restrictions on bringing in children from a particular country for the purposes of adoption may also be

---

[321]　art.16(1).

[322]　art.17, together with art.5.

[323]　The relevant legislation, described as "a legal minefield", is examined in *Re M (A Child) (Adoption: Placement outside Jurisdiction)* [2010] EWHC 1694 (Fam); [2011] Fam. 110.

[324]　s.1 of the Act provides an extensive checklist of considerations to which the court and the adoption agency must have regard.

[325]　Adoptions with a Foreign Element Regulations 2005 (SI 2005/392).

[326]　See *MN (India) v Entry Clearance Officer (New Delhi)* [2008] EWCA Civ. 38; [2008] 2 F.L.R. 87 for a discussion of the four different ways for a child to be granted clearance to enter the UK for the purposes of adoption, none of which were fulfilled in this case.

[327]　Adoption and Children Act 2002 s.83(8).

imposed by the Secretary of State on the grounds of public policy, including where that country is a Convention country.[328]

Taking children abroad for adoption

Where prospective adoptive parents, who are not domiciled or habitually resident in England and Wales,[329] intend to adopt a child under the law of another country outside the British Islands, the High Court may make an order giving them parental responsibility for that child.[330]

10–075

A child may not be taken out of the jurisdiction "for the purpose of adoption" unless such an order has been made.[331] This does not apply where a child is sent by a local authority to live outside the jurisdiction with the approval of the court.[332] The power to give such approval is not available where a local authority is placing a child for adoption with prospective adopters (para.19(9)) but where a child is sent abroad in circumstances in which adoption is one option being considered, this will not amount to being "placed for adoption".[333]

However, an order giving prospective adopters parental responsibility may not be made unless the child has had a home with the prospective adoptive parent, or in the case of adoption by a couple both of them, at all times during the preceding ten weeks.[334] The requirement has been criticised as placing too great a burden on prospective adopters from overseas; there is power[335] to vary or disapply the requirement, notably in the case of adoptions by natural relatives, but the power has not been exercised. However, the courts have interpreted the requirement in ways which assist potential adopters. In *Re G (A Child) (Adoption: Placement outside Jurisdiction)*,[336] the prospective adopters were family members resident in the United States; the adoptive mother spent ten weeks with the child in England, but the adoptive father could only spend three weeks. The Court of Appeal held that this was sufficient in the circumstances to satisfy the purposes of the Act. It was later held that the ten week period need not be within the jurisdiction.[337] In *Re G (A Child) (Adoption: Placement outside Jurisdiction)*, the Court of Appeal had said that the purpose of this requirement was to ensure that a relationship should begin to establish between the child and the potential adopters and for the authorities to have an opportunity to assess the suitability of those

10–076

---

[328] Children and Adoption Act 2006 ss.9–12; Adoptions with a Foreign Element (Special Restrictions on Adoptions from Abroad) Regulations 2008 (SI 2008/1807); special restrictions have been imposed for Cambodia (SI 2008/1808), Guatemala (SI 2008/1809), Haiti (SI 2010/2265) and Nepal (SI 2010/951).
[329] Adoption and Children Act 2002 s.84(2).
[330] *ibid.*, s.84(1).
[331] *ibid.*, s.85(1)(2); anyone arranging to remove a child without first being granted parental responsibility is guilty of an offence under s.85(4).
[332] Under Children Act 1989 Sch.2, para.19.
[333] *ibid.*, para.19(9); *C v M* [2008] EWHC 332 (Fam), approved in *Re A (A Child) (Adoption: Assessment Abroad)* [2009] EWCA Civ 41; [2010] Fam. 9.
[334] *ibid.*, s.84(4). The Adoptions with a Foreign Element Regulations 2005 (SI 2005/392) reg.10, contains further requirements which must be fulfilled prior to removal.
[335] Adoption and Children Act 2002 s.86.
[336] [2008] EWCA Civ 105; [2008] Fam 97.
[337] *Re A (A Child) (Adoption: Assessment Abroad)* [2009] EWCA Civ 41; [2010] Fam. 9.

potential adoptive parents, but in *Re A (A Child) (Adoption: Assessment Abroad)* it held that there was no reason for those opportunities for assessment to be in England.

Recognition of foreign adoptions

Adoptions in the British Isles

10–077   There never has been any doubt that adoption orders made in Scotland would be recognised in England without question, and this is now expressly enacted.[338] It is also expressly provided that adoption orders made in Northern Ireland, the Channel Islands and the Isle of Man shall be recognised in England and Scotland.[339]

Overseas adoptions

10–078   Provisions dating from 1968, now contained in s.87 of the Adoption and Children Act 2002, empower the Secretary of State to specify as "overseas adoptions" any adoption effected under the law of any country outside the British Islands. The intention was to recognise adoptions made in countries whose adoption law is broadly similar to our own, and they are specified by Order.[340] They include most of the Commonwealth (exceptions include India and Bangladesh), all western European countries, Yugoslavia, Greece, Turkey, Israel, South Africa, China, and the United States. Under this Order, there need be no juristic link of any kind, such as domicile, between the adopters and the country where the adoption was made. The only qualifications are that the adoption must have been effected under statutory law and not under common law or customary law; that the adopted person had not attained the age of 18 and had not been married; and that recognition must not be contrary to public policy. Subject to this, recognition is automatic.[341]

Convention adoptions

10–079   Section 66 of the Adoption and Children Act 2002, implementing art.23 of the Convention, provides for the recognition of adoptions under the Hague Convention of 1993. Although the Convention covers only adoptions that create a permanent parent-child relationship,[342] it does provide for such adoptions (called in some systems of law "simple adoptions") which do not sever the legal relationship between the child and its natural parents, to be converted into full adoptions by the law of the Contracting State.[343] The 1999 Act establishes a

---

[338] Adoption and Children Act 2002 s.105.
[339] s.106 of the 2002 Act for Northern Ireland, and s.108 of the 2002 Act and regulations made under this section in respect of the Channel Islands and the Isle of Man.
[340] See SI 1973/19 and amending Orders, under review in 2012.
[341] Adoption and Children Act 2002 ss.66 and 67.
[342] art.2(2).
[343] arts 26 and 27.

procedure under which the High Court can direct that a Convention adoption should be recognised in England as having more limited effects on the status of the child than a full adoption, so for example enabling the child to succeed to the estate of its natural parent.[344]

Other adoptions

The recognition in England of other adoptions, that is, adoptions other than those made in the British Isles and other than "overseas" or "Convention" adoptions, still depends on the common law. So many adoptions have been specified as "overseas adoptions" that there is little geographical scope left for the common law to operate in, but it will still apply to adoptions made, e.g., in certain eastern European countries; Middle Eastern countries other than Turkey and Israel; Pakistan, Japan and a few Central and South American countries.[345] It will also apply to adoptions made in countries designated in the "overseas adoptions" context where the adoptions were effected under the customary or common law of countries, or involved the adoption of adults.

10–080

The majority of the Court of Appeal in *Re Valentine's Settlement*[346] laid it down, in the words of Lord Denning M.R., that at common law "the courts of this country will only recognise an adoption in another country if the adopting parents are domiciled there and the child is ordinarily resident there".[347] Danckwerts L.J. agreed with the Master of the Rolls, except that he was "not sure" whether the ordinary residence of the child was a requirement for recognition. In that case, the Court of Appeal refused to recognise two South African adoption orders made in respect of two children who were assumed to be resident and domiciled in South Africa, because the applicants were domiciled in what was then Southern Rhodesia (now Zimbabwe) and there was evidence that the Southern Rhodesian courts would not recognise the South African adoptions. There are indications in the judgments that the adoptions would have been recognised without difficulty if they had been recognised by the Southern Rhodesian courts.[348] So, perhaps we can say, on the analogy of the common law rule as to the recognition of foreign divorces in *Armitage v Att-Gen*,[349] that at common law a foreign adoption will be recognised in England if the adopters were domiciled in the foreign country, or if it would be recognised in the country where the adopters were domiciled. However, in light of the Adoption and Children Act 2002 providing for the additional connecting factor of habitual residence for the prospective adopters, it

---

[344] Adoption and Children Act 2002 s.88.

[345] An Indian adoption was recognised under the common law in *D v D (Foreign Adoptions)* [2008] EWHC 403 (Fam); [2008] 1 F.L.R. 1475.

[346] [1965] Ch. 831 at 843 and 846. Earlier cases are *Re Wilson* [1954] Ch. 733; *Re Wilby* [1956] P. 174; and *Re Marshall* [1957] Ch507.

[347] At that time the residence of the child in England was one of the jurisdictional requirements for adoption. This is no longer so. Hence it seems unlikely that the ordinary residence of the child in the foreign country will continue to be necessary for the recognition of foreign adoptions at common law.

[348] [1965] Ch. 226 at 234, per Pennycuick J.; p.855, per Salmon L.J.

[349] [1906] P. 135; above, para.9–037.

is arguable that the rule in *Re Valentine's Settlement* should be extended to cover cases where the adopters were habitually resident in that country.[350]

Public policy

10–081   In *Re Valentine's Settlement*, Lord Denning M.R. entered one caveat[351]: the foreign adoption should not be recognised if recognition would be contrary to public policy. It is more than usually important to keep this factor in mind when deciding whether to recognise a foreign adoption, because the laws of some foreign countries differ so widely from English law as to the objects and effects of adoption. Hence, if the adoption was made for some ulterior object other than the welfare of the child, some at least of its effects might have to be denied recognition in England. But the facts would have to be extreme before public policy demanded the total non-recognition of a foreign adoption for all purposes. If, to take an improbable but striking example, the law of a foreign country allowed a bachelor of 50 to adopt a spinster of 17, an English court might hesitate to give the custody of the girl to her adoptive parent; but that might be no reason for not allowing her to succeed to his property as his "child" on his death. A mere difference between the foreign law and English domestic law should not be sufficient for withholding recognition on this ground. In particular, the fact that the adopted person was over the age of 18, or that the adoption was not made by court order,[352] should not prevent recognition. A system of law which is prepared to recognise polygamous marriages and extra-judicial divorces should not be too squeamish about recognising foreign adoptions. The recognition in England of "overseas adoptions" may be refused on the ground of public policy[353]; but of course the recognition of adoptions made elsewhere in the British Isles may not.

Declarations as to foreign adoptions

10–082   Provision was made in the Family Law Act 1986 for declarations as to the validity of foreign adoptions.[354] Such a declaration may be sought only by an applicant whose status as an adopted child of any person depends on whether the child has been adopted by that person by either a Convention adoption, an overseas adoption as defined in the Adoption and Children Act 2002, or by an adoption recognised by the law of England and Wales and effected under the law of any country outside the British Islands. The declaration that the applicant is or is not the adopted child of a named person by virtue of such an adoption determines the position of the applicant for the purposes of s.67 of the 2002 Act which deals with the status conferred by adoption.

The jurisdictional rules correspond to those applying to other declarations in family matters. So English courts have jurisdiction if (and only if) the applicant is

---

[350] See Murphy, *op. cit.*, p.231.
[351] [1965] Ch. 831 at p.842. cf. Salmon L.J. at p.854.
[352] Adoption and Children Act 2002, s.66(1)*(e)* assumes that a foreign adoption can be recognised at common law although not made by court order.
[353] Adoption and Children Act 2002 s.89.
[354] Family Law Act 1986 s.57, as amended by the Adoption and Children Act 2002 Sch.3, para.49.

domiciled in England on the date of the application or was habitually resident in England throughout the period of one year ending with that date.[355]

---

[355] Family Law Act 1986 s.57(3).

CHAPTER 11

CONTRACTS

There is an appreciable difference in texture between the rules of the conflict of **11–001** laws dealing with matters of family law and those, about to be examined, in the field of commercial contracts. This is no accident but the product of significant differences between the underlying topics.

So, in the field of marriage and divorce the relevant legal rules need to be such as will enable the status of the parties to be established with as much certainty as possible. That is important both to the parties themselves and to the state, whose interest is evidenced by the requirements in most legal systems of publicity and registration both for the creation and the dissolution of marriages. Although it is a point hard for young lovers to accept, there is a dry legal sense in which every marriage is the same. A standard set of legal rights and duties (or in the case of the matrimonial property régime, a range of options) applies to each and every marriage entered into under a particular legal system. In terms of the conflict of laws, this is reflected in the rules as to jurisdiction and the recognition of marriages and divorces, rules which have a certain precision, even rigidity. It is only in the complex areas of child custody and financial arrangements that there is any real scope for tailoring the outcome to the particular circumstances of the case.

By contrast there is much less state interest in the ephemeral commercial transactions, often entered into with little or no formality, which give rise to contractual obligations. Contracts are almost infinitely varied. It is unlikely that a mechanical choice of law rule that is appropriate for a contract to sell land would be equally appropriate for a contract of employment, or a contract for the carriage of goods by sea. The problems that may arise are very numerous, as may be seen by looking at the table of contents of any book on the domestic law of contract. It is unlikely that a choice of law rule will be equally appropriate for questions of offer and acceptance, capacity of the parties, formalities, and illegality.

11–002   All of this has the effect, in almost every legal system, of leading to choice of law rules as to contractual obligations which are characterised by flexibility, and by sensitivity both to the particular circumstances of the contract and to the nature of the issue that has arisen between the parties. This was very clearly so in the English case law which followed the approach of the common law. The civil law approach, with its emphasis on legal certainty, is reflected in European legislation and this led Advocate General Bot to write in one context[1] that "legal certainty and foreseeability of the applicable law have taken preference over the flexibility of application of the conflict rule"; but, as we shall see, the EU Regulation retains many elements of flexibility.

THE ENGLISH COMMON LAW APPROACH

11–003   In England, the flexible rule that until 1991 governed most issues was known as the "proper law of the contract". In speaking of it, Lord Wright explained[2]:

> "English law in deciding these matters has refused to treat as conclusive, rigid or arbitrary criteria such as *lex loci contractus* [the law of the place in which the contract was made] or *lex loci solutionis* [the law of the place of performance], and has treated the matter as depending on the intention of the parties to be ascertained in each case on a consideration of the terms of the contract, the situation of the parties, and generally on all the surrounding facts. It may be that the parties have in terms in their agreement expressed what law they intend to govern, and in that case *prima facie* their intention will be effectuated by the court. But in most cases they do not do so. The parties may not have thought of the matter at all. Then the court has to impute an intention, or to determine for the parties what is the proper law which, as just and reasonable persons, they ought [to] or would have intended if they had thought about the question when they made the contract."

In the common law approach developed by the nineteenth-century English judges, the "proper law of the contract" was the system of law by reference to which the contract was made: the law chosen by the parties, or that with which the transaction had its closest and most real connection.[3]

Party autonomy

11–004   The power of the parties to select the law which is to govern their contract, the principle of "party autonomy", can be seen as the conflict of laws aspect of freedom of contract or of the market autonomy. In so far as parties are free to enter into whatever contractual bargains they think fit, that freedom is not complete unless they can chose the law by reference to which their agreement

---

[1] Case C-133/08 *Intercontainer Interfrigo SC v Balkenende Oosthuizen BV* [2009] ECR I-9687, footnote 11 to the Opinion.

[2] *Mount Albert Borough Council v Australasian Temperance and General Assurance Society* [1938] A.C. 224 at 240. For the development of this approach and the importance formerly given to the law of the places of contracting and performance, see McClean, De Conictu Legum (2000) 282 Hague *Recueil des cours*, Ch.V; Nygh, Autonomy in International Contracts (Clarendon Press, Oxford, 1999).

[3] See *Bonython v Commonwealth of Australia* [1951] A.C. 201, per Lord Simonds at 209.

will be construed.[4] In practical terms, by an express selection of the proper law, the parties relieved the court of the difficult task of ascertaining it when the facts were nicely balanced between two systems of law. To allow them to do so injected some certainty into the common law approach, which was otherwise open to the criticism that it could take a law-suit to determine what law governed. But the principle of party autonomy took root even in the rather different soil of civil law countries, so that by 1980 when it was enshrined in the Rome Convention, it was already part of the law of all the then Member States of the European Community.[5]

Absence of choice by the parties

In the absence of choice, express or implied, by the parties, the courts determined the proper law by identifying the system of law with which the transaction had its closest and most real connection.[6] In this inquiry:

> "many matters have to be taken into consideration. Of these the principal are the place of contracting, the place of performance, the places of residence or business of the parties respectively, and the nature and subject matter of the contract".[7]

11–005

The Assunzione[8] is an instructive illustration of the difficulties inherent in such an open-textured approach: the facts were so nicely balanced between French and Italian law that the Court of Appeal had to use a very delicate pair of scales in order to determine the proper law.

> The contract was one for the carriage of wheat from Dunkirk to Venice on board an Italian ship. The charterers were an organisation of French grain merchants. The wheat was shipped under an exchange agreement between the French and Italian governments, but the Italian shipowners did not know this. The contract was negotiated by correspondence between brokers in France and brokers in Italy. It was formally concluded in Paris in the English language and in an English standard form. Freight and demurrage were payable in Italian currency in Italy.

It was held unanimously that Italian law was the proper law of the contract. The decisive factor was that both parties had contractual obligations to perform in Italy.

The common law rules here outlined remain in force in many Commonwealth countries, but in England they almost wholly gave way first to the provisions of the Rome Convention on the Law Applicable to Contractual Obligations 1980,

11–006

---

[4] For possible limitations at common law on the freedom to choose the governing law, see *Vita Food Products Inc. v Unus Shipping Co* [1939] A.C. 277.
[5] See the official Explanatory Report on the Convention, the Giuliano and Lagarde report, [1980] O.J. C283 at pp.15–16.
[6] cf. the notion of the "centre of gravity" of a contract: *Auten v Auten*, 124 N.E.2d 99 (N.Y. C.As, 1954), a notion sometimes also used in European cases: Bundesgerichtshof, May 7, 1969 (VIII ZR 142/68, DB 1969, 1053); Case C-280/90 *Hacker v Euro-Relais GmbH* [1992] E.C.R. I-1111, Opinion of Advocate General Darmon, para.33; Case C-133/08 *Intercontainer Interfrigo SC v Balkenende Oosthuizen BV* [2009] ECR I-9687, Opinion of Advocate General Bot.
[7] *Re United Railways of the Havana and Regla Warehouses Ltd* [1960] Ch. 52 at 91.
[8] [1954] P. 150.

given effect by the Contracts (Applicable Law) Act 1990, and now to those of the Rome I Regulation, European Parliament and Council Regulation No 593/2008 of June 17, 2008 on the law applicable to contractual obligations[9] which has "(Rome I)" as part of its formal title. The abandonment of the common law rules was not universally popular. A distinguished commentator wrote as the 1990 Act was coming into force:

> "The Act replaces one of the great achievements of the English judiciary during the last 140 years or so, an achievement which produced an effective private international law of contracts, was recognised and followed in practically the whole world and has not at any time or anywhere led to dissatisfaction or to a demand for reform".[10]

The United Kingdom played a full part in its negotiation of the Rome I Regulation but initially chose not to be bound by it[11]; as the final text met most of the UK's concerns, it then agreed to accept the Regulation.[12]

THE ROME CONVENTION AND THE ROME I REGULATION[13]

11–007 The Rome I Regulation applies to contracts concluded after December 17, 2009.[14] It is a revision of the Rome Convention of 1980, the provisions of which apply to contracts made on or before that date.[15] It is designed to be consistent both with the Brussels I Regulation and with the Rome II Regulation.[16] It is necessary, in what follows, to deal fully with both the Convention and the Regulation: the Convention will still be relied on in contract disputes for a number of years, the interpretive case law of the European Court of Justice (ECJ) on the provisions of the Rome Convention has only just started to emerge,[17] and much of the text of the Regulation is in fact simply taken over from the Convention.

---

[9] O.J. L 177/6, 4.7.2008.

[10] Mann, (1991) 107 L.Q.R. 353.

[11] See *Rome I—Should the UK opt in?* Consultation Paper CP05/08. See also Ruiz Abou-Nigm, "Rome I: Evolution or Status Quo?" in Fernandez Arroyo and Gonzalez Martin (eds), *Tendencias y relaciones del derecho internacional privado americano actual (Jornadas de la ASADIP 2008)* (Porrua, Mexico 2010) 553.

[12] Implementing rules are contained in the Law Applicable to Contractual Obligations (England and Wales and Northern Ireland) Regulations 2009 (SI 2009/3064).

[13] See Plender and Wilderspin, *The European Private International Law of Obligations* (3rd edn, Sweet & Maxwell, 2009) and Bělohlávek, *Rome Convention/Rome I Regulation* (Juris, 2010).

[14] Regulation, art.28.

[15] For the thinking of the Commission which led to the adoption of the Regulation, see its Green Paper on the conversion of the Convention into a Community instrument and its modernisation, COM/2002/0654 final.

[16] European Parliament and Council Regulation No 864/2007 of 11 July 2007 on the law applicable to non-contractual obligations (Rome II) (as to which see chapter 12, below): Rome I Regulation, Recital (7).

[17] The first reference for a preliminary ruling of the ECJ on the interpretation of the Convention was made in Case C-133/08 *Intercontainer Interfrigo SC v Balkenende Oosthuizen BV* [2009] ECR I-9687.

Interpretation

An explanatory report on the Rome Convention by Professors Mario Giuliano   **11–008**
and Paul Lagarde was published in the *Official Journal*,[18] and the Contracts
(Applicable Law) Act 1990 enables this to be considered in interpreting the
Convention. There is provision in an appended Protocol (which came into force
in 2004) giving the ECJ jurisdiction to rule on the interpretation of the
Convention,[19] and any question of interpretation which is not referred to the ECJ
must be determined in accordance with the principles laid down by, and any
relevant decision of, the ECJ.[20] The Court will be able to rule on the
interpretation of the Rome I Regulation under the usual rules applying to
European legislation. Where the language of the Convention is carried over into
the Regulation, decisions on the Convention will naturally be relied on also in
relation to the Regulation.

Scope

The rules of the Rome Convention are declared to apply to "contractual   **11–009**
obligations in any situation involving a choice between the laws of different
countries".[21] A "choice" exists, in effect, whenever there is a foreign element
which might lead to the application of a particular law; it may, for example, be
the residence of a party to the contract, the place of performance, or the fact that
the parties have chosen a particular law as applicable.[22] The Regulation text uses
a different formulation: it is to apply, "in situations involving a conflict of laws,
to contractual obligations in civil and commercial matters"[23]; there seems to be
no change in the meaning, though the Regulation makes an explicit exclusion of
revenue, customs and administrative matters.

Both the Convention and the Regulation treat the notion of "contractual
obligations" as self-explanatory, but in fact it is far from being unproblematic. As
in the case of art.5 of the Brussels I Regulation,[24] the ECJ may well have to
clarify the boundary between, for example, contractual and tortious obligations.[25]

A related difficulty concerns the word "obligations". That might be read to
limit the scope to cases where the parties were actually bound, obliged, by the
terms of their apparent agreement, and to exclude cases in which the contract was
void. Such a reading cannot be correct, for many articles are concerned with the
very question of the validity of the contract: it would be absurd to argue that the
Convention or the Regulation was in some sense inapplicable if, under its rules,

---

[18] [1980] O.J. C283.
[19] See Sch.3 of the 1990 Act and O.J. C334/1, 30.12.2005.
[20] s.3(1).
[21] Convention, art.1(1).
[22] See Giuliano-Lagarde report, p.10.
[23] Regulation, art.1(1).
[24] See Case C-26/91 *Jakob Handte GmbH v TMCS* [1993] E.C.R. I-3967 (product liability claim
based on implied warranty theory of liability held tortious for the purposes of the Brussels
Convention); and see above, para.4–021 and 4–028.
[25] See Czepelak, (2011) 7 J.Priv.Int.L. 393.

the contract were invalid. It is expressly provided that the applicable law governs "the consequences of nullity of the contract".[26]

11–010
The countries whose law may be made applicable are not limited to Member States (or to Contracting States to the Convention); it is expressly provided that a law specified by the Convention or Regulation must be applied whether or not it is the law of such a state.[27] So the rules apply where the countries relevant to a contractual dispute are, for example, England, New Zealand and Ontario. Under the Convention, the law chosen had to be the law of a state: there could not be a reference to the customs of international trade (often referred to as the *lex mercatoria*),[28] nor to the rules of an international convention, nor to Sharia law.[29] The position is not changed under the Regulation so far as the applicable law is concerned, but Recital (13) states that the Regulation does not preclude parties from incorporating by reference into their contract a non-State body of law or an international convention. This means that the terms of such a body of law or convention may become the text of the contract, but issues arising will be a matter for the applicable law of some state.[30]

In the case of federal or composite states in which each territorial unit (such as Ontario) has its own rules of law in respect of contractual obligations, each territorial unit is treated as a "country" for the purposes of the Convention and the Regulation.[31]

11–011
A federal or composite state is not bound to apply the Convention or Regulation to conflicts solely between the laws of different units within that state.[32] The United Kingdom is, of course, such a state. Section 2(2) of the 1990 Act provides that the Convention rules are to apply in the case of conflicts between the laws of different parts of the United Kingdom. It would have made for needless complexity to retain the common law rules for cases involving, say, a choice only between England and Scotland, but to apply the Convention if the choice of

---

[26] Convention, art.10(1)(e); Regulation, Art.12(1)(e). The Convention provision was not given effect in English law by the 1990 Act, because most of those consequences, and in particular the recovery of moneys paid under a void contract, were classified in English law as falling under the law of restitution rather than the law of contract. The Regulation provision does, of course, apply in England.

[27] Convention, art.2; Regulation, art.2.

[28] The Commission's Proposal (COM (2005) 650, para.3.2.) provided for the possibility of choosing non-national rules of law such as the Unidroit Principles of International Commercial Contracts, the Principles of European Contract Law, or the European Common Frame of Reference, but not the *lex mercatoria* or the like, as these concepts were not sufficiently precise. The European Parliament asked for the deletion of references to non-national systems of law in the interests of legal certainty.

[29] *Shamil Bank of Bahrain EC v Beximco Pharmaceuticals Ltd* [2004] EWCA Civ 19; [2004] 1 W.L.R. 1784 (clause reading "Subject to the principles of Glorious Sharia'a, this agreement shall be governed by and construed in accordance with the laws of England" treated as choice of English law); *Halpern v Halpern* [2007] EWCA Civ 291; [2007] 2 Lloyd's Rep. 56; *Musawi v R E International (UK) Ltd* [2007] EWHC 2981 (Ch); [2008] 1 All E.R. (Comm) 607.

[30] cf. Inter-American Convention on the Law Applicable to International Contracts (Mexico 1994) (CIDIP-V). Art.7(1) allowing the choice of any law, including a non-national system of law such as the Unidroit Principles. On the comparison between the Inter-American Convention and the Rome I Regulation see Albornoz, (2010) 6 J.Priv.Int.L. 23.

[31] Convention, art.19(1); Regulation, art.22(1).

[32] Convention, art.19(2); Regulation, art.22(2).

Dutch law were perceived as available on the same facts. A similar provision is made in relation to the Regulation, with an express exclusion of insurance contracts.[33]

Exclusions

Article 1(2) of each instrument expressly excludes certain matters from its scope. Family law is excluded, for the relevant considerations there are quite different from those applying in the commercial area. So are subjects like company and insurance law,[34] where there is much other harmonisation activity. It was found that some other matters could not readily be accommodated within the system of the Convention (arbitration agreements and bills of exchange, each classified in different ways in different Member States; and trusts, known to few such States). The list of exclusions is such that in English law some matters of contract, notably arbitration agreements, remain governed by the common law rules.[35] **11–012**

Most of the exclusions are stated in absolute terms: **11–013**

(1)   what might be described by way of shorthand as family law obligations; the language differs as between the Convention and the Regulation. The Convention speaks of:

> contractual obligations relating to wills and succession, rights in property arising out of a matrimonial relationship, and rights and duties arising out of a family relationship, including maintenance obligations in respect of illegitimate children.

and the Regulation, more elaborate at this point, has two relevant exclusions:

> (b)   obligations arising out of family relationships[36] and relationships deemed by the law applicable to such relationships to have comparable effects,[37] including maintenance obligations;
>
> (c)   obligations arising out of matrimonial property regimes, property regimes of relationships deemed by the law applicable to such relationships to have comparable effects to marriage, and wills and succession.

(2)   obligations arising under bills of exchange, cheques and promissory notes and other negotiable instruments to the extent that the obligations under such other negotiable instruments arise out of their negotiable character; **11–014**

---

[33] See Law Applicable to Contractual Obligations (England and Wales and Northern Ireland) Regulations 2009 (SI 2009/3064) reg.5. In relation to Rome I Regulation, art.7 on insurance contracts, see the Financial Services and Markets Act 2000 (Law Applicable to Contracts of Insurance) Regulations 2009 (SI 2009/3075).

[34] See the Commission's 2002 Green Paper, para.3.2.2ff for an analysis of the complex position which has developed in the insurance field resulting in the partial exclusion in art.1(2)(j) of the Reg.

[35] See, e.g., *Haugesund Kommune v Depfa ACS Bank* [2010] EWCA Civ 579; [2011] 1 All E.R. 190 (legal capacity of companies).

[36] "Family relationships" covers parentage, marriage, affinity and collateral relatives: Regulation, Recital (8).

[37] The "comparable effects" provisions are to be interpreted in accordance with the law of the Member State seised of the case: Regulation, Recital (8).

here the text is unchanged in the Regulation,[38] the Recitals to which specify that bills of lading are included to the extent that the obligations under the bill of lading arise out of its negotiable character.[39]

(3) arbitration agreements[40] and agreements on the choice of court[41];

(4) company law issues,[42] i.e., questions governed by the law of companies and other bodies, corporate or unincorporated, such as the creation, by registration or otherwise, legal capacity, internal organisation or winding up of companies and other bodies, corporate or unincorporated and the personal liability of officers and members as such for the obligations of the company or body[43];

11–015 (5) the question as to whether an agent is able to bind a principal, or an organ to bind a company or body, corporate or unincorporated, to a third party;

(6) the constitution of trusts and the relationship between settlors, trustees and beneficiaries; and

(7) in the Regulation only, obligations arising out of dealings prior to the conclusion of a contract: the Recitals explain that these obligations are covered by art.12 of the Rome II Regulation[44]; and

(8) certain contracts of insurance; the Regulation has more elaborate provisions as to insurance, which are considered below,[45] covering risks situated (in the understanding of the *lex fori*) in the territories of the Member States.

11–016 Two other exclusions are expressed in more qualified terms:

(9) questions involving the status or legal capacity of natural persons, without prejudice to one provision which forms art.11 of the Convention and art.13 of the Regulation[46];

(10) evidence and procedure, without prejudice to another specific provision, which forms art.14 of the Convention and art.18 of the Regulation.[47]

---

[38] See Garcimartín Alférez, (2009) 5 J.Priv.Int.L.85 on the question of whether certain types of financial instruments that are regarded as negotiable instruments are within this exclusion or not.

[39] Regulation, Recital (9). See Boonk, [2011] L.M.C.L.Q. 227.

[40] See Arzandeh and Hill, (2009) 5 J.Priv.Int.L. 425; and Yüksel, (2011) 7 J.Priv.Int.L. 149.

[41] For jurisdiction clauses (i.e. "agreements on the choice of court"), see above, paras 4–060ff and 5–061.

[42] For proposed further harmonization of conflict of laws rules on the law applicable to companies, see *The Stockholm Programme—An open and secure Europe serving and protecting the citizens* (O.J. C115/1, 4.5.2010) and its implementing Action Plan (COM (2010) 171 final).

[43] See *Haugesund Kommune v Depfa ACS Bank* [2010] EWCA Civ 579; [2011] 1 All E.R. 190. The text follows the Regulation, but the changes from the Convention text are very minor drafting matters only.

[44] Regulation, Recital (10).

[45] See below, paras 11–046ff. Excluded from the Regulation by art.1(2) are insurance contracts arising out of operations carried out by organisations other than undertakings referred to in art.2 of Directive 2002/83/EC concerning life assurance the object of which is to provide benefits for employed or self-employed persons belonging to an undertaking or group of undertakings, or to a trade or group of trades, in the event of death or survival or of discontinuance or curtailment of activity, or of sickness related to work or accidents at work.

[46] See below, paras 11–065ff.

[47] See below, paras 17–010ff.

THE CHOICE OF THE GOVERNING LAW

The heart of both the Convention and the Regulation is to be found in articles 3 **11–017** and 4. Article 3 embodies the principle of "party autonomy", giving the parties freedom to select the law which is to govern the contract. As the Giuliano-Lagarde Report observes, this simply reaffirms a rule embodied in the private international law of all the then Member States of the Community.[48] The recitals to the Regulation affirm the principle that "The parties' freedom to choose the applicable law should be one of the cornerstones of the system of conflict-of-law rules in matters of contractual obligations".[49]

Article 4 provides a set of rules for determining the governing law in the absence of a choice by the parties; it is at this point that there is the most significant divergence between Convention and Regulation.

There is in principle no room for the doctrine of *renvoi*[50] in the context of the Convention or the Regulation, art.20 of the Regulation stipulating:

> The application of the law of any country specified by this Regulation means the application of the rules of law in force in that country other than its rules of private international law, unless provided otherwise in this Regulation.[51]

The law chosen by the parties

Article 3(1) of the Regulation provides that a contract is to be governed by the **11–018** law chosen by the parties. The choice must be express or clearly demonstrated (at this point the Convention has "demonstrated with reasonable certainty") by the terms of the contract or the circumstances of the case.

It would have been possible for the drafters to have taken a hard line. The inclusion of a choice of law clause is such an everyday matter in international contracts that its absence should take one straight to the rules in art.4 as to the position where there is an absence of choice. That would be to ignore commercial realities. Not every international commercial contract receives the attentions of lawyers (still less of skilled lawyers). It is quite possible for an express choice of law to be omitted, while the terms of the contract (by their reference to related transactions,[52] or to a recognised standard form or the practices of a particular market,[53] or as to arbitration) can quite properly be interpreted as pointing clearly to the parties' assumption that the law of a particular country will govern.[54] Where there has been an established course of dealing between the parties, fresh contracts may be entered into quite informally: "Could you send us more of the

---

[48] Report, p.15, with full citations.

[49] Regulation, Recital (11).

[50] See below, paras 18–023ff.

[51] cf. Convention, art.15.

[52] e.g., *FR Lürssen Werft GmbH & Co. KG v Halle* [2010] EWCA Civ 587; [2011] 1 Lloyd's Rep. 265.

[53] e.g., the presumption that a re-insurance policy is governed by the same law as the related insurance policy; see *Wasa International Insurance Co. v Lexington Insurance Co.* [2009] UKHL 40; [2010] 1 A.C. 180.

[54] See the Giuliano-Lagarde report, at p.17.

same, please?" Legal rules must in these matters reflect commercial realities and expectations; hence the reference above to "the circumstances of the case".

11–019 Difficult questions can be asked about the situation in which words in the contract may or may not amount to an express choice of law, and the law which should govern this question of construction. But it is suggested that these questions will seldom need to be answered. The important question is whether art.3(1) has been satisfied; if it is, nothing turns on whether the choice was express or not. The "boundary question" is one of an essentially factual nature: have the parties clearly demonstrated a choice of applicable law? Only if the answer is "no" will art.4 apply. The need for a *clear* demonstration of such a choice may be seen as stricter than the Convention's requirement of demonstration "with reasonable certainty"; the European Commission, commenting on practice under the Convention, observed that "the German and English courts, perhaps under the influence of a slightly more flexible form of words, and under the influence of their previous solutions, are less strict about discerning a tacit choice than their European counterparts",[55] and the new language in the Regulation seeks to eliminate this variation in practice.

It is this factual question, with attention being paid not only to the wording of the contract but to all the circumstances of the case, that enables the courts to examine the practical realities just referred to: relevant trade practices, the use of standard forms developed in particular countries where there is special expertise but used worldwide,[56] and the previous course of dealings between the parties. So, in the Convention case of *Egon Oldendorff v Libera Corp (No.2)*[57] there was no choice of law clause in a contract between German and Japanese companies, but their use of a well-known English standard form of charterparty and the presence of a clause specifying arbitration in England was held to demonstrate the choice of English law as the applicable law.

Qui elegit iudicem elegit ius?

11–020 Recital (12) to the Regulation declares that an agreement between the parties to confer on one or more courts or tribunals of a Member State exclusive jurisdiction to determine disputes under the contract should be one of the factors to be taken into account in determining whether a choice of law has been clearly demonstrated. This reflects long-standing English practice, and the only puzzling feature is the limitation to courts in Member States. In practice, a selection of the courts of New York as having exclusive jurisdiction is just as significant as the choice of the courts of France or Germany. The choice of a particular court is usually supported by very different reasons from those which support a choice of law, so it cannot be automatically inferred from a choice of court that the parties

---

[55] Green paper, para.3.2.4.2. The similarity between the Convention and the English common law approach was stressed by Mance L.J. in *American Motorists Insurance Co. v Cellstar Corp.* [2003] EWCA Civ 206; [2003] I.L.Pr. 370.

[56] The expertise of the London insurance market is one example: *Gan Insurance Co. Ltd v Tai Ping Insurance Co. Ltd* [1999] 2 All E.R. (Comm) 54.

[57] [1996] 1 Lloyd's Rep. 380.

chose the *lex fori* to govern their contract.[58] This is not to say that choice of the *lex fori* might not be a sensible and cost-effective choice, but it should be an informed and deliberate one by the parties. In some scenarios, the parties will agree on the jurisdiction of the courts in a "neutral" country because they wish to avoid proceedings before the courts in the country of the eventual counter-party. In these cases, the choice of forum is not necessarily connected to the choice of law and a presumption in favour of the parallelism between choice of court and choice of law would not lead to an appropriate law to govern the contract.

A common problem, in this as in other areas of the law of contract, is the use by the parties of standard conditions which are mutually inconsistent. There will be no express choice of law within art.3 unless the court can find a consensus between the parties, and the use of inconsistent terms,[59] or the clear rejection of a proffered choice of law clause,[60] indicates a lack of consensus.

Division of or change in the governing law

By their choice, the parties can select the law applicable to the whole or a part only of the contract.[61] This allows *depéçage*, a splitting of the contract between different legal systems. This can be done by reference to different duties of performance or, presumably, different numbered clauses. But there may be problem cases in which the two chosen laws cannot logically be reconciled in their application to a particular situation, for example, repudiation for non-performance[62]; in such a case there can be no effective choice by the parties, and the court would have to rely on art.4.   **11–021**

It is possible for the parties to change the governing law, either by altering their own expressed choice or by making a choice where previously they had not done so.[63] However, any variation by the parties of the law to be applied made after the conclusion of the contract will not prejudice its formal validity (that is, where the contract was formally valid at its inception under the Convention or Regulation rules,[64] any additional formal requirements of the new governing law will be ignored) or adversely affect the rights of third parties.

---

[58] This presumption was rejected by the House of Lords in *Compagnie d'Armement Maritime SA v Compagnie Tunisienne de Navigation SA* [1971] AC 572 at 596.

[59] See *Iran Continental Shelf Oil Co v IRI International Corp.* [2002] C.L.C. 372 (revsd [2002] EWCA Civ 1024, but not on this point).

[60] Asin *Land Rover Exports Ltd v Samcrete Egypt Engineers and Contractors SAE* [2001] EWCA Civ 2019; [2002] C.L.C. 533 (choice of law clause in draft agreement crossed out by one party).

[61] Convention, art.3(1); Regulation, art.3(1). This is to be distinguished from an arrangement under which the parties agree that the law applicable depends upon stated circumstances (the law of State A on one contingency, of State B on another); such "floating" choice of law clauses appear perfectly valid.

[62] An example in the Giuliano-Lagarde Report, p.17.

[63] Convention, art.3(2); Regulation, art.3(2). See *ISS Machinery Services Ltd v Aeolian Shipping SA, The Aeolian* [2001] EWCA Civ 1162; [2001] 2 Lloyd's Rep. 641 (successive contracts dealing with supply and then provision of spare parts for machine governed by different laws; no evidence that choice of law in second contract intended to change law governing the first contract).

[64] These are in art.9 of the Convention and art.11 of the Regulation; see below, para.13–034.

Freedom of choice and mandatory rules

11–022   There is no requirement that the chosen law need have any real connection with the parties or the subject matter of their contract.[65] That this is so is apparent from art.3(3) but that same provision qualifies the complete freedom of choice.[66] The provision is more elegantly drafted in the Regulation, where it reads:

> Where all other elements relevant to the situation at the time of the choice are located in a country other than the country whose law has been chosen, the choice of the parties shall not prejudice the application of provisions of the law of that other country which cannot be derogated from by agreement.[67]

In the Convention text the provisions which cannot be derogated from by agreement are described as "mandatory rules", and this caused some problems as that phrase seems to be used in two different senses within the English text of the Convention. The concept is further discussed below, as the Regulation now speaks of "overriding mandatory provisions".[68] However, the concept is not a difficult one: the Unfair Contract Terms Act 1977 familiarised English lawyers with the idea that certain types of liability under English law cannot be excluded by a contractual term. In that sense, the liability rules are mandatory.

11–023   Such rules may serve many purposes. They may relate to the socio-economic policies of states, for example in the field of competition or "anti-trust" law; exchange control designed to protect the national economy or its currency; laws designed to protect the environment. Or they may seek to regulate the contents of private contracts, requiring the inclusion of certain types of term, or prohibiting exclusion or exemption clauses or the imposition of unreasonable sanctions in penalty clauses. They may be designed to protect the interests of those seen as economically weak, such as workers (with rules as to health and safety at work and to safeguards from unfair dismissal) or consumers (with rules designed to help them in disputes with suppliers of goods and services). Or they may serve more general interests such as the proper administration of justice or the uniform regulation of an international industry such as aviation.[69]

Article 3(3) envisages a situation in which all elements of the factual situation are connected with Country A, the law of which contains a relevant rule which cannot be derogated from by agreement. The parties, for whatever reason, agree that the law of Country B is to govern their contract. They have that freedom of choice, and art.3(3) does not remove it; the law of Country B will indeed be the governing law. However, the non-derogable rules of Country A will also apply, and within its scope will override any different rule in the law of Country B.

---

[65] cf. the issue at common law in *Vita Food Products In. v Unus Shipping Co Ltd* [1939] A.C. 277.

[66] See also Regulation, art.3(4), a similar rule as to non-derogable rules of Community law.

[67] The redraft was intended to make no substantial change: Regulation, Recital (15).

[68] See para.11–069ff.

[69] See McClean, De Conflictu Legum (2000) 282 Hague Receuil des cours), Ch.V.

The provision speaks of "all other elements relevant to the situation". What this **11–024** may mean can be considered in the light of facts based on those of an Australian case[70]:

> X is an estate agency which specialises in selling retirement homes in the South of Queensland, advertising widely in newspapers circulating in the holiday areas of Queensland where potential purchasers may be staying. A contract is entered into which carries a commission much in excess of the maximum amount allowed under Queensland legislation; that legislation cannot under the law of Queensland be excluded by a contractual term. X's conditions of doing business specify that the law of Hong Kong should govern.

If all the elements are connected only with Queensland, there is no difficulty. If the estate agency is a company incorporated under the law of Hong Kong, or for that matter of New South Wales, or the purchase is made by a couple retiring from their present home in Tasmania, the factual elements are no longer all connected to Queensland. This raises the question, to which there is as yet no clear answer, as to whether the adjective "relevant" is to be interpreted so as to enable some minor non-Queensland elements to be ignored and the non-derogable rule applied.

Article 3(4) of the Regulation protects in the same manner the imperative norms of European law.[71]

Incorporation (by reference) of foreign law

A distinction must be drawn between the parties' express selection of the **11–025** applicable law and their incorporation of some of the provisions of a foreign law (other than the applicable law) as a term or terms of the contract. It is open to the parties to an English contract to agree that their rights and liabilities shall be determined in accordance with the relevant provisions of the French Commercial Code. The effect is not to make French law the applicable law but rather to incorporate the French law provisions as contractual terms into an English contract. This is a convenient "shorthand" alternative to setting out the French provisions verbatim. It often happens that statutes governing the liability of a carrier, such as the Carriage of Goods by Sea Act 1971, are incorporated by what is known as a "paramount clause" in a contract governed by a law other than that of which the statute forms part. The statute then operates not as a statute but as a set of contractual terms agreed upon by the parties.[72]

---

[70] *Golden Acres Ltd v Queensland Estates Pty Ltd* [1969] Qd.R. 378 (affd. on other grounds (1970) 123 C.L.R. 418). See *Caterpillar Financial Services Corp v SNC Passion* [2004] EWHC 569 (Comm); [2004] 2 Lloyd's Rep. 99; *Emeraldian Ltd Partnership v Wellmix Shipping Ltd, Guangzhou Iron & Steel Corp Ltd* [2010] EWHC 1411 (Comm); [2011] 1 Lloyd's Rep. 301.

[71] See *Ingmar GB Ltd v Eaton Leonard Technologies Inc* [2000] E.C.R. I-09305. The inclusion of a provision on the applicability of European imperative norms in Art.3 has been criticised. See Boele-Woelki and Lazić, 'Where Do We Stand on the Rome I Regulation?' in Boele-Woelki and Grosheide (eds) *The Future of European Contract Law, Liber Amicorum E H Hondius* (Kluwer, 2007) at 31. In their opinion it would have been better to deal with this issue in the general provision dealing with overriding mandatory rules (art.9).

[72] The practice is not free from difficulties as the statute incorporated may not be an ideal "fit" to the facts of the particular contract: see *Adamastos Shipping Co. Ltd v Anglo-Saxon Petroleum Co* [1959] A.C. 133; *Seven Seas Transportation Ltd v Pacifico Union Marina Corp, The Oceanic Amity* [1984] 2

The distinction between incorporation of foreign law by reference and an express choice of the applicable law is seen most clearly if there is a change in the law between the time of making the contract and its performance. The applicable law is a living law and must be applied as it is when the contract is to be performed and not as it was when the contract was made.[73] Thus, legislation passed in the country of the applicable law may have the effect of modifying or discharging the contractual obligation, e.g. by reducing the rate of interest[74] or declaring a gold value clause invalid.[75] On the other hand, where a foreign statute is incorporated in a contract as a contractual term, it remains part of the contract, although as a statute it may have been amended or repealed.

Applicable law in the absence of choice: the Convention

11–026   As the rules of the Convention and of the Regulation diverge at this point, they must be dealt with separately.

In the Convention, if there is no choice by the parties, the governing law is determined by the complex rules set out in art.4. The starting point is the clear principle set out in art.4(1):

> To the extent that the law applicable to the contract has not been chosen in accordance with art.3, the contract shall be governed by the law of the country with which it is most closely connected.

In this context, as in art.3, there is room for *depéçage*: there is a, notably guarded, provision that "nevertheless" a severable part of the contract which has a closer connection with another country may "by way of exception" be governed by the law of that other country.[76] The Court of Appeal has held that this contemplates distinct provisions within a contract, which can be treated as separate from the rest of the contract.[77]

11–027   If art.4 had stopped at that point, it would have reflected the English common law position; but the authors of the Convention felt obliged to limit its flexibility. They felt it essential to give the courts more guidance as to the identification of the law of the country of closest connection. So art.4(2) provides:

> Subject to the provisions of paragraph 5 of this article, it shall be presumed that the contract is most closely connected with the country where the party who is to effect the performance which is characteristic of the contract has, at the time of conclusion of the contract, his habitual residence, or, in the case of a body corporate or unincorporate, its central administration. However, if the contract is entered into in the course of that party's trade or profession, that country shall be the country in which the principal place of business is situated

---

All E.R. 140. The distinction between incorporation by reference and choice of law is not always easy: *Shamil Bank of Bahrain EC v Beximco Pharmaceuticals Ltd* [2004] EWCA Civ 19; [2004] 1 W.L.R.1784.

[73] *Re Helbert Wagg & Co Ltd's Claim* [1956] Ch. 323 at 341; *Rossano v Manufacturers Life Insurance Co* [1963] 2 Q.B. 352 at 362.

[74] *Barcelo v Electrolytic Zinc Co of Australasia Ltd* (1932) 48 C.L.R. 391.

[75] *R v International Trustee for the Protection of Bondholders A/G* [1937] A.C. 500.

[76] Convention, art.4(1).

[77] *Bank of Scotland v Butcher* [1998] N.P.C. 144.

or, where under the terms of the contract the performance is to be effected through a place of business other than the principal place of business, the country in which that other place of business is situated.

This paragraph is best approached in a number of stages:

(1)   The first stage is the identification of the "party who is to effect the performance which is characteristic of the contract". This idea, made fashionable by its use in Swiss legal texts,[78] is explained in the Giuliano-Lagarde Report as one which "links the contract to the social and economic environment of which it will form a part".[79] It identifies a particular category of contract, an exercise more appealing to the civil law mind than that formed by the common law.

11–028

In the normal case, one party to a contract provides consideration in the form of money. The performance which is characteristic of the contract is:

> "the performance for which the payment is due, i.e. depending on the type of contract, the delivery of goods,[80] the granting of the right to make use of an item of property, the provision of a service, transport, insurance,[81] banking operations,[82] security, etc. which usually constitutes the centre of gravity and the socio-economic function of the contractual transaction".[83]

If A pays B to act as the distributor of A's goods in a particular country, the characteristic performance of this distribution contract would seem to be that of B. The facts are seldom as simple as that, and the Court of Appeal has held on one set of facts that it was the supplier of the goods rather than their distributor who effected the characteristic performance.[84] There may, of course, be cases, such as complex financial services transactions, where this sort of analysis is unhelpful. A later provision in art.4 takes care of that problem.[85]

---

[78] See the Law on Private International Law of 1987, art.117; Vischer, "The Concept of Characteristic Performance reviewed" in Borras (ed.), *E Pluribus Unum: Liber Amicorum Georges A L Droz* (1996), 499; and Mankowski, "The Principle of Characteristic Performance Revisited Yet Again" in Boele-Woelki et al (eds), *Convergence and Divergence in Private International Law – Liber Amicorum Kurt Siehr* (2010), 433.

[79] p.20.

[80] e.g., the supply of whisky in *William Grant & Sons International Ltd v Marie Brizard Espana SA* 1998 S.C. 537.

[81] e.g., work as an insurance broker as in *Hogg Insurance Brokers Ltd v Guardian Insurance Co Inc.* [1997] 1 Lloyd's Rep. 412.

[82] In the case of a contract between a bank and one of its customers, the bank will provide the characteristic performance, but (see point (iii), below) the location of the branch holding the account may be relevant: *Sierra Leone Telecommunications Co Ltd v Barclays Bank Plc* [1998] 2 All E.R. 821 at 826–827. More complex banking cases can require very careful analysis, often involving the use of agency concepts with the agent as the party regarded as providing the characteristic performance. See, e.g., *Bank of Baroda v Vysya Bank* [1994] 2 Lloyd's Rep. 87 (confirmation of letters of credit).

[83] Giuliano-Lagarde Report, p.20.

[84] *Print Concept GmbH v GEW (EC) Ltd* [2001] EWCA Civ 352, criticised (it is submitted correctly) by Hill (2004) 53 I.C.L.Q. 325 at 335–336.

[85] Convention, art.4(5), considered below, para.11–030.

(2)   Having identified the relevant party, it must be determined whether in entering into the contract he was acting in the course of his trade or profession,[86] which is a matter of fact that will usually, but perhaps not always, present little difficulty.

11–029   (3)   If he was so acting, then it is to be presumed that the country with which the contract is most closely connected is that in which the party's principal place of business is situated.[87]

If, however, under the terms of the contract the performance is to be effected through some other place of business, the country is that in which that other place of business is situated. Plainly, a contractual term that performance by a London-based company was to be effected through its Rome office would come within this type of case. It is not wholly clear whether the Convention phrase "under the terms of the contract" would be satisfied by a term expressly requiring performance in Italy (in circumstances normally requiring action by a local representative) but making no reference to a place of business there. A stricter test was applied in *Ennstone Building Products Ltd v Stanger Ltd (No. 2)*[88]:

> E, an English company, supplied stone for use in building work. S, also an English company, provided testing and consultancy services through offices in England (its head office), Wales and Scotland. E supplied stone for a building in Edinburgh, but technical problems arose. A member of E's staff visited S's Scottish office, and it was agreed that S would conduct tests and report. A dispute arose and E brought a claim against S in England. The key issue was whether Scottish or English law applied; under Scottish law the claim might be time-barred.

The Court of Appeal held that unless a term of the contract would be broken by performance through a particular place of business, the last part of art.4(2) would not apply. The parties had anticipated performance of the contract through the defendant's Scottish office, but there was no contractual requirement to that effect. Article 4(2) therefore pointed to the country of the defendant's principal place of business, namely England.[89]

(4)   If the relevant party was not acting in the course of his trade or profession, the presumption is that the country with which the contract is most closely connected is that in which, at the time of the conclusion of the contract, he had his habitual residence, or in the case of a "body" its central administration.

---

[86] Note that this is the question; not whether *in effecting the characteristic performance* he would be so acting.

[87] Note that the test is as stated; the presumption in art.4(2) always identifies a place *of business*; the place *of performance* as such is not relevant for this purpose (though it may of course be crucial for the purposes of jurisdiction under art.5(1) of the Brussels I Regulation: see paras 4–026ff).

[88] [2002] EWCA Civ 916; [2002] 1 W.L.R. 1141.

[89] cf. the different view tentatively advanced in *Iran Continental Shelf Oil Co v IRI International Corp* [2002] EWCA Civ 1024 per Clarke L.J. at para.[65].

Disregarding the presumption: Article 4(5)

The presumption created by art.4(2)[90] has a limited effect. It does not apply if the **11–030** characteristic performance cannot be determined; more significantly, it is to be disregarded if it appears from the circumstances as a whole that the contract is more closely connected with another country.[91]

The English courts, unlike some in other Member States, are used to a flexible test of this sort, and might be expected to resort to the presumptions only in "tie-break" situations. The English cases seem in general to confirm that assessment. In the earliest case, the presumptions pointing to the application of the law of State A were disregarded because the relevant transaction was part of linked series of transactions which as a whole were governed by the law of State B.[92]

Morrison J. in *Definitely Maybe (Touring) Ltd v Marek Lieberberg Konzertagentur GmbH*[93] referred to the fact that, under the common law approach, little weight would be given to the place of business or residence of a party and much more weight to the place of performance; he spoke of "a natural tendency to wish to maintain the old, well-developed common law position where factors were weighed and attempts were made to ascertain the true intention of the parties". Article 4(2) reverses the order of priority. In *Definitely Maybe*:

> DM, agents with a principal place of business in England, arranged with MLK, a German company, for the rock band Oasis to appear at two concerts in Germany. The group appeared, but without its lead guitarist, Noel Gallagher. MLK refused to pay the agreed fee. The issue of jurisdiction depended on what law governed. DM was the party effecting characteristic performance of the contract.

Morrison J. felt that prima facie the contract was nonetheless most closely **11–031** connected with Germany. What weight, then, had to be given to the presumption? His answer was "due" weight. The burden of proof was on the party seeking to have the presumption disregarded to establish factors which pointed to another country. This would be more readily achievable where the place of performance was different from the place of the performer's business. "But in carrying out what must be regarded as a comparative exercise, due weight must be given to the factor identified in Art.4(2)." In the instant case, and despite his observation that giving wide effect to art.4(5) would render the presumption in art.4(2) of no value, Morrison J. held that this burden had been discharged, and German law applied.

A similar approach can be seen in the later case of *Land Rover Exports Ltd v Samcrete Egypt Engineers and Contractors SAE*[94]:

---

[90] And the special presumptions in Convention, art.4(3)(4), to be considered below.
[91] Convention, art.4(5).
[92] Which just happened to be England: *Baroda v Vysya Bank* [1994] 2 Lloyd's Rep. 87.
[93] [2001] 1 W.L.R. 1745.
[94] [2001] EWCA Civ 2019; [2002] C.L.C. 533, followed in *Commercial Marine & Piling Ltd v Pierse Contracting Ltd* [2009] EWHC 2241 (TCC); [2010] 1 All E.R. (Comm) 1087. See also *British Arab Commercial Bank plc v Bank of Communications* [2011] EWHC 281 (Comm); [2011] 1 Lloyd's Rep. 664.

LR appointed T its distributor in Egypt. S, with a principal place of business in Egypt, entered into a contract of guarantee with LR guaranteeing, inter alia, T's debts. S was sued on the guarantee. As S was the party whose performance was characteristic of that contract, the presumption in art.4(2) clearly pointed to the law of Egypt. The Court of Appeal disregarded the presumption, applying English law as the place of payment under the guarantee was in England.[95]

11–032   It is difficult not to see these decisions as interpreting the Convention text to make it accord with the pre-Convention common law. There is in some other Contracting States a very different view of the relationship between arts 4(2) and 4(5). The best known example is the Dutch case of *Société Nouvelle des Papeteries de l'Aa v BV Maschinefabrieke BOA.*[96] The case involved the supply of machinery by a Dutch company, which clearly provided the characteristic performance. Delivery was to a French company in France; payment was in francs; the contract was negotiated in France. The Dutch court held that the presumption in art.4(2) should be disapplied only if, in the light of special factors, the country of habitual residence (or principal place of business) of the party carrying out the characteristic performance had "no real value as a connecting factor".

In the process that led to the adoption of the Rome I Regulation, the European Commission's Green Paper commented on the differing views as to the strength of the presumption in art.4(2). It expressly favoured the Dutch view:

"Given the letter and spirit of the Convention, the courts might reasonably be expected to begin with the presumption of Art.4(2). Only if it emerged that the law designated is not appropriate because other circumstances clearly militate in favour of another law would the court then use the 'exception clause'."[97]

Immovables

11–033   Special presumptions apply in certain cases. To the extent that the subject matter of a contract is a right in immovable property, or a right to use immovable property, it is presumed that the contract is most closely connected with the country where the immovable property is situated[98]; this reflects the usual position at common law.

Applicable law in the absence of choice: the Regulation

11–034   Article 4 of the Regulation contains much more precise and detailed rules in the case in which the parties have not chosen the applicable law. The notion of "characteristic performance" is much less important. So is the notion of "the closest connection". There are no presumptions as such, but a series of rules each applying to a different type of contract with a limited power to depart from the

---

[95] A second reason was that the place of performance by LR of its contract with T was also in England, but it is difficult to see the relevance of that.

[96] Hoge Raad, September 25, 1992; see Struycken, [1996] L.M.C.L.Q. 18. cf. the facts of the common law case of *The Assunzione* (above, para.11–005).

[97] Green Paper, para.3.2.5.3, which canvassed various means of ensuring that its preferred approach is generally adopted.

[98] Convention, art.4(3).

relevant rule. The policy, hard fought over in the negotiations, is that the conflict-of-law rules should be highly foreseeable, but that the courts should retain a degree of discretion to determine the law that is most closely connected to the situation.[99] The rules[100] are as follows:

(a) a contract for the sale of goods shall be governed by the law of the country where the seller has his habitual residence.   **11–035**

No further definition is given of "sale of goods" but it (and "provision of services" in the following rule) are to be interpreted in the same way as in art.5 of the Brussels I Regulation.[101]

To apply this rule, and some others, it is necessary to have a clear provision as to the meaning of habitual residence.[102] Article 19 accordingly provides that, for the purposes of the Regulation, the habitual residence of companies and other bodies, corporate or unincorporated, is the place of central administration; and the habitual residence of a natural person acting in the course of his business activity is his principal place of business.[103] In each case, the facts are taken as at the time of the conclusion of the contract.[104] However, where the contract is concluded in the course of the operations of a branch, agency or any other establishment, or if, under the contract, performance is the responsibility of such a branch, agency or establishment, the place where the branch, agency or any other establishment is located is to be treated as the place of habitual residence.[105]

(b) a contract for the provision of services shall be governed by the law of the country where the service provider has his habitual residence;

(c) a contract relating to a right in rem in immovable property or to a tenancy of immovable property shall be governed by the law of the country where the property is situated;

(d) notwithstanding point (c), a tenancy of immovable property concluded for temporary private use for a period of no more than six consecutive months shall be governed by the law of the country where the landlord has his habitual residence, provided that the tenant is a natural person and has his habitual residence in the same country;

(e) a franchise contract shall be governed by the law of the country where the franchisee has his habitual residence;   **11–036**

(f) a distribution contract shall be governed by the law of the country where the distributor has his habitual residence;

(g) a contract for the sale of goods by auction shall be governed by the law of the country where the auction takes place, if such a place can be determined;

---

[99] Regulation, Recital (16).
[100] Regulation, art.4(1).
[101] Regulation, Recital (17).
[102] Recital (39) refers to inappropriateness of having three criteria, as in art.60 of the Brussels I Regulation on the domicile of companies and other bodies.
[103] Regulation, art.19(1).
[104] Regulation, art.19(3).
[105] Regulation, art.19(2).

(h)   a contract concluded within a multilateral system which brings together or facilitates the bringing together of multiple third-party buying and selling interests in financial instruments, as defined by art.4(1), point (17) of Directive 2004/39/EC, in accordance with non-discretionary rules and governed by a single law, shall be governed by that law.[106]

11–037   The problem with this type of list is that some contracts may not be covered at all, and other contracts may combine elements of two or more entries. In both these cases, the regulation provides that the contract is to be governed by the law of the country where the party required to effect the characteristic performance of the contract has his habitual residence.[107] A very common illustration would be a contract for the sale of machinery which also provided for the seller to carry out regular servicing of the machinery for a number of years. This combines the sale of goods (point (a)) and the supply of services (point (b)). Both those rules identify the habitual residence of the seller/provider of services, and it will be obvious that he is to affect the characteristic performance of the contract.

Departing from these rules

11–038   The policy that the courts should retain a degree of discretion, to determine the law that is most closely connected to the situation, means that these rules cannot always be followed. The regulation provides that where it is clear from all the circumstances of the case that the contract is manifestly more closely connected with a country other than that indicated by those rules, the law of that other country is to apply.[108] The Recitals indicate that account should be taken, inter alia, of whether the contract in question has a very close relationship with another contract or contracts.[109] The word "manifestly" is a signal to the courts to use this power only in very clear cases.[110] The emphasis placed on the habitual residence of one party, even with the special understanding of habitual residence in branch and agency cases, may identify a state very little connected with the substantial purpose of the contract. It remains to be seen how the courts use this power.

There is one further escape clause. Where the facts are such that the law applicable cannot be determined by using the rules in art.4(1) and (2), the contract is governed by the law of the country with which it is most closely connected.[111]

---

[106] See Recital (18).
[107] Regulation, art.4(2).
[108] Regulation, art.4(3).
[109] Regulation, Recital (20).
[110] On the standard required by the Regulation as compared to the Convention, see Dickinson, [2010] L.M.C.L.Q. 27.
[111] Regulation, art.4(4).

Contracts of carriage[112]

The Convention and the Regulation contain special rules applying to contracts for the carriage of goods. This applies to contracts the main purpose of which is the carriage of goods, even if they are classified as charterparties under national law.[113] In the Convention a special presumption favours the country in which, at the time the contract was concluded, the carrier had its principal place of business if it was also the country in which the place of loading or the place of discharge or the principal place of business of the consignor was situated.[114] This rule is replaced in the Regulation by a similar rule, making use of the concept of habitual residence, to which provisions dealing with the carriage of passengers are added.

11–039

(a)   In the case of the carriage of goods (including single-voyage charter parties and other contracts the main purpose of which is the carriage of goods)[115] where the parties have not chosen the applicable law, the law applicable to a contract for the carriage of goods is the law of the country of habitual residence of the carrier, provided that the place of receipt[116] or the place of delivery or the habitual residence of the consignor is also situated in that country. If those requirements are not met, the law of the country where the place of delivery as agreed by the parties is situated applies.[117] "Consignor" means any person who enters into a contract of carriage with the carrier and the term "the carrier" should refers to the party to the contract who undertakes to carry the goods, whether or not he performs the carriage himself.[118]

(b)   The passenger provisions are more complicated. The freedom of the parties to select the applicable law is limited. They (and in reality that means the carrier) may select only the law of the country where (a) the passenger has his habitual residence; or (b) the carrier has his habitual residence; or (c) the carrier has his place of central administration; or (d) the place of departure is situated; (e) the place of destination is situated. Where the parties have not chosen the applicable law, the law applicable is the law of the country where the passenger has his habitual residence, provided that either the place of departure or the place of destination is situated in that

11–040

---

[112] See Morse, "Contracts of Carriage and the Conflict of Laws" in Boele-Woelki et al (eds), *Convergence and Divergence in Private International Law—Liber Amicorum Kurt Siehr* (2010), 463. See also Kenfack, 2009 Clunet 3.

[113] Case C-133/08 *Intercontainer Interfrigo SC v Balkenende Oosthuizen BV* [2009] ECR I-9687 at paras 33–35 of the judgment.

[114] Convention, art.4(4).

[115] Regulation, Recital (22).

[116] This may not be the same as the place of loading referred to in the Convention: a carrier may collect the goods at a place distant from that at which the goods are loaded on to the vehicle that is to carry them.

[117] Regulation, art.5(1). In the words of Advocate General Bot in Case C-133/08 *Intercontainer Interfrigo SC v Balkenende Oosthuizen BV* [2009] ECR I-9687, "legal certainty and foreseeability of the applicable law have taken preference over the flexibility of application of the conflict rule" (para.65 of the judgment).

[118] Regulation, Recital (22).

country. If these requirements are not met, the law of the country where the
carrier has his habitual residence applies.[119]

(c)   In each case, where it is clear from all the circumstances of the case that the
        contract, in the absence of a choice of law, is manifestly more closely
        connected with a country other than that indicated in these rules, the law of
        that other country applies.

In relation to contracts for the carriage of goods, the matter may well fall
within one or other of the well-established international transport conventions,
which not affected by the Regulation.[120]

Consumer contracts

11–041   It is part of the policy of the Rome I Regulation,[121] as it was of the Convention,[122]
that the weaker parties to contracts should be protected by conflict-of-law rules
that are more favourable to their interests than the general rules. This principle is
strongly established in Europe but equally strongly rejected in the United States.
In the Community texts, it is applied to consumers, insurance policy-holders and
employees. So far as consumers are concerned, the Regulation contains a fairly
extensive revision of the Convention text, so the two must be dealt with
separately.

Consumer contracts under the Convention

11–042   The Convention rules, set out in art.5, can usefully be compared with the special
rules as to jurisdiction set out in arts 15 to 17 of the Brussels I Regulation.[123]

Article 5 applies to a contract[124] the object of which is the supply of goods or
services to a person ("the consumer") for a purpose which can be regarded as
being outside his or her trade or profession,[125] or a contract for the provision of
credit for that object. The text of the Convention is silent as to the nature of the
other party (the supplier or the source of credit) and also lacks the emphasis,
found in the Giuliano-Lagarde report, on whether the consumer appears to be, or
holds himself out to be, acting outside his trade or profession.

Where the requirements of art.5(1) are met on these points, a choice of law
made by the parties will not have the result of depriving the consumer of the

---

[119] Regulation, art.5(2).

[120] Regulation, art.25. Member States had a duty to notify the EU Commission of the Conventions
referred to in art.25 by June 17, 2009. See the list in [2010] OJ C343/4. The UK has notified no
Conventions.

[121] Regulation, Recital (23).

[122] See Giuliano-Lagarde report, p.23.

[123] See above, paras 4–053ff, where several issues raised by both sets of provisions are examined.

[124] But not to a contract of carriage (except an inclusive tour contract providing for a combination of
travel and accommodation: art.5(5)); or a contract for the supply of services where the services are to
be supplied to the consumer exclusively in a country other than that in which he or she is habitual
resident: art.5(4).

[125] The Giuliano-Lagarde report, at p.23, argues that the purchase of equipment for use in a
professional activity will not be a consumer activity; cf. above, para.4–053.

protection afforded to him by the mandatory rules[126] of the law of the country in which he has his habitual residence,[127] if one of the following sets of circumstances applies:

(1) in that country the conclusion of the contract was preceded by a specific invitation addressed to him or by advertising, and he had taken in that country all the steps necessary on his part for the conclusion of the contract; or

(2) the other party or his agent received the consumer's order in that country; or

(3) the contract was for the sale of goods and the consumer travelled from that country to another country and there gave his order, provided that the consumer's journey was arranged by the seller for the purpose of inducing the consumer to buy.[128]

Where a consumer contract entered into in any of these circumstances contains no choice of the applicable law, then, notwithstanding art.4, it is governed by the law of the country in which the consumer has his or her habitual residence.[129]

Except in the relatively unusual cases within sub-paragraph (3), the Convention gives no protection to the increasingly common "mobile consumer", who travels to a country other than that of habitual residence to make a purchase or receive a service.

11–043

In effect, the seller has to have entered into the market-place in the consumer's country, and to have done so in specific ways. The increased availability in all European countries of newspapers and journals primarily directed at a market in another country, the appearance of satellite television channels serving whole continents or indeed most of the world, and the growth of e-commerce all make some of the ideas in art.5 seem distinctly dated. As the European Commission observed in its Green Paper[130]:

> "The criteria selected no longer seem adapted to the development of new distance selling techniques. To determine whether or not a contract is within the scope of Art.5, it is always necessary to locate it in space by reference to an aspect such as advertising, the signing of a contract or the receipt of an order."

In addition, this solution is no longer in harmony with art.15 of the [Brussels I] Regulation, under which consumer protection provisions apply where a company directs its business activities towards the Member State of the consumer's residence and a contract is concluded within the framework of these activities, whatever distance selling technique is used.

---

[126] See above, para.11–022. The reference would seem to be to mandatory rules as defined in art.3(3) of the Convention.
[127] In matters not within the scope of any mandatory rules, the choice of law will be effective.
[128] Convention, art.5(1)(2).
[129] art.5(3).
[130] para.3.2.7.2.

Consumer contracts under the Regulation

11–044   Article 6 of the Regulation provides[131] that a contract concluded by a natural person for a purpose which can be regarded as being outside his trade or profession (the consumer) with another person acting in the exercise of his trade or profession (the professional) shall be governed by the law of the country where the consumer has his habitual residence, provided that the professional:

(a)   pursues his commercial or professional activities in the country where the consumer has his habitual residence; or

(b)   by any means, directs such activities to that country or to several countries including that country;

and the contract falls within the scope of such activities.[132] If the requirements in points (a) or (b) are not fulfilled, applicable law is determined under the general rules in arts 3 and 4.[133]

11–045   So far as the concept of "directed activity"[134] in point (b) is concerned, Recital (24) asserts that it must be interpreted harmoniously in the Brussels I Regulation and the Rome I Regulation, and cites the joint declaration by the Council and the Commission (on art.15 of the Brussels I Regulation) that:

> "the mere fact that an Internet site is accessible is not sufficient for Article 15 to be applicable, although a factor will be that this Internet site solicits the conclusion of distance contracts and that a contract has actually been concluded at a distance, by whatever means. In this respect, the language or currency which a website uses does not constitute a relevant factor".

The parties may choose the law applicable to contract which does meet those requirements but such a choice cannot deprive the consumer of the protection afforded to him by provisions that cannot be derogated from by agreement by virtue of the law of the consumer's habitual residence.[135]

Certain types of contract which might seem to fall within the consumer contract category are excluded from the effect of these rules. They are contracts for the supply of services where the services are to be supplied to the consumer exclusively in a country other than that in which he has his habitual residence; contracts of carriage other than a contract relating to package travel[136]; contracts

---

[131] Without prejudice to the rules in art.5 (carriage) and art.7 (insurance).
[132] Regulation, art.6(1).
[133] Regulation, art.6(3).
[134] See Gillies, Electronic Commerce and International Private Law (Ashgate, 2008); Tang, Electronic Consumer Contracts in the Conflict of Laws (Hart Publishing, 2009); Tang, (2010) 6 J.Priv.Int.L. 225; and Fawcett, Harris and Bridge, International Sales of Goods in the Conflict of Laws (O.U.P., 2005), pp.1217–1321. See also *Pammer v Reederei Karl Schluter GmbH & Co KG* Case (C-585/08) (joined with case C-144/09); [2012] All E.R. (EC) 34.
[135] Regulation, art.6(2).
[136] See Council Directive 90/314/EEC of June 13, 1990 on package travel, package holidays and package tours.

relating to a right in rem in immovable property or a tenancy of immovable property other certain timeshare contracts[137]; and certain contracts relating to financial instruments.[138]

Insurance contracts

One of the aims of the Rome I Regulation was to draw together relevant rules in a single instrument, and this was partially successful in the case of insurance contracts. Reference will not be made here to the complex position before the regulation.   **11–046**

Article 7 of the Regulation applies to insurance contracts covering a "large risk", whether or not risk covered is situated[139] in a Member State, and to all other insurance contracts covering risks situated inside the territory of the Member States.[140] It does not apply to reinsurance contracts.[141] A "large risk" is defined by reference to an earlier Directive[142] and includes such things as risks relating to damage to or loss of, railway stock, aircraft, ships, vehicles, goods in transit, and export and instalment credit. An insurance contract covering a large risk is governed by the law chosen by the parties, and to the extent that the applicable law has not been so chosen, by the law of the country where the insurer has his habitual residence. Where, however, it is clear from all the circumstances of the case that the contract is manifestly more closely connected with another country, the law of that other country applies.[143]

In the case of all other insurance contracts, the ability of the parties (in practice the insurer) to select the governing law is limited. The parties may select only: **11–047**

(a)   the law of any Member State where the risk is situated at the time of conclusion of the contract;

(b)   the law of the country where the policy holder has his habitual residence;

(c)   in the case of life assurance, the law of the Member State of which the policy holder is a national;

(d)   for insurance contracts covering risks limited to events occurring in one Member State other than the Member State where the risk is situated, the law of that Member State; or

(e)   where the policy holder of a contract falling under this paragraph pursues a commercial or industrial activity or a liberal profession and the insurance contract covers two or more risks which relate to those activities and are

---

[137] See European Parliament and Council Directive 94/47/EC of October 26, 1994 on the protection of purchasers in respect of certain aspects of contracts relating to the purchase of the right to use immovable properties on a timeshare basis.

[138] Regulation, art.6(4). See Recitals (26)–(31).

[139] For the location of risks, see regulation, art.7(6) and the Directives there cited.

[140] Where such insurance contracts cover risks situated outside the Member States, the general rules in arts 3 and 4 will apply subject to any special rules in the specialised Directives.

[141] Regulation, art.7(1).

[142] The First Council Directive 73/239/EEC of July 24, 1973 on the co-ordination of laws, regulations and administrative provisions relating to the taking-up and pursuit of the business of direct insurance other than life assurance, art.5(d).

[143] Regulation, art.7(2).

situated in different Member States, the law of any of the Member States concerned or the law of the country of habitual residence of the policy holder.

Where, in the cases set out in points (a), (b) or (e), the Member States referred to grant greater freedom of choice of the law applicable to the insurance contract, the parties may take advantage of that freedom. To the extent that the law applicable has not been chosen by the parties, the contract is governed by the law of the Member State in which the risk is situated[144] at the time of conclusion of the contract.[145]

11–048   Where under the law of a Member State, insurance of a risk is compulsory, (a) the insurance contract shall not satisfy the obligation to take out insurance unless it complies with the specific provisions relating to that insurance laid down by the Member State that imposes the obligation. Where the law of the Member State in which the risk is situated and the law of the Member State imposing the obligation to take out insurance contradict each other, the latter prevails; and (b) by way of derogation from the usual rules (those in art.7(2) and (3)), a Member State may lay down that the insurance contract is to be governed by the law of the Member State that imposes the obligation to take out insurance.[146]

Individual employment contracts

11–049   Article 6 of the Convention and art.8 of the Regulation contain broadly similar provisions dealing with individual employment contracts. There is no attempt to define "employment", though the Giuliano-Lagarde Report[147] observed that de facto employment situations (where, for example, the employer fails to issue any formal contract of employment) are included.

As a matter of general principle, the law most relevant to employment is that of the country in which the employee works. That statement fails, however, to reflect the fact that individual employees may work in several countries; they may have one fixed base but visit other countries for shorter or longer periods, but may also have a pattern of work which makes it difficult to identify any place as the base from which they work; and the employer may be located in a quite different country, having recruited the employee in yet another. The Regulation deals rather better with this range of fact-situations than does the Convention.

Under the Convention, an individual employment contract is, in the absence of choice in accordance with art.3, governed (a) by the law of the country in which the employee habitually carries out his work in performance of the contract, even

---

[144] For this purpose, where the contract covers risks situated in more than one Member State, the contract is to be considered as constituting several contracts each relating to only one Member State: art.7(5).
[145] Regulation, art.7(3).
[146] Regulation, art.7(4).
[147] At p.26.

if temporarily employed in another country[148]; or (b) if the employee does not habitually carry out his work in any one country, by the law of the country in which the place of business through which he was engaged is situated[149]; unless it appears from the circumstances as a whole that the contract is more closely connected with another country, in which case the contract is to be governed by the law of that country.[150] These provisions were examined in the first case to reach the ECJ on employment contracts under the Rome Convention, *Koelzch v Luxembourg*.[151]

> K was a German lorry driver employed by the Luxembourg subsidiary of a Danish company. The employer's business was the transport of flowers and other plants from Denmark to destinations situated mostly in Germany, but also in other European countries, by means of lorries stationed in Germany but registered in Luxembourg. The employer had no seat or offices in Germany. K's contract contained a clause selecting Luxembourg law as the applicable law and another giving exclusive jurisdiction to the courts of Luxembourg. After K was dismissed, he sued first in Germany (the German courts holding that they had no jurisdiction) and then in Luxembourg. K argued that under art.6 of the Convention [substantially reproduced in art.8 of the Rome I Regulation] the mandatory rules of German law applied, notwithstanding the choice of Luxembourg law, as he habitually carried out his work in performance of the contract in Germany.

The ECJ as whether in a situation where the employee works in more than one country, but returns systematically to one of them, that country must be regarded as that in which the employee habitually carries out his work. Despite the argument that to interpret art.6(2)(a) so as to cover such a case would render art.6(2)(b) meaningless, the court drew on the case-law under the Brussels I Regulation and answered in the affirmative. art.6(2)(b), referring to the place of business through which the employee was engaged, is to be applied only in cases where the court is able to determine the country in which the work is habitually carried out. That is the effect of art.8(3) of the Rome I Regulation and the ECJ chose to apply the Regulation rule in interpreting the Convention.

In determining where an employee habitually carries out the work, a court:

11–050

> "must, in particular, find in which state is situated the place from which the employee carries out his transport tasks, receives instructions concerning his tasks and organises his work, and the place where his work tools are situated. It must also determine the places where the transport is principally carried out, where the goods are unloaded and the place to which the employee returns after completion of his tasks".[152]

In *Voogsgeerd v Navimer*,[153] the interpretation of "the country in which the place of business is situated through which an employee was engaged", within the meaning of art.6(2)(b) of the Convention was at stake. The ECJ held that art.6(2) requires first to establish whether the employee, in the performance of the contract, habitually carries out the work in the same country, which is the country

11–051

---

in which or from which, in the light of all the factors which characterise that activity, the employee performs the main part of the obligations towards the employer. If that cannot be established under that provision,[154] Article 6(2)(b) must be understood as referring exclusively to the place of business which engaged the employee and not to that with which the employee is connected by his or her actual employment.

A choice of law clause included in an individual contract of employment does not have the result of depriving the employee of the protection afforded by the mandatory rules of the law which would be applicable under the rules just stated in the absence of choice.[155] Examples in English law will include the statutory provisions as to such matters as maternity leave and redundancy.

Under the Regulation, to the extent that the law applicable to the contract has not been chosen by the parties, the contract is governed by the law of the country "in which or, failing that, from which" the employee habitually carries out his work in performance of the contract. The country where the work is habitually carried out shall not be deemed to have changed if he is temporarily employed in another country.[156] It is only where the law applicable cannot be determined under these rules that contract is governed by the law of the country where the place of business through which the employee was engaged is situated.[157] Where it appears from the circumstances as a whole that the contract is more closely connected with a country other than that identified by these rules, the law of that other country applies.[158] Where there is a choice of law by the parties, it does not deprive the employee of the protection afforded to him by provisions that cannot be derogated from by agreement under the law that, in the absence of choice, would have been applicable under the rules just stated.[159]

The protection of the weaker party

11–052   There is no doubt that the object of these special provisions is the protection of the weaker party. Neither the Convention nor the Regulation deals satisfactorily with the situation that can arise in which the law chosen by the parties offers *better* protection to the weaker party than the law apparently preferred by the legislative texts. It is not at all improbable that both legal systems will have mandatory (or non-derogable) rules designed to protect consumers or employees, and one or other system may afford better protection on particular issues. As Morse has well observed, it would "hardly accord with common sense to say the consumer is 'deprived' of the protection of the mandatory rules of the law of his habitual residence if he is better off than he would have been had those rules been applied".[160] It is therefore arguable that the clear policy underlying the legislation

---

[154] art.6(2)(a).
[155] Convention, art.6(1). This was relevant in both *Koelzch v Luxembourg* and the *Voogsgeerd* case.
[156] Regulation, art.8(2).
[157] Regulation, art.8(3).
[158] Regulation, art.8(4).
[159] Regulation, art.8(1).
[160] (1992) 41 I.C.L.Q. 1 at 8.

requires the rules to be applied with a flexibility uncharacteristic of the continental approach to texts of this sort, and that the more protective set of rules should always be applied.

That does not even begin to exhaust the difficulties surrounding this matter. Given that one legal system may provide better protection on certain aspects (in an employment context, for example, it may have more fully developed rules on redundancy than on maternity leave), is the employee to be able to pick and chose, to select the law most favourable on the particular facts? Or might it be argued that both systems of law are to be applied, given cumulative effect so that the weaker party gets double protection?[161] It has to be admitted that the texts provide no answer, and the ECJ may have to give a further example of its capacity for creative interpretation.

SCOPE OF THE APPLICABLE LAW

The use of the term "applicable law" must not mislead the reader into supposing that the law so described necessarily governs all issues concerning a particular contract. That this is not the case is evident from the partial exclusion from its scope of questions of capacity, already noted.[162] The applicable law does, however, govern many questions, including the interpretation of the contract[163] and some other matters which require comment.

11–053

Performance

Article 10 of the Convention and art.12 of the Regulation each make two references to "performance". This is listed as one of the matters governed by the applicable law[164] but it is also provided that:

11–054

> in relation to the manner of performance and the steps to be taken in the event of defective performance regard shall be had to the law of the country in which performance takes place.[165]

This latter provision does not displace the applicable law; the court is merely to "have regard to" the law of the place of performance. This is explained in the Giuliano-Lagarde Report[166] as empowering the court to consider the relevance of that law and, in its discretion, to apply it in whole or in part so as to do justice between the parties. Such unusual flexibility is the more striking given the uncertainty which surrounds the distinction between "performance" proper and "the manner of performance".

At common law there was a familiar, if not clear-cut, distinction between the "substance of the obligation" and the "method and manner of performance". It

11 055

---

[161] See on this set of issues Philip, in North, *op. cit.*, (1982) at 99; Kaye, New Private International Law of the European Community (Dartmouth, Aldershot, 1993), at 213.
[162] See paras 11–016 and 11–065.
[163] Convention, art.10(1)(a); Regulation, art.12(1)(a).
[164] Convention, art.10(1)(b); Regulation, art.12(1)(b).
[165] Convention, art.10(2); Regulation, art.12(2).
[166] p.33.

was well established that the proper law of the contract governed the substance of the obligation; so, for example, in *Mount Albert Borough Council v Australasian Temperance and General Assurance Society*[167]:

> A New Zealand borough corporation borrowed £130,000 in 1926 from an insurance company incorporated in Victoria and carrying on business in Australia and New Zealand. To secure the loan the borough corporation issued debentures charged on the borough rates, and therefore on New Zealand land. The proper law of the contract was New Zealand law. Interest on the debentures at the rate of five and two-third per cent was payable in Victoria. In 1931, during the Great Depression, a Victorian statute reduced the rate of interest on all mortgages to 5 per cent. It was held that this statute did not apply to the debentures, although Victoria was the place of performance, because New Zealand law was the proper law of the contract.

11–056   It was also clear that excuses for non-performance such as the doctrine of force majeure were matters for the proper law. However, in establishing that proposition, the Court of Appeal, in *Jacobs v Credit Lyonnais*[168] said that the law of the place of performance might well regulate the "method and manner" of performance; but this was confined to matters of detail, matters which do not affect the substance of the obligation. If, for instance, under an English contract a seller undertook to deliver goods in Paris "during usual business hours", it would presumably be for French law to say what business hours were usual; but English law would determine whether performance was excused by frustration or to what extent the seller was liable for defects in the goods delivered. If, by an English contract, an English seller agreed to sell goods in Lisbon to an American buyer for export to East Germany, Portuguese law would say whether an export licence was required and whether the goods had to be cleared through the customs, but English law would determine whether the seller or the buyer was under a duty to obtain the licence, and if no licence was obtained, which party had broken the contract or whether the contract had been frustrated.[169] If a New York contract made between an Australian and a Canadian provided for the payment of dollars in London, New York law would determine whether this means American or Australian or Canadian dollars (money of account), i.e. the extent of the debtor's indebtedness, but English law would determine whether payment might or had to be made in dollar bills or could be made in pound notes (money of payment), i.e. how the debtor's obligation was to be performed.

It is, however, clear that the distinction drawn in the Convention and the Regulation cannot be interpreted in quite this way. They make two references to performance, one referring to it as being governed by the applicable law, and it is in that context that the Giuliano-Lagarde Report mentions "conditions relating to the time and place of performance".[170] The second reference, to the "manner and method" category, or perhaps we should say "sub-category", is one in which other rules may be applied as a matter of discretion. This is an area in which clarification must be awaited from the courts.

---

[167] [1938] A.C. 224.
[168] (1884) 12 Q.B.D. 589.
[169] *Pound & Co Ltd v Hardy & Co Inc* [1956] A.C. 588.
[170] p.32.

Consequences of breach

The applicable law governs, *within the limits of the powers conferred on the court*   **11–057**
by its procedural law, the consequences of breach, including the assessment of
damages *in so far as it is governed by rules of law*.[171] This tortuous language
reflects a hard-fought compromise, and its effects are not easily stated. The
difficulty lies in the qualifications italicised above.

In general, the type of remedies which are to be made available, be they
damages, injunctions, or orders for specific performance, will be determined by
reference to the applicable law. However, and this is the point of the first
qualification, a court will not be required to make an order unknown to its legal
system or (less clearly) to make an order that its procedures regard as
inappropriate, e.g., an order of specific performance in the context of an
employment contract. So far as the assessment of damages is concerned, one
aspect of that exercise, the actual "quantification" (e.g. what amount of money is
appropriate in the case of the loss of a right foot?) is traditionally regarded as a
matter for the court of trial, as one for the *lex fori* or simply a question of factual
estimation. The effect of the second qualification seems to be to leave that
practice unchanged, but to give effect to rules of the applicable law that impose a
maximum sum that can be awarded in any particular circumstances, for example
by limiting the liability of a carrier to a certain maximum or making similar
provision in respect of compensation for wrongful dismissal. Again, this area
awaits clarification by the ECJ.

Extinguishing obligations, prescription and limitation of actions

These matters are governed by the applicable law.[172] So far as limitation of   **11–058**
actions is concerned, this reflects the position reached in English law in the
Foreign Limitation Periods Act 1984; that the limitation rules of the *lex causae*
govern.[173]

PARTICULAR TOPICS

Material validity

Provisions in art.8 of the Convention and art.10 of the Regulation address the   **11–059**
question of "material validity" a term which includes a number of matters which
English writers would more readily see as concerned with the "formation" of the
contract, e.g., offer and acceptance.

So, the existence and validity of a contract, or of any term of a contract, is to
be determined by the law which would govern it under the Convention or
Regulation if the contract or term were valid.[174] This is to apply what is
sometimes called "the putative applicable law", ascertained by applying the usual

---

[171] Convention, art.10(1)(c); Regulation, art.12(1)(c) (emphasis added).
[172] Convention, art.10(1)(d); Regulation, art.12(1)(d).
[173] See below, para.17–023.
[174] Convention, art.8(1); Regulation, art.10(1).

rules as set out in arts 3 and 4. It involves giving weight to any choice of law made by the parties, even though the legal existence or validity of the instrument in which that choice is expressed is *ex hypothesi* doubtful.

Illegality

11–060   One aspect of material validity is the question of illegality. At common law, the English courts had held that performance of a contract was excused (i) if it had become illegal by the proper law of the contract or (ii) necessarily involved doing an act which was unlawful by the law of the place where the act had to be done.[175] If the contract were governed by English law, the latter aspect of this rule could be seen as an application of the rule of English domestic law as to the effect of supervening illegality. It was never finally established whether there was an independent rule of the conflict of laws under which illegality could be a matter for the law of the place of performance.[176] This issue would only arise were the English court faced with a contract governed by the law of State A (not England), performance of which was illegal by the law of the place of performance, State B.

The position now is that illegality is a matter for the applicable law. This still means that where the applicable law is English, the English rule as to supervening illegality will apply. This can be illustrated by the facts of the pre-Convention case of *Ralli Brothers v Compania Naviera Sota y Aznar*[177]:

> A contract, governed by English law, for the carriage of jute by sea from Calcutta to Barcelona provided for the payment of freight on delivery of the cargo at Barcelona at the rate of £50 per ton. After the date of the contract, but before the arrival of the ship, a Spanish decree fixed the maximum freight on jute at £10 per ton and made it illegal to pay more. The shipowners' action to recover the difference between £10 and £50 per ton was dismissed.

The decision would be the same today, on the basis that illegality, performance and discharge of contractual obligations are all matters for the applicable law—English law—and by applying the rule of English domestic law as to the effect of supervening illegality. However, as will be seen, rules of the country in which a contract is to be performed may in some circumstances be given direct effect.[178]

Consent

11–061   Another aspect of material validity is that of consent; a contract cannot exist unless the parties consent to be bound by it, either by a positive giving of consent or, in some situations, by tacit acceptance. The latter possibility, in effect that in some legal situations silence may be held to indicate consent, has given rise to a great deal of debate. In practice the issue is likely to arise in less extreme circumstances, where the law as to the giving of consent varies as between the countries concerned.

---

[175] *Libyan Arab Foreign Bank v Bankers Trust Co* [1989] Q.B. 728.

[176] See *Zivnostenska Banka v Frankman* [1950] A.C. 57 at 59 per Lord Reid, but cf. the different view expressed by Lord Reid in a companion case, *Kahler v Midland Bank* [1950] A.C. 24 at 28.

[177] [1920] 2 K.B. 287.

[178] See below for "overriding mandatory provisions": paras 11–069ff.

The general view is that it would be unfair to deem someone to have consented when his or her actions (or silence) would not have this effect under that person's "own" law. The Community instruments express this thought, and identifies the country of a party's habitual residence[179] as the relevant one: a party may rely upon the law of the country in which he has his habitual residence to establish that he did not consent[180] if it appears from the circumstances that it would not be reasonable to determine the effect of his conduct in accordance with the putative applicable law.[181] "Reasonable" defies further definition, though it has been said that in applying it in this context the courts should take a "dispassionate, internationally minded approach".[182]

Formal validity

"Form" is defined in the Giuliano-Lagarde Report[183] as including "every external **11–062** manifestation required on the part of a person expressing a will to be legally bound, and in the absence of which such expression of will would not be regarded as fully effective". This clearly includes a requirement that a contract is valid only if it is in writing, or witnessed in a particular way, or drawn up before a notary, or registered; though on the last point, the notion of form does not include questions as to what may be required to make a term binding on third parties.

The Convention and Regulation favour the formal validity of agreements by listing a number of laws, compliance with the requirements of any of which will establish formal validity. The rules are somewhat confusingly set out, but their effect can be stated as follows:

(1) It always suffices to comply with the formal requirements of the applicable law.[184]

(2) A contract concluded between persons who are in the same country is formally valid if it satisfies the formal requirements of the law of that country.[185] The development of electronic means of communication means that it is not always possible for one party to know the whereabouts of the other, but this lack of knowledge is immaterial.

(3) A contract concluded between persons who are in different countries is **11–063** formally valid if it satisfies the formal requirements of the law of either of those countries,[186] or (under the regulation only) the law of the country where either of the parties had his habitual residence at that time.[187]

---

[179] Even in the case of corporations or other business associations.

[180] He is provided with a shield, not a sword; he can avoid being bound but not create a binding obligation.

[181] Convention, art.8(2); Regulation, art.10(2).

[182] *Egon Oldendorff v Libera Corp* [1995] 2 Lloyd's Rep. 64 at 70.

[183] p.29.

[184] Convention, art.9(1)(2); Regulation, art.11(1)(2).

[185] Convention, art.9(1); Regulation, art.11(1).

[186] Convention, art.9(2); Regulation, art.11(2).

[187] Regulation, art.11(2).

(4)   For the purposes of these rules, where a contract is concluded by an agent, the country in which the agent acts is the relevant country.[188]

(5)   However, none of the above rules can be relied on the case of consumer contracts within the relevant provisions of the Convention or Regulation.[189] The formal validity of such contracts is governed by the law of the country in which the consumer has his or her habitual residence.[190]

11–064 (6)   A contract, the subject matter of which is a right in immovable property or a right to use immovable property, remains subject to the mandatory (or non-derogable) requirements of form of the law of the country where the property is situated, if by that law those requirements are imposed irrespective of the country where the contract is concluded and irrespective of the law governing the contract.[191]

(7)   Finally, and most obscure to the English reader, "a unilateral act [in the Convention, an act] intended to have legal effect relating to an existing or contemplated contract" is formally valid if it satisfies the formal requirements of the law which governs or would govern the contract, or of the law of the country where the act was done,[192] or, under the Regulation, of the law of the country where the person by whom it was done had his habitual residence at that time.[193] The Giuliano-Lagarde Report gives as examples notices of termination or of repudiation.[194]

Incapacity

11–065 In general, questions of capacity are excluded from the scope of the Convention and of the Regulation, and are therefore still governed by the common law rules. The Community texts do contain one limited provision. In a contract concluded between persons who are in the same country (not necessarily in one another's presence), a natural person (as opposed to a company or other entity) who would have capacity under the law of that country may invoke his incapacity resulting from another law only if the other party to the contract was aware of this incapacity at the time of the conclusion of the contract or was not aware thereof as a result of negligence.[195] The stringent requirements of this article will be noted, and also the fact that it is concerned only with the right of a person to invoke his own incapacity; were the other party to raise capacity issues, the common law rules would apply.

There is, however, an extraordinary dearth of English authority on the question of what law governs capacity to make a contract. There is only one decision (dating from 1800) and a few stray and contradictory *dicta*.

One approach, which has long seemed old-fashioned, is to regard a person's capacity to contract as an emanation of status and therefore as governed by the

---

[188] Convention, art.9(3); Regulation, art.11(1)(2).
[189] i.e. those to which Convention, art.5 or Regulation, art.6 applies.
[190] Convention, art.9(5); Regulation, art.11(4).
[191] Convention, art.9(6); Regulation, art.11(5).
[192] Convention, art.9(4); Regulation, art.9(3).
[193] Regulation, art.9(3).
[194] p.29.
[195] Convention, art.11; Regulation, art.13.

law of the person's domicile. Another is to consider it as a factor determining the validity of the contract and therefore as governed by its proper law. There is general agreement among writers that in this context the proper law must be ascertained objectively, i.e. by applying the test of closest connection. Any other view would lead to the unacceptable result that a child could confer capacity on himself or herself by agreeing that some more favourable system than the objectively ascertained proper law should govern the contract.[196]

A hypothetical case illustrates the difficulty of deciding between the law of the domicile and the proper law of the contract: **11–066**

> A domiciled Ruritanian aged 20 buys goods on credit from a London shop. Could he refuse to pay for them on the ground that by Ruritanian law minority ends at 21 and contracts made by minors cannot be enforced against them?

Here we have a conflict of policy between Ruritanian law, anxious to protect its domiciliary (or national) from making an improvident bargain, and English law, which we may assume to be the putative proper law. Most students coming fresh to this topic say that the Ruritanian should be held liable because commercial convenience requires this result. In the great majority of cases this answer is surely correct. If we assume that the Ruritanian minor is in England, art.11 of the Rome Convention or art.13 of the Rome I Regulation will usually secure that result.

But if we change the facts and suppose (a) that the Ruritanian minor never left Ruritania, the contract being concluded by correspondence, or by email; (b) that the shopkeeper opened negotiations by sending him a catalogue depicting, e.g., attractive-looking motor-bikes or electric guitars; (c) that the letter of acceptance was posted in Ruritania; and (d) that the shop was owned and managed by Ruritanians, then the case for applying English law becomes progressively weaker. But in the normal case, where the contract is made *inter praesentes* in the London shop and the shop is English-owned and managed, then the case for applying English law is strong. It would lead to inconvenience and injustice if the validity of an ordinary contract made in England, of which English law was the putative proper law, were allowed to depend on the law of one party's foreign domicile with which the other party could not be expected to be familiar.

There may of course be no real conflict between the law of the domicile and the proper law of the contract. If we reverse the facts and suppose that a domiciled Englishman aged 20 buys goods on credit from a shop in Ruritania, and that law is the putative proper law, it could be plausibly argued that the customer is not entitled to the protection of English law, because by that law he is of full age, nor of Ruritanian law, because he is not a Ruritanian. If so, the contact should be valid and the Englishman liable. We have here what the Americans call a false conflict[197]; if this is recognised, there is no problem.   **11–067**

---

[196] cf. *Cooper v Cooper* (1888) 13 App. Cas. 88 at 108, where Lord Macnaghten said: "It is difficult to suppose that Mrs. Cooper could confer capacity on herself by contemplating a different country as the place where the contract was to be fulfilled".
[197] For false conflicts, see below, para.19–038.

So far as the practice of the courts is concerned, dicta favouring the law of the domicile can be quoted,[198] but they were all delivered in cases concerning capacity to marry or to make a marriage settlement, and they have been much criticised. Although the place of contracting is commonly regarded as of little importance, as in modern commercial practice it may be fortuitous, dicta may also be cited in favour of the law of the place of contracting,[199] and so can one Scottish case[200] where a contract made in Scotland by a minor domiciled in Ireland was held valid. In a Canadian case,[201] a husband and wife, domiciled in Quebec but resident for many years in Ontario, made a separation agreement in Ontario. When sued in Ontario for arrears of maintenance due under the agreement, the husband's executor pleaded that by the law of their domicile the spouses had no capacity to make such a contract. The court rejected this defence on the ground that capacity to contract is governed by the proper law of the contract. The court said that had the parties been resident as well as domiciled in Quebec, and had made the contract during a short visit to Ontario, "it would be against common sense to decide the parties' capacity by Ontario law". This dictum is perhaps more significant than the decision itself.

11–068   In one English case,[202] there is an indication that the judge would have held that incapacity was governed by the proper law, but the matter did not directly arise.

In view of what has been said, the law which an English court would apply to the question is obviously anybody's guess. The best solution, it is suggested, is to say that if a person has capacity either by the proper law of the contract or by the law of his domicile and residence, then the contract is valid, so far as capacity is concerned.

RESTRICTIONS ON THE REACH OF THE APPLICABLE LAW

Overriding mandatory provisions of the forum

11–069   One of the more troublesome aspects of the Rome Convention was its treatment of "mandatory rules". The phrase was used in two senses, and we have already encountered one, that of rules which cannot be derogated from by agreement between the parties. The second sense is clarified in the Regulation which speaks of "overriding mandatory provisions" and provides a definition:

> Overriding mandatory provisions are provisions the respect for which is regarded as crucial by a country for safeguarding its public interests, such as its political, social or economic

---

[198] *Sottomayor v De Barros (No.1)* (1877) 3 P.D. 1 at 5 (criticised in *Sottomayor v De Barros (No.2)* (1879) 5 P.D. 94 at 100, and in *Ogden v Ogden* [1908] P. 46 at 73); *Re Cookes Trusts* (1887) 56 L.J. Ch. 637 at 639; *Cooper v Cooper* (1888) 13 App.Cas. 88 at 99, 100 and 108.
[199] *Male v Roberts* (1800) 3 Esp. 163 (the nearest English case to a decision on the matter); *Simonin v Mallac* (1860) 2 Sw. & Tr. 67; *Baindail v Baindail* [1946] P. 122 at 128 (both cases of marriage). In *Republica de Guatemala v Nunez* [1927] 1 K.B. 669 at 689–690 and 700–701, Scrutton and Lawrence L.JJ. refused to decide between the *lex domicilii* and the *lex loci contractus*, because they coincided.
[200] *McFeetridge v Stewarts and Lloyds Ltd*, 1913 S.C. 773. See especially at p.789, per Lord Salvesen.
[201] *Charron v Montreal Trust Co* (1958) 15 D.L.R. (2d) 240.
[202] *Bodley Head v Flegon* [1972] 1 W.L.R. 680.

organisation, to such an extent that they are applicable to any situation falling within their scope, irrespective of the law otherwise applicable to the contract under this Regulation.[203]

This definition is based on the decision of the ECJ in *Arblade*.[204] English writers have used the expression "overriding statutes", legislative rules which override or preclude the normal rules of choice of law.[205] The European Commission had earlier explained in its Green Paper that:

"What is special about [this type of rule] or *lois de police*,[206] is that the court does not even apply its conflict rules to see what law would be applicable and assess whether its content might be repugnant to the public policy of the forum but automatically applies its own law."[207]

Both the Convention[208] and the Regulation provide, albeit in different language, that nothing they contain restricts the application of the overriding mandatory provisions of the law of the forum.[209] These provisions allow English courts to continue to apply the overriding provisions of English statutes. So, the Trade Union and Labour Relations (Consolidation) Act 1992[210] and the Employment Rights Act 1996[211] both provide that "for the purposes of this Act it is immaterial whether the law which (apart from this Act) governs any person's employment is the law of the United Kingdom, or of a part of the United Kingdom, or not". This does not mean that the Acts apply to all contracts of employment in the world, regardless of their connection with the United Kingdom, because another section of each Act lays down that certain of its provisions do not apply where under his contract of employment the employee ordinarily works outside Great Britain.[212] What it does mean is that the draftsman, instead of enacting (or leaving it to be assumed) that the Act only applies when the law governing the contract of employment is that of some part of the United Kingdom, has cut across the normal rules of the conflict of laws and laid down his own rules for the application of the Act. His method has two advantages. First, it prevents the parties evading the Act by choosing a foreign law as the law of the contract of employment. Second, it secures the benefits of the Act to employees who work in the United Kingdom for foreign employers and whose contracts of employment might well be governed by foreign law.

11–070

---

[203] Regulation, art.9(1).

[204] Cases C-369/96 and C-374/96 [1999] E.C.R. I-8453 at para.31. See for criticism by (one of the negotiators of Rome I, Hellner, (2009) 5 J.Priv. Int. L. 447 at 460.

[205] An example is the Carriage of Goods by Sea Act 1971: *The Hollandia* [1983] 1 A.C. 565.

[206] The term used in the heading to art.7 in the French text of the Convention.

[207] Green Paper, para.3.2.8.1.

[208] Convention, art.7(2): "Nothing in this Convention shall restrict the application of the rules of the law of the forum in a situation where they are mandatory irrespective of the law otherwise applicable to the contract".

[209] Regulation, art.11(2).

[210] s.289, re-enacting earlier legislation, on which see Mann, (1966) 82 L.Q.R. 316; Hughes, (1967) 83 L.Q.R. 180; Unger, (1967) 83 L.Q.R. 427 at 428–433; Mann, (1972–73) 46 B.Y.I.L. 177 at 136–137.

[211] s.204(1).

[212] 1992 Act s.285; 1996 Act s.215, re-enacting earlier legislation, which is also discussed in the articles cited above. For other and so very difficult cases, see *Ravat v Halliburton Manufacturing & Services Ltd* [2012] UKSC 1.

11–071 An even more important example is provided by the Unfair Contract Terms Act 1977.[213] That Act imposes severe restrictions on the validity of exemption clauses in many kinds of contract. The provisions of the Act are mandatory: the parties cannot contract out of them.[214] To prevent them from doing so indirectly by selecting a foreign law as the applicable law, s.27(2) provides that the Act has effect notwithstanding any contract term purporting to apply the law of some country outside the United Kingdom, if (a) the term appears to have been imposed wholly or mainly for the purpose of enabling the party imposing it to evade the application of the Act; or (b) in the making of the contract one of the parties dealt as consumer[215] and was then habitually resident in the United Kingdom, and the essential steps necessary for the making of the contract were taken there.[216] Section 27(2)(a) is a novelty in that it introduces for the first time a doctrine of evasion of law into English law.

Overriding mandatory provisions of other states

11–072 What has been more controversial is the effect of overriding mandatory provisions of third states,[217] i.e., states which are neither the forum nor the state whose law is the applicable law. The Rome Convention has a provision on this subject which was not given effect in the law of England. Article 7(1) reads as follows:

> When applying under this Convention the law of a country, effect may be given to the mandatory rules of the law of another country with which the situation has a close connection, if and in so far as, under the law of the latter country, those rules must be applied whatever the law applicable to the contract. In considering whether to give effect to these mandatory rules, regard shall be had to their nature and purpose and to the consequences of their application or non-application.

Although there are cases in which this sort of provision could be useful (for example a case falling just outside art.3(3) because not every element was connected with the same country), the vagueness of this provision both in failing to identify the class of country which might be thought to have "a close connection" and in giving a discretion ("effect may be given") without any real guidance as to its exercise, rendered it unacceptable to the United Kingdom. The European Commission cites one English case as illustrating the circumstances addressed by art.7(1). It is *Regazzoni v K C Sethia (1944) Ltd*[218] in which the House of Lords held a contract designed to evade the Indian legislation prohibiting trade with South Africa unenforceable. However, the basis of the

---

[213] See, e.g., *Trident Turboprop (Dublin) Ltd v First Flight Couriers Ltd* [2009] EWCA Civ 290; [2010] Q.B. 86.

[214] Unless a contract is an "international supply contract" as defined in s.26. That definition follows closely the definition in the Uniform Laws on International Sales Act 1967.

[215] "Dealt as consumer" is widely defined by s.12.

[216] For a comment on s.27 of the 1977 Act, see Mann, (1978) 27 I.C.L.Q. 661.

[217] See Dickinson, (2007) 3 J.Priv.Int.L. 53; Kunda, Internationally Mandatory Rules of a Third Country in European Contract Conflict of Laws (Rijeka Law Faculty, 2007); Hellner, (2009) 5 J.Priv. Int. L. 447.

[218] [1958] A.C. 301.

decision was English public policy, and the contract was governed by English law, so reliance on a provision akin to art.7(1) would not have been necessary.

The Rome I Regulation contains a more restricted provision, which is of course part of the law of the United Kingdom: **11–073**

> Effect may be given to the overriding mandatory provisions of the law of the country where the obligations arising out of the contract have to be or have been performed, in so far as those overriding mandatory provisions render the performance of the contract unlawful. In considering whether to give effect to those provisions, regard shall be had to their nature and purpose and to the consequences of their application or non-application.[219]

This is much more specific: it is limited to the rules of the country of performance, and to the rules of that country which make performance illegal. The resulting provision is consistent with English courts' practice prior to the entry into force of the Regulation.

Ordre public

Even if there is no overriding statute, the English courts have one route open to them to apply English law rather than the rules of the applicable law as identified by the Convention or the Regulation. Article16 of the Convention and art.21 of the Regulation contain a text, familiar in international agreements, allowing the application of a rule of the law of any country specified by the Convention to be refused if such application is "manifestly incompatible with the public policy *(ordre public)* of the forum".   **11–074**

Public policy has been characterised as a "last-ditch weapon"[220] wielded at the *end* of the forum's choice of law process to resist the application of the rule which that process has identified (unlike the overriding mandatory provisions which operate to prevent that process operating). Although public policy may be invoked to protect broadly-defined interests, it is "targeted" in the sense that it is the application of the foreign rule to the particular case which is opposed, not the foreign rule as such.

In *Duarte v The Black and Decker Corp.*[221] the public policy exception was raised in relation to a contract of employment. The mandatory rules referred to in art.6(1) of the Convention (specific provisions whose overriding purpose was to protect employees) did not extend to cover the English law on restrictive covenants in employment contracts. However, it was held that art.16 of the Rome Convention allowed the claimant employee to rely on English public policy to disregard a restrictive covenant governed by the law of Maryland, since the employee was working in England and the non-compete covenant was invalid and unenforceable under English law.

---

[219] Regulation, art.9(3).
[220] Jackson, "Mandatory Rules and Rules of *Ordre Public* in North", *op. cit.*, (1892) p.62.
[221] [2007] EWHC 2720 (Q.B.); [2008] 1 All E.R. (Comm) 401.

Voluntary Assignment and contractual subrogation

11–075 Article 12 of the Rome Convention and art.14 of the Rome I Regulation deal with voluntary assignment.[222] The issue has become vital to the financial services sector in transactions such as securitisation and factoring.[223] However, the effectiveness of cross-border assignments raises long-vexed questions. The leading English case is *Raiffeisen Zentral Bank Osterreich AG v An Feng Steel Co Ltd*,[224] where the Court of Appeal decided that art.12(2) of the Convention covers "issues both as to whether the debtor owes monies to and must pay the assignee (their 'relationship') and under what 'conditions', e.g. as regards the giving of notice".

Article 12 of the Rome Convention reads as follows:

> "1. The mutual obligations of assignor and assignee under a voluntary assignment of a right against another person ('the debtor') shall be governed by the law which under this Convention applies to the contract between the assignor and assignee.
> 2. The law governing the right to which the assignment relates shall determine its assignability, the relationship between the assignee and the debtor, the conditions under which the assignment can be invoked against the debtor and any question whether the debtor's obligations have been discharged."

11–076 Article 14 of the Regulation provides:

> "1. The relationship between assignor and assignee under a voluntary assignment or contractual subrogation of a claim against another person (the debtor) shall be governed by the law that applies to the contract between the assignor and assignee under this Regulation.
> 2. The law governing the assigned or subrogated claim shall determine its assignability, the relationship between the assignee and the debtor, the conditions under which the assignment or subrogation can be invoked against the debtor and whether the debtor's obligations have been discharged.
> 3. The concept of assignment in this article includes outright transfers of claims, transfers of claims by way of security and pledges or other security rights over claims."

The scope of the rule has been extended in the Regulation, as a result of which the provision also governs contractual subrogation. In comparison to its predecessor, the Regulation has made it clear that the law applicable to the contract between assignor and assignee also governs the property aspects of an assignment; however, it does not cover questions of effectiveness and priorities in relation to third parties.[225]

---

[222] See Le Verhagen and Van Dongen, (2010) 6 J.Priv.Int.L.1.

[223] See Hartley, (2011) 60 I.C.L.Q. 29 and Møllmann [2011] L.M.C.L.Q. 262.

[224] [2001] EWCA Civ 68; [2001] Q.B. 825.

[225] A very controversial issue in the negotiations on the Rome I Regulation (finalised in 2008) was the effect of assignments upon third parties. The Commission undertook to prepare and submit a report on the question of the effectiveness of an assignment or subrogation of a claim against third parties, and the priority of the assigned or subrogated claim over a right of another person (art.27(2)). The Commission's report was due on June 17, 2010 but had not been published at the time of writing.

CHAPTER 12

TORTS AND OTHER NON-CONTRACTUAL OBLIGATIONS

As every law student knows, the law of torts is a core component not only of a **12–001** law degree course but of the common law; yet for centuries the law of torts was almost ignored in the conflict of laws. Story, in his major nineteenth-century treatise on the conflict of laws, did not refer to torts at all. Even the sixth edition of Dicey, published in 1949, contained only nine pages on torts compared with 175 pages on contracts. There is more to be said now, and developments in EU law place torts within a larger category; hence the compendious title to this chapter. Those same developments have, alas, made the topic more difficult.

All that calls for some explanation. As a matter of history, the law of torts is largely a creation of the twentieth century, a response to enormous changes in the manufacture and distribution of products and in transport and communication. Before that century, there was little to say about the law of torts even in domestic English law, and it is unsurprising that the same should be true of the conflict rules. In more recent times globalisation has meant that the area we know as "torts" has become much more important. Dangerous electrical machinery may cause fatal accidents in countries far removed from its place of manufacture; pharmaceutical products have caused babies to be born without arms or legs thousands of miles from the laboratory where the drugs were made. Foreign business travel and tourism has increased enormously: accidents occur and people are injured or killed far from home. Satellite television programmes and websites can be seen all over the world: private reputations sometimes suffer. Especially in the United States, torts has become a favourite topic in the field of choice of law: in American writing, torts cases have come to be the focus of the discussion of methodological issues in the conflict of laws, or (in simpler language) the discussion of why courts apply foreign law, and on what basis they choose it.[1]

Unlike the law of contract, the law of torts lacks a single focus. Its content is very disparate, and different legal systems use the concept in different ways and to protect a range of interests which may vary from country to country. So in some countries, the protection of privacy is a function of this branch of the law whereas in England a law of privacy is still work in progress. The common law uses tort remedies, in the guise of detinue, conversion or wrongful interference with goods, as a means of trying title to movable property; such an idea is quite alien to civil law systems which use a different legal category, often derived from the Roman law *vindicatio*, for that purpose.

For EU legislation, the category of "torts" seemed problematic and that of "non-contractual obligation" was preferred. The demarcation of the boundaries of that new category will take some time but it clearly includes most of what English law regards as "torts".

12–002   The development of the English rules of the conflict of laws as to torts was not only slow but also unsatisfactory. There were few cases of any significance, and a leading decision of the House of Lords[2] created more uncertainty than clarity. In 1995, Parliament intervened and enacted new rules in Pt III of the Private International Law (Miscellaneous Provisions) Act of that year. Statutory reform was, however, incomplete: actions for defamation were excluded altogether. That Act is in turn being replaced by European legislation in the form of the Rome II Regulation, formally European Parliament and Council Regulation (EC) No 864/2007 of July 11, 2007 on the law applicable to non-contractual obligations[3] which has "(Rome II)" in its full title. These developments draw on a set of ideas debated over the years and outlined in the paragraphs that follow.

THE LAW OF THE PLACE OF THE TORT

12–003   In the course of the twentieth century, most legal systems developed conflicts rules which applied, or at least gave pride of place to, the law of the place of the tort, the *lex loci delicti*. In 1994, a survey by the Law Commission showed that

---

[1] See Currie, *Selected Essays on the Conflict of Laws* (Duke University Press, Durham NH, 1963), Chs 3, 7 and 14; Cavers, *The Choice of Law Process* (University of Michigan Press, Ana Arbor, 1965), Chs 1, 2 and 6; Hancock, *Torts in the Conflict of Laws* (University of Michigan Press, Ana Arbor, 1942); Stromholm, *Torts in the Conflict of Laws* (Norstedt, Stockholm, 1961); Kahn-Freund (1968) 124 Hague *Recueil des Cours*, 5 (a profound and penetrating study from the point of view of comparative law); Morse, *Torts in Private International Law* (North Holland, Amsterdam, 1978); McClean, *De Conflictu Legum* (2000) 282 Hague *Recueil des Cours*, Ch.VI.
[2] *Boys v Chaplin* [1971] A.C. 356.
[3] O.J. L 199/40, 31.7.2007.

the law of the place of the tort was the primary choice of law rule in almost all European countries, though the notion of the "place of the tort" was differently expressed and some countries[4] allowed the application of another law if that were more favourable to the injured party.[5] In the nineteenth century, some writers, notably Savigny,[6] had argued for the application of the *lex fori*, the law of the court seised of the case. English common law gave some weight to the *lex fori*, but except in countries which still follow the unreformed English doctrine, the use of the *lex fori* has been abandoned as impractical and unjust.[7]

The adoption of the law of the place of the tort as the prevailing doctrine reflected in part ideas as to the "territoriality" of law. It seemed natural to many lawyers to argue that the law of the place where events occur is the only law that can attribute legal consequences to them, an argument seen by some to follow from the, now long-abandoned, "vested rights" theory.[8] In what was for a century the leading English case, Willes J. paid lip-service to this argument when he said that "the civil liability arising out of a wrong derives its birth from the law of the place, and its character is determined by that law".[9]

A more pragmatic argument in favour of applying the law of the place of the tort is that it usually accords with the legitimate expectations of the parties.[10] The law of torts attaches certain liabilities to certain kinds of conduct and to the creation of certain social risks. Those engaging in activities that may involve liability should be able to calculate the risks they are incurring, and to insure against them. Everyone should be entitled to adjust his or her conduct to the law of the country in which the conduct is to take place. The ancient adage "when in Rome, do as the Romans do" becomes, in modern life, "when in Rome see that your insurance policy covers the risks against which Romans insure".[11]

CERTAINTY OR FLEXIBILITY

However, there are strong arguments against a mechanical application of the law of the place of the tort to each and every issue arising out of each and every kind of tort. The very notion of "the place of the tort" raises questions. It may be difficult to determine, as in cases where the defendant's acts take place in one country, and the ensuing harm to the claimant is sustained in another. Even if the

12–004

---

[4] Germany and Hungary.
[5] See HL Paper (Session 1194–95) 36, at pp.19–22; Morse, (1984) 32 Am.Jo.Comp.L. 51.
[6] *System des heutigen roemische Rechts* (1849), Vol. 8, pp.275 et seq
[7] See the decision of the Canadian Supreme Court in *Tolofson v Jensen* (1995) 120 D.L.R. (4th) 289 applying the law of the place of the tort as an invariable rule, and those of the High Court of Australia in *Pfeiffer Pty Ltd v Rogerson* (2000) 172 ALR 625, noted Olbourne, [2002] C.L.J. 537 (adopting the same approach in an intra-Australian context) and *Regie National des Usines Renault SA v Zhang* [2002] 187 ALR 1, noted Smart, (2002) 118 L.Q.R. 512 (reserving the issue in international cases).
[8] See Holmes J. in *Slater v Mexican National Ry* (1904) 194 U.S. 120 at 126, and *Western Union Telegraph Co v Brown* (1914) 234 U.S. 542 at 547. cf. Cardozo J. in *Loucks v Standard Oil Co of New York*, 224 N.Y. 99; 120 N.E. 198, 200 (1918): "A tort committed in one state creates a right of action that may be sued upon in another unless public policy forbids". For the theory, see para.19–010.
[9] *Phillips v Eyre* (1870) L.R. 6 Q.B. 1 at 28.
[10] An argument accepted in the High Court of Australia in *Pfeiffer Pty Ltd v Rogerson* (2000) 172 ALR 625 at 645.
[11] Kahn-Freund (1968) 124 Hague *Recueil des Cours*, 44.

location is clear-cut, the place of the tort may be fortuitous. This is particularly true in transport accidents. An aircraft may disintegrate in flight, or may be forced off its course by bad weather and crash in a country in which neither the passengers nor the airline contemplated that the journey would end. A road accident may occur in Switzerland involving English and Italian lorry drivers: it might just as well have occurred in Italy or France.

The most important point, however, is that the application of the law of the place of the tort regardless of the habitual residence of the tortfeasor and the victim, and regardless of the type of issue and the type of tort involved, may lead to results which seem wholly inappropriate. If, for instance, a Scotsman employed by a Scottish firm, negligently driving his employer's lorry, causes the death of another Scotsman employed by the same firm who is a passenger in the lorry, so committing a tort under both English and Scots law, there is hardly a strong case for applying English law to the Scottish widow's claim for compensation, just because the accident happened at Shap in England, a mere 40 miles south of the border.[12]

Considerations of this kind led Dr Morris to suggest, in 1949, that tort liability should be governed by "the proper law of the tort", the law of the country with which the tort had its closest and most real connection.[13] The gist of this theory is that, while in many, perhaps most, situations there would be no need to look beyond the place of the tort, we ought to have a conflict rule broad enough and flexible enough to take care of the exceptional situations as well as the more normal ones; otherwise the results will begin to offend our common sense. It was suggested that a proper law approach, which the common law had used with great success in the field of contract, would, if intelligently applied, furnish a much-needed flexibility and enable different issues to be segregated, thus allowing a more adequate analysis of the social factors involved. It was also suggested that a proper law approach would facilitate a more rational solution of the problems that arise when acts are done in one country and harm ensues in another.

12–005   The proper law thesis can take a stronger or a weaker form. The stronger version places great emphasis on the virtue of flexibility, and argues that the primary choice of law rule should be that of the proper law. A court following that approach would start with a blank sheet of paper and examine the factors connecting the tort to particular countries without reference to any presumption giving priority to any one factor.[14] This stronger form of the proper law thesis was adopted by the American Law Institute's *Restatement Second of the Conflict of Laws*. The leading section on torts provides that "the rights and liabilities of the parties with respect to an issue in tort are determined by the local law of the state which, as to that issue, has the most significant relationship to the occurrence and the parties".[15]

---

[12] These are the facts of *M'Elroy v M'Allister*, 1949 S.C. 110.

[13] (1949) 12 M.L.R. 248, commenting on *M'Elroy v M'Allister*, above; and (in more detail) (1951) 64 Harv.L.Rev. 881. See also Nygh, (1977) 26 I.C.L.Q. 932.

[14] An analogy would be the application in a contract case of art.4(1) of the Rome I Regualtion without reference to the presumption in art.4(2); see para.11–026.

[15] *Restatement*, s.145.

On the other hand, the stronger form of the proper law doctrine has been criticised by some because it sacrifices the advantages of certainty, predictability and uniformity of result which are claimed to follow from the application of the law of the place of the tort. It is also said that the analogy from contract is not useful because the parties to a contract can avoid uncertainty by choosing the proper law,[16] whereas liability in tort is usually unexpected: road accidents are by definition never planned. Predictability of result may not be such an important factor in the law of torts as it is in the law of contract or the law of property but it is important in practice because it facilitates the lawyer's task of advising the client and negotiating a settlement.

The balance of argument may favour the weaker form of the proper law thesis. This accepts the value of having a clear rule, such as the application of the law of the place of the tort, to be applied in the majority, and perhaps the great majority, of cases. But it also stresses the value of flexibility: where a proper law analysis identifies another law with which the tort (or some issue in a tort case) is much more closely connected, it should be possible for a court to apply that other law.

Before the Rome II Regulation

The Rule in *Philips v Eyre*

It is necessary to give some account of the common law developments in England: they profoundly influenced later legislation, and the rule they produced still applies in defamation cases.   **12–006**

In 1870, the common law rule was formulated in a celebrated dictum by Willes J. in *Phillips v Eyre*[17]:

> "As a general rule, in order to found a suit in England for a wrong alleged to have been committed abroad, two conditions must be fulfilled. First, the wrong must be of such a character that it would have been actionable if committed in England. Secondly, the act must not have been justifiable by the law of the place where it was done."

This dictum was treated by later courts almost as if it were a statutory provision, but their struggles with its interpretation are now happily of little consequence.[18] The Rule in *Phillips v Eyre* came eventually to be understood as a rule of "double actionability". Its first limb was that a claim brought in England on a tort committed abroad would fail unless the conduct complained of was actionable as a tort by English domestic law. Its second limb was that the claim would also fail if there were no civil liability under the law of the place of the tort as between the actual parties to the litigation.

It is the first limb, the application of the *lex fori*, which is the distinctive feature   **12–007**
of the Rule. Its survival for over a century is one of the oddities of English legal history. Nowhere else in the English conflict of laws did a claimant have to surmount a double hurdle and show that the claim was valid not only by the

---

[16] *Boys v Chaplin* [1971] A.C. 356, per Lord Hodson at pp.377–378; per Lord Wilberforce at p.391.
[17] (1870) L.R. 6 Q.B. 1 at 28–29.
[18] See, e.g., *Machado v Fontes* [1897] 2 Q.B. 231; *McLean v Pettigrew* [1945] 2 D.L.R. 65.

appropriate foreign law, but also by English domestic law. The requirement effectively closed the doors of the English court to every action in tort not recognised by English domestic law, even when the only connection with England was that the defendant had moved there after the tort was committed. It was roundly criticised over the years but when the House of Lords had an opportunity to consider the matter in *Boys v Chaplin*,[19] they expressed unanimous approval of this aspect of the rule, despite Lord Wilberforce's concession that it "bears a parochial appearance; that it rests on no secure doctrinal principle; that outside the world of the English-speaking common law it is hardly to be found."[20] The House of Lords showed not only an obstinate conservatism on this point, but "a predilection for the sole application of English law, whatever the tort and wherever committed."[21]

The second limb of the rule, referring to the law of the place of the tort, was relatively uncontroversial. Its effect can be seen from the facts of *Phillips v Eyre*[22] itself.

> An action for assault and false imprisonment was brought in England on the basis of events in Jamaica said to be the responsibility of the defendant, who was Governor of Jamaica. The defendant pleaded that the acts complained of were done by him in the course of suppressing a rebellion which had broken out, and that his acts were subsequently declared lawful by an Act of Indemnity passed by the island legislature.

The Court of Exchequer Chamber held that as the actions of the defendant were not legally wrongful in the law of Jamaica, there was no liability in the law of the place of the tort and so the action failed. After the speeches of the Law Lords in *Boys v Chaplin*,[23] it was clear that the second limb would be satisfied if there were civil liability between the parties in the law of the place of the tort. There was no requirement that the defendant's conduct be classified as tortious by the foreign law; it was sufficient if by that law the defendant's liability to pay damages was contractual, quasi-contractual, quasi-delictual, proprietary or sui generis.[24]

A more flexible approach

12–008   In *Boys v Chaplin*[25]:

> The plaintiff and defendant were both normally resident in England but temporarily stationed in Malta in the British armed services. While both were off duty, the plaintiff, riding as a pillion passenger on a motor scooter, was seriously injured in a collision with a car negligently driven by the defendant. By the law of Malta, he could only recover special damages for his

---

[19] [1971] A.C. 356.
[20] At p.387.
[21] McGregor, (1970) 33 M.L.R. 1 at 5.
[22] (1870) L.R. 6 Q.B. 1.
[23] [1971] A.C. 356.
[24] Lord Hodson at p.377 and Lord Wilberforce at p.389 both required "civil liability" (not tortious liability).
[25] [1971] A.C. 356.

expenses and proved loss of earnings, which in the circumstances amounted to no more than £53. By English law, he could recover general damages for pain and suffering, i.e., a further £2,250.

The plaintiff recovered the full sum, totalling £2,303. It is not at all easy to identify the ratio decidendi. In part the difficulty arises from the fact that the appeal raised two quite distinct issues. The first is essentially one of the classification of questions as to the heads of damage. The House of Lords held, surely correctly but by the slimmest of majorities, that the question as to available heads of damage—the extent of liability in terms of economic loss, pain and suffering, loss of amenities of life, etc. was a substantive issue governed by the applicable choice of law rule rather than a procedural issue governed by the *lex fori*.[26]

That left the second issue before the House of Lords, the correct choice of law rule. It is difficult to find any proposition that commanded the support of a majority. Academic and professional opinion identified the speeches of Lord Hodson and, especially, Lord Wilberforce as authoritative, and later courts have associated *Boys v Chaplin* with their approach. It can be seen as embracing the weaker form of the proper law thesis. In essence, the "general rule" expounded by Willes J. in *Phillips v Eyre* was made subject to exceptions: it might be departed from where the facts of the case so required. Lord Wilberforce began with what he described as a well-understood rule covering the majority of normal cases, but he saw the desirability of making that rule flexible enough to take account of varying interests and considerations of policy presented by the presence of particular foreign elements. A particular issue might be governed by the law of the country that, with respect to that issue, had the most significant relationship with the occurrence and the parties.[27] It was important to segregate the relevant issue and to consider whether, in relation to that issue, the general rule ought to be applied or whether, "on clear and satisfactory grounds", it should be departed from.

In *Boys v Chaplin* such grounds were held to exist because both parties were normally resident in England and only temporarily present in Malta. If both parties, or only the defendant, had been Maltese, the decision would have been different.[28] If the issue had been whether the defendant was absolutely liable or liable only for negligence, the case for applying Maltese law would have been much stronger.

12–009

The outcome in *Boys v Chaplin* was the application of the law of the forum, but the exception to the general rule was not in terms limited to cases where it would result in the application of that law. Might it be used to secure the application of the law of the place of the tort, or of a third country? In *Red Sea Insurance Co Ltd v Bouygues SA*,[29] a Privy Council case on appeal from Hong Kong, it was held that it could: on the facts and using the new flexibility, the whole case, and not just one limited issue, was held to be properly governed by

---

[26] See the analysis of the speeches in *Boys v Chaplin* in *Harding v Wealands* [2004] EWCA Civ 1735; [2005] 1 All E.R. 415.

[27] per Lord Hodson at p.380; per Lord Wilberforce at pp.390–392.

[28] per Lord Hodson at p.379; per Lord Wilberforce at pp.389 and 392.

[29] [1995] 1 A.C. 190, applied in *Pearce v Ove Arup Partnership Ltd* [2000] Ch. 403.

the law of the place of the tort. Before the uncertainties this decision produced could be worked out in further, and no doubt expensive, litigation, there was introduced into Parliament what became the Private International Law (Miscellaneous Provisions) Act 1995 Pt III of which reformed the law in this field.

The 1995 Act

12–010   The general effect of Pt III of the Private International Law (Miscellaneous Provisions) Act 1995 was to abolish the double actionability rule and substitute a statutory general rule applying the law of the place of the tort with an exception derived from the common law developments in *Boys v Chaplin*[30] and *Red Sea Insurance Co Ltd v Bouygues SA*.[31]

Section 11(1) established a new "general rule": "The general rule is that the applicable law is the law[32] of the country in which the events constituting the tort in question occur". However, the common law flexibility developed in *Boys v Chaplin*[33] and *Red Sea Insurance Co Ltd v Bouygues SA*[34] was retained in the 1995 Act, where the new general rule could be "displaced" when the special circumstances of the case so required. Section 12 of the Act reads almost as a statutory restatement of the common law development, though one operating in a changed context. It provides:

(1)   If it appears, in all the circumstances, from a comparison of:
    (a)   the significance of the factors which connect a tort with the country whose law would be the applicable law under the general rule; and
    (b)   the significance of any factors connecting the tort with another country,
    that it is substantially more appropriate for the applicable law for determining the issues arising in the case, or any of those issues, to be the law of the other country, the general rule is displaced and the applicable law for determining those issues or that issue (as the case may be) is the law of that other country.
(2)   The factors that may be taken into account as connecting a tort with a country for the purposes of this section include, in particular, factors relating to the parties, to any of the events which constitute the tort in question or to any of the circumstances or consequences of those events.

The analysis required by s.12(1) was quite sophisticated. It required the court, as a first step, to identify the factors connecting "the tort" to particular countries.[35] The court had then to consider the possibility of the displacement of

---

[30] [1971] A.C. 356.
[31] [1995] 1 A.C. 190.
[32] i.e., the internal law, not including choice of law rules, so excluding *renvoi*: 1995 Act s.9(5), and see Ch.18, below.
[33] [1971] A.C. 356.
[34] [1995] 1 A.C. 190, applied *Pearce v Ove Arup Partnership Ltd* [2000] Ch. 403.
[35] *Roerig v Valiant Trawlers Ltd* [2002] EWCA Civ 21; [2002] 1 W.L.R. 2304, per Waller L.J. at para.[12]; *Harding v Wealands* [2004] EWCA Civ 1735; [2005] 1 All E.R. 415, per Waller L.J. at para.[12].

the general law "for determining the issues arising in the case, or any of those issues", so that the displacement need not identify a new applicable law for the tort as a whole but might do so for a single issue (e.g. whether one spouse may sue the other in tort). As will be seen, the Rome II Regulation is less sophisticated, or perhaps more straight-forward, in this respect. It may be noted, finally, that many factors could be taken into account. They included "factors relating to the parties": the length and closeness of the links between a party and the countries concerned and the existence or otherwise of a relationship between the parties before the tort occurred.[36]

THE ROME II REGULATION

Discussion of a European instrument on the law applicable to non-contractual obligations as a counterpart to the Rome Convention began in 1998. A preliminary draft was prepared in 2002, building on work by the European Private International Law Group, and a formal Proposal was submitted by the Commission in July 2003.[37] Despite some sharp criticisms, notably by the EU Committee of the House of Lords,[38] the proposal made good progress and eventually emerged as the Rome II Regulation in July 2007. It applies from January 11, 2009[39] but to "events giving rise to damage which occur after its entry into force"[40]; as the entry into force and the application of a Regulation are not necessarily the same, it is possible that the Regulation applies where the events giving rise to the damage occurred on or after August 20, 2008. The Regulation does not apply to Denmark and "Member State" must be understood as excluding Denmark.

12–011

INTERPRETATION

The European Court will have competence to interpret the Regulation in accordance with the usual rules applying to EU legislation. This jurisdiction is likely to have a particular importance in the case of this Regulation: as the Recitals recognise, the concept of a non-contractual obligation itself varies from one Member State to another and so must be understood as an autonomous concept.[41] The substantive scope and provisions of the Regulation are intended to

12–012

---

[36] This factor was absent in *Boys v Chaplin* (see per Diplock L.J., [1968] 2 Q.B. 1 at 44); it has been very important in American cases applying a proper law approach, e.g., *Babcock v Jackson*, 191 N.E.2d 279 (1963).

[37] COM(2003) 427 final. See Dickinson, *The Rome II Regulation: A Commentary* (Oxford: O.U.P., 2009).

[38] *The Rome II Regulation*, Eighth Report, Session 2003–2004 (HL Paper 66).

[39] art.32.

[40] art.31. See Case C-412/10 *Homawoo v GMF Assurances S.A.* [2012] I.L.Pr. 2 (date of claim irrelevant); *Alliance Bank JSC v Aquanta Corporation* [2011] EWHC 3281 (Comm) (favouring date of damage rather than date of events causing damage; cf. art.4(1) cited below).

[41] Recital (11), which adds the specific observation that the conflict-of-law rules set out in this Regulation should also cover non-contractual obligations arising out of strict liability.

be consistent with the Brussels I Regulation and "the instruments dealing with the law applicable to contractual obligations", meaning the Rome Convention and the Rome I Regulation.[42]

The countries whose law may be made applicable are not limited to Member States; it is expressly provided that a law specified by the Regulation must be applied whether or not it is the law of such a State.[43] The law of a country means the rules of law in force in that country other than its rules of private international law; i.e., *renvoi* is excluded.[44]

In the case of federal or composite states in which each territorial unit has its own rules of law in respect of non-contractual obligations, each territorial unit is treated as a "country" for the purposes of the Convention and the Regulation.[45] A federal or composite State is not bound to apply the Convention or Regulation to conflicts solely between the laws of different units within that State.[46]

SCOPE

12–013 The Regulation applies, in situations involving a conflict of laws, to non-contractual obligations in civil and commercial matters. "Civil and commercial matters" will no doubt be given the same meaning as in the Brussels I Regulation[47]; expressly excluded are revenue,[48] customs and administrative matters and the liability of the State for acts and omissions in the exercise of State authority (*acta iure imperii*).[49]

Although there is no definition of "non-contractual obligations", there is, under that heading, a definition of "damage". It covers any consequence arising out of tort/delict,[50] unjust enrichment, *negotiorum gestio* or *culpa in contrahendo*.[51] Some of these terms will be unfamiliar not only to many readers of this book but to English lawyers generally. *Negotiorum gestio*[52] concerns unauthorised interference in the affairs of another, a sort of unauthorised agency, in which the intervenor is entitled to recover the expenses incurred and to a degree of immunity. *Culpa in contrahendo* relates to pre-contractual matters, but is dealt with under Rome II and not Rome I. Recital (30) explains that for the purposes of the Regulation it is an autonomous concept and should not necessarily be interpreted within the meaning of national law. It should include the violation of

---

[42] Recital (7).
[43] art.3.
[44] art.24. For *renvoi*, see further, Ch.18.
[45] art.25(1).
[46] art.25(2).
[47] See para.4–013.
[48] So, for example, claims for unjust enrichment based on the payment of tax where the demand for payment was ultra vires (as in *Woolwich Equitable Building Society v I.R.C.* [1993] 1 A.C. 70) do not fall within the Regulation.
[49] art.1(1). Claims arising out of *acta iure imperii* include claims against officials who act on behalf of the State and liability for acts of public authorities, including liability of publicly appointed office-holders: Recital (9).
[50] The "tort/delict" usage continues throughout; for convenience we shall refer simply to "tort".
[51] art.2(1).
[52] Sheehan, (2006) 55 I.C.L.Q. 253.

the duty of disclosure and the breakdown of contractual negotiations.[53] The Regulation deals with anticipated events in that it applies to non-contractual obligations that have not yet arisen but are likely to arise[54]; and similarly references to an event giving rise to damage includes events giving rise to damage that are likely to occur; and references to damage include damage that is likely to occur.[55]

Exclusions

Article 1(2) lists a number of matters which are excluded from the scope of the Regulation. Many are identical to those listed in the corresponding provision in the Rome I Regulation, and similar reasons apply[56]; but it must be admitted that it is difficult to identify what "non-contractual obligations" could arise in some of the listed cases. The matters excluded are: **12–014**

(a) non-contractual obligations arising out of family relationships[57] and relationships deemed by the law applicable to such relationships to have comparable effects[58] including maintenance obligations;

(b) non-contractual obligations arising out of matrimonial property régimes, property régimes of relationships deemed by the law applicable to such relationships to have comparable effects to marriage, and wills and succession;

(c) non-contractual obligations arising under bills of exchange, cheques and promissory notes and other negotiable instruments to the extent that the obligations under such other negotiable instruments arise out of their negotiable character;

(d) non-contractual obligations arising out of the law of companies and other bodies corporate or unincorporated regarding matters such as the creation, by registration or otherwise, legal capacity, internal organisation or winding-up of companies and other bodies corporate or unincorporated, the personal liability of officers and members as such for the obligations of the company or body and the personal liability of auditors to a company or to its members in the statutory audits of accounting documents[59];

(e) non-contractual obligations arising out of the relations between the settlors, trustees and beneficiaries of a trust created voluntarily[60];

(f) non-contractual obligations arising out of nuclear damage;

(g) non-contractual obligations arising out of violations of privacy and rights relating to personality, including defamation.

---

[53] See further para.12–029 below.

[54] art.2(2).

[55] art.2(3).

[56] See para.11–012 *et seq*.

[57] "Family relationships" covers parentage, marriage, affinity and collateral relatives: Recital (10).

[58] The "comparable effects" provisions are to be interpreted in accordance with the law of the Member State seised of the case: Recital (10).

[59] The reference to the liability of auditors has no equivalent in the Rome I Regulation.

[60] The Rome I Regulation does not specify that the trust be created voluntarily; it was more important here to exclude constructive trusts.

The last exclusion was particularly controversial and the debates reflected those in Britain which led to the exclusion of defamation from the 1995 Act. Article 30(2) of the Regulation requires the Commission, not later than December 31, 2008, to submit a study on the situation in the field of the law applicable to non-contractual obligations arising out of violations of privacy and rights relating to personality, taking into account rules relating to freedom of the press and freedom of expression in the media, and conflict-of-law issues related to Directive 95/46/EC.[61] The deadline was not met.

There is one further limited exclusion.[62] The Regulation does not apply to evidence and procedure, without prejudice to arts 21 and 22.[63]

PARTY AUTONOMY

12–015 The Regulation adopts the notion of party autonomy, applying in the field of non-contractual obligations ideas more familiar in relation to contract disputes. At first sight the notion of a choice of law agreement in relation to a tort might seem improbable: the parties will not have foreseen the events giving rise to the claim. A choice of law agreement *after* the event may, however, be entirely sensible; and, as we have seen, the term "non-contractual obligations" is wider than "torts".

So in most cases,[64] the parties may agree to submit non-contractual obligations to the law of their choice by an agreement entered into *after* the event giving rise to the damage occurred.[65] Where all the parties are pursuing a commercial activity, effect will be given to an agreement freely negotiated *before* the event giving rise to the damage occurred.[66] The choice must be expressed or demonstrated with reasonable certainty by the circumstances of the case and must not prejudice the rights of third parties.

As in the case of contractual obligations, i.e. under the Rome I Regulation,[67] there are limitations on the parties' freedom of choice. Where all the elements relevant to the situation at the time when the event giving rise to the damage occurs are located in a country other than the country whose law has been chosen, the choice of the parties does prejudice the application of provisions of the law of that other country which cannot be derogated from by agreement.[68]

---

[61] European Parliament and Council Directive 95/46/EC of October 24, 1995 on the protection of individuals with regard to the processing of personal data and on the free movement of such data.
[62] art.1(3).
[63] See Ch.17.
[64] Not in the context of unfair competition: art.6(4); nor that of the infringement of intellectual property rights: art.8(3).
[65] art.14(1)(a).
[66] art.14(1)(b).
[67] See para.11–022.
[68] art.14(2); art.14(3) deals with the application of such rules in EU law.

TORTS

The primary rule

Article 4 of the Rome II Regulation contains general rules applicable to torts, **12–016** saving certain other types of non-contractual obligation for later treatment. The primary rule is that in art.4(1):

> The law applicable to a non-contractual obligation arising out of a tort shall be the law of the country in which the damage occurs irrespective of the country in which the event giving rise to the damage occurred and irrespective of the country or countries in which the indirect consequences of that event occur.

The policy behind this provision is set out in the Recitals. They note that the principle of the *lex loci delicti commissi* (the law of the place of the tort) is the basic solution for non-contractual obligations in virtually all the Member States, though the practical application of the principle where the component factors of the case are spread over several countries varies.[69] A connection with the country where the direct damage occurred (*lex loci damni*) strikes a fair balance between the interests of the person claimed to be liable and the person sustaining the damage, and also reflects the modern approach to civil liability and the development of systems of strict liability.[70] The law applicable should be determined on the basis of where the damage occurs, regardless of the country or countries in which the indirect consequences could occur, and so, in cases of personal injury or damage to property, the country in which the damage occurs should be the country where the injury was sustained or the property was damaged respectively.[71] As Andrew Smith J. observed in *Hillside (New Media) Ltd v Baasland*,[72] this provides no guidance in cases in which financial loss is suffered in more than one country.

The question of where a tort should be located has been much debated. This **12–017** question has been encountered in the context of the Brussels I Regulation, where it was possible for the European Court to give the claimant the option of locating the tort at the place where there occurred the damage *or* the event giving rise to that damage.[73] Such an option is not available when a single applicable law is to be identified. There is no difficulty where all the events, except the bringing of the action, occur within one country. It is not so simple when the defendant's act takes place in one country, and the ensuing harm is inflicted on the claimant in another: for example, the defendant negligently manufactures poisoned chocolates in country A which are bought, perhaps at an airport,[74] in country B and consumed in country C, with the result that the consumer dies in country D. The first *Restatement* contained a rule of thumb that "the place of wrong is in the state

---

[69] Recital (15).
[70] Recital (16).
[71] Recital (17).
[72] [2010] EWHC 3336 (Comm).
[73] Case 21/76 *Bier v Mines de Potasse d'Alsace* [1976] E.C.R. 1735; [1978] Q.B. 708.
[74] It will be immaterial whether the sale is before or after passing through immigration controls; the notice 'UK Border' is important for immigration purposes but not for choice of law.

where the last act necessary to make an actor liable for an alleged tort takes place".[75] This "last event" rule focuses on the question when the tort is constituted, and that is not necessarily the same question as where it should be located. Moreover, the "last event" rule is not easy to apply, as the facts just given illustrate. For this and other reasons, the "last event" approach has been cogently criticised by writers.[76]

Section 11(2) of the Private International Law (Miscellaneous Provisions) Act 1995 sought at least to minimise the difficulties. It provided that where elements of the events giving rise to the claim occurred in different countries, the applicable law for a cause of action in respect of personal injury was that of the country where the individual was when he or she sustained the injury; and for a cause of action in respect of damage to property, the law of the country where the property was when it was damaged. This is the same approach as is adopted in the Rome II Regulation, though the specific rules are in the Recitals and not the text of the Regulation.

Article 4(1) excludes a reference to the law of the country or countries in which only the indirect consequences of an event. This is similar to the *Dumez* principle developed in the context of the Brussels I Regulation.[77]

The common habitual residence exception

12–018   The law of the place of the tort does not have unqualified sway under the Regulation. Where the person claimed to be liable and the person sustaining damage both have their habitual residence in the same country at the time the damage occurs, the law of that country applies.[78] Whether this would apply on facts similar to those in *Boys v Chaplin*[79] depends on the meaning to be given to "habitual residence", and the Regulation gives only a limited answer. Article 23 provides that, for the purposes of the Regulation, the habitual residence of companies and other bodies, corporate or unincorporated, is the place of central administration[80]; however, where the contract is concluded in the course of the operations of a branch, agency or any other establishment, or if, under the contract, performance is the responsibility of such a branch, agency or establishment, the place where the branch, agency or any other establishment is located is to be treated as the place of habitual residence.[81] The habitual residence of a natural person acting in the course of his or her business activity is the principal place of business.[82] The parties in *Boys v Chaplin* were both off-duty, so

[75] s.377.
[76] Rheinstein, (1944) 19 Tulane L.Rev. 4 at 165; Cook, *Logical and Legal Bases of the Conflict of Laws* (Harvard University Press, Cambridge MA, 1942), Ch.13; Morris, (1951) 64 Harv.L.Rev. 881 at 887–892; Webb and North, (1965) 14 I.C.L.Q. 1314.
[77] See Case 220/80 *Dumez France v Hessische Landesbank* [1990] E.C.R. I- 49 and para.4–040.
[78] art.4(2).
[79] [1971] A.C. 356; see para.12–008.
[80] art.23(1).
[81] art.23(1).
[82] art.23(2).

the Regulation offers the courts no guidance, and the European Court is likely to develop an autonomous meaning of habitual residence to cover such non-business cases.

The 'more closely connected' exception

Article 4(3) contains a more general exception to the primary rule: **12–019**

> Where it is clear from all the circumstances of the case that the tort is manifestly more closely connected with a country other than that indicated in paragraphs 1 or 2, the law of that other country shall apply. A manifestly closer connection with another country might be based in particular on a pre-existing relationship between the parties, such as a contract, that is closely connected with the tort in question.

Again the policy is explained in the Recitals, as combining legal certainty and the need to do justice in individual cases.[83] The latter is the basis for the "escape clause" in art.4(3).[84]

Experience with a similar escape clause in the Rome Convention showed that national courts differed in the use they made of it. Common law courts, with a tradition of using a "close connection" test, more often used the escape clause. It remains to be seen how the present escape clause is used.

How might these rules work?

The English cases, decided under the common law rule or the 1995 Act, cannot   **12–020** be relied on in the interpretation of the Regulation but their facts can be used to explore how the new rules might work in practice.

In *Boys v Chaplin*,[85] the country in which the damage occurred was undoubtedly Malta. The common law general rule was displaced as the only people involved were British subjects, normally resident in England and only temporarily present in Malta as part of their duties in the British Forces. None of the speeches in the House of Lords examined the facts any more closely: we have no idea how long the parties had been in Malta, and we know virtually nothing about their vehicles and the purposes of their journeys. If the parties were found to have been habitually resident in England at the relevant time, which seems unlikely, the exception in art.4(2) would apply.[86] If not, the only basis for applying English law would be under art.4(3), but there seems very little upon which to base any argument that the tort was manifestly more closely connected with England than with Malta.

Were the facts of *Harding v Wealands*[87] to recur, the arguments to be deployed might be similar under the Regulation but they would take a different shape.

---

[83] Recital (14).
[84] Recital (18).
[85] [1971] A.C. 356.
[86] As would the special issues as to the level of compensation examined in Recital (33); see below, para.12–031.
[87] [2004] EWCA Civ 1735; [2005] 1 W.L.R. 1539. This aspect of the case was not examined in the speeches in the later appeal to the House of Lords: [2006] UKHL 32; [2007] 2 A.C. 1.

H was English. He met W in Australia and she later came to live with him in England. After some seven months, W returned to New South Wales on what was intended to be a five-week visit. She was soon joined by H. While they were travelling in New South Wales, in W's own car which was registered and insured in New South Wales, W lost control of the car, which rolled over. H was rendered tetraplegic. He returned to England some months after the accident: he would require special care in England for the rest of his life. W travelled to England with him, and the claim form was served on her in England before her eventual return to Australia.

Reversing the trial judge, who had given great weight to the fact that the parties were at the time of the accident habitually resident in England and in a settled relationship there, the Court of Appeal held that the general rule under the 1995 Act, pointing to the law of New South Wales, should *not* be disapplied. W's links with New South Wales were much more significant than her links with England. W was a citizen of Australia driving on a New South Wales driving licence, and the accident occurred in New South Wales. Under the Regulation, a finding that the parties were both habitually resident in England would attract art.4(2), under which English law would be applicable. The argument about displacement would then be whether that result should be averted by holding that the tort was manifestly more closely connected with New South Wales; such an argument might well succeed.

12–021 One contrast between the position under the 1995 Act and that under the Regulation is illustrated by *Roerig v Valiant Trawlers Ltd*[88]:

A Dutchman was killed in an accident on a trawler registered in England (so that the place of the tort was deemed to be England) and owned by an English company, a subsidiary of a Dutch company. The skipper was English, but at the relevant time the crew was operating under a Dutch fishing master. The trawler had sailed from, and was to return to, a Dutch port. The deceased's partner sued in England under the Fatal Accidents Act 1976 on her own behalf and that of their children; they all lived in the Netherlands. Under English law, any damages would be reduced by the value of any benefits received on account of the death; under Dutch law there was no such reduction.

There was no dispute about liability, to which the Court of Appeal would have applied English law under the general rule of s.11 of the Act. The argument advanced, unsuccessfully, in the case was whether Dutch law could be applied to a particular issue, that of damages for loss of dependency. Under the Regulation, the question is what law applies to the tort as a whole; art.4 does not allow the issues to be disaggregated. In the actual case, counsel did not seek to advance the argument that the tort as such was more closely connected with the Netherlands, which would be the issue under art.4(3).

Torts taking place on ships or aircraft are generally treated as located in the State of registration of the ship or aircraft. There is little authority on the point, and it may be that the "more closely connected" exception would be likely to be found applicable in many such cases.

In the common law case of *Johnson v Coventry Churchill International Ltd*[89]:

---

[88] [2002] EWCA Civ 21; [2002] 1 W.L.R. 2304.
[89] [1992] 3 All E.R. 14.

The plaintiff, an English joiner, entered into what was held to be a contract of employment with the defendant, an English company which placed English personnel seeking to work abroad. The plaintiff worked in Germany and was injured on a building site when the plank on which he was crossing a trench collapsed. This would give rise in English law to liability for breach of the employer's duty to provide a safe system of work, but there would be no liability in German law in the absence of a wilful, as opposed to negligent, breach.

It was held that the then general rule of double-actionability would be displaced in favour of the application of English law. The parties were both English, the contract was expressly made subject to English law,[90] and the judge found that the fault which gave rise to the accident arose from decisions taken in England that safety issues were not the defendants' concern. Justice to the plaintiff seemed to dictate the application of English law, and as the defendants could, and in fact had, taken insurance cover against any liability under that law, they would not be disadvantaged. Under the Regulation, Germany is plainly the country in which the damage occurred but there would seem a strong case, based on the contractual relationship, for invoking art.4(3) and holding that the tort was manifestly more closely connected with England than with Germany. The analysis undertaken in the actual case, and especially the references to the liability insurance, might not be fully appropriate in the new legal context.

Product liability

The Regulation contains specific rules for certain types of tortuous liability, in the belief that in those cases "the general rule does not allow a reasonable balance to be struck between the interests at stake".[91] The first of these special cases is that of product liability. In that context the Recitals contain the unexceptionable but fairly unhelpful declaration that the choice of law rules in matters of product liability should meet the objectives of fairly spreading the risks inherent in a modern high-technology society, protecting consumers' health, stimulating innovation, securing undistorted competition and facilitating trade.[92] It is not at all clear, to give one of a number of possible examples, how the choice of law rules adopted, or indeed any conceivable choice of law rules, can stimulate innovation.

12–022

The rules in art.5 are in the form of a "cascade", a device quite familiar in civil law systems. Unless the parties share a common habitual residence, in which case the law of that country applies by virtue of art.4(2), the applicable law is (a) the law of the country in which the person sustaining the damage had his or her habitual residence when the damage occurred, if the product was marketed in that country; or, if the product was not so marketed, (b) the law of the country in which the product was acquired, if the product was marketed in that country; or, if the product was not so marketed, (c) the law of the country in which the damage occurred, if the product was marketed in that country. In many cases, these three countries will in fact be the same, but it is quite possible for a person

---

[90] The claim was brought exclusively in tort; the contract was merely a part of the factual background.
[91] Recital (19).
[92] Recital (20).

habitually resident in State A to buy a product at an airport in State B and consume it, with harmful effects, in State C. The Regulation assumes that a product will have been marketed in some country, but if the defendant could not reasonably foresee the marketing of the product, or a product of the same type, in the country the law of which is applicable under the cascade, the law of the country in which the defendant is habitually resident applies.[93] It is not clear what meaning is to be given to the notion of "marketing": it might refer to a process of stimulating interest amongst potential users of the product, e.g., by advertising, but is perhaps more likely to refer simply to the entry of the product into the "stream of commerce" in the particular country.

There is a 'more closely connected' exception, worded as in art.4(3).[94]

Unfair competition and acts restricting free competition

12–023   Unfair competition may have general effects on the market or affect a specific competitor. The general approach in the Regulation is to identify as the law applicable to non-contractual obligations the law of the country in which the damage occurs.[95] That principle is no less appropriate in the special context of unfair competition, and can readily be applied where only one specific competitor is affected, as for example passing-off and some cases of inducing breach of contract.[96] Where the effects are more general, as with misleading advertisements, some clarification is needed,[97] and art.6(1) applies the law of the country where competitive relations or the collective interests of consumers are, or are likely to be, affected.[98]

Similarly, the law applicable to a non-contractual obligation arising out of a restriction of competition is the law of the country where the market is, or is likely to be, affected.[99] "Restriction of competition" is interpreted in Recital (23) as covering prohibitions on agreements between undertakings, decisions by associations of undertakings and concerted practices which have as their object or effect the prevention, restriction or distortion of competition within a Member State or within the internal market, as well as prohibitions on the abuse of a dominant position within a Member State or within the internal market, where such agreements, decisions, concerted practices or abuses are prohibited by European law or that of a Member State.

The law applicable under art.6 may not be derogated from by an exercise of party autonomy, i.e., an agreement within art.14.[100]

---

[93] art.5(1).
[94] art.5(2).
[95] art.4(1).
[96] This is the effect of art.6(2).
[97] See Recital (21).
[98] art.6(1).
[99] art.6(3)(a). See art.6(3)(b) for the cases in which the market is, or is likely to be, affected in more than one country.
[100] art.6(4).

Environmental damage

Another case in which special provision is made is that of environmental damage, **12–024** meaning adverse change in a natural resource, such as water, land or air, impairment of a function performed by that resource for the benefit of another natural resource or the public, or impairment of the variability among living organisms.[101] The primary rule in art.4(1) applies with one qualification: the person seeking compensation for environmental damage may choose to base his or her claim on the law of the country in which the event giving rise to the damage occurred.[102]

Infringement of intellectual property rights

It was formerly thought that the English court had no jurisdiction to entertain **12–025** claims for infringement of foreign intellectual property rights, irrespective of whether issues of title or validity were involved. This was based on the *Mocambique* rule (which principally concerns jurisdiction over issues relating to foreign land)[103] and the act of state doctrine.[104] In *Lucasfilm Ltd v Ainsworth*[105] this understanding was not challenged so far as it was limited to patents and other intellectual property rights dependent on the grant or authority of a foreign state, and to cases where what is in issue is the validity of the patent, as opposed to its infringement. The Supreme Court held, however, that, in the case of a claim for infringement of copyright, the claim is one over which the English court has jurisdiction, provided that there is a basis for in personam jurisdiction over the defendant.

Where the claim can be heard in England, the choice of law rules will be those in the Rome II Regulation, which apply the *lex loci protectionis*, the law of the country for which protection is claimed.[106] For the purposes of the Regulation, the term "intellectual property rights" includes copyright, related rights, the sui generis right for the protection of databases and industrial property rights.[107] In the case of an infringement of a unitary EU intellectual property right, the law applicable, for any question that is not governed by the relevant EU instrument, is the law of the country in which the act of infringement was committed.[108] The law applicable under art.8 may not be derogated from by an exercise of party autonomy, i.e., an agreement within art.14.[109]

---

[101] Recital (24). An illustration would be the facts of Case 21/76 *Bier v Mines de Potasse d'Alsace* [1976] E.C.R. 1735; [1978] Q.B. 708.
[102] art.7.
[103] See para.13–012.
[104] Both as applied notably by the High Court of Australia in *Potter v Broken Hill Pty Co Ltd* (1906) 3 C.L.R. 479.
[105] [2011] UKSC 39; [2012] 1 A.C. 2008.
[106] art.8(1).
[107] Recital (26).
[108] art.8(2).
[109] art.8(3).

Industrial action

12–026 There is wide diversity in the law of the different Member States on such matters as the legal status of trades unions and the liabilities which may flow from certain types of "industrial action" such as a strike or a lock-out. The Regulation is drafted so as to respect national law[110] but does contain a choice of law rule. If the parties have a common habitual residence (as will very often be the case) the law of that country will apply.[111] Otherwise, the law applicable to a non-contractual obligation in respect of the liability of a person in the capacity of a worker or an employer or the organisations representing their professional interests for damages caused by an industrial action, pending or carried out, is the law of the country where the action is to be, or has been, taken.[112]

UNJUST ENRICHMENT

12–027 Article 10 deals with cases of unjust enrichment.[113] Such cases are by their nature quite varied, and that fact is reflected in the text of the Regulation which attempts a categorisation with three different rules.

If a non-contractual obligation arising out of unjust enrichment, including payment of amounts wrongly received, concerns a relationship existing between the parties, such as one arising out of a contract or a tort, that is closely connected with that unjust enrichment, it is governed by the law that governs that relationship.[114] In English law, claims for unjust enrichment very commonly involve sums of money paid on the basis of a mistaken belief in liability, either contractual or tortuous, or in respect of consideration that has totally failed, and they will clearly fall within this provision. A not dissimilar case is that set out in section 7(4) of the Torts (Interference with Goods) Act 1977: "if a converter of goods pays damages first to a finder of the goods, and then to the true owner, the finder is unjustly enriched unless he accounts over to the true owner . . . ; and then the true owner is unjustly enriched and becomes liable to reimburse the converter of the goods." It remains to be seen how the terms "relationship ... arising" and "closely connected with" are interpreted. In the case of a man left injured by the roadside after an assault upon him, a passer-by who tends his wounds and takes him to a nearby inn, paying the inn-keeper to look after him, is entitled under some systems of law to recover his expenses from the injured man. There has clearly been a tort, but not one directly involving the passer-by. There is no (pre-)existing relationship between the passer-by and the injured man, so that it is not possible to identify a law governing such a relationship.

Where the applicable law cannot be determined on the basis of that rule and the parties had their habitual residence in the same country when the event giving rise to unjust enrichment occurred, the law of that country applies.[115] Taking the

---

[110] See Recitals (27) and (28).
[111] art.9 applies art.4(2) in this case.
[112] art.9.
[113] See Chang, (2008) 57 I.C.L.Q. 863.
[114] art.10(1).
[115] art.10(2).

last example, were the kind passer-by to come from Samaria, not "the same country", this rule, too, would be inapplicable. Cases of proprietary restitutionary claims, for example where A's property or its proceeds comes into B's hands and A is able to assert a constructive trust or "trace" the goods, will often fall under this rule. The test of a common habitual residence may not seem entirely appropriate in such cases; its use avoids what can be a difficult issue under the next following rule, of deciding *where* the unjust enrichment occurred, but it will be necessary to decide what is often almost the same question: *when* it occurred.

Where the applicable law cannot be determined on the basis of either or those rules, the law of the country in which the unjust enrichment took place applies.[116]

There is an escape clause in the case of the obligation being manifestly more closely connected with a country other than that identified in these rules: in that case the law of that other country applies.[117]

NEGOTIORUM GESTIO

A similar "cascade" applies in the case of *negotiorum gestio*, a non-contractual **12–028** obligation arising out of an act performed without due authority in connection with the affairs of another person. So, the law governing the relevant relationship existing between the parties; or, failing that, the law of the country in which the parties both had their habitual residence when the event giving rise to the damage occurred; or, failing that, the law of the country in which the act was performed.[118] There is an escape clause in the case of the obligation being manifestly more closely connected with a country other than that identified in these rules: in that case the law of that other country applies.[119]

CULPA IN CONTRAHENDO

In this context, that of a non-contractual obligation arising out of dealings prior to **12–029** the conclusion of a contract, regardless of whether the contract was actually concluded or not, the primary rule is that the obligation is governed by the law that applies to the contract or that would have been applicable to it had it been entered into.[120] Where the applicable law cannot be determined on the basis of that rule, it is (a) the law of the country in which the damage occurs, irrespective of the country in which the event giving rise to the damage occurred and irrespective of the country or countries in which the indirect consequences of that event occurred; or (b) where the parties had their habitual residence in the same country at the time when the event giving rise to the damage occurred, the law of that country; or (c) where it is clear from all the circumstances of the case that the non-contractual obligation arising out of dealings prior to the conclusion of a

---

[116] art.10(3).
[117] art.10(4).
[118] art.11(1)–(3).
[119] art.11(4).
[120] art.12(1).

contract is manifestly more closely connected with a country other than that identified in (a) and (b), the law of that other country.[121]

REACH OF THE APPLICABLE LAW

12–030   The applicable law identified under the Regulation governs a wide range of issues. Article 15 sets out a long, but non-exclusive,[122] list:

(a)   the basis and extent of liability, including the determination of persons who may be held liable for acts performed by them;

(b)   the grounds for exemption from liability, any limitation of liability and any division of liability;

(c)   the existence, the nature and the assessment of damage or the remedy claimed;

(d)   within the limits of powers conferred on the court by its procedural law, the measures which a court may take to prevent or terminate injury or damage or to ensure the provision of compensation;

(e)   the question whether a right to claim damages or a remedy may be transferred, including by inheritance;

(f)   persons entitled to compensation for damage sustained personally;

(g)   liability for the acts of another person;

(h)   the manner in which an obligation may be extinguished and rules of prescription and limitation, including rules relating to the commencement, interruption and suspension of a period of prescription or limitation.

12–031   Point (c) calls for some comment. In the context of contractual obligations, both the Rome Convention and the Rome I Regulation provide that the applicable law governs, *within the limits of the powers conferred on the court by its procedural law*, the consequences of breach, including the assessment of damages *in so far as it is governed by rules of law*.[123] The language of point (c) contains no such qualifications, and it seems that all aspects of the assessment of damages, including quantification, are referred to the applicable law. At common law, questions of liability and of heads of damage were matters for the governing law, but the matter of "quantification", arriving at a sum of money which compensates for the loss of a limb, for pain and suffering, the reduction in earning power, or whatever, was always been regarded as procedural, and so a matter for the *lex fori*. That was affirmed in *Boys v Chaplin*[124] and accepted as applying under the 1995 Act in *Roerig v Valiant Trawlers Ltd*,[125] but the position is changed by the Regulation.

This seems to be confirmed by Recital (33), which refers to one piece of unfinished business, road traffic cases. It declares that "according to the current

---

[121] art.12(2).

[122] "Shall govern, *in particular*..."

[123] Rome Convention, art.10(1)(c); Rome I Regulation, art.12(1)(c) (emphasis added). See para.11–057.

[124] [1971] A.C. 356.

[125] [2002] EWCA Civ 21; [2002] 1 W.L.R. 2304.

national rules on compensation awarded to victims of road traffic accidents, when quantifying damages for personal injury in cases in which the accident takes place in a State other than that of the habitual residence of the victim, the court seised should take into account all the relevant actual circumstances of the specific victim, including in particular the actual losses and costs of after-care and medical attention." The issue of compensation for the victims of road traffic accidents is to be the subject of a study, originally due by the end of 2008, on all options, including insurance aspects, for improving the position of cross-border victims, which would pave the way for a Green Paper.[126] By 20 August 2011 the Commission was due present a study on the effects of the Regulation with respect to the Hague Convention of May 4, 1971 on the law applicable to road traffic accidents. As is all too often the case, these deadlines have proved meaningless.

Rules of safety and conduct

Despite the extensive reach of the applicable law, the Regulation recognises that in assessing the conduct of the person claimed to be liable, account must be taken, as a matter of fact and in so far as is appropriate, of the rules of safety and conduct which were in force at the place and time of the event giving rise to the liability,[127] even where the non-contractual obligation is governed by the law of another country.[128] "Rules of safety and conduct" means all regulations having any relation to safety and conduct, including, for example, road safety rules in the case of an accident.[129]   **12–032**

Direct action against the insurer of the person liable

The person having suffered damage may bring his or her claim directly against the insurer of the person liable to provide compensation if the law applicable to the non-contractual obligation or the law applicable to the insurance contract so provides.[130]   **12–033**

Subrogation

Where a person (the creditor) has a non-contractual claim upon another (the debtor), and a third person has a duty to satisfy the creditor, or has in fact satisfied the creditor in discharge of that duty, the law which governs the third person's duty to satisfy the creditor determines whether, and the extent to which, the third person is entitled to exercise against the debtor the rights which the creditor had against the debtor under the law governing their relationship.[131]   **12–034**

---

[126] See the Commission Statement made when the Regulation was adopted.
[127] art.17.
[128] See Recital (34).
[129] *ibid.*
[130] art.18. For the position in the U.K, see the European Communities (Rights against Insurers) Regulations 2002 (SI 2002/3061).
[131] art.19.

Multiple liability (i.e., contribution)

12–035   If a creditor has a claim against several debtors who are liable for the same claim, and one of the debtors has already satisfied the claim in whole or in part, the question of that debtor's right to demand compensation from the other debtors is governed by the law applicable to that debtor's non-contractual obligation towards the creditor.[132] The effect of this can be seen from this example:

> A, who is habitually resident in England, sustains damage in France. He has a claim in tort against B, also habitually resident in England, and C, who is habitually resident in Germany. The claim against B will be governed by English law, under the common habitual residence rule in art.4(2). If B pays damages, B's claim for contribution from C will also be governed by English law.

Formal validity of "unilateral acts"

12–036   Article 21 provides that a unilateral act intended to have legal effect and relating to a non-contractual obligation shall be formally valid if it satisfies the formal requirements of the law governing the non-contractual obligation in question or the law of the country in which the act is performed. The meaning of this provision is obscure, at least to an English reader. In the contractual sphere, the term "unilateral act" can apply to formal notice of denunciation or rescission and there are analogous circumstances in some legal systems in relation to non-contractual obligations.[133]

Burden of proof

12–037   The law governing a non-contractual obligation under the Regulation applies to the extent that, in matters of non-contractual obligations, it contains rules which raise presumptions of law or determine the burden of proof.[134]

LIMITS ON THE REACH OF THE APPLICABLE LAW

12–038   As in the case of the Rome I Regulation, there are certain limits on the reach of the applicable law. They are briefly noted here, as the principles have been discussed in the Rome I context. Article 16 provides that nothing in the Regulation restricts the application of the provisions of the law of the forum in a situation where they are mandatory irrespective of the law otherwise applicable to the non-contractual obligation.[135] Article 26 contains the usual *ordre public* provision, that the application of a provision of the law of any country specified by the Regulation may be refused only if such application is manifestly incompatible with the public policy (*ordre public*) of the forum.[136]

---

[132] art.20.
[133] For the proof of such acts, see art.22(2).
[134] art.22(1).
[135] cf. para.11–069.
[136] See para.11–074.

Actions in defamation

Neither the Regulation nor the 1995 Act applies to claims in defamation.[137] They remain governed by the common law rule, that of double actionability subject to the flexibility derived from *Boys v Chaplin*.[138] This meets the concerns of the press and other media: the continued relevance of the law of the forum via the first limb of the common law rule means that the defences of fair comment and qualified privilege remain available even where publication takes place abroad, and this goes some way to mitigate the advantages of England as a forum for defamation plaintiffs.[139]

12–039

---

[137] Regulation, art.1(2)(g); 1995 Act s.13(1). Defamation is defined for this purpose in s.13(2): it includes claims for libel, slander, slander of title, slander of goods or other malicious falsehood.
[138] See above, para.12–008.
[139] See Hartley, (2010) 59 I.C.L.Q. 25.

CHAPTER 13

PROPERTY

This chapter examines the conflict of laws rules relating to property, rules which **13–001** are generally much easier to grasp than those found in English domestic law. We need first to examine the way in which property is classified for the purposes of the conflict of laws. This involves distinctions between movables and immovables, and between tangible and intangible movables; the meaning of these terms will be explored shortly. The choice of law rules for each category (and in the case of immovables, some special rules as to jurisdiction) are then examined. Finally, we will examine the effect of governmental acts such as nationalisation.

The death of an individual will, and his or her marriage may, have a general effect on that individual's property rights. These are considered elsewhere[1]; the focus of this chapter is on specific as opposed to general transfers of property.

THE DISTINCTION BETWEEN MOVABLES AND IMMOVABLES

In English domestic law, the leading distinction between proprietary interests in **13–002** things is the historical and technical distinction between realty and personalty. In the English rules of the conflict of laws, however, the leading distinction between things is the more universal and natural distinction between movables and immovables.[2] This approach produces rules which "work" even when the other system of law involved is one in which the English distinction between realty and personalty is unknown. "In order to arrive at a common basis on which to

---

[1] See, for matrimonial property regimes, Ch.14; for succession, Ch.15.
[2] *Freke v Carbery* (1873) LR 16 Eq. 461; *Duncan v Lawson* (1889) 41 Ch.D. 394; *Re Hoyles* [1911] 1 Ch. 179; *Macdonald v Macdonald*, 1932 SC (HL) 79. See, generally, Falconbridge, *Selected Essays on the Conflict of Laws* (Canada Law Book, Toronto, 2nd ed., 1954), Ch. 21; Cook, *Logical and Legal Bases of the Conflict of Laws* (Harvard University Press, Cambridge, 1942), Ch.2; Robertson, *Characterization in the Conflict of Laws* (Harvard University Press, Cambridge, 1940), pp.190–212; Smith, (1963) 26 M.L.R. 16.

determine questions between the inhabitants of two countries living under different systems of jurisprudence, our courts recognise and act on a division otherwise unknown to our law into movable and immovable".[3]

The importance of the distinction between movables and immovables is most apparent in the context of succession, because succession to movables is governed (in general) by the law of the deceased's domicile, whereas succession to immovables is in general governed by the *lex situs* (the law of the country of the location) of the property.[4]

Immovable property is essentially land, but different systems of law may characterise things as movable or immovable in different ways. In all systems, some physically movable things are so closely connected with the land that for legal purposes they are characterised as immovables. Thus, in English domestic law the title deeds to land and the keys of a house are characterised as real estate and therefore as immovable. In Scots law, the old form of security known as the heritable bond[5] was characterised, at least for some purposes, as immovable; and this was recognised by the English courts.[6] There may, therefore, be a conflict between the law of the forum and the law of the country in which the property is located (the *lex situs*) as to whether a particular thing is movable or immovable. In such a situation, it is well settled that it is the *lex situs* that determines the characterisation.[7]

Examples

13–003   For the purposes of the conflict of laws, leasehold interests in land in England are classed as interests in immovables,[8] and it is quite immaterial that English domestic law regards them as personal estate. The same is true of a mortgagee's interest in land in England, including the right to repayment of the debt.[9] But in Australia and New Zealand it is equally well settled that a mortgagee's interest in land is an interest in a movable, on the theory that the debt is the principal thing and the security only an accessory.[10]

Until the Trusts of Land and Appointment of Trustees Act 1996[11] a trust for sale of land notionally converted the interests of the beneficiaries from real estate to personal estate. On the conflicts plane, however, this application of the

---

[3] *Re Hoyles* [1911] 1 Ch. 179 at 185, per Farwell L.J.

[4] Below, Ch.15. The attempts made in this book to avoid the more arcane Latinisms must exclude the very convenient expressions *situs* and *lex situs* in relation to property.

[5] A bond for a sum of money to which is joined, for the creditor's further security, a conveyance of land or of heritage, to be held by the creditor in security of the debt.

[6] *Jerningham v Herbert* (1829) 4 Russ 388 at 395; *Re Fitzgerald* [1904] 1 Ch. 573 at 588.

[7] *Re Hoyles* [1911] 1 Ch. 179; *Re Berchtold* [1923] 1 Ch. 192 at 199; *Macdonald v Macdonald*, 1932 SC (HL) 79 at 84; *Re Cutcliffe* [1940] Ch. 565 at 571. The *situs* of property is not always self-evident: see Dicey, Morris and Collins (14th edn, 2006), Rule 120.

[8] *Freke v Carbery* (1873) LR 16 Eq. 461; *Duncan v Lawson* (1889) 41 Ch.D. 394; *Pepin v Bruyere* [1900] 2 Ch. 504.

[9] *Re Hoyles* [1911] 1 Ch. 179.

[10] *Re ONeill* 1922] N.Z.L.R. 468; *Re Young* [1942] V.L.R. 4; *Re Williams* [1945] V.L.R. 213; *Haque v Haque (No.2)* (1965) 114 C.L.R. 98 at 133 and 146; *Re Greeneld* [1985] 2 N.Z.L.R. 662.

[11] s.3(1).

doctrine of conversion was treated by the English courts as irrelevant: the beneficiaries' interests were treated as immovables.[12]

Change in situs

Difficult problems arise if things that are physically movable are moved from a jurisdiction which regards them as legally immovable to a jurisdiction which regards them as legally movable. Logically, the new *lex situs* should determine their character. In *Re Middleton's Settlement,*[13] the proceeds of sale of Irish settled land were reinvested in English securities. It was held that for purposes of taxation the securities were situated in England. It seems to follow from that decision that, had it been necessary to determine for purposes of the conflict of laws whether the English stocks and shares were, as a matter of legal classification, movable or immovable, they would have been held to be movable. Under Irish law, a statutory doctrine of conversion[14] would treat them as land, but the property was no longer in Ireland.[15]

13–004

IMMOVABLES

Jurisdiction over immovables

Most legal systems accept that jurisdiction over immovable property is properly exercised exclusively by the courts of the country in which the land is situated. This principle is accepted in the Brussels I Regulation,[16] which gives exclusive jurisdiction, regardless of the domicile of the parties, "in proceedings which have as their object rights in rem in immovable property, or tenancies of immovable property" to the courts of the Member State in which the property is situated.[17]

13–005

This provision has proved surprisingly troublesome. One of the easier questions is its effect where a single land-holding straddles an international boundary. The European Court has held that in such a case separate actions will have to be brought in each Member State in respect of the parcel of land in that State, unless perhaps the land in one State is a very small fraction of the whole.[18]

---

[12] *Re Berchtold* [1923] 1 Ch. 192. Compare the position of capital money arising under a sale of settled land, deemed by the Settled Land Act 1925 s.75(5) to be "land" and so necessarily treated on the conflicts plane as an immovable: *Re Cutcliffe* [1940] Ch. 565. The Trusts of Land and Appointment of Trustees Act 1996 prevented the creation of any further settlements under the Settled Land Act 1925.

[13] [1947] Ch. 583; affirmed sub nom. *Midleton v Cottesloe* [1949] A.C. 418.

[14] Settled Land Act 1882 s.22(5) (then unrepealed in its application to Ireland).

[15] What does make the result seem distinctly odd is that a similar rule was part of English law; but s.75(5) of the Settled Land Act 1925 did not apply to that case because the capital money did not arise "under this Act".

[16] Council Regulation No. 44/2001. For the other jurisdictional rules of the Regulation, see Ch.4. Similar rules are found in the Lugano Convention.

[17] art.22(1).

[18] Case 158/87 *Scherrens v Maenhout* [1988] E.C.R. 3791. See Hartley, (1989) 17 E.L.Rev. 57.

Actions based on rights in rem

13–006   More fundamental difficulties concern the concepts of "rights in rem" and "tenancy". The former concept has very clear and precise meanings in many civil law systems, where the types of interest in land which may exist are strictly limited. In English law, the use of the trust device means that almost any interest may be created as a term of the trust. The respective positions of trustee and beneficiary as legal and beneficial owner of land are not easily accommodated in the language of the Regulation.

The European Court explored this issue in *Webb v Webb*[19]:

> George Webb provided money with which his son Lawrence bought a flat in Antibes, France. The flat was used as a holiday home by both father and son. A dispute arose between father and son. The son claimed that the flat had been given to him by his father. The father claimed that the son held the flat on trust for him and sought an order that the son should transfer the legal ownership to him.

In one sense, the object of the proceedings was that George Webb should acquire full ownership, a right in rem, of the property; hence, it was argued that only the French courts had jurisdiction. The European Court held, however, that for the provision as to exclusive jurisdiction[20] to apply it was not sufficient that the action involved a right in rem; it had to be *based on* a right in rem. The father was not asserting that he already had such a right, enforceable against the whole world, but only a right as against his son.

13–007   A similar result was reached in the context of a matrimonial dispute in *Prazic v Prazic*[21]:

> H began divorce proceedings in France. W, anxious for the case to be heard in England, tried to begin divorce proceedings there but failed under the Brussels IIa Regulation as the French court was the court first seised. W next tried to bring a claim relating to certain property the couple had bought in London, relying on the Trusts of Land and Appointment of Trustees Act 1996 and art.22 of the Brussels I Regulation.

The Court of Appeal refused to accept the art.22 argument: W was asserting an equitable right in personam and not a right in rem.[22]

The boundaries of the concept of actions based on rights in rem were explored in two contrasting cases. In *Re Hayward*,[23] a trustee in bankruptcy claimed to be entitled, as legal owner, to a half-share of a villa in Spain: the Spanish courts had exclusive jurisdiction. A different result was reached in *Reichert v Dresdner Bank*[24]:

---

[19] Case C–292/92, [1994] E.C.R. I–1717; [1994] Q.B. 696. See Briggs, (1994) 110 L.Q.R. 526.
[20] Then art.16(1) of the Brussels Convention; now art.22(1) of the Regulation.
[21] [2006] EWCA Civ 497; [2006] 2 F.L.R. 1128.
[22] The Court of Appeal also thoroughly disapproved of the attempt to rely on the 1996 Act when divorce proceedings were under way.
[23] [1997] Ch. 45.
[24] Case C–115/88, [1990] E.C.R. I–27. See also Case C–343/04 *Land Oberösterreich v EZ as* [2006] E.C.R. I–4557 (action for injunction against nuisance not a dispute having as its object rights in rem in

Mr and Mrs R, German nationals residing in Germany, owned a property in Antibes, France. By a deed executed in a notary's office in France, they made a gift of the property to their son who also resided in Germany. A German bank, a creditor of Mr and Mrs R, brought in the French courts an *action paulienne*, seeking a declaration that the gift was void as a fraud on the creditors.

The bank asserted that the French courts had jurisdiction under the predecessor of art.22(1); the bank's argument failed, for the dispute was really concerned with the respective rights of creditors, not title to property.

Tenancies

The concept of "a tenancy" is not defined but in some civil law systems leases fall outside the category of rights in rem and require separate mention in the text. It is not possible to read into the Regulation some of the distinctions, used for various purposes in English law, between a short-term letting and a longer lease, or between a contract to grant an interest and its actual grant.[25] In some cases the European Court has adopted a restrictive approach to the scope of art.22(1). So, in *Sanders v Van der Putte*[26] where the dispute concerned a florist's shop, it was held that there was no exclusive jurisdiction because the lease was essentially of the business carried out in the shop rather than of the shop as a building. Similarly, package holiday contracts fall outside art.22(1) even if they include accommodation not owned by the travel company.[27] But short-term holiday lets and time-share arrangements have been held to be within art.22(1).[28]

13–008

In *Rosler v Rottwinkel,*[29] a German landlord made a holiday cottage in Italy available on a short-term let. He brought an action in the German courts against the tenant claiming compensation under the terms of the lease for damage done to the property and sums due for gas and electricity, and also damages in respect of his own holiday in a neighbouring property, ruined by the behaviour of the defendants. The European Court held that the Italian courts had exclusive jurisdiction, applying to all the obligations of the parties under the lease, including any action for the recovery of possession, to collect rent or other charges due, and the cost of necessary repairs. The jurisdiction did not extend to issues only indirectly related to the lease, such as the claim for the ruined holiday.

The application of the exclusive jurisdiction rule to short-term holiday lettings was seen as undesirable, and some are now excluded. The Regulation provides that in the case of proceedings which have as their object tenancies of immovable

13–009

immovable property; although the basis of such an action is the interference with a right in rem in immovable property, the real and immovable nature of that right was, in such a context, of only marginal significance).

[25] See *Jarrett v Barclays Bank plc* [1999] Q.B. 1.
[26] Case 73/77, [1977] E.C.R. 2383.
[27] Case C–280/90 *Hacker v Euro-Relais GmbH* [1992] E.C.R. 1111.
[28] Case 241/83 *Rosler v Rottwinkel* [1985] E.C.R. 99; [1986] Q.B. 33; *Jarrett v Barclays Bank plc* [1999] Q.B. 1.
[29] Case 241/83, [1985] E.C.R. 99; [1986] Q.B. 33. See also Case C–8/98 *Dansommer v Gotz* [2000] E.C.R. I–93; [2001] 1 W.L.R. 1069 (exclusive jurisdiction covered an action brought by a tour operator, not the owner of the relevant property, against a tenant for damages for taking poor care of premises and causing damage to holiday accommodation).

property concluded for temporary private use for a maximum period of six consecutive months, the courts of the Member State in which the defendant is domiciled also have jurisdiction, provided that the tenant is a natural person (i.e. not a corporation) and that the landlord and tenant are domiciled in the same Member State.

Claims in contract and concerning rights in rem

13–010 A different provision of the Regulation enables the court of the *situs* of immovable property, where it is possible under the *lex situs* to combine an action relating to a contract with an action (against the same defendant, one domiciled in a Member State) relating to rights in rem in the property (for example an action both to enforce a mortgage debt and to obtain an order for the sale of the property), the courts of the *situs* may hear the former together with the latter, even if they would not otherwise have jurisdiction over the contractual action.[30]

Limits on jurisdiction

13–011 It follows from the above that where the land in question is situated in England and the issues fall within the scope of the Regulation or the Lugano Convention, the English courts will have jurisdiction. If the land is in England and the Regulation and Convention do not apply, the English court may take jurisdiction by allowing service out of the jurisdiction under the Civil Procedure Rules on the basis that the whole subject matter of a claim relates to property within the jurisdiction.[31] Where the land is in another part of the United Kingdom or another Member State or State party to the Lugano Convention, the jurisdiction of the English court will be excluded. If the land is in some other State, or the issue is not within the scope of the Regulation or the relevant Convention, it is still necessary to explore what is known as the *Moçambique* rule.

The *Moçambique* rule: title to foreign land

13–012 As a general rule, English courts have no jurisdiction to entertain a claim for the determination of the title to, or the right to possession of, any immovable situated outside England.[32] The origins of this rule have been traced to the ancient common law practice whereby juries were chosen from persons acquainted with the facts of a case, who therefore decided questions of fact from their own knowledge and not from the evidence of witnesses. In order that the right jury might be empanelled it was necessary to lay the venue exactly. The consequence was that English courts had no jurisdiction to entertain actions where the facts occurred abroad. This led to such inconvenience that the rule was evaded by the

---

[30] art.6(4).
[31] C.P.R., r.6.36 and PD 3.1(11).
[32] *British South Africa Co. v Companhia de Moçambique* [1893] A.C. 602.

fiction of *videlicet*, i.e. by the untraversable allegation[33] that a foreign place was situated in, e.g., the parish of St Marylebone.[34]

Unfortunately, this relaxation applied only to "transitory" actions, that is, actions where the facts might have occurred anywhere (e.g., for breach of contract). It did not apply to local actions, where the facts could only have occurred in a particular place (e.g., actions relating to foreign land).[35]

The rules as to venue were abolished by the Judicature Act 1873, and accordingly it was then arguable that there was no longer any reason for English courts not to decide questions of title to foreign land, or at least grant damages for trespass to such land. But in the leading case of *British South Africa Co v Companhia de Moçambique*[36] the House of Lords decided that:

13–013

> "the grounds upon which the courts have hitherto refused to exercise jurisdiction in actions of trespass to lands situated abroad were substantial and not technical, and that the rules of procedure under the Judicature Acts have not conferred a jurisdiction which did not exist before".

Unfortunately, neither Lord Herschell nor Lord Halsbury, who delivered speeches in that case, vouchsafed a hint as to what these "substantial" grounds were.

The facts of the case were as follows:

> The plaintiff, a Portuguese chartered company, alleged that it was in possession of large tracts of lands in southern Africa, and that the defendant, an English chartered company, by its agents wrongfully broke and entered and took possession of the lands and ejected the plaintiff company therefrom. The plaintiff claimed (1) a declaration that it was lawfully in possession of the lands; (2) an injunction restraining the defendant from asserting any title to the lands; (3) £250,000 damages for trespass. The defendant pleaded that because the lands were outside the jurisdiction the statement of claim disclosed no cause of action.

In the Court of Appeal the plaintiff formally abandoned claims (1) and (2), and that court by a majority declared that the High Court had jurisdiction over claim (3). The House of Lords unanimously reversed that judgment and dismissed the action.

13–014

Section 30 of the Civil Jurisdiction and Judgments Act 1982 provides that English courts have jurisdiction to entertain proceedings for trespass to or other torts affecting foreign land, unless the proceedings are principally concerned[37] with a question of title to, or the right to possession of, the land. This section reverses the much-criticised decision of the House of Lords in *Hesperides Hotels Ltd v Aegean Turkish Holidays Ltd*[38] where the House refused to limit the

---

[33] i.e., one that could not be denied.

[34] Holdsworth, *History of English Law*, Vol. 5, pp.140–142.

[35] For an attempt by Lord Mansfield to circumvent this distinction, see cases on land in "uncivilised" parts of Canada cited in *Mostyn v Fabrigas* (1774) 1 Cowp 161. The rule was re-asserted in *Doulson v Matthews* (1792) 4 T.R. 503 at 504.

[36] [1892] 2 Q.B. 358; [1893] A.C. 602.

[37] This imprecise expression has been held to be "a matter of judgment, one of fact and degree": *Re Polly Peck International plc (No.2)* [1998] 3 All E.R. 812 at 828.

[38] [1979] A.C. 508.

Moçambique rule to cases where title or the right to possession was in issue, conceding only that it did not prevent an action for damages for trespass to the contents of a building situated abroad.

Effect of the Brussels I Regulation

13–015   It is possible that the Brussels I Regulation has affected the position. If the defendant is domiciled in England, so that an English court has jurisdiction in a civil and commercial matter under art.2 of the Regulation, can it refuse to exercise jurisdiction on the ground that the land is situated abroad, in a non-Member State? Strict logic would suggest a negative answer, but policy arguments, including the clear policy of the Regulation in respect of disputes as to title to land, strongly support the continued right of the English court to decline jurisdiction in these circumstances. This latter view has been supported, albeit obiter, by the Court of Appeal.[39] In the decision of the European Court of Justice in *Owusu v Jackson*[40] that the plea of forum non conveniens was generally unavailable where the English court had jurisdiction under art.2, the precise issue as to foreign land was expressly reserved, as it was not raised by the facts before the court. In *Lucasfilm v Ainsworth*[41] (which was primarily concerned with intellectual property rights) the Court of Appeal held in effect that the *Moçambique* rule was not affected by art.2 and *Owusu v Jackson*. On appeal, the view of the Supreme Court on other issues meant that it did not address that specific matter.[42]

Scope of the Moçambique rule

13–016   If the *Moçambique* rule is one of policy, as the House of Lords insisted, the better opinion would seem to be that it cannot be waived by any agreement between the parties.[43]

The common law rule is subject to two not very well defined exceptions, both of which are derived from the practice of Courts of Equity. These will now be considered.

First exception: contracts and equities

13–017   If the court has jurisdiction in personam over a defendant, either because of presence in England when a claim form is served, or because of submission to the jurisdiction, or because the court grants permission to serve the claim form out of the jurisdiction under the Civil Procedure Rules, the court has jurisdiction to entertain an action against the defendant in respect of a contract or an equity

---

[39] *Re Polly Peck International plc (No.2)* [1998] 3 All E.R. 812 at 829–830.
[40] Case C–281/02, [2005] E.C.R. I-1383; [2005] Q.B. 801.
[41] [2009] EWCA Civ 1328; [2010] Ch. 503.
[42] [2011] UKSC 39; [2011] 4 All E.R. 817.
[43] *The Tolten* [1946] P. 135 at 166. Contrast *The Mary Moxham* (1876) 1 P.D. 107 at 109 and *Re Duke of Wellington* [1948] Ch. 118, where waiver seems to have been allowed: but the latter case would now fall under the second exception to the rule, and the former would raise no jurisdictional problem in view of s.30 of the Civil Jurisdiction and Judgments Act 1982.

affecting foreign land. In considering the scope of this exception, s.30 of the Civil Jurisdiction and Judgments Act 1982 must be borne in mind: there is no need to rely on this exception if proceedings are not principally concerned with a question of title to, or the right to possession of, the land.

Courts of Equity have, from the time of Lord Hardwicke's decision in *Penn v Baltimore*,[44] exercised jurisdiction in personam in relation to foreign land against persons locally within the jurisdiction of the English court in cases of contract, fraud and trust.[45] The facts of that case (slightly simplified) were as follows:

> Penn was the owner of the then province of Pennsylvania. Lord Baltimore was the owner of the then province of Maryland. They made a contract to settle the boundaries between the two provinces. Lord Hardwicke decreed specific performance of the contract.

The obligations which the courts will thus enforce are not easily brought under one head. "They all depend", said Parker J., "upon the existence between the parties to the suit of some personal obligation arising out of contract or implied contract, fiduciary relationship or fraud, or other conduct which, in the view of the Court of Equity in this country, would be unconscionable, and do not depend for their existence on the law of the locus of the immovable property".[46]

13–018

The jurisdiction is substantially confined to cases in which there is either a contract or an equity between the parties. Examples of contracts are claims by a lessor to recover rent due under a lease of foreign land,[47] or claims by a vendor or purchaser of foreign land for specific performance of a contract of sale.[48] Examples of equities are claims to redeem[49] or foreclose[50] a mortgage on foreign land, or to prevent a creditor from purchasing foreign land at an undervalue by making unfair use of local procedure,[51] or to reclaim gifts made under undue influence,[52] or for a declaration that the defendant holds foreign land as trustee.[53]

The decided cases have emphasised the following general points:

13–019

(a)　The jurisdiction cannot be exercised if the *lex situs* would prohibit the enforcement of the decree. "If, indeed", said Lord Cottenham, "the law of the country where the land is situate should not permit, or not enable, the defendant to do what the court might otherwise think it right to decree, it would be useless and unjust to direct him to do the act".[54] What this means is far from clear. In the very case in which Lord Cottenham was speaking, a mortgagee by deposit of title deeds was held entitled to priority over the mortgagor's unsecured creditors, although by the *lex situs* of the land the deposit gave him no lien or equitable mortgage over the land at all.

---

[44] (1750) 1 Ves. Sen. 444.
[45] *Pattni v Ali* [2006] UKPC 51; [2007] 2 A.C. 85.
[46] *Deschamps v Miller* [1908] 1 Ch. 856, 863.
[47] *St. Pierre v South American Stores Ltd* [1936] 1 K.B. 382.
[48] *Richard West and Partners Ltd v Dick* [1969] 2 Ch. 424.
[49] *Beckford v Kemble* (1822) 1 S. & St.7.
[50] *Toller v Carteret* (1705) 2 Vern. 494; *Paget v Ede* (1874) LR 18 Eq. 118.
[51] *Cranstown v Johnston* (1800) 5 Ves. 277.
[52] *Razelos v Razelos (No.2)* [1970] 1 W.L.R. 392.
[53] *Cook Industries Inc. v Galliher* [1979] Ch. 439.
[54] *Re Courtney, ex p. Pollard* (1840) Mont & Ch. 239 at 250.

(b)   The jurisdiction cannot be exercised against strangers to the equity unless they have become personally affected thereby. But it is difficult to determine what degree of privity prevents a defendant being a stranger to the equity. If A agrees to sell foreign land to B, but instead conveys it to C who has notice of the contract, C is a stranger to the equity against whom the jurisdiction cannot be invoked.[55] But if a company creates an equitable charge on foreign land in favour of debenture-holders, and sells the land to a purchaser "subject to the mortgage lien or charge now subsisting", and the purchaser expressly undertakes to pay the debentures and interest thereon, the court has jurisdiction to entertain an action by the debenture-holders against the purchaser to enforce their security.[56] The distinction between buying land with notice of a contract and buying land subject to a charge seems to be a tenuous one, not easily reconcilable with equitable doctrines of constructive notice.

(c)   The jurisdiction cannot be exercised if the court cannot effectively supervise the execution of its order. For this reason the court will not order a sale of foreign land at the instance of a mortgagee.[57] But it will order the foreclosure of a mortgage,[58] decree specific performance of a contract to sell foreign land,[59] and make an order for the inspection of foreign land.[60]

13–020   (d)   The jurisdiction cannot be exercised unless there is some personal equity running from the plaintiff to the defendant. Thus, in *Re Hawthorne*,[61] by reason of an intestacy the title to a house in Dresden was in dispute between A and B. B sold the house and received part of the purchase-money. A brought an action against B to make him account for the purchase-money, but it was held that the court had no jurisdiction. And in *Deschamps v Miller*[62]:

> A man and woman, domiciled in France, married there. Their marriage contract adopted a matrimonial property régime including community of after-acquired property under French law. The husband acquired land in India, where he went through a bigamous ceremony of marriage with Q, and settled the land on trusts for the benefit of Q and her children. After the deaths of the husband and wife the plaintiff, their only son, brought an action against the trustees of the settlement claiming his share of the land in India under French law. It was held that the court had no jurisdiction.

The equitable jurisdiction is anomalous and, as Lord Esher said,[63] "seems to be open to the strong objection that the court is doing indirectly what it dare not do directly". In the early cases in which the jurisdiction was invoked, the land was situated within British colonies with ill-developed court systems. In modern times, it is difficult to rely on any such rationale. A modern judge could hardly

---

[55] *Norris v Chambres* (1861) 29 Beav. 246; 3 D.F. & J. 583.
[56] *Mercantile Investment Co. v River Plate Co.* [1892] 2 Ch. 303.
[57] *Grey v Manitoba Rly Co.* [1897] A.C. 254.
[58] *Paget v Ede* (1874) LR 18 Eq. 118, criticised by Falconbridge, *op. cit.*, pp.618–620.
[59] *Richard West and Partners Ltd v Dick* [1969] 2 Ch. 424.
[60] *Cook Industries Inc. v Galliher* [1979] Ch. 439.
[61] (1883) 23 Ch.D. 743.
[62] [1908] 1 Ch. 856.
[63] *Companhia de Moçambique v British South Africa Co.* [1892] 2 Q.B. 358 at 404–405.

say, as Shadwell V.C. once said, "I consider that in the contemplation of the Court of Chancery every foreign court is an inferior court".[64]

Second exception: estates and trusts

If the court has jurisdiction to administer a trust[65] or the estate of a deceased person, and the property includes movables or immovables situated in England and immovables situated abroad, the court has jurisdiction to determine questions of title to the foreign immovables for the purposes of the administration. This formulation of the exception is based upon that of Dicey, Morris and Collins[66] because it has never been precisely formulated by English judges, though it has been approved by the Court of Session and referred to without dissent by the Court of Appeal.[67] But the existence of the exception can scarcely be doubted. The principal authority on which it rests is the case of *Nelson v Bridport*[68]:

13–021

> The King of the Two Sicilies granted land in Sicily to Admiral Nelson for himself and the heirs of his body, with power to appoint a successor. By his will, which dealt also with property in England, the Admiral devised the land to trustees in trust for his brother William for life with remainders over. After the Admiral's death, and in the lifetime of William, a law was passed in Sicily abolishing entails and making the persons lawfully in possession of such estates the absolute owners thereof. Taking advantage of this law, brother William devised the land to his daughter Lady Bridport. The remainderman under the Admiral's will claimed to be entitled to the land. The court assumed jurisdiction.

Here, it will be noticed, there was no contract, no fiduciary relationship and no equity between the parties: nothing in the report suggests that they were other than complete strangers to each other. There was nothing but a mere naked question of title to foreign land, and therefore the case could not possibly have fallen under the first exception discussed above.

This second exception is also supported by a number of other cases.[69] These cases cannot be explained on the ground that the jurisdictional objection was waived because, as we have seen, the better opinion is that the *Moçambique* rule cannot be waived; and in any case it is difficult to see how waiver could be allowed in cases where the interests of minors or of unborn persons are involved. The cases may perhaps be justified on the ground that the court can make its adjudication effective indirectly through its control of the trustees or of the other assets situated in England.

---

[64] *Bent v Young* (1838) 9 Sim. 180 at 191.
[65] It may be that this should now be confined to trusts arising under wills or intestacies, since these are excluded from the Brussels I Regulation, whereas inter vivos trusts might fall within art.22(1), above, para.4–046.
[66] (14th edn, 2006), Rule 122(3)(b).
[67] *Jubert v Church Commissioners for England*, 1952 SC 160 at 162; *Polly Peck International plc (No.2)* [1998] 3 All E.R. 812, at 828.
[68] (1846) 8 Beav. 547.
[69] *Hope v Carnegie* (1866) LR 1 Ch. App. 320; *Ewing v Orr-Ewing* (1883) 9 App Cas. 34; *Re Piercy* [1895] 1 Ch. 83; *Re Moses* [1908] 2 Ch. 235; *Re Stirling* [1908] 2 Ch. 344; *Re Pearses Settlement* [1909] 1 Ch. 304; *Re Hoyles* [1911] 1 Ch. 179; *Re Ross* [1930] 1 Ch. 377; *Re Duke of Wellington* [1948] Ch. 118.

Immovables: choice of law

13–022   One of the most deeply-rooted principles of the English conflict of laws, and of the corresponding rules in other legal systems, is that all questions relating to immovables are governed by the *lex situs*. The proposition may seem an almost self-evident one, for land can never be moved, and can be dealt with only in a manner permitted by the *lex situs*. Coupled with the *Moçambique* rule, the application of the *lex situs* ensures that virtually all disputes in the English courts about title to land are governed by English law.

However, the *situs* rule has been subjected to devastating academic criticism[70] on the ground that it is much too broad, hopelessly undiscriminating, and careless of the important policies of domestic law. Admittedly it achieves certainty, uniformity and symmetry in the law, and is easy to apply; but as we shall see it can lead to extremely harsh and inconvenient results. The first of the critics was Cook, who pointed out that when a court sitting at the *situs* of the land is confronted by a document (e.g., a deed or will) executed abroad by a person domiciled abroad, the real question is: should the court apply to such a document the same rule of decision that it would apply to a purely domestic document. He argued cogently that in matters of form, capacity, and matrimonial property it should not, but that in matters of essential validity it should.

13–023   Cook's analysis was carried several stages further by Hancock who, in an important series of articles, argued that, apart from questions of the marketability or use of land, the *situs*-forum should not necessarily apply the domestic law of the *situs* but should consider whether that law, properly interpreted and understood, was intended to apply to foreign-executed documents or to persons domiciled abroad.

The arguments of Cook and Hancock have not persuaded English judges to reconsider their traditional reliance on the *situs* rule as an all-embracing formula by which, in the absence of statute or judicial precedent to the contrary, all questions relating to land must be governed. But it may be pointed out that, long before Cook and Hancock, it was held that a foreign marriage contract or settlement (even if it was not express but was imposed or implied by foreign law) could affect the devolution of land in England[71]; that wills of immovables are, as a general rule, interpreted by reference to the law of the testator's domicile[72]; that now by statute a will of immovables must be treated as properly executed if its execution conformed to the law of the country where it was executed, or where the testator was domiciled or habitually resident, or of which he or she was a national.[73]

---

[70] Cook, *op. cit.,* Ch.10; Hancock, (1964) 16 Stanford L. Rev. 561; (1965) 17 Stanford L. Rev. 1095; (1966) 18 Stanford L. Rev. 1299; (1967) 20 Stanford L. Rev. 1; Weintraub, (1966) 52 Cornell L.Q. 1; Morris, (1969) 85 L.Q.R. 339.

[71] *Re De Nicols (No.2)* [1900] 2 Ch. 410; below, para.14–015.

[72] See below, para.15–029.

[73] Wills Act 1963 s.1; below, para.15–019.

Renvoi

Nearly all writers on the conflict of laws agree that, in the rare cases where an   **13–024**
English court is dealing with a question of title to land situated abroad, it should
apply whatever system of domestic law the *lex situs* would apply,[74] and there are
cases in which this has been done.[75] In other words, this situation is one in which
it is justifiable to apply the doctrine of *renvoi* in order to achieve uniformity with
the *lex situs*.[76] Uniformity with the *lex situs* is important because in the last resort
the land can only be dealt with in a manner permitted by that law. Consequently,
any decision by a non-*situs* court which ignored what the courts of the *situs* had
decided or would decide might well be of no value.

In what follows, it should be noted that the effect of grants of administration
on immovables, succession to immovables, and marriage are reserved for
separate discussion in later chapters.

Formal validity

There appears to be only one reported English case in which the formal validity   **13–025**
of a deed affecting land has been considered. In *Adams v Clutterbuck*,[77] a
domiciled Englishman conveyed to a purchaser domiciled in England a right of
shooting over land in Scotland. The conveyance was made in England by an
instrument in writing but not under seal. The law of England required such
conveyances to be under seal, but the law of Scotland did not. It was held that the
conveyance was valid.

Insofar as the instrument is to have effect as a contract, its formal validity is
governed in the case of contracts concluded on or before December 17, 2009 by
the Rome Convention as given effect by the Contracts (Applicable Law) Act
1990 and in respect of contracts concluded after that date by European Parliament
and Council Regulation 593/2008 on the law applicable to contractual obligations
("Rome I"). The only special rule is that in art.9(6) of the Convention and (in a
slightly different draft) in art.11(5) of the Regulation. The rule in its Regulation
wording is that a contract the subject matter of which is a right in rem in
immovable property or a tenancy of immovable property is subject to the
requirements of form of the law of the country where the property is situated if by
that law (a) those requirements are imposed irrespective of the country where the
contract is concluded and irrespective of the law governing the contract; and (b)
those requirements cannot be derogated from by agreement.

Essential validity

Although all the cases concern wills, there can be no doubt that the essential   **13–026**
validity of a deed affecting land in England is also governed by English law. That

---

[74] Falconbridge, *op. cit.*, pp.141 and 217–220; Cook, *op. cit.*, pp.264 and 279–280; Lorenzen, *op. cit.*,
p.78; Hancock, (1965) 17 Stanford L. Rev. 1095 at 1096, n.4.
[75] *Re Ross* [1930] 1 Ch. 377; *Re Duke of Wellington* [1947] Ch. 506.
[76] See below, para.18–038.
[77] (1883) 10 Q.B.D. 403.

law will determine what estates can legally be created,[78] what are the incidents of those estates,[79] whether gifts to charities are valid,[80] and whether the interests given infringe the rule against perpetuities or accumulations.[81]

On the other hand, the material or essential validity of a contract affecting land is governed either by the Rome Convention or the Rome I Regulation.[82] Under the Convention, if the parties have not chosen the governing law, that law will be determined by art.4.[83] Article 4(3) provides that, to the extent that the subject matter of the contract is a right in immovable property or a right to use immovable property, it is presumed that the contract is most closely connected with the country in which the immovable is situated. Although this presumption will not apply if it appears from the circumstances as a whole that the contract is more closely connected with another country,[84] the likely result is that the *lex situs* will apply in almost every case. The Rome I provisions are likely to have the same effect. Article 4(1)(c) of the Regulation provides that a contract relating to a right in rem in immovable property or to a tenancy of immovable property is governed by the law of the country where the property is situated; but art.4(3) adds that where it is clear from all the circumstances of the case that the contract is manifestly more closely connected with another country, the law of that other country applies.

Capacity: land in England

13–027 There appears to be no reported case in which the English court has had to consider the question of capacity to transfer land in England when the transferor was domiciled abroad.[85] The relevant considerations are well illustrated by the American case of *Proctor v Frost*[86]:

> A married woman domiciled in Massachusetts became surety in that state for her husband and gave as security a mortgage on land she owned in New Hampshire. The mortgagee brought proceedings in New Hampshire to foreclose the mortgage. The mortgagor's defence was that by a New Hampshire statute a married woman could not become surety for her husband.

The New Hampshire court rejected this defence on the ground that "the primary purpose of the statute was not to regulate the transfer of New Hampshire real estate, but to protect married women in New Hampshire from the consequences of their efforts, presumably ill-advised, to reinforce the credit of embarrassed husbands". This decision seems sound and sensible; but the reasoning is not entirely satisfactory because it emphasises the place where the mortgage was executed and not where the mortgagor was domiciled. The mortgagor was surely

---

[78] *Nelson v Bridport* (1846) 8 Beav. 547.
[79] *Re Miller* [1914] 1 Ch. 511.
[80] *Duncan v Lawson* (1889) 41 Ch.D. 394; *Re Hoyles* [1911] 1 Ch. 179.
[81] *Freke v Carbery* (1873) LR 16 Eq. 461.
[82] See para.11–007.
[83] See para.11–026.
[84] As a result of applying art.4(5) of the Convention.
[85] Issues as to capacity are generally excluded from both the Rome Convention and the Rome I Regulation.
[86] 89 N.H. 304; 197 A. 813 (1938).

outside the scope of the New Hampshire statute, not because she executed the mortgage in Massachusetts but because she was domiciled there.[87]

If the laws of the two states had been reversed and the mortgagor was incapable of making the mortgage by the law of her domicile (Massachusetts), but capable by the *lex situs* (New Hampshire), there would have been something to be said for applying the *lex situs* and holding the mortgage valid, at any rate if the mortgagee was domiciled and resident in New Hampshire. New Hampshire mortgagees ought not to be deprived of their security because of some lurking incapacity in the law of the mortgagor's domicile.

    Capacity to take (as opposed to transfer) land in England is governed by English domestic law. Perhaps the most striking illustration of this principle is the former rule, abolished in 1870,[88] that an alien could not own land in England. A more modern, but still obsolete, illustration is afforded by *Att-Gen v Parsons*,[89] where the House of Lords held that a company incorporated in the Republic of Ireland could not hold land in England without a licence in mortmain from the Crown.

13–028

Capacity: land abroad

The question what law governs capacity to transfer land situated abroad came before the Court of Appeal in *Bank of Africa v Cohen*,[90] where the *lex situs* was applied. The reasoning is, however, most unsatisfactory.

13–029

> A married woman, domiciled and resident with her husband in England, executed a deed in England whereby she agreed to mortgage land in Johannesburg to an English bank as security for past and future advances by the bank to her husband. The bank sought specific performance of the deed. The mortgagor's defence was that by South African law a married woman was incapable, with limited exceptions inapplicable in the instant case, of becoming surety for her husband. The trial judge found as a fact that she knew quite well what she was doing.

It was held that her capacity to make the contract was governed by South African law and the contract was therefore void. This decision seems unjust. The bank was left without security for advances made on the strength of the mortgagor's promise; and she was allowed to break her promise with impunity although she knew quite well what she was doing. The court made no attempt to ascertain either the policy of the South African law, or whether a South African court would have applied South African domestic law to this very case. Had it done so, it might well have discovered that the South African law laid down a policy not for South African land but for South African married women, and that the defendant was outside the scope of that law because she was domiciled in England. Moreover, the court was dealing not with a mortgage but with a contract to make a mortgage. If, as seems likely, the law governing the contract (at that date, the proper law of the contract) was English law, what was there to prevent

---

[87] The reasoning is criticised on this ground by Cook, p.275, n.48, and Hancock, (1967) 20 Stanford L.Rev. 1 at 31, though both writers approve the result.

[88] Naturalisation Act 1870 s.2.

[89] [1956] A.C. 421.

[90] [1909] 2 Ch. 129; criticised by Falconbridge, *op. cit.*, p.629.

the court from making a decree of specific performance? The court made no attempt to determine the proper law of the contract, but baldly asserted that the defendant's capacity was governed by the *lex situs,* and mechanically applied the domestic provisions of that law.

TANGIBLE MOVABLES

13–030   We now turn to examine the question of what law governs the validity of particular transfers of movables and the effect on the proprietary interests of the parties and those claiming under them.[91] By a "particular" transfer is meant, for example, a transfer by way of sale, gift, pledge, hire-purchase, or conditional sale. We are not concerned with general transfers made on occasions such as marriage or death: these are considered elsewhere.[92]

It is convenient to consider first the transfer of what are called "tangible movables", i.e. chattels, ordinary objects such as furniture, cars, or jewellery. But much property is intangible: simple contract debts, shares in companies, intellectual property rights, and so on. Diverse in nature, they are referred to collectively as "intangible movables" and are considered in a later part of this chapter.

Where the *situs* remains constant

13–031   In simple cases where the *situs* of the chattel remains constant at all material times, the *lex situs* governs the validity and effect of the transfer.[93] There is a consistent line of authority to that effect. "I do not think", said Maugham J., "that anyone can doubt that, with regard to the transfer of goods, the law applicable must be the *lex situs.* Business could not be carried on if that were not so".[94] "There is little doubt", said Devlin J., "that it is the *lex situs* which, as a general rule, governs the transfer of movables when effected contractually".[95] "The proper law governing the transfer of corporeal movable property", said Diplock L.J. "is the *lex situs*".[96] More recently, the authorities were reviewed and the principle reasserted by Moore-Bick J. in *Glencore International AG v Metro Trading International.*[97] Applying the *lex situs* has the great advantage of

---

[91] See Lalive, *The Transfer of Chattels in the Conflict of Laws* (1955); Zaphiriou, *The Transfer of Chattels in Private International Law* (1955); Chesterman, (1973) 22 I.C.L.Q. 213.

[92] Below, Chs.14 and 15.

[93] *Inglis v Usherwood* (1801) 1 East 515; *City Bank v Barrow* (1880) 5 App.Cas. 664; *Inglis v Robertson* [1898] A.C. 616; *Government of the Islamic Republic of Iran v Barakat Galleries Ltd* [2007] EWCA Civ 1374; [2008] 1 All E.R. 1177. The same principle applies to the acquisition of title in newly-created goods: *Glencore International AG v Metro Trading International* [2001] 1 Lloyd's Rep. 284 at 296.

[94] *Re Anziani* [1930] 1 Ch. 407 at 420.

[95] *Bank voor Handel en Scheepvaart NV v Slatford* [1953] 1 Q.B. 248 at 257.

[96] *Hardwick Game Farm v Suffolk Agricultural Poultry Producers Association* [1966] 1 W.L.R. 287 at 330; affirmed by the House of Lords [1969] 2 A.C. 31.

[97] [2001] 1 Lloyd's Rep. 284. See also *Macmillan Inc v Bishopsgate Investment Trust plc (No.3)* [1996] 1 W.L.R. 387 (title to shares in a company).

certainty because, except where goods are in transit from one country to another,[98] it is likely to be easily ascertainable.

The *lex situs* rule governs not only questions of ownership but also the location of a possessory title. The Court of Appeal has accepted that the *lex situs* governs the question whether a party has an immediate right to the possession of goods for the purpose of establishing a claim in tort for conversion.[99]

It is of course possible to argue for the application of some other law than that of the *situs*. It would plainly be inappropriate to apply a law identified by reference to characteristics of the parties, such as their domicile or place of business.[100] Nor in modern conditions would it be sensible to apply the law of the place in which the relevant transaction occurs, for this can be purely fortuitous. The claims of the law governing the transaction by which the transfer is effected may seem stronger. A transfer may be invalid as a transfer yet valid as an executory agreement to transfer; there are advantages in recognising the links between the contractual and proprietary issues.

The issue was very fully examined in *Glencore International AG v Metro Trading International*.[101] Counsel for the claimants argued that when issues relating to the passing of property arose as between the immediate parties to a contract, English law ought to resolve any conflict between the terms of the contract and the *lex situs* by recognising and giving effect to the contract in accordance with its governing law in preference to the *lex situs*. In rejecting this argument, Moore-Bick J. referred to the two main justifications for the *lex situs* rule: that it accords with the natural expectations of reasonable men and facilitates business, and indeed was required by considerations of commercial convenience; and that it reflects the practical realities of control over movables. He did not favour an exception in those cases involving only the two parties to the contract: consistency of principle requires that the same rule should apply whether or not third party interests were affected. The very nature of title to movables is that it gives the person in whom it is vested rights which can be maintained against all other parties. Questions of title are most likely to be of importance when one party to the transaction became insolvent, where the interests of third parties in the form of a general body of creditors may clearly be affected. Practical control over movables can ultimately be regulated and protected only by the state in which they are situated and the adoption of the *lex situs* rule in relation to the passing of property recognized that fact. That is just as true in relation to the passing of property between the parties to the transaction as it is in relation to the passing of property between one or other of them and a third party.

13–032

---

[98] Slade J. in *Winkworth v Christie Manson & Woods Ltd* [1980] 1 Ch. 496, quoted with evident approval a rule that where goods are in transit, and their *situs* is casual or not known, a transfer which is valid and effective by its proper law will be valid and effective in England: see now Dicey, Morris and Collins, *op cit*, at the Exception to Rule 124.

[99] *Government of the Islamic Republic of Iran v Barakat Galleries Ltd* [2007] EWCA Civ 1374; [2008] 1 All E.R. 1177 (where the point was agreed by counsel for both parties).

[100] Early continental writers held that *mobilia sequuntur personam* (movables follow the person) but this is nowhere followed today.

[101] [2001] 1 Lloyd's Rep. 284. The complex facts involved dealings in the United Arab Emirates (the *situs*) with oil the subject of contracts governed by English law. *Glencore* was approved on this point in *Dornoch Ltd v Westminster International BV* [2009] EWHC 1782 (Admlty).

It is also the case that a transfer may be by way of a gift, so that the transferor is under no contractual obligation at all.[102] There may be two independent transfers, each governed by the law of a different country, e.g., where the title to goods is in dispute between an unpaid seller and a pledgee from the purchaser.[103] Moreover, a problem may arise although there has been no transfer at all. For instance, A finds B's ring in Scotland, takes it to England, and possesses it there for a period sufficient to extinguish B's title under the English, but not the Scottish, Statute of Limitations.

Renvoi

13–033 An issue addressed in a number of cases but which still awaits a definitive ruling from an appellate court, is the availability of *renvoi* in applying the *lex situs*. It was rightly said in *Glencore International AG v Metro Trading International*[104] that:

> "if the *lex situs* rule rests, at least in part, on a recognition of the practical control exercised by the State in which they are situated, there is something to be said for applying whatever rules of law the Courts of that state would actually apply in determining such questions".

It was not necessary to resolve the issue on the facts, and the point had also been left unresolved in the earlier case of *Winkworth v Christie Manson & Woods Ltd*.[105] More recent cases, examined in a later chapter,[106] show a strong judicial disinclination to accept the application of *renvoi* in this context.

Public policy

13–034 There is at least one exception to the *lex situs* rule: the English court may decline to give effect to the relevant rules of the *lex situs* on the ground of public policy.[107] A second exception has been suggested, that of want of good faith on the part of the person acquiring title[108]: the existence of any such exception, at least as distinct from public policy considerations, was doubted by Moore-Bick J. in the *Glencore* case.[109]

---

[102] See *Cochrane v Moore* (1890) 25 Q.B.D. 57 (where, however, the *lex situs* was not pleaded).
[103] See, e.g., *Inglis v Robertson* [1898] A.C. 616.
[104] [2001] 1 Lloyd's Rep 284.
[105] [1980] 1 Ch. 496. cf. *McMillan Inc v Bishopsgate Investment Trust plc (No.3)* [1996] 1 W.LR 387 (at first instance: *renvoi* held inapplicable, but a case on priority in respect of intangibles; the *renvoi* issue was not taken on appeal).
[106] See paras 18–023ff.
[107] *Winkworth v Christie Manson & Woods Ltd* [1980] 1 Ch. 496; *Glencore International AG v Metro Trading International* [2001] 1 Lloyd's Rep. 284.
[108] *Winkworth v Christie Manson & Woods Ltd* [1980] 1 Ch. 496.
[109] *Glencore International AG v Metro Trading International* [2001] 1 Lloyd's Rep. 284 at 295.

Where the *situs* changes

Much more complicated problems arise if the *situs* of the goods does not remain **13–035** constant at all material times, so that a choice has to be made between two or more *leges situs*. For example, a car is delivered to a hirer in England under a hire-purchase contract, taken by the hirer to France, and sold there to a purchaser in circumstances which give the purchaser a good title under the general doctrine of French law *en fait de meubles, la possession vaut titre.*[110]
The leading English case is *Cammell v Sewell*[111]:

> A, a domiciled Englishman, bought some timber in Russia and shipped it to England in a Prussian ship. The ship was wrecked off the coast of Norway. B, the master of the ship, sold the timber in Norway to C in circumstances which gave C a good title by the law of Norway, but not by English law. C brought the timber to England. It was held that C's title conferred by the *lex situs* prevailed over that of A.

Cammell v Sewell was followed in *Winkworth v Christie*[112] where works of art were stolen from the plaintiff's house in England, taken to Italy without his knowledge or consent, and there sold to the second defendant, an Italian, who sent them to the first defendant in England to be auctioned. By Italian law the second defendant had a good title. It was held that Italian law governed.

Cammell v Sewell is usually cited for the proposition that the English owner's **13–036** title, validly acquired in Russia where he bought the timber, was lost by what happened in Norway. But it also decides that the Norwegian buyer's title, validly acquired in Norway, was not lost when he brought the timber to England. This second aspect of the case is just as important as the first; and it leads to the following distinction[113]:

> A title to a tangible movable acquired or reserved [under the *lex situs*] will be recognised as valid in England if the movable is removed from the country where it was situated at the time when such title was acquired, unless and until such title is displaced by a new title acquired in accordance with the law of the country to which it is removed.

For the sake of clarity, let us call the country of the first *situs* X, and the country of the second *situs* Y. The law can be stated in four propositions.

(a) A title to goods acquired in X will be recognised in England if the goods **13–037** are subsequently removed to Y, until some new title validly acquired in Y overrides the title acquired in X. If no such new title is acquired in Y after the removal of the goods to Y, the fact that the title acquired by the law of X would not have been acquired by the law of Y is immaterial, for the goods were in X at the material time. This is the result of the decision in *Cammell v Sewell*[114]:

---

[110] French Civil Code, art.2279.
[111] (1860) 5 H. & N. 728.
[112] [1980] Ch. 496.
[113] See Dicey, Morris and Collins, *op. cit.*, r.125.
[114] (1860) 5 H. & N. 728 at 742–743; cf. *Todd v Armour* (1882) 9 R. 901.

"If, according to Norwegian law, the property passed by the sale in Norway to Clausen as an innocent purchaser, we do not think that the subsequent bringing of the property to England can alter the position of the parties".

(b) If a new title is acquired under the law of Y after the removal of the goods to Y, which has the effect of overriding prior titles, the title previously acquired under the law of X is displaced. It was for this reason that A's Russian title was displaced by C's Norwegian title in *Cammell v Sewell,* since the sale by the master of the ship had by Norwegian law the effect of overriding prior titles. It was for this reason that A's English title was displaced by C's Italian title in *Winkworth v Christie,* since the sale by the thief had by Italian law the effect of overriding prior titles. Other instances of transactions which override prior titles in English domestic law are sales by a mercantile agent under statutes such as s.2 of the Factors Act 1889, and sales by a buyer in possession with the consent of the seller under statutes such as s.25 of the Sale of Goods Act 1979.[115] That the goods were removed to Y without the owner's consent makes no difference: "We do not think that goods which were wrecked here would on that account be less liable to our laws as to market overt[116] or as to the landlord's right of distress, merely because the owner did not foresee that they would come to England".[117]

13–038 (c) The difficult intermediate case is where A has acquired or reserved a title to goods in X, and B, the person in possession of the goods, takes them to Y, where they are sold by B to a purchaser, the sale not being one which overrides prior titles, or attached by B's creditors, not being creditors claiming a paramount lien. By the law of X, the owner's title prevails over that of the purchaser or creditors; by the law of Y, it does not. But the reason it does not is quite different from that in paragraph (b) above. Here the purchaser or creditors are not saying to A: "Our title prevails over yours because the sale to or attachment by us overrides all prior titles by the law of Y". They are saying: "Our title prevails over yours because your title, validly acquired or reserved by the law of X, was not validly acquired or reserved by the law of Y".

In this situation, most of the English, American and Canadian cases uphold the title of the owner A against that of purchasers from or creditors of B.[118] The reason is simple: since the goods were in X when A's title was reserved, the law of X should govern that reservation of title. As the matter was put in the *Glencore* case,[119] English law recognises the effect which the

---

[115] *Cammell v Sewell,* cited above, at p.744; *Alcock v Smith* [1892] 1 Ch. 238 at 267; *Embiricos v Anglo-Austrian Bank* [1905] 1 K.B. 677; *Century Credit Corporation v Richard* (1962) 34 D.L.R. (2d) 291; *Price Mobile Home Centres Inc. v National Trailer Convoy of Canada* (1974) 44 D.L.R. (3d) 443; *Re Fuhrmann and Miller* (1977) 78 D.L.R. (3d) 284; *Maden v Long* [1983] 1 W.W.R. 649.

[116] The special rules under which overriding title was acquired on a sale in market overt were abolished in England in 1995.

[117] *Cammell v Sewell,* above, at p.745.

[118] *Simpson v Fogo* (1863) 1 H. & M. 195; *Goetschius v Brightman* (1927) 245 N.Y. 186; 156 N.E. 660; *Industrial Acceptance Corporation v La Flamme* [1950] 2 D.L.R. 822; *Rennie Car Sales v Union Acceptance Corporation* [1955] 4 D.L.R. 822.

[119] *Glencore International AG v Metro Trading International* [2001] 1 Lloyd's Rep. 284 at 295–296.

lex situs gives to a transaction, but does not recognise any attempt by the *lex situs* to re-characterise a transaction which occurred when the goods were situated within another country.

Very often the law of Y differs from the law of X in that it requires hire-purchase **13–039** or conditional sales contracts to be registered in Y. There is an observable tendency for courts, even courts in Y, to hold that the statutory registration requirements of the law of Y are confined to domestic transactions,[120] or can be satisfied if A registers soon after he becomes aware that the chattel has been removed to Y, even though this may not be until after it has been sold there to a purchaser.[121] Thus, in a leading American case[122]:

> A & Co., a Californian corporation, sold a motor car in California to B, a Californian resident, on hire-purchase terms. It was agreed that title should remain with A until the price was fully paid and that until then B would not remove the car out of California. Before the price was fully paid, B took the car to New York without A's knowledge or consent and sold it there to C, a bona fide purchaser. By the law of California, A's title was superior to any title derived from B on resale, even to an innocent purchaser for value. By the law of New York, all such reservations of title were void against subsequent purchasers in good faith unless the contract was registered in New York. The contract never was so registered. The New York Court of Appeals held that A & Co.'s title was good against C.

It follows from what has been said that whether A loses his title when his goods **13–040** are removed to Y and dealt with there depends entirely on why the law of Y would say that his title is lost.[123] It may do so, generally speaking, for one of two reasons: either because it says that an event which has occurred in Y has the effect of overriding prior titles, or because it does not recognise that the transaction whereby A acquired or reserved his title in X had this effect by the law of Y. In the former case, the law of Y governs, and A's title is lost, because the law of Y *(lex situs)* determines the effect of the transaction in Y when the goods were in Y, and the law of X is irrelevant to that transaction. In the latter case, the law of X governs, and A retains his title, because the law of X *(lex situs)* determines the effect of the transaction in X when the goods were in X, and the law of Y is irrelevant to that transaction. This conclusion is the necessary consequence of the proposition advanced in paragraph (a) above. If A acquires a valid title to goods in X, we have seen that A's title is upheld if the goods are removed to Y, even though A would not have acquired a good title by law of Y. Thus, if B removes A's goods to Y, A's title is still good. If B now sells the goods in Y to C, there is no reason why B should be capable of passing a better title than he has himself, unless the law of Y attributes this special effect to the sale there.

This distinction was drawn very clearly in a Canadian case[124]:

---

[120] See, e.g., *Goetschius v Brightman* (1927) 245 N.Y. 186; 156 N.E. 660.

[121] *Rennie Car Sales v Union Acceptance Corporation*, above; *McAloney v McInnes and General Motors Acceptance Corporation* (1956) 2 D.L.R. (2d) 666. See Davis, (1964) 13 I.C.L.Q. 53.

[122] *Goetschius v Brightman* (1927) 245 N.Y. 186; 156 N.E. 660.

[123] See Morris, (1945) 22 B.Y.I.L. 232, 238–246.

[124] *Century Credit Corporation v Richard* (1962) 34 D.L.R. (2d) 291 at 293–294; cf. *Traders Finance Corporation v Dawson Implements Ltd* (1959) 15 D.L.R. (2d) 515. Contrast *Industrial Acceptance Corporation v La Flamme* [1950] 2 D.L.R. 822, approved in *Century Credit Corporation v Richard*, but distinguished on the ground that the court overlooked s.25(2) of the Ontario Sale of Goods Act.

A & Co. sold a motor car in Quebec to B, a resident of Quebec, under a conditional sales contract which provided that the car should remain the property of A & Co. until the price was fully paid. Before the price was fully paid, B took the car to Ontario without the knowledge or consent of A & Co. and sold it there to C, a resident of Ontario, who had no knowledge of A & Co.'s rights in the car. The law of Ontario required conditional sales contracts to be registered; the law of Quebec did not. The Ontario Court of Appeal held that A & Co.'s title would have prevailed against C, but for the fact that B was a person who had agreed to buy goods and was in possession of them with the consent of the seller and could therefore pass a good title to C under s.25(2) of the Ontario Sale of Goods Act.

13–041   In the course of his judgment, Kelly J.A. said:

> "If the laws of Ontario were to seek to invalidate [A & Co.'s] title by refusing to recognise that the transaction which took place in Quebec had the effect of continuing the title in [A & Co.], this attempt of Ontario law to invalidate a transaction taking place in Quebec would be bad because the validity of a Quebec transaction must be determined by the laws of Quebec, the *lex situs* . . . However, if the laws of Ontario provide that a later transaction which takes place wholly within Ontario has the effect of overriding prior titles, then since Ontario does not seek to give its laws any extra-territorial effect the laws of Ontario prevail and the title created under the laws of Ontario displaces the title reserved in the Quebec transaction".

(d) In the situations so far discussed, it has been assumed that the law of Y affords greater protection to purchasers and creditors than the law of X. The reverse side of the usual picture is presented when chattels are taken into Y and dealt with there in circumstances which deprive the owner of title by the law of X, but not by the law of Y. Suppose that A delivers a chattel in State X to B, a broker, for the purposes of sale, but reserving title: no title is to pass to B. B takes the chattel to State Y and there sells it to C. By the law of State Y, A's reservation of title is good as against third parties. In the law of State X, the circumstances of the transaction are such that A's title was extinguished. A has good title, for the law of State X was not the *lex situs* at the time of the relevant transaction.[125]

13–042   A valiant effort was made by counsel in *Raiffeisen Zentralbank Österreich AG v Five Star General Trading LLC*[126] to argue that the *lex situs* rule applied equally to intangible movables. The argument was rejected, not least because the allocation of a *situs* to an intangible is necessarily quite artificial.[127] (There are rules which do that, for example the rule that a debt is regarded by English law as located where it is enforceable).[128] Equally unsuccessful was the argument that in the case of intangibles there could be the same distinction as can be drawn in the

---

[125] See *Cline v Russell* (1908) 2 Alta. L.R. 79; *Rennie Car Sales v Union Acceptance Corporation* [1955] 4 D.L.R. 822; Morris, (1945) 22 B.Y.I.L. 232, 246–247.

[126] [2001] EWCA Civ 68; [2001] Q.B. 825; Briggs, (2001) 72 B.Y.I.L.. 461.

[127] In the *Raiffeisen* case, the *situs* was said to be France the claim being on insurers resident in France. The deed of assignment was expressly governed by English law.

[128] See *Hillside (New Media) Ltd v Baasland* [2010] EWHC 3336 (Comm).

context of tangibles: that between the contractual and proprietary aspects of transactions.[129] The various issues are clearly governed by the Rome Convention or its successor the Rome I Regulation.

The *Raiffeisen* case also confirmed the significance of another distinction, that between voluntary and involuntary assignments. There are processes (such as garnishment, considered more fully below)[130] under which the debtor is obliged to pay not the original creditor, A, but some other person, and that transfer is involuntary on the part of A. An example is an attachment of earnings order, under which an employer must pay part of an employee's salary to satisfy a court order. Voluntary assignments, but not involuntary assignments, are now governed by art.12 of the Rome Convention and, in respect of contracts concluded after December 17, 2009, art.14 of the Rome I Regulation. As the Court of Appeal observed in the *Raiffeisen* case, the difference between the consensual and non-consensual cases is such that it is neither surprising nor inconvenient that they have different choice of law rules.

Identifying the issues

The voluntary assignment of an intangible movable can raise a number of different issues, some of which can be illustrated by using the example of a simple contract debt, one created by a transaction between A (the creditor) and B (the debtor). By a further transaction, A assigns the benefit of the debt to C.[131]   **13–043**

One set of questions concerns the validity of that second transaction, as between A and C. Logically, that will be governed by the law applicable to that transaction. But there are other questions which cannot be referred to that law.

One is the prior question whether the debt is assignable at all, a question that can only be answered by reference to the law which governs the creation of the debt, the law applicable to the original transaction between A and B. Another issue is that of priorities, were A to assign the same debt, in separate transactions, to C and to D: has C or D the better claim? The issue (which may be simply a question of which transaction came first, but may involve a consideration of further steps such as giving notice to B or making an entry on a register of some sort) cannot be resolved by reference to the law governing either of the competing assignments. It is best also referred to the law applicable to the original transaction between A and B.

---

[129] For discussion of this and related issues, see Moshinsky, (1992) 108 L.Q.R. 591; Struycken, [1998] L.M.C.L.Q. 345.

[130] See para.13–049.

[131] There are of course many more complex cases, and there may be special considerations in, for example, the field of intellectual property and in relation to various forms of financial instruments.

Intrinsic validity

13–044   The intrinsic validity of a voluntary assignment is governed by art.14(1) of the Rome I Regulation[132]: the relationship between assignor and assignee under a voluntary assignment or contractual subrogation of a claim against another person (the debtor) is to be governed by the law that applies under the Regulation to the contract between the assignor and assignee.[133] "Contractual subrogation" involves the creation of subrogation rights by contract, notably in an insurance context. It is clear that art.14(1) govern the proprietary as well as the contractual issues as between assignor and assignee.[134]

This law will govern issues as to the formal and essential validity of the assignment. The question of the capacity of the parties to make or to take under the assignment is more difficult; neither the Convention nor the Rome I Regulation addresses this issue.[135] It was considered in the leading case of *Republica de Guatemala v Nunez.*[136]

> In 1906, the President of Guatemala deposited £20,000 in a London bank. In 1919 in Guatemala, he assigned this sum to his illegitimate son, Nunez, a minor domiciled and resident in Guatemala. By English law the assignment was valid in all respects. By the law of Guatemala it was formally invalid and a minor could not accept a voluntary assignment unless a tutor had been appointed by a judge on his behalf; this was not done.

13–045   Unfortunately, the judges gave different reasons for their decision that the assignment was governed by Guatemalan law, and only Scrutton and Lawrence L.JJ. distinguished between the various grounds of invalidity. On the capacity point, both these judges held that the issue was governed either by the law of the domicile or by the law of the country in which the assignment took place. So do the judgments of Day and Wills JJ. in *Lee v Abdy*[137]:

> H, domiciled in Cape Province, insured his life with an English insurance company and assigned the policy to his wife in Cape Province. The assignment was valid by English law but void by the law of the Cape as a gift between husband and wife. It was held that Cape law governed and that the assignment was void.

However, there can be no doubt that in the *Guatemala* case Guatemalan law was the law applicable to the assignment and that in *Lee v Abdy* it was the law of the Cape. It is submitted that the governing law of the assignment is a far better test of capacity than either the law of the domicile or the law of the place of the

---

[132] cf. the rather different language of the Rome Convention, art.12, providing that the mutual obligations of the assignor and assignee are governed by the law which under the Convention applies to the contract between the assignor and assignee.

[133] art.14(3) offers a partial definition of the concept of assignment, as including outright transfers of claims, transfers of claims by way of security and pledges or other security rights over claims.

[134] See Recital (38) to the Regulation and T.C. Hartley, (2011) 60 I.C.L.Q. 29.

[135] Save for the special rule in art.11 of the Convention and art.13 of the Regulation; see paras 11–065ff.

[136] [1927] 1 K.B. 669.

[137] (1886) 17 Q.B.D 309.

assignment. It also produces a result harmonising with the principle in art.12(1) and applying to other aspects of the mutual obligations of the assignor and assignee.

Assignability

In some systems of law some kinds of debts cannot be assigned at all, for obvious reasons of social policy: e.g. policies of life insurance, future wages, pensions, maintenance payable to a wife or child. By art.14(2) of the Rome I Regulation, the assignability of a right is determined by "the law governing the right", in the case of a contractual right that applying under the other provisions of the Convention.[138]

13–046

Other issues

The same rule determines the relationship between the assignee and the debtor, the conditions under which the assignment or subrogation can be invoked against the debtor and whether the debtor's obligations have been discharged.[139] This category of issues would seem to include such questions as the need for notice of the assignment to be given to the debtor, whether the assignee takes subject to equities, the effect of the debtor paying the assignee instead of the assignor, and that, once much debated, as to the priority between competing assignments of the same right.

13–047

That priority issues are included seems to have been the opinion of the Court of Appeal in *Raiffeisen Zentralbank Österreich AG v Five Star General Trading LLC*[140] but the debates surrounding the drafting of the Rome I Regulation suggest otherwise. The Commission's original proposal included a rule under which the issue of priority would be governed by the law of the country where the assignor was habitually resident. This rule could have been difficult for financial institutions to operate and was dropped; though the Commission is to return to the issue.[141] In its consultation document on whether the United Kingdom should opt in to the Regulation, the Ministry of Justice assumed that the Rome Convention did not address the issue and that national law governed. English law would seem to subject the priority issue to the law of the original claim, which happens to be the law identified by art.14(2) of the Regulation.[142]

---

[138] The Rome Convention, art.12(2), is to the same effect.

[139] *Raiffeisen Zentralbank Österreich AG v Five Star General Trading LLC* [2001] EWCA Civ 68; [2001] Q.B. 825, declining to follow a Dutch decision, *Brandsma v Hansa Chemie AG* (Hoge Raad, May 16, 1997, N.J. 1998 No. 585) which gave a wider effect to art.12(1) (see Struycken, [1998] L.M.C.L.Q. 345 and more generally A. Flessner and H. Verhagen, *Assignment in European Private International Law* (2006)).

[140] [2001] EWCA Civ 68; [2001] Q.B. 825.

[141] See Regulation, art.27(2) on the duty to report on the matter.

[142] See *Kelly v Selwyn* [1905] 2 Ch. 117.

Legal subrogation

13–048   Although not really a case of assignment, similar issues may arise where a person (the creditor) has a contractual claim against another (the debtor) and a third person has a duty to satisfy the creditor, or has in fact satisfied the creditor in discharge of that duty. Article 15 of the Rome I Regulation provides that in such cases, the law which governs the third person's duty to satisfy the creditor determines whether and to what extent the third person is entitled to exercise against the debtor the rights which the creditor had against the debtor under the law governing their relationship.[143]

GARNISHMENT: THIRD-PARTY DEBT ORDERS

13–049   The determined expulsion of traditional language from the Civil Procedure Rules means that "garnish" will soon be a forgotten term, depriving authors of the chance to deploy jokes of a culinary variety. The Rules now speak of "third-party debt orders": orders by which a judgment creditor secures the payment to him of money which a third party (referred to in the older cases as the garnishee), who is within the jurisdiction, owes to the judgment debtor.[144] A similar process (called arrestment in Scotland) is allowed by the laws of other countries. In a purely domestic case, the third party is of course effectively discharged from further liability once he has paid the judgment creditor. To that extent it amounts to an assignment of the debt, but it is not a voluntary assignment and is not affected by the Rome Convention or the Rome I Regulation.

The English court will have jurisdiction to make an order only if the third party is within the jurisdiction of the court.[145] Mere temporary presence at the time the initial "interim third-party debt order" is made may suffice, as will submission to the jurisdiction by a person physically absent.[146]

In some cases the third party is in double jeopardy. This can be illustrated by the facts of *Société Eram Shipping Co Ltd v Compagnie Internationale de Navigation*[147]:

> Eram, a Romanian company, obtained judgment against A Co. and B (the judgment debtors, both resident in Hong Kong) in the French courts. The judgment was registered for enforcement in England. The judgment debtors had an account with the third party, a Hong Kong bank,[148] to which Hong Kong law applied. Eram obtained an interim third party debt order in England requiring, in effect, the bank to apply the money in the account to pay the sums due under the French judgment.

---

[143]   Rome Convention, art.13 is to similar effect.
[144]   C.P.R. r.72.1(1).
[145]   *ibid.*
[146]   *SCF Finance Co. Ltd v Masri (No.3)* [1987] Q.B. 1028.
[147]   [2003] UKHL 30; [2004] A.C. 260, noted Rogerson, [2003] C.L.J. 576, Briggs, (2003) 74 B.Y.I.L. 511. See also the speeches in *Deutsche Schachtbau-und Tiefbohrgesellschaft mbH v Shell International Petroleum Co. Ltd* [1990] 1 A.C. 295, where the debt was situated in England.
[148]   The Hong Kong bank had branches in England and so was within the jurisdiction for the purpose of the Rules.

The difficulty for the bank was that the courts in Hong Kong would not recognise   **13–050**
a third party debt order made in England in relation to a debt situated in Hong
Kong; as the House of Lords admitted, that was not "an unusual or idiosyncratic
rule but one which reflects general international practice". The bank might
therefore find that it had paid money in accordance with the third party debt
order, but that under the law of Hong Kong this payment would not discharge its
obligations to the judgment-debtor.

The House of Lords held that it was not open to the English court to make an
order in circumstances, such as those of the *Eram* case, where it is clear or
appears that the making of the order will not discharge the debt of the third party
to the judgment debtor according to the law governing that debt.

The *Eram* decision was followed in a companion case decided on the same
day, *Kuwait Oil Tanker SAK v Qabazard*[149] which also concerned the effect of
provisions in the Lugano Convention, found also in the Brussels I Regulation.
Article 22 of the latter provides:

"The following courts shall have exclusive jurisdiction, regardless of domicile:

...

5. in proceedings concerned with the enforcement of judgments, the courts of the Member
State in which the judgment has been or is to be enforced".

The judgment creditors sought a third-party debt order in respect of bank   **13–051**
accounts in Switzerland.[150] The House of Lords held that Switzerland was the
state in which the judgment was being enforced, and therefore the Swiss courts
had exclusive jurisdiction. It follows from this decision and the *Eram* case that
the English courts (a) have no jurisdiction to make a third party debt order where
the debt is located in a Member State or a state party to the Brussels or Lugano
Convention, and (b) will not make an order when the law of the State in which
the debt is located will not recognise payment under the order as discharging the
third party's obligations to the judgment debtor.

This is an area in which the European Community may take action. A Green
Paper published in 2006 raised the possibility of creating a European order for
the attachment of bank accounts.[151] An attachment order issued in one Member
State would be recognised and enforceable throughout the European Union
without the need for a declaration of enforceability.

There is surprisingly little English authority on the converse question, namely,
when will effect be given by English courts to a foreign garnishment order.
Clearly, if no effect is given, there may be a risk that the third party will be
compelled to pay the debt twice. Here again it seems that the test is whether the
debt is situated, in other words properly recoverable, in the foreign country where
the order was made.[152]

---

[149] [2003] UKHL 31; [2004] 1 A.C. 300.
[150] As in the *Eram* case, the Swiss bank had a branch in England and so was present within the
jurisdiction.
[151] COM(2006) 618 final.
[152] See *Rossano v Manufacturers Life Insurance Co. Ltd* [1963] 2 Q.B. 352 at 374–383; *Deutsche
Schachtbau v Shell International Petroleum Co. Ltd* [1990] 1 A.C. 295 at 354.

GOVERNMENTAL SEIZURE OF PROPERTY

13–052   It is the practice of some governments to seize private property on various pretexts and in the supposed interests of the state, often with inadequate compensation payable to the owners, and sometimes with no compensation payable at all. The issue can be one of considerable political and economic importance, especially in the context of foreign investment.[153] The state may nationalise foreign companies, or requisition or expropriate property: nothing seems to turn on the precise terminology used.

Difficult questions in the conflict of laws are presented if such decrees purport to have extra-territorial effect, or if the property affected by the decree is later brought to England. The questions tend also to be associated with two important principles which are discussed elsewhere in this book. These are: first, the principle that English courts will not enforce directly or indirectly a foreign penal law[154]; and, secondly, the principle that English courts have in general no jurisdiction to entertain an action which affects a foreign sovereign's interest in property.[155]

The principle on which English courts proceed when deciding whether to recognise foreign governmental decrees purporting to seize private property is comparatively simple to state but often difficult to apply. The principle is that the decree will be recognised as having deprived the owner of property if the property was within the territory of the foreign state at the time of the decree,[156] but not otherwise.[157] The application of the principle in any particular case involves answering three questions. First, what was the legal situation of the property at the time of the decree? Secondly, did the decree purport to affect property situate at that place? Thirdly, is the decree a part of the law of a place which the English courts can recognise? These three questions will now be discussed in turn.

The situation of property

13–053   The property may be movable or immovable, tangible or intangible. Artificial rules have to be adopted in order to ascribe a location, a *situs,* to intangible things or choses in action. The general principle is that choses in action are situated where they are properly recoverable. Thus, a simple contract debt is situated where the debtor resides and can be sued and presumably keeps his or her

---

[153] See Asante, (1988) 37 I.C.L.Q. 588.
[154] Above, para.3–010.
[155] Above, para.6–002.
[156] *Luther v Sagor* [1921] 3 K.B. 532; *Princess Paley Olga v Weisz* [1929] 1 K.B. 718; *Re Banque des Marchands de Moscou* [1952] 1 All E.R. 1269; *Jabbour v Custodian of Israeli Absentee Property* [1954] 1 W.LR 139; *Re Helbert Wagg & Co Ltd's Claim* [1956] Ch. 323 at 344–349; *Williams & Humbert Ltd v W & H Trade Marks (Jersey) Ltd* [1986] A.C. 368.
[157] *Lecouturier v Rey* [1910] A.C. 262; *The Jupiter (No.3)* [1927] P. 122, 250; *Re Russian Bank for Foreign Trade* [1933] Ch. 745 at 766–767; *Government of the Republic of Spain v National Bank of Scotland,* 1939 S.C. 413; *Frankfurther v W. L. Exner Ltd* [1947] Ch. 629; *Novello & Co. Ltd v Hinrichsen Edition Ltd* [1951] Ch. 595; *Bank voor Handel en Scheepvart NV v Slatford* [1953] 1 Q.B. 248; *Att-Gen of New Zealand v Ortiz* [1984] A.C. 1; affd. on other grounds *ibid.*, p.41.

assets.[158] This is so even if the contract provides for payment at another place.[159] There may of course be a number of countries in which the debtor can be sued, and it may well be that the residence of a company for this purpose can be equated with its domicile for the purposes of the Civil Jurisdiction and Judgments Act 1982. If the debtor resides in more countries than one, and the creditor either expressly or impliedly stipulates for payment at one of them, then the debt will be situated there.[160] If there is no such stipulation, the debt is situated at that place of residence where it would be paid in the ordinary course of business. Shares in a company are situated where, as between the shareholder and the company, they can be effectively dealt with according to the law under which the company was incorporated. Thus, if shares are transferable only upon a register they will be situated at the place where the appropriate register is kept.[161] Where they are transferable upon more than one register they will be situated at the register where they would be dealt with in the ordinary course by the registered owner.[162] Intellectual property rights owe their origin to the law of a particular country, and are said to be situated in that country.[163]

Tangible objects are, as a general rule, legally situated where they physically are. But ships and aircraft may be an exception. There are dicta indicating (though somewhat faintly) that a ship on the high seas is deemed to be situate at her port of registry.[164] But this applies only to ships on the high seas. When a ship is in territorial or national waters, the artificial *situs* is displaced by the actual *situs*, and the ship is treated like any other chattel.[165] Hence, a foreign governmental decree requisitioning a ship registered in that foreign State will not be recognised if, at the time of the decree, the ship is in an English port.[166] What has been said about ships may also be true of aircraft. An aircraft in flight over the high seas or over a no man's land such as the North Pole or the Antarctic might well be held to be situate in its country of registration [167]

[158] *New York Life Insurance Co v Public Trustee* [1924] 2 Ch. 101; *Deutsche Schachtbau v Shell International Petroleum Co Ltd* [1990] A.C. 295.

[159] *Re Helbert Wagg & Co Ltd's Claim* [1956] Ch. 323.

[160] *Jabbour v Custodian of Israeli Absentee Property* [1954] 1 W.LR 139 (insurance by English company of property in Israel; company resident in both England and Israel; debt held situated in Israel).

[161] *Brassard v Smith* [1925] A.C. 371; *R. v Williams* [1942] A.C. 541.

[162] *R. v Williams*, above; *Treasurer of Ontario v Aberdein* [1947] A.C. 24; *Standard Chartered Bank Ltd v I.R.C.* [1978] 1 W.L.R. 1160.

[163] *Lecouturier v Rey* [1910] A.C. 262; *Novello & Co. Ltd v Hinrichsen Edition Ltd* [1951] Ch. 595.

[164] *The Jupiter* [1924] P. 236 at 239; *The Cristina* [1938] A.C. 485 at 509.

[165] *Trustees Executors and Agency Co. Ltd v IRC* [1973] Ch. 254.

[166] *Government of the Republic of Spain v National Bank of Scotland*, 1939 SC 413; *Laane v Estonian State Cargo and Passenger Line* [1949] 2 D.L.R. 641.

[167] *Blue Sky One Ltd v Mahan Air* [2010] EWHC 631 (Comm).

The interpretation of the decree

13–054 Whether the decree purports to affect the property in question can only be answered by interpreting the decree. There is an observable tendency for English courts to hold whenever possible that the decree does not purport to have extra-territorial effect,[168] since this will often provide an easy answer to the dispute between the parties.

Recognition of the foreign act

13–055 If the seizure is to be recognised in England it must have some standing in the law of the place where it occurs; forcible seizure by a revolutionary mob will not be recognised. But what is one day a revolutionary mob may the next day be the effective government of an existing or a newly independent State. It was formerly the convenient practice of the United Kingdom Government to accord recognition to foreign governments, either de jure or de facto. The courts would recognise an act of a foreign government accorded at least de facto recognition, even if the recognition came after the act in question.[169] The acts of an unrecognised government might be given effect if it could be treated as a subordinate body set up by another (recognised) government; this approach was applied to acts of the former East German Government as a subordinate body of the Soviet Union.[170] However, in 1980 the United Kingdom Government announced that it would no longer accord recognition to governments, although it would continue to accord recognition to states in accordance with international practice.[171] For the purposes of legal proceedings, the attitude of the Government as to whether a new régime qualified to be treated as a government would have to be inferred from the nature of the dealings, if any, that the Government might have with it, and in particular whether it dealt with the régime on a normal government-to-government basis.[172] In *Republic of Somalia v Woodhouse Drake and Carey (Suisse) SA,*[173] the absence of such dealings was taken into account, along with other factors such as the extent of the control exercised by the "interim government" whose acts were in issue.

---

[168] e.g., *Lecouturier v Rey* [1910] A.C. 262; *The Jupiter (No.3)* [1927] P. 122, 145; *Re Russian Bank for Foreign Trade* [1933] Ch. 745 at 767.

[169] *Luther v Sagor* [1921] 1 K.B. 456.

[170] *Carl Zeiss Stiftung v Rayner & Keeler Ltd (No.2)* [1967] 1 A.C. 853. See also *Gur Corp v Trust Bank of Africa Ltd* [1987] Q.B. 559.

[171] For the complications ensuing, see *R. (Kibris Turk Hava Yollari) v Secretary of State for Transport* [2009] EWHC 1918 (Admin.); [2010] 1 All E.R. (Comm) 253 (re the so-called Turkish Republic of N Cyprus).

[172] See (1980) 51 B.Y.I.L. 367–368; Warbrick, (1981) 30 I.C.L.Q. 568, 576–592.

[173] [1993] Q.B. 54.

Property within the confiscating state

If a foreign decree is entitled to recognition under these principles, the effect to be **13–056** given to it depends upon the location of the property it purports to seize. It will operate to affect rights to property if the property is within the territory of the foreign state and the foreign state has reduced the property to possession.[174] The leading case is *Luther v Sagor*[175]:

> A & Co., a Russian company, had a factory or mill in Russia where in 1919 they had a large stock of manufactured boards. The Soviet Government promulgated a decree vesting the property of all sawmills and woodworking establishments in the state. In reliance on this decree State officials seized A & Co.'s timber and sold it to B, an American firm carrying on business in London. B imported the timber into England. A & Co. claimed a declaration that the timber was their property. Roche J. granted the declaration, on the ground that His Majesty's Government had not recognised the Soviet Government as the government of a sovereign State. B appealed. Before the hearing of the appeal the Foreign Office informed B's solicitors that His Majesty's Government recognised the Soviet Government as the de facto government of Russia. The Court of Appeal gave judgment for B.

The principle in *Luther v Sagor* was accepted and applied by the House of Lords in *Williams & Humbert Ltd v W & H Trade Marks (Jersey) Ltd.*[176] The underlying dispute in that case concerned the "Dry Sack" sherry trademark which had belonged to the plaintiff English company, a wholly-owned subsidiary of R, a Spanish company. The Spanish Government compulsorily acquired all the shares in R and this act was recognised as effective. It did not seek to change the ownership of the shares in the English company; they remained the property of R (though of course the English company was now subject to the control of R's new owner, the Spanish authorities).

Property outside the confiscating state

The approach of the English courts to foreign decrees is quite different where the **13–057** property is outside the territorial limits of the foreign state. As Lord Templeman put it in *Williams & Humbert Ltd v W & H Trade Marks (Jersey) Ltd*[177]:

> "There is undoubtedly a domestic and international rule which prevents one sovereign state from changing title to property so long as that property is situate in another state. If the British government purported to acquire compulsorily the railway lines from London to Newhaven and the railway lines from Dieppe to Paris, the ownership of the railway lines situate in England would vest in the British government but the ownership of the railway lines in France would remain undisturbed."

Accordingly, the English courts will not give effect to a foreign decree so far as it purports to deal with rights in property in England.

---

[174] *Brokaw v Seatrain UK Ltd* [1971] 2 Q.B. 476; *Government of the Islamic Republic of Iran v Barakat Galleries Ltd* [2007] EWCA Civ 1374; [2009] Q.B. 22.
[175] [1921] 3 K.B. 532. See also *Princess Paley Olga v Weisz* [1929] 1 K.B. 718.
[176] [1986] A.C. 368.
[177] [1986] A.C. 368. See also *Kuwait Airways Corp v Iraqi Airways Co. (Nos 4 and 5)* [2002] UKHL 19; [2002] 2 A.C. 883.

Public policy

13–058   In *Bank voor Handel en Scheepvaart NV v Slatford*,[178] Devlin J., after an exhaustive review of the authorities, refused to give effect to a decree of the Netherlands Government-in-exile in England which purported to transfer to the state the property in England and elsewhere of persons resident in enemy-occupied Holland. He refused to follow the anomalous decision in *Lorentzen v Lydden & Co Ltd*[179] where effect had been given to a not dissimilar decree of the Norwegian Government-in-exile; that case, which is no longer good law, was based on the desirability of enforcing an act of an allied Government acting at a critical time in its, and England's, history. Devlin J. rejected the idea that the English court should consider what he described as "the political merits" of such a decree. The same view was taken by the Court of Appeal in *Peer International Corp v Termidor Music Publishers Ltd*[180]: the court refused to give any weight to an argument that, because a Cuban decree was made for "benevolent" reasons, it should be treated as having effect on property in England. A public policy exception to the principle that a foreign decree cannot affect property in England was rejected for a set of reasons advanced by counsel and accepted by the Court of Appeal:

> "(1) it would subordinate English property law to that of a foreign state; (2) the rule would be founded and would operate by reference to public policy which could change from time to time and could be uncertain; (3) it would require the English courts to assess the merits of the foreign legislation; (4) it would lead to intractable problems when the property was situated in a third state; (5) it would require the court to balance one public policy against the public policy that states do not interfere with property situated abroad, and (6) it would lead to great uncertainty."

13–059   There are, however, grounds upon which the English courts may refuse to recognise or to give effect to a foreign decree, even in cases where the property was in the foreign state at the time of the decree. They were analysed by Nourse J. at first instance in *Williams & Humbert Ltd v W & H Trade Marks (Jersey) Ltd*,[181] an analysis subsequently adopted by the Court of Appeal.[182] English law will not recognise certain foreign confiscatory laws: those which are discriminatory on grounds of race, religion or the like and constitute a grave infringement of human rights.[183] Similarly, the English courts will not recognise decrees which discriminate against British nationals in time of war by purporting to confiscate their movable property situated in the foreign State.[184] Nor will the English court enforce a foreign law confiscating property in a foreign State if the law is categorised as penal.[185]

---

[178] [1953] 1 Q.B. 248.
[179] [1942] 2 K.B. 202.
[180] [2003] EWCA Civ 1156; [2004] Ch. 212.
[181] [1986] A.C. 368.
[182] See *Settebello Ltd v Banco Totta & Acores* [1985] 1 W.L.R. 1050.
[183] See *Oppenheimer v Cattermole* [1976] A.C. 249.
[184] *Wolff v Oxholm* (1817) 6 M. & S. 92; *Re Fred Krupp A.G.* [1917] 2 Ch. 188; *Re Helbert Wagg & Co. Ltd's Claim* [1956] Ch. 323 at 345.
[185] *Banco de Vizcaya v Don Alfonso de Borbon y Austria* [1935] 1 K.B. 140.

However, Nourse J. held that there was no additional category of decrees which would be denied recognition merely because they purport to confiscate the property of particular individuals[186] or categories of individuals.[187] There also seems to be no place in modern English law for an argument that a decree should be denied recognition or enforcement because no compensation, or inadequate compensation, is payable to the owner under the decree. In one case,[188] Scott L.J. considered that a decree providing for only 25 per cent compensation was obviously penal. In two later cases,[189] Nazi decrees directed against Jewish businesses were treated as penal not so much because the owners of the businesses were Jews as because the decrees were confiscatory and no compensation was payable. On the other hand, in *Luther v Sagor*[190] and *Princess Paley Olga v Weisz*[191] the decrees were not treated as penal although no compensation at all was payable. The better view would seem to be that whether or not compensation is payable is irrelevant.[192] This is certainly the more convenient view: it would be a thankless task for a court to have to decide what amount of compensation is adequate, and whether a promise to pay compensation at some time in the future is worth more than the paper it is written on.

---

[186] cf. *Banco de Vizcaya v Don Alfonso de Borbon y Austria* [1935] 1 K.B. 140, which Nourse J. would rest on the fact that the decree was penal in the criminal law sense; *The Rose Mary* [1953] 1 W.L.R. 246, as explained in *Re Helbert Wagg & Co Ltds Claim* [1956] Ch. 323 at 346, an explanation rejected by Nourse J.

[187] See the decree confiscating the property of the House of Romanov mentioned in *Princess Paley Olga v Weisz* [1929] 1 K.B. 718 at 722. The plaintiff's property was not caught by the decree because her marriage to the Grand Duke Paul was morganatic.

[188] *A/S Tallina Laevauhisus v Estonian State SS Line* (1947) 80 Ll.L.R. 99 at 111. cf. *Laane v Estonian State Cargo and Passenger Line* [1949] 2 D.L.R. 641.

[189] *Frankfurther v WL Exner Ltd* [1947] Ch. 629; *Novello & Co Ltd v Hinrichsen Edition Ltd* [1951] Ch. 595.

[190] [1921] 3 K.B. 532.

[191] [1929] 1 K.B. 718.

[192] See especially the judgments of Devlin J. in *Bank voor Handel en Scheepvaart NV v Slatford* [1953] 1 Q.B. 248 at 258 and 260–263, and of Upjohn J. in *Re Helbert Wagg & Co Ltd's Claim* [1956] Ch. 323 at 349 (declining to follow *The Rose Mary* [1953] 1 W.L.R. 246, a decision of the Supreme Court of Aden which concerned facts of some political sensitivity and so enjoyed more attention than it deserved).

CHAPTER 14

MATRIMONIAL PROPERTY

Had this book been written in a civil law country, the heading would undoubtedly   14–001
have been "matrimonial property régimes". To the bewilderment of some civil
lawyers, England has no such régime, or rather, none in the civilian sense. Since
the Married Women's Property Act 1882, marriage as such has had no effect in
English law on the property of the spouses. Both parties remain separately
entitled to the property owned by them at the time of the marriage or acquired
afterwards, unless they choose to regulate their property rights by a marriage
contract or settlement.

Such a contract or settlement will govern the respective property rights of the
parties, but no such contract can exclude the court's discretion to make
appropriate orders if the marriage should end in divorce (or annulment). In the
leading case of *Granatino v Radmacher*,[1] the Supreme Court swept away the old
rule that agreements providing for the future separation of the parties to a
marriage were contrary to public policy. But it held that it remained the case that
it was for the court to determine the appropriate ancillary relief when a marriage
came to an end. The court could give some weight to a pre-nuptial agreement and
would make an order in terms similar to those of the agreement when, but only
when, it was fair to do so. It was for English law to govern the exercise of this
discretion, even if there were a pre-nuptial agreement governed by some other
law.

When in this chapter reference is made to a marriage contract or settlement, this   14–002
means an agreement as to the rights of the parties during their marriage. On the
death of a party, that agreement will of course determine what property forms part
of the deceased's estate. We are not, however, here concerned with any
adjustment to the position an English court may make after divorce.

The position is very different in many continental European countries, in nine
of the United States,[2] and under the Roman-Dutch law applied in South Africa.
There, a system of community of property exists under which marriage has the

---

[1] *Granatino v Radmacher* [2010] UKSC 42; [2011] 1 A.C. 534.
[2] Arizona, California, Idaho, Louisiana, Nevada, New Mexico, Texas, Washington, and Wisconsin:
see Darie, (1993) 42 I.C.L.Q. 855.

effect of vesting the property, owned by either spouse at the time of the marriage or acquired during its subsistence, in both of them jointly; and pre-nuptial contracts may have binding effect on divorce.

14–003 There are many different systems of community property,[3] but for present purposes they may be divided into three main types: full (or universal) community, community of gains (acquests), and community of chattels and gains. In full community, which exists in the Netherlands and South Africa, the community extends to all movables and to immovables acquired during the marriage, and the husband has wide powers of administration over the property; there is a tendency in modern law, however, to restrict them. In community of gains, which applies now in Spain, in some of the United States, in many Eastern European countries, and—since 1965 in a very attenuated form—in France, the community is confined to property acquired during the marriage otherwise than by gift or inheritance. The husband usually has powers of administration, but the wife may have power to deal with her earnings or her separate property. The mixed form, the community of gains and chattels, comprises all chattels whether owned at the time of the marriage or acquired during its subsistence, but only such land as the spouses acquired during the subsistence of the marriage through work or thrift. It does not apply to land held by either spouse at the time of the marriage or acquired during its subsistence through inheritance or gift. This is the classic form of community under the original French Civil Code of 1804 but has been abolished not only in France itself but also in countries such as Belgium and Luxembourg where the 1804 Code formerly applied. "Deferred community" or "participation", which exists in the Scandinavian countries, Germany, Quebec and elsewhere, is a system of separation of property: no assets are held as joint assets during the marriage, but when the marriage is dissolved, either by death or divorce, the law provides for each spouse (or the estate of a deceased spouse) to receive a specified share of their combined assets or in the increase in those assets during the marriage.

14–004 Nearly all systems of community property régime allow the spouses to contract out of the system if they so desire, and in most systems the failure of the spouses to do so means that they become subject to the standard community régime provided by law. The effect of this often is that the spouses adopt the standard régime by a kind of tacit consent.

In the conflict of laws, the effect of marriage on the property of the spouses differs in accordance with whether there is or is not a marriage contract or settlement between them.[4] Most of the English cases are concerned with the former situation, and English authority on the latter is sparse.

---

[3] Law Com. Working Paper No. 42, Family Property Law (1971); Rheinstein and Glendon, Int. Ency. Comp.L., Vol.4, Ch.4; Marsh, *Marital Property in the Conflict of Laws* (University of Washington, Seattle, 1952).
[4] The validity of this distinction is denied by Goldberg, (1970) 19 I.C.L.Q. 557.

WHERE THERE IS NO MARRIAGE CONTRACT OR SETTLEMENT

A hundred years ago, the rule applying in this type of case was seen as wholly unproblematic: **14–005**

> "It is not necessary to cite authorities to show that it is now settled that, according to international law as understood and administered in England, the effect of marriage on the movable property of spouses depends (in the absence of any contract) on the domicile of the husband in the English sense."[5]

Today, however, this is one area of the conflict of laws where it is difficult to state the position with any certainty.

One element in the current uncertainty concerns the parties' freedom of choice: the scope in this context of "party autonomy". It is argued in the current edition of *Dicey, Morris and Collins* that "if the parties to a marriage are entitled to regulate their matrimonial régime directly by contract [that is, a marriage contract or settlement stating the respective property rights of the parties], it would be strange if they were unable to do so by making a contract to determine the governing law". And that "if they are entitled to choose the governing law by means of an express contract, why should they not be entitled to do so by means of an implied contract?"[6] The courts have not endorsed, or indeed even considered, these arguments, and it is not at all clear how one would discern an "implied contract" selecting the governing law. Where the parties have not entered into a marriage contract or settlement to govern their property rights, they may well have given no thought at all to the matter and it would be wrong to find any implied contract. So, even if the arguments advanced in *Dicey, Morris and Collins* are seen as persuasive, there must still be a rule that can be applied in the absence of choice by the parties.

So far as movables are concerned, there is general agreement that the governing   **14–006**
law (whether it applies in the absence of or regardless of choice by the parties) is the law of the "matrimonial domicile". But there is much less certainty about the meaning of "matrimonial domicile". Before 1956 there was a difference of opinion on that point between Dicey and Cheshire. Cheshire's view, which was consistent with his theory on the law governing capacity to marry, was that it meant the intended matrimonial home, the domicile which the husband and wife intended to acquire and did acquire within a reasonable time after the marriage. If, for instance, a man domiciled in England married a woman domiciled in South Africa, and the husband and wife flew to South Africa immediately after the ceremony, intending to make it their matrimonial home, Cheshire would say that South Africa, not England, was their matrimonial domicile, and that South African law should determine the effect of their marriage on their movable property. But, as Dicey pointed out, there was no conclusive English authority in favour of this view, and there were practical difficulties in its application. What if the husband and wife did not fly to South Africa until a month, or a year, after the ceremony? Where was the line to be drawn? Were the rights of the spouses to remain in suspense until they actually acquired a new domicile in pursuance of

---

[5] *Re Martin* [1900] P. 211 at 233, per Lindley M.R.
[6] Dicey, Morris and Collins, *The Conflict of Laws* (14th edn, 2006), para.28–019.

their pre-matrimonial intention? Dicey concluded that the safer rule to adopt was that the matrimonial domicile meant the husband's domicile at the time of the marriage, except perhaps in a clear case where the domicile is changed very shortly after the marriage.

14–007 In 1956, in *Re Egerton's Will Trusts*,[7] Roxburgh J. considered the rival views and preferred that of Dicey. Since the change of domicile in that case did not take place until two years after the marriage, the judge's observations about the effect of an immediate change of domicile were (as he pointed out) obiter. Nevertheless he made it clear that the law of the intended matrimonial domicile could apply only in very special circumstances, for example where the change of domicile followed immediately on the marriage and the spouses were at that time without means.[8]

After that decision, it was again regarded as settled law that it was the law of the husband's domicile at the time of the marriage which governed its effect on the movable property of the spouses. The selection of the husband's rather than the wife's domicile was then entirely natural, for at common law the wife acquired the husband's domicile as a direct result of the marriage. The abolition of that rule by the Domicile and Matrimonial Proceedings Act 1973 raised questions that were not previously relevant. If, for example, a woman domiciled in State A marries a man domiciled in State B (each retaining those domiciles after the marriage); the woman brings to the marriage considerable property, mostly in the form of investments in companies established in State A, but the man has only very limited savings; and the matrimonial home is, at least initially, established in State A, there seems little merit in applying the law of the husband's domicile to determine the matrimonial property régime.

14–008 It would be consistent with *Re Egerton's Will Trusts* to interpret the term "matrimonial domicile" as being *in the usual case* the domicile of the husband. It is not possible to be very clear as to the circumstances that would justify a departure from this presumption, but the example just used suggests some factors that might be relevant. A different approach, giving more weight to the expressed or implied intentions of the parties, or making an objective assessment of the country with which the issue had the closest and most real connection,[9] would be a more radical break with past orthodoxy. All that can be said is that, despite the long tradition of applying the law of the husband's domicile, further development of the law is possible and indeed overdue.

---

[7] [1956] Ch. 593.

[8] At pp.604–605. See the similar decision by the Appellate Division of the Supreme Court of South Africa in *Estate Frankel v The Master*, 1950 (1) S.A. 220, after an elaborate argument in which counsel cited cases from all over the world and the opinions of jurists from the sixteenth century onwards.

[9] Hartley in Fawcett (ed.), *Reform and Development of Private International Law* (Oxford University Press, Oxford, 2002), p.226, uses the term "the centre of gravity of the marriage", presumably at the time of the marriage.

Change in the matrimonial domicile

What happens if the matrimonial domicile (however defined) changes during the marriage? It is a disputed question whether such a change of domicile alters the governing law. The prevailing doctrine in mainland Europe and in South Africa is the doctrine of *immutability,* according to which the rights of the spouses "are regulated once and for all by the law of the domicile of marriage".[10] In the United States, on the other hand, the prevailing doctrine is the doctrine of *mutability,* according to which the rights of the spouses to after-acquired movables are regulated by the law of the domicile at the time of acquisition.[11]

14–009

English law is not yet committed either to the doctrine of mutability or to the doctrine of immutability.[12] In *Lashley v Hog,*[13] the House of Lords held (on appeal from the Court of Session) that a change of domicile from England to Scotland carried with it the application of Scots law. On the other hand, in *De Nicols v Curlier*[14] the House of Lords held that, on a change of domicile from France to England, the French system of community of goods continued to apply to movables acquired by the husband and wife after they had become domiciled in England. The House of Lords evidently regarded *Lashley v Hog* as an embarrassing rather than a helpful decision. They distinguished it on two grounds: (1) in *De Nicols v Curlier* the effect of marriage without an express contract was assumed to be that an implied contract was imposed on the parties by French law, whereas there was no such contract in *Lashley v Hog*[15]; and (2) in *Lashley v Hog* the question was not one of matrimonial property law at all but of the law of succession.[16] If the first ground of distinction is the one to be preferred, it means that *De Nicols v Curlier* belongs exclusively to the next section of this chapter, and that we are left with *Lashley v Hog* as our only authority on mutability versus immutability. The first ground of distinction was adopted by the majority of their Lordships, but some eminent writers have preferred the second.[17] It is therefore an open question as to whether an English court will apply the doctrine of mutability or immutability in the event of a change of domicile, and in the absence of a contract express or implied.

14–010

The doctrine of immutability does not produce satisfactory results if the spouses are forced to change their domicile by political or economic pressure. It does not seem reasonable that refugees, who have acquired a domicile of choice in England or elsewhere after their marriage, should continue to be governed for the

14–011

---

[10] *Brown v Brown,* 1921 A.D. 478, 482.
[11] Restatement s.258. If, however, the after-acquired movables represent property acquired under an earlier matrimonial property régime, that régime will apply, so mutability is heavily qualified.
[12] See Hartley in Fawcett (ed), *op. cit.,* pp.219–224.
[13] (1804) 4 Paton 581; analysed by Goldberg, (1970) 19 I.C.L.Q. 557, 580–584.
[14] [1900] A.C. 21.
[15] *ibid.,* per Lord Macnaghten at pp.34 and 36; per Lord Shand at p.37; per Lord Brampton at p.44.
[16] *ibid.,* per Lord Halsbury at p.29; per Lord Morris at p.36.
[17] Westlake, *Private International Law* (7th edn, 1925), p.74; Foote, *Private International Law* (5th edn, 1925), p.355; Falconbridge, *Selected Essays on the Conflict of Laws,* p.106; cf. Mann, (1954) 31 B.Y.I.L. 217 at 224–226. This view was take by a United States court which held that *De Nicols v Curlier* was authority for the application of mutability in English law: *Estate of Charnia v Shulman,* 608 F. 3d 67 (1st Cir, 2010).

rest of their lives by the law of their matrimonial domicile, perhaps the one country in the world which they will never revisit. Moreover, the doctrine of immutability may give rise to difficult questions of characterisation, and may require the court to draw delicate distinctions between questions of matrimonial property law and questions of the law of succession. Take, for example, a case in which the husband and wife were married while domiciled in France and were subject to the French system of community, and the husband died intestate domiciled in England. French law would (if the doctrine of immutability were applied) determine how much of the common movable property of the spouses belonged to the husband at the time of his death. English law, as the law governing succession to movables, would determine what proportion of the husband's movables passed to the wife by reason of his intestacy.[18] The result might be to give the wife a much larger share than she would have got if either French law alone or English law alone had governed the property rights of the spouses from the time of the marriage. Under English law, she would have acquired no rights in her husband's movables by reason of the marriage, but only by reason of his death intestate; under French law, she would have had no rights on his death intestate except to her share of the community property. In the converse case of a change of domicile from England to France, she might get nothing.[19] This is because by French law community of gains is constituted by a marriage under French law, and not by married people coming to France and settling there. It must begin from the day of the marriage.[20]

Immovables

14–012 There is very little authority on the effect of marriage on the immovable property of the spouses in the absence of a contract express or implied. It seems that the *lex situs* governs. In *Welch v Tennent*[21] a husband and wife were married in 1877 (i.e., before the Married Women's Property Act 1882). They were domiciled in Scotland. The wife owned land in England, which she sold with her husband's concurrence, and the proceeds of sale were paid to him. The parties then separated and the wife took proceedings in the Scottish courts asking for a declaration that the proceeds of sale were not subject to her husband's *jus mariti*. The House of Lords, reversing the Scottish courts which had applied Scots law, held that English law applied and that the proceeds of sale belonged to the husband.

Claims by third parties

14–013 It is arguable that the subtle questions surrounding the use of the matrimonial domicile test are inappropriate in cases in which the dispute is not primarily about the relative rights of the parties to a marriage but about the claims of third parties,

---

[18] See *Beaudoin v Trudel* [1937] 1 D.L.R. 216.
[19] See Lipstein, (1972) 135 *Recueil des Cours*, 209; Kahn-Freund, (1974) 143 *Recueil des Cours*, 377–380.
[20] *De Nicols v Curlier* [1900] A.C. 21 at 33; cf. *Re Egerton's Trusts* [1956] Ch. 593, 600.
[21] [1891] A.C. 639.

for example on the bankruptcy of one of the spouses. In such a case, the creditors will seek to enforce their claims against any property vested in the bankrupt spouse, but excluding property that spouse holds as trustee as opposed to beneficially. The question is whether the interests of the other spouse under some matrimonial property régimes also defeat the creditors. Hartley has suggested[22] that for this purpose the respective rights of the spouses should be governed not by the otherwise applicable matrimonial property régimes but by the *lex situs* of the property, both movable and immovable. Although Hartley claims that this approach is the only way in which justice can be done to the parties, it seems that the underlying policy question is one of priorities: are the other spouses' claims to be preferred to or subordinated to those of third parties. The courts have yet to address such issues.

WHERE THERE IS A MARRIAGE CONTRACT OR SETTLEMENT

If there is a marriage contract or settlement, the terms of the contract (assuming it to be valid) govern the rights of the husband and wife to all property within its terms which are then owned or subsequently acquired, notwithstanding any subsequent change of domicile. Whether any particular property, for example after-acquired property, is within its terms is a question of construction of the contract. **14–014**

The rule applies even if the contract is implied by law. Thus, in the leading case of *De Nicols v Curlier*[23]:

> H and W, French citizens domiciled in France, married there without a marriage contract. There was evidence that by French law the effect was the same as if they had made an express contract incorporating the system of community of goods. At the time of the marriage they had no means whatever, but nine years later they emigrated to England with joint savings of £400, and acquired an English domicile. They set up a small restaurant called the Café Royal in Regent Street, London, which prospered exceedingly. H died having by his will given all his real and personal estate on trust for sale and to hold the proceeds on trust for W for life, and then for his daughter and her husband and children. He left about £600,000 worth of property in England and about £100,000 worth of wine in France.

Dissatisfied with the provision made for her by H's will, W claimed that despite the change of domicile and the provisions of the will she was entitled to one-half of H's property under the system of community of goods. It was arranged that the argument should be confined in the first instance to the effect of the change of domicile on the testator's movables only. The House of Lords held that W was entitled to the half-share she had claimed. **14–015**

When the summons came on for further argument as to the effect of the change of domicile on the testator's immovables in England, Kekewich J. held in *Re De Nicols (No.2)*[24] that the wife was also entitled to one-half of the immovables. He was pressed with s.4 of the Statute of Frauds 1677, which provided that no action should be brought on an oral contract for the sale or other

---

[22] In Fawcett (ed), *op. cit.*, at pp.232–234.
[23] [1898] 1 Ch. 403; [1898] 2 Ch. 60; [1900] A.C. 21.
[24] [1900] 2 Ch. 410. For a full critique of aspects of Kekewich J.'s reasoning in distinguishing *Lashley v Hog*, see Hartley in Fawcett (ed), *op. cit.*, at pp.221–224.

disposition of an interest in land. But he followed (and perhaps extended) earlier cases deciding that the section did not apply to a partnership.

This unorthodox decision is supported by an earlier one of Stirling J. in *Chiwell v Carlyon,*[25] where the facts were similar except that at the time of their marriage the parties were domiciled in South Africa. The husband acquired land in Cornwall. The question was whether this land was subject to the South African system of community. Stirling J. sent a case for the opinion of the Supreme Court of Cape Colony under the British Law Ascertainment Act 1859. In other words, he decided that the rights of the spouses in the English land were governed by South African law. The South African court gave an opinion that by South African law the English land was held in community, whether or not the spouses had acquired an English domicile. Stirling J. then gave judgment in accordance with this opinion.

14–016   This notion of an "implied contract" is sharply criticised as "both impractical and contrary to principle" by the editors of *Dicey Morris and Collins.*[26] It was, however, defended and applied in a careful judgment of the New South Wales Court of Appeal in *Murakami v Wiryadi.*[27]

In *Re De Nicols (No.2)* and *Chiwell v Carlyon,* it was clear that the French and South African systems of community included land situated outside France and South Africa respectively. In *Callwood v Callwood,*[28] there was no evidence that, under the law of the Danish West Indian island where the parties were domiciled, the Danish system of community extended to land situated outside the island. Consequently, it was held that when the husband acquired land in the British Virgin Islands, it was not subject to community.

The essential validity, interpretation and effect of the marriage contract or settlement are governed by its proper law.[29] The search for the proper law of a marriage contract or settlement is generically similar to the search, under the common law rules formerly applying, for the proper law of an ordinary commercial contract. Because of the nature of the subject matter, the weight to be given to the various factors is different. In the absence of an express selection of the proper law by the parties, the most important single factor is undoubtedly the matrimonial domicile, though perhaps it is putting the matter too strongly to say that there is a presumption in favour of this law. Subject to what has been said above, the matrimonial domicile means the husband's domicile at the time of the marriage.[30] Other factors which may have to be considered, and which frequently point to some other law, are: the fact that the settled property belonged to the wife or her family, and that her domicile before or after the marriage was different from the husband's[31]; the language and legal style of the settlement[32]; the fact

---

[25] (1897) 14 S.C. 61. The case is unreported in England.

[26] (14th edn, 2006), para.28–023.

[27] [2010] NSWCA 7. The court observed, at para.111, "There is a hint of an academic turf battle in this analysis – conflicts scholars resenting the intrusion of contracts scholars".

[28] [1960] A.C. 659; criticised by Unger (1967) 83 L.Q.R. 427, 440–441.

[29] The Rome I Regulation does not apply to contractual obligations relating to rights in property arising out of a matrimonial relationship: see above, para.11–013.

[30] See para.14–006.

[31] *Van Grutten v Digby* (1862) 31 Beav. 561; *Re Megret* [1901] 1 Ch. 547; *Re Bankes* [1902] 2 Ch. 333; *Re Fitzgerald* [1904] 1 Ch. 573; *Re Mackenzie* [1911] 1 Ch. 578.

that its provisions are invalid by the law of the matrimonial domicile[33]; the place of management of the trust[34]; the place of residence of the trustees[35]; the place of investment of the securities.[36] Since the last two factors may change, the relevant time for giving effect to them is the date of the settlement.[37]

The case of *Duke of Marlborough v Att-Gen*[38] illustrates the application of the law of the matrimonial domicile:

14–017

> H, the ninth Duke of Marlborough, who was domiciled in England, married W, the daughter of a wealthy New Yorker. A marriage settlement in English language and form was made whereby W's father settled $2½ million and covenanted that his executors would settle a further $2½ million after his death. The settlement comprised included no English property at all. (Evidently it is an expensive business to marry an English Duke.) The settled property was and remained invested in American securities. One trustee was English and the other American. The settlement contained ancillary clauses which were meaningless (but not invalid) by New York law. The question was whether or not English estate duty was payable on the death of H. The Court of Appeal held that the proper law of the settlement was English law and that estate duty was payable.

The case of *Re Bankes,*[39] which is typical of many others, illustrates the application of some other law:

> H, domiciled in Italy, married W, domiciled in England. A marriage settlement in English language and form was made whereby property belonging to W, which was invested in English securities, was vested in English trustees. By Italian law the settlement was invalid (a) because it was not executed before a notary (a question of form), and (b) because it altered Italian rules of succession (a question of essential validity). It was held that the proper law of the settlement was English law, and that it was valid.

There can be no doubt that the parties are free to choose the proper law by an express clause in the settlement, at any rate if the transaction has a substantial connection with the selected law.[40] "As a general rule the law of the matrimonial domicile is applicable to a contract in consideration of marriage. But this is not an absolute rule. It yields to an express stipulation that some other law shall apply".[41]

14–018

There is very little authority on the essential validity and interpretation of a marriage settlement comprising immovables. In *Re Pearse's Settlement,*[42] an English marriage settlement contained a covenant by the wife to settle her after-acquired property. She acquired land in Jersey. By the law of Jersey no trusts of land were permitted and all transfers thereof had to be for value. It was held that the land in Jersey was not caught by the covenant.

---

[32] *Re Megret,* above; *Re Bankes,* above; *Re Fitzgerald,* above; *Re Mackenzie,* above; *Re Hewitts Settlement* [1915] 1 Ch. 228.

[33] *Re Bankes,* above; *Re Fitzgerald,* above.

[34] *Re Cloncurry's Estate* [1932] I.R. 687.

[35] *Van Grutten v Digby,* above; *Re Megret,* above; *Re Cloncurry's Estate,* above.

[36] *ibid.*

[37] *Re Hewitt's Settlement,* above; *Duke of Marlborough v Att-Gen* [1945] Ch. 78.

[38] Above; criticised by Morris, (1945) 61 L.Q.R. 223.

[39] [1902] 2 Ch. 333.

[40] *Montgomery v Zari,* 1918 S.C. (H.L.) 128.

[41] *Re Fitzgerald* [1904] 1 Ch. 573 at 587.

[42] [1909] 1 Ch. 304.

A marriage settlement will be formally valid if it complies with the formalities prescribed by either the law of the place where it was executed[43] or the proper law.[44]

14–019 The question as to which law governs capacity to make a marriage settlement is rather more difficult. On principle, capacity should be governed by the proper law of the settlement. That is the law which, at common law, governed capacity to make a commercial contract, and there seems no reason for a different principle to be applied here. It is sometimes said, however, that capacity to make a marriage settlement is governed, not by the proper law (which as we have seen is usually, but not necessarily, the law of the matrimonial domicile), but by the law of the domicile of the party alleged to be incapable. According to this view, the capacity of an English girl under eighteen years of age to make an antenuptial settlement prior to her marriage with a domiciled foreigner would be governed by English law. The three cases usually cited for this proposition are *Re Cooke's Trusts*,[45] *Cooper v Cooper*[46] and *Viditz v O'Hagan*.[47] It is submitted that, properly considered, these cases lay down no such proposition but, on the contrary, decide that capacity is governed by the proper law.[48]

In *Re Cooke's Trusts*:

> A domiciled English woman aged under 21 made a notarial contract in French form prior to her marriage with a domiciled Frenchman. She died domiciled in New South Wales having by her will given all her property to X. Her children attacked her will on the ground that the contract gave them vested rights in her property.

14–020 Stirling J. rejected their claim on the ground that her capacity to make the contract was governed by English law as the law of her antenuptial domicile and that by English law the contract was "void". But the value of this case as an authority is impaired by the erroneous assumption made by the court as to English domestic law. In English domestic law (and the law of Ireland is the same), marriage settlements made by minors are not void but voidable in the sense that they are binding on the minor unless the minor repudiates them within a reasonable time after attaining the age of majority.

In *Cooper v Cooper*[49]:

> A domiciled Irish girl aged under 21 married a domiciled Scotsman in Dublin. By an antenuptial contract made in Scottish form, the husband covenanted to pay her a small annuity if she survived him and the wife accepted this in full satisfaction of her rights as a Scottish widow. 36 years later the husband died domiciled in Scotland and the wife claimed to repudiate the contract.

14–021 The House of Lords held that she was entitled to do so. It is true that Lord Halsbury and Lord Macnaghten gave as their reason for this conclusion that the

---

[43] *Guepratte v Young* (1851) 4 De G. & Sm. 217.
[44] *Van Grutten v Digby* (1862) 31 Beav. 561; *Viditz v O'Hagan* [1899] 2 Ch. 569; *Re Bankes* [1902] 2 Ch. 333.
[45] (1887) 56 L.T. 737.
[46] (1888) 13 App.Cas. 88.
[47] [1900] 2 Ch. 87.
[48] See Morris, (1938) 54 L.Q.R. 78.
[49] (1888) 13 App.Cas. 88.

wife was an infant by Irish law when she made the contract. But it is impossible to accept these statements at their face value. For Lord Halsbury said that by Irish law an infant's marriage settlement contracts are "void",[50] and Lord Macnaghten said that Mrs Cooper's contract was "voidable" in the sense that it was binding on her until she repudiated it, which she had elected to do.[51] Yet in *Edwards v Carter*[52] (which was not a case on the conflict of laws), the House of Lords held that a minor's marriage settlement contract was neither void, nor voidable whenever the minor chose to repudiate it, but voidable only within a reasonable time after the minor had attained his majority. The House of Lords further held that it was too late for the minor to repudiate when he attained the age of 26, yet Mrs Cooper was allowed to repudiate at the age of 54. It is plain that there is a direct inconsistency between *Cooper v Cooper* and *Edwards v Carter* which cannot be reconciled, unless we assume that Scots law as the law of the matrimonial domicile as well as Irish law as the law of the wife's antenuptial domicile exerted an influence on the decision in the former case. The true position would appear to be that by Irish law the contract was voidable for a short time only, but by Scots law it was voidable forever, because any ratification by Mrs Cooper would have been revocable as a donation between husband and wife.[53] Therefore she had never had capacity to make a binding contract.

In *Viditz v O'Hagan*[54] the Court of Appeal expressly adopted this view of *Cooper v Cooper*. The facts were that: **14–022**

> A domiciled Irish girl aged under 21 married a domiciled Austrian. She made an antenuptial settlement in English form, settling her property on the usual trusts of an English marriage settlement. 29 years later the husband and wife, still domiciled in Austria, purported to revoke the settlement by a notarial act made in Austria in Austrian form. By Austrian law such revocation was valid notwithstanding the birth of children.

It was held that the revocation was valid, because the wife never possessed capacity to make an irrevocable settlement either before or after her marriage. Two passages from Lord Lindley's judgment are instructive. Speaking of the case before him, he said[55]:

> "By the Austrian law she was unable to ratify or confirm this contract; she could always repudiate it, but could never ratify it, i.e. deprive herself of the right to repudiate it. This was the case in *Cooper v Cooper*, but it was not so in *Edwards v Carter*."

And speaking of *Cooper v Cooper* he said[56]:

> "In that case a lady did succeed in repudiating a marriage settlement made when she was an infant after the lapse of much more than a reasonable time, if you shut out of consideration the change of her domicile between the execution of the settlement and the repudiation."

---

[50] At p.99.
[51] At pp.107–108.
[52] [1893] A.C. 360.
[53] See per Lord Watson at p.106.
[54] [1900] 2 Ch. 87.
[55] At p.96.
[56] At p.98.

14-023 The clear inference from the concluding words in this passage is that in Lord Lindley's view the House of Lords in *Cooper v Cooper* did not "shut out of consideration" the law of Scotland. If so, *Cooper v Cooper* is no authority for the proposition that capacity to make a marriage settlement is governed by the law of the domicile of the party alleged to be incapable. It is therefore submitted that such capacity is governed by the proper law of the contract, which means, in this connection, the system of law with which the contract is most closely connected, and not the law intended by the parties. As Lord Macnaghten said in *Cooper v Cooper*,[57] "it is difficult to suppose that Mrs Cooper could confer capacity on herself by contemplating a different country as the place where the contract was to be fulfilled".

The lowering of the age of majority in English law from 21 to 18[58] has of course reduced the practical significance of the problem here discussed.

INTERNATIONAL AND EUROPEAN DEVELOPMENTS

Hague Convention

14-024 In 1978, the Hague Conference on Private International Law agreed a Convention on the Law Applicable to Matrimonial Property Régimes. Only three states ratified the Convention. The primary rule was that the matrimonial property regime was governed by the internal law designated by the spouses before marriage, chosen from a restricted list: the law of any state of which either spouse was a national at the time of designation; the law of the state in which either spouse had his or her habitual residence at the time of designation; and the law of the first state where one of the spouses established a new habitual residence after marriage. The spouses could also designate, with respect only to immovables, the law of the place where the immovables were situated.[59] They may also provide that any immovables which may subsequently be acquired shall be governed by the law of the place where such immovables are situated. In the absence of any choice by the spouses, and with certain exceptions, the applicable law was that of the state in which both spouses establish their first habitual residence after marriage.[60] The spouses could change the governing law during their marriage.[61]

Proposed European Union Regulation

14-025 In March 2011, the Commission published a proposal for a Council Regulation on jurisdiction, applicable law and the recognition and enforcement of decisions in matters of matrimonial property régimes.[62] This builds upon the Hague Convention but, as its title indicates, has a much wider scope.

---

[57] (1888) 13 App. Cas. 88 at 108.
[58] Family Law Reform Act 1969 s.1(1).
[59] art.3.
[60] art.4.
[61] art.6.
[62] COM(2011) 126 final.

On jurisidiction, the proposed regulation would give jurisdiction to a court seised of an application concerning the succession of a spouse under the proposed Regulation on succession or of application for divorce, judicial separation or marriage annulment under the Brussels IIa Regulation. In other cases, jurisdiction would be given to the courts of the Member State of the spouses' common habitual residence, or failing that, of the last common habitual residence if one of them still resides there, or, failing that, of the defendant's habitual residence, or failing that, of the nationality of both spouses or, in the case of the United Kingdom and Ireland, of their common "domicile". Both parties might also agree that the courts of the Member State whose law they have chosen as the law applicable to their matrimonial property régime in accordance with the Reguation should also have jurisdiction.

On choice of law, the proposed Regulation allows the spouses to select the law of **14–026** the state of their habitual common residence; or of the state of habitual residence of one of the spouses; or of the state of which one of them is a national. In the absence of a choice by the spouses, the applicable law would be the law of the state of the spouses' first common habitual residence after their marriage or, failing that, the law of the state of the spouses' common nationality at the time of their marriage or, failing that, the law of the state with which the spouses jointly have the closest links, taking into account all the circumstances, in particular the place where the marriage was celebrated. There would be provision for change in the applicable law.

A decision given in a Member State under the proposed Regulation would be recognised in the other Member States without any special procedure being required. Certain grounds for non-recognition are specified.

In June 2011 it was announced that the United Kingdom did not propose to opt into this Proposal.

CHAPTER 15

SUCCESSION AND THE ADMINISTRATION OF ESTATES

In their treatment of the estates of deceased persons, English law and the systems   **15–001**
based on it differ widely from modern civil law systems. In English law the
general principle is that no one is entitled to deal with the property of a deceased
person without first obtaining the authority of the court.[1] If the deceased made a
will appointing an executor who is willing to act, the necessary authority is
acquired by the executor obtaining a grant of probate of the will. If the deceased
died intestate, the necessary authority is acquired by some person (for example
one of the next of kin, or a creditor) obtaining a grant of letters of administration.
Where there is a will but no executor, the letters of administration are "with will".
The executors or administrators (generically called the personal representatives)
succeed to the property of the deceased, and are bound to clear the estate of debts,
duties and expenses; this is the process of administration of the estate. The
personal representatives then distribute the surplus among the persons entitled
under the deceased's will or intestacy. Issues of "succession" concern this
beneficial distribution of the net surplus of the estate.

In civil law countries, the general rule is that the property of a deceased person
passes directly to the deceased's heirs or universal legatee; personal representatives in the English sense need not be appointed and when personal
representatives are appointed, their duties are usually of a supervisory nature,
quite different from those of English personal representatives.[2] But, whatever the
foreign law may say, no property in England may pass directly to a foreign heir or
universal legatee: an English grant must be obtained.

---

[1] *New York Breweries Co Ltd v Att-Gen* [1899] A.C. 62. There are statutory exceptions, e.g.
Administration of Estates (Small Payments) Act 1965.
[2] See *Re Achillopoulos* [1928] Ch. 433. In 2009, the European Commission published a Proposed
Regulation on succession and wills; see para.15–034.

ADMINISTRATION OF ESTATES

English grants of administration

15–002   The practice concerning grants of administration is governed by the Non-Contentious Probate Rules 1987 as amended. These give wide discretion to the court, in practice the officials of the probate registries. Disputes concerning the administration of estates, however, are the subject of proceedings in the Chancery Division.

Until 1932, the English court could make a grant only if there were property of the deceased situated in England. This restriction could be very inconvenient. When a person died domiciled in England but leaving property in a civil law country, the foreign court would sometimes refuse to make a grant of representation until a grant had been obtained in England. If the deceased left no property in England, the result was an impasse.[3] The Administration of Justice Act 1932[4] therefore provided that the court should have jurisdiction to make a grant in respect of any deceased person, even if the deceased left no property in England. But if there is no property of the deceased in England and the deceased died domiciled abroad, the court is very reluctant to make a grant.[5]

Separate wills

15–003   Testators sometimes make separate wills disposing of their property in England and abroad. If one instrument confirms the other, they both together constitute the last will of the testator, and an executor seeking a grant of representation must take probate of both. But if the wills are independent of each other, the practice is to admit only the English will to probate unless there is some reason for also making a grant of probate in respect of the foreign will.[6]

Person to whom the grant will be made

15–004   When a person dies domiciled in a foreign country, the court will make a grant in the first instance to the person entrusted with the administration of the estate by the court of the deceased's domicile.[7] If there is no such person, for example because no application for a grant has yet been made in the country of the domicile or because its courts do not appoint personal representatives in the English sense, the grant will be made to the person entitled to administer the

---

[3] *In the Goods of Tucker* (1864) 3 Sw. & Tr. 585.
[4] s.2(1). This Act was repealed by the Senior Courts (formerly Supreme Court) Act 1981 Sch.7, but in substance kept alive by s.25(1).
[5] *Aldrich v Att-Gen* [1968] P. 281, 295.
[6] *Re Wayland* [1951] 2 All E.R. 1041.
[7] Non-Contentious Probate Rules 1987 r.30(1)(a) (r.30 is amended, as to the titles of the officers acting, by SI 1991/1876). The English administration is said to be "ancillary" to the "principal" administration in the domicile.

estate by the law of the domicile.[8] But the making of such a grant is discretionary, and the court may make a grant to such other person as it thinks fit, either because there is no one who qualifies under these rules or because there are special circumstances which appear to require it.[9]

If the deceased left a formally valid will in English or Welsh which names an executor as such, or which describes (in any language) the duties of a named person in terms which according to English law are sufficient to constitute an executor "according to the tenor", probate may be granted to that person.[10] If the law of the domicile restricts the powers of the representative to a fixed period from the death of the deceased, such restriction will be disregarded in England.[11]

The foreign personal representative must be a person to whom a grant can properly be made in English law. Thus, the court will not make a grant to a foreign personal representative who is a minor.[12] And if there is a minority or a life interest arising under a will or intestacy, the court must normally[13] make a grant to not less than two individuals or a trust corporation; it will therefore not make a grant to a single individual even if that individual is entitled to administer the estate by the law of the domicile.[14]

15–005

Under the Consular Conventions Act 1949, the court may make a grant to a consular officer of a foreign State to which the Act has been extended by Order in Council, if a national of that state is entitled to a grant of probate or administration in respect of property in England, is not resident in England, and has not by an attorney applied to the court for a grant.

Effect in England of Scottish, Northern Irish and Commonwealth grants

Scottish and Northern Irish grants

Section 1 of the Administration of Estates Act 1971 provides that where a person dies domiciled in Scotland or Northern Ireland, a Scottish "confirmation" or Northern Ireland grant will be treated without further formality as if it had originally been made by the English High Court. There are of course reciprocal provisions for the direct recognition of English grants in Scotland and Northern Ireland,[15] and as between Northern Ireland and Scotland.[16]

15–006

---

[8] Non-Contentious Probate Rules 1987 r.30(1)(b). Where the English estate consists wholly of immovables, a grant limited thereto may be made to the person who would have been entitled if the deceased had died domiciled in England: Non-Contentious Probate Rules 1987 r.30(3)(b).

[9] Non-Contentious Probate Rules 1987 r.30(1)(c); *In the Goods of Kaufman* [1952] P. 325; see also *Practice Direction* [1953] 1 W.L.R. 1237.

[10] Non-Contentious Probate Rules 1987 r.30(3)(a).

[11] *In the Estate of Goenaga* [1949] P. 367, a case difficult to reconcile with *Laneuville v Anderson* (1860) 2 Sw. & Tr. 24; see Morris, (1950) 3 Int.L.Q. 243; Lipstein, (1949) 26 B.Y.B.I.L. 498.

[12] *In the Goods of HRH the Duchesse d'Orleans* (1859) 1 Sw. & Tr. 253.

[13] See Senior Courts (formerly Supreme Court) Act 1981 s.114(2), under which the court has a discretionary power to make a grant to one individual if it thinks fit.

[14] See Non-Contentious Probate Rules 1987 r.30(2).

[15] Administration of Estates Act 1971 ss.2(1) and 3(1).

[16] Administration of Estates Act 1971 ss.2(2) and 3(1).

Commonwealth grants

15–007 Under the Colonial Probates Act 1892, a grant of representation made in a country to which the Act has been applied by Order in Council may be sealed with the seal of the probate registry and will thereafter have the same effect as an English grant. The Act has been applied to almost the whole Commonwealth.[17] The Act does not require that the deceased should have been domiciled in the country where the grant was made, but the probate registry has a discretion whether or not to reseal. Unless there are special reasons, a grant not made by the court of the domicile will not be resealed unless it was made to a person who would have been entitled to an original grant in England, e.g. as an executor named in a will written in English or Welsh, or as the person entitled to administer the estate by the law of the domicile.[18]

Effect of an English grant

15–008 An English grant vests in the personal representatives all property of the deceased, movable or immovable, which at the time of the death is situated in England[19]; and also, probably, any movables of the deceased which are brought to England after that time.[20] But, although there is no authority on the point, it would be consistent with principle to recognise the title of a third party who under the *lex situs* had obtained a good title to such movables before they were brought to England.[21] Even if the deceased died domiciled in England, an English grant does not of its own force vest in the personal representatives any property which is and remains outside England: at most it gives the personal representative a "generally recognised claim" to be appointed as such by the courts of the country where the movables are situated.[22]

An English personal representative may legitimately take such steps as are open to him or her to recover property of the deceased wherever situated. Whether there is a positive duty to recover assets situated outside England is less clear. Usually the English personal representative will be unable to recover such assets without first obtaining a grant of representation from the foreign court. Anyone attempting to deal with foreign assets without a grant may be liable as an executor *de son tort* under the foreign law. In practice, therefore, an English personal representative will be concerned with foreign assets only if the deceased died domiciled in England, since only in such a case has the English personal representative a "generally recognised claim" to a grant from the foreign court. If there are sufficient assets in England to pay the debts and duties, an English personal representative is not obliged to collect a specifically bequeathed chattel

---

[17] See the Colonial Probates Act Application Order 1965 (SI 1965/1530), SI 1976/579 (Vanuatu), and SI 1997/1572 (continued application to Hong Kong Special Administrative Region). The Act continued to apply to South Africa during the period when that country was outside the Commonwealth.

[18] Non-Contentious Probate Rules 1987 r.39(3).

[19] Administration of Estates Act 1925 s.1.

[20] *Whyte v Rose* (1842) 3 Q.B. 493 at 506, per Parke B.

[21] See above, para.13–035.

[22] *Blackwood v R* (1882) 8 App.Cas. 82, 92.

situated abroad, and may simply assent to its vesting in the legatee and leave the latter to bear the expense of bringing it home[23] or paying any foreign duty which it may have attracted.[24]

A personal representative will be liable to account for assets under an English **15–009** grant only if he or she received them in the character of English personal representative. An English personal representative who also has a grant from a foreign court is not accountable in England qua personal representative for assets recovered in that capacity.

Choice of law

The administration of a deceased person's estate is governed wholly by the law of **15–010** the country in which the personal representative obtained the grant.[25] Every question as to the admissibility of debts and as to the priority in which debts are to be paid is governed by the *lex fori*. Foreign creditors rank equally with English creditors, whether the English administration is principal or ancillary.[26] The only difference is that the English ancillary administrator need not advertise for foreign claims.[27]

Administration does not include the distribution of surplus assets to beneficiaries under the deceased's will or intestacy. That is a matter of succession. If the deceased died domiciled abroad, the English administration is ancillary to that which takes place in the country of the domicile, and the English ancillary personal representative will normally hand over the surplus to the principal representative appointed by the courts of the domicile.[28] However, the court has a discretionary power to restrain the English personal representative from so doing. This power has been exercised where the domiciliary representative would have applied the surplus to pay debts which by English domestic law were statute-barred[29]; or would have distributed the surplus in accordance with a will which by the English rules of the conflict of laws had been revoked.[30] In both these cases the court ordered the English representative not to hand over the assets but to distribute them to the persons entitled under English law.

---

[23] *Re Fitzpatrick* [1952] Ch. 86.
[24] *Re Scott* [1915] 1 Ch. 592.
[25] *Preston v Melville* (1841) 8 Cl. & F. 1.
[26] *Re Kloebe* (1884) 28 Ch.D. 175.
[27] *Re Achillopoulos* [1928] Ch. 433 at 445.
[28] *Re Achillopoulos* [1928] Ch. 433; *In the Estate of Weiss* [1962] P. 136.
[29] *Re Lorillard* [1922] 2 Ch. 638; approved by Lord Simonds in *Government of India v Taylor* [1955] A.C. 491 at 509.
[30] *Re Manifold* [1962] Ch. 1.

Foreign personal representatives

15–011   A foreign personal representative who wishes to represent the deceased in England must obtain an English grant.[31] Anyone else intermeddling with the assets of the deceased incurs all the liabilities but none of the privileges of such a representative.[32] However, a foreign personal representative who has obtained a judgment against a debtor of the estate in the foreign country can enforce the judgment in England in a personal capacity without taking out an English grant.[33]

A foreign personal representative without an English grant cannot be made liable in England for property held or acts done in the capacity of foreign representative.[34] The foreign personal representative may be liable in England through acts attracting liabilities as a debtor or trustee, for example by entering into a contract in England in respect of the estate, or by making an improper investment[35]; and, by intermeddling with English assets, will become liable as an executor *de son tort*.[36]

SUCCESSION

15–012   When the estate of a deceased person has been fully administered, that is to say when all debts, duties and expenses have been paid, the question arises by what law the beneficial distribution of his or her net estate is to be governed. As a general rule, succession to immovables is governed by the *lex situs*, and succession to movables by the law of the deceased's last domicile. Few qualifications need to be made to these propositions so far as intestate succession is concerned. But in succession under wills it may sometimes be necessary to look at the law of the testator's domicile at the date on which the will was executed; other laws are made relevant by statute if the question is one of formal validity.

Intestate succession

Movables

15–013   It has been settled law for over 200 years that intestate succession to movables is governed by the law of the deceased's last domicile.[37] This subject to the application of *renvoi*, which has been developed very largely in this context.[38]

---

[31] *Carter and Crosts Case* (1585) Godb. 33; *Tourton v Flower* (1735) 3 P. Wms. 369; *New York Breweries Co Ltd v Att-Gen* [1899] A.C. 62; *Finnegan v Cementation Co Ltd* [1953] 1 Q.B. 688.

[32] *New York Breweries Co Ltd v Att-Gen* [1899] A.C. 62. cf. the recognition of a foreign trustee in bankruptcy as a matter of course.

[33] *Vanquelin v Bouard* (1863) 15 C.B. (N.S.) 341; *Re Macnichol* (1874) L.R. 19 Eq. 81.

[34] *Jauncy v Sealey* (1686) 1 Vern. 397; *Beavan v Hastings* (1856) 2 K. & J. 724; *Flood v Patterson* (1861) 29 Beav. 295; *Degazon v Barclays Bank International* [1988] F.T.L.R. 17.

[35] *Harvey v Dougherty* (1887) 56 L.T. 322.

[36] *New York Breweries Co Ltd v Att-Gen.* [1899] A.C. 62.

[37] *Pipon v Pipon* (1744) Amb. 799; *Somerville v Somerville* (1801) 5 Ves.750.

[38] See para.18–023.

But this rule applies only to succession in the strict sense of that term. It does not apply to the right of the Crown or of a foreign government to take ownerless property as bona vacantia or under a *jus regale*.[39] The title to movables so claimed is governed by the *lex situs* and not by the law of the deceased's last domicile. Thus, if a person dies intestate domiciled in a foreign country and without next of kin, and the foreign state claims his or her movables in England as ownerless property, the Crown's claim to the movables as *bona vacantia* will be preferred.[40] In such a case the foreign state claims not by way of succession but because there is no succession. It is otherwise, however, if the foreign state claims as *ultimus heres* (last heir)[41] under the foreign law and not under a *jus regale*. In such a case there is a true claim of succession which is governed by the law of the domicile, and the claim of the foreign State will be preferred to that of the Crown.[42]

Immovables

According to the traditional rule of the English conflict of laws, intestate succession to immovables is governed by the *lex situs*. This was confirmed, albeit with reluctance, in *Re Collens*.[43]   **15–014**

The scission principle

The "scission" principle under which intestate succession to immovables is governed by the *lex situs* has been abandoned by almost all countries outside the common law world. The principle made some sense before 1926 when there were two systems of intestate succession in English domestic law, one for realty and the other for personalty. It makes no sense today when England and all other countries in the world have adopted one system of intestate succession for all kinds of property. It has been more fully argued elsewhere[44] that the "scission" principle has outlived its usefulness in England and should be abandoned in favour of the law of the intestate's domicile.   **15–015**

---

[39] Both these concepts allow the Crown or the State to take ownerless property as, in effect, a prerogative right.

[40] *Re Barnett's Trusts* [1902] 1 Ch. 847; *Re Musurus* [1936] 1 All E.R. 1666.

[41] A typical civil law code will list heirs in an order of priority, with the state as the final heir in default of all others.

[42] *Re Maldonado's Estate* [1954] P. 223. This is an extreme example of characterisation in accordance with the *lex causae* (below, para.18–010) and as such it has been much criticised: see Gower, (1954) 17 M.L.R. 167; Cohn, (1954) 17 M.L.R. 381; Lipstein, [1954] Camb. L.J. 22. The decision does seem to treat the form of the foreign law as more important than its substance.

[43] [1986] Ch. 505. The existence of the rule was assumed in *Balfour v Scott* (1793) 6 Bro. P.C. 550; *Brodie v Barry* (1813) 2 v & B. 127, 131; *Dundas v Dundas* (1830) 2 Dow & Cl. 349; *Freke v Carbery* (1873) L.R. 16 Eq. 461; *Duncan v Lawson* (1889) 41 Ch.D. 394; *Re Berchtold* [1923] 1 Ch. 192; and *Re Cutcliffe* [1940] Ch. 565.

[44] Morris, (1969) 85 L.Q.R. 339.

The Hague Conference on Private International Law at its Sixteenth Session in 1988 drew up a Convention on the Law Applicable to Succession to the Estates of Deceased Persons, which adopts the unitary approach[45]; having received only one ratification, it is a dead letter.

The retention of the *situs* rule frequently frustrates the intention of Parliament. For when Parliament passes a modern statute on intestate succession, it seeks to give effect to what the average intestate would have wished to do with his or her property, if he or she had made a will. What average intestate? Surely the obvious answer is, an English intestate if the statute applies to England, and a Scottish intestate if the statute applies to Scotland; and indeed legislative action follows sample surveys of wills conducted on this basis.

15–016 Even within the United Kingdom there are striking differences between the English, Scottish, and Northern Ireland laws of intestate succession, particularly with regard to the rights of the surviving spouse. In England, a surviving spouse is now entitled to a statutory legacy of £250,000 if the intestate left issue and £450,000 otherwise.[46] A similar rule is found in Northern Ireland. Suppose that a man dies intestate domiciled in Northern Ireland leaving a widow and no issue, and leaving movables in Northern Ireland worth £200,000 and land in England worth the same amount. Would the widow be entitled to two statutory legacies, one under the English and a second under the Northern Ireland legislation, thereby leaving nothing for the next of kin (perhaps the mother of the intestate)?

It should not be supposed that this is a mere hypothetical case, far removed from reality. In *Re Collens*[47]:

> C died intestate domiciled in Trinidad and Tobago leaving a substantial estate there, another in Barbados, and a comparatively small estate, including some land, in England. After litigation in Trinidad between his widow and G, his ex-wife, G accepted $1 million in full settlement of her claims against the Trinidad estate. G then successfully asserted a claim to the statutory legacy (then only £5,000) under English law.

The Vice-Chancellor reached this conclusion with regret, and expressed the hope that the Law Commission would review the "scission" principle in the light of the criticisms made of it by Dr Morris.

Wills

Capacity

15–017 The law of the testator's domicile determines whether the testator has personal capacity to make a will of movables.[48] "Personal capacity" is here used to denote such questions as whether a minor or a married woman or a person suffering from

---

[45] See the very full Explanatory Report by D. W. M. Waters, *Actes et Documents de la 16e Session*, p.525.

[46] Administration of Estates Act 1925 s.46(1)(i) para.(3), as amended by Intestates' Estates Act 1952 s.1, Family Provision Act 1966 s.1(1)(b), and SI 2009/135.

[47] [1986] Ch. 505. See also *Re Rea* [1902] Ir. R. 451 and *Re Ralston* [1906] V.L.R. 689.

[48] *In bonis Maraver* (1828) 1 Hagg. Ecc. 498; *In bonis Gutteriez* (1869) 38 L.J.P. & M. 48; *In the Estate of Fuld (No.3)* [1968] P. 675 at 696.

bodily or mental illness[49] can make a valid will. It does not include what are sometimes called questions of proprietary capacity, for example, whether a testator can leave property away from his or her spouse and children. Such questions are best regarded as questions of material or essential validity and will be dealt with later under that heading.[50]

There is no difficulty in applying the principle stated above if the testator's domicile is the same at the date of death as at the date of the will. But if the domicile changes between these two dates, and the two laws differ, it is necessary to choose between them. It is submitted that, on principle, the law of the domicile at the date of the will should govern.[51] Hence, if the testator makes a will at the age of 18 while domiciled in a country where minority ends at 21 and minors cannot make wills, and dies domiciled in England, the will would be void. Conversely, if the testator makes a will at the age of 18 while domiciled in England, and dies domiciled in a country where minority ends at 21 and minors cannot make wills, the will should be valid. It may be noted that by English domestic law (and presumably by the domestic laws of other countries) a testator must have personal capacity to make a will at the date when the will is made, and capacity at the date of death is neither necessary nor sufficient.

So far as capacity to *take* movables under a will is concerned, it has been held **15–018** that a legacy can be paid to a legatee who is of age to receive it by the law of his or her domicile or by the law of the testator's domicile, whichever happens first.[52]

There is no English authority on what law governs capacity to make a will of immovables. Probably the *lex situs* would be held to govern.[53] This seems to have been the assumption in *Re P (Statutory Will)*[54] where the deceased was domiciled in California and the court ordered the making of a statutory will dealing with immovable property in England as the deceased lacked capacity under the Mental Capacity Act 2005.

Formal validity

At common law, a will of immovables had to comply with the formalities **15–019** prescribed by the *lex situs*,[55] and a will of movables had to comply with the formalities prescribed by the law of the testator's last domicile.[56] This latter rule led to much inconvenience and hardship when, for example, the domicile of the testator changed after the execution of the will, or the testator became mortally ill while travelling in a country other than that of his or her domicile. After various

---

[49] *In the Estate of Fuld (No.3)*, above.
[50] Below, para.15–026.
[51] Most writers adopt this view: Story s.465; Savigny s.377; Wolff s.557; F. A. Mann (1954) 31 B.Y.I.L. 217 at 230–231. *Re Lewal's Settlement* [1918] 2 Ch. 391 supports the statement in the text; but that was a case on the exercise of a power of appointment by will.
[52] *Re Hellman's Will* (1866) L.R. 2 Eq. 363.
[53] See *Bank of Africa v Cohen* [1909] 2 Ch. 129, above, a case on capacity to transfer land *inter vivos*.
[54] [2009] EWHC 163 (Ch); [2010] Ch. 33.
[55] *Coppin v Coppin* (1725) 2 P. Wms.291; *Pepin v Bruyere* [1900] 2 Ch. 504.
[56] The leading case is *Bremer v Freeman* (1857) 10 Moo. P.C. 306.

attempts by the courts[57] and Parliament[58] to remedy the situation, the modern law was enacted in the Wills Act 1963, which gives effect to the Hague Convention of 1961 on the Formal Validity of Wills.[59]

Section 1 of the Act provides that a will shall be treated as properly executed if its execution conformed to the internal law in force in the territory where it was executed, or in the territory where, at the time of its execution or of the testator's death, he was domiciled or had his habitual residence, or in a State of which, at either of those times, he was a national. This section applies to wills of movables and to wills of land; and s.2(1)(b) additionally provides that a will of immovables shall be treated as properly executed if its execution conformed to the internal law in force in the territory where the property was situated.

Under s.1, if a testator is domiciled in one country, habitually resident in a second, and a national of a third, and changes all three between the time of execution of the will and the time of death, there are no fewer than six systems of law by which the formal validity of the will may be tested, or seven if the testator makes the will in a yet different country. This should be enough to save most wills from formal invalidity so far as the conflict of laws is concerned. There is no requirement in the Act that all the testamentary instruments executed by a testator must conform to the same system of law. Hence, a will and six codicils could each derive its formal validity from a different system.

The law of the testator's nationality

15–020 The reference to the law of the testator's nationality is an even greater innovation than the reference to the law of habitual residence. If the testator is a national of a federal or composite state comprising many countries, like the United States of America or the United Kingdom, there is an obvious difficulty in ascertaining his nationality for the purposes of the Act. Section 6(2) attempts to solve this problem. It provides as follows: (a) if there is in force throughout the state in question a rule indicating which of its systems of internal law can properly be applied in the case in question, that rule shall be followed; but (b) if there is no such rule, the system shall be that with which the testator was most closely connected at the relevant time.[60]

It is not easy to imagine circumstances in which the provisions of s.6(2)(a) will be applicable, or to assign a precise meaning to the provisions of s.6(2)(b). One has to think of a testator who is, for example, a British citizen or a citizen of the United States of America, who is domiciled and habitually resident elsewhere and who makes a will elsewhere, the will being formally invalid by the law of the

[57] *Collier v Rivaz* (1841) 2 Curt. 855; *In bonis Lacroix* (1877) 2 P.D. 94. This, as a matter of history, is how the doctrine of *renvoi* obtained a foothold in English law, obviously as an escape device: see para.18–028.
[58] The notoriously ill-drafted Wills Act 1861 (Lord Kingsdown's Act).
[59] The Act was based on the recommendations in the Fourth Report of the Private International Law Committee, Cmnd. 491 (1958). For comments on the Act, see Kahn-Freund, (1964) 27 M.L.R. 55; Morris, (1964) 13 I.C.L.Q. 684. On the Convention, see Neels, (2007) 56 I.C.L.Q. 613.
[60] "The relevant time" is defined (very obscurely) as the time of the testator's death where the matter is to be determined by reference to circumstances prevailing at his death, and the time of execution of the will in any other case.

place where it was made and of the testator's domicile and habitual residence, so that it is necessary to invoke the law of the testator's nationality in order to admit the will to probate. Section 6(2)(a) can rarely help in circumstances like these, because it is doubtful if there is a composite State in the world which has a uniform conflicts rule but different rules of domestic law for the formal validity of wills. Certainly the United Kingdom has not, nor has the United States. And as for s.6(2)(b), how can we determine whether our hypothetical testator is "most closely connected" with, England or Scotland or New York or California, when *ex hypothesi* he or she is domiciled and habitually resident outside the United Kingdom or the United States?

The only possible answer seems to be, look and see where the testator keeps the   **15–021** bulk of the property. This answer will not help if, as is likely in the circumstances here envisaged, the property is kept in the country where the testator is domiciled or habitually resident, and not in the State of nationality. It might have been more sensible to make the formalities of the *lex situs* available for wills of movables, as they are for wills of immovables.[61] The reference to the law of the nationality will not work for British or American citizens: but it does them no obvious harm and will be beneficial in relation to citizens of many other countries.

Wills made on ships and aircraft

The law of the country where the will was executed is given an extended meaning   **15–022** in the case of wills made on board a vessel or aircraft "of any description". In addition to the law of the place where the vessel or aircraft happens to be (including, no doubt, the country in whose territorial waters the vessel is sailing or the country over which the aircraft is flying), s.2(1)(a) of the Act allows as an alternative the internal law in force in the territory with which, having regard to its registration (if any) and other relevant circumstances, the vessel or aircraft may be taken to have been most closely connected. This will normally be the law of the flag or, in the case of ships wearing flags like the Red Ensign, the law in force at the port of registration. The cautious drafting is presumably designed to allow for exceptions in the case of flags of convenience. There is no requirement that the vessel or aircraft should be in motion when the will is made. Hence a will formally valid by French law would be admissible to probate in England if executed on board a French ship alongside in an English port, or on board a French aircraft on the runway at Heathrow Airport.

Changes in the relevant law

Section 6(3) of the Wills Act 1963 provides that regard is to be had to the formal   **15–023** requirements of a particular law at the time of execution, but that this is not to prevent account being taken of an alteration of the law affecting wills executed at that time if the alteration enables the will to be treated as properly executed. Thus, retrospective alterations in the law are relevant if they *validate* a will, but irrelevant if they *invalidate* it. This subsection is not in terms confined to

---

[61] s.2(1)(b).

alterations in the law made before the death of the testator; and there is no reason to read into it words that are not there.[62]

Special requirements as to form

15–024 Under some foreign systems of law, certain classes of testators can make wills only in a special form. For example, testators over 16 and under 18 years of age may be able to make wills only in notarial form. It has long been controversial among continental jurists whether such provisions relate to form or to capacity. Section 3 of the Wills Act 1963 settles this question by providing that where a law in force outside the United Kingdom falls to be applied (whether in pursuance of the Act or not), any requirement of that law whereby special formalities are to be observed by testators answering a particular description, or witnesses to the execution of the will are to possess certain qualifications, shall be treated as a formal requirement, notwithstanding any rule of that law to the contrary. So, if a German national, domiciled and habitually resident in Germany and aged seventeen, makes a will in Germany in holograph form, the will would not be admitted to probate in England because it was not made in notarial form as required by German law. If, however, the will had been made in France and was formally valid by French law, it would be admitted to probate: the testator had capacity by the law of his domicile, and the will was formally valid by the law of the country where it was executed.

Renvoi

15–025 It will be seen that the Act refers throughout to the "internal law" of the various systems which it allows. Thus, any reference to another system from the conflicts rules of the systems of law authorised by the Act is excluded. But the Act does not abolish, either expressly or by implication, the doctrine of *renvoi* in relation to the formal validity of wills, nor the rule of common law that the formal validity of a will of movables is governed by the law of the testator's last domicile.[63] Hence, if a British citizen with an English domicile of origin and an Italian domicile of choice makes a will of movables which is formally valid by English domestic law but formally invalid by Italian domestic law, and it is proved that the Italian courts would regard the will as formally valid, it could be admitted to probate in England by way of *renvoi* from Italian law instead of under sections 1 and 6(2) of the Act.

Material or essential validity

15–026 The material, or essential, validity of a will of movables, or of any particular gift of movables contained therein, is governed by the law of the testator's domicile at the time of death.[64] The term material or essential validity includes such

---

[62] If this is right, the subsection renders *Lynch v Provisional Government of Paraguay* (1871) L.R. 2 P. & M. 268 obsolete. See below, para.18–055.

[63] For *renvoi*, see below, para.18 –023.

[64] *Whicker v Hume* (1858) 7 H.L.C. 124; *Dellar v Zivy* [2007] EWHC 2266 (Ch); [2007] I.L.Pr. 868.

questions as whether the testator must leave a certain proportion of his estate to his children or widow,[65] and whether gifts to attesting witnesses are valid.[66] But if the will bequeaths property on trusts, any question as to whether the trust offends against a rule against perpetuities or accumulations is determined by the law governing the trust under the Recognition of Trusts Act 1987 and not by the law governing the validity of the will.[67]

The material or essential validity of a gift by will of immovables is governed by the *lex situs*. That law will determine what estates can legally be created,[68] what are the incidents of those estates,[69] whether gifts to charities are valid,[70] and whether the testator is bound to leave a certain proportion of his estate to his children or widow.[71]

Closely analogous to the question whether a testator is bound to leave a certain proportion of the estate to his or her spouse or children (as is the case under the laws of Scotland, France and many continental European countries) is the question whether the court can make an order for the payment of part of the income of the estate to any dependants (as it can in England under the Inheritance (Provision for Family and Dependants) Act 1975). In England the statute itself limits the court's power to cases where the testator died domiciled in England, whether the property is movable or immovable.[72]

Construction (or interpretation)

The construction of a will of movables is governed by the law intended by the testator. In the absence of indications to the contrary, this is presumed to be the law of the testator's domicile at the time the will was made[73]; but this is only a rebuttable presumption.[74] An illustration is provided by *Dellar v Zivy*[75]:   **15–027**

> Z, French by nationality, lived in England for many years managing the UK subsidiary of the family company. His will disposed of French shares, and in it he declared himself to be domiciled in England. In fact, he may well have retained his French domicile of origin, but the making of the declaration, the use in the will of the trust for sale, unknown in French law, and the direction that English solicitors be consulted over the administration of the estate all made it clear that he intended the will to be interpreted in accordance with English law.

A change of domicile between the time the will was made and the time of the testator's death does not affect the construction of the will:

---

[65] *Thornton v Curling* (1824) 8 Sim. 310; *Campbell v Beaufoy* (1859) Johns. 320; *Re Groos* [1915] 1 Ch. 572; *Re Annesley* [1926] Ch. 692; *Re Ross* [1930] 1 Ch. 377; *Re Adams* [1967] I.R. 424.
[66] *Re Priest* [1944] Ch. 58; see now Wills Act 1968.
[67] See para.16–007.
[68] *Nelson v Bridport* (1846) 8 Beav. 547.
[69] *Re Miller* [1914] 1 Ch. 511.
[70] *Duncan v Lawson* (1889) 41 Ch.D. 394; *Re Hoyles* [1911] 1 Ch. 179.
[71] *Re Hernando* (1884) 27 Ch.D. 284; *Re Ross* [1930] 1 Ch. 377.
[72] Inheritance (Provision for Family and Dependants) Act 1975 s.1(1). See, e.g., *Cyganik v Agulian* [2006] EWCA Civ 129; [2006] 1 F.C.R. 129.
[73] *Anstruther v Chalmer* (1826) 2 Sim. 1; *Re Fergusson* [1902] 1 Ch. 483; *Re Cunnington* [1924] 1 Ch. 68.
[74] *Bradford v Young* (1885) 29 Ch.D. 617; *Re Price* [1900] 1 Ch. 442 at 452 and 453; *Re Adams* [1967] I.R. 424.
[75] [2007] EWHC 2266 (Ch); [2007] I.L.Pr. 868.

"If a question arises as to the interpretation of the will, and it should appear that the testator has changed his domicile between making his will and his death, his will may fall to be construed according to the law of his domicile at the time he made it".[76]

This is reinforced by s.4 of the Wills Act 1963, which provides that the construction of a will shall not be altered by reason of any change in the testator's domicile after the execution of the will.

15–028 The term "construction" includes not only the meaning of words and phrases used by the testator, but also the way in which the law fills up gaps in the dispositions when the testator has failed to foresee and provide against certain events (for example, that one of several named residuary legatees might predecease the testator). This of course is not construction in the sense that it has reference to the intentions of the actual testator, for *ex hypothesi* the testator never had in mind the events which have happened. But it is construction in the sense that the law supposes that the average testator would wish the gap to be filled in a particular way.

A good instance of construction in accordance with the law of the testator's domicile is afforded by *Re Cunnington,*[77] where a British subject domiciled in France made a will in the English language and form in which he gave his residue on trust for division between ten named legatees, most of whom resided in England. Two of these legatees predeceased him. It was held that their shares were divisible among the survivors in accordance with French law, and did not lapse to the next of kin as they would have done by English domestic law. Again, if a testator domiciled in one of the United States were to give legacies expressed in dollars to legatees resident in Canada and Australia, there can be little doubt that the amount of the legacies would be calculated in American dollars.[78]

If a testator domiciled in England gives movables to the "heirs" or "next of kin" of a person who died domiciled in a foreign country, should the heirs or next of kin be ascertained in accordance with English law or the law of the foreign country? The English courts have adopted the former solution,[79] and the Scottish courts the latter.[80] The view of the Scottish courts seems preferable. For surely the question is not "Who would have been A's next of kin if he had died domiciled in England?" but rather "Who are A's next of kin having regard to the fact that he died domiciled abroad?"[81]

15–029 There is no reason to suppose that a different general rule applies to the construction of wills of immovables. However, the use of technical language of the *lex situs* may indicate an intention that its law should govern the construction of the will.[82] Difficult problems arise when the testator devises land in two different countries and aims at producing identical results by the use of the technical language of one system of law only. The court, when interpreting the will in accordance with the law of the testator's domicile, will endeavour to see

---

[76] *Philipson-Stow v I.R. C.* [1961] A.C. 727 at 761 per Lord Denning.
[77] [1924] 1 Ch. 68.
[78] *Saunders v Drake* (1742) 2 Atk. 465.
[79] *Re Fergusson's Will* [1902] 1 Ch. 483.
[80] *Mitchells Trustee v Rule* (1908) 16 S.L.T. 189; *Smiths Trustee v Macpherson*, 1926 S.C. 983.
[81] *Smith's Trustee v Macpherson*, 1926 S.C. 983 at 991–992, per Lord Sands.
[82] *Bradford v Young* (1885) 29 Ch. D. 617 at 623.

that the dispositions will operate in the country in which the land is situated to the fullest extent possible under the *lex situs*.[83] But if the *lex situs* makes it illegal or impossible to give effect to the terms of the will as construed by the law of the testator's domicile, then the *lex situs* will prevail.[84]

Revocation

The question as to what law determines whether a will has been revoked is one of considerable nicety.[85] A will may be revoked either (a) by a later will or codicil, or (b) by some other testamentary mode of revocation, for example in English domestic law by burning, tearing or destroying, or (c) by a change of circumstances, for example in English domestic law by the subsequent marriage of the testator, or in some other systems by the testator's subsequent divorce or by the birth of children. Each of these modes requires separate discussion.

15–030

Revocation by later will or codicil

A later will or codicil may revoke an earlier will either expressly or by implication. It may do so expressly, as when the testator says "I hereby revoke all testamentary dispositions heretofore made by me". In such a case the question whether the second instrument revokes the first depends on the intrinsic validity of the second will, especially with regard to the capacity of the testator and the formal validity of the will.[86] Both these matters have already been discussed.[87] It may be added that under s.2(1)(c) of the Wills Act 1963 a later will, in so far as it revokes an earlier will or any provision therein, will be treated as properly executed if its execution conformed to any law by reference to which the revoked will would be so treated. So, if the testator is domiciled in one country, habitually resident in a second, and a national of a third, and changes all three between the execution of the earlier and the later will, and again between the execution of the later will and the time of death, there may be a choice of nine systems of law for the formal validity of the revoking (as opposed to the disposing) provisions of the later will, or eleven if the wills are made in different countries.

15–031

However, if one will deals only with property in a foreign country and is made in foreign form, and the other deals only with property in England, the later will does not necessarily revoke the earlier one even if it contains a revocation clause.[88]

If the later will does not contain an express revocation clause, it may nevertheless revoke the first will by implication, for example if it is described as a "last" will (though this is not sufficient by English domestic law), or if its provisions cannot stand with those of the earlier will, as when the earlier will gives property to A and the later will gives the same property to B. In such cases,

---

[83] *Studd v Cook* (1883) 8 App.Cas. 577 at 591, per Lord Selborne.
[84] *Re Miller* [1914] 1 Ch. 511; *Philipson-Stow v I.R.C.* [1961] A.C. 727 at 761.
[85] For comparative material, see Neels (2007) 56 I.C.L.Q. 613.
[86] *Cottrell v Cottrell* (1872) L.R. 2 P. & M. 397; *Re Manifold* [1962] Ch. 1.
[87] Above, para.15–017 *et seq.*
[88] *Re Wayland* [1951] 2 All E.R. 1041; *Re Yahunda's Estate* [1956] P. 388.

the question is one of construction and is governed prima facie by the law of the testator's domicile at the time of making the later will.

Other testamentary modes of revocation

15–032 The question as to whether a will is revoked by burning, tearing or destroying or the like is no doubt governed by the *lex situs* in the case of immovables or by the law of the testator's domicile in the case of movables. If the testator's domicile is the same at all material times there is no difficulty. But if the domicile changes between the date of the alleged act of revocation and the date of death, and the two laws differ, it is necessary to determine which law governs. They may differ, for example, because in English law the will must be destroyed in the presence of the testator,[89] but in other systems (such as Italian law[90]) this is not necessary. If a testator domiciled in Italy writes to the solicitor who holds the will instructing the solicitor to destroy it, and by Italian law this amounts to an effective revocation, it is thought that the will would be revoked even if the testator died domiciled in England. For the will is effectively revoked by the law of the testator's domicile: it ceases to exist as a will just as though it had never been made, so that there is no will upon which English domestic law can operate. The converse case is perhaps more difficult: a testator domiciled in England writes to the solicitor instructing him to destroy his will, and dies domiciled in Italy. Here again it is thought that the law of the testator's domicile at the date of the alleged act of revocation would govern, with the result that the will would not be revoked. For at the time when the act was done there was no revocation in law, and at the time when the act might have amounted to revocation in law the act did not in fact occur. There is however no English authority on either of these questions.[91]

Revocation by subsequent marriage

15–033 In English domestic law a marriage revokes any previous will made by either party to the marriage.[92] In the laws of most other countries (including Scotland) it does not. It is well settled that the question as to whether a will is revoked by subsequent marriage is governed by the law of the testator's domicile at the time of the marriage. Thus in the leading case of *Re Martin*,[93] a lady domiciled in France made a will, married a domiciled Englishman (thereby, as the law then stood, acquiring an English domicile by operation of law), and died domiciled in France: it was held that her will was revoked. Conversely, in *In the Estate of Groos*[94] a lady domiciled in Holland made a will, married a domiciled Dutchman, and died domiciled in England: it was held that her will was not revoked.

---

[89] Wills Act 1837 s.20.

[90] See *Velasco v Coney* [1934] P. 143.

[91] See Mann (1954) 31 B.Y.B.I.L. 216 at 231.

[92] Wills Act 1837 s.18, as substituted by Administration of Justice Act 1982 s.18, where some exceptions are stated.

[93] [1900] P. 211.

[94] [1904] P. 269. cf. *In bonis Reid* (1866) L.R. 1 P. & M. 74; *Westerman v Schwab*, 1905 S.C. 132.

Of course, a subsequent marriage will not revoke a will if the marriage is void under English rules of the conflict of laws, for example because the parties are within the prohibited degrees of consanguinity or affinity.[95] But it will revoke a will if the marriage is voidable.[96]

EUROPEAN DEVELOPMENTS

Within the European Union, the Commission has published a Proposal for a Regulation on succession and wills,[97] put forward on the dubious basis that by eliminating obstacles to the free movement of persons it will advance the proper functioning of the internal market. Many of its provisions, for example those on *lis pendens* and on recognition and enforcement, are based on those in the Judgments Regulation.

15–034

On jurisdiction, the proposed rule of "general jurisdiction" is that "the courts of the Member State on whose territory the deceased had habitual residence at the time of their death shall be competent to rule in matters of successions"[98]; "habitual residence" is undefined. That court would be able in appropriate cases to transfer the case to the courts of the state whose law had been chosen by the deceased as the applicable law.[99] Where the habitual residence of the deceased at the time of death was not located in a Member State, various courts in the Member States would be able to exercise a "residual jurisdiction".[100]

On choice of law, the proposed general rule is that the law applicable to the succession as a whole, i.e. to movables and immovables alike, would be that of the state in which the deceased had his or her habitual residence at the time of death.[101] There would, however, be an element of party autonomy, in that a person would be free to choose as the law to govern the succession as a whole the law of the state whose nationality he or she possessed.[102] Article 19 defines the scope of application of the governing law very widely, including "any obligation to restore or account for gifts and the taking of them into account when determining the shares of heirs",[103] the so-called "claw-back" provision. The proposed Regulation as a whole would not apply to the "constitution, functioning and dissolving of trusts".[104]

The effect of the proposed Regulation on the administration of estates is not entirely clear. Article 21(2) provides that the law applicable to the succession under the Regulation "shall be no obstacle to the application of the law of the Member State in which the property is located where it subjects the administration and liquidation of the succession to the appointment of an administrator or executor of the will via an authority located in that Member

15–035

---

[95] *Mette v Mette* (1859) 1 Sw. & Tr. 416.
[96] *Re Roberts* [1978] 1 W.L.R. 653.
[97] COM(2009) 154 final, 14.10.2009; see Lein, (2009) 11 Yb.P.I.L. 107.
[98] art.4.
[99] art.5.
[100] art.6.
[101] art.16.
[102] art.17.
[103] art.19(1)(j).
[104] art.1(3)(i).

State". However, the law applicable to the succession would govern the determination of the persons, such as the heirs, legatees, executors or administrators of the will, who would be likely to be appointed to "administer and liquidate the succession". The Regulation would introduce a European Certificate of Succession, the use of which would not be obligatory; it would "constitute proof of the capacity of heir or legatee and of the powers of the executors of wills or third-party administrators".[105]

Doubts as to the impact of the proposed Regulation on English practice, especially its "claw-back" provision, led the United Kingdom to decide in December 2009 not to opt into this Proposal.

---

[105] art.36.

CHAPTER 16

TRUSTS

The trust is perhaps the most distinctive contribution made by English law to the   **16–001**
science of general jurisprudence. It is therefore surprising that there was at
common law a dearth of authority on what law governs the validity and
administration of trusts in the conflict of laws. Those issues are made all the more
important by the fact that although many countries in the civil law tradition have
legal devices that serve some of the purposes for which trusts arc used, none have
a fully-developed trust on the English model. The position was transformed by
the enactment of the Recognition of Trusts Act 1987 which gave effect in the law
of the United Kingdom to the Hague Convention on the law applicable to trusts
and on their recognition of January 10, 1986,[1] and was later complicated by the
appearance of the Rome II Regulation.[2] In what follows, the Convention and its
implementation in England are considered first, and then the rather difficult
question of the, limited, impact of the Rome II Regulation.

The Hague Convention's authors had an ambitious aim, to "establish common
provisions on the law applicable to trusts and to deal with the most important
issues concerning the recognition of trusts",[3] for a variety of legal systems, some
of which had a highly developed law of trusts, some of which were wholly
without the trust, and others again had devices analogous to the trust in function
or structure. This diversity required the inclusion of a description of the trust in
the Convention as a means of indicating the range of legal institutions within its
scope, and also to exclude from the scope of the Convention some uses of the

---

[1] The text, with certain omissions, is scheduled to the 1987 Act. For commentaries, see the official
Explanatory Report by von Overbeck, *Actes et Documents de la 15e Session*, p.370; Hayton, (1987)
36 I.C.L.Q. 260; Harris, *The Hague Trust Convention* (Hart Publishing, Oxford, 2002); Gaillard and
Trautman, (1987) 35 Am.J.Comp.L. 307.
[2] European Parliament and Council Regulation No.864/2007, [2007] O.J. L 199, p.40.
[3] Preamble. As Harris observes, the choice of law rules have more in common with those for
contracts than property: see Fawcett (ed.), *Reform and Development of Private International Law*
(Oxford University Press, Oxford, 2002) 187.

trust familiar to English lawyers but not clearly linked to property interests, for example constructive trusts used as a form of remedy.[4]

16–002   The Convention describes the trust as the legal relationship created, inter vivos or on death, by a person, the settlor, when assets have been placed under the control of a trustee for the benefit of a beneficiary or for a specified purpose.[5] It applies only to trusts created voluntarily and evidenced in writing.[6] Some resulting trusts will be included, such as those arising where a trustee continues to hold property after the exhaustion of express trusts[7] but it is far from clear whether other types of resulting trusts, even if later evidenced in writing, will be caught.[8] Trusts created by judicial decisions are not included, but Contracting States are free to extend the provisions of the Convention to such trusts.[9]

The Recognition of Trusts Act 1987 adopts the principles of the Convention. Although the Convention itself came into effect in 1992, and then only as between three States,[10] the Act applies to trusts regardless of the date on which they were created[11] but this does not affect the law to be applied to anything done or omitted before August 1, 1987.[12] Section 1(2) of the Act applies the Convention's provisions not only in relation to the trusts described in arts 2 and 3 but also in relation to any other trusts of property arising under the law of any part of the United Kingdom or by virtue of a judicial decision, whether in the United Kingdom or elsewhere.[13] The first of these extensions is in very general terms, and will include trusts created orally and never evidenced in writing, and trusts created by statute or under statutory powers[14]; the only requirement is that the trust must "arise under the law of" some part of the United Kingdom, a requirement which may prove unclear in some types of case. The second extension, to trusts created by judicial decisions, indicates no pre-requisites for the recognition of the decision in question. It was designed to enable the United Kingdom to meet its obligations under the Brussels Convention 1968, now replaced by the Brussels I Regulation.[15] In its operation in respect of decisions reached outside the Member States, the English courts will, it seems, require the decision to be capable of recognition in England under the applicable rules as to foreign judgments.

---

[4] See Hayton, (1987) 36 I.C.L.Q. 260 at 264.

[5] art.2(1). The last phrase will include charitable trusts and Scottish public purpose trusts.

[6] art.3.

[7] See von Overbeck, Explanatory Report, para.51.

[8] cf. Hayton, (1987) 36 I.C.L.Q. 260 at 263–264.

[9] art.20, not reproduced in the 1987 Act.

[10] Australia, Italy and the United Kingdom. There are now 12 Contracting States.

[11] art.22.

[12] Recognition of Trusts Act 1987 s.1(5). The position resulting from a combination of this provision and art.22 was described with some restraint as "obscure" in *Armenian Patriarch of Jerusalem v Sonsino* [2002] EWHC 1304.

[13] See Barnard, [1992] C.L.J. 474.

[14] See e.g. Law of Property Act 1925 ss.34–36 (co-ownership); Administration of Estates Act 1925 s.33 (trust for sale on intestacy), in each case as amended by Trusts of Land and Appointment of Trustees Act 1996.

[15] Brussels I Regulation, art.5(6) (action against settlor, trustee or beneficiary of a trust created by the operation of a statute, or by a written instrument, or created orally and evidenced in writing, in the courts of the member state in which the trust is domiciled); *Gómez v Gómez-Monche Vives* [2008] EWCA Civ 1065; [2009] Ch. 245; Harris, [2011] 14 Trusts and Trustees 236.

Some trusts, for example a trust created orally in the Irish Republic, fall outside **16–003** the scope of the Recognition of Trusts Act 1987. This does not mean that such trusts will be invalid or incapable of recognition. The principles applicable to trusts generally before the coming into force of the 1987 Act will continue to apply in such cases; the Act is consistent with what limited authority exists as to the position at common law,[16] and it is likely that the courts will seek to ensure that no inconsistencies develop in future.

There is an important distinction between questions relating to the settlement, will, or other instrument which operates inter alia to vest property in trustees and questions relating to the validity and operation of the trust provisions contained in it. In the negotiations at The Hague, delegates used the expression "rocket-launcher" for the former type of question, as opposed to the "rocket" of the trust itself. The Hague Convention, and so the 1987 Act, does not apply to what it styles "preliminary issues", those falling into the former category[17]; an English court will continue to deal with those issues under the existing rules of the conflict of laws. If in the case of a testamentary trust the testator had no capacity to make the will or the will is formally invalid or has been revoked, it will not be admitted to probate and any trust contained therein will fail. Similarly, a marriage contract or settlement may fail because of incapacity or invalidity in point of form. The essential validity of a gift of movables contained in a will is governed by the law of the testator's domicile at the time of his or her death[18]; that law will determine, e.g., whether the testator is free to deal in the will with the whole of his or her estate or whether a testator's powers are limited by a rule that a fixed proportion of the property must go to the spouse and children.[19] A will of movables or immovables will be interpreted in accordance with the law intended by the testator, which in the absence of any indication to the contrary, is presumed to be the law of the testator's domicile at the time the will is made.

THE GOVERNING LAW

Articles 6 and 7 of the Hague Convention, as given effect by the Recognition of **16–004** Trusts Act 1987, contain two rules as to the law governing the validity, construction, effects and administration of a trust. The primary rule[20] is that a trust is governed by the law chosen by the settlor. The choice must either be express or be implied in the terms of the instrument creating or the writing evidencing the trust interpreted, if necessary, in the light of the circumstances of the case.[21] There is no doubt that at common law a settlor was able to select the

---

[16] *Att-Gen v Campbell* (1872) L.R. 5 H.L. 524; *Duke of Marlborough v Att-Gen (No.1)* [1945] Ch. 78; *Iveagh v I.R. C.* [1954] Ch. 364; *Chellaram v Chellaram* [1985] Ch. 409. See Evans, (1986) 102 L.Q.R. 28; Wallace, (1987) 36 I.C.L.Q. 454.

[17] art.4.

[18] See para.15–026.

[19] *Thornton v Curling* (1824) 8 Sim. 310; *Re Annesley* [1926] Ch. 692; *Re Ross* [1930] 1 Ch.377; *Re Adams* [1967] I.R. 424.

[20] art.6. For change of the governing law, see art.10 and para.16–005, below.

[21] It is only when determining whether there is an *implied* choice that resort may be had to the circumstances of the case: *Tod v Barton* [2002] EWHC Ch. 264 at para.[33].

governing law of a trust.[22] A testator or settlor domiciled in England is free to set up a trust governed by some foreign law, and conversely such a person domiciled in a foreign country may establish an English trust.[23]

If the settlor makes no choice of the governing law, or selects some law which does not provide for trusts or the category of trust involved,[24] the secondary rule applies. This is that the trust is governed by the law with which it is most closely connected.[25] The same rule appears to apply at common law.[26] In cases within the 1987 Act, the ascertainment of the law with which a trust is most closely connected involves making reference in particular to four factors:

(a)   the place of administration of the trust designated by the settlor;
(b)   the *situs* of the assets of the trust;
(c)   the place of residence or business of the trustee; and
(d)   the objects of the trust and the places where they are to be fulfilled.[27]

16–005   There is among these factors "a certain implicit hierarchy",[28] but also a considerable overlap as (a) and (c) will usually coincide. Although not expressly stated in the Hague Convention, it is clear from other provisions of the Convention[29] that these factors are to be considered as at the moment of creation of the trust.[30]

Despite the identification of the four factors, the court must carry out a careful examination of all the circumstances. For example, in *Chellaram v Chellaram*,[31] a case decided before the Act, the settlor and beneficiaries were all domiciled in India. However, the parties were found to have contemplated that the trust would be administered in England; the assets of the trust were shares in a holding company in Bermuda, the underlying assets being in 12 countries (none of which was India); the trustees were either ordinarily resident in, or closely connected with, England; and the purpose of the whole arrangement was to avoid Indian taxation and exchange control regulations. The court was not required to resolve the question as to whether the proper law was Indian or English, a question which would be made no easier by the guidance in the 1987 Act: the factors there set out

---

[22]   See *Este v Smyth* (1854) 18 Beav. 112 at 122; *Re Hernando* (1884) 27 Ch.D. 284 at 292–293; *Re Fitzgerald* [1904] 1 Ch. 573 at 587.
[23]   See e.g. *Att-Gen v Campbell* (1872) L.R. 5 H.L. 524. cf. *Mayor of Canterbury v Wyburn* [1895] A.C. 89. See *Re Pollak's Estate* [1937] T.P.D. 91, as explained in *Chellaram v Chellaram* [1985] Ch. 409 at 431–432.
[24]   See art.6(2).
[25]   art.7(1). As Harris observes, the choice of law rules have more in common with those for contracts than property: see Fawcett (ed.), *op. cit.*, 187.
[26]   *Duke of Marlborough v Att-Gen (No.1)* [1945] Ch.78 at 83; *Iveagh v I.R.C.* [1954] Ch. 364; *Chellaram v Chellaram* [1985] Ch. 409.
[27]   art.7(2).
[28]   von Overbeck, Explanatory Report, p.386.
[29]   See art.10 dealing inter alia with changes in the governing law.
[30]   cf. von Overbeck, Explanatory Report, p.387. cf. *Chellaram v Chellaram (No.2)* [2002] EWHC 632 (Ch); [2002] 3 All E.R. 17: for jurisdictional purposes, the applicable law falls to be determined at the date of the proceedings.
[31]   [1985] Ch. 409. See also *Armenian Patriarch of Jerusalem v Sonsino* [2002] EWHC 1304.

will be taken into account in cases not falling within the Act.[32] Other factors, also relied on in the cases at common law[33] can also be weighed in applying art.7. These will include the domicile of the settlor, especially if the trust is created by a will or a marriage settlement,[34] the legal style of the trust instrument, the domicile of the beneficiaries, and the place of execution of the trust deed.

The weight to be given to all these factors, whether or not listed in art.7, must vary with the circumstances. The *situs* of the assets of the trust may deserve little weight: the movables included in a trust are usually intangible, e.g., stocks, shares and bonds; and the *situs* of an intangible movable is a fiction. The place where a trust deed is executed may not be sufficiently related to the substance of the transaction; it may be fortuitous, or worse still, carefully contrived so as to take advantage of a favourable law.   **16–006**

Article 5 of the Convention provides that the Convention does not apply to the extent that the law specified by Chapter II as the applicable law does not provide for trusts or the category of trusts involved. This provision, as given effect in the 1987 Act, seems not to have been considered by an English court. If the Convention does not apply for the reason stated, recourse would be had to the common law. Whether a court applying the common law to identify the governing law would have regard to the fact that one possibly applicable law did not provide for trusts is an unresolved question.[35]

The freedom of choice given to the settlor is qualified by art.18 which allows the provisions of the Convention to be disregarded when their application would be manifestly incompatible with public policy. At common law, it seems that the settlor's freedom of choice might similarly be subject to the requirements of English public policy; for example, an English court would presumably not allow a settlor creating an essentially English trust to evade the English rule against perpetuities by selecting, as the proper law of the trust, the law of some foreign country where the rule does not apply.[36]

SCOPE OF THE GOVERNING LAW

he law identified by arts 6 or 7 of the Convention governs the validity of the trust, its construction, its effects, and the administration of the trust.[37] In particular it governs: **16–007**

---

[32] In *Chellaram v Chellaram (No.2)* [2002] EWHC Ch. 632; [2002] 3 All E.R. 17 at paras [164]–[167], Lawrence Collins J. considered it "likely" that Indian law governed. See also *Martin v Secretary of State or Work and Pensions* [2009] EWCA Civ 1289.

[33] See the analysis by Wallace, (1987) 36 I.C.L.Q. 454 at 468 469.

[34] See especially *Iveagh v I.R.C.* [1954] Ch. 364 (domicile of settlor and beneficiaries decisive, despite execution of settlement and location of assets in England).

[35] See *Berezovsky v Abramovich* [2011] EWCA Civ 153 at [108]ff.

[36] See also art.13, which is not included in the text as given effect by the 1987 Act. It provides that no state is bound to recognise a trust the significant elements of which (except for the choice of the applicable law) i.e., the place of administration and the habitual residence of the trustee, are more closely connected with states which do not have the institution of the trust or the category of trust involved.

[37] art.8(1).

the appointment, resignation and removal of trustees, the capacity to act as a trustee, and the devolution of the office of trustee;

the rights and duties of trustees among themselves;

the right of trustees to delegate in whole or in part the discharge of their duties or the exercise of their powers;

the power of trustees to administer or to dispose of trust assets, to create security interests in the trust assets, or to acquire new assets;

the powers of investment of trustees;

restrictions upon the duration of the trust, and upon the power to accumulate the income of the trust;

16–008   the relationships between the trustees and the beneficiaries including the personal liability of the trustees to the beneficiaries;

the variation or termination of the trust;

the distribution of the trust assets; and

the duty of trustees to account for their administration.[38]

So far as the appointment of trustees is concerned, there is no legal bar to the appointment of trustees resident abroad as trustees of an English trust: but such an appointment is improper except in exceptional circumstances, e.g., where all the beneficiaries have become resident in the foreign country concerned.[39] On the other hand there is no power to appoint the English Public Trustee as trustee of a foreign trust, even though all the beneficiaries are domiciled and resident in England, the trust property is situated in England, and the trustees who wish to retire from the trust are all resident in England.[40]

16–009   It is desirable that a trust should be treated as a unit and that the trusts of all the property comprised therein should be governed by a single law. The fact that some of the property is movable and some immovable does not necessarily defeat this policy.

In *Re Fitzgerald*[41] the Court of Appeal held that a marriage settlement in Scottish form made by a lady domiciled in Scotland before her marriage to a domiciled Englishman was governed by Scots law. Most of the settled property (to the amount of £13,200) was invested in Scottish heritable bonds, i.e. in immovables; the only movable was a sum of £500 in cash. One reason given by Cozens-Hardy L.J. for holding that Scots law was the proper law was the following:

"It can scarcely be denied that the *lex loci* – i.e., the law of Scotland – must apply to the extent of the £13,000. There was £500 cash belonging to the lady which was paid over to the trustees for investment. It seems to me that this sum cannot fairly be treated as intended to be subject to a different law from that which is applicable to the bulk of the property".

---

[38] art.8(2).

[39] *Meinertzhagen v Davis* (1844) 1 Coll.N.C. 335; *Re Smith's Trusts* (1872) 20 W.R. 695; *Re Liddiard* (1880) 14 Ch.D. 310; *Re Whitehead's Trusts* [1971] 1 W.L.R. 833.

[40] *Re Hewitt's Settlement* [1915] 1 Ch. 228.

[41] [1904] 1 Ch. 573.

But if the trust property had consisted of £13,000 worth of movables and a cottage in England worth £500, the same reasoning inverted would have led to the conclusion that the land in England was subject to the same law as the movables, i.e., Scots law.

Similarly, it seems advisable to avoid a rigid distinction between the validity, interpretation and effect of a trust on the one hand and questions of "administration" on the other. It has sometimes been suggested that the latter should be governed by the law of the place of administration of the trust. Such a rigid distinction was rejected in *Chellaram v Chellaram*,[42] but as in the case of the manner of performance of a contract,[43] regard must be had to the law of the place of administration so far as the detailed procedures for the administration of the trust are concerned. In a similar context, it has been held that the English courts will not administer a foreign charity under the supervision of the court, nor will they settle a scheme for such a charity.[44] They may, however, authorise an application to the appropriate foreign court to frame such a scheme.[45] But if the foreign objects of an English charitable trust fail, the court will direct an application of the trust funds cy-près.[46]

16–010

The Hague Convention gives effect to these policies, but also admits the possibility of *depeçage*. Article 9 provides that a severable aspect of the trust, particularly matters of administration, may be governed by a different law. A deliberate choice by the settlor of two different laws to govern different issues or different types of property will therefore be respected.

Cases at common law before the 1987 Act established that the proper law of the trust governed the material or essential validity of the trust,[47] its interpretation,[48] and its effect, e.g. the question whether a beneficiary can alienate his or her interest in the trust and whether that interest can be reached by the beneficiary's creditors.[49]

RECOGNITION OF TRUSTS

The Recognition of Trusts Act 1987, despite its Short Title, is, like the Hague Convention to which it gives effect, primarily about the law applicable to trusts. Where a trust is valid under the governing law (and where no "preliminary issue" can be raised as to the validity of the will or trust instrument) its recognition necessarily follows. Article 11(1) of the Convention, which provides that a trust created in accordance with the law specified in the Convention must be recognised as a trust, is almost tautologous. However;

16–011

---

[42] [1985] Ch. 409.
[43] See para. 11-054.
[44] *Provost of Edinburgh v Aubrey* (1754) Ambler 256; *Att-Gen v Lepine* (1818) 2 Swanst. 181; *Emery v Hill* (1826) 1 Russ. 112; *New v Bonaker* (1867) L.R. 4 Eq. 655.
[45] *Re Fraser* (1883) 22 Ch.D. 827; *Re Marr's Will Trusts* [1936] Ch. 671.
[46] *Re Colonial Bishoprics Fund* [1935] Ch. 148.
[47] *Lindsay v Miller* [1949] V.L.R. 13; *Augustus v Permanent Trustee Co (Canberra) Ltd* (1971) 124 C.L.R. 245. cf. art.8(2)(f) for the similar position under the 1987 Act.
[48] *Perpetual Executors and Trustees Association of Australia Ltd v Roberts* [1970] V.R. 732; cf. art.8(1).
[49] *Re Fitzgerald* [1904] 1 Ch. 573; cf. art.8(1).

"judges of civil law countries . . . might stand perplexed before the pure and simple affirmation that a trust . . . should deploy effects in their countries . . . It is necessary that [the Convention should] indicate at least on the principal points, what recognition will consist of and what the effects will be that the trust will deploy".[50]

Accordingly, art.11 provides that recognition implies,

"as a minimum, that the trust property constitutes a separate fund, that the trustee may sue and be sued in his capacity as trustee, and that he may appear or act in this capacity before a notary or any person acting in an official capacity."

16–012   Further, in so far as the law applicable to the trust requires or provides, recognition implies in particular:

(a)   that personal creditors of the trustee can have no recourse against the trust assets;

(b)   that the trust assets do not form part of the trustee's estate upon his insolvency or bankruptcy;

(c)   that the trust assets do not form part of the matrimonial property of the trustee or his spouse nor part of the trustee's estate upon his death; and

(d)   that the trust assets may be recovered when the trustee, in breach of trust, has mingled trust assets with his own property or has alienated trust assets.

However, the rights and obligations of any third party holder of the assets remain subject to the law determined by the choice of law rules of the forum.[51] These provisions, like the description of the trust in art.2, concentrate on the position of the trustee, and deal less than satisfactorily with that of beneficiaries. In particular a beneficiary's right to trace trust assets is restricted, especially where the relevant assets are situated in a country the law of which does not have the concept of the trust.[52]

16–013   An important practical aspect of the recognition of trusts is the inclusion of trusts in registers of title, a matter of some difficulty in civil law countries. Article 12 seeks to facilitate such registration, but only in so far as this is not prohibited by, or inconsistent with, the law of the state where registration is sought.

The effect of art.11, and indeed of the Hague Convention as a whole, is qualified by the savings for mandatory rules in arts 15 and 16, of which the former is remarkable for the looseness of its drafting. It provides that the Convention "does not prevent" the application of the law designated by the conflicts rules of the forum, in so far as it cannot be derogated from by voluntary act, "relating in particular"[53] to various matters: the protection of minors and incapable parties; the personal and proprietary effects of marriage; succession rights, testate and intestate, especially the indefeasible shares of spouses and relatives; the transfer of title to property and security interests in property; the

---

[50]   von Overbeck, Explanatory Report, p.377.

[51]   art.11(2)(3). See Harris in Fawcett (ed.), *op. cit.*, at 196–197.

[52]   See Hayton, (1987) 36 I.C.L.Q. 260 at 275–276; Harris, (2002) 73 B.Y.B.I.L. 65.

[53]   The Court of Appeal emphasised in *Charalambous v Charalambous* [2004] EWCA Civ 1030; [2004] 2 F.C.R. 721 that "the liberation from Arts 6 and 8 which Art.15 provides" was not limited to the six specified cases.

protection of creditors in matters of insolvency; and the protection, in other respects, of third parties acting in good faith.[54]

If recognition of a trust is prevented by the application of art.15, the court is directed to try to give effect to the objects of the trust by other means.[55] Article 16 similarly protects the mandatory rules of the forum.

VARIATION OF TRUSTS

Under s.1(1) of the Variation of Trusts Act 1958, the High Court or a county court[56] has power to approve any arrangement varying or revoking all or any of the trusts on which the property is held under any will, settlement or other disposition. In cases decided before the Recognition of Trusts Act 1987 it was held that this jurisdiction was unlimited, applying even to trusts governed by a foreign law[57] but that an English court would hesitate before exercising its jurisdiction in such cases.[58] In cases within the Recognition of Trusts Act 1987, the variation of trusts is one of the matters governed by the law identified by arts 6 or 7 as the law governing the trust.[59] This is a choice of law rule and does not directly affect the jurisdiction of the English courts, but it may make it more likely that an English court would disclaim the exercise of jurisdiction, treating the courts of the relevant foreign country as a more appropriate forum. Such an approach was expressly contemplated in *Re Pagets Settlement*.[60] There Cross J., while accepting that he had jurisdiction to vary a settlement assumed to be governed by the law of New York, said:

16–014

> "Where there are substantial foreign elements in the case, the court must consider carefully whether it is proper for it to exercise the jurisdiction. If, for example, the court were asked to vary a settlement which was plainly a Scottish settlement, it might well hesitate to exercise its jurisdiction to vary the trusts, simply because some of, or even all, the trustees and beneficiaries were in this country. It may well be that the judge would say that the Court of Session was the appropriate tribunal to deal with the case".

It is important that the power of a divorce court to vary a settlement made by the parties to a marriage, under s.24 of the Matrimonial Causes Act 1973 after granting a decree, and under s.17 of the Matrimonial and Family Proceedings Act 1984 after a foreign decree, should be exercised in accordance with the English *lex fori* as part of the whole range of powers exercisable in those contexts. The Recognition of Trusts Act 1987 does not affect that position.[61]

16–015

The law applicable to the validity of the trust determines whether that law, or the law governing a severable aspect of the trust, may be replaced by another

---

[54] art.15(1).

[55] art.15(2).

[56] County Courts Act 1984 s.23(b).

[57] *Re Ker's Settlement* [1963] Ch. 553.

[58] *Re Paget's Settlement* [1965] 1 W.L.R. 1046; *Mubarak v Mubarak* [2007] EWHC 220 (Fam); [2007] 2 F.L.R. 364.

[59] Hague Convention, art.8(2)(h).

[60] [1965] 1 W.L.R. 1046 at p.1050.

[61] *Charalambous v Charalambous* [2004] EWCA Civ 1030; [2004] 2 F.C.R. 721 (noted Harris, (2005) 121 L.Q.R. 16), applying the principle in art.15.

law.[62] The governing law may be changed by the court on an application under the Variation of Trusts Act 1958. In *Re Seale's Marriage Settlement*[63] it was held that the court has power under the Variation of Trusts Act 1958 to approve an arrangement revoking the trusts of an English settlement, substituting the trusts of a foreign settlement and appointing a foreign trustee. In that case the husband and wife and their children had all emigrated to Canada many years before the application was made to the court. But in *Re Weston's Settlements,*[64] the Court of Appeal refused to approve a similar arrangement where the settlor and his two sons (on whom the settlements in question had been made) emigrated from England to Jersey a bare three months before the application was made. Although the parties' evidence that they intended to remain permanently in Jersey was uncontradicted, the court obviously disbelieved it: the application was "an essay in tax avoidance naked and unashamed".

16–016   In that case it appeared that there was no Trustee Act in force in Jersey and that the courts there had never made an order executing the trusts of a settlement, though there was also evidence that they would probably do so if required. But the inexperience of the Jersey courts in matters of trusts does not prevent the English court from approving a revocation of an English settlement and the substitution of a Jersey settlement in a proper case. Thus in *Re Windeatt*[64] the court made such an order. It distinguished *Re Weston's Settlements* on the ground that the life tenant had been living in Jersey for nineteen years before the application was made, that she was probably domiciled there, and that her children were born there.

The powers of the court to vary trusts under the Matrimonial Causes Act 1973 and the Variation of Trusts Act 1958 extend to trusts of immovables as well as to trusts of movables.

THE EUROPEAN REGULATIONS

16–017   The Rome I Regulation on the law applicable to contractual obligations[65] does not apply to the constitution of trusts or the relationship between settlors, trustees and beneficiaries.[66] The Rome II Regulation on the law applicable to non-contractual obligations[67] is prima facie of greater relevance. In that Regulation there is also an exclusion dealing with trusts, but it is in qualified terms: "non-contractual obligations arising out of the relations between the settlers, trustees and beneficiaries of a trust created voluntarily".[68] It will be recalled that the scope of the Hague Convention is limited to trusts created voluntarily and evidenced in writing,[69] and the earlier discussion of the effect of that provision is equally applicable to the Rome II Regulation exclusion. The

---

[62] Hague Convention, art.10.
[63] [1961] Ch. 574.
[64] [1969] 1 Ch. 223.
[65] European Parliament and Council Regulation 593/2008, [2008] O.J. L177 at p.6.
[66] Rome I Regulation, art.1(2)(h).
[67] European Parliament and Council Regulation No.864/2007, [2007] O.J. L 199 at p.40.
[68] Rome II Regulation, art.1(2)(e).
[69] art.3.

intention is clearly that where the Convention applies, it prevails over the Regulation, and art.28(1) of the Regulation gives effect to that intention. However, the Recognition of Trusts Act 1987, as we have seen, has a scope wider than that of the Convention and goes beyond even the extension to trusts created by judicial decision, an extension expressly allowed by the Convention.[70] There are therefore some trusts within the 1987 Act but beyond the scope of the Convention to which the Rome II Regulation will apply. The courts have yet to grapple with the implications of this awkward conclusion.

---

[70] Convention, art.20.

THE CONDUCT OF INTERNATIONAL LITIGATION

This Chapter is concerned with some of the processes involved in a cross-border, **17–001** and so a conflicts, case. It describes an important part of the context within which conflicts issues arise, although of course many cases that raise issues in the conflict of laws do not lead to litigation.

SUBSTANCE AND PROCEDURE

There is an important rule, found in all systems of the conflict of laws, that all **17–002** matters of procedure are governed exclusively by the law of the court seised of the case, the *lex fori*. Every legal system has its own ways of dealing with cases, for example in settling which judges sit to hear the case and how far the procedure is oral as opposed to written. It would be quite impracticable to have different kinds of process for cases containing foreign elements and for purely domestic cases. This means that an English court will apply to a case containing foreign elements any rule of English law which, in its view, is procedural, and will refuse to apply any rule of foreign law which, in its view, is procedural. That needs to be balanced by a loyal application of foreign law insofar as it governs the substance of the case as the *lex causae*.

That principle is well established but the line between substance and procedure is a difficult one to draw. It is of course a question of characterisation; and we shall see how controversial that doctrine is.[1] At one time it was possible to say that "English lawyers give the widest possible extension to the meaning of the term 'procedure'".[2] The risk inherent in this approach was that it might well defeat the whole object of the conflict of laws by denying a remedy where one

---

[1] Below, para.18–002.
[2] Dicey, 1st edn (1896) at p.712.

should exist or, conversely, by allowing claims which should be rejected. Academic writing and the development of European Union law have done much to change the approach.[3]

17–003 In principle, the line between substance and procedure should be drawn with some regard for the reason for drawing it. Cook[4] suggested as a practical test: "How far can the court of the forum go in applying the rules taken from the foreign system of law without unduly hindering or inconveniencing itself?" Cook also pointed out that the line between substance and procedure may have to be drawn in one place for the purposes of the conflict of laws and in another place in other contexts, e.g., for the purpose of the rule that statutes affecting procedure are, but statutes affecting substance are not, presumed to have retrospective effect. This is not to say that the distinction may not be drawn in the same place for many purposes: it is merely to deny that it must necessarily be drawn in the same place for all purposes.

The primary object of the rule that procedural matters are governed by the *lex fori* is to obviate the inconvenience of conducting the trial of a case containing foreign elements in a manner with which the court is unfamiliar, and which may indeed simply be impracticable given other features of local practice. If, therefore, it is possible to apply a foreign rule, or to refrain from applying an English rule, without running into that sort of difficulty, those rules should not necessarily be characterised as procedural for the purposes of the conflict of laws.

One effect of European legal developments on English practice has been to shift the balance between substance and procedure at a number of points. The process began with the Rome Convention given effect in England by the Contracts (Applicable Law) Act 1990, which applied the law governing the contract to cover some issues which at common law would be matters of procedure governed by the *lex fori*; the resulting position is maintained in the Rome I Regulation. In the context of non-contractual obligations, there are similar rules in the Rome II Regulation. Their effect is noted at the relevant points in the discussion which follows.

PARTIES

17–004 Earlier editions of this book contained the general proposition that it is for the *lex fori* to determine who are the proper parties to proceedings. Such a general proposition can no longer be sustained, as many issues related to the identity of the proper parties will fall to be decided by reference to some other law.

So, where the issue is whether a potential party has legal personality, the English court will accept the view of the law of the country in which the entity is established. A business association created under Swiss law and having legal personality under that law (though as a partnership it would not have such

---

[3] See Carruthers, (2004) 53 I.C.L.Q. 691.
[4] Cook, *Logical and Legal Bases of the Conflict of Laws* (Harvard University Press: Cambridge MA, 1942), p.166.

personality in English law) has been held entitled to sue in England.[5] A rather more surprising example is that of an Indian temple, also held to be a competent claimant.[6]

In many contexts, the question of the identity of the proper parties cannot be distinguished from the underlying question of liability, who is liable to whom, which is clearly governed by the *lex causae*, the law governing the relevant contract, tort or other claim. The Rome II Regulation spells this out in the context of non-contractual obligations: the law applicable under the Regulation governs the determination of persons who may be held liable for acts performed by them[7]; the question whether a right to claim damages or a remedy may be transferred, including by inheritance[8]; persons entitled to compensation for damage sustained personally[9]; and liability for the acts of another person.[10]

There remain, however, some issues as to the proper parties which are merely procedural and so a matter for the *lex fori*. That law determines who may take steps as an administrator of an estate of a deceased person, foreign-appointed representatives not being recognised for this purpose.[11] A similar question is whether the person sued is the proper defendant to the action. In some foreign systems of law a defendant cannot be sued unless and until some other person has been sued first. For instance, in some foreign systems a creditor cannot sue an individual partner without first suing the firm and exhausting its assets, or cannot sue a surety without first suing the principal debtor. Such rules are in sharp contrast to the rule of English law that any partner may be sued alone for the whole of the partnership debts, and that a surety may be sued without joining the principal debtor. Even under the Rome II Regulation it seems that the question is whether such a rule of foreign law is substantive or procedural. If the *lex causae* regards the defendant as under no liability whatever unless other persons are sued first, the rule is substantive and must be applied in English proceedings; the Regulation governs the determination of persons who may be held liable for acts performed by them.[12] If on the other hand the *lex causae* regards the defendant as liable, but makes the defendant's liability conditional on other persons being sued first, then the rule is procedural and is ignored in English proceedings.[13]

17–005

[5] *Oxnard Financing S.A. v Rahn* [1998] 1 W.L.R. 1465.
[6] *Bumper Development Corp v Commissioner of Police for the Metropolis* [1991] 1 W.L.R. 1362.
[7] art.15(a).
[8] art.15(e).
[9] art.15(f).
[10] art.15(g). See Schoeman, [2010] L.M.C.L.Q. 81.
[11] See *Kamouh v Associated Electrical Industries International Ltd* [1980] Q.B. 199 (where the same approach was applied to the administration of an absentee's property).
[12] art.15(a). See the common law cases of *General Steam Navigation Co v Guillou* (1843) 11 M. & W. 877 and *The Mary Moxham* (1876) 1 P.D. 107.
[13] *General Steam Navigation Co v Guillou*, above; *Bullock v Caird* (1875) L.R. 10 Q.B. 276; *Re Doetsch* [1896] 2 Ch. 836; *Subbotovsky v Waung* [1968] 3 N.S.W.R. 261, affirmed on other grounds, *ibid.*, at p.499. This rule is criticised by Wolff, *Private International Law*, 2nd edn (Oxford: Clarendon Press, 1950), p.240.

SERVICE OF PROCESS

17–006   Where proceedings are commenced in the English courts, it is for English law as the *lex fori* to determine whether there has been good service of the claim form. The law of the country in which service is to be effected cannot, however, be ignored. The law of any state may properly exercise control over actions taking place on its territory. States in the civil law tradition tend to see service of process as an exercise of the judicial power of a state, and are reluctant to permit within their borders an expression of the sovereignty of another state. For example, in Switzerland service on behalf of the claimant of foreign process without the permission of the Swiss authorities is an offence.[14]

Rule 6.40(4) of the Civil Procedure Rules provides that "Nothing in [the relevant rule, r.6.40(3)] or in any court order authorises or requires any person to do anything which is contrary to the law of the country where the claim form or other document is to be served". If service is effected in a way that contravenes this principle, the English court does have a discretion nonetheless to allow service to stand, but will do so only in "a very strong case", for example where there was an express representation by the defendant that the method of service adopted was lawful.[15] In 'truly exceptional cases' the English court may achieve the same result by dispensing with service.[16]

Official assistance may be available in the service of process, either under a bilateral Civil Procedure Convention between the United Kingdom and the country in which service is to be effected, or the Hague Convention on the service abroad of judicial and extra-judicial documents of 1965.[17] Within the European Union, Parliament and Council Regulation 1393/2007 of 13 November 2007 deals with the service in the Member States of judicial and extrajudicial documents in civil or commercial matters.[18] It provides a mechanism for service via transmitting and receiving agencies in each Member State and governs whether the method of service is valid and when service took place.[19]

MAREVA OR FREEZING INJUNCTIONS

17–007   A freezing injunction is one restraining a defendant from dealing with or disposing of or removing from the jurisdiction any or all of his assets, to prevent their dissipation. It takes the name by which is commonly known from one of the first cases in which such an injunction was granted, *Mareva Compania Naviera*

---

[14] *Ferrarini SpA v Magnol Shipping Co Inc., The Sky One* [1988] 1 Lloyd's Rep 238; and see *Bentinck v Bentinck* [2007] EWCA Civ 175; [2007] 2 F.L.R. 1.

[15] *Ferrarini SpA v Magnol Shipping Co Inc., The Sky One* [1988] 1 Lloyd's Rep 238.

[16] C.P.R., r. 6.16. See *Phillips v Symes (No. 3)* [2008] UKHL 1, *sub nom Phillips v Nussberger* [2008] 1 W.L.R. 180 (essential document omitted by misunderstanding from a bundle of documents served in Switzerland); *Olafsson v Gissurarson (No 2)* [2008] EWCA Civ 152; [2008] 1 W.L.R. 2016 (personal service in Iceland; Icelandic law was not complied with as addressee not asked to sign a receipt for the documents).

[17] See McClean, *International Co-operation in Civil and Commercial Matters*, 3rd edn, (Oxford: Oxford University Press, 2012).

[18] For text see OJ L 324/79, 10.12.2007. It replaced an earlier Regulation (SI 1348/2000) which was in turn based on a draft Convention signed in 1997 but never in force.

[19] *Tavoulareas v Tsavliris* [2004] EWCA Civ 48, [2004] 1 Lloyd's Rep 445.

S.A. v International Bulkcarriers S.A.[20] The purpose of the injunction is to prevent a potential defendant from thwarting the claimant's plans by moving assets from one country to another. As part of English procedural law, the power to grant such injunctions applies to many cases where the *lex causae* and the primary jurisdiction is that of a foreign country.

It was once the case that a freezing injunction could not be granted unless the English court had jurisdiction over the merits of the case.[21] This limitation was removed by statutory intervention, first by s.25(1) of the Civil Jurisdiction and Judgments Act 1982 which enabled the High Court to grant interim relief where proceedings had been or were to be commenced in a Contracting State to the Brussels or the Lugano Convention. This provision was extended in 1997 to apply to proceedings commenced or to be commenced in any country.[22]

Similarly, it was thought at one time that a freezing injunction was a remedy only available against foreign defendants, perhaps because in such cases the risk of assets being removed was usually greater and more obvious.[23] It was however accepted by the Court of Appeal in 1980 that an injunction could properly be granted even if the defendant was based in England if in the circumstances there was a danger of the assets being removed,[24] and this was put beyond doubt by s.37(3) of the Senior Courts (formerly Supreme Court Act) 1981.

Again, the Court of Appeal formerly held that an injunction had to be limited to **17–008** the assets of the defendant within the jurisdiction of the court,[25] but since 1989 the courts have made "worldwide" freezing injunctions.[26] The terms of a worldwide injunction do however provide that it applies only to a limited class of persons outside the jurisdiction and does not, in respect of assets located outside the jurisdiction,

> "prevent any third party from complying with what it reasonably believes to be its obligations, contractual or otherwise, under the laws and obligations of the country or state in which those assets are situated or under the proper law of any contract between itself and the Respondent; and any orders of the courts of that country or state, provided that reasonable notice of any application for such an order is given to the Applicant's solicitors".[27]

The Court of Appeal has set out five considerations which the court should bear in mind, when considering the question whether it is inexpedient to make an order[28]:

---

[20] [1975] 2 Lloyd's Rep. 509. For the history, see McClean (1996) 260 Hague *Receuil des cours* 22–35.

[21] *Siskina v Distos Compania Naviera S.A.* [1979] A.C. 210. See *Mercedes Benz A.G. v Leiduck* [1996] A.C. 284.

[22] SI 1997/302.

[23] This was the explanation offered by Megarry V.C. in *Barclay-Johnson v Yuill* [1980] 1 W.L.R. 1259.

[24] *Prince Abdul Rahman Bin Turki Al Sudairy v Abu Taha* [1980] 1 W.L.R. 1268.

[25] *Ashtiani v Kashi* [1987] Q.B. 888.

[26] *Babanaft International C. S.A. v Bassatne* [1990] Ch. 13; *Republic of Haiti v Duvalier* [1990] Q.B. 202; *Derby & Co Ltd v Weldon (No.1)* [1990] Ch. 48.

[27] C.P.R. Practice Direction 25A, Annex, para 20.

[28] *Motorola Credit Corp v Uzan* [2003] EWCA Civ 752; [2004] 1 W.L.R. 113.

17–009 Firstly, whether the making of the order will interfere with the management of the case in the primary court, e.g. where the order is inconsistent with an order in the primary court or overlaps with it. Secondly, whether it is the policy in the primary jurisdiction not itself to make worldwide freezing/disclosure orders. Thirdly, whether there is a danger that the orders made will give rise to disharmony or confusion and/or risk of conflicting inconsistent or overlapping orders in other jurisdictions, in particular the courts of the state where the person enjoined resides or where the assets affected are located. If so, then respect for the territorial jurisdiction of that state should discourage the English court from using its unusually wide powers against a foreign defendant. Fourthly, whether at the time the order is sought there is likely to be a potential conflict as to jurisdiction, rendering it inappropriate and inexpedient to make a worldwide order. Fifthly, whether, in a case where jurisdiction is resisted and disobedience to be expected, the court will be making an order which it cannot enforce.

A worldwide freezing order will usually contain an undertaking by the party who obtained the order not to seek to enforce it in another jurisdiction without the permission of the court.[29]

EVIDENCE

17–010 "The law of evidence", said Lord Brougham, "is the *lex fori* which governs the courts. Whether a witness is competent or not; whether a certain matter requires to be proved by writing or not; whether certain evidence proves a certain fact or not; that is to be determined by the law of the country where the question arises, and where the court sits to enforce it".[30] On the other hand,

> "it is not everything that appears in a treatise on the law of evidence that is to be classified internationally as adjective law, but only provisions of a technical or procedural character for instance, rules as to the admissibility of hearsay evidence or what matters may be noticed judicially."[31]

Thus, the *lex causae* generally determines what are the facts in issue[32]; and it may do so by providing that no evidence need, or may, be given as to certain matters, for instance as to compliance, or failure to comply, with certain formalities of a marriage ceremony. Such provisions are substantive.[33] On the other hand the *lex fori* determines how the facts in issue must be proved.

To this last principle there are important exceptions. Article 18 of the Rome I Regulation provides that the law governing a contractual obligation under the Regulation applies to the extent that, in matters of contractual obligations, it contains rules which raise presumptions of law or determine the burden of proof. A contract or an act intended to have legal effect may be proved by any mode of proof recognised by the law of the forum or by any of the laws referred to in

---

[29] For the considerations governing the grant of permission, see *Dadourian Group International Inc v Simms* [2006] EWCA Civ 399; [2006] 1 W.L.R. 2499.

[30] *Bain v Whitehaven and Furness Rly* (1850) 3 H.L.C. 1 at 19.

[31] *Mahadervan v Mahadervan* [1964] P. 233 at 243, per Simon P.

[32] *The Gaetano and Maria* (1882) 7 P.D. 137.

[33] *Mahadervan v Mahadervan*, above.

art.11 of the Regulation under which that contract or act is formally valid, provided that such mode of proof can be administered by the forum. Similar provisions are found in the Rome II Regulation dealing with non-contractual obligations.[34]

Admissibility

Questions as to the admissibility of evidence are decided in accordance with the **17–011** *lex fori*.[35] Thus a document may be received in evidence by the English court although it is inadmissible by the *lex causae*.[36] Conversely, copies of foreign documents admissible by the *lex causae* are only admissible in England if they comply with English law as to the admissibility of copies.[37]

A distinction has been drawn between extrinsic evidence adduced to interpret a written document, e.g., a contract, and extrinsic evidence adduced to add to, vary or contradict its terms. The admissibility of the former is a question of interpretation, governed by the law applicable to the contract; the Rome I Regulation affirms this principle in cases to which it applies.[38] The admissibility of the latter is, subject to the exceptions in the Rome I Regulation, a question of evidence governed by the *lex fori*.[39] Thus in *St Pierre v South American Stores Ltd*[40] a question arose as to the meaning of the covenant to pay rent contained in a lease of land in Chile and governed by Chilean law. It was held that evidence of negotiations prior to the contract and of subsequent writings was admissible, although it was inadmissible by English law. On the other hand, in *Korner v Witkowitzer*[41] the plaintiff sued to recover arrears of pension due under a contract governed by Czech law. In order to obtain leave to serve notice of the writ out of the jurisdiction he had to prove that the contract was broken in England. It was held that evidence of an oral agreement whereby the plaintiff was to receive his pension in the country in which he might be living when it accrued was inadmissible, since this would be to vary the terms of the written agreement.

---

[34] art.22.

[35] *Yates v Thompson* (1835) 3 Cl. & F. 544; *Bain v Whitehaven and Furness Ry.* (1850) 3 H.L.C. 1.

[36] *Bristow v Sequeville* (1850) 5 Exch. 275.

[37] *Brown v Thornton* (1837) 6 Ad. & El. 185. For an exception, see the Evidence (Foreign, Dominion and Colonial Documents) Act 1933, as amended by s.5 of the Oaths and Evidence (Overseas Authorities and Countries) Act 1963 (Orders in Council may provide for admissibility of official and properly authenticated copies of foreign public registers).

[38] Rome I Regulation, art.12(1)(a); (at common law:) *St. Pierre v South American Stores Ltd* [1937] 1 All E.R. 206, 209; affd. [1937] 3 All E.R. 349.

[39] *Korner v Witkowitzer* [1950] 2 K.B. 128 at 162–163; affirmed *sub nom. Vitkovice v Korner* [1951] A.C. 869.

[40] [1937] 1 All E.R. 206 at 209; affd. [1937] 3 All E.R. 349.

[41] [1950] 2 K.B. 128; affd. [1951] A.C. 869.

Requirement of written evidence

17–012 Section 4 of the Statute of Frauds 1677 provided that "no action shall be brought" on a number of contracts unless the agreement, or some note or memorandum thereof, was in writing. Section 4 now applies only to contracts of guarantee.[42] In the famous (or notorious) case of *Leroux v Brown*[43] it was held that s.4 contained a rule of procedure and therefore prevented the enforcement in England of an oral contract governed by French law which could have been sued upon in France. Although the decision has never been overruled,[44] it would seem to have been overtaken by the provisions in the Rome I Regulation already referred to. It deserves a mention because it illustrates how *not* to approach the distinction between substance and procedure. To characterise the section as procedural merely because it says "no action shall be brought" is to regard the form of the section as more important than its substance. To characterise it as procedural for the purposes of the conflict of laws, merely because it had previously been characterised as procedural for some purposes of English domestic law, is to lose sight of the purpose of the characterisation.

Witnesses

17–013 Whether a witness is competent or compellable appears to be a matter for the *lex fori*.[45] If the question depends, as it often does, on the matrimonial status of a witness (because for example a spouse may not be a compellable witness to testify against the other spouse), the question of status must be referred to the appropriate *lex causae* before the English rule of evidence can be applied.

Burden of proof

17–014 Subject once again to the far-reaching effect of the provisions in the Rome I and Rome II Regulations, it seems that in English law questions relating to the burden of proof are matters for the *lex fori*.[46] Yet there is much to be said for treating them as substantive, as the outcome of a case can depend on where the burden of proof lies. As Lorenzen says, "the statement that courts should enforce foreign substantive rights but not foreign procedural laws has no justifiable basis if the so-called procedural law would normally affect the outcome of the litigation".[47]

---

[42] Law Reform (Enforcement of Contracts) Act 1954 s.1.

[43] (1852) 12 C.B. 801.

[44] See *Irvani v G. and H. Montage GmbH* [1990] 1 W.L.R. 667 and the cases there discussed; the Statute of Frauds was ultimately held inapplicable on the facts.

[45] *Bain v Whitehaven and Furness Rly* (1850) 3 H.L.C. 1 at 19.

[46] *The Roberta* (1937) 58 Ll.L.Rep. 159 at 177; *In the Estate of Fuld (No.3)* [1968] P. 675 at 696–697.

[47] Lorenzen, *op. cit.*, p.134.

Presumptions

Presumptions are of three kinds: presumptions of fact, and rebuttable and **17–015** irrebuttable presumptions of law. Presumptions of fact arise when, on proof of certain basic facts, the trier of fact may, but need not, find the existence of a presumed fact. Presumptions of fact have, strictly speaking, no legal effect at all, and need not be considered here. So far as presumptions of law are concerned, the Rome I and Rome II Regulations provide that in the case of contractual and non-contractual obligations within the scope of the regulations, the law governing the obligation applies to the extent that it contains, in the substantive law as opposed to the law of procedure, rules which raise presumptions of law.[48] No distinction is drawn between presumptions of law which are rebuttable and those which are irrebuttable; the rule appears to apply to both categories.

That distinction does, however, need to be observed when considering the position at common law. Irrebuttable presumptions of law arise when, on proof of the basic facts, the trier of fact *must* find the presumed fact in any event. An example is the presumption of survivorship contained in s.184 of the Law of Property Act 1925. It is now generally agreed that, even for the purposes of domestic law, irrebuttable presumptions of law are rules of substance, and this is also true for the purposes of the conflict of laws.[49] Rebuttable presumptions of law arise when, on proof of the basic facts, the trier of fact must find the presumed fact unless the contrary is proved. For the purposes of the conflict of laws such presumptions must be divided into those which only apply in certain contexts, and those which apply in all types of case. Examples of the first type are the presumptions of resulting trust, advancement, satisfaction and ademption, and the presumptions contained in s.2 of the Perpetuities and Accumulations Act 1964 to the effect that a female under the age of 12 or over the age of 55 cannot have a child. All these are thought to be so closely connected with the existence of substantive rights that they ought to be characterised as rules of substance.

Examples of the second type of rebuttable presumptions are the presumptions of marriage, legitimacy,[50] and death. It is uncertain whether these presumptions are rules of substance or rules of procedure. In cases involving presumptions of marriage the courts have applied the *lex causae* whenever that law was proved[51]; and the most recent dictum on the subject treats such a presumption as a rule of substance.[52]

Obtaining evidence abroad[53]

In countries in the common law tradition the preparation of a case for trial is the **17–016** private responsibility of the parties. In contrast to this approach, many civil law countries view the obtaining of evidence as part of the judicial function, and the

---

[48] Rome I Regulation art.18(1); Rome II Regulation art.22(1).
[49] *Re Cohn* [1945] Ch. 5.
[50] Much weakened by s.26 of the Family Law Reform Act 1969.
[51] *Hill v Hibbit* (1871) 25 L.T. 183; *De Thoren v Att-Gen* (1876) 1 App.Cas. 686; *Re Shephard* [1904] 1 Ch. 456.
[52] *Mahadervan v Mahadervan* [1964] P. 233, 242.
[53] See McClean, *op. cit.*, Ch.3.

actions of agents of a foreign court may be seen as offending the sovereignty of the state in its judicial aspect. If evidence is to be obtained in such countries, official intervention will normally be required, though bilateral and multilateral civil procedure conventions may exist to regulate and simplify the procedures.

English law makes ample provision enabling parties to English proceedings to obtain evidence abroad. The powers given are exercised with the greatest discretion,[54] partly because of the sensitivities of other countries but also to avoid unnecessary expense, delay and inconvenience. The court acts under its general power to order depositions to be taken before an examiner, with appropriate disclosure of documents before the examination takes place.[55] The procedure usually adopted involves the issue of a Letter of Request to the judicial authorities of the foreign country asking the foreign court to take the required evidence or arrange for it to be taken.[56]

Increasing numbers of countries, including the United Kingdom, are parties to the Hague Convention on the Taking of Evidence Abroad in Civil and Commercial Matters 1970, which establishes clear procedures and improves the flow of information between Contracting States. Within the European Union, Council Regulation No. 1206/2001 of 28 May 2001 on cooperation between the courts of Member States in the taking of evidence in civil and commercial matters provides a procedure designed to ensure the swift production of evidence available in another Member State.

Obtaining evidence in England for use abroad

17–017 There is no objection in English law to the taking of evidence required for use in foreign proceedings without the intervention or permission of an English court or official agency. Such intervention will be required if measures of compulsion are required against an unwilling witness. However, the oath may only be administered in England with lawful authority. A person appointed by a court or other judicial authority of a foreign country does have power to administer oaths in the United Kingdom for the purpose of taking evidence in civil proceedings carried on under the law of that foreign country,[57] and a foreign diplomatic agent or consular officer has a general power to administer oaths in accordance with the law of the foreign country concerned.[58]

The High Court may order the taking of evidence in England at the request of a foreign court or tribunal under the Evidence (Proceedings in Other Jurisdictions) Act 1975. Although the Act was passed to enable the United Kingdom to ratify the Hague Convention on the Taking of Evidence Abroad in Civil and Commercial Matters 1970, it does not reproduce the provisions of the Convention. The Act is drafted so as to apply to all requests for assistance whether or not made under the Convention.

---

[54] *Settebello Ltd v Banco Totta & Acores* [1985] 1 W.L.R. 1050; *Charman v Charman* [2005] EWCA Civ 1606; [2006] 1 W.L.R. 1053; *Honda Giken Kogyou Kabushiki Kaisha v KJM Superbikes Ltd* [2007] EWCA Civ 313.
[55] C.P.R., r.34.8.
[56] C.P.R., r.34.13.
[57] Oaths and Evidence (Overseas Authorities and Countries) Act 1963 s.1.
[58] Consular Relations Act 1968 s.10(1).

When an application is made to the High Court under the Act, the court must be **17–018** satisfied that the evidence is to be obtained for the purposes of civil proceedings which have either been instituted before the requesting court or whose institution before that court is contemplated.[59] In this context "civil proceedings" means "proceedings in any civil or commercial matter".[60] Given that there is in this context no internationally acceptable definition of a "civil or commercial matter", the English court must satisfy itself that the proceedings concern a civil or commercial matter under the laws of both the requesting and requested countries.[61] For the purposes of English law, "proceedings in any civil matter" includes all proceedings other than criminal proceedings, and "proceedings in any commercial matter" fall within "proceedings in any civil matter". So far as the law of a requesting country is concerned, reference is to be made to the law and practice of that country, having regard to the manner in which classification is ordinarily made in that country.[62] In English law, fiscal matters are properly within the category of "civil and commercial", and a request by a foreign country for assistance in obtaining evidence to be used in the enforcement of the revenue law of that country in proceedings before the courts of that country, does not constitute direct or indirect enforcement of the revenue law of a foreign State.[63]

The English court may not order any steps to be taken unless they are steps which could be required to be taken by way of obtaining evidence for the purposes of English civil proceedings.[64] Where the foreign court seeks the disclosure of documents, there are clear limitations on what may be ordered. What is sought must be evidence, and not merely information which might suggest a line of enquiry leading to evidence: "fishing expeditions" are not allowed.[65] On a request for oral evidence to be taken, the test is whether there is good reason to believe that the intended witness has knowledge of matters in issue so as to be likely to be able to give evidence relevant to those issues.[66]

The Protection of Trading Interests Act 1980, which was enacted primarily in the context of hostility to the United States' anti-trust jurisdiction, provides that the English court must refuse to make an order in response to a foreign court's request if it is shown that the request infringes the jurisdiction of the United Kingdom or is otherwise prejudicial to the sovereignty of the United Kingdom. A certificate signed by or on behalf of the Secretary of State to the effect that the request is such an infringement or is so prejudicial is conclusive.[67]

The Secretary of State may also give directions for prohibiting compliance with **17–019** certain orders of foreign courts or authorities requiring any person in the United

---

[59] Evidence (Proceedings in Other Jurisdictions) Act 1975 s.1(b).
[60] Evidence (Proceedings in Other Jurisdictions) Act 1975 s.9(1).
[61] *Re State of Norway's Application (Nos 1 and 2)* [1990] 1 A.C. 723, where the history of UK legislation since the Foreign Tribunals Evidence Act 1857 is examined. See Mann, (1989) 105 L.Q.R. 341.
[62] *Re State of Norway's Application (Nos 1 and 2)* [1990] 1 A.C. 723.
[63] *Re State of Norway's Application (Nos 1 and 2)* [1990] 1 A.C. 723.
[64] Evidence (Proceedings in Other Jurisdictions) Act 1975 s.2(3).
[65] Evidence (Proceedings in Other Jurisdictions) Act 1975 s. 2(4); *Re State of Norway's Application (Nos. 1 and 2)* [1990] 1 A.C. 723.
[66] *First American Corp v Sheikh Zayed Al-Nahyan* [1999] 1 W.L.R. 1154.
[67] Protection of Trading Interests Act 1980 s.4.

Kingdom to produce any commercial document not within the territorial jurisdiction of the foreign country, or to provide commercial information compiled from such documents, or to publish any such document or information.[68] A direction may be given if it appears to the Secretary of State that a requirement infringes the jurisdiction of the United Kingdom or is otherwise prejudicial to the sovereignty of the United Kingdom, or if compliance with it would be prejudicial to the security or foreign relations of the United Kingdom.[69]

NATURE OF THE CLAIMANT'S REMEDY

17–020   At common law, the nature of the remedy is a matter of procedure to be determined by the *lex fori*. Thus if the claimant is by the *lex causae* entitled only to damages but is by English law entitled to specific relief, e.g., specific performance or an injunction, that type of remedy is available in England.[70] Conversely, an English court will not grant specific relief where to do so is contrary to the principles of English law.[71]

Although an action in England will not fail merely because the claim is unknown to English law, it will fail if English law has no appropriate remedy for giving effect to the plaintiff's alleged foreign right. Thus in *Phrantzes v Argenti*[72]:

> A Greek daughter who had just been married claimed that by Greek law her father was under an obligation to provide her with a dowry. Her claim failed, not because it was unknown to English law, but because by Greek law the amount of the dowry was within the discretion of the court and varied in accordance with the wealth and social position of the father and the number of his children, and with the behaviour of the daughter. The English court therefore had no remedy for giving effect to the Greek claim.

Here again, the principle that the nature of the remedy is a matter for the *lex fori* is affected by the provisions of the Rome I and Rome II Regulations. The law applicable by virtue of the Rome I Regulation governs, within the limits of the powers conferred on the court by its procedural law,[73] the consequences of breach, including the assessment of damages so far as it is governed by rules of law.[74] The law applicable by virtue of the Rome II Regulation governs the existence, the nature and the assessment of damage or the remedy claimed, and, within the limits of powers conferred on the court by its procedural law, the measures which a court may take to prevent or terminate injury or damage or to ensure the provision of compensation.[75]

Where the Regulations apply, the distinction formerly drawn between remoteness of damage, which has always been treated as a question of substance

---

[68] Protection of Trading Interests Act 1980 s.2(1). See *British Airways Board v Laker Airways Ltd* [1985] A.C. 58.

[69] Protection of Trading Interests Act 1980 s.2(2).

[70] *Baschet v London Illustrated Standard* [1900] 1 Ch. 73; *Boys v Chaplin* [1971] A.C. 356 at 394, per Lord Pearson.

[71] Consider *Warner Brothers Pictures v Nelson* [1937] 1 K.B. 209 where, however, foreign law was not pleaded.

[72] [1960] 2 Q.B. 19.

[73] i.e., the forum court is not required to make an order unknown to its legal system.

[74] Rome I Regulation art.12(1)(c) replacing the Rome Convention, art.10(1)(c).

[75] Rome II Regulation art.15(c), (d).

governed by the *lex causae*, and measure or quantification of damages, seen as a question of procedure governed by the *lex fori*,[76] is inapplicable: the assessment of damages is a matter for the *lex causae*.

Judgments in foreign currency

Prior to 1975 it had been regarded as settled law for nearly 400 years that an English court could not give judgment for the payment of an amount expressed in foreign currency. The reason was that the sheriff could not be expected to know the value of foreign currency (currency-conversion websites not having been invented) and thus could not enforce any money judgment by execution unless it was expressed in pounds sterling. The rule was re-asserted by a unanimous House of Lords in 1961 in *Re United Railways of the Havana and Regla Warehouses*,[77] where Lord Denning declared, "If there is one thing clear in our law, it is that the claim must be made in sterling and the judgment given in sterling. We do not give judgments in dollars any more than the United States courts give judgments in sterling".[78]

17–021

This rule was an unjust rule, because it made an anomalous and unnecessary exception to the principle of "nominalism". If a debt is expressed in foreign currency, both parties expect to measure their rights and obligations in terms of that currency and no other. The creditor should bear the risk of a depreciation of that currency after the date of maturity of the debt; the debtor should bear the risk of its appreciation. Most English judges remained impervious to the injustice of the rule until sterling depreciated in terms of the foreign currency, rather than the other way round as in the earlier cases.

In 1975 the House of Lords in *Miliangos v George Frank (Textiles) Ltd*[79] discarded the rule, and overruled its own previous decision in *Re United Railways*, and held that judgment could be given for an amount expressed in foreign currency or the sterling equivalent at the date when the court authorises enforcement of the judgment in terms of sterling.

17–022

> The action was by a Swiss seller against an English buyer for the price of goods sold. The price was quoted in Swiss francs and Swiss law was the proper law of the contract. The sterling equivalent of the price was £42,000 in 1971 when payment was due and (owing to the depreciation of the pound) £60,000 in 1974 at the date of the hearing. The House of Lords held that the Swiss seller was entitled to the larger sum.

As a precedent, the decision in the *Miliangos* case was expressly confined to claims for a liquidated debt expressed in foreign currency in cases where the proper law of the contract was that of a foreign country and where the money of account and payment was that of that country or possibly of some third country outside the United Kingdom. The House of Lords declined to review the whole field of the law regarding foreign currency obligations, leaving it open to future

---

[76] *Boys v Chaplin* [1971] A.C. 356 (where the House of Lords had to determine the proper characterisation of rules as to recoverable heads of damage, and held that they went to substance).
[77] [1961] A.C. 1007.
[78] At pp.1068–1069.
[79] [1976] A.C. 443.

discussion whether the same rule should apply to claims for damages for breach of contract or for tort. But a spate of cases rapidly clarified the scope of the decision. It is now clear that the court can give judgment for payment of an amount in foreign currency as damages for breach of contract[80] or for tort.[81] It can also do so on making an award under s.1(3) of the Law Reform (Frustrated Contracts) Act 1943 for the restoration of a valuable benefit to the claimant.[82] It has also been held that the principle of *Miliangos* applies even though the contract is governed by English law.[83] But there must of course be some foreign element. In the case of a liquidated debt, it is presumably sufficient if the debt was expressed in foreign currency. In the case of damages for breach of contract or for tort, the test adopted by the House of Lords is that damages can be awarded in a foreign currency if that was the currency in which the loss was effectively felt or borne by the person suffering it, having regard to the currency in which he or she generally operates or with which he or she has the closest connection.[84] In the case of restitution for unjust enrichment, the award will be made in the currency in which the defendant's benefit can be most fairly and appropriately valued.[85]

STATUTES OF LIMITATION

17–023   The common law distinguishes two kinds of statutes of limitation: those which merely bar a remedy and those which extinguish a right.[86] This common law rule was well-established, although it has been subjected to searching judicial criticism, doubting whether the distinction between "right" and "remedy" provided an acceptable basis on which to proceed.[87] Statutes of the former kind are procedural, while statutes of the latter kind are substantive. In general, the English law as to limitation of actions has been regarded as procedural,[88] but ss.3(2), 17 and 25(3) of the Limitation Act 1980 are probably substantive since they expressly extinguish the title of the former owner. Sometimes a statute creates an entirely new right of action unknown to the common law and at the same time imposes a shorter period of limitation than that applicable under the general law. An example is the Civil Liability (Contribution) Act 1978: where a person becomes entitled to a right to recover contribution under s.1 of that Act, the limitation period is two years.[89] There is Scottish, Australian and American

---

[80] *Jean Kraut A/B v Albany Fabrics Ltd* [1977] Q.B. 182; *Services Europe Atlantique Sud v Stockholm Rederiaktiebolag Svea* [1979] A.C. 685.

[81] *The Despina R* [1979] A.C. 685.

[82] *B.P. Exploration Co (Libya) Ltd v Hunt (No.2)* [1979] 1 W.L.R. 783 at 840–841.

[83] *Barclays Bank International Ltd v Levin Brothers (Bradford) Ltd* [1977] Q.B. 270; *Services Europe Atlantique Sud v Stockholm Rederiaktiebolag Svea* [1979] A.C. 685.

[84] *The Despina R* [1979] A.C. 685; *Services Europe Atlantique Sud v Stockholm Rederiaktiebolag Svea* [1979] A.C. 685.

[85] *B.P. Exploration Co (Libya) Ltd v Hunt (No.2)* [1979] 1 W.L.R. 783.

[86] *Phillips v Eyre* (1870) L.R. 6 Q.B. 1 at 29; *Black-Clawson Ltd v Papierwerke Waldhof-Aschaffenberg A.G.* [1975] A.C. 591, 630.

[87] See the dissenting judgments in *McKain v R. W. Miller & Co (South Australia) Pty. Ltd* (1991) 174 C.L.R. 1.

[88] *Williams v Jones* (1811) 13 East 439; *Ruckmaboye v Mottichund* (1851) 8 Moo.P.C. 4.

[89] Limitation Act 1980 s.10.

authority in favour of the view that such special periods of limitation are substantive, even if they are contained in a different statute from that which creates the right.[90]

At common law, the English courts used the same distinction between right and remedy in characterising foreign statutes of limitation, with results which were far from happy. The Foreign Limitation Periods Act 1984, based on recommendations by the Law Commission,[91] adopts the general principle, subject to an exception based on public policy where the court finds that there would be "undue hardship" to a person who is or might be a party,[92] that the limitation rules of the *lex causae* are to be applied in actions in England. English limitation rules are not to be applied unless English law is the *lex causae* or one of two *leges causae* governing the matter.[93] The applicable provisions of the foreign *lex causae* are defined to include both procedural and substantive rules with respect to a limitation period.[94] English law as the *lex fori* does, however, determine whether, and the time at which, proceedings have been commenced,[95] and so whether the proceedings were commenced within the time-limit.

Under the Rome I Regulation, the applicable law governs the various ways of extinguishing obligations, and prescription and limitation of actions[96]; under the Rome II Regulation a fuller provision to similar effect subjects to the applicable law the manner in which an obligation may be extinguished and rules of prescription and limitation, including rules relating to the commencement, interruption and suspension of a period of prescription or limitation.[97] These provisions achieve the same result as the Foreign Limitation Periods Act 1984. In each case application of the governing law may be refused if its application would be manifestly contrary to English public policy[98]; this, it is submitted, is a stricter test than that applied under the 1984 Act.

17–024

---

[90] For a comparative study, see Harder, (2011) 60 I.C.L.Q. 659.
[91] Law Com. No. 114 (1982).
[92] 1984 Act s.2. See *The Komninos S* [1990] 1 Lloyd's Rep. 541; *Harley v Smith* [2010] EWCA Civ 78.
[93] s.1(1)(2). Foreign torts were, until the coming into force of Pt III of the Private International Law (Miscellaneous Provisions) Act 1995, an example of the "two *leges causae*" situation.
[94] Foreign Limitation Periods Act 1984 s.4.
[95] Foreign Limitation Periods Act 1984 s.1(3).
[96] Rome I Regulation art.12(1)(d).
[97] Rome II Regulation art.15(h). See SI 2008/2986.
[98] Rome I Regulation art.21; Rome II Regulation art.26.

CHAPTER 18

SOME TECHNICAL PROBLEMS

As promised, or threatened, in the first chapter,[1] some matters of fundamental   **18–001**
importance and great difficulty have been reserved for discussion at the end of the
book. These are characterisation (on which there is a measure of agreement on
the solution, but no clarity as to the identity of the problem), the incidental
question (which is incapable of any overall solution), *renvoi* (on which the
English courts have thus far adopted a common approach, one that unfortunately
lacks merit), and the whole issue of the time factor in the conflict of laws. These
matters will be examined in turn.

CHARACTERISATION

The issue of characterisation[2] has been regarded by many continental and some   **18–002**
English and American writers as a fundamental problem in the conflict of laws. It
was 'discovered' independently and almost simultaneously by the German jurist
Kahn[3] and the French jurist Bartin[4] at the end of the nineteenth century, and was
introduced to American lawyers by Lorenzen in 1920[5] and to English lawyers by
Beckett in 1934.[6]

---

[1] Above, para.1–019.
[2] There is a vast literature on this subject and the following is only a selection: Lorenzen, *Selected Articles on the Conflict of Laws* (New Haven: Yale University Press, 1947), Chs. 4 and 5; Beckett, (1934) 15 B.Y.B.I.L. 46; Robertson, *Characterisation in the Conflict of Laws* (Cambridge MA: Harvard University Press, 1940); Falconbridge, *Selected Essays on the Conflict of Laws*, 2nd edn, (Toronto: Canada Law Book, 1954), Chs 3–5; Wolff, *Private International Law* (Cambridge MA: Harvard University Press, 1942), ss.138–157; Cook, *Logical and Legal Bases of the Conflict of Laws*, Ch.8; Rabel, *Conflict of Laws: A Comparative Study* (Ann Arbor: University of Michigan Press, 1947), Vol. I, pp.47–72; Inglis, (1958) 74 L.Q.R. 493 at 503–516; Kahn-Freund, (1974) 143 Hague *Recueil des cours*, 369–382; Forsyth (2006) 2 J.Priv.I.L. 425.
[3] (1891) 30 Jhering's Jahrbücher 1.
[4] (1897) Clunet 225, 466 and 720.
[5] (1920) 20 Col.L.Rev. 247; reprinted in Lorenzen, Ch.4.
[6] (1934) 15 B.Y.B.I.L. 46.

Nature of the problem

18–003   The conflict of laws exists because there are different systems of domestic law. But systems of the conflict of laws also differ. Yet all systems have at least one thing in common. They are expressed in terms of juridical concepts or categories, and localising elements or connecting factors. This may be seen by considering some typical rules of the English conflict of laws familiar from earlier chapters of this book: "succession to immovables is governed by the *lex situs*"; "the formal validity of a marriage is governed by the law of the place of celebration". In these examples, succession to immovables and formal validity of marriage are the categories, while *situs* and place of celebration are the connecting factors.

In the majority of cases it is obvious that the facts must be subsumed under a particular legal category, that a particular conflict rule is available, and the connecting factor indicated by that conflict rule is unambiguous. But sometimes it is not obvious. Even if the forum and the foreign country have the same conflict rule and interpret the connecting factor in the same way, they may still reach different conclusions because they characterise the question in different ways. For instance, the forum may regard the question as one of succession, while the foreign law may regard the same question as one of matrimonial property. That is the problem of characterisation.

18–004   Two illustrations will show the precise nature of the problem.

(1)   A woman buys a ticket in London for a train journey from London to Glasgow. She is injured in an accident in Scotland. Is her cause of action for breach of contract, in which case English law may govern as the law applicable to the contract, or for tort, in which case Scots law may apply? By which law, English or Scots, is this question to be answered?[7] Or, as the issues are now governed by European Union Regulations, is there an autonomous European rule that might apply?

(2)   A Frenchman under the age of 21 marries an Englishwoman in England without obtaining the consent of his parents as required by French law. The French and English conflict rules agree that the formalities of marriage are governed by the law of the place of celebration (English law), and also that the husband must have capacity to marry by his personal law (French law).[8] But is the issue in the case one of formalities (in which case the French rule will be irrelevant) or of capacity (in which case the French rule will be apply and the marriage will be void for want of capacity)?[9] Or, analysing the question in different terms, is the French rule to be characterised as one dealing with formalities (and so inapplicable) or with capacity?

---

[7] See *Horn v North British Rly* (1878) 5 R. 1055; *Naftalin v L.M.S. Rly*, 1933 S.C. 259.

[8] The fact that the personal law means the law of the nationality in France and the law of the domicile in England is immaterial if we assume that the husband was French by nationality and French by domicile

[9] *Ogden v Ogden* [1908] P. 46.

The subject-matter of characterisation

Before we go further, we need to ask what exactly is it that we characterise? In earlier editions of this book, Dr Morris argued that in illustration (1) above, the answer was the nature of the cause of action; in illustration (2) the relevant rule of French law. In practice, attempts to characterise particular rules of law can produce serious difficulties. **18–005**

An example is provided by *Re Cohn*[10]:

> A mother and daughter, both domiciled in Germany but resident in England, were killed in an air raid on London by the same high explosive bomb. The daughter was entitled to movables under her mother's will if, and only if, she survived her mother. By the English conflict rules, succession to movables is governed by the law of the domicile, but questions of procedure are governed by the *lex fori*. By s.184 of the Law of Property Act 1925, the presumption was that the elder died first; but by Art.20 of the German Civil Code the presumption was that the deaths were simultaneous.

Uthwatt J. first decided that the English presumption was substantive, not procedural, and therefore did not apply. He next decided that the German presumption was also substantive and not procedural, and therefore did apply. He reached this conclusion for himself by examining the terms of Art.20 in its context in the German Civil Code, uninfluenced by the characterisation placed upon it by the German courts or by the characterisation which he had already placed upon s.184. Had he reached different conclusions, the difficulties latent in his approach would have become obvious. If s.184 had been characterised as substantive and Art.20 as procedural, then neither rule would have applied.[11] If, on the other hand, s.184 had been characterised as procedural and Art.20 as substantive, both rules would apply: the court would have been faced with conflicting presumptions and would have had to choose between them.

It seems better to say that what has to be characterised is the issue in the case, the "question in issue".[12] As Auld L.J. put it in *Macmillan Inc. v Bishopsgate Investment Trust plc (No.3)*[13] (where the issue concerned a claim viewed as either restitutionary or proprietary): **18–006**

> "The proper approach is to look beyond the formulation of the claim and to identify ... the true issue or issues thrown up by the claim and defence. This requires a parallel exercise in classification of the relevant rule of law."

"Parallel" cannot mean "simultaneous". Although Forsyth has argued,[14] in effect, that the issues can be identified only via the relevant rules of law, it seems more accurate to say that the relevant rule can only be discovered by the process

---

[10] [1945] Ch. 5; discussed by Morris, (1945) 61 L.Q.R. 340.

[11] The practical result would be that those interested in the daughter's estate would not have been entitled to the mother's movables, because they would have been unable to prove that the daughter survived her mother.

[12] See *Macmillan Inc. v Bishopsgate Investment Trust plc (No.3)* [1996] 1 W.L.R. 387, where the different members of the court use various terms to express the point.

[13] *Macmillan Inc. v Bishopsgate Investment Trust plc (No.3)* [1996] 1 W.L.R. 387 at 407.

[14] (1998) 114 L.Q.R. 141.

of characterisation of the issue. As we have seen, the typical conflicts statement is that issue A is governed by rule B, and the logical approach is one that starts with the issue.

Various solutions

18–007   Although various compromise solutions have been advocated, the principal contenders are characterisation by the *lex fori* and by the *lex causae*. These, together with one other approach, will be examined in turn.

Lex fori

18–008   The great majority of continental writers follow Kahn and Bartin in thinking that, with certain exceptions,[15] characterisation should be governed by the law of the forum, the *lex fori*.

The strongest reason for relying on characterisation by the *lex fori* is that the exercise is essentially concerned with identifying the relevant legal category and so the applicable English conflicts rule, leading in turn to the identification of the governing law. Any reference to potentially-applicable foreign law (except perhaps to inform an understanding of legal concepts) is premature until that has been done.

The continental writers tend to argue their case in terms of the characterisation of rules of law rather than issues. They assert that the forum should characterise rules of its own domestic law in accordance with that law, and should characterise rules of foreign law in accordance with their nearest equivalents in its own domestic law. This is in substance what was done in *Ogden v Ogden,* illustration (2), above.

18–009   The main argument in favour of this view is that if the foreign law were allowed to determine in what situations it is to be applied, the law of the forum would lose all control over the application of its own conflict rules, and would no longer be master of its own house. The main objections to this view are as follows. In the first place, to argue by analogy from a rule of domestic law to a rule of foreign law is to indulge in mechanical jurisprudence of a particularly objectionable kind, and may result in the forum seriously distorting the foreign law, applying it in cases where it would not be applicable and vice versa, so that the law applied to the case is neither the law of the forum nor the foreign law nor the law of any country whatever. In the second place, this view breaks down altogether if there is no close analogy to the foreign rule of law or institution in the domestic law of the forum.

---

[15] One of Bartin's exceptions was the characterisation of interests in property as interests in movables or immovables, which he said must be determined by the *lex situs*.

Lex causae

A few continental writers[16] believe that characterisation should be governed by   **18–010**
the *lex causae*, i.e. the appropriate foreign law. According to Wolff,[17] "every legal
rule takes its characterisation from the legal system *to which it belongs"*.

This view was in substance adopted in *Re Maldonado*,[18] where the Court of
Appeal had to decide whether the Spanish Government's claim to the movables
in England of a Spanish intestate who died without next of kin was a right of
succession (in which case the Spanish Government was entitled to the movables)
or a *jus regale* (in which case the English Crown was entitled to them). The court
held that this question must be decided in accordance with Spanish law, with the
result that the Spanish Government was entitled. The argument in favour of this
view is that to say that the foreign law governs, and then not apply its
characterisation, is tantamount to not applying it at all.

But this view is open to even more serious objections than the first one. In the
first place, it is a circular argument to say that the foreign law governs the process
of characterisation before the process of characterisation has led to the selection
of the foreign law. Secondly, if there are two potentially applicable foreign laws,
why should the forum adopt the characterisation of one rather than the other?

Analytical jurisprudence and comparative law

Other writers[19] argue that the process of characterisation should be performed in   **18–011**
accordance with the principles of analytical jurisprudence and comparative law.
This view has its attractions, because judicial technique in conflicts cases should
be more internationalist and less insular than in domestic cases.

But the objections to this view are that there are very few principles of
analytical jurisprudence and comparative law of universal application: "international agreement on analytical concepts is a utopia".[20] While the study of
comparative law is capable of revealing differences between domestic laws, it is
hardly capable of resolving them. For instance, comparative law may reveal that
parental consents to marriage are sometimes regarded as affecting formalities and
sometimes as affecting capacity to marry, or that statutes of limitation are
sometimes treated as procedural and sometimes as substantive: but how can
comparative law determine the way in which these matters should be
characterised in a particular case? Moreover, the method proposed seems quite
inconsistent with the pragmatic spirit and traditions of the common law. There is
no reported case in which this method has been adopted by an English court.

---

[16] e.g., Despagnet, (1898) Clunet 253; Wolff, *op. cit.*, ss.138–157.
[17] At p.154 (Wolff's italics).
[18] [1954] P. 223; above, para.15–013.
[19] e.g. Rabel, *op. cit.*, Vol. I, pp.54–56; Beckett, (1934) 15 B.Y.B.I.L. 46 at 58–60.
[20] Kahn-Freund, *op. cit.*, p.227.

An internationalist approach?

18–012 In *Macmillan Inc. v Bishopsgate Investment Trust plc (No.3)*[21] the Court of Appeal characterised property by the *lex fori*, though the parties were agreed on that point. Auld L.J. did, however, place an important gloss on the *lex fori* approach:

> "However, classification of an issue and rule of law for this purpose, the underlying principle of which is to strive for comity between different legal systems, should not be constrained by particular notions or distinctions of the domestic law of the *lex fori*, or that of the competing system of law, which may have no counterpart in the other's system. Nor should the issue be defined too narrowly, so that it attracts a particular domestic rule under the *lex fori* which may not be applicable under the other system".

18–013 This seems to be a call for an "internationalist" application of the *lex fori*.[22] It is certainly the case that for some purposes of the conflict of laws, the English courts use categories unknown in domestic law (preferring, for example, the distinction between movables and immovables to the domestic division of property into realty and personalty).

It is far from clear how far this notion can be generalised in the characterisation process, and its limitations were exposed in its examination by a sharply divided Court of Appeal in *Haugesund Kommune v Depfa ACS Bank*.[23] The case concerned the capacity or power of Norwegian municipalities to enter into certain types of financial transaction. Aikens L.J. (with whom Pill L.J. agreed) characterised the issue as one of the "capacity" of a corporation. He continued, referring to the relevant rule in Dicey, Morris and Collins[24]:

> "The rule as framed assumes that the legal concept of 'capacity' has a commonly understood content and significance so far as concerns non-English corporations. But because this is a conflict of laws rule, the corporations to be considered may, by definition, be non-English, and matters concerning their constitution may be governed by laws other than English law. That is the case here. As Mance L.J. points out in his judgment in *Raiffeisen Zentralbank Österreich AG v Five Star Trading LLC*,[25] classes or categories of issues which are recognised by English conflicts rules are man-made, not natural; they have no inherent value beyond their purpose of assisting in the selection of the most appropriate law to deal with them. They may need redefinition or modification. That must be so whether the conflicts rule is one agreed internationally, as with the Rome Convention, or is the product of the English common law."

18–014 In Aikens L.J.'s view, what was said by Auld L.J. about legal issues was equally applicable to the legal concepts that go to make up issues, and so to the concept of "capacity". It would be legal parochialism to insist that the legal concepts used to make up the rule had to conform to English common law concepts. "Capacity" had to be given a broader, "internationalist", meaning and not be confined to the narrow definition accorded by domestic English law.

---

[21] [1996] 1 W.L.R. 387.
[22] For some similar notions in the theoretical literature, see Forsyth (1998) 114 L.Q.R. 140 at 153–156.
[23] [2010] EWCA Civ 579; [2012] 2 W.L.R. 199.
[24] Rule 162(1) in the 14th edn, 2006.
[25] [2001] Q.B. 825.

Etherton L.J. was scathing. To say, with Auld L.J., that the underlying purpose of classification for settling a conflict of laws rule is "to strive for comity between competing legal systems" said nothing as to what the limits of such comity should be as a matter of policy. Aiken L.J.'s analysis led to a result which was counter-intuitive to an English lawyer and judge, was in marked contrast to the English law concept of corporate capacity, was not consistent with a sound policy objective, and was capable of producing bizarre consequences. Given the context, of contracts governed by English law, there was no authority which required giving the word "capacity" any meaning other than its meaning in domestic English jurisprudence.

Conclusions

English law is relatively rich in cases raising questions of characterisation,[26] but poor in judicial discussion of the problem. It is well settled that the *lex situs* determines the characterisation of property.[27] But apart from that, it cannot be said that English courts have adopted any consistent theory of characterisation in accordance with the *lex fori,* of which *Ogden v Ogden*[28] is perhaps the most celebrated example, or in accordance with the *lex causae,* exemplified by *Re Maldonado.*[29]

18–015

It remains to add that, in the opinion of some writers, the problem of characterisation has no practical significance and its importance has been exaggerated. It is true that conflicts of characterisation have arisen in relatively few cases, and that the process of characterisation is frequently simple and even obvious. But in some cases it is difficult, and these are the cases which have been most discussed and the results of which have been received with least enthusiasm. Hence the problem of characterisation does seem to have practical importance as well as academic interest; and some knowledge of its nature is essential for any serious student of the conflict of laws.

---

[26] In addition to the cases discussed in the text, see *Leroux v Brown* (1852) 12 C.B. 801 (Statute of Frauds 1677 s.4: substance or procedure); *Re Martin* [1900] P. 211 at 240 (Wills Act 1837 s.18: testamentary or matrimonial law); *Re Wilks* [1935] Ch. 645 (Administration of Estates Act 1925 s.33(1): administration or succession); *Re Priest* [1944] Ch. 58 (Wills Act 1837 s.15: formal or essential validity of wills); *Apt v Apt* [1948] P. 83 (proxy marriages: formal validity or capacity to marry); *Re Kehr* [1952] Ch. 26 (Trustee Act 1925 ss.31 and 32: administration or succession); *In the Estate of Fuld (No.3)* [1968] P. 675 at 696–697 (onus of proof of testamentary capacity: substance or procedure). For other examples, see Robertson, *op. cit.*, pp.164–188 and 245–279; Falconbridge, *op. cit.*, pp.73–123; Beckett (1934) 15 B.Y.B.I.L. 46 at 66–81.
[27] Above, para.13–002.
[28] [1908] P. 46.
[29] [1954] P. 223.

18–016 A problem similar to that of characterisation was discovered or invented by the German jurist Wengler in 1934.[30] It is called the incidental question,[31] and it arises in this way.

Suppose that an English court is considering a main question that has foreign elements, in the course of which other subsidiary questions, also having foreign elements, arise incidentally. Suppose that by the appropriate rule of the English conflict of laws, the main question is governed by the law of a foreign country. Should the subsidiary questions be governed by the English conflict rule appropriate to such questions, or should they be governed by the appropriate conflict rules of the foreign law that governs the main question? An illustration will make this clearer.

Suppose that a testator domiciled in France gives movables in England to his "wife". The main question here is the succession to the movables, governed by French law, the law of the testator's domicile. The incidental question is the validity of the marriage, which may in turn depend on the validity of some previous divorce. Should these questions be referred to the English or the French rules of the conflict of laws relating to the validity of marriages and the recognition of divorces?

18–017 In order that a true incidental question may squarely be presented, three conditions must be fulfilled. First, the main question must by the English conflict rule be governed by the law of some foreign country. Second, a subsidiary question involving foreign elements must present itself and be capable of arising in its own right or in other contexts, and for which there is a separate conflict rule. Third, the English conflict rule for the determination of the subsidiary question must lead to a different result from the corresponding conflict rule of the country whose law governs the main question. Such cases are rare. Thus, in a case of succession to movables, the first condition would not be satisfied if the deceased died domiciled in England. The third condition would not be satisfied if a testator domiciled abroad gave a legacy to his or her legitimate children, but the English and the foreign conflict rule agreed that the children were or were not legitimate.[32]

Decisions, or even *dicta*, involving the incidental question in English, Commonwealth or American case law, are extremely rare.

18–018 In *Schwebel v Ungar*[33]:

---

[30] Wengler, (1934) 8 Rabel's Zeitschrift, 148–251; Robertson, *op. cit.*, Ch.6; Wolff, *op. cit.*, ss.196–200; Gotlieb, (1955) 33 Can. Bar Rev. 523–555; Wengler, (1966) 55 Rev. Crit. 165–215; Hartley, (1967) 16 I.C.L.Q. 680–691; Gotlieb, (1977) 26 I.C.L.Q. 734.

[31] This term was used by Wolff and is considered the most suitable English expression. The French and German terms are, respectively, "*question préalable*" and "*Vorfrage*".

[32] cf. *Doglioni v Crispin* (1866) L.R. 1 H.L. 301.

[33] (1963) 42 D.L.R. (2d) 622; (1964) 48 D.L.R. (2d) 644; discussed by Lysyk (1965) 43 Can. Bar Rev. 363; approved by Simon P. in *Padolecchia v Padolecchia* [1968] P. 314 at 339. The facts *of Schwebel v Ungar* are misstated by Gotlieb in (1977) 26 I.C.L.Q. 734 at 775 and 793.

> A husband and wife, both Jews, were domiciled in Hungary. They decided to emigrate to Israel. While en route to Israel they were divorced by a Jewish ghet (or extra-judicial divorce) in Italy. This divorce was not recognised by the law of Hungary (where they were still domiciled) but was recognised by the law of Israel. The parties then acquired a domicile in Israel, and the wife while so domiciled went through a ceremony of marriage in Toronto with a second husband, who subsequently petitioned the Ontario court for a decree of nullity on the ground that the ceremony was bigamous.

The main question here was the wife's capacity to remarry, which by the conflict rule of Ontario was governed by the law of Israel. The incidental question was the validity of the divorce. This was not recognised as valid by the conflict rule of Ontario but was recognised as valid by the conflict rule of Israel. The Supreme Court of Canada, affirming the decision of the Ontario Court of Appeal, held that the remarriage was valid, because by the law of her antenuptial domicile the wife had the status of a single woman. Thus, the incidental question was determined by the conflict rule of Israeli law, the law governing the main question, and not by the conflict rule of the forum.

In *R. v Brentwood Marriage Registrar*[34]:   **18–019**

> An Italian husband married a Swiss wife and later obtained a divorce from her in Switzerland, where they were both domiciled. After the divorce the wife remarried. The husband wanted to marry, in England, a Spanish national domiciled in Switzerland. But the Registrar refused to marry them because in his view there was an impediment. By Swiss law, capacity to marry is governed by the law of the nationality; and Italian law did not recognise the divorces of Italian nationals.

The main question here was the husband's capacity to remarry, which by the English conflict rule was governed by Swiss law, the law of his domicile. The incidental question was the validity of the divorce. This was recognised as valid by the English conflict rule; but was not recognised by the Swiss conflict rule as entitling the husband to remarry. The Divisional Court upheld the Registrar's objections to the remarriage. Thus the incidental question was determined by the conflict rule of Swiss law, the law governing the main question, and not by the conflict rule of the forum.

The actual decision in *R. v Brentwood Marriage Registrar* would now be different because s.50 of the Family Law Act 1986 provides that where a foreign divorce (or nullity decree) is recognised in England, the fact that the divorce is not recognised elsewhere shall not preclude either party from remarrying in England or cause the remarriage of either party to be regarded as invalid in England.[35]

In *Baindail v Baindail*,[36] Lord Greene M.R., in the course of a discussion of the   **18–020**
extent to which polygamous marriages might be recognised in England, said:

> "If a Hindu domiciled in India died intestate in England leaving personal property in this country, the succession to the personal property would be governed by the law of his domicile; and in applying the law of his domicile effect would have to be given to the rights of any children of the Hindu marriage and of his Hindu widow".

---

[34] [1968] 2 Q.B. 956.
[35] See above, para.8–029.
[36] [1946] P. 122 at 127.

Thus, this dictum recognises that the incidental questions of the validity of the marriage and the legitimacy of the children would be governed by Indian law (the law governing the main question, of succession) and not necessarily by the English conflict rule.

In *Haque v Haque*,[37] a succession case on appeal from Western Australia, the High Court of Australia applied the conflicts rule of the *lex successionis* (Indian law) and not that of the *lex fori* to determine the formal validity of a marriage celebrated in Western Australia.

Thus the weight of English, Canadian, and Australian authority (so far as it goes) seems to indicate that the incidental question is usually determined by the conflict rule of the foreign law governing the main question and not by the conflict rule of the forum.

18–021 The writers who have discussed the incidental question are equally divided in opinion between those who think it should be determined by the conflict rule of the foreign law and those who think it should be determined by the conflict rule of the forum.[38] They usually discuss the classic case of the testator domiciled in France who gives movables in England to his "wife". The writers who take the first view mentioned above emphasise that the question is not the abstract question, "was the claimant the wife of the deceased?" but rather, "was she his wife according to the law of his domicile at the time of his death and as such entitled to succeed to his movables under his will?" Those who take the second view emphasise that since *ex hypothesi* the incidental question is capable of arising in its own right or in other contexts than the one before the court, and has conflict rules of its own available for its determination, the court (if it applied the foreign-conflict rule) might have to give a decision contrary to its own conceptions of justice, and different from what it would have decided if the question had been presented to it in some other form. Thus, if the husband had petitioned for nullity on the ground of consanguinity, the court would have applied its own conflict rules, and might have dismissed the petition and held the marriage valid. But if the wife claimed to succeed to the husband's movables on his death, the court, if it applied the conflict rule of the law governing succession, might have to hold that she was not entitled to succeed because the marriage was invalid.

The first view harmonises well with the tendency of English courts to decide questions of succession to movables in the same way as the courts of the deceased's domicile would decide them, so as to promote uniformity of distribution. But this international harmony has to be purchased at the price of internal dissonance: sometimes the price may seem too high.

18–022 Suppose, for instance, that a Mexican national domiciled in England obtains a divorce from his wife in the English court. The divorce is, of course, valid in England, but it is not valid in Mexico. After the divorce the husband, while still domiciled in England, marries a second wife. He dies intestate domiciled in Mexico leaving movables in England. By the English conflict rule the succession to these movables is governed by Mexican law as the law of the intestate's

---

[37] (1962) 108 C.L.R. 230.
[38] See the analysis in Gotlieb, (1977) 26 I.C.L.Q. 734, 751–760.

domicile (main question); and by Mexican law the intestate's wife is entitled to a share: but which wife is entitled, the first or the second or neither (incidental question)? By Mexican law, the first wife is entitled, because she was never validly divorced and therefore the husband's remarriage was invalid. But the English court might well be reluctant to deny the validity of its own divorce decree, and if it were, the second wife should be entitled.

Such cases show that the problem of the incidental question is not capable of a mechanical solution and that each case may depend on the particular factors involved. As one writer puts it, "there is really no problem of the incidental question, but as many problems as there are cases in which incidental questions may arise".[39] Like the problem of characterisation, the incidental question is seldom discussed by courts, but it does seem to involve a fundamental problem which is necessarily present in certain types of case.

RENVOI

Nature of the problem

The problem of *renvoi*[40] arises whenever a rule of the conflict of laws refers to the "law" of a foreign country, but the conflict rule of the foreign country would have referred the question to the "law" of the first country or to the "law" of some third country. Suppose, for instance, that a British citizen dies intestate domiciled in Italy, leaving movables in England; and that by the English conflict rule, succession to movables is governed by the law of the domicile (Italian law), but by the Italian conflict rule succession to movables is governed by the law of the nationality (English law). Which law, English or Italian, will regulate the distribution of the English movables? This is a relatively simple case of remission from Italian law (the law identified by the English choice of law rule, the *lex causae*) to English law (the law of the forum or *lex fori*). Had the intestate been a German instead of a British citizen we should have had a more complicated case of transmission from Italian to German law. It will be as well to focus attention on cases of remission at the outset.[41]

18–023

The literature identifies three solutions to the problem. As will become clear, they would be better described as "approaches" rather than solutions. The debate has tended to assume that there is an answer to the whole issue of *renvoi*; a very significant Australian decision challenges that assumption, and in consequence the terms in which the issue has been examined hitherto. Whether or not the Australian view gathers support, the traditional terms need to be understood.

---

[39] Gotlieb, above, at p.798.
[40] There is an immense literature on this subject, and the following is only a selection: Wolff, *op. cit.*, ss.178–195; Falconbridge, *op. cit.*, Chs 6–10; Cook, *op. cit.*, Ch.9; Lorenzen, *op. cit.*, Chs 2, 3, 5; Morris, (1937) 18 B.Y.B.I.L. 32; Griswold, (1938) 51 Harv.L.Rev. 1165; Inglis, (1958) 74 L.Q.R. 493; Kahn-Freund, *op. cit.*, 431–437; Briggs, (1998) 47 I.C.L.Q. 877; *op. cit.*, Kassir, *Réflexions sur le renvoi en droit international privé comparé* (Bruylant, Brussels, 2002).
[41] Transmission is briefly considered below, para.18–044.

The internal law solution

18–024   The English court might apply the purely domestic rule of Italian law applicable to Italians, disregarding the fact that the intestate was a British citizen, which is in any case irrelevant in the English conflict of laws. This method requires proof of Italian domestic law, but not of its choice of law rules. It has been recommended (obiter) by two English judges on the ground that it is "simple and rational",[42] but rejected in another case after a comprehensive review of the authorities.[43]

Partial or single renvoi theory

18–025   The English court might accept the reference back from Italian law and apply English domestic law, disregarding the fact that the intestate was domiciled in Italy. This process is technically known as "accepting the *renvoi*".[44] This method requires proof of the Italian conflict rules relating to succession, but not of the Italian rules about *renvoi*. It is the practice in many of the countries of continental Europe,[45] but it is not the current doctrine of the English courts.

Total or double renvoi

18–026   The English court might decide the case in the same way as it would be decided by the Italian court. If the Italian court would refer to English "law" and would interpret that reference to mean English domestic law, then the English court would apply English domestic law. If on the other hand the Italian court would refer to English "law" and interpret that reference to mean English conflict of laws and would "accept the *renvoi*" from English law and apply Italian domestic law, then the English court would apply Italian domestic law. This method requires proof not only of the Italian conflict rules relating to succession but also of the Italian rules about *renvoi,* requiring a high degree of expertise from witnesses (and creating a risk that the experts will disagree).

How this theory works in practice can best be seen by comparing two leading cases. In *Re Annesley*[46]:

> T, a British subject of English domicile of origin, died domiciled in France in the English sense, but not in the French sense.[47] She left a will that purported to dispose of all her property. By French law, T could dispose of only one-third of her property because she left two surviving children. Evidence was given that a French court would refer to English law as T's

---

[42] *Re Annesley* [1926] Ch. 692 at 708–709, per Russell J.; *Re Askew* [1930] 2 Ch. 259 at 278, per Maugham J.

[43] *Re Ross* [1930] 1 Ch. 377 at 402.

[44] This expression must be distinguished from accepting the doctrine of the *renvoi*, which the forum may do without necessarily accepting the first reference back. The former expression means stopping the game of tennis with the return of serve. The latter means continuing the game until the other player gets tired of it.

[45] Including Austria, France, Germany, Monaco, Spain and Switzerland; by contrast, Denmark, Greece, Italy, the Netherlands, and Norway reject *renvoi*.

[46] [1926] Ch. 692.

[47] Because she had not obtained authority to establish her domicile in France as required by Art.13 of the Civil Code (since repealed).

national law and would accept the *renvoi* back to French law. French domestic law was applied and T's will was only effective to dispose of one-third of her property.

In *Re Ross*,[48] on the other hand: 18–027

> T, a British subject domiciled in Italy, died leaving movables in England and Italy and immovables in Italy. She left two wills, one in English and the other in Italian. By her English will she gave her property in England to her niece X. By her Italian will she gave her property in Italy to her grand-nephew Y, subject to a life interest to his mother X. She left nothing to her only son Z. Z claimed that by Italian law he was entitled to one-half of T's property as his *legitima portio*. By the English conflict rules, the validity of T's will was governed by Italian law as the law of her domicile in respect of movables and by Italian law as the *lex situs* in respect of immovables. Evidence was given that an Italian court would refer to English law as T's national law in respect of both movables and immovables, and would not accept the *renvoi* back to Italian law. English domestic law was applied and Z's claim was rejected.

Origin and development

The doctrine of *renvoi* obtained a foothold in English law in 1841 via cases on the   18–028
formal validity of wills. In that context, three factors favoured its recognition. First, the English conflict rule was at that time unduly rigid. It insisted on compliance with one form and one form only for wills, that of the testator's last domicile.[49] Second, in neighbouring European countries (where people of English origin were likely to settle) there was a more flexible conflict rule, which allowed compliance with the forms prescribed by either the testator's personal law or the law of the place where the will was made. Third, there was a judicial bias in favour of upholding wills which admittedly expressed the last wishes of the testator and were defective only in point of form.

The fountain-head of authority is *Collier v Rivaz*,[50] where the court had to consider the formal validity of a will and six codicils made by a British subject who died domiciled in Belgium in the English sense, but not in the Belgian sense.[51] The will and two of the codicils were made in Belgian form and were admitted to probate in England without argument. Four of the codicils were opposed because they were not made in local Belgian form, though they were made in English form. Upon proof that by Belgian law the validity of wills made by foreigners not legally domiciled in Belgium was governed by "the laws of their own country", Sir H. Jenner admitted these codicils to probate, remarking that "the court sitting here to determine it, must consider itself sitting in Belgium under the peculiar circumstances of this case". He did not consider the possibility that a Belgian court might have accepted the *renvoi* from English law and applied Belgian domestic law.

So the doctrine of *renvoi* was invoked, obviously as an escape device, in order to   18–029
get round the rigidity of the English conflict rule. The fact that the will and the two codicils made in Belgian form were admitted to probate as well as the four

---

[48] [1930] 1 Ch. 377.
[49] The law has since been amended, first by the Wills Act 1861, and then by the Wills Act 1963. See above, para.15–019.
[50] (1841) 2 Curt. 855.
[51] Because he had not obtained the authority of the Belgian Government to establish his domicile in Belgium as required by art.13 of the Code Napoléon.

codicils made in English form means that the English conflict rule was interpreted as a rule of alternative reference either to the domestic rules or to the conflict rules of Belgian law. A rule of alternative reference, while practicable for the formal validity of wills, is impracticable for the essential (or intrinsic) validity of wills or for intestacy. In such cases the court must choose between the domestic rules and the conflict rules of the foreign law. It cannot apply both, for it must decide whether or not the testator had disposing power, whether or not the deceased died intestate, and if so who were the next of kin. It is one thing to uphold a will if it complies with the formalities prescribed by either the domestic rules or the conflict rules of the foreign law. It is quite another thing to allow the next of kin entitled under the domestic rules of the foreign law to share the property with the next of kin entitled under its conflict rules.

Collier v Rivaz was disapproved in *Bremer v Freeman*,[52] where on almost identical facts the Privy Council refused to admit to probate the will of a British subject who died domiciled in France in the English sense, but not in the French sense, on the ground that it was made in a form acceptable in English but not in French law.

18–030 Until 1926, the few decisions and dicta which recognised the *renvoi* doctrine were all consistent with a theory of partial or single *renvoi*. That is to say, the English court first referred to the conflict rules of the foreign law and then applied the domestic rules either of English law or of the law of a third country,[53] without considering the possibility that the foreign court might accept the *renvoi* from English law and apply its own domestic law. In *Re Annesley*,[54] Russell J. introduced the doctrine of double or total *renvoi* (but without citing any authority or giving any reasons for doing so) and applied French domestic law as the law of the domicile on the ground that a French court would have done so by way of *renvoi* from English law. He expressed his personal preference for reaching this result by a more direct route, that is, by the application of French domestic law in the first instance without any *renvoi* at all[55]; but this part of his judgment has not been followed.[56] This theory of double *renvoi* is of course quite different from the theory of single or partial *renvoi* because, by inquiring how the foreign court would decide the case, it envisages the possibility that the foreign court might "accept the *renvoi*" and apply its own domestic law, as happened in *Re Annesley*.

18–031 Confusion between the two theories was, however, introduced by an obiter dictum of the Privy Council in *Kotia v Nahas*,[57] which appeared to speak in terms of single or partial *renvoi*. It was the principal authority relied upon for the application of the *renvoi* doctrine in *Re Duke of Wellington*[58]:

---

[52] (1857) 10 Moo. P.C. 306 at 374; followed in *Hamilton v Dallas* (1875) 1 Ch.D. 257 (partial intestacy).
[53] As in *Re Trufort* (1877) 36 Ch.D. 600, and *Re Johnson* [1903] 1 Ch. 821, a much criticised decision.
[54] [1926] Ch. 692.
[55] At pp.708–709.
[56] *Re Ross* [1930] 1 Ch. 377 at 402. See, however, *Re Askew* [1930] 2 Ch. 259 at 278.
[57] [1941] A. C. 403 at 413.
[58] [1947] Ch. 506; affirmed on other grounds, [1948] Ch. 118; discussed by Morris, (1948) 64 L.Q.R. 264; Jennings, (1948) 64 L.Q.R. 321; Mann, (1948) 11 M.L.R. 232; Falconbridge, *op. cit.*, pp.229–232.

The testator, who was a British subject domiciled in England, made a Spanish will giving land and movables in Spain to the person who should fulfil two stated qualifications, and made an English will giving all the rest of his property on trust for the person who should fulfil one of the qualifications. At his death there was no person who fulfilled both qualifications, and questions arose as to the devolution of the property in Spain. It appeared that Spanish law, as the *lex situs* of the land, referred questions of succession to the national law of the testator and would not accept the *renvoi* back to Spanish law. Wynn Parry J. therefore applied English domestic law and held that the gift in the Spanish will failed for uncertainty and that the Spanish property fell into the residue disposed of by the English will.

However, it was nowhere stated that the construction of the Spanish will would have been different in Spanish domestic law; and, indeed, if the construction of the Spanish will was the only point at issue, it would seem that English domestic law should have been applied without any reference to Spanish law because the testator was domiciled in England.[59] One of the counsel engaged in the case later furnished the information that by Spanish domestic law the testator could in the circumstances only dispose of half of his property and that the other half passed to his mother as heiress. It may be that this is the explanation of the decision; but it must be admitted that there is no trace of this to be found in the report. Whatever may have been the reason for referring to Spanish law, it is clear that the judge, although he relied mainly on a dictum enunciating a theory of single *renvoi*, was in fact adopting a theory of double *renvoi*. Otherwise, there would have been no occasion to inquire whether Spanish law would "accept the *renvoi*" from English law, an inquiry which occupied much space in the judgment.

General conclusion from the English cases

The history of the *renvoi* doctrine in English law is the history of a chapter of accidents. The doctrine originated as a device for mitigating the rigidity of the English conflict rule for the formal validity of wills. The passing of Lord Kingsdown's Act in 1861 rendered this mitigation no longer necessary, at any rate in cases where the testator was a British subject. But the doctrine was applied in cases falling within that Act, and was extended far beyond its original context to cases of intrinsic validity of wills and to cases of intestacy. In 1926, the theory underlying the doctrine underwent a significant change, but no authorities were cited nor reasons given for making the change.[60] Two of the cases that have been relied upon as establishing the doctrine have been subsequently overruled or dissented from.[61] In three other cases, the decision would have been the same if the court had referred to the domestic rules of the foreign law in the first instance.[62] And in three further cases,[63] none of the parties was concerned to argue that the foreign law meant foreign domestic law. It follows that the whole

18-032

---

[59] See above, para.15–027.
[60] *Re Annesley* [1926] Ch. 692.
[61] *Collier v Rivaz* (1841) 2 Curt. 855, see above, paras 20–20; *Re Johnson* [1903] 1 Ch. 821, see *Re Annesley* [1926] Ch. 692 at 705; *Re Askew* [1930] 2 Ch. 259 at 272.
[62] *Re Annesley* [1926] Ch. 692; *Re Askew* [1930] 2 Ch. 259; *In the Estate of Fuld (No.3)* [1968] P. 675.
[63] *Re Johnson* [1903] 1 Ch. 821; *Re O'Keefe* [1940] Ch. 124; *Re Duke of Wellington* [1947] Ch. 506. In *Re O'Keefe*, the originating summons did not even suggest the possibility that Italian domestic law was applicable.

question of *renvoi* can be reviewed by any appellate court. In *Macmillan Inc v Bishopsgate Investment Trust plc* at first instance,[64] Millet J. noted that the *renvoi* doctrine had often been criticised, and said:

> "It is probably right to describe it as largely discredited. It owes its origin to a laudable endeavour to ensure that like cases should be decided alike wherever they are decided, but it should now be recognised that this cannot be achieved by judicial mental gymnastics but only by international conventions".

The issue was not pressed on appeal,[65] and a later court noted Millet J.'s observations but nonetheless applied the doctrine.[66]

It is certainly the case that the English doctrine was formulated before many important developments in the methodology of the conflict of laws, notable the recognition of the significance of "mandatory rules". Those developments point to a need for the reconsideration of the nature and purpose of the doctrine.

An Australian approach

18–033 That reconsideration must take into account the judgments of the High Court of Australia in *Neilson v Overseas Projects Corporation of Victoria Ltd*[67]:

> N's husband was employed by an Australian company to work on a project in China. N went with him, and was injured when she fell down the stairs of the flat provided by the company. The company, as occupier, was in breach of the duty of care it owed N, but a limitation of actions issue arose. The law of Western Australia referred liability to the law of the place of the tort, China, but Chinese law provided that where the parties are nationals of the same country, the law of their own country "maybe applied."

The High Court of Australia was divided and the case is made more difficult by the inadequacy of some of the evidence as to Chinese law. All the judgments repay study; what follows is an exposition of the leading judgment by Gummow and Hayne JJ.

Their Honours examined the development of the *renvoi* doctrine and described how, in their words, "metaphorical references to renvoi ('return' or 'reference back') entered the English legal lexicon",[68] the problem being presented, artificially, as if some dialogue occurred between jurisdictions. Would a foreign jurisdiction to whose law the forum had referred, "refer" the issue back to the forum and say that forum law should be applied? Would the forum "accept" the reference back? In their Honours' view, scholarly debate had "focused more upon theoretical explanations for the method of solution than upon the principal and essentially practical concern of the courts, which is to decide the controversies that are tendered by the parties for decision."[69]

---

[64] [1995] 1 W.L.R. 978.
[65] [1996] 1 W.L.R. 387.
[66] *Glencore International AG v Metro Trading International Inc.* [2001] 1 Lloyd's Rep. 284.
[67] [2005] HCA 54; (2005) 233 C.L.R. 331. See Briggs, [2006] L.M.C.L.Q. 1; Dickinson (2006) 122 L.Q.R. 183.
[68] At para.86.
[69] At para.87.

They argued that the most important premise was that the rules adopted should, **18–034** as far as possible, avoid parties being able to obtain advantages by litigating in a particular (in the instant case, an Australian) forum which could not be obtained if the issue were to be litigated in the courts of the jurisdiction whose law is chosen as the governing law. A party could gain an advantage by litigating in the courts of the forum rather than the courts of the foreign jurisdiction only if the forum were to choose to apply only *some* of the law of that foreign jurisdiction. (In the terms of the traditional debate, this is to reject the internal law solution, which was favoured by the dissenting judge, McHugh J.).

Their second premise was that certainty and simplicity are desirable characteristics; they cite Kahn-Freund[70] as saying that the intellectual challenge presented by questions of conflict of laws is its main curse, and that in this field dogmatism must yield to pragmatism.[71] To take no account of what a foreign court would do when faced with the facts of the case would not assist the pursuit of certainty and simplicity, because it would require the law of the forum to divide the rules of the foreign legal system, which must be assumed to be intended to constitute an integrated system of interdependent rules, between those rules that are to be applied by the forum and those that are not. They illustrate this with a worked example[72]:

> "A foreign legal system may make separate provision for the kinds of loss sustained by a person as a result of a traffic accident, recoverable from the party whose negligence caused that loss, according to whether the negligent party was a national of, or domiciled in, that foreign country. The differences may reflect not only different insurance arrangements for 'local' drivers from those applying to others but also different social security and health arrangements. That is, the foreign legal system may also make provision in its social security and health legislation for giving larger benefits to those who are nationals of, or domiciled in, the country than the benefits allowed to others. If the Australian choice-of-law rules look only to the 'domestic' law of that country, what account is to be taken of these different social security and health provisions in deciding the extent of the liability to an Australian citizen of the Australian employer of a negligent 'local' driver sued in an Australian court? Is reference to be made only to the foreign law that deals with recovery of damages? Is reference to be made to the social security and health provisions? Any division that is made is necessarily an incomplete and incoherent reflection of the law of that place."

The argument seems to be leading to the double *renvoi* solution, but their **18–035** Honours reject the traditional scholarly analyses as not providing a sure footing upon which to construct applicable rules. They reject the traditional distinction between a foreign legal system's rules of "domestic law" and its choice of law rules[73]:

> "Choosing a single overarching theory of *renvoi* as informing every question about choice of law would wrongly assume that identical considerations apply in every kind of case in which a choice of law must be made. But questions of personal status like marriage or divorce, questions of succession to immovable property, questions of delictual responsibility and questions of contractual obligation differ in important respects. Party autonomy may be given much more emphasis in questions of contract than in questions of title to land. Choice of governing law may be important in creating private obligations by contract but less important

---

[70] Kahn-Freund, *General Problems of Private International Law*, 1976, p.320.
[71] Kahn-Freund, *General Problems of Private International Law*, 1976, p.290.
[72] At para.95.
[73] At para.99.

when the question is one of legal status. Choosing one theory of *renvoi* as applicable to all cases where a choice of law must be made would submerge these differences."

In the field of tort, the Australian choice-of-law rule applies the law of the place of the tort, the *lex loci delicti*. In that context, their Honours held that the *lex loci delicti* is the whole of the law of that place. If the foreign jurisdiction would choose to apply the law of the forum, and not the law of the place where the wrong was committed, the forum should apply its own law. If the law of the place where the wrong was committed would look to a third jurisdiction to provide the relevant law governing the resolution of substantive questions, the forum should look to and apply the law of that third jurisdiction. Scholars (and they include Dr Morris) whose writings showed great antipathy to *renvoi* did accept that the doctrine should be invoked if it is plain that the object of the relevant choice of law rule, in referring to a foreign law, will on balance be better served by construing the reference to foreign law as including the conflict rules of that law. A choice of law rule for foreign torts which requires reference to and application of the *lex loci delicti*, without exception, was such a case.[74]

It is perhaps a fair summary to say that the case endorses the application of a double *renvoi* approach if, but only if, the nature of the dispute and the underlying purpose of the forum's choice-of-law rule justify its application.

Scope of the doctrine in England

18–036   The English *renvoi* doctrine has been applied to the formal[75] and intrinsic[76] validity of wills and to cases of intestate succession.[77] It has been applied when the reference has been to the law of the domicile,[78] the law of the place where a will was made,[79] and the law of the place where an immovable was situated (*lex situs*).[80] Outside the field of succession, it seems to have been applied only to legitimation by subsequent marriage[81] and, with unfortunate results, in the context of child abduction.[82] There are indications that it might be applied to the formal validity of marriage[83] and to capacity to marry.[84] It no longer applies to the formal validity of wills in cases falling within the Wills Act 1963. *Renvoi* is excluded by the Rome Convention, its successor (the Rome I Regulation),

---

[74] At paras 109–111.

[75] *Collier v Rivaz* (1841) 2 Curt. 855; *In the Goods of Lacroix* (1877) 2 P.D. 94; *In the Estate of Fuld (No. 3)* [1968] P. 675.

[76] *Re Trufort* (1887) 36 Ch. D. 600; *Re Annesley* [1926] Ch. 692; *Re Ross* [1930] 1 Ch. 377; and (perhaps) *Re Duke of Wellington* [1947] Ch. 506.

[77] *Re Johnson* [1903] 1 Ch. 821; *Re O'Keefe* [1940] Ch. 124; *Haji-Ioannou v Frangos* [2009] EWHC 2310 (QB); [2010] 1 All E.R. (Comm) 303 (were the doctrine was applied, without any discussion, to intestate succession to rights under a judgment).

[78] *Collier v Rivaz*; *Re Trufort*; *Re Johnson*; *Re Annesley*; *Re Ross*; *Re Askew*; *Re O'Keefe*; *In the Estate of Fuld (No.3)*, all cited above.

[79] *In the Goods of Lacroix*, above.

[80] *Re Ross*, above; *Re Duke of Wellington*, above.

[81] *Re Askew*, above.

[82] e.g., *Re J.B. (Abduction) (Rights of Custody: Spain)* [2003] EWHC 2130, [2004] 1 F.L.R. 976.

[83] *Taczanowska v Taczanowski* [1957] P. 301 at 305 and 318; above, para.8–008.

[84] *R. v Brentwood Marriage Registrar* [1968] 2 Q.B. 956; above, para.8–029.

reflecting the common law rule that "the principle of *renvoi* finds no place in the field of contract",[85] and, in the field of tort, by the Rome II Regulation.

Even in the sphere in which the doctrine has been most frequently applied, namely succession to movables and immovables, it must be stressed that for every case which supports the doctrine there are hundreds of cases in which the domestic rules of the foreign law have been applied as a matter of course without any reference to its conflict rules, though it must be admitted that most of these can be explained on the ground that no one was concerned to argue that the reference to foreign law included its rules of the conflict of laws. There is, therefore, no justification for generalising the few English cases on *renvoi* into a general rule that a reference to foreign "law" always means the conflict rules of the foreign law, and no justification for the statement that "the English courts have generally, *if not invariably,* meant by "the law of the country of domicile" the whole law of that country".[86]

Much of the discussion of the *renvoi* doctrine has proceeded on the basis that the choice lies in all cases between its absolute acceptance and its absolute rejection. Even before *Neilson v Overseas Projects Corporation of Victoria Ltd,*[87] it was clear that in some situations the doctrine is convenient and promotes justice, and that in other situations the doctrine is inconvenient and ought to be rejected. In some situations the doctrine may be a useful means of arriving at a result which is desired for its own sake; but often this is because the English conflict rule is defective. For instance, if the court wishes to sustain a marriage which is alleged to be formally invalid, or to promote uniformity of distribution in a case of succession to movables where the deceased left movables in more countries than one, or to avoid conflicts with the *lex situs* in a case of title to land or conflicts with the law of the domicile in a case involving personal status, then the doctrine of *renvoi* may sometimes be a useful (though troublesome) device for achieving the desired result. On the other hand, in all but exceptional cases the theoretical and practical difficulties involved in applying the doctrine outweigh any supposed advantages it may possess. The doctrine should not, therefore, be invoked unless it is plain that the object of the English conflict rule in referring to a foreign law will on balance be better served by construing the reference to mean the conflict rules of that law.[88]

When will this be so? A number of types of case can be considered in which the arguments for *renvoi* have been advanced:

18–037

---

[85] The leading common law authority was *Re United Railways of the Havana and Regla Warehouses Ltd* [1960] Ch. 52 at 96–97 and 115.

[86] *Re Ross* [1930] 1 Ch. 377 at 390, per Luxmoore J. (italics added).

[87] [2005] HCA 54; (2005) 233 C.L.R. 331. See Briggs, [2006] L.M.C.L.Q. 1; Dickinson (2006) 122 L.Q.R. 183.

[88] See Lawrence Collins J. in *Barros Mattos v MacDaniels Ltd* [2005] EWHC 1323 (Ch) at [108] citing language to this effect in *Dicey, Morris and Collins.*

Title to land situated abroad[89]

18–038 If the question before the English court is whether a person has acquired a title to land situated abroad, the court (in so far as it has jurisdiction to deal with the matter at all) will apply the *lex situs*, the law of the place where the land is situated. One of the reasons for applying the *lex situs* is that any adjudication which was contrary to it would in most cases be a *brutum fulmen*, a waste of judicial breath, since in the last resort the land can only be dealt with in a manner permitted by the *lex situs*.

This reason requires that the *lex situs* should be interpreted to mean the law that the *lex situs* would apply. Suppose, for instance, that a British citizen domiciled in England dies intestate leaving land in Spain; and that by Spanish domestic law X is entitled to the land, but that Spanish courts would apply English domestic law according to which Y is entitled. It would be manifestly useless for an English court to decide that X was entitled to the land, because X could never recover it from Y in Spain.[90] However, the Wills Act 1963 excludes *renvoi* even in the case of immovables so far as the formal validity of wills is concerned.

Movables

18–039 A similar argument suggests that when the English court applies the *lex situs* to determine the title to movables situated abroad, it should interpret the *lex situs* broadly so as to include whatever the courts of the *situs* have decided or would decide. However, the argument is not so strong as in the case of land, because the movables may be taken out of the jurisdiction of the foreign court; the application of the *renvoi* doctrine in this type of case was rejected in *Islamic Republic of Iran v Berend*,[91] in which Eady J. referred with some approval to the non-dogmatic approach taken in *Neilson v Overseas Projects Corporation of Victoria Ltd*.[92] In *Dornoch v Westminster International N.V.*,[93] Tomlinson J., having reviewed the earlier dicta, thought that were he to apply *renvoi* in a case involving movables he would be "rowing against a strong tide". He would be reluctant to apply in a commercial context, concerning marine insurance and title to a ship, a doctrine "hitherto applicable only in fields such as the formal and intrinsic validity of wills, intestate succession and legitimation by subsequent marriage when in the fields of contract, tort, restitution and trusts a deliberate decision has apparently been taken to eschew the doctrine of *renvoi*." Having referred to the Australian approach, the judge refused to reach a definitive answer to the *renvoi* issue, given the incomplete evidence of the foreign law then available to him. Finally, in *Blue*

---

[89] See Falconbridge, *op. cit.*, pp.141 and 217–220; Cook, *op.cit.*, pp.264 and 279–280; Lorenzen, *op. cit.*, p.78.

[90] For this reason it is thought that the decision in *Re Ross* [1930] 1 Ch. 377 was correct so far as the immovables were concerned, subject to what is said later about the difficulty arising from the reference by the foreign law to the national law of a British citizen.

[91] [2007] EWHC 132; [2007] 2 All E.R. (Comm) 132.

[92] [2005] HCA 54; (2005) 233 C.L.R. 331. See Briggs, [2006] L.M.C.L.Q. 1; Dickinson (2006) 122 L.Q.R. 183.

[93] [2009] EWHC 1782 (Admlty); [2009] 2 Lloyd's Rep. 420.

Sky One Ltd. v Mahan Air[94] Beatson J. rejected the use of *renvoi* in a commercial context (the mortgage of an aircraft located abroad). He criticised elements in Tomlinson J.'s reasoning, and by implication that of the High Court of Australia in *Neilson*:

> "to leave the applicability of the *renvoi* doctrine to a case by case analysis depending on the identification of the policy behind the private international law of the particular country under consideration is likely to lead to a very uncertain legal regime. Indeed it could lead to a Tennysonian wilderness of single instances. Moreover, as Fentiman states,[95] it would mean 'that the identity of the applicable law cannot be known without a judicial determination, even in a case where the location of the property is known to the parties'."

So title to movables is one area in which the use of *renvoi* is excluded.

Formal validity of marriage

Factors similar to those which originally favoured the application of the *renvoi* doctrine as a device for sustaining the formal validity of wills also favour its application as a device for sustaining the formal validity of a marriage celebrated abroad. These factors are, first, a rigid rule of the English conflict of laws which normally requires compliance with the law of the place of celebration (the *lex loci celebrationis*); secondly, a more flexible rule in neighbouring European countries (where English people frequently get married) which allows compliance with either the *lex loci* or the personal law of the parties; and thirdly, a strong judicial bias in favour of the validity of marriage. There is, however, no English case which actually sustains the validity of a marriage on the ground that it was formally valid by the law which the *lex loci celebrationis* would apply. But it is a legitimate inference from *Taczanowska v Taczanowski*[96] that such a marriage would be upheld. This does not mean that a marriage would be held formally invalid for failure to comply with the formalities prescribed by whatever system of domestic law would have been referred to by the conflict rules of the *lex loci celebrationis*. It merely means that a marriage may be formally valid if the parties comply with the formalities prescribed by either the domestic rules of the *lex loci celebrationis*, or by whatever system of domestic law the *lex loci celebrationis* would apply. Thus, the reference to the *lex loci celebrationis* in the case of formalities of marriage is an alternative reference to either its conflict rules or its domestic rules, just as it was in the case of formalities of wills.

18–040

Certain cases of transmission[97]

Where the foreign law referred to by the English court would refer to a second foreign law, and the second foreign law would agree that it was applicable, the case for applying the second foreign law is strong.

18–041

---

[94] [2010] EWHC 631 (Comm).
[95] International Commercial Litigation (Oxford: Oxford University Press, 2010), para.5.57.
[96] [1957] P. 301 at 305 and 318.
[97] Griswold, (1938) 51 Harv.L.Rev. 1165 at 1190; Lorenzen, *op. cit.*, pp.76–77; cf. *Re Trufort* (1887) 36 Ch.D. 600; *R. v Brentwood Marriage Registrar* [1968] 2 Q.B. 956.

Thus, if a German national domiciled in Italy died leaving movables in England, and Italian and German law both agreed that German domestic law was applicable because the *propositus* was a German national, the English court should accept that situation and apply German domestic law. For the practical advantages of deciding the case the way the Italian and German courts would decide it (especially if the *propositus* left movables in Italy and Germany as well as in England) seem to outweigh the theoretical disadvantages of this mild form of transmission.

If, on the other hand, the second foreign law would not agree that it was applicable, then there seems no reason for it to be applied. Thus, if a Danish national domiciled in Italy died leaving movables in England, and Italian law would apply the law of the nationality, while Danish law would apply the law of the domicile, neither law recognising any *renvoi* from the other, then the English court should apply Italian domestic law, thus ignoring *renvoi* altogether.[98]

Difficulties in the application of the doctrine

18–042   It remains to discuss certain difficulties in the application of the English *renvoi* doctrine, emphasised by Beatson J. in *Blue Sky One Ltd. v Mahan Air*.[99] These are as follows.

Unpredictability of result

18–043   The doctrine makes everything depend on "the doubtful and conflicting evidence of foreign experts".[100] Moreover, it is peculiar to this theory of *renvoi* that it requires proof, not only of the foreign choice of law rules, but of the foreign rules about *renvoi* and there are few matters of foreign law about which it is more difficult to obtain reliable information. In continental countries, decided cases, at least of courts of first instance, are not binding as authorities to be followed, and doctrine changes from decade to decade. Consequently, we find Wynn Parry J. saying in *Re Duke of Wellington*[101]:

> "It would be difficult to imagine a harder task than that which faces me, namely, of expounding for the first time either in this country or in Spain the relevant law of Spain as it would be expounded by the Supreme Court of Spain, which up to the present time has made no pronouncement on the subject, and having to base that exposition on evidence which satisfies me that on this subject there exists a profound cleavage of legal opinion in Spain and two conflicting decisions of courts of inferior jurisdiction".

The English cases show that the effect of acquiring a domicile in a foreign country may sometimes be to make the foreign domestic law applicable,[102] sometimes English domestic law,[103] sometimes the law of the domicile of

---

[98] Wolff, *op. cit.*, p.203.
[99] [2010] EWHC 631 (Comm).
[100] *Re Askew* [1930] 2 Ch. 259 at 278, per Maugham J, cited with approval in *Blue Sky One Ltd v Mahan Air* [2010] EWHC 631 (Comm) at [178].
[101] [1947] Ch. 506 at 515.
[102] *Re Annesley* [1926] Ch. 692; *Re Askew* [1930] 2 Ch. 259.
[103] *Re Ross* [1930] 1 Ch. 377.

origin,[104] and sometimes the law of yet a fourth country.[105] There is no certainty that different results will not be reached in any future case in which the same foreign laws are involved, because foreign law is a question of fact and has to be proved by evidence in each case. Moreover, if the evidence of foreign law is misleading or inadequate, the English court may reach a result which is unreal or unjust to the point of absurdity.

Thus, in *Re O'Keefe*[106] the intestate had lived in Italy for the last 47 years of her **18–044** life and was clearly domiciled there. Yet the effect of the English *renvoi* doctrine was that her movables were distributed not in accordance with the Italian domestic law with which she might be expected to be most familiar, and in reliance on which she may have refrained from making a will, but in accordance with the domestic law of the Irish Free State, of which she was not a citizen, which only came into existence as a political unit during her long sojourn in Italy, and which she had never visited in her life except for a "short tour" with her father 60 years before her death. The only possible justification for such a result is that it may have enabled the movables in England to devolve in the same way as the movables in Italy. But of course in many cases uniformity of distribution is unattainable so long as some systems of law refer to the national law and others to the law of the domicile. For instance, uniformity of distribution would be impossible on any theory if an Italian national died intestate domiciled in England, for the English and Italian courts would each distribute the movables subject to its control in accordance with its own domestic law.

The national law of a British citizen

The most frequent occasion for applying the *renvoi* doctrine has been the conflict **18–045** between English law, which refers succession to movables to the law of the domicile, and the laws of some continental countries, which refer to the law of the nationality. If the *propositus* is a British or an American citizen, the foreign court's reference to his or her national law is meaningless, for there is no such thing as a "British" or "American" or even a "Canadian" or "Australian" law of succession, nor, conversely, is there any such thing as "English" nationality. If the English court decides for itself how the foreign court might be expected to interpret its reference to the national law of a British citizen, as has been done in some cases, it is not necessarily deciding the case as the foreign court would decide it. Thus in *Re Johnson*[107] and *Re O'Keefe*[108] it was assumed, without any evidence of foreign law, that the national law of a British subject meant the law of his domicile of origin. If, on the other hand, the English court allows a foreign expert witness to assume that the national law of a British citizen is English law,

---

[104] *Re Johnson* [1903] 1 Ch. 821; *Re O'Keefe* [1940] Ch. 124.

[105] *Re Trufort* (1887) 36 Ch.D. 600; *R. v Brentwood Marriage Registrar* [1968] 2 Q.B. 956.

[106] [1940] Ch. 124; a much criticised decision. The short unreserved judgment has given rise to "a flood of writings in all corners of the world, but particularly in Italy": Nadelmann, (1969) 17 Am. J. Comp. L. 418 at 444.

[107] [1903] 1 Ch. 821.

[108] [1940] Ch. 124 at 129: "Italian lawyers cannot say what is the meaning of the law of the nationality when there is more than one system of law of the nationality".

as has been done in other cases,[109] it is basing its decision on a manifestly false premise. Thus in *Re Ross*[110] the evidence was that "the Italian courts would determine the case on the footing that the English law applicable is that part of the law which would be applicable to an English national [sic] domiciled in England". In *Re Askew*,[111] the expert witness stated: "I am informed and believe that John Bertram Askew was an Englishman [sic]. Therefore English law would be applied by the German court". Of course it can be argued that if the English court seeks to discover what decision the foreign court would reach, the grounds on which the foreign court would arrive at its decision are irrelevant.

Circulus inextricabilis

18–046   As we have seen,[112] the effect of applying the doctrine of double *renvoi* is to make the decision turn on whether the foreign court rejects the *renvoi* doctrine altogether or adopts a doctrine of single or partial *renvoi*. But if the foreign court also adopts the doctrine of double *renvoi,* then logically no solution is possible at all unless either the English or the foreign court abandons its theory, for otherwise a perpetual *circulus inextricabilis* would be created. So far, this difficulty has not yet arisen, because English courts have not yet had occasion to apply their *renvoi* doctrine to the law of a country that adopts the same doctrine. (That, in turn, is due to the fact that most Commonwealth countries, which are likely to adopt the double *renvoi* doctrine, also follow the English choice of law rules, so that a reference back to English law from the law of such a country is unlikely.) Yet the possibility remains, and the *circulus inextricabilis* cannot surely be dismissed as "a (perhaps) amusing quibble".[113] "With all respect to what Maugham J. said in *Re Askew*," said the Private International Law Committee, "the English judges and the foreign judges would then continue to bow to each other like the officers at Fontenoy".[114] It is hardly an argument for the doctrine of double *renvoi* that it will only work if the other country rejects it.

In *Neilson v Overseas Projects Corporation of Victoria Ltd*,[115] Gummow and Hayne JJ. considered the possibility of what they called "an infinite regression of reference." Their Honours held that there was no evidence suggesting that China would apply a "double *renvoi*" approach, but recognised that the problem could arise. They seem to favour the application of the law of the forum in such a case.[116]

---

[109] e.g., *Re J.B. (Child Abduction) (Rights of Custody: Spain)* [2003] EWHC 2130; [2004] 1 F.L.R. 976.
[110] [1930] 1 Ch. 377 at 404.
[111] [1930] 2 Ch. 259 at 276.
[112] Above, para.18–026.
[113] *Re Askew* [1930] 2 Ch. 259 at 267, per Maugham J.
[114] First Report (1954) Cmd. 9068, para.23(3).
[115] [2005] HCA 54; (2005) 233 C.L.R. 331. See Briggs, [2006] L.M.C.L.Q. 1; Dickinson (2006) 122 L.Q.R. 183.
[116] At paras 130–134.

Conclusion

As a purely practical matter it would seem that a court should not undertake the **18–047** onerous task of trying to ascertain how a foreign court would decide the question, unless the situation is an exceptional one and the advantages of doing so clearly outweigh the disadvantages. In most situations, the balance of convenience surely lies in interpreting the reference to foreign law to mean its domestic rules. Although the doctrine of *renvoi* was favoured by Westlake[117] and Dicey,[118] the great majority of writers, both English and foreign, are opposed to it. Lorenzen said: "Notwithstanding the great authority of Westlake and Dicey, it may reasonably be hoped that, when the doctrine with all its consequences is squarely presented to the higher English courts, they will not hesitate to reject the decisions of the courts that have lent colour to *renvoi* in the English law".[119] There is no case which prevents the Court of Appeal (still less the Supreme Court) from reviewing the whole problem, and it is submitted that such a review is long overdue.

The time factor

The conflict of laws deals primarily with the application of laws in terms of **18–048** geography, of place. Yet as in other branches of the law, so in the conflict of laws, problems of time cannot altogether be ignored. There is a considerable continental literature on the time factor in the conflict of laws, and a growing awareness of the problem by English-speaking writers[120] though, as might be expected, the English courts have dealt with it in a somewhat empirical fashion.

Three different types of problem have been identified by writers. The time factor may become significant if there is a change in the content of the conflict rule of the forum (called *le conflit transitoire* by French writers), or in the content of the connecting factor (which the French call *le conflit mobile*), or, most important of all, in the content of the foreign law to which the connecting factor refers. These will now be discussed in turn.

Changes in the conflict rule of the forum

A change in the conflict rule of the forum does not differ from a change in any **18–049** other rule of law and its effect must therefore be ascertained in accordance with the familiar English rules of statutory interpretation and of judicial precedent.

Judge-made law is retrospective in operation, whereas statute law is usually prospective. Very strange consequences sometimes follow from a retrospective

---

[117] Ch.2.

[118] 3rd edn, Appendix I.

[119] Lorenzen, *op. cit.*, p.53. The sentence was first published in 1910, but the learned author left it unchanged in 1947.

[120] See F. A. Mann (1954) 31 B.Y.I.L. 217; Grodecki, (1959) 35 B.Y.B.I.L. 58; Spiro, (1960) 9 I.C.L.Q. 357; Rabel, *op. cit.*, Vol. 4, pp.503–519; Grodecki, *International Encyclopaedia of Comparative Law* (Nijhoff, Tübingen, 1976), Vol. III, 8; Pryles, (1980) Monash U.L. Rev. 225; Fassberg, (1990) 39 I.C.L.Q. 856.

alteration in a conflict rule of the forum by judicial or legislative action, especially in the field of family relations. Thus, the English conflict rule for the recognition of foreign divorces was radically altered by judicial action in 1953[121] and again in 1967,[122] and by legislative action in 1971[123] and 1986.[124] In *Hornett v Hornett*[125]:

> A man domiciled in England married in 1919 a woman domiciled before her marriage in France. They lived together in France and England until 1924, when the wife obtained a divorce in France. The husband heard about this divorce in 1925. He then resumed cohabitation with his wife in England until 1936, when they parted. No children were born of this cohabitation. In 1969 the husband petitioned for a declaration that the divorce would be recognised in England.

18–050 Although it could not have been recognised before 1967, the divorce was recognised under the new judge-made rule declared by the House of Lords in that year.[126]

If we alter the facts a little, the consequences of this retrospective alteration of the conflict rule are startling:

(1) If children had been born of the resumed cohabitation between the parties after the divorce, they would have been legitimate when born, but rendered illegitimate by the subsequent recognition of the decree.

(2) If the husband had gone through a ceremony of marriage with another woman in 1945, his second marriage had been annulled for bigamy in 1950, and his second wife had then remarried, would the result of recognising the divorce in 1971 be to invalidate the nullity decree and also the second wife's second marriage?

(3) If the husband had died intestate in 1940, and a share in his property had been distributed to his French wife as the surviving spouse, would she have had to return it when the new conflict rule declared by the House of Lords in 1967 validated her French divorce?

Changes in the connecting factor

18–051 From the temporal point of view, the connecting factor in a rule of the conflict of laws may be either constant or variable. It may be of such a character that it necessarily refers to a particular moment of time and no other, or it may be liable to change so that further definition is required. For instance, a conflict rule which referred the question of capacity to make a will to the law of the testator's domicile would be meaningless unless it defined the moment of time at which the domicile was relevant.

---

[121] *Travers v Holley* [1953] P. 246.

[122] *Indyka v Indyka* [1969] 1 A.C. 33.

[123] Recognition of Divorces and Legal Separations Act 1971.

[124] Family Law Act 1986 ss.44–49; for the retrospective effect of the relevant provisions see Recognition of Divorces and Legal Separations Act 1971 s.52.

[125] [1971] P. 255; discussed by Karsten, (1971) 34 M.L.R. 450.

[126] See the powerful arguments adduced by Latey J. in the court of first instance and by Russell L.J. (dissenting) in the Court of Appeal in *Indyka v Indyka* [1967] P. 233 at 244–245 and 262–263.

Examples of constant connecting factors in the English conflict of laws include the *situs* of an immovable, the place where a marriage is celebrated, a will executed, or a tort committed, and the domicile of a corporation.[127] Examples of varying connecting factors include the *situs* of a movable, the flag of a ship, and the nationality, domicile or residence of an individual.

In these cases, it is simply a question of formulating the most convenient and just conflict rule, and the time factor, though it cannot be disregarded, is not the dominant consideration. For this reason, it has been doubted whether it is appropriate to treat a change in the connecting factor as a problem of time in the conflict of laws.[128]

Changes in the *lex causae*

Changes in the *lex causae* present much the most important and difficult problems of time in the conflict of laws, especially when the change purports to have retrospective effect. The overwhelming weight of opinion among writers is that the forum should apply the *lex causae* in its entirety, including its transitional rules. This is certainly the prevailing practice of courts on the mainland of Europe. It is arguably the prevailing practice of the English courts, although there is one case, *Lynch v Provisional Government of Paraguay,*[129] which is often cited for the contrary proposition.

18–052

Much confusion has resulted from ambiguous formulations of the conflict rule, and these in turn have suffered from a failure to distinguish between constant and variable connecting factors. If, for example, the forum's conflict rule says that succession to immovables is governed by the *lex situs,* the connecting factor is constant, no further definition is required, and it is natural and proper for courts to apply the *lex situs* as it exists from time to time. But if the forum's conflict rule says that succession to movables is governed by the law of the deceased's domicile, the connecting factor is variable, and further definition is required to make the rule more precise. So the words "at the time of his death" are added in order to define the time at which his domicile is relevant. The effect of this is to exclude reference to any earlier domicile, but courts have sometimes assumed that the effect is also to exclude retrospective changes in the law of the domicile made after the death of the deceased. This assumption seems unnecessary and improper, for the two questions are really quite distinct.

Although it must be emphasised that the problem is always basically the same, namely, should the forum apply or disregard subsequent changes in the *lex causae,* it will be convenient to deal with it under the following heads arranged according to subject matter: succession to immovables; succession to movables; torts; discharge of contracts; and validity of marriage. In conclusion, something will be said on the extent to which public policy may occasionally induce the forum to refuse recognition to foreign retrospective laws.

18–053

---

[127] A corporation, unlike an individual, cannot at common law change its domicile.
[128] See Grodecki, (1959) 35 B.Y.B.I.L. 58.
[129] (1871) L.R. 2 P. & D. 268.

Succession to immovables

18–054   In *Nelson v Bridport*[130]:

> The King of the Two Sicilies granted land in Sicily to Admiral Nelson for himself and the heirs of his body, with power to appoint a successor. By his will the Admiral devised the land to trustees in trust for his brother William for life with remainders over. After the Admiral's death, and in the lifetime of William, a law was passed in Sicily abolishing entails and making the persons lawfully in possession of such estates the absolute owners thereof. Taking advantage of this law, brother William devised the land to his daughter, from whom it was claimed by the remainderman under the Admiral's will.

In giving judgment for the defendant, Lord Langdale M.R. took it for granted that he had to apply the law of Sicily as it existed from time to time and not as it was at the time of the original grant or at the time of the Admiral's death.

Succession to movables

18–055   However, an opposite result was reached in *Lynch v Provisional Government of Paraguay*[131]:

> A testator who had been dictator of Paraguay died domiciled there having by his will left movable property in England to his mistress, the plaintiff. Two months after his death, but before probate of the will had been granted in England, there was a revolution in Paraguay, and the new Government passed a decree declaring all the testator's property wherever situate to be the property of the state and depriving his will of any validity in England or elsewhere. This decree purported to relate back to the time of the testator's death. The plaintiff applied for a grant of probate as universal legatee under the will.

Her application was opposed by the new government. The Government's opposition was bound to fail, because the decree was penal[132] and because property in England could not be confiscated by a foreign government.[133] But Lord Penzance, in granting probate to the plaintiff, preferred to rest his judgment on the ground that English law adopts the law of the domicile "as it stands at the time of the death" and does not undertake to give effect to subsequent retrospective changes in that law. In support of this proposition he quoted Story's formulation that succession to movables is governed by the law of the domicile "at the time of the death", without appearing to realise that the last six words were intended to qualify "domicile" and not "law", and that Story never considered the effect of subsequent retrospective changes in the law.

18–056   Lord Penzance's manifest inclination to uphold the will on the peculiar facts of the case is understandable, but his wide formulation has been much criticised by writers[134] on the ground that it failed to give effect to the transitional law of the *lex causae,* and appeared to do so irrespective of the content of that law. If, for

---

[130] (1846) 8 Beav. 547.
[131] (1871) L.R. 2 P. & D. 268.
[132] See *Banco de Viscaya v Don Alfonso de Borbon y Austria* [1935] 1 K.B. 140.
[133] See above, para.13–057.
[134] See Mann (1954) 31 B.Y.B.I.L. 217 at 234; Grodecki (1959) 35 B.Y.B.I.L. 58 at 67–69, where various interpretations of the decision are discussed.

example, the will had been defective in point of form, say, because the law of Paraguay required all wills to be witnessed by a notary public, and after the testator's death it was discovered that a witness, though practising as a notary, was not qualified to do so, and the will had been validated by retrospective legislation in Paraguay, it is hard to suppose that Lord Penzance would have thought it "inconvenient and unjust" to give effect to that legislation.

The decision was followed without much discussion in the curious case of *Re Aganoor's Trusts*[135]:

> A testatrix died in 1868 domiciled in Padua having by her will given a settled legacy to A for life and if he died without children to B for life and then to B's children living at B's death. This was valid by the Austrian law in force in Padua in 1868; but on September 1, 1871, the Italian Civil Code came into force and forbade trust substitutions, dividing the ownership between the persons in possession on that date and the first persons entitled in remainder who were born or conceived before then. B died in 1891 leaving children. A died in 1894 without children.

It was held that the settled legacy was valid and that the change in the law in force in Padua made after the death of the testatrix would be ignored. This result is diametrically opposite to that which was reached in *Nelson v Bridport*.[136]

If it is true that in succession to movables no account is to be taken of subsequent changes in the *lex causae* made after the death of the testator, that proposition is subject to an important qualification so far as the formal validity of wills is concerned. For s.6(3) of the Wills Act 1963 provides that retrospective alterations in the *lex causae* made after the execution of the will are relevant in so far as they validate but irrelevant in so far as they invalidate the will. This enactment is not in terms confined to alterations in the law made before the death of the testator, and there seems no reason to read into it words that are not there.

18–057

Torts

In *Phillips v Eyre*, already discussed in the context of torts[137]:

18–058

> An action for assault and false imprisonment was brought in England against the ex-Governor of Jamaica. The acts complained of took place in Jamaica while the defendant was engaged in suppressing a rebellion which had broken out in the island. The acts were illegal by the law of Jamaica as it stood at the time of the tort; but the defendant pleaded that they had been subsequently legalised by an Act of Indemnity passed in Jamaica with retrospective effect.

The Court of Exchequer Chamber gave effect to this defence. It follows from this decision that even in 1870 English law had no objection to foreign retrospective legislation as such; and what was true in 1870 must be even more true today when retrospective legislation has become a more familiar phenomenon in English domestic law. It will be noted that the Court of Exchequer Chamber adopted a wholly different approach from that of Lord Penzance in *Lynch*'s case.

---

[135] (1895) 64 L.J.Ch. 521; criticised by Mann, (1954) 31 B.Y.BI.L. 217 at 234; Grodecki (1959) 35 B.Y.B.I.L. 58 at 69–70.
[136] (1846) 8 Beav. 547.
[137] (1870) L.R. 6 Q.B. 1.

It is thought that a similar result would follow from the application of the rules in the Rome II Regulation, given the approach, already noted,[138] prevalent in European legal systems generally.

Discharge of contracts

18–059   The discharge of a contractual obligation is a matter for the applicable law, determined under the Rome I Regulation. There seems little doubt that this means the applicable law as it exists from time to time, so that legislation enacted in the country of the applicable law after the date of the contract may have the effect of discharging or modifying the obligations of the parties. This was certainly the case under the common law rules in respect of changes in the content of the proper law of the contract.[139]

In *Adams v National Bank of Greece*[140] the House of Lords refused to apply a Greek law which purported retrospectively to exonerate a Greek bank from liability under an English contract of guarantee. The House was not unanimous in its reasons for reaching this conclusion[141]; but the main reason seems to have been that since the proper law of the contract was English, no Greek law could discharge one party's obligation thereunder.[142] In other words, Greek law was not the *lex causae*. The case is noteworthy in the present context because all five Law Lords went out of their way to approve the principle of *Lynch*'s case.[143] But only Lord Tucker based his judgment squarely on that decision, and Lord Reid was not satisfied that it should be applied to a case like the one before him. This is surely the better view.

Validity of marriage

18–060   In *Starkowski v Att-Gen*[144]:

> H1 and W, both Roman Catholics domiciled in Poland, went through a ceremony of marriage in Austria in May 1945 in a Roman Catholic church. They lived together until 1947, when they separated, having acquired a domicile of choice in England. In 1950 W went through a ceremony of marriage in England with H2, a Pole domiciled in England. In May 1945 a purely religious marriage without civil ceremony was void by Austrian law. But in June 1945 a law was passed in Austria retrospectively validating such marriages if they were duly registered. By some oversight, the marriage between H1 and W was not registered until 1949, by which time they had acquired a domicile in England and separated.[145]

---

[138] At para.18–052.

[139] See, e.g., *Re Chesterman's Trusts* [1923] 2 Ch. 466 at 478; *Perry v Equitable Life Assurance Society* (1929) 45 T.L.R. 468; *De Beeche v South American Stores Ltd* [1935] A.C. 148; *R. v International Trustee for the Protection of Bondholders AG* [1937] A.C. 500; *Kahler v Midland Bank Ltd* [1950] A.C. 24; *Re Helbert Wagg & Co. Ltd's Claim* [1956] Ch. 323 at 341–342.

[140] [1961] A.C. 255.

[141] See, for a detailed analysis of the judgments, Grodecki, (1961) 24 M.L.R. 701 at 706–714.

[142] See, in particular, the judgment of Lord Reid and that of Diplock J. in the court of first instance: [1958] 2 Q.B. 59.

[143] [1961] A.C. 255.

[144] [1954] A.C. 155.

[145] Mann thought that the breakdown of the marriage before the registration of the Austrian ceremony should have led the House of Lords to an opposite conclusion: (1954) 31 B.Y.B.I.L. 217 at 243–245. But this seems unacceptable for the reasons given by Grodecki, (1959) 35 B.Y.B.I.L. 58 at 75–76.

The House of Lords held that the Austrian ceremony was valid and the English ceremony was bigamous and void. Lord Reid stated the question to be decided as follows: "Are we to take the law of that place [of celebration] as it was when the marriage was celebrated, or are we to inquire what the law of that place now is with regard to the formal validity of that marriage?" He answered the question by saying "There is no compelling reason why the reference should not be to that law as it is when the problem arises for decision".[146] Lord Cohen[147] distinguished the *Lynch* case somewhat faintly on the ground that it involved a remotely different subject matter. Lord Tucker[148] agreed with Barnard J. in the court of first instance[149] that *Lynch*'s case would have been of more assistance if the second ceremony had preceded the registration of the first. But these distinctions are illusory because, as is shown by Lord Reid's formulation quoted above, the problem was basically the same. The House of Lords adopted a different approach and surely a preferable one from that of Lord Penzance in *Lynch*'s case.

Public policy

The prevailing practice of the English courts thus seems to be to apply the *lex causae* as it exists from time to time and to give effect if need be to retrospective changes therein. But the consequences of giving effect to retrospective changes in the law are sometimes so extraordinary that public policy must occasionally impose qualifications and exceptions. There is an almost complete lack of English authority on this question. The discussion that follows is therefore highly speculative. It will throw the problem into the clearest possible relief if we consider some variations on the facts of the *Starkowski* case and consider what decision an English court might be expected to reach.   **18–061**

(1) If the Austrian marriage had been valid originally but had later been retrospectively invalidated by Austrian legislation, it would seem that, on grounds of policy, the marriage should be held valid in England.

(2) If either party had obtained an English nullity decree annulling the Austrian marriage for informality before it was registered, it would seem that the foreign retrospective legislation should not be allowed to invalidate the English nullity decree.[150]

(3) What would the position have been if the English ceremony had preceded   **18–062** and not followed the registration of the Austrian ceremony? The majority of the House of Lords expressly left this question open in the *Starkowski* case.[151] It is thought that the English ceremony should have been held valid. A similar point was decided by the British Columbia Court of Appeal in *Ambrose v Ambrose*[152]:

---

[146] [1954] A.C. 155 at 170 and 172.
[147] At p.180.
[148] At p.175.
[149] [1952] P. 135 at 144.
[150] See *Von Lorang v Administrator of Austrian Property* [1927] A.C. 641 at 651, per Lord Haldane.
[151] [1954] A.C. 155 at 168, 176 and 182.
[152] (1961) 25 D.L.R. (2d) 1; criticised by Castel, (1961) 39 Can. Bar Rev. 604, by Hartley, (1967) 16 I.C.L.Q. 680 at 699–703; and by Grodecki, *op. cit.*, Vol. III, Ch.8, para.34(1).

A wife obtained an interlocutory judgment for divorce from her first husband in California, where they were domiciled, on 25 November 1930. This judgment could become final, and so entitled either party to remarry, at the expiration of one year, either on the application of either party or on the court's own motion. It was not in fact made final until 1939. Meanwhile, in 1935, the wife went through a ceremony of marriage in the State of Washington with her second husband, who was domiciled in British Columbia. They lived together in British Columbia until 1956, when they separated. The wife then took advantage of a Californian statute passed in 1955 and obtained an order from the Californian court in 1958 which retrospectively back-dated the divorce to 25 November 1931, the earliest date on which final judgment could have been obtained. The second husband then petitioned for nullity in British Columbia on the ground that the second ceremony was bigamous.

18–063 The court granted a decree. It distinguished *Starkowski v Att-Gen* on two grounds. First, the defect in that case was formal and could be corrected by the law of the place of celebration, which remained constant throughout; whereas the defect in the *Ambrose* case related to capacity to marry, a matter which was governed by the law of the wife's antenuptial domicile: but she ceased to be domiciled in California in 1939, and was therefore domiciled in British Columbia, and not in California, when she obtained her order from the Californian court in 1958.[153] Second, in *Starkowski v Att-Gen* the retrospective validation of the Austrian ceremony preceded the English ceremony, whereas in the *Ambrose* case the Washington ceremony preceded the retrospective validation of the Californian divorce.

---

[153] In Canadian law, the domicile of a married woman was the same as that of her husband, but a woman whose marriage was void acquired the domicile of the man if she lived with him in the country of his domicile. Therefore W remained domiciled in California until her divorce from H1 was made final in 1939, whereupon she became domiciled in British Columbia because she had been living there with H2 since 1935 on the ground that she was married to him.

CHAPTER 19

THEORIES AND METHODS

In the opening chapter of this book, there was a brief discussion of the   **19–001**
justification for the conflict of laws, and for the application in some cases by the
courts of the forum state of rules derived from a foreign legal system. The
justification offered was a pragmatic one: a desire to do justice between the
parties to the dispute, an exercise informed by perceptions of what the parties, or
the wider public, would expect or feel to be an appropriate outcome. The point
was also made, in discussing the term "private international law", that there is no
single system of conflict of laws rules: they differ from country to country. There
is a fairly well-defined set of *questions* which constitute the subject, but the
answers are those of individual legal systems. Each legal system draws on its
own tradition and experience in making a judgment as to what is just, or
appropriate, or meets the legitimate expectations of the parties.

There are some matters of fact which every legal system has to take into
account in developing its rules of the conflict of laws. An obvious example
concerns land: from the earliest times, it has been recognised that land cannot in
practice be dealt with except in accordance with the rules, or at least the
mandatory rules, of the *lex situs*. We have seen, too, how developments in
transport and communications have deprived the place in which the parties enter
into a commercial contract of much of its former significance. In other areas,
however, the content of legal rules is less clearly influenced by external factors
and more by the internal logic of the law itself, for example in fixing the precise
boundary between contract and tort. There is nothing inherent in the conflict of
laws which dictates a "correct" answer, or which enables one to say that the
approach taken by a particular legal system is or is not in accord with principle. It
is true that academic commentators or even official law reform agencies may
criticise a rule. They may believe it arose through some historical misunderstanding, or by some accident of litigation or legislation. It may be said to produce
inconvenient or capricious results. But until the law is changed, it follows from
state sovereignty that it remains in force and immune from effective challenge.

The reader's growing familiarity with the English rules of the conflict of laws as   **19–002**
they have been examined in the central chapters of this book may have
encouraged a belief that the pragmatic English approach is wholly unproblematic,
that it reflects an understanding accepted always and everywhere. This final

chapter will serve as a timely corrective. It examines alternative theoretical approaches that have been advanced, and some methodologies which are radically different from those used in England.

THEORIES

19–003   It is appropriate to begin with two of the founding fathers of our subject, Huber and Savigny. They each believed that there were principles of private international law of universal validity, from which the subject could be developed logically and scientifically.

Huber

19–004   Ulrich Huber (1636–1694) was successively a professor of law and a judge in Friesland. He was the author of the shortest treatise ever written on the conflict of laws[1] (only five quarto pages), but his influence on its development in England and the United States has been greater than that of any other foreign jurist.

Huber laid down three maxims "for solving the difficulty of this particularly intricate subject". They are as follows[2]:

(1)   The laws of each state have force within the limits of that government, and bind all subject to it, but not beyond.
(2)   All persons within the limits of a government, whether they live there permanently or temporarily, are deemed to be subjects thereof.
(3)   Sovereigns will so act by way of comity that rights acquired within the limits of a government retain their force everywhere so far as they do not cause prejudice to the power or rights of such government or of its subjects.

19–005   In his first two maxims Huber states, more clearly than anyone before him, that all laws are territorial and can have no force and effect beyond the limits of the country where they were enacted, but that they bind all persons within that country, whether native-born subjects or foreigners. It was this insistence on the territorial nature of law that made Huber's doctrines so congenial to English and American judges. Then, in his third maxim, Huber offers, almost casually, two explanations of the apparent paradox that, despite the doctrine of territorial sovereignty, foreign law is applied beyond the territory of its enacting sovereign. His first explanation is that this is done simply by the tacit consent of the sovereign in whose territory the foreign law is applied. His second explanation is that what is enforced and applied is not foreign law as such but the rights to which the foreign law gives rise. Such thinking was to be expressed by later

---

[1] *De Conflictu Legum* (1689). For translation and comment, see Lorenzen, *Selected Articles on the Conflict of Laws* (New Haven CT: Yale University Press, 1947), Ch.6; Davies, (1937) 18 B.Y.B.I.L. 49. Perhaps it is not fanciful to suggest that Huber's practical illustrations, which are such a feature of his work, were used as a model by Dicey and by the American Law Institute's *Restatements*.
[2] Section 2.

writers in terms of the doctrines of comity and of vested rights, discussed below. The third maxim also contains the seeds of the doctrine of public policy, discussed in Chapter 3.

Savigny

The most influential writer on the conflict of laws in the civil law tradition (perhaps in any tradition) was Friedrich Carl von Savigny, who was born in Frankfurt in 1779 and died in 1861. He has been described as "a prince among the intellectuals of his age".[3] His treatment of the subject became very well known in England through the translation by William Guthrie,[4] with the title *A Treatise on the Conflict of Laws and the Limits of their Operation in Respect of Place and Time.*

19–006

Savigny wrote[5]:

> "It is the function of the rules of law to govern legal relations. But what is the extent or sphere of their authority? What legal relations (cases) are brought under their control? The force and import of this question becomes apparent when we contemplate the nature of positive law, which does not happen to be one and the same all over the world, but varies with each nation and state; being derived in every community, partly from principles common to mankind, and partly from the operation of special agencies. It is this diversity of positive laws which makes it necessary to mark off for each, in sharp outline, the area of its authority, to fix the limits of different positive laws in respect to one another. Only by such demarcation does it become possible to decide all the conceivable questions arising from the conflict of different systems of positive law in reference to the decision of a given case.
> The converse mode of procedure may also be followed, in order to find the solution of such questions. When a legal relation presents itself for adjudication, we seek for a rule of law to which it is subject, and in accordance with which it is to be decided; and since we have to choose between several rules belonging to different positive systems, we come back to the sphere of action marked off for each, and to conflicts resulting from such limitation. The two modes of procedure differ only in the points from which they start. The question itself is the same, and the solution cannot turn out differently in the two cases".

This exercise of "fixing the limits of different positive laws in respect to one another" is taken forward using a simple analysis of the subject matter of legal rules. They deal with *persons*, "their capacity for rights and capacity for acting, or the conditions under which they can have rights and acquire rights", and *legal relations*, including rights to specific things or to whole estates (i.e., succession), obligations and family relations.[6] Savigny concludes from this analysis that "the rule of law applicable to every given case is determined . . ., first and chiefly, by the subjection of the person concerned to the law of a certain territory".[7]

19–007

The assumption behind all this is surely that there is a single and correct answer to private international law questions. That is even plainer in Savigny's reformulation of the object of the exercise: "to ascertain for every legal relation

---

[3] By Wieacker in his *Privatrechtsgeschichte der Neuzeit*, in the translation by Weir (as *A History of Private Law in Europe*, Clarendon Press, Oxford, 1995) p.304.
[4] Published by T. & T. Clark, Edinburgh, 2nd edn, 1880.
[5] *ibid.*, 344; in Guthrie's translation, pp.47–48.
[6] *ibid.*, para.345; p.56.
[7] *ibid.*, para.345; p.57.

(case) that law to which, in its proper nature, it belongs or is subject"[8]; or "to ascertain, for the legal relations of every class, to what territory it belongs, and therefore, as it were, to discover its seat", an inquiry to be based on "a comparative view of the legal relations themselves".[9]

Story and the doctrine of comity[10]

19–008   In 1857 Joseph Story, a professor at Harvard University and a justice of the United States Supreme Court, published his *Commentaries on the Conflict of Laws, Foreign and Domestic.*[11] It is a remarkable work, combining exposition of the case-law developed in England and in the United States with lengthy quotations from the leading writers in the civil law tradition. It has been described as "the most remarkable and outstanding work on the conflict of laws which had appeared since the thirteenth century in any country and in any language".[12]

There is an ambivalence in Story's treatment of the nature of the conflict of laws. Although he cites extensively from their writings, his opinion of the civilians of continental Europe is distinctly unflattering. "Their works . . . abound with theoretical distinctions, which serve little other purpose than to provoke idle discussions, and with metaphysical subtleties which perplex, if they do not confound, the inquirer".[13] There speaks the authentic voice of the pragmatic common lawyer!

19–009   Story took over Huber's doctrine of comity and made it the basis of his own system[14]:

> "The true foundation on which the subject rests is that the rules which are to govern are those which arise from mutual interest and utility; from the sense of the inconveniences which would arise from a contrary doctrine; and from a sort of moral necessity to do justice in order that justice may be done to us in return".

In England, Story's doctrine of comity was rejected by Dicey on the following grounds[15]:

> "If the assertion that the recognition or enforcement of foreign law depends upon comity means only that the law of no country can have effect as law beyond the territory of the sovereign by whom it was imposed, unless by permission of the state where it is allowed to operate, the statement expresses, though obscurely, a real and important fact. If, on the other hand, the assertion that the recognition or enforcement of foreign laws depends upon comity is meant to imply that . . . when English judges apply French law, they do so out of courtesy to

---

[8] *ibid.*, para.348; p.70
[9] *ibid.*, para.361; p.139.
[10] See Lorenzen, *op. cit.*, pp.138–139, 158–160, and 199–201; Cheatham, (1945) 58 Harv.L.Rev. 361 at 373–378; Anton, *Private International Law* (W. Green and Son, Edinburgh, 1970), pp.21–24; Yntema, (1966) 65 Mich.L.Rev. 1.
[11] (Little, Brown and Co., 2nd ed., 1985).
[12] Lorenzen, *op. cit.*, pp.193–194. But for a ruthless attack on Story's postulates, which were an extension of those of Huber, see Cook, *Logical and Legal Bases of the Conflict of Laws* (Harvard University Press, Cambridge MA, 1942), Ch.2.
[13] para.11; p.10.
[14] Story, *op. cit.*, s.35.
[15] Dicey, *The Conflict of Laws* (London: Stevens and Sons, 1896), p.10.

the French Republic, then the term 'comity' is used to cover a view which, if really held by any serious thinker, affords a singular specimen of confusion of thought produced by laxity of language. The application of foreign law is not a matter of caprice or option; it does not arise from the desire of the sovereign of England, or of any other sovereign, to show courtesy to other states".

More recently Collins has traced the abandonment of the comity doctrine as a basis for private international law,[16] but he observes that while it may be discredited in the eyes of text-writers it thrives in judicial decisions. The theory has performed, and may still perform, a useful function in freeing the conflict of laws from parochialism, and in making our judges more internationalist in outlook and more tolerant of foreign law than they might otherwise have been.

Dicey and the theory of vested rights[17]

Dicey's treatise *The Conflict of Laws* was first published in 1896, though it had been in preparation since 1882. Dicey identified in Savigny, Bar, and other continental writers a theoretical approach, aiming to show what ought of necessity to be in any given case the rule of private international law. He admitted that the advantages of such an approach might be underrated by English lawyers "to whose whole conception of law it is at bottom opposed". But he then went on to identify its weakness[18]:

19–010

> "it rests on the assumption, common to most German jurists, but hardly to be admitted by an English lawyer, that there exist certain self-evident principles of right whence can be deduced a system of legal rules, the rightness of which will necessarily approve itself to all competent judges".

There is some irony in the fact that Dicey's survey concludes with the formulation of a set of General Principles of the subject.[19]

In Dicey's view, the growth of choice of law rules was "the necessary result of the peaceful existence of independent nations combined with the prevalence of commercial intercourse": these conditions compelled judges of every nation "by considerations of the most obvious convenience" to apply foreign laws.[20] Noting, and perhaps overstating, the similarity between the rules adopted in practice in different countries, Dicey explained this by the asserting that courts everywhere had in mind the same object. "All, or nearly all, the rules as to choice of law, which are adopted by different civilised countries, are provisions for applying the principle that rights duly acquired under the law of one country should be recognised in every country".[21]

---

[16] Collins, in Fawcett (ed.), *Reform and Development of Private International Law* (Oxford: Oxford University Press, 2002), Ch.4.

[17] See Dicey, 3rd edn, pp.11 at 23–33; Beale, *Treatise on the Conflict of Laws* (New York: Baker, Voorhis & Co., 1935), Vol. 3, pp.1967–1975; Cheatham, (1945) 58 Harv.L.Rev. 361 at 379–385; Carswell, (1959) 8 I.C.L.Q. 268.

[18] Dicey, *op. cit.*, pp.18–19.

[19] cf. the observation by Cook, *op. cit.*; p.6, that both Story and Dicey do at times, without being fully conscious of it, revert to the theoretical method which professedly they had abandoned.

[20] Dicey, *op. cit.*, p.8.

[21] Dicey, *op. cit.*, p.12.

19–011 This leads to Dicey's General Principle No. 1:

> "Any right which has been duly acquired under the law of any civilised country is recognised and, in general, enforced by English courts, and no right which has not been duly acquired is enforced or, in general, recognised by English courts".[22]

Savigny had many years before considered a not dissimilar proposition "that local law should always be applied by which vested rights shall be kept intact".[23] He dismissed it in a single sentence: "This principle leads into a complete circle; for we can only know what are vested rights, if we know beforehand by what local law we are to decide as to their complete acquisition".[24] Dicey acknowledged this criticism, but had no real answer to it.

It was left to Beale, the Reporter of the American Law Institute's first *Restatement of the Conflict of Laws*, to elevate the vested rights theory into a dogma and make it the theoretical basis of his system. Obsession with this theory led Beale to make some surprisingly trenchant statements, for example[25]:

> "The question whether a contract is valid can on general principles be determined by no other law than that which applies to the acts [of the parties], that is, by the law of the place of contracting ... If ... the law of the place where the agreement is made annexes no legal obligation to it, *there is no other law which has power to do so.*"

19–012 The vested rights theory has been effectively destroyed by Arminjon[26] in France and by Cook[27] and Lorenzen[28] in the United States. Cook was trained as a physical scientist and he was something of a philosopher as well as a lawyer. Probably no more incisive mind than his has ever been applied to the problems of the conflict of laws. Certainly it is true that he "discredited the vested rights theory as thoroughly as the intellect of one man can ever discredit the intellectual product of another".[29] Objections to the vested rights theory include the following:

(1) As Savigny noted long ago, the theory "leads into a complete circle; for we can only know what are vested rights if we know beforehand by what local law we are to decide as to their complete acquisition".[30]

---

[22] Dicey, *op. cit.*, pp.23–24. There is a fascinating discussion (*ibid.*, p.30) about which countries could be regarded for this purpose as "civilised". France, the United States and Mexico qualified; but not Turkey and China. Dicey indicates no criteria.

[23] para.361; p.147.

[24] para.361; p.147.

[25] Beale, *op. cit.*, vol. 2, p.1091 (italics added).

[26] (1933) II Hague *Recueil des cours*, 5–105.

[27] (1924) 33 Yale L.J. 457; reprinted in Cook, *op. cit.*, Ch.1. See also Chs 13 and 14.

[28] 1924) 33 Yale L.J. 736; reprinted in Lorenzen, *op. cit.*, Ch.1. See also pp.104–111.

[29] Currie, *Selected Essays on the Conflict of Laws* (Duke University Press, Durham NC, 1963), p.6, cf. Cavers, Book Review of Cook, (1943) 56 Harv.L.Rev. 1170, 1172: "the author's technique has enabled him to destroy the intellectual foundations of the system to the erection of which Professor Beale devoted a lifetime".

[30] Savigny, *op. cit.*, p.147. Yntema, (1953) 2 Am.Jo.Comp. Law 297 at 313 states that Dicey "does not appear to have considered Savigny's objection that the principle [of vested rights] is circular". This is wrong, because Dicey quoted Savigny's statement (3rd edn, p.33), though his attempt to refute it is unconvincing.

(2)   The theory assumes that for every situation in the conflict of laws there is one[31] and only one "jurisdiction" which has power to determine what legal consequences should follow in the given situation. It therefore led to the formulation of broad mechanical rules which had to be applied in order to select the relevant "jurisdiction", regardless of the content of its law and regardless of the social and economic considerations involved.

(3)   The theory derived whatever plausibility it had from simple cases where all   **19–013**
the facts occurred in one country but the action was brought in another. If the facts are distributed between two foreign countries, or between one foreign country and the forum, the case presents a problem in the conflict of laws not only for the forum but also for the foreign country or countries concerned and indeed for any court in the world. Hence it is impossible to tell what rights have been acquired under the foreign law unless the forum inquires how the foreign court would decide this very case. This introduces the problem of *renvoi,* which according to the first Restatement[32] (but not according to Dicey[33]) is ordinarily to be rejected. Dicey, it would seem, "stuck to the logic of the vested rights theory to the bitter end".[34]

(4)   It is undeniable that the courts may decline, for a variety of reasons, to enforce the claimant's rights under the foreign law. Examples are cases in which the forum's public policy is invoked, or in which the forum classifies the foreign rule as procedural.

The demolition of the vested rights theory was Cook's great contribution. In his   **19–014**
original article,[35] published in 1924, which was never adequately answered and not at all by Beale, he discussed the famous case of *Milliken v Pratt,*[36] to which we shall return later in this chapter:

> A married woman, domiciled in Massachusetts, in that state signed and gave to her husband an offer addressed to the plaintiff in Maine, offering to guarantee payment by her husband for goods to be sold to him by the plaintiff. The husband posted the letter to the plaintiff in Maine, and the plaintiff accepted the offer there by sending the goods from that state. By the law of Massachusetts, a married woman had no capacity to make a contract of guarantee; by the law of Maine she had. The Massachusetts court held that the law of Maine governed because the contract was made there, and therefore the lady was liable.

Cook pointed out that, for the Maine court as well as for the Massachusetts court, this case presented a problem in the conflict of laws; and that the Massachusetts court could not have enforced a Maine-created right unless it undertook to discover how a Maine court would have decided this very case, which (since it contented itself with ascertaining the domestic law of Maine) it did not.

In the United States, the *Restatement Second* has abandoned the vested rights theory and all its consequences. No longer is it said that the validity of a contract and the question of liability for torts are governed by the law of the place where

---

[31]   The theory affords no guidance when the cause of action arose, e.g., on the high seas.

[32]   ss.7, 8.

[33]   3rd edn, Appendix 1.

[34]   Cook, *op. cit.,* p.371.

[35]   (1924) 33 Yale L.J. 457; reprinted in Cook, *op. cit.,* Ch.1.

[36]   125 Mass.374 (1878).

the contract was made or the tort committed. Instead, the Restatement lays down that both these questions are determined by "the local law of the state which has the most significant relationship to the occurrence and the parties".[37]

The local law theory[38]

19–015 Cook's positive contribution to doctrine in the conflict of laws is usually known as the local law theory. His method, congenial to an English lawyer, was not to start with preconceived ideas about the nature of law, but to proceed inductively by a method of scientific empiricism, stressing what the courts have done rather than what the judges have said. Noting the inescapable fact that in a case such as *Milliken v Pratt*[39] the court enforced a Massachusetts-created right and not a Maine-created right, and feeling the need to reconcile the application of foreign law with the doctrine of territorial sovereignty, Cook concluded that the forum always enforced rights created by its own law. In his own words[40]:

> "The forum, when confronted by a case involving foreign elements, always applies its own law to the case, but in doing so adopts and enforces as its own law a rule of decision identical, or at least highly similar though not identical, in scope with a rule of decision found in the system of law in force in another state or country with which some or all of the foreign elements are connected, the rule so selected being in many groups of cases, and subject to the exceptions to be noted later, the rule of decision which the given foreign state or country would apply, not to this very group of facts now before the court of the forum, but to a *similar but purely domestic group of facts involving for the foreign court no foreign element* . . . The forum thus enforces not a foreign right but a right created by its own law".

19–016 Cook's theory was at first enthusiastically received in England, but enthusiasm has since waned. The theory seems sterile because there really is no need to reconcile the application of foreign law with the doctrine of territorial sovereignty, as Cook – no less than the protagonists of the vested rights theory – assumed.[41] For the law of England includes not only the domestic law of England but also its rules of the conflict of laws, which are just as much part of English law as the law of contract or the law of torts. Hence, it is no abdication of English sovereignty to apply foreign law in English courts if the English rules of the conflict of laws lay down that foreign law is applicable. To say that in such a case the English court is not applying foreign law but enforcing rights acquired under foreign law (vested rights theory), or modelling its rule of decision on that of the foreign law (local law theory), is really to play with words.

The reader may well conclude that the theoretical debates of the past centuries have made little real progress. There must remain practical questions as to how the courts actually go about the business of deciding case which have international aspects. To these methodological questions we now turn.

---

[37] *Restatement Second*, s.145 (torts); s.188 (contracts). This is subject (in contracts) to a choice of law by the parties: ss.186 and 187.

[38] See Cook, *op. cit.*, Ch.1; Cheatham, (1945) 58 Harv.L.Rev. 361 at 385–391.

[39] 125 Mass.374 (1878), the facts of which are given above.

[40] Cook, *op. cit.*, pp.20–21 (his italics). Cook derived this local law theory from Judge Learned Hand's judgment in *Guinness v Miller* 291 F. 769 (1923), but cf. Cavers, (1950) 63 Harv.L.Rev. 822 on the differences between the two approaches.

[41] See Cook, *op. cit.*, p.51 at n.9, where he accepted Story's version of Huber's first two axioms.

METHODS

Jurisdiction-selecting rules or rule-selecting rules?

The typical rules of the conflict of laws select a particular country whose law will **19–017** govern the matter in question, irrespective of the content of that law. They do not select a particular rule of law. Theoretically at least, the court does not need to know what the content of the foreign law is until after it has been selected.[42] But that approach is not the only possible one.

Cavers

In 1933, Cavers published an important article[43] in which he deplored the **19–018** "jurisdiction-selecting" technique (as he called it) of the traditional conflict of laws system. He pointed out that to apply the law of a particular jurisdiction without regard to the content of that law was bound to lead to injustice in the particular case and to generate false problems. "The court is not idly choosing a law; it is determining a controversy. How can it choose wisely without considering how that choice will affect that controversy?"[44] The court's duty is to reach a result which is a just one in the particular case and so it should not close its eyes to the content of the two conflicting rules of law.

As an illustration of what he had in mind, Cavers posed a hypothetical case based on *Milliken v Pratt,*[45] but with the laws of the two states reversed. Suppose that a married woman domiciled in Massachusetts makes a contract in Maine, and that by the law of Massachusetts she has capacity to make such a contract, but that by the law of Maine she has not. Does it make sense to say that the law of the place of contracting governs and therefore the contract is void? Surely not: for the Maine law was intended to protect married women domiciled or resident in Maine, not married women domiciled or resident in Massachusetts. The problem is therefore a false one.

At first sight Cavers's thesis seems an attractive one. Yet on closer inspection **19–019** certain doubts arise. They are as follows:

(1)   As he admitted in his original article,[46] the thesis may not be workable in international conflicts as opposed to interstate conflicts within the United States, because in the former situation "the application of mechanical rules of law may be regarded as necessary to save the alien litigant from xenophobia. Discretion is a safe tool only in the hands of the disinterested. Such disinterestedness may more readily be credited to courts within the bounds of a federal union".

---

[42] There are cases in which neither the judge nor the reporter tells us what difference there was between the two systems of law between which a choice had to be made. Instances are: *Chatenay v Brazilian Submarine Telegraph Co* [1891] 1 Q.B. 79; *Re Duke of Wellington* [1947] Ch. 506; *The Assunzione* [1954] P. 150; *Tzortzis v Monark Line A/B* [1968] 1 W.L.R. 406.

[43] (1933) 47 Harv.L.Rev. 173.

[44] At p.189.

[45] 125 Mass.374 (1878); above, para.19–014.

[46] (1933) 47 Harv.L.Rev. 173 at 203.

(2)   If the courts are invited to choose between two competing rules of law without being given any guidance as to the principles which should influence their choice, there is a danger that they will choose what they consider to be "the better rule". There is an observable tendency for some American courts to do just that.

(3)   To expect the courts to discard the accumulated experience of centuries and to abandon the traditional system of the conflict of laws altogether is asking a great deal. Cavers envisaged that in course of time a new body of rules would emerge from the decisions of the courts if his thesis were adopted.[47] In his later writings he saw no objection to a jurisdiction-selecting rule if it is the product of two decisions choosing on policy grounds between competing rules in cases in which the law-fact patterns are reversed, provided the way in which it was put together is kept in mind.[48]

19–020   In 1965, Cavers took this last idea further in his book *The Choice of Law Process*. The central theme of the book is the presentation of seven "principles of preference" as guides for a court in cases where the conflict of laws is neither false nor readily avoidable.[49] Five of these principles relate to torts and two to contracts and conveyances. Cavers disclaimed any idea that his seven principles were intended to form a complete system even in these two fields of law. He also emphasised that if a particular case did not fall within any of his principles, this did not mean that a contrary choice of law must be made: it simply meant that the case posed a different problem from that covered by the principle and therefore required further consideration.

Cavers' five principles in the field of torts are as follows:

(1)   Where the law of the state of injury sets a higher standard of conduct or of financial protection than the law of the state where the defendant acted or had his home, the former law should be applied.[50]

(2)   Where the law of the state in which the defendant acted and caused an injury sets a lower standard of conduct or of financial protection than the law of the plaintiff's home state, the former law should be applied.[51] A sub-principle, not given a number, provides that if both plaintiff and defendant have their homes in a state or states other than the state of injury and the law of the state of injury sets a lower standard of financial protection than that afforded by the law or laws of the parties' home state or states, the law of that home state which affords the lower degree of protection should be applied.[52]

---

[47] (1933) 47 Harv.L.Rev. 173 at 193 *et seq.*
[48] (1963) 63 Col.L.Rev. 1219 at 1225–1226; Cavers, *The Choice of Law Process* (Ann Arbor: University of Michigan Press, 1965), p.9, n.24.
[49] Cavers, Chs 5, 6, 7 and 8. For comments on his method, see Reese, (1966) 35 Fordham L.Rev. 153; Ehrenzweig, (1966) 80 Harv.L.Rev. 377; Baade, (1967) 46 Tex.L.Rev. 14 at 156–175; Scoles, (1967) 20 Jo.Leg.Ed. 111; von Mehren, (1975) 60 Cornell L.Rev. 927 at 952–963; Westmoreland, (1975) 40 Mo.L.Rev. 407 at 423–427 and 459–460; Leflar, *American Conflicts Law*, 3rd edn (Indianapolis: Bobbs-Merrill Co., 1977), s.95.
[50] Cavers, *op. cit.*, pp.139–145.
[51] pp.146–157.
[52] pp.157–159.

(3)   Where the state in which the defendant acted has established controls   **19–021**
      (including civil liability) over the kind of conduct in which the defendant
      was engaged when he caused a foreseeable injury to the plaintiff in another
      state having no such controls, the law of the former state should be
      applied.[53]
(4)   Where the law of a state in which a relationship between two parties has its
      seat has imposed a standard of conduct or of financial protection on one
      party for the benefit of the other which is higher than that of the state of
      injury, the law of the former state should be applied.[54]
(5)   Where the law of a state in which a relationship between two parties has its
      seat has imposed a standard of conduct or of financial protection on one
      party for the benefit of the other which is lower than that of the state of
      injury, the law of the former state should be applied.[55]

Cavers proposed no principles of preference for any fields of law other than torts   **19–022**
and contracts and conveyances. But of course there are many other fields in
which his method might be used, marriage for example. Despite Cavers's own
statement to the contrary,[56] it is difficult to believe that his theory will work in
international situations. He has articulated some of those choice-influencing
factors to which judges consciously or unconsciously resort. But in an
international case, how could a judge express a preference for the rules adopted
by one country or another when those countries are not component parts of a
federal system but are linked only by diplomatic relations or (perhaps) by a
common cultural heritage?

  The truth may well be that many of the traditional rules of the conflict of laws
are the product of the type of process he describes. Take, for example, the rule
that the formal validity of a marriage is governed by the law of the place of
celebration. As it stands, this rule is a somewhat arid statement. In order to give it
colour and texture, we need to split it up into its component parts, distinguishing
between cases where the law of the place of celebration holds the marriage valid
and cases where it holds the marriage void. We may also have to distinguish
between cases where the marriage is celebrated in England and cases where it is
celebrated abroad. We then find that our simple arid rule can be expanded into
four propositions:

(a)   A marriage celebrated in England in accordance with the formalities   **19–023**
      prescribed by English domestic law is valid.
(b)   A marriage celebrated in England not in accordance with the formalities
      prescribed by English domestic law is void.

---

[53] pp.159–166.
[54] pp.166–177.
[55] pp.177–180. But Cavers disapproves of this as a principle, and says that it would probably not
achieve general acceptance. The decisions of the New York Appellate Division in *Kell v Henderson*,
270 N.Y.S. 2d 552 (1966), of the Supreme Court of Wisconsin in *Conklin v Horner*, 38 Wis. 2d 468,
157 N.W. 2d 579 (1968) and of the Supreme Court of Minnesota in *Milkovich v Saari*, 295 Minn. 155,
203 N.W. 2d 408 (1973) are inconsistent with it.
[56] Cavers, *op. cit.*, pp.viii, 117, 119n.

(c)   A marriage celebrated abroad in accordance with the formalities prescribed by the law of the place of celebration is valid.

(d)   A marriage celebrated abroad not in accordance with the formalities prescribed by the law of the place of celebration is void.

But, and this is the point of the present discussion, that final proposition was found to be too harsh, and so a number of exceptions to it have been created on policy grounds, some by statute and some by the courts.[57] So if we make the distinctions noted above, and bear in mind the exceptions to proposition (d), our simple, arid rule for the formal validity of marriage assumes a much less mechanical air.

19–024   It does not seem necessary to abandon the whole existing system of the conflict of laws, with its apparatus of concepts and rules, as long as it yields acceptable results. The particular history of the development of the rules of the conflict of laws in the United States, where the influence of the vested rights theory led to the appearance of some indefensible rules, may have made a radically new approach inevitable. Elsewhere, there is no such urgent need, and it makes for economy of thought (and that means in practice judicial time, and so expense) to be able to apply a conflict rule instead of having to think out each problem afresh each time it arises. The great value of Cavers's contribution is that it does enable the "false conflict" to be identified and avoided. This is a matter which will be considered in more detail later in this chapter.

Currie: governmental interest analysis

19–025   An even more revolutionary opponent of the traditional system than Cavers was Brainerd Currie. In his opinion, "we would be better off without choice of law rules".[58] In a series of challenging articles, he inveighed again and again against "the system"; and he had some very hostile things to say about it. He deployed a rich array of adjectives: conceptualistic, irrational, mindless, ruthless, wretched, spurious, futile, arbitrary, hypnotic, mystical, intoxicating. The existing system was characterised as an apparatus, a machine, a field of sophism, mystery and frustration: "it has not worked and cannot be made to work".

Currie began his attack on "the system" by an analysis in depth of *Milliken v Pratt*.[59] Noting that the policies of the two states concerned were in conflict, he identified the policy of Massachusetts law as designed to protect Massachusetts married women, and the policy of Maine law as designed to protect the security of transactions by giving effect to the reasonable expectations of the parties. He then demonstrated with the aid of a number of ingenious tables that the application of the law of the place of contracting generated more false problems than there were real ones, and then solved the false problems, more often than not, in an obviously unacceptable way, by defeating the interests of both the states concerned, or by defeating the interests of one without advancing the interests of the other. He did not draw from this the conclusion which Cook had

---

[57] See above, para.8–009.

[58] Currie, *Selected Essays on the Conflict of Laws*, p.183.

[59] 125 Mass.374 (1878); see above, para.19–014. Currie's article now appears as Ch.2 of his book.

drawn,[60] namely, that the law of the domicile would be a better solution of the problem than the law of the place of contracting. He admitted that the application of this law would eliminate the false problems. But he rejected it on the grounds that "domicile is an intolerably elusive factor in commercial transactions"[61]; and that the application of the law of the domicile "would be commercially inconvenient and would consistently prefer the 'obsolete' to the 'progressive' policy".[62]

Instead, Currie proposed a radical new method for solving conflicts problems which would dispense with traditional conflict rules altogether. The latest statement of his thesis is as follows[63]:   **19–026**

(1) When a court is asked to apply the law of a foreign state different from the law of the forum, it should inquire into the policies expressed in the respective laws, and into the circumstances in which it is reasonable for the respective states to assert an interest in the application of those policies. In making these determinations the court should employ the ordinary processes of construction and interpretation.

(2) If the court finds that one state has an interest in the application of its policy in the circumstances of the case and the other has none, it should apply the law of the only interested state.[64]

(3) If the court finds an apparent conflict between the interests of the two states it should reconsider.[65] A more moderate and restrained interpretation of the policy or interest of one state or the other may avoid conflict.[66]

(4) If, upon reconsideration, the court finds that a conflict between the legitimate interests of the two states is unavoidable, it should apply the law of the forum.[67]   **19–027**

(5) If the forum is disinterested, but an unavoidable conflict exists between the laws of two other states, and the court cannot with justice decline to adjudicate the case, it should apply the law of the forum – until someone comes along with a better idea.

Currie claimed that acceptance of his "governmental interest" analysis would dispense not only with traditional conflict rules but also render obsolete such doctrines as *renvoi*, characterisation and public policy, which he regarded as devices required to make "the system" work.

Before we attempt to evaluate this revolutionary thesis, a few words of explanation are required. First, Currie was adamant that if the forum and the   **19–028**

---

[60] Cook, *op. cit.*, Ch.16.

[61] Currie, *op. cit.*, p.103.

[62] Currie, *op. cit.*, p.180.

[63] (1963) 63 Col.L.Rev. 1233 at 1242–1243. Other succinct statements of his thesis appear in Currie, *op. cit.*, pp.183–184 and 188–189.

[64] This, says Currie, is what the court did in *Babcock v Jackson*, 12 N.Y. 2d 473, 191 N.E. 2d 279 (1963).

[65] This proposition formed no part of Currie's earlier statements of his position. It was added later.

[66] See para.19–030, below.

[67] This, says Currie, is what the court did in *Kilberg v Northeast Airlines*, 9 N.Y. 2d 34; 172 N.E. 2d 526 (1961).

foreign state concerned each had an interest in the application of its law, the law of the forum must be applied, even though the foreign state had the greater interest. He refused to concede that the forum was entitled to weigh the interests of the two states. His reason was that assessment of the respective values of the competing legitimate interests of two sovereign states, in order to determine which is to prevail, is a political function of a very high order. This is a function that should not be committed to courts in a democracy. It is a function that the courts cannot perform effectively, for they lack the necessary resources.[68]

Second, as he himself admitted, Currie's method afforded no intellectually satisfying solution of "the intractable problem of the disinterested third state", that is cases where the forum has no interest in the outcome, but two foreign states have conflicting interests. He discussed this problem several times in his book,[69] and later devoted a special article to it.[70] In that article he minimised the practical importance of the problem by noting that actual cases involving it are extremely rare. He suggested that if possible the forum should avoid the problem by declining jurisdiction on *forum non conveniens* grounds; or, if that proved impossible, by construing it away by finding that the interest of one of the two foreign states did not really exist.[71] Lacking either of these solutions, the forum should either apply the law which it thinks Congress would apply if it legislated on the question, or should apply the law of the forum. He said, "If I were a judge I think I should prefer application of the law of the forum as the bolder technique. But then, I am a pretty old-fashioned fellow".[72] His contempt for traditional rules of the conflict of laws was such that he would not apply them even in this situation.

19–029   Old-fashioned or not, Currie's avowed object was to reduce the conflict of laws garden to ashes.[73] His ideas have been widely but not universally accepted in the United States, not only by academics but also by courts; European writers, however, are more sceptical.[74] The following are among the difficulties which acceptance of his theory would present to an English court:

(1)   The conflict of laws deals mainly with private law and is concerned with the interests of private persons and not with the interests of governments. It may be doubted whether governments are really interested in having their law applied in a conflict of laws situation, unless indeed the government of

---

[68] Currie, *op. cit.*, p.182.

[69] Currie, *op. cit.*, pp.62–64, 120–121, 606–609 and 720–721.

[70] Currie, (1963) 28 Law and Contemporary Problems 754.

[71] This is what the court did in *Reich v Purcell* 63 Cal. 2d 31; 432 P. 2d 727 (1967).

[72] (1963) 28 Law and Contemporary Problems 754 at 780.

[73] Currie, *op. cit.*, p.185.

[74] For a selection of comments on Currie's theory, see Hill, (1960) 27 U. of Chi.L.Rev. 463 (for Currie's reply, see Ch.12); Ehrenzweig, *Conflict of Laws* (St. Paul MN: West Publishing Co., 1962), pp.348–351; (for Currie's reply, see (1964) Duke L.J. 424 at 435–436); Leflar, *op. cit.*, s.92; Kegel, (1964) Recueil des Cours, II, 95, 180–207; Reese, (1964) I Hague *Recueil des cours* 315, 329–333; Reese, (1965) 16 U. of Tor.L.J. 228; Chief Justice Traynor, (1965) Duke L.J. 426; Cavers, *op. cit.*, pp.72–75, 96–102; Baade, (1967) 46 Tex.L.Rev. 141–151; Kahn-Freund, (1968) II Hague *Recueil des cours*, 5, 56–61; (1974) III *Recueil des cours*, 147, 413–415; von Mehren, (1975) 60 Cornell L.Rev. 927 at 935–941; Westmoreland, (1975) 40 Mo.L.Rev. 407 at 421–423 and 455–459; Fawcett, (1982) 31 I.C.L.Q. 189.

a country is a party to the action: and even then it may suit its purpose to argue that the foreign law and not its own should be applied.

(2)   Over one-third of Currie's book is devoted to a discussion of how his method is affected by the American Constitution, and in particular by the clauses dealing with full faith and credit, due process of law, privileges and immunities and equal protection of the laws.[75] Transplanted to a different environment, it is difficult to see how his theory would work in the absence of constitutional checks and balances.

(3)   It may be doubted whether Currie's refusal to concede that the forum is entitled to weigh its interests in the balance against those of the foreign state concerned is really consistent with his later and more refined view that, if the forum is confronted by an apparent conflict, it may be able to avoid the conflict by a "moderate and restrained interpretation" of its policy or that of the foreign state. For what is this but weighing in disguise?[76]   **19–030**

(4)   If the forum has an interest in the application of its law that cannot be construed away by a "moderate and restrained interpretation of its policy", Currie's method requires that the law of the forum should be applied, even if some other state has a much greater interest, and even if the result is to disappoint the reasonable expectations of the parties. Thus the interest of the forum prevails over all other considerations. And, as he freely admitted, his method sacrifices the goal of uniformity of result irrespective of the forum in which the action is brought, which has always been regarded as one of the most important objectives of the conflict of laws. For if there is a true conflict, and each state applies its own law as Currie's method requires, then the result will depend on the plaintiff's choice of forum. For this reason his method has been criticised as unduly orientated in favour of the *lex fori* and in favour of plaintiffs.

(5)   Currie's method requires that the "interest" of the forum and of the foreign state should be easily identifiable by counsel and court. This requirement is only fulfilled in the simplest of cases. In one of his articles,[77] Currie took nearly 40 pages to identify the policy behind a North Carolina statute of 1933 which prohibited actions on the personal covenant by certain kinds of mortgagee after foreclosure proceedings.   **19–031**

It is unrealistic to suppose that the purposes behind substantive rules of law are so clear, so unambiguous, and so singular that we can hope to discover them in the course of a trial with some degree of certainty and without risk of error. This is true of the substantive rules of the forum, and even more true of the substantive rules of foreign law. A rule of law is often the outcome of conflicting social, economic, political and legal pressures. It is an amalgam of conflicting interests. It does not express unequivocally a single "governmental interest" to the exclusion of all others. If it is an ancient rule of law, its original purpose may be lost in the mists of antiquity; and its continuance may simply be due to inertia or to lack of

---

[75] Currie, *op. cit.*, Chs 5, 6, 10, 11. It may be noted that aliens as well as American citizens are within the protection of the due process and equal protection clauses.

[76] Currie's answer to this criticism is to be found in Currie, *op. cit.*, pp.604–606, and in (1963) 28 Law and Contemporary Problems, 754, 756–761.

[77] Reprinted as Ch.8.

Parliamentary time to abolish it. Hence, what Currie said about the weighing of interests applies equally to the determination of policies: "it is a function that the courts cannot perform effectively, for they lack the necessary resources".[78]

(6) To expect the courts to abandon choice of law rules, and proceed on a case-by-case basis through governmental interest analysis, seems futile. Because of the doctrine of precedent, cases decided on the basis of governmental interest are bound to yield choice of law rules. These rules may differ from the traditional ones, but they are still rules, and as such are binding on the courts in future cases. Hence, as has been well said, "trying to throw away choice of law rules is like trying to throw away a boomerang".[79]

However, in spite of these criticisms, it must freely be admitted that Currie, like Cavers, did perform a useful service in enabling us to identify and avoid false problems. These will be discussed in more detail later in this chapter.

Comparative impairment

19–032 The Californian courts have adopted a variant on Currie's method which deserves separate treatment here. We have seen that if the forum and the foreign state each has an interest in the application of its law, Currie was adamant that the law of the forum must be applied, even if the foreign state has the greater interest. But the Californian courts have adopted a theory which involves the weighing of interests. A striking example is afforded by *Bernhard v Harrah's Club*[80]:

> In that case, the Supreme Court of California held that a Nevada tavern keeper was vicariously liable under a Californian statute for serving too much liquor to a drunken guest, who negligently injured the plaintiff in California while driving back to her home in that state, even though Nevada law imposed no such liability. The court found that California's interest in protecting its residents would be very seriously impaired if the defendant was held not liable, while Nevada's interest in protecting its tavern keepers would not be so seriously impaired if the defendant was held liable, at least if (as in the instant case) it had actively solicited Californian custom by advertising there.

If Nevada had been the forum it seems most unlikely that its courts would have agreed that Californian law was applicable. Yet the Californian courts on the whole apply their doctrine of comparative impairment in an even-handed way. In *Offshore Rental Co v Continental Oil Co*[81]:

> The plaintiff was a Californian corporation with its main place of business in California and places of business in other states, including Louisiana. A key employee of the plaintiff was injured in Louisiana owing to the defendant's negligence. The plaintiff sued for loss of services. Such an action was maintainable in California but not in Louisiana. The Supreme Court of California applied the law of Louisiana because it found that Louisiana's interest would be the more gravely impaired if its law was not applied.

---

[78] Currie, *op. cit.*, p.182, quoted above, para.19–028.
[79] Rosenberg, (1967) 67 Col.L.Rev. 459 at 464. cf. Cavers, *op. cit.*, p.74.
[80] 16 Cal. 3d 313; 546 P. 2d 719 (1976).
[81] 22 Cal. 3d 157; 583 P. 2d 721 (1978).

But as with governmental interest analysis in its more usual form, the process of   **19–033**
weighing interests is a complex one, with unpredictable outcomes. One more
example can be used to illustrate this. In *Industrial Indemnity Co v Chapman*[82]:

> IIC, a Californian company, brought an action in California against C, an Illinois law firm,
> alleging professional negligence, in the form of negligent advice received and acted upon in
> Texas where IIC was engaged in negotiating a very large transaction. The action was
> time-barred under the statutes of limitations in California and Texas, but not that of Illinois.

The court held that all three states had legitimate interests in having their law
applied. California had an interest in seeing its residents recover (which actually
pointed to the application of Illinois law) but what was seen as a stronger interest
in stopping stale claims. Texas was interested as the State where the alleged
negligence occurred. Illinois was seen as having an interest in regulating its
attorneys, but this was in effect disregarded as no evidence was presented that the
regulation of lawyers was a motivating factor in the formulation of the Illinois
rule.[83] The action therefore failed.

Choice-influencing factors

In 1952, Cheatham and Reese published an article in which they listed and   **19–034**
commented on a number of policies which they believed should guide the courts
in deciding choice of law questions and in formulating rules for the choice of
law.[84] The American Law Institute adopted these policies (with some
modifications) in the *Restatement Second of the Conflict of Laws,* of which Reese
was Reporter.

    Section 6 of the *Restatement* says that in the absence of direct guidance from a
relevant statute, the factors to be weighed by a court include the following:

(1)   *The needs of the interstate and international systems.* Choice of law rules   **19–035**
       should seek to further harmonious relations between states and nations and
       to facilitate commercial intercourse between them.
(2)   *The relevant policies of the forum.* Every rule of law, whether embodied in
       a statute or in judge-made law, was designed to achieve one or more
       purposes. Therefore a court should have regard for these purposes in
       determining whether to apply its own rule or the rule of another country in
       the decision of a particular issue.
(3)   *The relevant policies of other interested states.* The forum, says the
       Restatement Second, should give consideration not only to its own relevant
       policies but also to those of all other interested states. It should seek to
       reach a result that will achieve the best possible accommodation of these
       policies. It is usually desirable that the state whose interests are most deeply
       affected should have its law applied.

---

[82] 22 F. 3d 1346 (5th Cir., 1994).

[83] In discussing a new Illinois statute, the court argued that as its effect was to shorten the time within
which an aggrieved client could sue an allegedly negligent lawyer, the statute could not have been
concerned to extend greater protection to the public from errant lawyers.

[84] 52 Col.L.Rev. 959 (1952). See also Reese, (1963) 28 Law and Contemporary Problems 679;
(1964) I Hague *Receuil des cours* 315, 340–356.

19–036 (4) *The protection of justified expectations.* As a general rule, a person is entitled to expect that conduct regulated in accordance with the law of one country (for example, the country in which the conduct takes place) will not be called in question in another country.

(5) *The basic policies underlying the particular field of law.* Situations sometimes arise where the policies of the interested states are largely the same but there are minor differences between their relevant local rules. In such instances, there is good reason for the court to apply the local law of that state which will best achieve the basic policy, or policies, underlying the particular field of law involved.

(6) *Certainty, predictability and uniformity of result.* These values, says the *Restatement*, are important in all areas of the law; and to the extent that they are attained in choice of law, forum-shopping will be discouraged.

19–037 (7) *Ease in the determination and application of the law to be applied.* Ideally, choice of law rules should be simple and easy to apply. Pushed to its logical conclusion, this policy would result in there being but one single rule, namely, that all cases should be decided in accordance with the *lex fori*. Hence, this policy should not be over-emphasised, since it is obviously of greater importance that choice of law rules should lead to desirable results. However, this policy does furnish the justification for applying the *lex fori* to questions of procedure.

A number of courts in the United States have made use of this approach, or the similar development of a list of choice-influencing considerations produced by Leflar.[85] The generality of the language used in defining these factors, even with the explanations offered by their authors, makes them difficult to use. It is hard to see an English court having much patience with an argument based upon them.

False conflicts and foreign law as datum

19–038 As we have seen, the great merit of the methods of Cavers and Currie is that they enable false problems to be identified and avoided. What are these false problems, or false conflicts as they are more usually called, and how can they be identified?[86] The trouble is that no two writers agree on what constitutes a false conflict. Still, there is a large measure of agreement that false conflicts include the following:

(1) The first class consists of cases where two countries have different laws, but one of them was obviously not intended to apply to the case in hand. Examples are: *Milliken v Pratt*[87] with the laws of the two states reversed (because the protective policy of Maine was not intended to apply to

---

[85] (1966) 41 N.Y.U.L. Rev. 267; (1966) 54 Calif.L.Rev. 1584. They are summarised in Leflar, *op. cit.*, ss 103–107.

[86] Perhaps the most comprehensive survey is that by Westen, (1967) 55 Calif.L.Rev. 74, where copious references to the literature are given. For shorter statements, see Cavers, *op. cit.*, pp.89–90; Leflar, *op. cit.*, s.93. The whole notion of false conflicts is criticised by Kahn-Freund, (1974) III Hague *Recueil des cours*, 259–268.

[87] 125 Mass.374 (1878); above, para.19–014.

Massachusetts married women); the Englishman aged 20 who buys goods in a Ruritanian shop, minority ending in Ruritanian law at 21; *Babcock v Jackson*[88] (which concerned an Ontario statute limiting the liability of a host-driver giving a free lift to a passenger, because the Ontario statute was not intended to apply to New York hosts, guests and insurance companies); *Haumschild v Continental Casualty Co*[89] (because the Californian rule of interspousal immunity was not intended to apply to Wisconsin spouses). By contrast, the converse of each of these cases poses a true conflict: a married woman domiciled and resident in Massachusetts makes a contract in Maine which she is incapable of making by Massachusetts law (*Milliken v Pratt*); a Ruritanian aged 20 buys goods in an English shop; an Ontario host negligently injures an Ontario guest in New York[90]; an Illinois husband negligently injures an Illinois wife in Wisconsin.[91] The difference between false and true conflicts of this class can easily be perceived even by those who are sceptical of governmental interest analysis. In this situation, to say that one country's law was not intended to apply is only another way of saying that it had no interest in applying its law to the case.

(2) The second class consists of cases where the laws of two countries are the same or would produce the same result. In an earlier chapter, we noted some examples where a conflict of characterisation leads to the law of neither country being applied.[92] A rather different illustration is provided by an Australian case *Koop v Bebb*[93]:   **19–039**

> The infant plaintiffs brought an action in the Supreme Court of Victoria for damages for the death of their father, who was a passenger in a motor vehicle driven by the defendant and who was killed as a result of the defendant's negligence. The accident occurred in New South Wales (where all parties were resident) and the father died in hospital in Victoria. Both Victoria and New South Wales had enacted legislation based on Lord Campbell's Act which permitted specified dependants to recover damages for the loss of their breadwinner. The statutes of the two states did not differ in any relevant respect.

Yet Dean J. held that the action failed because the Victorian statute did not apply to wrongful acts occurring outside Victoria. His decision was reversed by the High Court of Australia; but the judges were not unanimous in their reasoning, and they made heavy weather of what should have been a simple case.

(3) We have seen that, perhaps especially in cases of tort, the issues should be segregated and not necessarily resolved by reference to the same law.[94] This application of different laws to the separable issues is called *depeçage*. There is a danger that an undiscriminating court may segregate the issues   **19–040**

---

[88] 12 N.Y. 2d 473; 191 N.E. 2d 279 (1963).
[89] 7 Wis. 2d 130; 95 N.W. 2d 814 (1959).
[90] *Kell v Henderson*, 270 N.Y.S. 2d 552 (1966).
[91] *Zelinger v State Sand and Gravel Co*, 38 Wis. 2d 98; 156 N.W. 2d 466 (1968); cf. *Johnson v Johnson*, 107 N.H. 30, 216 A. 2d 781 (1966), where on similar facts an opposite result was reached.
[92] Above, para.18–005.
[93] (1951) 84 C.L.R. 629.
[94] See para.12–010 but cf. para.18–005.

improperly and so produce an unjust result which distorts the laws of both the countries concerned. In *Maryland Casualty Co v Jacek*[95]:

> "A husband, resident with his wife in New Jersey, negligently injured her while both were travelling in the husband's car in New York. The husband was insured under a policy issued in New Jersey which provided that the insurer would satisfy any claim which the husband might become "legally obligated to pay". By the law of New York, a wife could sue her husband in tort but could not recover on his insurance policy unless express provision to that effect was specifically included in the policy. By the law of New Jersey, the policy would be construed to cover the wife's injuries, but wives could not sue their husbands in tort. Thus, if all the facts had occurred in New Jersey, the wife would be unable to recover because she could not sue her husband in tort; if all the facts had occurred in New York, she would be unable to recover because the policy did not cover her injuries."

Yet a lower federal court in New Jersey held that the wife could recover, because in its view the law of New Jersey governed the construction of the policy, and the law of New York governed the question whether the wife could sue her husband in tort.[96] The result seems wrong because the laws of both States were concerned with the danger of collusive suits by husbands or wives against insurance companies. The New York law permitting suits between spouses was enacted at the same time as the New York law restrictively interpreting insurance policies. There was a clear connection between the two laws, as the New York courts had observed[97]:

> The purpose and policy of the legislature in making these simultaneous amendments is unmistakably clear. The object was to authorise personal injury actions between spouses, and at the same time to guard against the mulcting of insurance companies by means of collusive suits between husband and wife.

The federal court in New Jersey thus exploited the interstate situation unfairly, to the detriment of the insurance company.[98] Although the laws of the two states were different, the conflict was false.

19–041   (4)   Another type of false conflict is where foreign law is referred to not for a rule of decision but for a *datum*. Currie emphasised that his governmental interest analysis was confined to cases of the first class.[99] The notion of foreign law being referred to not to furnish the rule of decision but as a *datum* is perfectly familiar to English law. Perhaps the simplest illustration is afforded by foreign rules of the road. These are not rules of decision but rules of conduct, non-compliance with which may amount to negligence. The foreign rules of conduct are incorporated in the English cause of action for negligence, just as the terms of a foreign statute may be incorporated in an English contract.[100]

---

[95] 156 F.Supp. 43 (1957). cf. *Lillegraven v Tengs*, 375 P. 2d 139 (1962).

[96] The case was decided two years before *Haumschild v Continental Casualty Co* 7 Wis. 2d 130; 95 N.W. 2d 814 (1959), where the rule of the *lex loci delicti* in this situation was abandoned.

[97] *Fuchs v London and Lancashire Indemnity Co*, 14 N.Y.S. 2d 387, 389 (1940).

[98] Contra, Reese (1973) 73 Col.L.Rev. 58 at 67–68, who approves of the result in this case.

[99] Currie, p.178.

[100] cf. *The Halley* (1868) L.R. 2 P.C. 193 at 203.

Currie's idea of foreign law being referred to as a *datum* was very much wider than this. He said that if a widow claims workmen's compensation in New York for the death of her husband there, or claims to be entitled as his widow under a New York will or intestacy, and the validity of her marriage is governed by Italian law, then this is not a case in the conflict of laws at all, since New York law in both cases furnishes the rule of decision, and Italian law furnishes no more than a *datum*.[101] This extremely narrow conception of what constitutes a case in the conflict of laws is certainly not adopted in England. If it were, it would mean that our choice of law rules for the validity of marriage could only be treated as true choice of law rules in the context of petitions for a decree of nullity or for a declaration as to status, and not in any other context. Apparently Currie would regard *Simonin v Mallac*[102] as a case in the conflict of laws, because the validity of the marriage was in issue in nullity proceedings brought by the wife against the husband. But he would not regard *Ogden v Ogden*[103] as a case in the conflict of laws, because the invalidity of the marriage was asserted as a defence to the second husband's petition for nullity on the ground of bigamy. This distinction seems very artificial.

There are three points on which all the modern American conflicts experts are agreed: first, the vested rights theory is dead; secondly, the mechanical place of contracting and place of tort rules of the first *Restatement* have rightly been abandoned; and thirdly, conflicts problems must be resolved in a flexible manner, case by case and issue by issue. But there agreement stops. In fact none of the new American methods is suitable for adoption by English courts in international cases. We would do better to build on what is good in the traditional system, as the *Restatement Second* seeks to do, rather than to abolish that system altogether and start again. The growth of a corpus of private international law derived from the European Union can be seen as underlining that conclusion: the detailed rules may differ markedly from those of English common law, but the methodology is much the same. There is however one idea found in that European material which comes close to some of the American notions.   **19–042**

European insights

This idea is that of the mandatory rule. A particularly striking use of the idea was in art.7(1) of the Rome Convention, never given effect in English law and not reproduced in the Rome I Regulation: **19–043**

> When applying under this Convention the law of a country, effect may be given to the mandatory rules of the law of another country with which the situation has a close connection, if and in so far as, under the law of the latter country, those rules must be applied whatever the law applicable to the contract. In considering whether to give effect to these mandatory rules, regard shall be had to their nature and purpose and to the consequences of their application or non-application.

---

[101] Currie, pp.69–72 and 177–178.
[102] (1860) 2 Sw. & Tr. 67.
[103] [1908] P. 46.

American writers in the Currie tradition will recognise this type of approach. Both in their thinking and in art.7(1), a possibly relevant State X is identified not by any exercise of party autonomy, nor by any choice of law rule, but by the mere fact of having some connection with the facts of the case. The question is whether its interest in having its law applied is a factor which should be recognised and taken into account. In the Rome Convention, the issue presented itself as one small aspect of an essentially rule-based methodology, a context very different from the clean sheet on which governmental interest calculations are normally written.

19–044 The European idea is most clearly expressed in art.19 of the Swiss Federal Act on International Private Law of 1987, which provides that:

> Where interests that are, according to Swiss legal understanding, legitimate and clearly overriding so require, a mandatory rule (*disposition impérative*) of a law other than that designated by this Act may be taken into account where the facts have a close connection to that law.
> In arriving at a decision in accordance with Swiss legal understanding whether such a rule should be taken into account, reference is to be made to the purpose of the rule and the consequences which would follow from its application.[104]

A similar approach can be found in case-law in a number of countries, for example the well-known *Alnati* case[105]:

> A cargo of potatoes, originating in France, was carried aboard a Dutch-registered ship, the *Alnati*, from Antwerp, in Belgium, to Rio de Janeiro, Brazil. On arrival, part of the cargo was found to have been damaged. The bill of lading specified that the contract of carriage was governed by the law of the Netherlands, and contained an exemption clause limiting the liability of the carrier to a greater extent than the Hague Rules on carriage of goods by sea would permit. A claim was brought in the Dutch courts. The Netherlands had not ratified the Hague Rules but they were mandatory in Belgium.

19–045 The Dutch Supreme Court, the *Hoge Raad*, applied Dutch law. On the facts, Belgium was merely a country through which the goods passed: there was no compelling Belgian interest in the case. However, as a matter of principle, the *Hoge Raad* recognised that:

> it may be that, for a foreign state, the observance of certain of its rules, even outside its own territory, is of such importance that the courts take them into account, and hence apply them in preference to the law of another state which may have been chosen by the parties to govern their contract.

In other words, the mandatory rules of a third state, such as Belgium on the instant facts, might be applied where their importance to the policy of that legal system, and the strengths of the links between the case and that state, so required. It is an interesting example of a principle being established in a case in which that principle was found not to be applicable.

---

[104] See Bucher, "L'ordre public et le but social des lois en droit international privé" (1993) II Hague *Recueil des cours* 1993–II, 9 at 88: he renders *Sonderanknüpfung* in French as *rattachement spécial*.
[105] May 13, 1966, [1977] NJ 522.

Conclusions

Modern approaches to the methodology of the conflict of laws can be **19–046** bewildering in their variety. However, they do have some relatively simple lessons. The first is that choice of law rules should be flexible and should be flexibly applied. The second is that they should never be applied without some regard to the content of the foreign law. Those simple axioms, and the notion of false conflicts, may serve to preserve all that is best in the traditional rule-selecting approach and to prevent it ossifying and becoming too inflexible to cope with the massive changes in society and commerce noted at the very start of this book.

INDEX

This index has been prepared using Sweet and Maxwell's Legal Taxonomy. Main index entries conform to keywords provided by the Legal Taxonomy except where references to specific documents or non-standard terms (denoted by quotation marks) have been included. These keywords provide a means of identifying similar concepts in other Sweet and Maxwell publications and online services to which keywords from the Legal Taxonomy have been applied. Readers may find some minor differences between terms used in the text and those which appear in the index. Suggestions to *sweetandmaxwell.taxonomy@thomson.com.*

All references are to paragraph number

INDEX